REHAM KHAN

ISBN 978-191641-52-18
Printed and bound in Great Britain.
Published by SK Publications 2018

Contents

Acknowledgements

It is strange to write an acknowledgements section when there is hardly anyone to acknowledge. The sad fact is that this was a mountain that I had to climb largely on my own. No one wanted to tell my story. Everyone who took an interest was in it for other reasons. Eventually, even those who wanted to help found that they could not. There were too many complications. There were obstacles and opponents at every turn. This was too much and too scary for just about everyone. With so many things working against me, I probably should have just given up. But I did not. And I only needed one source of help.

This book would never have been completed had it not been for Sahir, my son. I would never have managed to organise it all by myself. We worked on it together, compiling passage after passage, chapter after chapter. It was a mammoth task. But we did it.

In bringing this book to you, Sahir was my only support. He kept me motivated and forced me to work harder. We would often stay up all night to get the job done. Sahir became an expert in editing, publishing, designing and countless other things. He single-handedly achieved what huge teams cannot. He displayed utter professionalism, and his tolerance of my totally unreasonable panic attacks was legendary.

Even Sahir's friends were supportive. Instead of complaining that he had no time to hang out, they got involved and gave us valuable feedback. These people offered more support than most people in my life ever have. I will not forget that.

Despite everything, this book was written. My story is ready to be told.

Preface

This is said to be 'the much-awaited book'. Awaited by those who fear what it will expose. Awaited by those who think it might just help their own political careers.

There will be many in the media who pick up this book simply to get some juicy content for their shows. But that is not why I write it.

Why do I write this book? Is it for revenge against certain people I have known? Is it to set the record straight? Is it to prove my innocence and incriminate others?

It is none of the above. It is the account of a public figure who also happens to be a human being, something the world seems to overlook.

This is the account of a mother who is responsible for three children of her own, as well as thousands of children who have no mother at all (another fact people seem keen to forget).

This is the account of a young girl who grew up very quickly. This is a story for my two daughters; a story that will tell them that the happiness they are looking for is within them. You are responsible for the smile on your face.

This is a story for my son: If you love a woman, she will give you her life. But if you hurt a woman, she will leave you for a much better life.

This is a story for those out there who think that there is no point going on anymore. To you I say this: You will see that there is every reason to get up, no matter how many times someone pushes you to the ground.

Prologue

The pine door burst open.

A tall man barged in. He saw the mother with the young child clinging to her under the crisp white linens. The thin, cruel lips were pursed tightly together on his long face. He stripped the duvet from the bed and grabbed the woman's thin wrists. In one swift movement, he dragged her to the floor. She fell to her knees. The little child cried out in terror. As the woman got up, she heard the familiar barrage of abusive words. But she realized that she was not afraid anymore.

The man did what he usually did, moving forward to punch her in the chest repeatedly. She heard herself scream for the first time in years. The man stepped back, as if surprised by any form of retaliation. The woman regained her bearings and stood in front of him. She threatened to call the police if he hit her again, but it had been twelve years and she had never reported him. She heard his laugh and screamed again, this time for her son.

"Sahir!!!"

As the man advanced towards her again, she warned him that she would call 999.

"Oh really! Let's see you do it then," he jeered.

He knew her inside out. He thought she did not have the courage to go through with it. He had her right where he wanted her. His wife had thought about leaving him every day for over twelve years. She would be certain by Friday. But as he left for work on Monday, she'd talk herself out of it. After all, it wasn't the sort of thing ladies did. How would her mother face society? What would people say?

She didn't look like a victim. Her lipstick was always in place. Her smile was always ready. She was young, confident and full of life. She had everything a woman could want. She lived in a five-bedroom house with en-suite bathrooms, a central staircase, four reception rooms, and a large conservatory. Not to mention the two luxury cars parked outside, one with her name on it. It was the perfect everything. She looked perfect. The house looked perfect. Her children looked perfect. They looked perfect together. But the reality was anything but perfect.

That night had hardly been the first time. There had been many times when a scene from a cheap soap opera was enacted in the country home. But something was different tonight. This woman was not the young teenager he had married long ago. This woman had changed. She ran out of the room and he chased her across the house and into her daughter's room. With the phone in her hand and adrenaline coursing through her, the woman made her move. She didn't even notice the toys on the floor digging into her feet as she dialled the number she had wanted to call for so long.

The man stood in the doorway and stared. The kids stood petrified, looking from one adult to the other. From the look on his face, it seemed he didn't believe her. He seemed certain she was bluffing. But then he heard her say, "Police. The Willows, South Street, North Kelsey".

He turned on his heel and disappeared. She locked the door behind him and sat down on the fairy-printed duvet of her daughter's bed. Her three kids huddled around her. She felt her bony chest hurt where he had punched her. Punching her straight in the chest was his style, almost a signature move. She could always sense his cowardice; how he would aim like a little boy who was scared. It was almost as if he expected a punch back. But she never retaliated. She barely even managed a whimper most of the time.

She remembered how he'd pinned her before, as he had many times. He was laughing as he forced himself on her.

"You are so pathetic!" he jeered. "Why don't you call 999? You can't even spit on me".

A single tear slid from her eye as she turned her head to one side. The only noise in the room was the banging of her head as it hit the headboard, over and over again. It was as if she was not human. She was but a vessel with a pole being driven into her, repeatedly. She was detached in that moment, as if she wasn't even there. Her soul was numb. But tonight, she felt it. The punch. The insult. The helplessness. She felt it all and she was shivering with anger and with fear.

She had always been a perfect prisoner. Why even bother retaliating? What was the point? Who would hear her? Who would come to save her?

No one ever did.

§

It was a cold night in 2005. Christmas was only a few weeks away and I had finally taken the first step. I had made the call. But I was shocked at what I'd done. The kids and I remained quiet until the doorbell rang. I heard my husband's footsteps on the wooden landing and then on the stairs. I looked out and saw him walking towards the door. In the minutes after the phone call, he had changed out of the denims that he lived in, put on a suit and combed his hair back neatly. He looked every bit the consultant psychiatrist he was paid to be by the NHS. I stared in disbelief at this transformation. I saw two police officers at the door. They asked him about the phone call. I slowly and awkwardly walked down the stairs. One policeman took my husband to the main lounge while the other one took me to the smaller living room. He shut the door and started by asking me my name. I smiled. It probably wasn't appropriate to the situation but it was what I always did. It's what I'd done my whole life. As I smiled and joked I thought to myself, 'Who is going to believe your story? You look fine. You don't look abused'.

But they believed me. They saw me shivering, despite my smile. The police officer's eyes were kind. He asked me general questions. He asked if I had family and friends. The other officer joined us and said that the doctor had insisted that he had only manhandled his wife, and not hit her. The doctor was asked to leave the property with the police and stay away for 48 hours.

A few weeks later, the same officer, Martin, came over to check on me. He told me how they were trained to pick up on subtle signs. He had noticed how Doctor Ijaz Rehman, my husband, had insisted on bringing him a cup of coffee in a mug that said '*World's Greatest Dad*' on it. I smiled and told him that it was actually a mug that had been left by a friend.

For a woman with no support, the greatest fear is the increase in risk after domestic violence is reported. I was terrified of the consequences, and by the prospect of Ijaz returning to us. This was a start; they had taken him away and told him not to return for 48 hours. But I resolved to never be helpless again.

It had taken a month of special prayers (*Istikhara*) to build up this resolve and courage. People often say to me, "But you are brave so it was easy for you". But I remember how scared I was until that first step. I guess it is easy to confuse cowardly acts taken with confidence and brave acts taken with fear. You become brave by doing brave acts.

I was a 32-year-old mother to three young kids, with no money, friends, or family. I had no job prospects and no man ready to step in and rescue me. But I had one thing which is far more important than all of that. I had hope.

Chapter 1

Life started off in Libya. I remember Libya as a happy place, characterised by the smell of fresh-baked baguettes, *khubz*, and huge Egyptian *chapattis*. This was a time when everyone had nothing but praise for the rather charismatic and revered Muammar Gaddafi. He was considered quite a heartthrob by the ladies (my mother's diary would open to a photograph of him). He was known for throwing out westerners on a whim, an action which would result in educated people like my mother filling in for English teaching positions, and even English radio stations. There were frequent mentions of his erratic temperament, but this was a man seen by most of those he was ruling as a strong leader; one who stood up to bullying and had miraculously survived numerous assassination attempts.

My parents, like many of my mother's family, left Pakistan in the late sixties. My dad was a young ENT surgeon who chose to move to Libya. My mother, ever the perfectionist, had already completed her family by then; she had a boy and a girl. But then...I happened. Perhaps being born in the Great Sahara has something to do with my ability to persevere and survive hardship. My mother certainly believed that I was a true Bedouin. I was born in the beautiful Mediterranean town of Ajdabia, in North Western Libya. We later moved to Benghazi. The society I recall was liberal. Women in traditional outfits walked side-by-side with ladies in skirts. In fact, the women had a very Parisian fashion sense, with face-nets, berets, and fishnet stockings all the rage.

Home life was peaceful and happy. Mummy and Daddy were happy. She would sing while cooking. I would help with the dishes. Surprisingly, I have a clear memory going back to when I was about four years old, with some flashes from when I was even younger, boosted by family albums of happy and prosperous times. Indians and Pakistanis enjoyed well-paid positions and a vibrant social life. I remember my mother being quite the fashionista: whether it was Western suits or Indian *sarees*, she was always beautifully elegant. She cut a striking picture. My sister, although a teenager at the time, was also very fashion-conscious, from fake eyelashes to huge flappers. My father was very fond of taking photographs of his beautiful wife and his daughters. I would never pose though. In every family photograph, my head would be turned the other way. My defiant, free-spirited nature was always right there.

My independent nature was something of a concern for my parents at times. As a two-year-old in our flat in Ajdabia, I decided one day that I was old enough to have my privacy. I decided to lock the bathroom door behind me, despite instructions not to do so. Unfortunately, locking the door for a toddler is a lot easier than opening it. I must have spent an awfully long time in there as I remember an abnormally long, black bathtub. However, I waited calmly, without even a whimper, while the family panicked outside.

Apparently, I was an unusual baby in that I never cried. I find it hard to believe that but everyone swears by it. I was apparently even taken to doctors to see if there was something wrong with me. I was probably just a quieter baby than my older brother, who cried enough to wake the neighbours up. The whole house would spend the evenings rocking and singing him to sleep. The favourite bedtime song was '*Munir Khan bunay ga sadr–i-Pakistan*' (Munir Khan will become President of Pakistan).

I stayed calm that day too, until eventually a young girl from next-door was recruited to climb in through the skylight and open the door from the inside. My parents were relieved, and I wasn't scolded. In fact, I only remember my mother being angry at me on two occasions at most. She didn't need to get angry. She could simply give me or my brother the look, and we would not step out of line. Her weapon of choice for getting us to behave was "I will not speak to you". For me and my brother, that was like a death sentence. It was the end of the world. It was an effective instrument of torture to get us to drink endless glasses of milk or excel in school.

With my own children, I found that my sudden, quiet disappointment worked so much better than persistent nagging or shouting, which generally falls on deaf ears. A talkative woman suddenly going quiet is a very clear sign of danger. I developed this mechanism to avoid saying anything hurtful. By simply allowing myself a few minutes to calm down, I would then be able to return and talk rationally about almost any issue. The kids could immediately recognise and correct their behaviour. Ugly arguments were never my style. Whether it was work issues or relationship issues, it was my style to get into the car and drive away and get it out of my system alone, without witnesses.

My father was a gentle soul, and never even so much as looked at us sternly. I was very much daddy's girl. Throughout his lifetime, I was his partner-in-crime when it came to eating out. My mother always insisted on very bland, healthy food at home, so Daddy and I would have lunch and ice-cream before coming home, but would always be caught because of the telltale signs of ice-cream on my school uniform. My father was popular in Libya too. I recall him being treated with utmost respect at work and in general. There was generally a respect for doctors, and the mere mention of his profession would result in people at car repair shops refusing to take money.

The Libyans were a loving lot, and fond of showering people with gifts. I remember several incidents where a reluctance to accept gifts was met with shock and genuinely hurt feelings. I remember my mother being asked to fill in as a substitute teacher in times when American or British teachers were thrown out. Her students kept bringing expensive gifts that my mother would refuse, resulting in tears. It wasn't only materially that Libyans expressed their love. Our landlords lived in the same compound as our family and an Indian family. They were not only good landlords but treated us like family. On one occasion, my mum came home to find my sister covered in hives and blisters. Apparently, the landlady had been waxing her own daughters with the traditional *halawa* wax (sugaring), and since Sweety was visiting, she got the works too.

Our other next-door neighbours were a Hindu family. The parents were both doctors and they had two boys. An *aya* (nanny) had been brought from India to look after the boys. My independent streak was once again visible as I refused to be kept locked away. One morning in an emergency, my parents left me at home alone for less than half an hour. When Tony and Joy from next door came over to play, they found me locked in the house. Not one to give up, I asked the younger one, Joy, who was about two years old, to crawl under the Venetian style blinds a couple of times to prise them open enough for me to slide out from underneath it. Mission accomplished, we went over to their home to play. We had not intended to stay for very long but soon became so engrossed with the train sets and the Kiri cheese sandwiches that we forgot to go back to my place. Meanwhile, my parents were having the scare of their lives trying to find their missing child. They had checked everywhere except with the next-door neighbours.

Although our Hindu neighbours were secular, I remember the *aya* taking our *arti* and applying *tilak* after her prayers. In addition to teaching us the Quran herself, my mother had taught us about all world religions. My own family were deeply religious Sunni Muslims. Both sides of my family were descendants of Ghurgushtan, the third son of Qais Abdur Rashid, the legendary father of the Pashtuns who brought Islam to our region. Qais is said to have travelled to Medina and been introduced by General Khalid bin Waleed to the Prophet Mohammad (PBUH). The holy Prophet (PBUH) is believed to have given Qais the name Abdul Rashid, the 'servant of the right-minded'. It is widely believed that Qais married Khalid bin Waleed's daughter, Sara, and returned to his birthplace of Zhob on the border between Baluchistan and Khyber Pukhtunkwa. His grave is in the Suleiman Mountains, also called Qais Baba Ghar.

My mother's family are Pannees, an Afghan tribe. They came even before the first Pashtun ruler of India, Behlol Lodhi, arrived in the region. They were asked by Lodhi to support him. They were horse and camel breeders at the time. My father's tribe, the Swatis (originally from Shalman in Afghanistan), came to Swat in the time of Mahmud Ghauri. Later, with Jalal Baba, they ousted the Turks from Hazara at the start of seventeenth century. Swatis have occupied the hills and plains ever since, and are the biggest land-owning group of the Mansehra and Battagram districts. My dad's side is Lughmani Swati, mainly settled in Baffa, Balakot, and Battagram. This Pashto speaking belt is very religious.

My father's family had a tradition of teaching Quran and *Tafseer*. However, being bound to pure Islamic teachings never meant bigotry or insensitivity to other religions or sects. All the women in the family were highly educated. My father's sisters were educated at Aligarh College in Delhi, before the partition of India into two states. It took two days by train from our village in Baffa in the North of Khyber Pukhtunkhwa. Both worked as educationists even before they were married. This progressive attitude meant the children in our family grew up in an environment that was neither bigoted nor intolerant.

To me, acceptance always came naturally. I was in for a shock years later when an older Pakistani lady would say to me, "It's bad enough when they go off with white boyfriends, but how can they go with a black man?" Such attitudes were nowhere near as uncommon as they should have been. Despite being rather dark ourselves, our societies were horribly racist towards blacks and dark-skinned people in our own communities, and perhaps still are. Even my own grandmother, who was a pale redhead herself, would complain if anyone got a touch of a tan or, God forbid, was born dark.

My ability to speak several languages developed through my exposure to several cultures and races from a young age. As the light-complexioned, rather talkative young child of a popular couple, I was spoiled by all in my parents' social circle in the Pakistani communities of Benghazi. The doting adults would teach me songs and jokes, and I would soak it all up. There are tape recordings of me as a three-year-old, telling jokes in Punjabi about *Sardars* (Sikhs), learned from Indian aunties. Punjabi was not my mother tongue, but a clear reminder of how many influences I had. My ability to memorise numbers and verses was enhanced by my mum, who had impressive general knowledge and was a huge fan of poetry. As an eight-year-old, I could recite *Shikwa* and *Jawabi-i-shikwa* by Dr Iqbal, the Ulysses of Urdu poetry.

It seems that someone had also fed me racist and religious bigotry at some point, as I vividly remember once making derogatory comments about Hindu gods while playing with my next-door neighbours. I didn't know what I was saying. My mother gently corrected me by telling bedtime stories of the Prophet Mohammad (PBUH) and his perseverance, even when attacked with stones by his own people.

As a child I required little supervision or rest. I was happy playing on my own with plasticine, or outside on bikes with the boys next-door. There wasn't much in the way of TV viewing in my life, but I do remember being enthralled by the film *The Message*, based on the life of our final prophet Hazrat Mohammad (PBUH). Night after night, I would watch it alone in the dining room where the TV was. I couldn't have been older than four or five. I don't remember watching standard TV or cartoons until I was a teenager. I was lucky to have an imagination, as well as parents who never used the TV as a babysitter. In fact, very few people can claim that they were as privileged as I was when it came to having attentive parents. My multi-talented mother was certainly an inspiration, and she gave us a head start over other children. Birthdays were large, elaborate affairs, and my mother baked the most fantastic cakes imaginable. Everything she did, she did to perfection. These high standards were also expected of us. Not disappointing her was what we cared about most. We would all grow out of it eventually, and she would finally come to accept that life is not about being perfect. To be imperfect is to be unique.

Money was good, and the quality of life was even better. If it hadn't been for my older sister growing up so quickly, my parents would have had no intention of returning. But, like it is with most expats, getting the daughter married off was a major motivating factor. My father wanted to move to England, but mum only liked it as a shopping destination. She persuaded him to move back to Pakistan instead.

One of my prized possessions in Libya was a shoebox of arts and crafts. It had bits and bobs and all sorts, with green shining foil crescents that I had cut out. In my excitement for our move, I had used the pieces of green and white to make the Pakistani flag. However, despite promises that it had been packed too, it was left behind. I could not tolerate that I had been lied to. I remember driving my mother mad with my persistent nagging to find those materials again. There is a strict code of conduct among Pashtuns (known as *Pukhunwali*) that ties us to high standards of hospitality and friendship. For deception, it advocates a fitting revenge. It may have been a small thing but, true to my roots, I did not forgive my parents for years for deceiving me.

Life in Pakistan should have been perfect. My mother had built her dream home in the city of Peshawar, right next door to the sister she had missed so much. This was the city where she had gone to college. But things were different now under the military dictatorship of Zia ul Haq. His involvement in the American war against the USSR in Afghanistan had literally changed the scenery. Afghan refugees were everywhere. For the elite, these poor people were destroying the peace of their leafy suburbs. We conveniently forgot that they were homeless because of us Pakistanis fighting the American war in Afghanistan. I remember buying cheese and oil from CSD (military stores) clearly stamped '*For Afghan Refugees - Not for resale*'. I also found a lovely friend in an Afghan refugee called Roohia. She told me the horrific story of how they had escaped the bombing in the middle of the night, and how the cash they stuffed into their socks was destroyed as they waded through water to reach safety.

Meanwhile, my mum and dad would have their only argument ever in front of me over the height of the boundary wall. My mother had built a 5-foot wall with decorative gaps in the middle. But the culture of the 80s was tilting more towards *purdah*. My mother eventually had to give in, and the wall was raised to a height of nine feet around the entire property, which had become the norm in those days. She brought it up resentfully every so often for years to come. She felt that her home had been turned into an ugly oppressive fort.

I had to deal with my own mini culture shock. Like many expat children, I refused to eat the local produce and dairy because of the unfamiliar smell and appearance. My weight loss was a huge concern for my family. But even to a child the differences between prosperous Libya and regressive Pakistan were so obvious. In fact, one of the first observations I had made about the country that my parents had missed so much was, "Your Pakistan is so *toota phoota* [broken]".

The Pakistan that they had returned to was crumbling, but the cracks were just beginning to appear.

§

We had left my shiny foil stars behind in Libya to come over to be with my older sister and brother, who had been sent to live with my mum's parents earlier. They had been in boarding schools in Malta, and as my sister blossomed into a stunning teenager, the decision to send her back to Pakistan was made. My brother was also packed off to live with my mother's parents. The move from Irish Catholic schooling straight into Pakistani culture meant the youngsters had to do a lot of unlearning, and a lot of quick cramming of new rules.

One major difference between Western and Eastern societies can be found in the terminology for close family members. In our society, there are several unique words that are used to display our affection to each other that go beyond the straightforward English terms of brother, sister, aunt, uncle, grandmother, grandfather, etc. We are accustomed to adding these kinds of terms to the end of everything, so that everyone receives this kind of respect. People we don't even know will have something simple like *Sahab* or *Sahiba* added to the end of their name (meaning sir/ma'am or Mr/Mrs). But for those we know and love, many more terms become available to us. Our people have ended up with a lot of different names for each other, borne out of respect and love. The suffix *–jee* (or alternatively *–jaan*) is a form of endearment reserved for those we hold dear. In fact, we are taught to refer to grown-ups as auntie or uncle even if they are not blood relatives.

There are several other terms too, like *chacha*, *chachi*, *taya*, *tayi*, *appa*, *appi*, *bhai*, *bhabhi*, etc. While I am a *khala* to my sisters's children, I am a *phuphi* to my brother's children, while my brother is a *mamoo* to our kids (and his wife a *mami*). The intricate system is further complicated by the fact that we will address random people as *bhai* or *baji* (meaning brother or sister) as a sign of respect. It was something my kids would find overwhelming but amusing. Major exceptions to this complicated set of titles were my parents, who both took ownership of more distinctive and easy nicknames. My father was known as Daddy to most of us, while my mother took on Barimummy (meaning the Big Mummy), inheriting the moniker from her own mother. Perhaps they were trying to be trendier than virtually everyone else in the world by not accepting some variation of grandfather and grandmother.

My grandfather, Dr Sher Bahadur Khan Pannee (who shared a striking resemblance with President field marshal General Ayub Khan) was considered a rather eligible bachelor, and was fondly known to all as Khanjee. He was the only son of an affluent Pashtun family, and a direct descendant of the Munir Khani tribe. His light complexion and hazel eyes added to his desirability. The local families were to be disappointed however, as the young doctor chose to marry a beautiful girl from Kasur, in Punjab. She was also from a Pashtun family belonging to the tribe of Batakzai from Kandahar, who had settled in the small hamlet of Kot Haleem Khan in Kasur. Everyone came to know her as Beejee.

The very pale-skinned Beejee of the Punjab had a classic oval face, with serenity reminiscent of the Mona Lisa. She belonged to a very rich, highly educated family, and was admired for her sophistication. My grandfather was a regular visitor to their house in his quest for knowledge of Islam and history. However, this marriage would produce no children, and an heir was vital for the Munir Khanis to continue their bloodline. (My grandfather was one of only two children, with his only sibling, a beautiful sister, having died of tuberculosis in her youth). After years of fighting off coordinated pressure from the rather authoritative mother and an insistent family, my Khanjee finally gave in. On the insistence of the family (and with the permission of his first wife), he entered into a second marriage to secure an heir.

This was what my sister Sweety was exposed to when she was sent to Pakistan. Her diaries from her time there are hilarious. The young teenager (who had been brought up overseas, away from family in a rather Western setting) quickly had to ditch her jeans for the loose *shalwar-kameez* that my grandfather preferred. The poor tailor would get horribly confused, as the teenager mimed to him to ignore my conservative grandfather's strict instructions to keep the outfits baggy and shapeless. Despite the strict atmosphere, she fell in love with the noisy households of Pakistan, and the extended families and staff. Later in life, Sweety would be working as a gender trainer. It surprised me that she would look back and describe the setup of my grandfather's home (with his two wives) so positively. When I'd ask her specific questions about her time there, she wouldn't be very helpful. Her response to every question was, "It was great, I loved it! The food was great! The people were great! Khanjee was great!"

The rather young second wife, Saadat Sultan, was my biological grandmother, but in our family, Beejee was always treated like a mother too, and was deeply respected by all the family. This was also encouraged by my grandmother (my own Barimummy). Sweety remembers how well the two wives got on with each other, describing them as close friends in a happy and harmonious home atmosphere. My mother, one of six children, had often told us how they all looked up to Beejee, who was full of wisdom and knowledge. Her status was never diminished in the household.

My Barimummy entrusted her first child, Iqbal Khan Pannee, to Beejee as soon as he was born. Beejee encouraged her own sister's marriage to a cousin of her husband. Her sister's children were considered very much part of the family too. Her niece was later married to the son of my uncle, Justice Abdul Hakeem Khan. It seems that the families had a positive experience, and further matrimonial matches within them were encouraged. However, besides my own marriage, there were no other unions with first cousins in the family, predominately due to an awareness of the possibility of genetic abnormalities.

The two ladies were poles apart. Beejee was an avid reader but loved her beauty routines too. My mother learned more about literature and skincare from her than her own mother. She fondly recalled how Beejee never went to bed without moisturising her feet. Beejee was very fond of wearing heavy jewellery and staying bedecked. Her *pazaibs* (anklets) were individually about 12 *tolas* (4 ounces) in weight. One of her beautiful *dawni* (headpieces) was given to my mother for her wedding, and handed down to Sweety. My Barimummy on the other hand, was a typical busy mum to six, with no time or inclination towards personal care. A tub of Nivea was all she used, and that too very rarely. The tall young woman had the added responsibility of a huge household, with an army of staff and extended family. And yet, the two wives of Dr Sher Bahadur Khan shared a lifelong friendship. Although much younger than Beejee, my own grandma survived her by only a year. Beejee's funeral was lovingly arranged by my Barimummy. According to my sister, a lot of credit went to Khanjee for maintaining fair and equal treatment of his wives, as prescribed by Islam.

Additionally, my Khanjee was known for helping the destitute, and a lot of widows and orphans were financially supported by him. This was very much a tradition his own mother had set. Although a very strict disciplinarian, his mother was a very loving and giving woman. My mother's nanny had been rescued as a young child from being sold into slavery. Bebe was of an Afridi origin, and soon became the overriding authority in the house. From housekeeping to managing finances, there wasn't much she could not do. Bebe was never treated like a servant. She was duly married off but chose to continue to live and work for us. She was given a generous piece of land near the main home, and her children were supported through high education. Today, they are professionals just like our own family members.

I was quite fond of Bebe. She had a habit of bringing me lots of colourful necklaces from her shopping trips. But she became my superhero after one incident. It was the evening, after my grandmother's funeral. My mum had fainted in her grief as usual, and I was (of course) the nurse. As I looked up, I saw Bebe approach us. She was holding a long wooden pole like a spear in her hand. Her tiny eyes glittered in the dimly lit room. She held her finger to her lips so I'd stay quiet. Like a Zulu warrior, in one swift movement she aimed at the corner of the bedhead and struck hard. My mum sat up, startled. We both looked down at the stone floor to see a viper, cut into two pieces. Bebe did not mess around.

The big kitchen was always full, and my chatty sister was often told off by my mother for sitting in the kitchen with the staff. It was a habit Sweety would maintain for the rest of her life; she was forever pampering the children of her staff like they were her own grandchildren. There was never any concept of inequality in our homes, and these have always been inherited values. One day, I would find myself with my own staff and household, and I would discover that my disregard and distaste for collecting wealth and assets would keep my staff worrying for me. There was a time when my cleaner came back from her holiday and delivered her mother's message to me: fire all the staff, move into a smaller property, and keep only one maid for myself. They felt that I should build a house for myself and save for my old age. I laughed and said, "How much older do you think I am likely to get? So far, so good".

My grandfather outlived both his wives, and remained mobile right to the end. Perhaps the wives became good friends because Khanjee spent much of his time studying and writing. His rather voluminous *'Tareekh-i-Hazara'* is considered the most authoritative historical account of our region of Hazara. He encouraged me to write to him, and the response would be full of corrections. Not only were grammatical errors not permitted, but ideas were expected to be refined too.

Regretfully, I had very little interaction with my mother's parents. They lived predominately in Abbottabad in their old age, and my grandfather's last days were in my aunt's home. Sweety however, enjoyed a close relationship with my maternal side, and was the apple of their eye. The first born in the family had the privilege of growing up around my uncles and aunts, who adored her. My mother would tell me of the huge picnics, with all the kids packed into the Dodge. My grandfather liked his cars, and it was important to get the new executive car in the market on his driveway. Sweety recalls an Opel Rekord in the 70s, as well as a red Volkswagen Beetle that was bought for my youngest aunt (and is still parked in one of the huge garages in Abbottabad).

The family had close friendships with the British, dating back to pre-partition days. Major Abbott, the first Deputy Commissioner of Hazara District (1849 to 1853), gave a certificate and an estate to the Chief of Paniah, Qaim Khan, who was my grandfather's great-uncle. He wrote fondly that Qaim Khan (along with his brothers, sons, and nephews) stood by his side throughout like his right hand. '*The chief of Paniah, Qaim Khan, demonstrated great courage and exhibited loyalty in the battle of 1949 against the Sikhs*,' he wrote, before continuing with '*Qaim Khan is a generous man and well respected in the whole district. I am parting with great sadness and regret in my heart with this loyal friend of mine*'.

The furniture, Royal Doulton china, and huge collection of rifles displayed around the towering property on Police Line Road were constant reminders of the close association with the British Raj. After serving as the Director of Health, the doctor retired as Deputy Inspector General of Jails in 1956. He continued to practice from his clinic, *Dar us Shifa* (House of Healing), in his home for several years afterwards. People still say that he was the finest surgeon of his time. His clinic was fascinating, with its classic-style laboratory of huge glass beakers and jars. He eventually turned his attention to tracing his roots, and his writing reflects his personal turmoil as he served the government while supporting the cause of a separate homeland for Muslims.

The anglicised influence was unshakeable for much of the family. His own two uncles emigrated to the U.S., and his only first cousin (born to an Italian mother in America) used the name Robert Joffrey instead of his Muslim name. He was the founder of the Joffrey Ballet, the first dance company to perform at the White House, at Jacqueline Kennedy's invitation. It went onto become the first ballet company to appear on American television, the first classical dance company to use multimedia, the first to create a ballet set to rock music, the first to appear on the cover of Time magazine, and the first company to have had a major motion picture based on it (Robert Altman's *The Company*).

My own three uncles chose to settle outside Pakistan. They maintained no links with the country. It was quite ironic really. Munir Khani wanted heirs so that their name would persist and their lands would be retained. But those heirs chose never to claim their inheritance or their family name. In fact, my older uncle Iqbal, who is more of a friend to me than an older relative, was very vocal with his concerns about my decision to return to Pakistan in later years. The accidents, heartbreak and insults I continually faced were to cause him further pain and anxiety. My older brother Munir, named after our valiant ancestor, would ask me how I coped with the problems in Pakistan.

I smiled and said, "I cope happily".

To me, such things were not problems, but challenges. Life is like an ECG. As long as there are highs and lows, we are alive. When it goes flat, death is pronounced. As the poet Ghalib would say, *"Moht sey pehley zindagi ghum sey nijaat paye kyun?* (Before death, how can life be free of worry?)".

It didn't have to be a male heir. It didn't have to be someone named Munir Khan who would tell the world of our bloodline and our tradition. The heir never needed to own lands or wield a sword. It could be a woman with no assets. All that was required was a woman who loved her roots, and conquered with her smile.

§

My brother had always found it difficult to adjust to life in Pakistan. Even as a young kid the arrangement wasn't working for him, so my parents were forced to move back earlier than they had initially planned. Sweety was stunning and marriage proposals had begun to pour in from a young age. After moving to Pakistan, I found myself interrogating suitors on a daily basis. I remember one eager young man trying to get inside info from me. "Can I ask you something?" he said, putting on the charm. I responded dryly, "You can ask all you want. I can choose not to answer".

Some of them never quite recovered from the questioning of this young, budding journalist, while others tried to buy me off with chocolates and comics. I was building up an impressive stash of *Archie* and *Richie Rich* comics but, needless to say, the bribes didn't work. I was never the type to care for 'gifts'. This was something that would continue to be true decades later. My loyalties couldn't be bought by material offerings. Love, of course, was different. I could give my life for love. That was the Pashtun way.

Ironically, after the huge push to get her married, my sister refused to say yes to anyone. There were *rishtas* (proposals) from nearly all the provinces, and a few from other nationalities too. She remained unmoved and focused on her graduation from Jinnah College for Women in Peshawar. She also completed a few semesters of Masters in Microbiology from Quaid-i-Azam University, Islamabad, and a few other courses besides, but she couldn't settle on her Prince Charming.

My father, brother and I found the almost-daily arguments between my mum and my sister emotionally draining. My arrival in the family, and the ultra-lenient attitude of my parents towards me, also wasn't appreciated by Sweety. My mother had been pushed into parenthood at a young age, and hadn't exactly built the best of relationships with her firstborn as a result. She was a teenager when she gave birth to Sweety, but had been in her thirties when she had me. She had clearly been cutting her teeth with the first child. She was an experienced parent by the time I arrived. My mum made me promise that I would never put her through the same thing when I navigated my own teenage years. I kept that promise, but made up for it in my adulthood instead.

The huge age gap between my siblings and I, as well as the fear of risking my mother's displeasure, meant I learned never to argue. To this day, I prefer to walk away instead of having a long, drawn-out confrontation. For a lot of my childhood I remember apologising profusely on behalf of my sister just to calm things down. My sister found me to be a very irritating presence as I was her polar opposite. People have always had trouble coping with my endless energy. Sweety would return from college and flop in the afternoon heat of Peshawar, only to be disturbed by the sound of me roller-skating up and down the long driveway. The afternoon sun couldn't deter me from play. She describes me as a constant noisy presence, and her complaints aroused little sympathy from my mum.

My level of activity required a lot of sugar. Everyone in my family has always had an incurable sweet tooth. I was always after some kind of snack, and there would be no biscuit jar in the house that I left full. My mother would make sure everyone got equal servings of ice cream, putting her aptitude for mathematics to good use when dividing the slab into five perfect pieces. Like normal humans, we would all eat our puddings when served. Except Sweety. She would hoard hers away, and it would torture me for days. Chocolates that were given to my brother and I were finished in a matter of seconds, while Sweety's would build into an impressive stash. Naturally, in the interest of making space in the freezer, and to save the chocolates from reaching their expiry date, I would lend a helping hand here and there. This would be met with blood-curdling screams from my older sister. The poor girl was expected to be the understanding older sibling.

There must have been a lot of pent-up anger toward me, the little monster. Indeed, one day when my parents were away and she was left to babysit, I received a resounding slap across the face (the only time I was ever smacked as a child!). Sweety recalls that the rest of that day was spent in terrible anxiety that I would tell on her. I never did, of course. I sometimes wonder if it might have been my annoying presence that finally led Sweety to go for marriage.

She finally settled on the most unlikely of candidates: a recommendation from my dad's sister of a family of apparently similar circumstances. The family had lived in Libya and England and the boy's father was an ENT surgeon, like my dad. The family was originally from Haripur but had settled in Rawalpindi. The term most flippantly used in Pakistan is the rather vague '*sharif*', which means 'respectable' when it comes to describing how suitable a prospective suitor's family is. In most cases, it means that the family is of the same sect and has money.

Even as a young adolescent, I could see how dramatically different this family was from ours. I quite liked their *desi nature*. In stark contrast to the reserved, ladylike demeanour of my mother, the mother-in-law seemed like Mrs Bennet from *Pride and Prejudice*. They were loud, expressive and different. The young man himself was nothing special. Nobody could quite see what Sweety saw in Khalid because he was not exactly God's gift to womankind in looks or personality. According to her, she liked him because he paid her no attention at all, unlike the rest of the world drooling at her feet. She would find out pretty soon what it was like to live with a man who never praises but is liberal with criticism.

Khalid was a wonderful big brother to me as he was to his own sisters, but with his wife, his behaviour left a lot to be desired. In private, he was affectionate to her, but in public he was aloof and distant. He clearly could not handle living with an exceptionally beautiful woman. He would demonstrate his insecurities through many snide and sarcastic jibes, even in front of me. Sweety would put up with his sarcasm, his violent mood swings, and even his reluctance to work for years on end. However, she would eventually give up and start to work as a schoolteacher to pay for her children's education and retain her sanity. Like many Pakistani parents, they stayed together for the children. When the boys left home, they separated.

Khalid died soon after, at the rather young age of 52. A three-minute cardiac arrest ended his rather uneventful life. Their youngest, Yousaf, was alone to deal with it all, as the older two brothers were now overseas. Yousaf was deeply affected by this sudden loss. He had to quickly grow into the young man his father had never been. He took on the responsibility of looking after his grieving grandmother and managing her affairs singlehandedly.

My nephew took after me. He also knew something about having to step up and take charge of a difficult situation in order to survive.

Chapter 2

The summer of 1985 was memorable. The twelve-year-old was finally allowed to move into a room of her own. Not only had this long-awaited independence been granted, but my passion for performance was finally being channelled, as I had managed to bag a children's show.

Almost a year earlier, a female producer at the only television network, PTV, had spotted me in a stage play produced by my mother for a women's charity in the Peshawar Club for the army. So impressed was Bushra Rafiq by my performance that she tracked me down and asked me in for an audition for a new puppet show she was launching on the state TV station. She had previously worked with the comedian, puppeteer and genius Farooq Qaiser. They needed a presenter for a children's program.

Bushra had seen me play the lead role in full makeup and ball gown. When I turned up in a frock and a ponytail, she was taken aback. They had been looking for a young lady, not a child. I wasn't even a very girly kind of girl. With an adoring older brother that I idolised, I was more likely to be seen with war paint on my face pretending to be Native American, fighting imaginary battles in the Wild West, rather than playing with dolls or experimenting with makeup. Nevertheless, she gave me a passage from a children's storybook to read out and I read it my way. People say that when I tell a story, I do it not only with the voices of the characters, but with full expression and complete immersion. Bushra was very creative when it came to using talent, and she fought the TV bosses for me to get the presenter position.

When I turned up on the set, I was given a *dupatta* to wear on top of the dress I wore, and was then caked in makeup. I was twelve but looked a lot older. In fact, I didn't look too different at twelve from how I would look at 44, but of course I lost the softness that the adipose layer gave me. I was a nightmare for the makeup artists as I hated makeup (especially eye makeup). I was an even bigger challenge for the PTV Urdu scriptwriters: I couldn't read Urdu very well and the big words just sounded wrong, so I improvised. It wasn't the prescribed Urdu for television. It was contemporary and anglicised, but the audience loved it. The catchphrase that became popular at the time was the result of me simply being my chirpy self on set. On the first day, the chief puppeteer (to keep me alert) sang out my nickname.

"Ms Reeeeeeeeeeeeema!"

I smiled and immediately sang back 'Jeeeeeee haan'. It was only a playfully affirmative response; a simple elongated and melodious "Yes!" But it quickly became popular with audiences and developed into something of catchphrase.

The long words and long recordings were not easy for a fidgety child, but the seniors kept me engaged with off-air gaffes and a constant stream of biscuits, a tradition which continues to this day. If you want Ms. Khan to stay chirpy, keep the biscuits coming!

I had positive and protective encounters with the adults I worked with on PTV. I discovered that one of the producers, the late Farukh Bashir *Sahab*, was so fatherly that he kept all the fan mail away from me since most of it was from boys. My mother would keep a hawk-like eye on the proceedings from the far end of the studio. She spent her entire summer chaperoning me, which I never realized or gave her credit for until much later. However, despite being a diligent and hyper-aware parent, she did not know that the risks to our children are far greater than we can comprehend. She perhaps felt that media was full of predators, so she was vigilant in TV studios. But in actual fact, abusers come in all sorts of guises.

Children in Pakistan are often sexually abused by home help, and it is still overlooked by lazy or status-conscious parents. Having a maid or a helper for your child is a symbol of prestige. Some slightly more concerned parents may employ older children to look after their young ones, and with no idea of the huge risk of not only accidents, but also of sexual exposure by those youngsters. The concept of paedophilia was alien to us while we were growing up. Often, our parents, in an effort to not pollute our minds, leave us unprotected to the dangers that we are exposed to as children.

My mother had always encouraged my performing abilities and, since I was a keen singer, she sent me for musical training at the established Abbasin Arts

Council in Peshawar. It was a group activity with other children and several musicians in a hall. From all angles, it could be regarded as a safe activity. The unsuspecting, carefree nine-year-old, who was a confident performer and the daughter of the President of the Children's Academy, was given preferential treatment by the boss. Everyone respected him. After all, he was an educated professional. I had been brought up with strict expectations of politeness and manners towards adults. To this day, that politeness is a burden, as I find it hard to get rid of people who may be boring me to death. I find it difficult to cut meetings short. But our children must be taught to NOT be polite if they feel uncomfortable.

There was something about this 'Uncle' which made me uneasy, but I could not fully comprehend what it was. After successfully evading offers of biscuits in his office, I was to discover why I did not like him on what is known as Iqbal Day. That day, our group was performing to a hall full of literary intellectuals at the Pearl Continental Hotel in Peshawar. The 'Uncle' came to get me from the ground floor, where we were all getting ready for the performance, and told me he was taking me upstairs to the hall as it was running late. He had brought me a bar of chocolate. I took the chocolate from the balding and ageing bureaucrat and walked with him to the lift. It was too short a walk to the lift for the nine-year-old to plan an escape. As we stepped into the lift, my sense of unease increased. As the doors closed, he asked, "Why do you think I like you so much?"

"Perhaps because you have no children of your own?" I responded.

"Why, you clever little girl" he said

The next 30 seconds would haunt me for years.

He bent down, and I felt his mouth on my lips. The thought of it makes my skin crawl to this day. It was such an awful feeling that I have to physically shake the image from my head even as I recall it. The image of that creepy man, with his afro-style frizzy hair at the back of his balding head, is etched into my memory. We need to tell parents and children that paedophiles come in suits too.

Fortunately for me, the lift opened on the first floor. It was a brief moment of violation that tortured me for years. I went on to perform in the tableau with not a step out of place, but I gave up my singing lessons forever. I did not know what had happened. I had no name for it, but I knew that it was very wrong and that I had to protect myself from it, and from him. I could not talk to any adult about it. The shame of what had happened was too much to confess. I was lucky that I could choose where I wanted to go and put my foot down, but many children may not have that liberty. They may not be able to avoid their maths or religious studies lessons because of strict parents. Do they have anyone they can talk to?

As an adult, I would actively campaign for this, in any way I could. This deep desire to protect children was rooted in another change. In the summer of 1985, I discovered another trait of mine: how much I loved babies. My first baby was my first nephew, Abubakr Khan, who arrived in August. With him arrived my chance to be a parent, and it would seem parenting came naturally to me. We were waiting at home when we got the news. As we reached the hospital, I saw my brother-in-law, Khalid *bhai*, sitting on the stairs of the hospital. It seemed as if the tall man had shrunk. I put a reassuring hand on his shoulder and felt him shivering. I went upstairs and the doctor pointed out Abubakr to me. He was the baby with the oblong head, thumb sucking noisily. I immediately bonded to him.

Nothing was difficult or scary for me. I took care of everything from clipping nails to giving him medicine. Abubakr and I became inseparable over the years; he was the younger sibling I had so desperately wanted. It not only prepared me for single-parenting, but reinforced my identity as a mother early on in life. I would be blessed with seven nephews, all of whom I am extremely close to. Along with my three children, they make my core circle of friends to this day. We tend to hang out together, and I end up assuming the role of agony aunt, quite literally.

People have often described me as ambitious, but my teachers always described me as uncompetitive. My goal in life was never to defeat others. I never cared who came first. What mattered more to me was achieving what I had set for myself, and moving forward as a person. I didn't have my eye on marks; I cared more about reading the book from the beginning to the end. Knowing everything was my motivation. Unlike the other girls, I never memorised past papers and the pre-prepared answers within them. Instead, I understood what I was studying. I wanted to learn.

Running after material success leaves people empty and unhappy. The diamond ring you must have for your hand will only put distance between you and your friends and will never give you a nice warm hug. Unlike sportsmen, winning medals and positions was immaterial to me. I wanted to win genuine respect and love, hoping to have just a few people around me who I could laugh with over cups of coffee and cake. Be wary of sycophants: they are boring and will never give good advice. Power-hungry, egotistical people are only ever surrounded by even greedier subordinates, who will all jump ship the minute the one they are on shows signs of sinking. We, as parents and society, put too much emphasis on achievement. We teach our kids that the love they receive is conditional: '*Bring me a trophy and I will love you more*'. My mother could be described as one of those parents, who wanted us to bring back medals. But it was my father's quiet influence, expecting nothing more of us than to be good and happy, that crushed her long list of material expectations.

After my three-month stint on TV, I was nominated for '*Best Child Star*' in the 6th PTV Awards. The award went to a three-year-old drama artist. She was the daughter of the famous TV star Laila Zuberi. Since I was not from a media family, it was great fun to rub shoulders with the TV stars we had watched from afar. While I looked around wide-eyed at the glamorous celebrities, my mother was focused on winning. I never understood her anger and disappointment at the result. I was secretly hoping to win of course, but not winning didn't affect me much. In fact, I learnt an important life lesson: that at times we really will want certain things or outcomes to go our way. But if and when they don't, and time passes, we will almost always look back on them and smile at just how worked up we'd got ourselves. Because nothing really matters. One day, you might be desperately waiting for someone's phone call or text. But with the passing of just a few months, you will realise that you managed to not only live without it, but also that whatever it was you were so hell-bent on getting (be it a person, job or anything else) probably just doesn't appeal to you anymore. It is absolutely true that life has better things planned for you than anything you can imagine. The only condition is that you persevere, preferably with a smile. Keep moving on from every disappointment with renewed hope, because things will get better. They always do.

My brief stint on TV as a child star meant that I had more friends almost overnight. The preceding years had been dominated by bullying from classmates and patronising comments from teachers. On one occasion, in year 5, I was embarrassed in class by Nadia for using the word 'object'. She insisted that the word did not exist in English. Everyone laughed at me. I burst into tears, more upset at her betrayal. The teachers were another issue. One of the biggest problems was that they would show blatant favouritism towards kids of politicians. The Saifullah family dominated local politics and business at the time. However, the Saifullah girls were lovely and humble considering they were surrounded by sycophancy. I didn't really think too deeply about it, but looking back, I was able to clearly see and understand how people's attitudes could change when you stumbled across fortune and fame. I was a happy-go-lucky child, and quite a late developer, with no interest in boys or romance until much later in life. Other girls would talk about boys and use sexual innuendos in conversation, which I struggled to understand.

I was always pretty naive when it came to boys. One day on the TV set, a young boy I had just interviewed walked over from across the large studio and pretended to pick up a book from the coffee table on the set. Without looking at me directly, he whispered, "Hello, how are you doing?" Decent girls did not talk to boys in this kind of society. It was definitely frowned upon. I was taken aback and gave him my trademark raised eyebrow. He didn't try it again. I didn't really get it but my inner moral police didn't like this covert behaviour much. My mother, for all her Westernised appearance, had given us very puritanical values, so I had a very uneventful teenage life. Working on the TV series not only taught me discipline, but I learned to apply makeup early on. I became so good that I ended up doing bridal makeup for everyone in our social circle, and became a pro at waxing, eyebrow shaping and hair styling. My mum found it very annoying that I would be spending so much time and energy making others look good, while ignoring my own appearance. My best friend Nadia had golden brown hair thanks to her Danish mother, but since both of us had spent all summer in the pool, the chlorine had ruined her hair. Every day for a couple of months after school, I would put an egg mask on her hair. The careful approach paid off, and soon the whole of Peshawar was raving about her glorious mane.

Nadia and I had a long, complicated relationship our entire lives. It all started when my mother cast me as Snow White in a charity performance, and Nadia was made to play the wicked queen. She was amazing, but I don't think she ever forgave me for taking the main role. My mother had painstakingly choreographed the whole thing, but her nepotism cost me a couple of years of resentment in school. It took a few years for us to finally become *BFFs*. By the summer of 1985, Nadia and I were officially best friends. Outside of school, we had been inseparable from day one, but the friendship would be unpredictable with long gaps in between, much like my TV career.

The TV makeup that I hated had caused another unforeseen problem. I looked much older than I was, and as the fan mail increased, so did my extended family's objections to a girl from our family being on the TV. I was told that it was drawing criticism from, and for, the family. I was told I would have to stop...so I did. I stopped working on TV, and stopped talking to all men, regardless of their age. I attributed the situation to men in our society, so I put a self-imposed ban on any communication with men. This meant that if anyone had even a remote interest in me, I would never find out. Decades later, my male buddies would tell me how men were scared of approaching me, which had resulted in very few offers of a romantic nature over the course of my life. Truth be told, I married everyone who pursued me, apart from one (who I very nearly married).

My teenage years were uneventful as far as romance was concerned. However, my theoretical knowledge of sex meant I would be holding court during recess. It all started when I got my period very late and no one had told me about it, so I walked down to the British Council library and obtained a book called *How To Tell Your Child About Sex*. I understood that my mother, for all her liberal appearance, could not bring herself to talk about delicate issues like biological changes and sex, so I handled it myself. I had no idea what sanitary napkins looked like so decided to make my own. It helped to be in a surgeon's household. My mother found out a few months later and I still remember her words: "*Beta*, if you don't tell mummy then who are you going to tell?"

And that was it. A pack of sanitary napkins in the bathroom would be waiting for me, and the birds and bees talk was never revisited. There was a reason for me becoming a Miss-Know-It-All. I had to know it all because I had to do it all myself. It would always be like that.

I educated myself about everything from conception to contraceptives to contraindications. All this knowledge was then imparted during recess to a willing audience. The girls had nicknamed me *Mor* (Pashto for mother). The lecture would be based on medical and accurate information, and delivered responsibly in a matter-of-fact fashion with no girly giggles. I recall taking a condom to school one day in Year 9 at the insistence of the hungry followers of my sex education class. My father used to hold free medical camps for the Afghan refugees, and I stumbled on a huge carton of condoms in his cupboard. As kids, I remember blowing them up as balloons, blissfully unaware of their intended use. Now, armed with the knowledge of that enlightening book, I opened the pack to a wide-eyed audience. We measured the length with a ruler, which was perhaps not advisable. As a result, I think we all agreed to remain celibate, and never to have sex, ever. Eventually, a defector from the group informed our form teacher, and I was called in for an explanation. I, of course, had a valid, logical answer ready and prepared. My mitigating skills were exceptional as always, and I convinced Miss Leena that this was something she should have done for us.

I found that the Irish Catholic sisters of the convent were far more conservative than even our Pakistani parents. We were not allowed to wear makeup or jewellery. No fashion or showbiz magazines were to be brought into school. We were not allowed to chew gum, even on the school bus. We were also subjected to regular random raids to confiscate romance novels like the popular *Mills and Boons*. My other unofficial best friend, Sauda (who has been wonderfully supportive all my life), was a keen reader of the *M&B* books, and when the gang got into any trouble in this regard, I would be the one relied upon to come up with an exit strategy. I was Sister Jacinta's library assistant, and she knew my reading habits well. I had never cared for trashy romance novels. I was obsessed with reading philosophy, political historical novels or biographies. From Confucius to *Mein Kampf,* I had read them all.

So, on that rather cold January day, when the sisters decided on a surprise raid, as the least likely suspect I knew straight away I wouldn't be scrutinised nearly as much as the others. When asked to leave our bags and walk out empty-handed from our classrooms, I quickly ripped open the lining of the coats of our tall basketball team-members and stashed the novels inside. We got away with it. The way a whole year's subscription of *Mills and Boons* somehow disappeared from the Year 10 classroom would forever remain a secret!

Ironically, though our parents and general society did not want us to know about our bodies or sex, two of us were married off that very year. In the next two years, all of our core group would be married, including the most unlikely candidate...me.

§

My father would enter the house smiling and offer greetings in his loud booming voice.

"*Asslam-u-alikaum jor takra khushaal*!" (Hello! Is everyone hale, hardy and hearty?)

We all would rush to greet him. He always came back home in a good mood, with confectionery in his hands. It could be coconut macaroons or traditional *jalebis*. He was seldom empty handed.

My father always addressed my mother as "Darling", which was surprising for my brother's wife. Even more shocking was the fact that he would greet his wife with a kiss when returning from a trip. This was also rather unusual in Pakistani culture, where affection towards spouses is restrained and frowned upon. Conversely, my future father-in-law would routinely be 'effing and blinding' at my mother-in-law right in front of us at the dinner table. Tears would rush to my eyes at her being humiliated in front of her daughter-in-law.

I have no memory of Daddy ever coming in saying he was tired or under stress - a rather surprising notion considering his life as a busy ENT surgeon with a diligent, old-style bedside manner. He would always be available to patients after carrying out an operation. It was only when I started working that I realised how amazing it was that he had managed to stay in a great mood for his family after those long, exhausting days.

In stark contrast to this, my father-in-law never once replied to a greeting or *salaam* from his children or daughters-in-law. I found it strange that my father-in-law (known to everyone as Major *Sahab* because he took early retirement), would pick up a long-distance phone call and not bother to reply. He would simply grunt and pass the phone to his wife. Even on our arrival from England in the holidays, he would simply unlock the front door, turn on his heel, and proceed back to his bedroom. There were no hugs, smiles or greetings.

My brother ended up being very much like my father used to be. He too had an air of authority about him generally, but with the women in the family he always had a gentle tone and a kind smile. I never once heard him shout in the home. Men who can face the world bravely do not need to raise their decibel level or their hand to a woman. They need no validation that they are man enough.

I was very much Daddy's proverbial princess, and thoroughly spoilt. My father would return from his morning prayers at the mosque and tap on my bedroom window to wake me for *Fajr*. Like most teenagers, I wasn't exactly a morning person. I would just dream that I had woken up and was praying. My mum always knew that I needed a second reminder, and would call out my name to get me to jump out of bed. On weekdays, it was usually just Daddy and I at the breakfast table, since we had an earlier start. I couldn't stand the smell of milk and egg yolks, and refused to eat breakfast cooked by the staff. But after several lectures on the importance of a good breakfast, I resolved the conflict by learning to make perfectly-scrambled eggs, egg custard and pancakes from scratch. Breakfasts on the weekends meant all of the family together. It was a jolly time with noisy chatting and an endless supply of buttered toast.

My Daddy made it a rule to personally take me to and from school. I was only ever picked up by a driver once in my entire school life. There was an awareness and a conscious effort not to leave children alone with staff. I would find my dad's cheerful demeanour quite annoying that early in the morning. Daddy was obsessive about personal hygiene and spent ages showering. My mum referred to the bathroom as his natural habitat. His arrival would be preceded by his perfume and cologne. He was always clean and always happy. He would sit behind the wheel, say his travel prayer, and then drive, peppering the journey with subtle life lessons. The pre-adolescent would be rolling her eyes as Daddy gently smiled and said, "Smile in the morning, smile all day". I would live by that beautiful adage my entire life.

The drive back home would start with Daddy buying us ice-cream cones. The swirls of chocolate and vanilla ice-cream dipped in melted chocolate would melt in seconds in the Peshawar heat. The daily treats would also include rotisserie-roasted lemon-garlic chicken. The final stop would be at the tandoor. I would happily munch on the crispy hot-baked wholemeal *dodai* bread all the way home.

As I'd sneak into the house I would inevitably be caught by my mum. She'd go through her horror at seeing my uniform covered in tell-tale ice cream stains and immediately turn on my dad. She would complain that he was spoiling me rotten and that she was worried for my future. She was right to be: I grew up believing all men were like him. But no man I ever met loved me like my Daddy did.

§

By Year 8, I had established my reputation as a performer, with regular morning mimicry of the previous night's TV offering. A television play called *Tanhaiyan* had taken the nation by storm. A new face, Marina Khan, had been introduced in it. The whole country had fallen in love with the young heroine for her very natural performances.

I caught a peek of her at a friend's house and then later met her at the 6th PTV awards. I had started taking the school bus occasionally by then. In the mornings, I would imitate her goofy acting in the play. On the awards night, as the ceremony finished and the crowd started to pour into the celebrity enclosure, Marina Khan grabbed me by the hand and led me into the safety of the green room. I don't know whether she recognised me from her visit to my friend's home in Peshawar, or just saw a young girl about to be attacked by adoring boys. I realised then that it is still possible for people who are successful to be genuinely nice people. She had no airs and graces and seemed not the least bit conscious that she was the darling of the nation.

After *Tanhaiyan*, Benazir Bhutto arrived on TV screens, and her anglicised English was too tempting not to mimic. It wasn't only the fact that she was the first female Muslim PM, but also that she was not a stereotypical Pakistani woman. In fact, I had the opportunity to see her in person at a friend's older sister's wedding. I vividly remember a rather tall woman walking briskly ahead of the men. The distance from the door of the hall to the stage took her less than a minute. Apparently, this is something I would later do myself: At a function in Taxila, in 2017, I would notice a particularly efficient man on security. I beckoned to him to come up to me, so he could also get a photo like the others. He thanked me and told me he had served with Benazir Bhutto, then added, "Ma'am, you walk even faster than Benazir". Men in Pakistan would frequently complain to my staff that they couldn't get good pictures because I would walk too fast.

As a young girl, I was irrepressible, and was always playing practical jokes on school mates. A fast runner and a featherlight teenager, I would force many heavier unfit seniors to move by running away with their shawls. They would try to catch me, but I was too quick for them. I would climb up onto the roof of the parked school buses and leave the shawls there. The best part of school was, of course, recess. Time management skills were crucial to fit everything into those thirty minutes. Busy people like me struggled to manage a bite to eat as well as a game of table tennis or badminton. I would also try to squeeze in a few minutes of baseball or basketball or whatever was on. My interest in singing and putting on plays also took a lot of my recess time. It left no time for standing in the unimaginably long queue at the tuck shop. The love of play overshadowed the need to eat.

I devised an alternate method of securing food. I knew Michael and his dad (who ran the tuck shop) were fond of me. I had successfully campaigned to saving their small business from shutting down by writing to the principal and explaining why we needed the tuck shop. They would save a piece of delicious freshy-baked Madeira cake and a stack of thinly-sliced lentil sandwiches for me. It was all washed down with ice-cold Coca-Cola in the traditional glass bottles.

Being the popular girl in school helped; there were many who would happily collect my order for me. No one in my core circle could get away with only buying food for themselves anyway; they would bring me my share or I would (very adorably) take my share. Nadia had a way of getting around it. She would take her retainer out of her mouth and slip it into her pocket the minute she saw me approaching. After touching the damp mouth-mould in her pocket a couple of times while looking for sweets or cash, I learned not to check her pockets again.

I was very busy with my socialising during break. There were several groups I hung out with. With my new-found recognition on television, and oodles of confidence, I was very much in demand. Everyone wanted to be my friend, but I don't think I ever really thought of anyone as a friend. By Year 8, Nadia and I were labelled 'best friends' as we spent so much time together after school. But during break, she was always indifferent towards me. She was a friend when it suited her. I had come to accept her need to be around the ultra-rich kids of politicians and industrialists.

I never confided in anyone, and certainly never broke down in front of anyone. That one incident with Nadia and the 'object' in Year 5 had shown me that people preferred a cheerful girl over a teary one. Never again did I cry in front of a stranger, except when my mother was pronounced dead. I would always deeply regret shedding tears in intimate relationships. It was perceived as a weakness that they could exploit. The world is a stage and we must wear makeup. Very few will value the real you, and those are the ones who will never give you a reason to cry.

Although I was popular, I can think of a few things that perhaps made me a little less lovable: I would never put on weight or get any acne, no matter how much I ate. Back then, I was blissfully unaware of any jealousy. Some girls would openly curse me to my face for having spotless skin, while others tried to put me down for my skinny physique. It all bounced off me. I never cared for anyone's opinion. As a pre-adolescent, I had actually prayed to *not* become curvy like some of my older family members. The sight of heaving, freckled bosoms was repulsive. God listened, and I remained flat-chested for much of my life. It wasn't until year 10 that I forced my mother to get me a bra. Meanwhile at school, my practical jokes continued. I would embarrass fellow classmates by pulling their elastic bra-straps at strategic times in a lesson. The noise was like a slingshot. Needless to say, though the class would giggle like mad, it was not appreciated by the victim.

Nadia enjoyed no immunity as my friend. We had desks in school which could be padlocked. I sat behind Nadia. One day, I slipped a padlock through the end of her long, thick, plaited hair, and shackled her to my desk, just behind her. When our rather adorable and much-tortured Home Economics teacher asked her to stand up to answer a question, poor Nadia couldn't get up because she was literally chained to my desk.

Our Home Economics teacher would suffer at the hands of most of our gang. She was rather voluptuous and would wear see-through outfits. Her choice of lacy underwear under diaphanous outfits would result in fits of giggles from us. She was a sweet soul and ignored it all. We never really appreciated her at the time since we were all besotted by our class teacher. Ms Nighat Afshan was an ordinary looking but exceptionally good-natured woman. She had won our loyalty not only because of her knowledge of science, but because she was totally involved in all aspects of our personality. She was invested in us. She cared. Sadly, she was diagnosed with cancer just before her marriage, which had already been long overdue. We weren't told about this, and reacted extremely badly to the unavoidable substitutes. No one measured up, but then again, we never gave anyone a chance. The Year 8s of 1986 managed to make eight teachers run for the hills in just a week.

No one explained to us why our favourite teacher had disappeared or if she would ever come back. We survived on unreliable rumours. The H.E. teacher happened to be around while we were so disturbed. We took great pleasure in arguing with her, and she patiently tried to help us. My fierce, blind loyalty to those who were insincere to me was spotted by her early on. After I stood up in class to defend Nadia one day, the teacher took me out and gently explained why I needed to not take risks for other people. She tried to warn me that not all people were worthy of my earnest support, but I did not listen. The friend in question would later abandon me on all key junctures of my life. My H.E teacher had perhaps been through it herself, and could recognise the vulnerability behind my tough, practical-joker exterior. But it would be thirty years before I learned to put myself first. We listen to people, but do we hear what they are saying?

By 1990, I had reluctantly joined Jinnah College for Women in Peshawar University. It was considered the best in the city, but I'd had set my heart on Kinnaird College in Lahore. However, my mother was terrified of sending me to the big city. She had heard stories that painted a rather liberal and bold image of Kinnaird girls. The former expat parent had not moved to Pakistan to take risks like that with her daughters, so she subtly manoeuvred me out of a move to a college in Lahore or Islamabad. Rather upset by this, I refused to apply to any college in Peshawar. My mother had to literally drag me to the principal's office at Jinnah College. The principal had the reputation of a dragon lady. She was an incredibly harsh woman, and widely hated for her abusive language. We were late for the application process, but my mother had an excellent reputation. She was immediately recognised by the Vice Principal from her own college days as the brainy, high-achieving daughter of Dr Sher Bahadur Khan. I cringed with embarrassment as I overheard my mother tell them how I would one day be an asset to their college.

On the first day of college, I was surprised to be welcomed as a bit of a celeb. I escaped without any bullying, which was normally the fate of freshers on their first day. And as time progressed, my fan following grew. However, this was predominately in the student core, especially the juniors, rather than the teaching faculty. The college was to quickly discover that I was hardly the nerdy, proper lady my dear mother had been in her time. For me, life was always about fun and laughter. Instead of toiling in the scorching sun of the compulsory NCC (National Cadet Corps training), something we were all supposed to endure, I would be found in the cool shade of the cafeteria, perfecting my skills with playing cards. There were more than enough adoring fans willing to sit in and complete my shifts for me. I enjoyed the training with guns, but sweating it out in the sun was not my style back then.

Juniors were in awe of me and my group. We were the best at everything, from academics to sports and dancing. Cooler still, we would routinely get into trouble with the college administration, although, on reflection, they do all seem like such petty issues. We would be fined for interrupting ongoing dance performances on the school stage with the intent of improvising over them. Juniors would draw images of me in chalk on my route to class. Poetry dedicated to me was chalked out in the school bathrooms. It all seems a bit excessive in retrospect.

The strictest teacher, Miss Chand Rehman, tried hard to restrain her smile at my free-spiritedness. Although she was a much-feared teacher to our seniors, she had a soft spot for me. In return, I was never late for her early class. Ms Rukhsana Iqbal, our English Literature teacher, had a phrase for me: "Reham is wanton like a stream. She cannot be contained". Although I didn't want to be a good student (and really tried hard not to be), it was teachers like these who made me so interested in studies that no one else in my core group of six girls would bother at all. Cheating was far from uncommon, and people like me didn't help the situation. The general understanding was "Reham will have read everything, let's leave it to her". There was no need for anyone to study.

By the end of Year 10, my friends were slowly being married off, one by one, every six months or so. As they returned to study after their weddings and in their pregnancies, cheating became a necessity for some. In one exam, for Faculty of Arts - Intermediate Level, I was moved to the far end of the hall by the invigilator so I would be left alone to complete my paper in peace. She could clearly see me being disturbed by constant kicks to my chair from the girl sitting behind me. After a welcome fifteen-minute period of peace, I nearly jumped out of my skin when I saw the same girl literally standing above me, asking me to explain what the word 'Thesmothete' meant in Thomas Hardy's novel *Far from the Madding Crowd*. The invigilator had to physically drag the girl away amid peals of laughter in the exam hall.

On one occasion, the principal sent me a message that a British girl would be sitting behind me, and that I should be helpful to her during the exam. Ironically, that girl had been sent back to Peshawar by expat parents for an arranged marriage. She was finding it hard to adjust to the conservative environment of Peshawar. The man she ended up marrying had put in a proposal to my family for me a year earlier. I had thought this man from Charsadda would not let me continue my education or have a career. Seeing him as a backward Pashtun, I had refused. A few years later, I bumped into the same girl. She had become a judge, and was madly in love with her rather progressive Pashtun husband, while I had found myself under lock-and-key in good old England.

In the 80s and 90s, Peshawar appeared to be quite conservative. However, we did have a very active underground fashion scene. Ladies-only fashion and variety shows were frequently arranged. There were several ladies clubs for the posh-toffs. I had been walking the catwalk since I was 13 in ladies-only fashion shows, like all the girls in our social circle. This was similar to the debutante balls in the West. It was very much a small elite class. Those who'd had exposure to the West lived in a world of their own. There was an overlap of the diplomatic circle into this class. There were also Christmas parties (all of us grew up being familiar with Christmas carols and traditions). A college friend of mine would recall fondly how I suggested strapless bras long before she even knew such things existed. Although I was brought up to be aware of what was happening in other countries and cultures, I was very conscious of my own traditions and culture.

I was nicknamed 'the hooded monster' in college. Scores of boys would line the road outside the college to eye the girls. Family and friends remember me wrapping the *chadar* methodically around myself, so no one could catch even the slightest glimpse of me. I believed all men were horrible perverts. My friends may have had no such qualms, but I had other priorities. Marriage was not on the cards for me, or so I thought.

As a 16-year-old, I was in a rush to start earning money and getting a career sorted. I reminded my mother of her own mother-in-law, and whenever annoyed by my restlessness and impatience she would address me as Zohra Jaan, her mother-in-law's name. Of course, I revelled in the labelling because my grandmother was my ideal woman. My grandmother was full of life and bounding with energy. Even later in life, when she wasn't very mobile, she had to know what everyone was up to, and controlled the household from her bed. By contrast, my mother was the kind of woman who spoke so slowly that it was pointless to make long distance phone calls to her as it would cost as much as an air ticket. My mother was very much the wise turtle of the household, who found all the rushing around to be dizzying.

I, on the other hand, was buzzing with enthusiasm and ideas, ready to set up a business empire rather than take it slow. I came up with a new idea every day, from setting up a female-only gym, to a home-delivery health food business. I wanted to make films too, and wrote an entire script one summer, based on *The summer of Katya*, much to my mother's horror. Boys and marriage were nowhere on the agenda.

But attitudes were changing rather rapidly under Zia, as were the laws. The elections he had promised to hold within 90 days never happened. He stayed put for ten years until his plane blew up in 1988. We also grew up during the time of the Afghan war, when the Mujahideen, Saddam Hussein, and Bin

Laden were heroes. Jihad was honourable, and Islamic Hudood Ordinance was imposed. The effects of the Islamisation introduced during the Zia years were to persist beyond his mysterious death. The fabric of society had changed, perhaps irreversibly.

My mother recalled how as teenagers in Peshawar it was possible for them to walk on Saddar Road without a *chadar*. But post-Zia, everything was different. My nephews from Islamabad would ask if there were any women in Peshawar, as they never saw any. The change had also permeated among our rather Americanised circle. My older sister got married at the age of 26, like most of her peer group, whereas I and nearly all my friends got married younger. Indeed, all my friends were married before they'd even left their teenage years. No one would bat an eyelid at a 15-year-old being married. And these were girls from educated privileged family backgrounds. It just seemed like the right thing to do at the time. My view on this could not be more different now. If I see any girl being married before she completes her education, the only reaction to expect from me is one of shock and protest.

Chapter 3

"MARRIAGE? ME? NEVER!!"

I was not meant to be married. Later in life, much would be written in the media about how I was a conniving, manipulative woman. People would say that I was the one with a plan and an ulterior motive. In reality, virtually everything that ever happened to me was accidental.

I was alone at home when my dad suddenly called me from his clinic, asking me to get ready to go to Abbottabad for his nephew's wedding. The rest of the family had gone a couple of days before. Daddy and I had stayed back because he had not been feeling too well. I wasn't very fond of the cousin who was getting married. They were a part of our family no one socialised with much because of their father's scary reputation. I particularly disliked that cousin because of his cheekiness and overt interest in my friends. I was going through a very religious phase and avoided mixed occasions. I had also started covering my head. I groaned loudly over the phone.

"Daddy, I have no clothes for the wedding. Do we have to?"

Daddy was clearly under emotional pressure from a sister he loved very much, and had been persuaded into attending the reception. I reluctantly got up to take a shower, sent the driver to pick my clothes up from the tailor, and we set off. The tailor had made a few mistakes in the stitching, but I could not refuse my dad's request. This would become a recognised fact: forcing me into doing something would result in me making no effort, to the annoyance of those forcing me.

We arrived at the groom's house with my hair still wet and tied in a loose bun, and a scowl on my face. As I entered the small four-bedroom house, a very thin man in a grey suit emerged from one of the bedrooms with black socks in his hand. I had never seen him before. I asked where my aunt was. He took one look at me and rather nervously called me by my older sister's nickname, "Sweety?"

He knew very well what Sweety looked like. She had attended the wedding celebrations the night before, and he had spent most of his childhood around her. Rather irritated at his stupidity, I responded, "No! It's Reham". My aunt emerged from behind him. I asked her if we could get ready somewhere and she rather bluntly responded "Nah. No place here". I said OK, turned on my heel, and left for the house of my other cousin, Zahid *bhai*, where the servants were promptly directed by him to open up the guest rooms for us. During the reception, the same thin man with his nervous movements kept popping in to the ladies' side. He was the groom's much older, unmarried brother.

Later that evening, all our cousins sat in the groom's drawing room singing songs. My older *phuphee*'s children and I had always been very close and would sing traditional folk songs together. The thin man was here also, prowling around. He wasn't really joining in but was eyeing us all from the corner of the room. It turned out that this thin man had recently qualified as a psychiatrist. Everyone kept going to him to ask about depression, insomnia, anxiety, and any other problem they were facing. I noticed how he struggled to remember the medical terms. When he forgot the correct term for a phobia for the umpteenth time, I could not help myself, and interjected, "It's Agoraphobia". He looked up, clearly impressed, and asked how I knew. I shrugged my shoulders and said that I was studying psychology. He then replied, "But people still use the wrong terminology and call it claustrophobia".

I got up and went to the toilet. When I returned, the topic of the conversation had changed to this man's marriage. He turned to my mother and said "*Mami jaan*, if you were to find me a girl then I would consider. My sisters and mother keep showing me strange girls". Someone asked him what kind of girl it was that most attracted him and he replied, "The film star Rekha is attractive". He then went on to talk about how women in Pakistan were still backward and not given any independence. And that was the conversation in the lounge full of people. No less. No more. We left.

The following day was the last reception. There was no conversation between this man and I. Exactly two days after this reception, my aunt and uncle came over and asked for my hand in marriage on behalf of their son. My mother was initially appalled at the idea. It was, after all, not only her in-laws, but also the son of a man everyone in the family and in his entire hometown disliked. She had seen how my aunt had suffered all her life at the hands of this man's temperament. He had allegedly been thrown out of the army because of his violent temper, and had punched my other aunt's husband during Hajj pilgrimage. However, my sister and sister-in-law (Munir's wife) had a soft spot for the suitor. My mother didn't mind him as such. She wanted to remove him from the environment and family she disliked. Her words at the time were, "I wouldn't mind if I could extract him like a strand of hair from butter".

My brother's wife really liked him. By contrast, my brother clearly disliked the idea but never vocalised his opinions. My father and brother are men whose displeasure is demonstrated by their silence, a trait which has earned them the respect of their families and friends. My late brother-in-law, however, pleaded with my mother repeatedly over long phone calls to reject the proposal.

In their sophistication, families like mine sometimes avoid open discussion and confrontation. This means that no one approaches an issue openly. This led me to being very open and honest with my children. I went for direct questions and straight advice. However, my father wasn't an overimposing figure, choosing to let my mother do most of the talking, while my mother was the epitome of ladylike grace and avoided direct, open conversations. She didn't particularly like my rather bold approach of calling a spade a spade. It's ironic that those who live with us are perhaps the ones who never really get to know us. Sometimes strangers know your heart better than you do yourself.

The whole process took another three months, but eventually I agreed. All I could think was, "There is nothing wrong with him I suppose". *Nothing wrong with him?* Now girls, that is no reason to marry someone. There should be everything right in a man before anyone even considers spending their evening with him, let alone their entire life. I gave myself away thinking, 'I guess he'll do'. You wouldn't pick a handbag on that basis. I was 18, the most popular girl in college, and was no economic burden on my parents. But still I felt that he was the best I deserved.

It is said that everything is connected in this universe. I discovered years later how my destiny was indeed connected to all the events in my life. The family had been thinking over the proposal until the day of the 1992 Cricket

World Cup final arrived. My father, the sport fanatic, would only ever look angry when Pakistan were playing. All of us were totally engrossed in the match. I remember praying feverishly for the win, when I was suddenly asked to leave the room: The cousin asking for my hand, Ijaz, had arrived unannounced with his family.

Apparently, it wasn't appropriate for me to be in the same room, watching the match with someone who was proposing to me. I remember muttering angrily and watching the last few moments through the clear glass door, swearing under my breath at this idiocy. I remember the jubilation after the match we had nearly lost, but won. I remember my mother being the first one to question why the captain had chosen to give himself all the credit for the win. His choice of words demonstrated his narcissism, she said. My mother had a very sharp, intuitive sense, and was very good at analysing people through body language and gestures. Sadly, our culture did not allow her to make full use of her abilities, even though my father never laid down any restrictions.

So euphoric was the nation that my family, who rarely ventured out to eat, decided to go to the only nearby 4-star hotel, the Pearl Continental, to celebrate. In that state of elation, it was somehow decided that the proposal would be accepted. On the 2nd of April, a day before my 19th birthday, I was officially engaged to be married to my first cousin, Ijaz ur-Rehman. I had been fasting, and, after the ring was put on my finger, we were left alone for a few moments in the drawing room of my home. I hid my nervousness with a confident smile while he lit a cigarette. His visible, nervous fidgeting did nothing to impress the teenager, who peered closely at his face and saw the grey sideburns for the first time.

He managed an uncomfortable smile and asked, "So when can I expect the next occasion to be?"

I immediately replied with a sour expression, pointing to the cigarette.

"Not any time soon if this goes on".

"Oh" he said, rather gallantly extinguishing the cigarette into the crystal ashtray. "There. Now, when can I expect it?"

"I think we should get to know each other, maybe. I want to pursue a professional career. I want to do a lot in life before I settle down".

To this, he replied, "And you can do that better in the West. We get married now, you can study after marriage. Do whatever you want to".

I pushed him further. "You know, my mother says I can continue my career in media after I get married".

"Your career in media?" he questioned

"Yes, I used to work on TV. Your dad was my biggest fan! And I am currently writing a film script".

"Really! Well, I suppose so, if that's what you want to do," he replied. But the 18-year-old missed the ominous sign of his discomfort at that announcement.

I was failing to shock this guy. He seemed keen. Why wasn't I sure? What was this feeling? He was giving all the right answers but I wasn't impressed. The next couple of months were spent staring at the pictures of the engagement. I remember trying to make myself fall for this guy. Love him. LOVE HIM. But still that unhelpful gut feeling would not go away.

Then the letters arrived. They were long, beautifully written, and laid down a good argument. He was telling me that this would work, that he would bend over backwards to make it work. "If you take one step towards me, I will take a hundred towards you," he wrote in one. I was touched. I was overwhelmed. In another letter, he insisted that love was mandatory for marriage. Love is indeed necessary, but love can neither be imposed nor demanded.

Then arrived the song collection. He told me his favourite was John Lennon's *Jealous Guy*. This should have set alarm bells ringing, but this 19-year-old knew nothing about men. I'd never held anyone's hand or snuck away to meet anyone. I had never been complimented. I had never talked to a man. I had no idea that well-rehearsed words and compliments are effortlessly repeated by playboys. They reuse the stuff that works.

My naivety didn't improve with age. At the age of 42, I'd fall for it all over again.

§

The answer to all our questions are in our dreams.

The concept of *Istikhara* (a special prayer when deliberating on a decision like marriage) is based on this. The answer lies within us: in our thoughts, our mood swings, and our lethargy. Our bodies are constantly screaming out to us that something is wrong but we refuse to listen. We listen to the whole world but never to our own heart.

My weight loss over the next couple of months was dramatic. By the wedding day, in July, I was just under 49kg. The sight of food would kill my hunger. I was scared. I wanted to get out of this, but had no courage to accept or say it. And then came the last day. I couldn't sleep at all. I was scared of just being alone with a man. I was petrified of having sex with a stranger, but society had taught me that it was perfectly normal. I knew everything yet nothing at all. I got myself so worked up that my hands were shaking while putting mascara on the following morning. My sister-in-law finally realised, and took the wand away to give me a hug. The problem with being a confident person is that no one suspects that you're scared. The life of a warrior is lonely.

The night of the wedding arrived. I waited and waited but there was no sign of the groom. He had stepped in earlier while I was praying, but had quickly left. To hide my nervousness from myself, I started to unpack and arrange the drawers. It was late when he finally came back. I was writing birthday cards to my friends. I was just a kid after all. He came in, also visibly nervous. He asked me to sit beside him on the bed. I had changed out of my bridal dress and was wearing a plain *shalwar-kameez*, which was closer to a nun's habit in terms of appeal. I sat down, my usual calm, confident exterior belying the child that wanted to run far away. His first comment was so unflattering that, in my shock, I wasn't even offended.

"You looked so thin. It looked like a *Dang* had walked in".

Dang is a Punjabi word for a long, thin pole. It was hardly the best start. He followed it by immediately starting to talk about his career and his boss. He talked nine to a dozen. I wasn't really following much of his monologue, and drifted off. I noticed once again how odd his mannerisms were. He kept talking about a 'Rayman'. It was a few days before I realised that he used an anglicised version of his surname to refer to himself. He was trying to impress me by telling me that he had passed his MRCPsych and that his female boss kept complimenting him. It wasn't working. He kept handing me papers from the briefcase on his knees. They were CVs and other documents. He also shoved a long narrow box in my direction. It took me a moment to realise it was a gift. A lightweight gold chain. I took it, quietly thinking that this was all a bit strange.

After an agonising hour or so, he decided to go to sleep. As he turned off the lights, he tried to hug me, and I felt a clumsy attempt at a kiss before he rolled over and fell asleep. I felt a huge sense of relief. I knew I had ventured into something very bizarre. It was a tad chilly as it had been raining but my new husband had decided to take *all* of the blanket. Finally, I got up to pray at *Fajr*, and took out a shawl to wrap myself in. It was a chilly start to a very cold marriage.

It had taken me just a few minutes to figure out that the man next to was very disturbed. The trouble is that by the time you get a chance to be that close to a man, it's already too late. There should be an emergency bell one can pull to jump off the train then and there. Sometimes, women just don't want to cause any trouble, so they go with the flow. It's like a lazy actor who gives it a shot despite being unhappy with the outfit and makeup. The set is all lit, and the crew is ready.

The following morning, I was woken up very early and rather rudely. I was told I had two hours to get ready for the *valima* reception. I don't remember a breakfast. All I remember is being bundled into the car and arriving at the venue long before the guests had arrived, without even something as simple as lipstick. Lipstick was borrowed from a guest who came to say hello to me in the room next to the wedding hall. With the lunch reception over, we returned to the home. I didn't see my husband all day. He seemed to be avoiding me and was not in a pleasant mood at all. I was puzzled.

Finally, late in the evening, Ijaz came to the bedroom. There was no small talk this time. No compliments, no romance, no time wasting. All I remember is a man I did not know very well trying to have sex with me. It was not what I had imagined or even heard of from my friends. It was what I had feared. The 33-year-old tried to consummate the marriage with a scared 19-year-old. He even commented, "Your heart is beating like a little bird". But that did not slow him down. All I remember is a wet, cold mouth. I did not stop him consciously but my body reacted as if it was a violation or transgression. The anger at his unsuccessful attempt was scary. He snarled at me. "If you weren't attracted to me, why the hell did you marry me?"

I did not know what to say or how to help the situation. 'Was it my fault? It must be my fault. How could I fix it?' My mind raced to try to think how I could calm him down but he looked very angry as he turned the lamp on. He reached over to the side table, took a cigarette, and lit it. He had promised to quit on my request after the engagement. Innocently and playfully, I took the cigarette from his hand, and said, "Well if you smoke then I will too".

It was the silly, nervous effort of a young girl trying to defuse the situation, but the response was earth-shattering.

"Look at you, behaving like a Hong Kongian slut!"

I was stunned into silence. In that moment, I gave up all hope of finding any love in my life. As he continued his vitriol, I just sat there, listening in shock. He went on for what seemed like an eternity before finally turning his back on me and turning off the lamp. I walked to the bathroom and locked the door. The window was open. I watched raindrops falling from the coloured fairy lights draped across the window, as fast as my tears. I stood in the window, staring out at a dark future ahead.

Ironically, after that horrific first experience which led to my husband labelling me 'frigid', he would raise suspicions on my virginity a few weeks later. An educated, older man from a medical background was insisting I hadn't bled enough. I could not believe what was happening to me daily. I remember walking out of the bedroom and sitting in the lounge after these wild accusations and insults. I would write down my feelings because I could not do much else. Those diary entries of a young, confused teenager from the summer of 1992 are painful to read. Leaving the room and sitting alone was also considered unacceptable, and would result in even more anger. Throughout my marriage, even looking sad was not allowed, let alone sulking. I could not smile, but then I was not allowed not to anyway. My husband would say that he loved my smile and wanted it on-demand, but my husband never did anything to put a smile on my face. I was never allowed to do anything but smile by those who professed to love me.

When I was about eight, my mother would often tell me to train my smile: not to smile cheek-to-cheek but to restrain it to something more demure. She told me to practice with the help of a mirror. I did it to please her and it certainly had an effect. That smile is perfect for magazine covers and I guess that was all that was required. The world, it seems, loves my practised, lopsided smile, but I miss the young girl whose smile almost reached her eyes.

Chapter 4

I read somewhere that if you can love the wrong person, imagine how much you would love the right person. People may think that it's sad that I wasn't loved by a man. But to me, the sad thing was that the men in my life didn't allow me to love them.

I think we have a desire to have someone in our life who we can express our love to. We long to say 'I love you' without even knowing whether we actually love someone. With the way our generation was brought up, we didn't really know much about sexual attraction or chemistry. I would have rewarded kindness with undying love. I was not looking for the most considerate man in the world, but someone who would at least allow me to pamper him, and want my attention.

As a newly-married 19-year-old, I was pushed away from showing affection by my first husband. Ijaz was not just my husband, he was the first man in my life. I would keep an ear out for the bell of the elevator to alert me to his arrival. I would rush to the door and hold it open to greet my husband with a welcoming kiss. We were the only ones on the top of that building so there were no prying eyes. As I would lean forward to kiss him, my husband would hold me back with his hands on my upper arms and pull his head back, with clear distaste on his face.

I initially thought that it must be my hair or my breath. I was convinced that there was something wrong with me. For the next twelve-and-a-half years, I would cook and then take a shower to make sure my hair didn't smell of curry. Ijaz also hated the sight of my hair on his sweater or on the floor. He would pick up a single strand of hair as if it was infected or belonged to an animal. I laughed it off but became very careful. I kept my hair tied away at home. Ijaz would insist on only freshly-cooked food, but would get irritated if the house smelt of curry. I had been given strict instructions on how the kitchen should be kept. No dishes were to be left out on the sink. Everything had to be dried and put away. All windows were to be left open during cooking, and internal doors had to be shut.

My mother had also been quite obsessional about cleaning so I took the instructions to heart. The kitchen was never a mess. Even when I was in labour, I made sure everything was spotless before I left to have the baby. Everyone would say our home was as perfect as a show home, which was an accurate description. It was not a home at all. It was just an immaculately-kept house. Homes are not built with perfectly-made beds and polished surfaces. A home is built with ruffled beds and uncontrollable laughter at silly spills. A home means loud laughs, no makeup, and the arms of your loved ones.

I was too young to not follow my husband's instructions. The instructions came with severe consequences. On the first day of our arrival in Billinge, Lancashire, Ijaz's friends received us. They dropped us at our new home and provided us with home-cooked food. The following day, Ijaz showed me how to cook a basic curry. Two days later, he invited friends for dinner. In a state of panic, I frantically looked for the book my sister had bought for me. It was Meera Taneja's *Pakistani Cooking*. That book saved me. I had never cooked curries before. I knew how to bake so I decided to focus on the oven. I put in a whole chicken and potatoes to roast. But the curry was not so easy. It wasn't that the recipe was hard to follow, but there were no pans. The beef refused to soften in the saucepans I was using.

I only knew how to make *kheer*, a Pakistani rice pudding, from a readymade mix. But when I put the milk to boil, it would scald. I was so scared that I hid the saucepan in the cupboard when I heard Ijaz coming. He walked in as I opened the door, and immediately asked what was burnt. He started sniffing the air and then marched into the kitchen. I said it was nothing but he started inspecting everything. He lifted lids, looked into the sink, and started inspecting the cabinets. Finally, he found the offending article. He clenched his jaw in anger. "First you burn it and then you hide it from me?"

It seems ridiculous to be afraid of a man for scalding a bit of milk in the bottom of a pan. But that girl was in a new, frightening situation. No one had ever shouted at that girl. That young girl felt like a criminal for scalding some milk. The girl was embarrassed and scared. The taming program had begun.

It was not that he wanted the perfect housewife, because I became that very quickly. He wanted power over me. He once sent me to the next-door neighbour to borrow some sugar. The instructions were very clear. I was not to deviate from them. But the neighbour had met me for the first time, and started chatting to me. A couple of nights before, her 7-year-old had been on her own, and had rung our doorbell in the middle of the night. I had comforted the scared child and tracked the mother to the hospital. She wanted to thank me, and offered me a cup of tea. I declined. I must have stood with her for 10 minutes at most, but when I came back the smile was wiped from my face in less than 10 seconds. Ijaz was outraged that I had not come back immediately. It took a couple of hours for me to calm him down with promises that I would never do such a thing again.

A week later, I was sent to buy a bottle of red sauce from the store downstairs. It was my first time in a shop after getting married, and I was in a new town. I knew it was not yet dinner time. I bought the sauce but stopped to look at the greeting cards like a typical teenager of my generation. I wanted to get my husband a romantic card. My older brother had been visiting, and accompanied me to the shop. When we returned upstairs, Ijaz asked my brother what had taken so long. He replied innocently and absentmindedly "Reham was looking at some stuff". It was the wrong thing to say. In private, I would receive a dressing down. If I had been told to get a bottle of sauce, that's all I was meant to do. I never bought that card for my husband in all those years together.

Ijaz had a huge issue with anyone that I adored or admired, especially those in my family. My older brother and eldest nephew were considered the geniuses of the family. But a good word about them led Ijaz to immediately ridicule them, and then to ridicule me. They both visited us only once, and their visits resulted in so much stress that even I didn't want them to visit again. Spending money on me and my kids was bad enough, but Ijaz did not take kindly to spending any money on my family. However, he would spend more than we had just to win over those he wanted to impress. In the end, his complexes and insecurities won out, and my attempts to reason with him failed altogether.

As I devoted myself to making sure everything was clean as expected, I stumbled on ill-kept secrets. In the writing desk was my new husband's true life partner: two bottles of alcohol, hidden away. Alcohol was not something I had seen while I was growing up. Alcohol is disapproved of, and not generally kept in the homes of Muslim families. I came from a family where the men did not even drink with friends outside of the home. I have always considered alcohol to be nothing more than a socially acceptable drug. I never touched the substance myself. When he came home, I questioned him softly. There was no shouting or screaming my end, just a simple question. His response to the new wife was two words.

"Stupid bitch".

I had also been raised in a home where the men never swore at anyone, let alone the women in the house. I must have stood there for ages, dead in my tracks, as he grabbed the whiskey and the vodka from my hands angrily and walked away. Unknown to me, I had stumbled on his darkest secret: His dependency on alcohol as a way out of a life he just couldn't cope with. I remember locking myself in the bathroom and quietly crying. At the time it was not the shock of realising he was a heavy drinker, but that I had married a man who clearly had no respect for women.

He returned after a few hours, much calmer than when he had left. There were no apologies. He took one look at my swollen eyes and suggested going down to the hospital canteen. The treat of eating mash and steamed vegetables was meant to do the trick. I ate quietly. It was clear to me what my life was going to be like.

I'd also discovered a huge bag full of pictures of his ex-girlfriend. Not only were the pictures never disposed of, but there were also frequent mentions of her. When I asked about university admissions, he suggested I do a beauty course like his ex, as that was apparently better for women than any professional degree. When I insisted that I was not interested in cosmetic beauty courses and wanted to pursue an undergraduate programme, he told me that he could not afford it as I would be classified a foreign student. My husband was on the salary of a senior registrar psychiatrist in the NHS. He had clearly promised my parents and I that I could continue my education. He'd even said that a British qualification was much better than the Pakistani degree I would be getting if we delayed the wedding. Left with no choice, I withdrew my application to

Liverpool University and focused instead on saving money as Ijaz demanded. He wanted to build his dream home in Pakistan, but when I married him he had a huge credit card bill to clear first. Even after we naturalised as British citizens and the cost of going to university was only £1100 per year, I was not allowed to pursue my studies.

On the fifth day after my wedding, his mother had complained to me that he had not contributed to the finances of the marriage. I was puzzled as all they'd had to do was the small, mandatory *valima* reception. We had not asked for anything, even waiving off the *Haq Mehr* (dower). I had inherited a lot of heavy heirlooms and jewellery from my parents so the groom's side's poor contribution went unnoticed. I got married on the 23rd of July. Within weeks, I was focused on saving. An entry in my diary from the 8th of August shows the budget I had made to clear his bills and reach his target. I started to plan to get him what he wanted. I wasn't going to rest until I achieved it.

I would lay the foundation to his dream. But to everyone's surprise, I would break away and face the world on my own only a few months after that.

§

Initially, the violence took the form of lots of stuff being thrown at me, along with tons of criticism. When a partner in an intimate relationship criticises, one tends to believe it. A younger woman in her first relationship is eager to please. Older men manipulate by snubbing and discouraging. Ijaz made disparaging remarks about my body, skin and weight. I was too tall, too skinny, too this, too that. There was apparently nothing beautiful about me.

Of course, that wasn't the case. He was just scared of complimenting me. He didn't want me to think I was beautiful because he did not want to lose me. Our own fears and insecurities stop us from accepting love. Ijaz had demons inside him. Everywhere we went, people would compliment me. But I would turn to my own man and there would be only negativity and abuse. When we would go for social events, he would be shouting and swearing so loudly in the car that my makeup would always be tear-stained, my face red with humiliation. But when we reached our destination, I would smile. And people would never seem to spot the smudged makeup or the red face. I remember walking into an event hoping not to be noticed, only to be told I was looking pink and healthy. It was almost funny.

What men don't realise is that you must tell your woman she is beautiful. She only wants to hear it from you, not from the rest of the world. Their words mean nothing to her. Your words pierce her heart. That's how you won her and that's how you will lose her. No man and no job can take your woman away if you are the man she is besotted with.

The first couple of months were a period of severe disciplining. I was put behind the wheel and told to drive without any knowledge of traffic rules. There was constant loud shouting if I did something wrong. His voice was loud when he spoke normally, so the decibel level was already above what I was used to. All the men in the family that I had grown up with were soft-spoken and gentle. I could only recall my father ever shouting once, at a thieving employee at work.

Ijaz's sudden loud screaming and punching of the ceiling and dashboard while I was trying to learn to drive usually came with threats that he would immediately divorce me. I hated every minute with this man, but the thought of divorce was unacceptable. Who would believe my story? I'd been the popular, confident girl in college. Everyone would blame me. I'd never looked like the woman people would feel sorry for.

In retrospect, the whole situation was ridiculous. I wanted to be as far away from this man as possible, but I feared the word divorcee being attached to my name so much that I stayed put. So dreaded was the D-word that my mother would refer to it as my 'separation' for years afterwards. I was a young girl without any qualifications. But even women with professional degrees stay in unhappy marriages to keep their mothers happy. A 30-year-old British-Asian woman working on human rights issues would one day tell me that she couldn't leave her husband because her mother had made it clear to her that our society viewed a divorcee as no better than a prostitute. This disapproval was shocking, but came even from the most educated mothers in our society.

I had married beneath my social class. Soon after we got married, my husband, annoyed by my well-heeled look, took me shopping; a pair of trainers, so I'd keep up with him, coupled with a T-Shirt and jogging bottoms was my only outfit for the rest of the year. When the Christmas sales arrived, I was allowed to go on my first solo shopping trip, and only then because I was now pregnant. Photos of the first few months of my marriage show the happy-go-lucky teenager sporting oversized men's jackets and sweaters. My appearance was the last thing on my mind. Just getting through the day was my aim. Respite came when Ijaz got a job at Guy's Hospital, London; the daily commute from Beckenham to Central London kept him away for most of the day.

The bookworm in me loved the fact that we lived on Elmers End, made famous in DH Lawrence's *Sons and Lovers*. I distracted myself from my unhappy marriage by walking to my true love every day - the local library. I was like a kid in a candy shop. It wasn't only the books, but also the freedom of walking alone, without any restrictions of Zia's Pakistan. In the controlled environment of Peshawar, stalkers would follow us home even when there was a chaperone. This was heaven. Like Cinderella I would vacuum the tiny one-bedroomed home from floor-to-ceiling while singing at the top of my voice.

But Ijaz hated it. Working in London meant waking up early, commuting on trains, and dealing with competitive workplaces. Hard work wasn't his style. The day started with him smashing his breakfast dish of fried eggs against the wall. After he left I would sit in front of the mirrored wardrobe and pretend to be a few years older and widowed. I was so young and naïve. I believed that he would eventually die since he was so much older than me. It was a childish fantasy but I knew no better back then. I did not have the courage to even think of divorce.

When things are wrong, our inner voice quietly whispers to us. But the louder voice of society suppresses it. My heart was telling me something was wrong before I signed on the dotted line. For months, my body rebelled against my decision but I chose not to listen. I was only eighteen and felt compelled to get married simply because all my friends were. A woman approaching thirty might have felt that her world was ending.

My experiences taught me that no man can ever protect or provide for you. Protection and financial security comes from the power that has created you. I see beautiful, amazing, young, and capable women settle for complete losers on a daily basis. It pains me to see these women compromising their dreams just because they have a fear of being left behind, particularly since those they are comparing themselves to are often unhappily married. I wish I could tell all the women in the world what I know: that marrying a man will not validate your existence. I wish I could say to them, "Recognise your worth yourself first. Only then will it be appreciated by others. Your own character and achievement will give you the dignity and respect that you think only marriage can provide".

A couple of days into my driving instruction, as I stopped at a roundabout to yield to the right, the stationary car was hit from the back by a tipsy driver. I was left with a severe whiplash but my husband, a health professional, put me straight back into the driving seat to take away the fear. He soon found out that I did not fear physical pain. It was nothing like the pain and humiliation of being shouted at when others could hear or see it. He preyed on this fear for years. He would constantly swear in Punjabi while we were shopping or sitting down to eat. One does not have to understand the language to figure out what is being said. I would get red-faced and my eyes would well up with tears. As my appetite for food or entertainment disappeared, his appetite for abuse increased. I was giving him what he wanted. A small man who is scared of the big bad world needs to feel he is big and powerful at home. Conversely, strong men can afford to whisper gently and smile at the women they love.

§

I had never understood the point of a honeymoon. The idea of going away to a beautiful location just after getting married made no sense to me. How could a newly married couple have their eyes or mind on anything but each other?

The point of a wedding day is to finally declare your commitment to spend the rest of your life with one person. The day should be intimate. The guest list should be small. Only those who are genuinely happy to see the two as a couple should be invited. Why invite dozens of guests who are only there to criticise or compare the wedding to others? The concept of an elaborate function was always lost on me.

My first wedding was, by Pakistani standards, a small gathering. It consisted of just one *nikkah* event, hosted by my parents, followed by the mandatory *valima* dinner, hosted by the groom's. I was against overspending on weddings and too many rituals. Since Ijaz was in debt, I never asked him to take me for a honeymoon. This set the tone for the next 12 years. No man would ever take me away for a romantic holiday.

The first month was a shock to the system, so a honeymoon did not really figure high on my priority list in any case. Ironically, it did not stop Ijaz from using the phrase "the honeymoon period is over" whenever there was an incident (which was pretty much daily).

However, Ijaz did take me out nearly every evening to explore a new nearby town. It was a good way of teaching me to drive and he did like the travelling. The only issue would be that I would have to take packed lunches, and buying souvenirs was not allowed. These kinds of trends continued for the rest of the marriage. Any and all forms of shopping were done by my husband, even clothes for the myself and the kids. I wasn't allowed to go shopping, nor was I given any money for personal expenses. I spent most of the first year of marriage in his shirts and jackets. But it didn't bother me much. There were far bigger issues to deal with than that.

Four months into the marriage, I decided to have a baby. Ijaz wasn't particularly keen but there was pressure from his parents. I set about getting tests for Rhesus factor, and getting my haemoglobin levels up. I conceived easily. The day I got my test result, I walked back home in the rain feeling a bit low. As I opened the front door, I heard the phone ringing. It was Sauda, my school friend. I broke the news to her immediately and she was genuinely pleased. However, the many insults and slurs from my husband had shaken my confidence. I cut across her uncontained excitement and heard myself mumble, "Will I be a good mother?"

Sauda, in her typical effervescent manner, exclaimed emphatically, "You, Reham, will be an amazing mother!"

It takes just a little encouragement from a kind person to help us up. I don't think she realised what a profound effect her simple sentence had on me. Those words held me together for my entire life.

On the contrary, Ijaz gave no response of happiness or excitement when I broke the news to him. And in that moment, I realised that I was in this alone. His lack of enthusiasm was puzzling. Perhaps deep down, we all know our limitations. As the pregnancy progressed, Ijaz remained uninterested in going to appointments. I even went alone to the ultrasounds.

During this time Ijaz's brother and family came to stay with us. We took them around sightseeing. It is customary for Asian families to entertain their guests. My first trimester was difficult, and my frequent throwing up interrupted our constant travelling, but I remained in high spirits and we all joked about it. I was always in a state of euphoria when pregnant, and managed to avoid illness.

The younger brother seemed very much the family man; an overly doting father and a devoted husband. I looked on enviously at them shopping together excitedly for their baby son and for each other. It all seemed so blissful and alien. On one occasion, they were so immersed in a shopping trip that they carried on with no need for any kind of break or lunch. They were completely oblivious to my continued reminders. I was the messenger, the link between them and my husband. I must have made two or three trips in and out of the shop, back and forth between the two brothers, with my husband swearing at me in the middle of the town centre in Croydon; telling me to drag the guests out as he was hungry and wanted to leave. Reasoning to a man shouting his head off in a situation like this is simply futile. For merely informing him that they were paying and on their way out, I received a swift "Fuck off" as he stormed off and left me feeling utterly humiliated in public.

I walked back into the shop, locked myself into the fitting room, and cried silently. When I emerged a few minutes later, with a calm and collected exterior, I told my brother-in-law that Ijaz had needed to attend to something. My brother-in-law was well aware of his sibling's temperament, and said out loud that he understood what would have happened, and that I needn't make excuses for my husband.

I had no money of my own, so I stayed until the couple decided to head back. I had no idea which bus would get us back but we found our way all the same. We reached home to find Ijaz inside the car, locked out of the house as he had left the keys with me. My brother-in-law let out a chuckle at this instance of karma, but I knew that this meant more trouble for me. Sure enough, it took an entire night of apologising for Ijaz to forgive me for my alleged insolence. He was my master and I was meant to walk when he wanted.

Months went by. I became the perfect housewife and a chef *par excellence*. The budgeting was exemplary, and the house spotless, but there were still only frowns. Even the expected arrival of a male baby did not help my approval rating. It would take me a while to realise that no matter what I did, I could never be perfect in my husband's eyes. The pregnancy kept me going. I had no one there for me, no one on my side, so was desperate to have a baby. I desperately wanted someone to fill my lonely existence, someone to talk to. After Sahir's birth, Ijaz would make fun of this very fact, for it wasn't until Sahir was over two years old that he finally started to speak.

During the pregnancy, we settled into the accommodations at De La Pole Hospital, Willerby, and made the acquaintance of the lovely family of an Iraqi consultant doctor. Ijaz would always take me to interviews and the homes of his bosses. My conversational skills were used when required, but when a family got close to me, my ties with them were severed. Many people probably thought I was a snooty young girl who did not bother to maintain contact. I couldn't tell them about the controlled situation I was in, how I was a virtual prisoner in my own home. Instead of socialising, I helped Ijaz prepare for his first part of USMLE, an entrance exam for doctors trying to apply for residency in the U.S. It was fun to help him with the multiple-choice questions.

There was no understanding of rest periods and support while I was pregnant. I was expected to clean, cook and serve non-stop. A few days a week a very loving older Kashmiri lady used to stay over next door. She was a locum staff-grade psychiatrist, who would frequently voice her concern at my carrying the heavy bags of groceries into the house. Her concern was valid but I was young and was keeping myself fit and healthy throughout. Besides, I had no choice.

Ijaz would sit upstairs in the third bedroom. I was expected to deliver endless cups of tea and coffee up to him. The vacuum cleaner was heavy and would have to be carried up and down the stairs too. I hadn't put on much weight in the pregnancy but at the end of the seventh month, as I suddenly started getting bigger, it became harder to keep my balance. One day I lost that balance altogether and, along with a mug of hot coffee, fell from the very top of the steep, almost vertical staircase. The coffee splashed onto the wall and I slid all the way to the bottom of the stairs. There were no spindles to grab onto to halt my descent as I hurtled down, badly skinning my back and elbows en route. I was so worried about the baby that I felt absolutely no pain. Miraculously, the baby was fine, though the midwife gave me a stern telling off for carrying trays of drinks up and down such a staircase.

Before the birth, I made sure I passed my driving test. But the months of shouting and threatening during those awful lessons had taken the only thing I had: confidence. Like all people who are criticised non-stop, I also started losing confidence in myself. The more Ijaz told me I was incompetent, the more nervous I became, and the more mistakes I made. Surprisingly, it was the instructor that I took about five or so lessons from who reminded me of the faith we are supposed to have. The instructor asked me when I wanted to take the test, as if I was ready. He knew all I lacked was confidence, not ability. I responded with a jittery giggle. "I hope to take it next month, so I can drive before the baby arrives, *Insha'Allah*".

Insha'Allah is a word often used in the same context as 'hopefully', but it actually means something closer to 'If Allah wills it'. I didn't expect the white man sitting next to me to understand the meaning of the phrase. But to my surprise, he smiled gently at me and replied, "And Allah wills it".

Meanwhile Ijaz was driving my mother and I mad with his impatience. My mother had finally agreed to come over and stay with us on the repeated pleading of my husband. He wanted her to look after me, but I knew that she was not used to old, dinghy accommodations and no staff, so I was reluctant for her to come. I also did not want her to see how I lived because I knew she would be upset. And, as I predicted, my mother spent much of the time in shock and depression at my gruelling schedule.

She gently suggested I buy ready-made meals as my uncles had, and not cook *chappatis* at home. My mother was not used to seeing women slaving in the kitchen or in the home themselves. She couldn't understand why I lived on a shoestring budget with no home-help, even though we had a good income. I tried to reassure her that I enjoyed it and was well enough to do everything, but I found her silently crying into her pillow most afternoons. This was not the environment she had imagined for her baby, and certainly not a set-up she was used to. I stuck up for my husband's irrational behaviour, much to her annoyance.

Sahir arrived on the expected date of delivery. The big day came and, although I was not one bit scared, it was a very long, exhausting labour. By late evening, as the labour pains increased, Ijaz was already fed up. His typical constant ranting was enough to drain anyone's energy, and my mum, unused to this childish behaviour by a man, retired with a massive headache.

My mother was a delicate woman who had been treated with a lot of care by my father and her own family. We knew she got anxious very easily. For me, people often use phrases like "Nothing scares you" and "You have nerves of a stoic". I had grown up around women who panicked at everything, especially my mum, who needed smelling salts every so often. Someone had to be the strong one, the one to hold them when they'd faint at the drop of a hat. Besides, I was my mother's favourite and she couldn't see me in pain. As so it came to pass that my delivery was almost perfect comedy: me in full-on labour, blowing away my pains and smiling on through, just to reassure my mother I was fine so she wouldn't collapse, and all the while trying to block out Ijaz's ranting insistence that I couldn't do it and would certainly die.

In the end, Yvonne, the midwife, decided to throw them both out so we could get on with the business at hand. She held onto my hand and helped me through the prolonged labour until a healthy, seven-and-a-half-pound baby boy was safely in my arms. Yvonne's eyes were glistening with the tears behind her thick, rimmed glasses. She learned forward and whispered, "Well done girl!"

It was a perfect moment. I had what I wanted most: the privilege of being a mum. It was something I would always treasure deeply. Sahir was all I needed to give me renewed vigour. Never again would I be defeated by the irrational criticism I was subjected to. I would never lose hope.

I was pampered in the ward. It was probably because I was a very young mum for Beverley Westwood Hospital, or perhaps Yvonne had said something. On the 6th day after Sahir arrived, I joined a City and Guilds course for cosmetic makeup. It was the only thing Ijaz agreed on. I was happy to make friends my own age and get some brief respite. The girls on the course would often comment that I didn't look or behave like a stereotypical Pakistani. I wasn't sure what they expected Pakistanis to be. I explained that perhaps they had not seen many to realise we come in all shapes and sizes. A racial origin has nothing to do with being unfriendly. That is just a personality trait. I struck a friendship with a girl on the course named Alison, who would drop me back home every evening and give me tons of hand-me-downs for Sahir. I took them gladly because Ijaz had not given me enough money to buy even one set of baby-grows and vests. The cot was second-hand and he wouldn't agree to a pram, so only a pushchair was bought.

At that time, Ijaz was saving every penny to buy land in Pakistan to build his dream home. He basically wanted a replica of the White House. It was a dream shared by many Pakistanis. These 'wedding cake homes' were seen as a status symbol. Many Pakistani families would live on frugal budgets so that they could spend whatever they had left in their hometowns, and gain respect in their communities. The allure of the luxury of this dream home in the future, and the prospect of staying there for lavish holidays or comfortable retirement, would exist as these people sacrificed the needs of the present.

Ijaz came from a household that collectively suffered from a severe inferiority complex brought on by richer relatives. This dictated his behaviour to his wife and child in private, and led to his braggart behaviour in public. I, on the other hand, always believed in living in the moment; a deep sense that this life is just a blip was ingrained in me right from the start. Collecting assets and 'keeping up with the Joneses' was not my father's style. All three of us were never motivated by money. We would earn to provide comfort for our children. Ijaz, on the other hand, was brought up with a singular drive to save, hoard, and collect assets. The need to catch up with others meant he never enjoyed the run. As a child, I had only seen kindness and laughter in the family home. Ijaz had grown up with only the fear of being whipped with a belt and bombarded with a barrage of abuse. He did not know how to love because he had been treated unkindly as a child. There had been no patient parenting so he never learnt to be a tolerant adult.

The first few weeks of a baby in the home are the moments one cherishes the most, but they were made the most stressful time for me. Like many young mums, I was learning on the job, and like many newborn babies, Sahir cried. He would cry with colic pains for a couple of hours in the evenings. I was not unduly worried or tired of his crying, and was happy to rock him to sleep. But Ijaz could not tolerate the crying for longer than a minute. His reaction to the baby's crying made me panic all the more.

Ijaz had moved to the third bedroom at the far end of the house while my mother was in the bedroom next to me. My mother was shocked at this arrangement, but I preferred to keep Ijaz away. I knew his violent tendencies. He would frequently barge into the room on hearing the baby crying. On one occasion, he slapped the one-month old baby to get him to stop. He would often shove the baby under a running tap to shock him. I spent my time trying to keep him from snatching my baby away. Ijaz's anger would blind him, and he would do insane things like shaking the baby and throwing him onto the bed. He seemed like a man possessed.

Even when in a good mood, he did not understand the concept of handling a newborn baby gently. Home videos would show a careless attitude akin to that of a child handling a baby, rather than a responsible medical doctor. One night, in the presence of my mother, he poured the contents of an entire bottle of Dentinox (a colic medicine) straight into Sahir's mouth. The baby spluttered and started to choke on the thick viscous liquid. My mother tried to clear the baby's throat. Terrified, I ran downstairs to call 999. My mother stormed out of the room at this madness while Ijaz disappeared for the rest of the evening. Ijaz had tried his best to choke the baby, but luckily Sahir recovered. My mother took the next flight back home, infuriated by his behaviour. But she didn't once tell me to leave him or come home. Instead, the family distanced themselves from me, as if it were my fault I had a mad husband.

My in-laws arrived soon after my mother left, and stayed with us for a couple of months. Both of them were elderly and in poor health. My father-in-law was infamous for his dreadful temperament. He was suffering from health issues that most men get in their later years. It wasn't the best of times for him. My mother-in-law was a very submissive woman who had suffered at the hands of his temper all her life. She was a diabetic and very frail having never fully recovered from a stroke at a relatively young age. Although an unreasonable man, my father-in-law was rather fond of me and, ironically, criticised his own son whenever he exhibited identical behaviour with his own wife.

The father-son relationship was difficult. I ended up taking my father-in-law for appointments and his surgery on my own. The loud, abrasive man looked terrified but also grateful as I accompanied him all the way to the operation theatre. The added pressure of looking after in-laws was no real problem for me. I did it to the best of my limited abilities. But this elderly couple seemed genuinely pleased with their daughter-in-law's input. And on the upside, their stay meant far fewer tantrums from their son. There was the occasional swipe at my cooking, which was mainly dry meat dishes, typical of Pashtun households; quite unlike their own, where a more watery fare would have been the norm. But on the whole they caused no real problems for me at all, which a lot of daughters-in-law complain about in our culture. However, they couldn't understand certain things, like my breastfeeding of the baby, or why I wouldn't bottlefeed or give him sugary snacks. Sahir was two months old, and I came across as quite mad for not allowing him grown-up desserts, like *halwa* or ice-cream. I would return home to find videos of them giving him mints in my absence. I couldn't bridge the gap between our differing levels of awareness.

In her own house, my mother-in-law had been reduced to a puppet, without a voice or mind of her own. However, she could see that her son had turned into a husband and father she would never have wanted. But it was too late of course. Ijaz had never seen a woman stand up for herself or her children, and this had undoubtedly helped make him what he was.

Sahir was only seven months old when Ijaz announced that he was taking us camping to Europe. He'd bought a tent and we were to set off in a week. My father was seriously ill during this time but I did not have the right to look unhappy. My mother never understood or forgave me for going off to Europe while the family was going through this extremely tense period. The plan was to cover nine countries in one month, and do it on a budget. A duvet and pillows were packed, along with a gas stove and a pressure cooker. I had no idea what to expect; I was a young, inexperienced mum. I didn't know how hot it would get. Sahir seems exhausted and dehydrated in many pictures of the trip. The trip involved hours of driving and pitching tents every two days. I was young and full of energy, so I learnt to put up a tent, and also managed to cook a full Indian dinner of lamb curry and rice every night. However, Ijaz simply had no idea how to behave around a woman, let alone a mother and a child.

Although we were almost always exhausted and horribly sunburnt, both Sahir and I managed to keep smiles on our faces. But by the time we got to Venice, it was all too much for the camping planner himself. As I stood admiring the mouth-blown Murano glass in a shop window, Ijaz suddenly lost it completely and stormed off. Puzzled, I racked my brain to think of what I had said to offend him. I was writing a diary as we travelled, and was recording everything I saw. I spent too much time by his standards reading descriptions and taking in all the history. I have always been the sort of person who could spend a whole day in a museum or art gallery. As I read the history of Murano glass, I had muttered something along the lines of "I hope I could buy it someday, when we have a home" under my breath. Hearing this, Ijaz went ballistic, and left his wife and child right there, right in the middle of this breath-taking, romantic city.

Thinking that he would come back in a little while, I stayed put. After an hour or so, I realised that I had to find my way back to the campsite. I had no money on me, only a return ticket for the water bus. It was getting late and the Italian men were very 'friendly', so it wasn't an ideal situation for a young girl with a baby. I walked briskly away with my head down as they called out *Sei Bellisima*. I wandered in the narrow streets, trying to find my way back, thinking that they all looked the same. I wondered if this would ever change. Maybe one day I would be here with romance, serenading and someone to hold my hand. After all, Pandora was still left with a little hope, locked up inside her box, even when everything else had escaped.

I returned to the campsite, went into the tent, and did something I had never done before: I questioned his behaviour. He was outraged at my disobedience, but I felt braver after Sahir. I stood my ground and heard myself say aloud that his behaviour was unacceptable. Ijaz spat at me and threw the metal camping stool at my face. I blocked my face with my arm and heard myself say, "That's enough! I want to leave you! Right now! Give me my passport. I want to go home".

He threw the passport at me and walked out of the tent. I was shivering with fear and anger. It was the first time he had been physically violent with me. I knew it had only been a matter of time, but it hurt. Not the bruised arm but the insult...being spat at and treated like a captive. Like most abusive partners, he convinced me that it was my fault. And like most victims, I believed he would not do it again. But it wasn't him who was deceiving me. It was me deceiving myself, making excuses for my lack of courage. We blame others for our situation, but we only have ourselves to blame for putting up with a bad situation.

After my threat to leave, the rest of the trip was relatively calm. I had meant it, and he clearly didn't want to put it to the test. By the time we reached Paris (our last stop), he even let me go shopping. I bought a linen dress and he picked out linen trousers for me. I would keep them forever. I also kept all the cards and letters he ever wrote to me. I kept them in a box along with his pictures, which my daughter ripped out of albums. I wanted my children to be able to see my past and our history. I thought there would come a time when he would repent and wish to reconnect with his children. I thought he would realise that he'd had everything: a beautiful family, a home, and a job, and perhaps make amends. But he chose instead to go even further into his insanity.

Back in Paris, Ijaz was amazed that I knew my history and art so well. He described his first visit to Barcelona: he had seen a very long queue outside a small entrance and had wondered what the sign above meant. It read 'PICASSO'. Ijaz thought it was an ice cream parlour, and was surprised that I knew who Pablo Picssso was. I was surprised that this surprised him.

My fascination with galleries annoyed him so much that he walked out of the Louvre in Paris after just a few minutes. His walking out on us was something I was quickly becoming used to. I would take full advantage of these tantrums. I was going to see all the treasures I could. I remember spending hours looking at the art. Sahir was in my arms but I was determined to wrestle my way through the Japanese tourists clicking away and get close to the Mona Lisa. I also remember being transfixed by Leonardo's da Vinci's *The Virgin and Child.* For a moment, I was somewhere else entirely.

Chapter 5

It was the summer of 1995. Sahir and I had barely begun settling down in the port town of Goole when Dr Rehman announced he wanted to resign and move to Australia.

Although the hospital accommodation didn't really look like a home, it was all Sahir and I had. I had started working as an apprentice at a local hair salon as part of a program for adults returning to education or training. The job gave me respite from the shouting and swearing at home, and allowed me a chance to be around other women. I loved even the simple joy of buying a pizza slice from the local Co-op for lunch. The hairdressing wasn't really my cup of tea but listening to people was. While washing their hair, I would realise that we all have the same dreams and fears, regardless of our skin colour or origin. All the mothers, daughters and wives had issues I was familiar with. I especially enjoyed looking after our elderly clients. One of the younger girls would frequently, and rather casually, mention how her boyfriend would be physically abusive. This seventeen-year-old would turn up for work with a bruised eye. I was shocked to find that even girls in England, with rights given to them by law and society, would choose to live with abuse. I'd thought being a punching bag was limited only to women in our culture. There are many who still believe that it is all safe and fair for women living in the West.

I chose to seal my lips most nights while the doctor chose to assert his manliness. He had taken on the position of locum consultant, was thirty-six years of age with a one-year-old son. He had no money in the bank, no property, and no right to remain indefinitely in the UK. His much younger wife was still looking young and learning a new skill. She had settled well into life in the UK. Nothing fazed her. Soon she would be able to get a job and maybe even another man. She knew his insecurities by now, understood the demons inside him. He continually starved himself to maintain a slim physique. Little did he know that his wife only wanted a smile, not a 32-inch waistline. I didn't care that the house was tiny compared to my parents' home. I didn't care if I hardly had any clothes. I had Sahir. We were happy to be playing with the wild flowers in the hospital grounds.

One night, Ijaz snapped again and grabbed me by the throat. He dragged me through the entrance corridor and slammed me against the glass and wood door. I felt the chain of the door dig into my head. He had blood in his eyes as he tried to choke me. I let out a loud scream so he would stop. I knew there was a doctor on-call staying next door. It worked. He stopped immediately. The following morning, the elderly Sri Lankan doctor from next door walked over to our Nissan as I took Sahir out of his car seat. He tried to talk to me about this and that, but I could tell he just wanted to give me an opportunity to ask for help. There was concern and kindness in his eyes. However, instead of confiding in him, I just felt embarrassed to the core.

It wasn't just him who knew. My husband's family were also very familiar with their son's temper tantrums. During Ramadan, my sister-in-law and her daughter had stayed with us. I loved spending time with my in-laws. Some of my best memories are of holidays with my sister-in-law, brother-in-law, and their kids. They would make fun of Ijaz's weird habits. Having them around made life easier. We would privately joke about how menacing he looked in his trench coat, peering out of the window to pounce on us if we were late coming back home. Although they made fun of his controlling behaviour, they also secretly feared I would leave him or tell the world about him. His prowling, controlling personality was suffocating for his family but they did not have to live with him or listen to him on a daily basis, so they never really intervened.

However, I did overhear them trying to talk sense into him a few times, emphasising that he needed to control his anger and be gentler with his wife and kid. My sister-in-law had given a lot of liberty to her only daughter after her own divorce, and could empathise with me. I caught her reading my letters to my mother; she probably thought that I would be voicing my unhappiness to my family. But I had not confided in anyone. It was just too embarrassing. And more importantly, I thought it was all *my* fault: I was not good enough, not competent enough, and not beautiful enough. I always provoked him to lose his temper by not being perfect or perfectly behaved. I went along with all his rash behaviour, hoping that he would find the peace and happiness he desired.

Then, before I knew it, we were moving to Australia, a place far too big and too new for the 23-year-old. I had become accustomed to Yorkshire's warm politeness and helpful demeanours, with the familiar 'love' at the end of every other sentence. "Don't you worry, love," the hospital porters and workers would say to me whenever I wanted something done. After that, handling the coarseness of Western Australia was difficult. On my first day in Perth, I answered the door to find a man in just a vest and shorts.

"Is this Number 1?"

There was no 'Hello' or 'Good morning'. I replied politely that it was and he brought in a washing machine. As I held the door open for him, he bumped into a pillar and rather rudely remarked, "Dumb place to put a pillar," before shoving the still-packaged washing machine off a trolley and leaving it in the middle of the hallway.

I heard myself say, "Will you not take it to the laundry room for me?"

"Nah!" the man responded blithely.

"So you're just going to leave it here?" I protested feebly. "Will I have to install it myself? I am not familiar with these".

"It's dead easy! Don't be a dummer!" the man replied, unmoved by my concern. I stared at him in disbelief and quietly signed the clipboard he pushed in my direction.

In fact, Western Australia reminded me of Pakistan. The men stared and the estate agents used racist terms to describe the areas. The odd thing was there were a lot of British ex-pats in Perth, but they seemed to have somehow forgotten British political correctness. And I clearly was not the only one conscious of this Western Australia bluntness. The morning TV shows would teach etiquette for businessmen wishing to make progress when meeting delegations from Asian countries, clearly aware of a certain regional deficiency. However, as time passed, I discovered that the bluntness was just bad packaging for very friendly people. They did not have the manners of the British, but at least you knew exactly where you stood.

As if the hot, blistering sunshine and brashness were not enough, my husband had become even more violent. He now had a consultant position, and the much sought-after immigration was only weeks away. But it didn't improve his behaviour at all. Any sound from Sahir in the night would be met with a hysterical reaction. Whenever he was disturbed, Ijaz would jump on the bed, fists clenched. The image of that naked man threatening to hit the toddler became imprinted in my mind. I would escape to the spare room with Sahir and lock it. We would not come out until after he had left for work in the morning. Once, Sahir and I stayed out of his sight in the spare room for two whole days.

But the time alone was for bubble-baths, singing Bananas-in-Pajamas, and taking long walks to the local park. The carport was our art den. I would put a rug under it and cover the wheelie bins with paper to use them as easels. We would spend the afternoons rolling out *parathas* (a layered, puffy bread/pastry). I made the most of this time with the only source of happiness in my life: my son.

As the months went by, I accidentally managed to forge a friendship that would last a lifetime. There were very few Pakistani families in Perth, and very few Pakistani doctors. But we managed to meet a couple who were extremely hospitable towards us. The husband was from Haripur, Hazara, which we knew very well. He was jobless, and took his frustrations out on the family. The wife was a highly competent homemaker. She was an excellent cook and stitched beautifully. We somehow connected, and became very good friends in a very short space of time. She reintroduced me to the cinema, beginning by dragging me to the Bollywood blockbuster *Dilwale Dulhania Le Jayenge*. The rest of the six months or so in Perth were spent enjoying leisurely barbecues while singing *DDLJ* songs together.

Surprisingly, Ijaz allowed this friendship to continue. Perhaps Maheen appeared benign enough to him. But I think the reason we connected was that we both shared a desire to live life on our own terms. After years of putting up with a husband who did not deserve her love, loyalty, or intelligence, she was forced to divorce him (she caught him stealing her bank cards and then marrying another woman while on holiday in Pakistan). She was still heartbroken when this small, ugly and unfaithful man ditched her. But life had decided to reward her for her tolerance.

After leaving him, Maheen completed a Master's in International Relations and went onto become a diplomat. She also found the love she had only seen on screen for much of her life, bringing this gorgeous new husband over to Pakistan with her years later. When we met up once more, after twenty years, she was one of the few people to encourage me to get married again. Although that would be the last time I would see her, the laughs we shared during those extremely tough months in Perth will always be cherished memories.

1995 was an eventful and news-heavy year. One story dominating the news, even in Australia, was the marriage of a very young Jewish heiress to a former Pakistani cricketer. The middle-aged man in question was vaguely familiar to me; he was the hero of my husband's generation. My husband would even copy his hairstyle and mannerisms, as did many of his peers. The journalist in me was surprised at the coverage this was getting in the International press. There were always so many rich, society weddings in the UK after all. Perhaps it was because the man in question was about to launch a political career.

Though he had been admired by countless Pakistanis, I had never paid much attention to Imran Khan. I remembered that his bachelor status had been the topic of iconic comedy shows like *50/50*, and interviews on TV. I would end up in heated debates with older Pakistani men in our circle as we sat watching these interviews of their hero. Imran Khan came across as an arrogant, rude, and rather ill-mannered man. Even back then, I disliked this attitude of arrogance and female subjugation I could certainly relate to the young girl marrying this domineering older man. Imran Khan came across as everything I detested in a man, yet he was everything men like my husband aspired to be. A close friend even gifted me an Imran Khan coffee table book in an effort to convert me. I passed it on without reading it. Perhaps this was a mistake. Reading up on people who do not appeal to you can come in handy later in life.

If 1995 was the year of the marriage that would influence Pakistani politics and culture for more than 20 years, the following year would be the year of the royal divorces that would modernise the face of the British monarchy forever. The most photographed woman in the world, Princess Diana, showed that a perfectly obedient woman was not the ideal anymore. She spoke up. She broke her dignified, ladylike silence. She broke the royal rules. It was not only the establishment that hated her for speaking up. Diana's interview to Martin Bashir drew sharp criticisms from the men around me. Some particularly disgusting remarks came from my psychiatrist husband, who had a habit of describing everyone as borderline personality disorder in the first meeting (before moving onto labelling them bipolar in subsequent meetings). His repertoire of psychiatric terminology ended there.

In her interview, Diana maintained that she believed *someone* had to go out and love people. She was touching the hearts of everyone she met, seemingly desperate to fill her loneliness and compensate for the love she had been deprived of. Later that year, we would all see that going out and loving people in need was not allowed, but breaking someone else's marriage was perfectly permissible.

The Spice Girls entered our lives that year too, and we were introduced to the concept of *girl power*. They urged us to spice up our lives. They were real-life Powerpuff girls, each exuding their individuality and power. You could be sporty, posh, scary, a baby, or even ginger, and that was just fine. The stage was big enough for all of them. The message was clear to women all over the world: "If you wanna be my lover, you've gotta get with my friends". We watched, sang, and were unknowingly influenced by these subliminal messages of female empowerment.

As the friendship with Maheen progressed, our immigration application was nearing acceptance. The whole point of moving to Australia was to get permanent residency and stability, or so I was told. But as the days passed, and Ijaz's violent tantrums increased, he suddenly let slip that in the event of a breakdown of a relationship, immigration was granted to the dependant partner at the time of application. I didn't know where he had heard this, but the idea made my husband so nervous that he resigned unexpectedly. We were on a flight back to the UK within a year.

After a month of respite, the violence escalated again. My husband would regularly pin me down in bed with a kind of wrestling of the legs, and mock me to move. A week later, I discovered the cause of this nervousness: he had applied for a joint mortgage (apparently for tax purposes) and needed my signature. Just the idea of a 'joint' mortgage had sent my husband on a violent spree. He would try to mark his territory forcefully at night, and would twist my limbs in bed just for the fun of it in the mornings. And the verbal attacks became pretty much continuous.

In utter despair, I finally picked up the phone and confided in my mother. She was angry but offered no solution other than to 'handle him smartly'. I couldn't explain to her that you can't handle abuse smartly. She was outraged, but never said, "Come home to me". She insisted it was my fault from day one for being his personal maid, and cooking and cleaning like a slave. My mother, bless her soul, had no idea how the rest of the world lived. My lifestyle was alien to her. She was the eldest daughter of an affluent family. Even after her marriage, she was treated like a princess. My father was the perfect gentleman. He earned, and his wife chose how to spend, which is probably why he did so well in his life. Most women who are given responsibility invest money well, and never have to resort to retail therapy to settle scores with the husband.

I had not been given any responsibility. I had not asked for a house, and wasn't included in any of the decision-making. One day, I was driven to a house in North Ferriby, Hull, which the doctor had chosen with his secretary. It was a four-bedroom detached house. It was bought for around £100,000 in an upmarket area but needed a lot of repair. We moved into the house and immediately started on extensive repair work. I was miserable and the only joy in my life was Sahir. As he was nearing school-age, I planned another pregnancy. I kept hoping parenthood would calm Ijaz down and that the marriage would work after all. I also had no courage to leave him; my mother had clearly told me that she would not support any such step. With no friends or family, the 23-year-old decided to make the best of a bad situation. Before long, I was pregnant again. And it worked for a while. Ijaz calmed down. Not only during the pregnancy, but even for a little while after it. And very soon, I would have another beautiful little companion to bring me joy in this bleak world.

§

I remember how Sahir and I had waited for his baby sister. Her pregnancy had followed a rather turbulent couple of years with his father. Even getting pregnant a second time did not calm the monster in my husband entirely. A compliment to the hostess by a guest could still have bruising consequences. I remember the full-term pregnant woman trying to protect her bump from anything he could get his hands on. On one occasion, a massive bunch of keys was hurled at me with so much force that the resulting bruise covered much of my right thigh. It took a long time to fade away but its presence did at least serve as a reminder to him, and limited further incidents.

Through the pregnancy, the baby hardly moved. It was a sign of the quiet, undemanding child that would soon arrive. By the time the day finally came round, I had put my foot down and said no to guests. I didn't want any elderly guests to look after this time. The pains started in the early morning and Ijaz, tormented by the thought of another long labour last time, refused to take me to hospital until I was certain it was time. He looked at me calmly applying my eyeliner and said, "Women don't calmly put on makeup when it's the real thing. They scream the house down. It must be just Braxton Hicks".

He instead took me to a DIY store to take my mind off things. As the pains increased, I pleaded with him to be taken back home at least. For the next few hours, I was trying everything in the book to breathe away the pains. At one point, I had my head resting on the step of the staircase, with me doubled over with pain. As I tried to breathe away the pains, Ijaz returned from his squash game, and came up to say that Roger was asking if we could join them for the squash club dinner on Thursday. I looked up at him and snarled, "It looks like I am having a baby so no, we cannot join them on Thursday, and if I am not having a baby right now, chances are I will be in labour by Thursday!"

Ijaz was not used to me being so forceful. It seemed to do the trick. He agreed to take me to the hospital, but not without making a pit stop at the local McDonald's. He remembered feeling very hungry and having mediocre sandwiches the last time I was in labour. As he turned around to ask me what I would have, I burst into a sweat and cried, "Please take me to the hospital! It's time!" I felt the tears rushing out of my eyes amid the searing pain, and begged him. Poor Sahir peered worriedly through his round glasses as this madness played out in front of him.

It took ages to get to Hull Princess Royal Hospital from our home in North Ferriby, which was at the other end of the city. Ijaz dropped me off at reception while he went to park the car. As I stood in the reception area, the shift was changing. They asked me to wait but I had to shout, "Someone please help me!" I stood there and wailed helplessly, unable to sit or walk. There was no time to wait. As the midwife helped me onto the delivery table, I asked for gas and air.

"There isn't any time for that now my dear," she replied.

Ridha arrived within five minutes of me being taken to the room. She cried as if in protest as she arrived into this world, and continued loudly for a solid fifteen minutes. Rarely is a child so perfect at birth. She had no puffiness, and looked simply beautiful. Sahir entered the room, with an uneaten Happy Meal still in his hand, looking even more worried, while the overgrown kid claiming to be his father followed sheepishly behind.

Right from day one, Sahir was involved in helping me look after his new baby sister, and he was a natural. He did not have a jealous bone in his body. It was as if he realised his responsibility to his family from the start. His sisters would never feel the absence of a father figure. I didn't know what the future held of course, but I knew Sahir would always be there to help sort out any issues. Indeed, before long I'd be watching him sort everything for them, from schooling to travelling arrangements. Sahir shaped himself into the perfect big brother. This behaviour extended to family and friends as well; they would seek him out for everything, from exam help and career guidance to emotional support. It all started with Ridha.

Unlike Sahir, Ridha hardly cried or fidgeted. She was a very easy-to-handle baby. As long as she was fed and warm, she was happy, and slept for long periods of time. I made rapid progress on the repairs and decoration of the house, and my baby slept peacefully through it all. Ridha was also the perfect model. I would spend the day putting her in pretty frocks and taking photos. For Sahir and I, our world was complete. Even Ijaz loved showing off his rather light-skinned baby girl with auburn curly ringlets.

One day, only a few months after the birth, I took the car seat out with Ridha still strapped in it, sleeping peacefully. I went upstairs to the bathroom. When I came back downstairs, I saw that Ridha was not in her car seat. I panicked, but then I saw her in Sahir's arms. He was sitting on the sofa like a pro, with the baby cradled carefully as he confidently fed her water from her bottle. I took a picture of it to remind them both when they were older, but it was hardly necessary. He made sure we received regular reminders that he would always look out for his family. Ironically, I now believe that pictures rarely tell a story accurately. Years later, a young journalist who was interested in my story would ask to see albums from my marriage. His first reaction was, "You look happy. It looks like a good, happy family".

"It was meant to look like a happy family," I replied.

The perfect bay trees outside the front door and the hand-hemmed floor length curtains hid a horrible secret. The boy who would always be praised for his intelligence came from a place where he had always been ridiculed for being a duffer. He was physically abused, day after day and meal after meal, for any reason. Sometimes it was for something as silly as not finishing his bread. I spent my days and nights protecting Sahir from violent abuse. Ijaz's anger and aggression had increased once more. It was as if this was not even his own son. With the birth of Ridha, Sahir was no longer allowed to come into our bedroom. The child would come running in early in the morning looking for his mum, only to be hit, shouted at, and chased back out.

Mealtimes were horrific, with food being forced down the poor four-year-old's throat. I had strict instructions: the child must have a full fried egg with two slices of bread for breakfast, and at least one whole pitta bread with curry at meal times. Sahir would often throw up when force-fed, and it would lead to him being dragged by the hair and smacked in blind rage. It was assumed that the child was throwing up on purpose. Any remaining leftovers on the plate would trigger fresh abuse. On one occasion, I put a plate with some scraps of egg white into the sink. Ijaz shouted at me, took the camera out, and took a photograph of this horrific crime.

One of the main ways of forcing Sahir to finish his food was dragging him into the coat cupboard and locking him in the dark while setting the burglar alarm off. The minute-long bleeping sounds before the main alarm went off would be coupled with the child's screams and my pleading to let him out. Ijaz would put his hand on the handle and shove me away when I would try to step in to stop this madness. Sahir became terrified of the burglar alarm, and he remained phobic of loud sounds for many years.

We all just stayed out of the way for the most part, and I tried to make sure we followed the rules. The image of Sahir being dragged up the stairs by his shiny, dark, straight hair will always torture me. I would try to intervene and Ijaz would turn on me. Sahir was so terrorised during the day that he started getting night terrors. It was somehow not understood by the psychiatrist that the child was sleepwalking, and not sneaking out of bed at night to play games. I would find him out of his bed in the middle of the night, crying hysterically and banging his hands on the windows. He was clearly fast asleep and wouldn't recognise me. Ijaz would storm in and slap the child repeatedly to wake him up. I ended up sleeping on the floor next to Sahir's bed to prevent these violent incidents. Most of our lives were spent protecting each other, while Ridha learned to stay hidden in her room, away from any provocation.

We would be asked what we wanted to eat, but giving the wrong answer could result in an hour-long lecture on how I was corrupting the children by getting them used to Western food. There was a deep hatred of anything associated with white or Western culture. I was pronounced a bad mother. Serving pancakes or vegetarian sausages to the kids was deemed serious corruption and deviation from Eastern traditions. Conveniently, alcohol consumption for the patriarch of the house did not fall onto this list of corrupting evil Western practices.

Somehow, McDonald's also slipped through the net of *haram* Western food. If we so much as mentioned anything else, the furious yet hilarious outbursts could begin. Ironically, I had a problem with McDonalds myself as it did not serve halal meat, but Ijaz insisted on it. It was the only way he felt Sahir would put on weight. On one occasion, Sahir simply said that he preferred a Margherita pizza, which resulted in Ijaz suddenly rolling down his window and howling at passers-by at the top of his voice, "*Mein pizza nahi khaoon ga*!! [I WILL NOT EAT PIZZA!!]".

It certainly wasn't funny at the time but recalling these eccentricities and childish outbursts would eventually become a source of amusement for us. A grown-up man behaving like a baby was shocking and very embarrassing at the time. But finding amusement in the worst memories may be the best way to move on.

Ironically, my kids grew up to be more attached to our culture and tradition than most kids from Pakistani villages. In our house there has to be *haleem* and *aloo gosht* cooked regularly. And a month without *gol guppas* or *barfi* would mean employment of a complex system of couriers. The children are fluent in Urdu and understand Pashto and Punjabi. I never made an active effort. You don't have to force tradition down someone's throat. Let them fall in love with heritage themselves.

§

When Ijaz was not shouting and screaming, he reminded me a lot of Mr Bean. He was that sort of character.

I recalled how infrequently he laughed with me. But in retrospect, he did a lot of laughable things. In our new house, he had insisted on me sewing in blackout curtains behind the heavy, dark blue velvet curtains. The room was pitch-black. This would lead to a few very amusing incidents. With Ridha's arrival, I had less time on my hands to tidy up wardrobes every day. One day, Ijaz called me up at midday and said, "I'll be home in 20 minutes. Grab a pair of black shoes and stand at the gate. I'm running late".

I was puzzled and did as was told. As I handed him the shoes through the car window, he looked up at me with a sheepish smile. He told me that he had been sitting in his ward with the nurses in his typical casual style, with his legs stretched out in front of him. Ijaz was fidgety, and would find it difficult to focus in meetings. About halfway into this particular meeting, he'd noticed that he had one black and one brown shoe on. The nurses had been smirking but hadn't pointed it out. Although he was smiling in embarrassment at the time, he later blamed his absent-mindedness on me. The bizarre incidents were a part of his daily routine. But like the nurses, we thought it best not to laugh at these idiocies outright.

One of the phobias Ijaz had developed was the fear of being burgled. I was constantly being scolded for not removing the car's radio panel every time I parked, even inside the school. I would remove it and either put it under the seat or in the nappy bag. During his lunch break one day, Ijaz decided to make a quick shopping trip to the town centre. Having found a parking spot, he took off the radio panel and took it with him. But already in his hand were used tissues and a cigarette pack, which he threw into the rubbish bin in the shopping centre. As soon as he did so, he realised he had thrown in the radio panel along with the rubbish. Public bins in England are often fixed to the ground and closed from the top with narrow slots on all four sides, similar to a letterbox. Homeless tramps can occasionally be seen putting their arms inside to reach for leftover chips or cigarettes. There, in the middle of the city centre, the consultant doctor in a suit was caught with his arm stuck deep in the bin by his rather gossipy manager.

On another occasion, during his time as an illegal immigrant in the U.S., he was pulled over by the police for running a red light. Ijaz pleaded and a bribe was agreed upon. The officer told him to walk over to the police car and throw a $100 bill through the rolled-down back window of the vehicle. Ijaz, thinking he could outsmart the police, threw in a one-dollar bill instead, and drove off feeling very happy with himself. A week later, the same police officer pulled him over and gave him a ticket for over $400!

Calling our marriage a mismatch is perhaps an understatement, but the problem was never really his unawareness and coarseness. It was that he was consumed by an inferiority complex because of his age, looks, and lack of status. These things have never bothered me. A kind word is worth so much more than a diamond solitaire. Winning a woman's heart takes only a smile, a warm hand, or a rose. Ijaz needed a 'Mrs Rayman' to show to the world, just like he needed a brand-new Mercedes Benz with personalised number plates. The scared little boy had been deprived of a father who loved him unconditionally and a mother who would protect him. Ijaz was not taught love. He never understood that he should have married a woman he could connect with, perhaps someone of his own age group who spoke own his language.

Within a year of Ridha's birth, I found I was pregnant again. It would be my only unplanned pregnancy. It was medically categorized as 'threatened' right from the start. My body hadn't had the rest it needed, and I was losing weight rapidly. The daily violence towards Sahir and the added responsibility of another baby had taken a toll. As I approached the fifth month I started getting extremely exhausted, and there was some bleeding. One day, Ijaz found me lying down in the afternoon and told me clearly that this was not a household where women retired in the afternoons to rest. But returning to the gruelling schedule just resulted in more bleeding. The following week, my doctor advised me to not carry heavy objects and to take complete rest. When I showed this to my husband, he decided we would all take the next flight to Pakistan.

When we landed in Pakistan, I discovered that Ijaz had made plans to take his entire extended family to the hilly resort of Nathiagali for a holiday. I asked my brother and sister to drop by. It was a lovely time of board games and laughter, which Ijaz typically refused to join in with. But there was a problem: in England, I'd had only my own two to look after, but here I was the hostess to four families. Ridha was not familiar with the family, and, since there were no carpeted areas, I also ended up carrying her the whole time.

One evening we all ended up sharing one room as the booking had been messed up. In the middle of the night, Sahir had a night terror again, and I tried to quickly calm both my children so the others would not be disturbed. A few minutes later, I felt a slight jab in my abdomen. I got up to use the toilet. As soon as I entered the bathroom, my waters broke violently. I stumbled out, called my husband, and explained what had happened. Ijaz told me to go back to sleep. I sat back on my bed and wondered what to do. I was scared and started sobbing. My brother-in-law heard and asked what the matter was. I told him what had happened. He shook my husband awake and admonished him for telling me to go back to sleep. A car was arranged to take me to Abbottabad. Two days later, I miscarried my baby at five months.

It took me years to get over that. I'd just lost a baby. No one understood and no one cared. The most cruel comments came from other women. My mother-in-law declared that it was my fault for losing a baby boy. They felt I had been irresponsible and careless. My singing on holiday was declared to be the reason by my sister-in-law. As the years went by, even Ijaz noticed that my personality had changed. I had lost the bounce. I hardly spoke anymore. I suppose I had given up on expecting anything from anyone. My smile had faded.

I had applied to Hull University for a degree in Sociology, and managed to get a place on the course. The female tutor had taken one look at me, judged me by my appearance, and asked for an essay on a book on feminism by Alison Jaggar. I read the entire book and completed the assignment in two days. She was taken aback by my ability. However, Ijaz said he would not allow me to go to university. I had recently had my hair cut very short. When he saw the picture on my student card, he flew into a rage. He took the car keys from me and snapped the debit card he had given me in half. I tried to defy him but there was no way of financing the course. I remember getting in touch with the careers advice line, and being told that if I could prove I was separated and not a dependent, I would perhaps get help with tuition fees. I vividly remember the last two-pound coins I used to take the bus home from Hull University. It was raining. As I left the campus, I saw shiny faces with excited smiles around me. But the young woman sat at the back of the big red bus in the pouring rain was not smiling. Her smile had disappeared.

The words of the tutor rang in my ears for years. I'd told her that I could not take the course but masked the truth. She saw through my lies. "Reham, you must return to higher education. You have real ability!" she exclaimed. But my ability didn't matter. The education and freedom that I thought would come with getting married was to be denied.

Months went by. Ijaz got quite concerned. In a moment of madness, he entered me into a BBC talent search. Surprisingly, I was selected from hundreds of people, and asked to come in for an audition. He drove me all the way to the audition in Cardiff, swearing the whole way as usual. There wasn't a job at the end of it. It was just a competition which would be part of a program. I ended up being shortlisted as one of the final six. However, I mentioned in the interview that my husband was based in another county, and that I would not be able to stay over for recordings. Ijaz was relieved but the whole experience only reinforced his fear that I could leave him. Within a few months, he had sold the house I had painstakingly repaired and decorated. It was a recurring theme of my life.

It was a joint mortgage, and he was paranoid that he would have to give me a share. He would let these fears slip out every so often. The week after he sold our house, the UK property market boomed. The house that we had just sold was suddenly worth more than double the amount we had received for it. It was impossible not to find it funny. These little moments of black humour are all I could take from that marriage besides my beautiful children. Beyond that was just darkness.

Chapter 6

Ijaz slumped into a deep depression as we moved to a rundown area in Grimsby. The children had to leave their school as it was too far to commute. He would cry to me at night, wailing that he had been very unjust to the children. As we'd left the old property, Ijaz had spotted the children kissing the polished window-sills and waving goodbye to the rooms. My children weren't that attached to the house, and were equally happy in the squally, rat-infested accommodation in Grimsby. They had just made a little game of saying goodbye to it. But it was that image that stuck in Ijaz's head, and he repeatedly cursed himself for his drastic decision. As he cried to me later, he asked me why I didn't stop him.

I didn't laugh in his face as I probably should have done. It wasn't like I'd had any power to stop him. And I *had* tried to convince him that it was a mistake. Even his father had asked me to stop him from selling the house. Ijaz had announced categorically that if I did not sign, he would auction it off anyway. I'd conveyed the concern even though I wasn't particularly bothered. I had never attached myself to such things, and I could see the same values in my children. It was a house of bricks. It meant nothing to me, and I knew it was not mine. What's the point of fighting for something or someone that is not yours?

To add to his troubles, I was asked to come to Pakistan by his family to help arrange his niece's marriage. As his depression grew and he became almost docile, I announced to him that I would like to have another child to cement our marriage and start afresh, and quickly fell pregnant once more. By January, Ijaz had moved us into a beautiful converted barn in a place called Thornton Curtis, North Lincolnshire. It was in the middle of nowhere. As I grew bigger, I could no longer drive, so we were pretty much marooned. But we didn't mind Thornton Curtis. It was a rural location and a quaint setting. We lived beside a train track but the train was infrequent, so it didn't bother us at all. The children and I loved the freedom of the open fields, and the view of Thornton Abbey, which was just a stone's throw away. Sahir and I taught Ridha to ride a bicycle, and the afternoons were spent baking or playing badminton.

The last trimester was extremely uncomfortable, and I couldn't lie down straight in bed. However, the service demanded from the kitchen to 'the Den' never ceased. In retrospect, it seems strange how willing and happy I was to slave away, just so he wouldn't shout or throw stuff at us. It's funny how women get married for financial and physical security, but the only times I was surrounded by comfort and luxury were when I was single. It's mind-boggling how marriage turned me into a maid so quickly.

In fact, those six months at Thornton Curtis were by far the best time in the entire marriage, partially because his place of work was far away and he knew I could not drive. It was a cold house, and Ijaz kept himself locked up in his den with a live fire when at home. Sahir had to suffer a couple of hours a week of Ijaz trying to teach him to play cricket amid Punjabi swear words, but there was very little interaction overall. It was a big barn and it was easy to keep out of his way. Years later, the kids would often say that they wanted to go back and buy it someday. This attitude was in direct contrast to their thoughts on the next place in the UK that they would live. That house in Lincolnshire was inseparable from this man, but his relative absence from Thornton Curtis made the attitude of the kids easier to understand. Many of Sahir's memories of Thornton Curtis are happy ones, but notably, very few have any trace of my husband. It was as if he had retroactively Photoshopped Ijaz out of his memories.

Another reason that this house became a home might have been down to the arrival of my third child, Inaya. This delivery was different. I wasn't alone this time. I had Sahir and Ridha children around me. They had waited for this baby, and understood what having a baby meant. The night before, I persuaded him to leave for the hospital earlier than I had for Ridha. It was late when we arrived, and I promptly sent him back with the children. I knew he would be more trouble than help and we had no one to babysit the kids. The children left reluctantly but I told them that they could come back as soon as it was time. I caught the midwives exchanging looks at the doctor leaving his wife but I was thirty and didn't care anymore. It was a long labour. As morning approached, the midwife gave me plenty of opportunities to ask my husband to come but I declined.

Inaya arrived at 8am on the 8th of May 2003. She was a bonnie 9lb baby. After I had held her in my arms, I asked the midwives to call my husband. Both the children were dressed for school. Sahir had tears in his eyes. Sahir's sad face quickly turned into a smile on seeing his baby sister. When I asked why he was upset, Ridha piped in with the inside info as always. Apparently, their father had planned to send them to school. She showed me the lovely sandwiches Sahir had made for lunch. The midwife was hovering nearby and later remarked sarcastically, "Dr Rehman left last night with grey sideburns and came back with perfectly brown tinted ones for the family photos!"

I ignored her saccharine smile. This 30-year-old had come a long way from looking wistfully at couples holding hands or kissing goodbye at airports. I had accepted my single parent status. I was only married in the eyes of the world. There was no spouse and no partner. As I looked at my two older children with the new baby in that hospital room, it occurred to me that nothing and no one could bring a change to this relationship. Sahir, Ridha, and I were alone in our pain and our joy, but we were a family and didn't need anyone else.

The days went by but the new baby showed no signs of leaving her mother for a minute. She clung on to me for dear life. Even before the delivery there had been signs of the baby being nervous. She was kicking away frantically. Now out in the open, Inaya showed no signs of settling down. She would hold on to my hair with one hand and suck the thumb of her other hand feverishly. I couldn't leave the baby for a minute. Inaya refused to go to anyone else.

Research suggests that a growing foetus is affected by the mother's surroundings and moods. I noticed after Sahir's birth that the theme music of the Australian soap *Neighbours* had an immediate calming effect on him. Later, it was discovered that the mid-afternoon slot had a heavy following of pregnant women. I wasn't the only expectant mum who had been taking the odd relaxing break with the show.

Thornton Curtis was a time where the kids and I were left undisturbed for much of the day but I was growing older and there was more time for reflection.

I had realised that serving my husband on hand and foot while he growled from his den wasn't really a life for any self-respecting human being. I enrolled myself on an Open University course in Social Sciences to pursue a Sociology degree via long-distance learning. The course got me thinking about social order and the myth of the perfect post-fifties nuclear family model: The socially constructed image of the perfectly cosy family home with the 2.2 children, the perfect wife in the Gingham skirt posing with the modern washing machine, and the husband sitting comfortably, smoking away. I realised I'd been fed a certain narrative: broken homes are devastating and the purpose of life is to serve the husband's every need. The silent rebellion was taking root. The thought of raising another girl in this oppressive environment was deeply disturbing. I was in constant conflict with myself. At some level, I'd decided that this baby should be raised without fear, in a proper, loving home, but I had not yet developed the courage or figured out a way to walk out. As fate would have it, I was nudged along by a decision my husband took soon after Inaya's birth.

By August 2003, Ijaz had packed me off to a country that I had never thought I fitted in. With a two-month-old baby, I was sent to Pakistan to live in a place called Chak Shahzad. I had moved back to a country that apparently suppressed women's rights. But it was living in that land that finally made me realise that I had to get out of this marriage. Chak Shahzad was originally designed to be a poultry and vegetable scheme, but the wealthy had started moving there to build beautiful farmhouses. Ijaz, desperate to impress the cousins, put all the money he had (with some help from his father and my dad) into a 3-acre plot, which meant there was no money left to develop it. He also insisted on putting the children in a new, expensive school, so I had absolutely no money for expenses. Since it was not an established school, the children struggled with mostly inexperienced teachers, and there was horrific bullying by children of rich but poorly-educated backgrounds.

While we waited to put enough money together to build a house, I had to move into the old clinic on the property and convert it into a home for me and the kids. My in-laws came to live with me as it was considered unsafe at the time. There had been a couple of high-profile kidnappings. Luckily, the former President, Pervez Musharraf, had bought a property in the vicinity, and the security of the area improved somewhat. It wasn't a huge improvement though, as it was only Musharraf's imported cows that lived there.

The long route from Chak Shahzad Farms to sector I8 in the city became even longer as construction of a new road began. It took an hour to get to and from the school. Little Inaya would be screaming away in the car seat. Ijaz said that he could not afford staff, so I had to cook and drive myself. The newly dug-up road left only a narrow strip for driving on which tested everyone's patience. The morning commute was agonisingly long. Soon enough, I was to have the first of a series of accidents. New to Pakistani driving, and with British driving habits, I wasn't always prepared for erratic overtaking. Pakistani buses are called 'flying coaches' for a reason. The drivers are not known for putting their foot on the brake once they hit the road. One morning, a bus crashed right into us while trying to overtake. Thankfully, no one got hurt. What I had to put up with at home was far more painful.

The first month in Chak Shahzad was effectively spent in the role of an exterminator. The property had been uninhabited for years, and was surrounded by overgrown weeds and maize. Naturally, there were snakes, rats and lizards of humongous size. There was no water or gas. Initially, we had to borrow water from the next-door neighbours and use a hosepipe to fill our tank. The tanks had not been cleaned for years. The kids and I ended up with eye infections because of the dirty water.

The elderly couple next door were adorable, and constantly worrying for me. If I stopped by for a few minutes, the lady would insist on feeding me. They were a deeply religious family, and I was pleasantly surprised to find that they had sent their very young, unmarried daughter to the U.S. to study. Even today, many Pakistani families would not send their young girls to a foreign country alone to study or pursue a career. When I asked how they had managed to do this, the lady simply replied that her daughter had been consistently scoring better than the son in school, and they felt that Allah would question them if they were unjust to her. I remember thinking, 'This is what faith is all about. It's about being just and fair'. When the girl had completed her studies, she returned home to look after her elderly parents. That's the power of love. Trust your children and they will value your trust, and be bound by the freedom you give them.

Months went by and I began to see the difference in the children. It was an alien environment. The house was not ideal. The weather was hot. The language and culture were so different. We hardly had any money, and I'd sold some of my jewellery to get through the month. All the money Ijaz had sent from England was for developing the land. My mother gave me a cheque to carpet and furnish the house but it was difficult to ask my husband for money for monthly groceries. There was bullying at school but the kids were blossoming, because, uncomfortable as it was, it was a safe home. Our smiles were returning. Mornings rang with the sound of laughter. Sahir was becoming confident and coming out of his books. Ridha started leaving her Barbies for real people. They could smile and sulk with no fear of being attacked.

However, Pakistani homes are not always the safest. One night, after a long day of running around getting the electricity generator fixed and refuelled, I stepped out to light the water heater. In my absence, the gas cylinder had been delivered but hadn't been connected properly. As soon as I lit a match, the leaked gas ignited. My right hand, face, hair, and clothes caught fire. Luckily, my quick reflexes helped, and it took me less than a minute to put the fire out. It was nearly midnight and there was no one around. I didn't even bother to scream. The front of my shirt had burnt away so I rushed inside and called Sahir. My hand had crumpled up and felt like it was still on fire.

Sahir called the mother of a school friend. Saleha and her husband, Khaqan *bhai*, arrived within half an hour. They hadn't even changed out of their pyjamas. When I refused to leave without asking my husband first, Saleha decided to stay over. From that day on, Saleha looked after me more than anyone had ever done. That night, she held my hand in front of the air conditioning vent for hours. Early the next morning, she drove me to the dermatologist. On noticing the lecherous doctor eyeing my face more than my burnt hand, she quickly took me to a more professional specialist. She then called my husband herself, and essentially told him that she would not let me leave her home until my injuries had healed, unless he was prepared to come back himself or ask his sister to come and look after me and the kids. Ijaz wasn't allowed to protest. Saleha, realising that I was uncomfortable with handing my baby to the maids, changed nappies and fed Inaya herself. She spent hours pouring a healing herbal treatment over my hand, as prescribed by her own father. Had it not been for her, my hand would never have healed completely.

After this incident, she probed me further for information about my bizarre personal life but I said very little. Ijaz was impressed by their wealth, and was very compromising in front of them. However, he started suspecting Saleha's husband. He couldn't believe that anyone could care without an ulterior motive. After my hand had healed, Saleha and I became firm friends. We were inseparable, but I feared my paranoid husband. However, Saleha insisted on taking her husband everywhere.

As I went to get the car serviced at the Corolla dealership one morning, Ijaz called the house. Sahir picked up and soon had to explain where his mother was. Ijaz then asked if I'd gone on my own. The way he said it made Sahir think that saying yes would be the wrong answer. I wasn't allowed to go anywhere alone so the little boy didn't know what to say. He panicked, before blurting that I had gone with Khaqan *bhai*, thinking that Ijaz would be reassured that I had not only been accompanied, but also had a man to keep me safe.

When I returned, I got a call from an incensed Saleha, who demanded to know why Sahir had said I was out with Khaqan. I explained that Sahir got scared. She gave me an earful of how I needed to not run around being a maid to my husband, and also teach my children to be more cunning. Apparently Ijaz had called her to check where her husband had gone with me. When she replied that Khaqan was still in bed with her, he had hung up. While this was happening, I'd been sat in the dealership's waiting room, trying to avoid the shocked stares of men. In his anger, Ijaz had forgotten that I'd been only following his own instructions.

Years later, Saleha would exclaim, "If things were so bad, Reham, why didn't you have an affair in the whole year you were here? You could have found a nicer man!"

I'd laugh. "Saleha, you never left me alone for a minute, how could I have found a man?"

The odd thing was that the man who was desperate to not lose me never tried to keep me happy. The man who lived in perpetual fear that I would leave him left me alone for months in another country. In the end, it was not another man who whisked me away, but the realisation that I did not want my son to become the man his father was. There were great examples of good men and women around me. One such man was our builder. He will never know that his behaviour with his own daughter, and the way he fondly spoke about his wife, would give me the courage to take the step I had wanted to since day one. Even my conservative Pashtun maid walked away from her husband's harshness. Yet an anglicised woman, who was born to be free, was enduring unimaginable torture.

§

Ijaz's plan was failing on multiple levels. The sudden plan to send us to Pakistan ahead of 11+ exams was not received well by me. I knew Sahir had real potential. We had disturbed his education enough already because of Ijaz's volatile mood swings. His friend's wife back in England had advised me that if I pretended to be happy in Pakistan, Ijaz would soon call me back. But it is in my nature to adapt very quickly to new environments and culture. It probably had something to do with being the child of one parent who could not adapt to any change, and the other who adapted to every change. Both contributed to the way I could happily endure every change in environment effortlessly. The kids and I were genuinely far happier in Pakistan. Sending me away was meant to control me, but he was getting frustrated by the minute as I was left unsupervised for weeks on end.

His parents were meant to chaperone me but found it difficult to leave their own home. He was finding it difficult to part with his job because he needed to fund his ambitious plans to build his dream home: a copy of the White House. The only solution was for him to make surprise visits whenever he could afford to. His visits were short but exhausting. He was now not used to having a baby around, so Inaya's crying resulted in the same kind of violent episodes that Sahir had been a victim of. There would be loud shouting, with Ijaz grabbing the five-month-old from my arms and shaking her violently before flinging her onto the hard bed. I feared for her life and kept her away as much as I could. The gardener outside could hear everything clearly. One day, as I drove the gardener to the local garden centre, he hinted how a famous politician was awful to his lovely wife. He was only being sympathetic but I was ashamed to the core.

My sister's marriage wasn't going too well either. One day, I would pick up the phone to hear her crying on the other end. I could also hear a woman loudly cursing her, and the sound of hitting in the background. I begged my husband to go and pick her up. He initially refused to get involved but when my cousin Samina *baji* called to intervene, Ijaz agreed. Ijaz brought Sweety home but his displeasure was visible. She stayed with us for less than a week with her young eight-year-old. I had decided that I would not let my sister live in an abusive environment any longer. Her husband and mother-in-law had kicked her to the floor in front of the servants.

Sweety's eldest son was at the university. The middle one was completing his O-levels at the time. I knew I had to take a stand for her but no one in the family supported my stance. In the meantime, Ijaz's violence towards me went up a level. One night he sat on top of me with his thumbs pressed onto my windpipe, choking me. "I can kill you right now and no one will come to your rescue," he mocked. "Go on, scream! Scream for your brother. Who will come and save you?"

I made no sound. I understood that he was right. No one would come to save me, but what he did not know was that it taught me that I could save myself. Only I could rescue me.

Throughout my trials, I found the strength I needed to fight through prayer. After this escalation in violence, I started praying even more. During the last few nights of Ramadan, Muslims pray all night until *Sehr* or breakfast time. Throughout our marriage, Ijaz never showed physical affection, not even the odd hug or cuddle. He didn't even seem attracted to me, but forcing himself on me gave him a sense of control. There was one night when he knew I wanted to pray. I was wearing a black fitted-shirt in thick material. The shirt had no slits. I gently mentioned that I had just prepared for prayers but Ijaz would not take no for an answer. Maybe if I thought that this man loved me and wanted to make love to me, I would not have resisted. But listening to abuse all day hardly makes you receptive to any advances. I resisted. Angered by my insolence, he threw me on the bed in one swift movement. He ripped the seam on the right side of my dress and marked his territory like a dog out on the street. There were days where I would tell him that I was on my period but he would insist I was lying. The bloodied sheets never produced anything more than a sheepish expression. There was never an apology or any concern for my well-being. It was as if I were not human. I was his...a possession. An item to be used, to be punched, to be displayed.

We had the most perfect first birthday party for Inaya. I had booked a portion of a theme park. Saleha, Sweety and the other school mums had even more fun than the kids on the rides. Inaya was surrounded by love and laughter. As with Ridha's first, the father was missing but not missed by his absence. We celebrated Ridha's sixth birthday with Saleha in another theme park in Nathiagali. Ijaz's plan had failed. His wife and kids were really loving Pakistan. And then we were called back to spend the summer in the UK.

The night before the flight, Ridha, who was normally such a pleasant and docile child, was behaving out of character. We were at Saleha's for a dinner party. Her house was like a toy store, with paddling pools, bikes, skateboards, swings, and slides. As we stepped into the courtyard, Ridha rushed towards the two-seater swing. Despite my warnings, she walked straight into the swinging metal object. It came at her like wrecking ball and hit her face with full force. Blood spurted out of her mouth.

I scooped her up and screamed for Saleha. We left the guests and she drove us to the doctors while swearing away at the kids. That was classic Saleha: always jumping up to help but cursing nonstop while at it. We loved her ineffectual scolding. Thirty minutes and four stitches later Ridha emerged out of the hospital terrified at the thought of what her father would say. She was right to be. Ijaz took one look at her and immediately created a scene right there and then at Heathrow Airport. However, his behaviour was surprising in other ways. He had brought the kids their favourite snacks and blackcurrant juices. He would normally give us so much grief for asking for these treats. He was suddenly making a real effort. I couldn't understand why.

I drifted off to sleep towards the end of the long journey from Heathrow to North East Lincolnshire. Just before I nodded off, he said to me, "There is a house I want you to see. It is near the place you wanted Sahir to go to school".

"What, now?" I asked, jet-lagged.

"It won't take long. Just from the outside," he insisted.

I woke up as we pulled into a long driveway. I looked through the car window and saw that the dining furniture was identical to ours. Ijaz let me into the property. Puzzled, I looked at him. He just grinned back at me.

"You've bought it!"

He nodded triumphantly. This was not a summer break. We were not going back. I followed him in a daze, up the grand central staircase that I had always wanted in my house, and the reality finally sank in. It was time to snap out of this existence where I did not know which continent I would end up from one day to the next. I had no voice, no value... like a vase or a candlestick that could be moved around and had no significance at all. This might have looked like the house I always wanted, but it wasn't my home. It was time to move.

The 11+ exam was in a couple of months. If only it had been a test for how often a family relocated, because we had moved 11 times by then. Sahir had moved schools six times in ten years. The poor thing rose to the occasion and sat the test. Surprisingly, he didn't get a place at the excellent selective school. Ijaz went ballistic, blaming me for teaching him poorly. He blamed me for the hefty mortgage too. Apparently, it was my fault that he'd bought the house. He shouted at Sahir, calling him a piece of shit, a duffer, and a whole host of other names. I appealed the decision. We learned that Ijaz had failed to submit the appropriate paperwork on time, and that the pass mark for the test had been 220. Sahir had scored 259. Eventually, Sahir got the place he had earned. But Ijaz never once apologised for cursing his son.

We were now in an exceptionally large five-bedroomed house with en-suite bathrooms and a sauna room. From the large conservatory, there were uninterrupted views of the green paddocks. There were four reception rooms and a large kitchen which seemed perfect for baking with noisy children. But this was the house that we could not laugh in. It was the house where I had to hide my course books under the sofa in the conservatory. It was the house where the 54-inch TV could be disconnected if a 32-year-old woman was caught watching *Friends*. The computer in the study was password-locked. Wires would be pulled out on a whim. This man thought he owned us.

Saleha came to visit as soon as she heard I wasn't coming back. Ijaz turned on the charm while she stayed but after 3 days, she said to me, "I can't stay here. I will suffocate". I couldn't understand what was wrong. We had been so hospitable. She sat me down. "Reham, if you think people are friends with you because you are married to a doctor and live in a big house, you are mistaken. Your friends will be your friends even if you live in a tiny house. This is no life. You don't have a husband. I never see him around you, helping you, or spending time with you. He even eats on his own. What kind of life is this?"

I did not need Saleha's advice because I had already decided, but it helped me focus. The plan was to get a teaching job at the children's school in Pakistan, for which I needed a Bachelor's degree. I knew I was going to be sent back to Chak Shahzad in the summer. I decided I would not return. I secretly studied for my Bachelor of Arts degree over the next few months, and also started looking for a lawyer who could help get me and my kids out safely. When I flew back to Pakistan in 2005, I was sporting a large gash on my cheek, courtesy of my husband slamming a door in my face when he flew into a rage a couple of nights before. At our housewarming the following day, nearly a hundred guests of our mostly Pakistani social circle saw the fresh scar on my face. They chose not to ask any questions while I played the perfect hostess.

I returned to Pakistan and sat my exam in the same Peshawar I had fled from many years before as a teenager in search of better education. While in Pakistan, Saleha advised me to return to England as it would be unsafe for me and the children. She pointed out that it was common for ex-spouses to be violent, and there was the risk of child abduction following a divorce. Reluctantly, I returned. It would be another three months before I could be free, but it was coming. I had finally found a lawyer willing to represent me.

§

We visited Pakistan during the October half-term. This was following the devastating earthquake of 2005. Many British Pakistanis, particularly doctors, had also chosen to go to help with the relief effort. Pakistanis displayed exemplary commitment and unity through this catastrophe. Saleha and I helped in our personal capacity too, along with our friends. We focused on reuniting missing children with their families and finding solutions for orphaned ones. One of our friends was a TV producer who asked me to join the lifeline telethon to explain the relief effort on the local PTV station. Ijaz allowed me to join the program for an hour but then became very angry afterwards. He was confused, it seemed, about how he felt when people complimented his wife and her abilities. One day, he would come back and say, "It seems you have cast a spell on everyone. Everywhere I go they seem to be in love with you. Even stray dogs in the street seem to ask about you". The following day it would be a barrage of insults and abuse. In one of these fits, he threw our passports at my face and said, "I am not paying for you and your tickets to go back".

I saw the passports on the floor. I felt the urge to just pick them up immediately but fear was holding me back. I'd been waiting for this moment for what felt like forever. I was staring at them like a lizard staring at a dropped tail. And then I moved to pick them up. I never returned the passports to him. On my return to England, I immediately sent them to my solicitor for safe-keeping, so that the kids would be protected. Ijaz had frequently threatened to take my kids away if I walked out on him. Although a parental child abduction protocol had existed between the two countries since 2003, it had not been incorporated into Pakistani law. Back in 2005, Pakistan was not part of the Hague convention. Child abduction to Pakistan was not understood or paid much attention to. Significant steps have been taken since then. In December 2016, Pakistan finally became a contracting state to the Hague convention. The law came into force in March the following year. However, it is still very common for children to be abducted by a spouse (mostly by men during a divorce). In some cases for which my help was sought, Pakistani women who had been imported as wives would be sent back home by their British husbands, and the children would be kept in England.

I would travel to Pakistan years later, and encounter a very young child on the plane. He kept coming to my seat. His father seemed like a perfectly nice young man but was struggling with the child. I asked where the mother was and he told me that she had left them. I asked why he was going to Pakistan and he gave me a story with too many holes in it. I discovered that he was dropping his son off with his aunt in a remote village in Punjab. Despite improved laws, kids are used to blackmail spouses into staying in abusive situations.

I remember how Ijaz threatened me for the millionth time during that October half-term in our Chak Shahzad home. He was becoming increasingly insecure. There was no place on earth he could lock his wife away from the world that threatened to set her free from him. One day at breakfast, he screamed again: "If you walk out on me, you will never see your beloved kids anymore".

"Fine," I responded. "I will not put up with this madness anymore!"

Taken aback, he backed off. I looked across at the children with tears glistening in their eyes. The following morning, as he was shaving in the bathroom, he suddenly charged towards me, in full view of the children. He pushed me against the wall and put his razor on my neck. "Try leaving now!" he snarled. My voice was silent, but this time there was cold defiance in my eyes.

The fights were over petty things like money for bottled drinking water, or new school shoes. I sold most of my jewellery to buy basic necessities. I couldn't bear to see torn shoes on my son's feet. We were not poor. But the consultant psychiatrist's pay was not for nappies and water. It was only for expensive land and cars. In his mad race to catch up with his rich cousins, he would lose the most precious gems he had: his own beautiful children.

Chapter 7

The man didn't even sneak a look up at me as his rights were read out to him. My legs were shaking. But this was the last of him... or so I thought.

He immediately called his brother, colleagues, and his nephew, Shoaib. Shoaib spent the next few days trying to convince me to give his *chacha* another chance. That same night, a group of doctors and their wives arrived to talk me out of it. One of his friends, who had recently tied the knot, said, "Even my parents used to fight like this. These persistent quarrels are disturbing for kids". I saw him earnestly trying to salvage a marriage, but I just smiled gently and said, "Brother, you are a good and decent man. But this is not a fight. This is not a marriage. I have wanted to leave him for years. Please understand".

But no one understood. This kind man's young wife had much to thank me for: their whole marriage had been supported by me. My participation in their wedding would actually soon be used against me, as this young woman would quickly announce that the reason for my divorce would emerge in the shape of a sugar daddy. I had performed some of the dance routines at their wedding, which is traditional in our social circle. Footage of innocent moments like this would be spread by certain people, in a deliberate attempt to paint me as a woman with a shady past.

I didn't have a sugar daddy, or any other reason to file for divorce. That phantom man never appeared, and neither did an apology. The same people I had entertained day and night were now saying awful things to my face, and much worse behind my back. My husband's brother made angry phone calls, telling me to stop this nonsense. Ultimately, I had to remind him that the Prohibitive Steps Order against my husband included indirect harassment. Mutual older cousins of ours were dragged in, and, several transatlantic calls later, I'd upset many in the family with my unwavering stance.

Even my own immediate family was unsupportive, except for my older sister. She was the only emotional support I had, and maintained positive contact throughout the post-divorce period. My brother's wife, who I had considered my best friend, distanced herself from me completely; no letters, no phone calls. A complete black out. The letters from my mother during this period were also disturbingly negative. In retrospect, I have no idea how I survived this emotional blackmail. If I faced so much resistance, despite belonging to an educated and enlightened family, what must other girls be up against?

Somewhat surprisingly, it was mainly the women around me who put me through constant guilt-trips over my decision. One religious woman even suggested I stay with him, but turn off all my senses and treat him only as a paycheck. All I could say in response was, "What you're describing to me is prostitution".

Only a year after my divorce, many of the same women who had judged me, talked behind my back, and spread malicious gossip, came back to me for advice. Those who don't understand what you are going through will repent in time, as they will inevitably go through something similar. I would always pick up those random phone calls and try to help those dealing with abuse. Some would call that extremely forgiving, and others would call it stupidity. I didn't know how to act any other way.

One day, a professional doctor with a very supportive family in the UK, called me. She had completed her PLAB, a professional qualification to allow her to practice in the UK. She needed me for legal and emotional advice. In her second phone call, she asked me if I was in more or less mental anguish after leaving my husband. I was taken aback by her question. It suddenly dawned on me how I had never once regretted or even looked back at that decision. I explained to her gently that dealing with divorce was not like taking a standard dosage of paracetamol; everyone has different coping mechanisms and abilities. After about 15 minutes of discussion, she suddenly changed her tone and said, "Reham, I was given a very different impression of you by your friends. You are not at all the person they say you are. They have been saying all sorts of nasty things about you". I simply replied that they were work colleagues of my ex-husband, not my friends.

I hung up and pushed the conversation out of my mind. Just a few weeks later, I received a message: the woman who had been mentioned in that phone call as the one spreading gossip about me had lost her young daughter. That hit me right in the gut; I was devastated. The little girl had been very fond of me. I was popular with all the kids of our family friends, mainly because most of their parents were much older than me. I'd always found conversations about clothing and jewellery incredibly boring, so I ended up spending time with the kids instead.

The funeral was on a weekday. It was a three-and-a-half-hour drive. After the service, I went to their home. As soon as I walked through the door, the distraught mother rushed to me. She hugged me and sobbed uncontrollably. I held her in my arms as she repeatedly and loudly asked for forgiveness. I went red, and whispered in her ear, "Do you really think I could have wished any evil towards you?" She held my face and said she knew I wouldn't, which was why she needed forgiveness from me. "It was a Satanic whisper that drove me to it. I realise you are an angel".

That was even more embarrassing. I could do nothing but listen and try to be comforting. She wept loudly. The other ladies insisted that I let her cry. She had been in shock ever since the sad news. I had obviously never hoped that anything would befall that family. I didn't believe in anything like karma. I had no time to pay attention to what people might be saying about me. In the first six months after my divorce, I'd been so busy trying to make ends meet. When I left Ijaz, I had just 300 Pakistani rupees in my handbag, left over after a recent trip to Pakistan. Surviving on less than £5 was never going to be easy. My husband immediately emptied the savings accounts so the courts could not access his money. All properties in Pakistan were backdated as gifts to his sister. I'd had a joint account with my husband, and a debit card with a £50 withdrawal limit. I was thrown off that account within two months of my filing for a divorce.

I took all my rings to local jewellers but found it difficult to sell 24 carat gold items to non-Asian jewellery shops, as Pakistani jewellery isn't hallmarked. I sold many items to family and friends for a fraction of the value. I sold the car in Pakistan via a contact, which led to Ijaz immediately launching a criminal case against my brother, even though we had complete ownership of the car, and all the legal documentation. My mother was unhappy with me in turn, because my brother had been dragged into it. My quick-thinking solicitor ensured that I at least got the car in the UK via the courts. Had it not been for the car, my kids and I would have been left to starve. Though I hated resorting to it, I had to borrow £200 from a wealthy couple who lived in Appleby. I was keen to return the money to them as soon as possible. The doctor handed me the envelope in the local leisure centre with a rather cold air about him. It wasn't the money, but my decision to divorce that had garnered that response.

After three weeks of feeding the kids with whatever was at home, I made the rather embarrassing journey to the Jobcentre. It cost £10 in fuel to drive to Grimsby. I sat in the car park of the supermarket opposite the Jobcentre for fifteen minutes or so, trying to pluck up the courage to walk through the doors. It was a sense of shame coupled with the fear of walking past the young, tattooed boys on the dole. It turned out to be a highly educational process. I learned that scruffy young men will often open doors better than men in suits. As I walked in after all that anxiety, I discovered I was at the wrong centre. The correct Jobcentre for my postcode was in Lincoln. I grimaced, and prepared for another £10 hit to my limited finances.

'The Jobcentre is for all sorts of people,' I told myself as I walked into the one in Lincoln. The man I spoke to had kind eyes, and listened to my story in quiet amazement. He asked how I had survived the last month without any money. I smiled and simply said, "I've had plenty of practice of living on very little".

It was true. I was a competent cook who could come up with countless different dishes with the same few ingredients. We lived mainly with just the oil, rice and flour in the house. The kids were just relieved that there was no ugliness anymore. They were happy to be free.

I had no reservations, and wasn't planning to say no to any kind of job. I was happy to be canteen staff or a cleaner if nothing else was available. However, the man suggested young adult vocational centres. I'd always had an interest in care and rehabilitation of young children who had been deprived of secure home environments, so I was intrigued. Sadly, I was not ultimately considered for such a role. Perhaps my appearance was not the best indicator of my abilities or interest. Good looks can be limiting in several ways. For some jobs, my looks went against me. There is a general perception that an attractive woman may not be competent or intelligent, and may be high maintenance. My status as a doctor's wife was also a negative in the minds of employers.

The friendly careers advisor also suggested a position as a driving instructor. I seriously considered it, but had no capital to set it up. Instead, by February I was making a small income delivering shopping catalogues to people's homes and taking orders for a company called Kleeneze. Sahir and I put in hour after hour, happily delivering the catalogues and collecting orders in the freezing cold. I remember staying up late in the night with Ridha, putting slips into over a hundred catalogues. Each catalogue had to be delivered and then retrieved a week later, with whatever orders the residents had left inside - if they'd even opened them at all. Most people didn't even bother to put the catalogues back out. Perhaps they didn't realise that we had to buy these catalogues ourselves before distributing them. Sahir and I made a great team, but it was time-consuming and involved a lot of walking. With frozen fingers, we would try to salvage the catalogues left out in the rain and snow. It was a good early lesson for both of us on how businesses made money. We often forget to visualise what the job actually entails, or factor in time and effort. Sahir and I learned the hard way, but never complained.

One day I was invited in by one of the few good customers who ordered regularly. I was usually delivering soaps to him. He showed me around his property, which he had converted into a Bed and Breakfast hotel after he lost his job. He gave me detailed info on how to make money from existing resources. This B&B was in the middle of nowhere, and only I delivered to him. It was not a tourist spot, but the man had managed to get long-term clients by offering good deals to local construction firms for their employees. His attention-to-detail had won over the guests. As he walked me out, he added reassuringly, "You drive that Mercedes with the three kids in the back and have no issue going door-to-door. I see you going places young lady". It was another little thing that someone said to me that stayed with me forever. I realised how it was all connected. All I had to do was learn to read the signs.

In addition to catalogue delivery, I started offering mobile beautician services such as waxing and threading. I even enrolled to become a Body Shop home consultant, to sell their products. I went for any kind of job I could. Saturdays were for interviews and auditions for upcoming jobs. I could be doing an interview for a delinquent rehab centre in the morning and an audition for a Walls Ice Cream advert in the afternoon. In between the job-hunting, I would plan museum visits for the children. Sundays would be for cleaning and bulk cooking. The kids always helped with the household chores. Sahir soon graduated from cutting okra to learning how to make roast dinners in the convection oven. I would return home from a long day at work to find roast chicken and potatoes cooked perfectly by the 12-year-old. He became a culinary expert as he grew up, and would end up refusing to teach me the brownie recipe he'd perfected over the years. He took great pleasure in the fact that I had taught him so much but forgotten all these recipes myself.

Ridha found her voice overnight. She told us how scared she had been all those years. She would snuggle into my bed every night and tell me how she had hated the big house. She had been the perfect 'seen and not heard' kid for far too long. I didn't even know that she was so traumatised by what she had seen. She opened up after the divorce, both to us and to CafCass (Children and Family Court Advisory and Support Service) reporters trying to assess the situation and decide whether to recommend contact with her biological father. In the first few weeks, she made me check that the doors were locked securely over and over again. She was terrified that Ijaz might have a spare key, and would creep in while we were asleep. All I could do was assure her that he was not in the country.

§

It was a freezing February afternoon as the kids and I returned from school. Inaya had a high temperature. As soon as I entered the huge house, I turned to the phone beside the front door to call a doctor. It had been disconnected. I had no credit on my mobile phone. The oil and heating bill had not been paid either.

In these first two months after filing for divorce, I had come under intense emotional pressure and criticism by my mother, my cousins, and my husband's friends to not go ahead with the decision. A few had stopped speaking to me, thinking I was being insolent by not even wanting to talk about the issue. My mother wrote deeply disturbing letters to me that could have driven anyone mad with guilt, but I knew what I was doing. The constant pestering, especially by my husband's best friend, did mean I backed down a touch. He had pleaded with me not to proceed with the divorce and instead leave things as they were. He had assured me that if I did not actively proceed with the divorce or the domestic abuse charges, I could continue to live like this. Ijaz had begged him to convince me to just allow some time to think over the decision.

I had said to him, "Naeem *bhai*, I know this man. I know what he will do".

But he still insisted I back down. The conversation was sad yet funny, with Naeem imploring me, "I know he is the biggest SOB that ever was but please give him one more chance".

"You know, I asked him," Naeem continued. "'What about the kids? Why don't you appreciate the kids?' and he replied, 'I'm not cut out to be a dad'. I asked him 'Why don't you appreciate your beautiful wife' and he replied, 'I am not cut out to be a husband'. Then I said, 'Why don't you appreciate your job' and he replied, 'I am not cut out to be a doctor'.

Then I said, 'Why don't you appreciate that you live in England' and he replied, 'I'm not cut out to live with *goras* (Westerners)'".

I listened to his soliloquy, amused. "And yet you still want me to take this man back?" I said in amazement.

I was to regret this concession to my first husband years later, when he would go to the media and ask why I had not pressed charges. I had taken the judge's advice in my best interests: that if this man lost his job because of my charges, I would never get anything out of him. He knew my economic position, but he did not know the man I had lived with. I learned that one should always listen to their own heart. There is no greater wisdom than what you know.

I knew Ijaz would try to crush me economically to force me to take him back. He thought I couldn't survive without his salary. I would see similar tactics used on me throughout the rest of my life. There was no emotional connection here though, so I could throw myself into my new challenges with all my energy. I immediately enrolled for a post-graduate diploma in Broadcast Journalism at East Coast Media in Grimsby.

I had no idea that this short post-graduate course would cause me so many political headaches later in life. I would one day come under attack by people desperate to tear me down, with a claim that I had never undertaken this course. At the time, I would have laughed openly if someone had told me that this would be the cause of a huge controversy. But to be fair, I would have found any element of my future hysterical and ludicrous if I had been told. I simply wanted to improve my skills and learn as much about my chosen career line as I could, and I leapt at every opportunity. I wanted more of everything: from improving my diction and accent, to learning camerawork, editing and writing-to-pictures. Being a divorcee was not going to be easy, but I was trying to capitalize on everything that my new situation could offer me.

The course itself had been an attraction to students because of a one-week placement at the BBC. Ironically, the placement at the BBC convinced me that I never wanted to be part of that organisation. It also became the reason I never disclosed my private details or vulnerabilities to anyone ever again. As an intern, I was about to learn how women can go out of their way to damage other women for no apparent reason.

On my first day of my placement at Look North, I was interviewed by the editor, a woman in her mid-forties. She was obviously quite accomplished to have made it this far. She encouraged me to tell her everything about myself. I began by telling her how I had just come out of a serious domestic abuse situation and had three small kids. I told her in detail how I was juggling the course and a job. I explained how I could do odd hours - the late evening shift, and the early one since I did have childcare facilities - but, if possible, I would like to show my face at my other job a couple of times a week, as I couldn't afford to lose it. This was only a two-week placement. She had told me to be honest. I wanted to make it clear that I was committed.

The letter that this woman wrote to my tutor was far from complimentary. It described me as a woman who had childcare issues and could not give any time to her internship. Puzzled by the letter, the tutor asked me what had happened. I didn't know. I thought that I had performed well. I had shot a piece of news for breakfast, been appreciated by the producer for doing an in-depth bit of research on state boarding schools, and even managed to get them a celebrity sports guest for the show.

My tutor, a talented woman who had herself been treated unfairly by the same system, smiled at me. "And did you speak to the sports editor when arranging the sports guest?" she inquired. I nodded. She smiled again. "You do know she's sleeping with the sports editor?"

"How would I know that? Besides, what has that got to do with this scathing letter about me?" I replied, aghast.

"Reham, look at you. She got jealous!"

I was confused. Why would a senior editor think a young girl would steal her silver-haired boyfriend away? But back then I had seen very little of the big bad world outside. Even today I get very shocked when women hate me for no obvious reason or men think they have a chance in hell with me. A woman being single doesn't mean she is available.

After that experience, I never told anyone I had kids, or if there was a childcare emergency. Mothers with young children, or newly married women, are discriminated against in subtle ways, despite the laws. This would not be the last time I would work with the BBC. In the future, I would be seen as the woman least likely to get married or pregnant. I appeared to be a ruthless career woman who was only interested in her own progression. I never tried to dispel the myth. I was committed to my job, and never once called in sick. I was a mother to three young children. I couldn't afford to jeopardize it.

The course was ultimately irrelevant to my career anyway. I was only four months into it when I landed my first presenting job on a mainstream channel. Through the rest of my career I would do several other courses to hone my skills but no one ever put that in their headlines.

§

By May, my non-stop job search had paid off. Four months after my divorce, I'd managed to get a job at a channel called Legal TV. I had been sending out emails and filling in questionnaires right, left, and centre. Even in my lunch break at college, I would be searching for jobs. One day, I received an invitation from this channel, asking me to join them as a guest on a show. I was quite puzzled but replied, asking for details. They explained that it was a newly set-up channel that dealt with legal issues. I explained that I was not a solicitor but they had apparently liked my responses. I told them that I was training to be a broadcast journalist and was invited in for an interview.

This was February. I was struggling to pay heating-oil bills amounting to one hundred and twenty pounds. Finding money for the fuel to get to Birmingham for the interview was an additional challenge, but I did not want to turn down the opportunity. I remember being terrified of driving into Birmingham. Ijaz had made such a huge fuss when driving into big cities; he had proper panic attacks. He had definitely damaged my confidence. But as I drove into Aston with a printout of directions from the internet (this was before I could afford a satnav), I remember feeling very proud of myself for finding my way effortlessly. It was my 'One small step for woman, one giant leap for womankind' moment.

I could never have imagined how my life would change as I entered those studios and offices in an industrial estate in Aston. I didn't even have a showreel. The interview did not involve a screen test. Apparently, my legal and medical-negligence related knowledge impressed them. The interviewer said that they would get back to me, and mentioned the salary package. I was unsure whether he was giving me a monthly or an annual salary amount. I was so desperate that I didn't question it. I remember thinking to myself, 'If this is a monthly salary, it's exceptionally good. If it's an annual salary, it's ridiculous'. I said nothing and left.

A couple of months went by. I had not heard back from Legal TV, so I tried my luck with Asian channels. The first stop was the (now infamous) ARY. The head of programming was a friendly girl who didn't seem right for the position. She had more knowledge about European politics and good restaurants in Knightsbridge than programming. It emerged later that this girl, Ayesha Subhani, was a former diplomat's daughter. I proposed a program format to her where opinionated Asian aunties would sit and discuss sensitive, taboo issues with the audience. She loved the idea, and promised me a slot in April. I was unconvinced. Later, she called to say that she had forgotten that there were no April slots because of the Pakistan v Sri Lanka cricket series.

I ended up meeting Salman Iqbal, the son of the owner of ARY. All I remember from that meeting was a rather flustered Ayesha Subhani, stressing as the boss suddenly arrived at the office. They ushered me into another room, where, after the initial introduction, the man continued watching the cricket match on TV. I was rather annoyed by his lack of courtesy, and started texting and ignoring him too. He took the hint, turned to me, and asked a few questions about the show. I answered him sharply. The man was clearly used to people treating him like a god, and was taken aback by my curt replies.

I have never cared for men who are obsessed by their position, and have never hidden my disdain. It hasn't harmed me ever to show a man that I have no regard for people with more money than manners. Men are sometimes quick to pick up the signs that a woman is not interested; it quickly puts them in their place. It may not get you the job you were after, but one should never feel obliged to smile at a prospective (or current) employer. Not only do you maintain your integrity but you will end up with a better job if you don't get coerced into being used as eye candy or, worse still, sexual favours.

April went by and I finally got the offer that would transform me from a hesitant housewife into a fearless, driven social activist. One day in early May, I got the call I had been waiting for. The people at Legal TV called me for a second interview. I sat up all night researching the channel and relevant legal issues. The following day, I was directed to their main offices in Five Ways, Birmingham. I was thrown in at the deep end by being instructed to prepare the following day's program. The producers and directors were Polish, and struggling to follow the jargon-heavy legal content. I immediately gelled with them, and threw myself into the work. Unknown to me, the owner of the channel and his partners were wandering around in the huge office, and must have noticed my work. At the time I took them as staff. It would be a month before I learned who they actually were.

The first day that my content went on air, I was asked to co-host a segment of the show. As I sat there, I became acutely aware that the anchor had no idea what she was talking about. I had prepared questions and researched the answers. It seemed a very basic level of preparation to me, but after the show I was hired as a presenter. The girl who had hosted the show was fired. I felt awful that the young girl was kicked out. This was to be my first taste of the cut-throat business of TV ratings.

I worked for two weeks on probation. I was promised a salary after this period. To my dismay, I was then asked to do another two weeks for free. I refused. I asked to see the owner and was led into a huge office. The owner sat at a desk deeply engrossed in work with masses of files around him. The young, turbaned man looked up, offered a rather saccharine hello, and introduced himself as Mr Bal. There was no other chair in the room. It was time to make my voice heard, literally.

"I was sent up here for a meeting with you but, since there is no chair, we can't have a meeting," I said loudly.

The man immediately stood up, flustered, and blurted something silly about the lack of chairs. We had the meeting standing – both of us - which lasted a few minutes. I told him clearly that I expected to be paid after two weeks of probation, as agreed, and that I wouldn't be coming in the following day unless I was paid. I told him the figure I expected. He was rather shocked, but tried being friendly, proposing instead to show me the city in his car. I wasn't having any of that. I responded that I had plenty of friends to help me with exploring the city. A spin in his Bentley didn't interest me in the least. I made sure that he would never dare to make such a suggestion again.

I left the office and did not return as per my word. A week went by. The boss called me again and asked me to read a disparaging article written about the channel. He was aghast at the criticism (which was rather brutal), and asked if I would come to work. I quoted the figure again. He agreed. I continued in that same job for over two years, hosting their flagship show with impressive viewing figures. These were the days before Ofcom introduced rules on charging for phone calls to TV shows. The channel made a huge profit on the calls to these live shows. The popularity of this particular show grew and grew and the number of calls to the channel for advice shot through the roof. Overwhelmed, we had to use a call centre in India. Consequently, my bosses were extremely happy with my performance, if not my unsmiling demeanour to them. The show became very popular with legal firms across the country as it meant more business for their legal experts. I had final say on who could be on the guest list.

It is important to never underestimate your worth if you have done the work to prove it. Ironically, while I never let anyone undervalue me in my professional life, I tended to allow people to walk all over me in my personal relationships. Professionally, I made sound judgements on the people I chose to work with, but when it came to men in a romantic capacity, I was incapable of making informed choices. Anyone who chased me and professed undying love was good enough. Perhaps we make our professional choices based on maths and monetary benefits. It's numbers that convince us, not words that sway. And maybe it's safer that way.

Within a couple of weeks, I had settled into the tough routine at Legal TV and was enjoying myself. The Polish staff had a great work ethic, yet admired me for my energy and enthusiasm. They would line the bottom shelf of the coffee table with my favourite chocolates because they knew I didn't stop for lunch. My lunch was usually a doughnut on-the-go. I never had time to take off the trainers under my pinstriped powersuits. I would leave after classes for my diploma finished at 2pm, and drive to Birmingham in time for my 4pm live show. Makeup was a 3-minute affair: a light patting of face powder and a slick of gloss.

No one could ever have guessed that this young-looking, composed anchor tackling serious issues was a mother-of-three, had just come out of an abusive marriage, and had just raced into work with a 3-year-old in her arms. Inaya would play or sleep in the green room right next to the studio, separated by a glass door, where I could keep an eye on her. We were a big happy family. We all worked hard and laughed harder still. It was a great team effort. Dave, my utterly mad director, was white and English to the core, but married to a Turkish woman. The cameraman, Winston, was black and from Aston. Stewart Lawley, my buddy, was a citizen of the world. The producers were all Polish, the content producer Vijay was a young, fresh immigrant from India. It was a cultural melting pot. Dave and I developed a great camaraderie; he could see what others could not. I had told everyone that I had a boyfriend so no one would hit on me. To ward off advances, I explained that this boyfriend was a very religious, scary, bearded man. It was a joke in the office that my boyfriend belonged to the Taliban. But Dave could see through my excuses as I struggled with trivial daily occurrences like punctured tyres. He would make jabs at me, asking where this phantom Taliban boyfriend was when I needed him. My knight in shining armour would remain a phantom all my life. Punctured tyres would become less of an issue soon though. I commuted like crazy for 11 months and clocked up 155,000 miles on the car. The car got exhausted but my energy only increased.

Because of the show, I became the face of a leading personal injury firm, and popularised the catchphrase "Don't delay, Claim Today". One of their adverts was targeted at the Pakistani and Indian community and became extremely popular as I appeared in it next to The King of Bollywood, Shahrukh Khan. The commercial was shot in 2008 after an event at the Olympia, the London Mela, organised by a private Indian Channel. I hosted a stage for the stars to meet and greet the fans. Shahrukh Khan was the main attraction. I was impressed by his professionalism and his lack of arrogance; this was an educated, well-brought up man of a middle-class family; friendly, with polite restraint, and not one bit of the diva he could so easily have been.

The advert was a hit and was followed by one with cricket star Shahid Afridi. The cricketer is known for his typical Pashtun good looks and his mercurial batting style. During the recording, as he struggled with the words, his simplicity shone through. He was every bit the stereotypical, warm yet naïve Pashtun. As we walked out of the recording studio, the Pashtun cricketer saw the baby sleeping on the sofa in the green room.

"Whose lovely child is this?" he enquired.

"It's my daughter," I replied.

"You are married?" He was taken aback. "Where is the father?" he asked, incredulously.

"He's not around. I have two other children as well," I replied.

He mumbled a rather sympathetic 'Oh'. Even in that brief encounter, I could sense that he was a soft-hearted man. We didn't speak much after that. I didn't know it then, but we would run into each other again years later.

§

It was June 2007. We were preparing for Ridha's 10th birthday. I had bought her favourite cake and wrapped everything beautifully just as she liked. Ridha wasn't expecting a gift from her father, but the young girl got a surprise she would never forget: the four of us being thrown out of our home. I had gone down to the village post office. While I was gone, Ridha got the fright of her life as she watched three strange men trying to get into her house. I came back to find the bailiffs changing the locks on the door. The house was dismantled bit by bit in front of the three children. I had fought the eviction three times successfully, but Ijaz had now won. Coincidentally, a lawyer on the show had suggested a mortgage advisor only a few weeks earlier, and I had managed to get a 100% mortgage. Miraculously, we'd exchanged contracts in four weeks, but I was not prepared to move. I wasn't expecting eviction.

As the bailiffs emptied the rooms of furniture and white goods before the children's eyes, I got on the phone and called a man with a van. It cost £475. I had hardly any money left after all the other costs of getting on the property ladder. I had sold a necklace to pay for the land registry. The seller had demanded an additional thousand for the light fittings. I refused to pay as I didn't have the money. We arrived at the new property at 2am. The girls were fast asleep among all the clothes and toys packed into the car. Sahir, the ever-ready helper, jumped out and started to unload. None of the light switches in the house worked. I stood in the darkness, wondering 'What next?' All the light fittings had been taken, leaving only taped-over wires. Sahir found a table lamp to plug in. In the light shone by the 14-year-old, I made my way round our first real home.

Before we'd left the house Ijaz had just thrown us out of, I'd packed all his clothes, suits, and even his underwear neatly in suitcases for him to collect. A colleague of his rang me up and asked exasperatedly why I was not shredding his clothes in anger. She wondered what my secret was for remaining so calm. But I'd always understood that he had had a psychologically disturbed childhood, which I certainly did not want for my own children. To see a parent behaving hysterically, consumed by revenge and hatred, is not good for any child. I had moved on the minute we were safe, never to look back...until one day, a decade later, I would be forced to.

Chapter 8

From 2015 to 2018, there were constant rumours of a kiss-and-tell book making the rounds. While this was happening, a British friend said to me, "Reham, I think you should write a book that tells the story of how you became this gladiator that you are today. Your life story is so much more interesting than anyone knows. I would want to know how you did it all on your own".

Eventually, I would be in a position where people would come to work for me. There would be younger men who saw me as a mother-figure, who would feel very angry at the hardship I'd had to bear. They would see the person off-camera and feel protective. I'd always tell them that, while I'd had experiences which were not pleasant, those experiences had made me who I am. I had trained in the best boot camps possible, and been prepared me for what I was sent to do. I owe everything to those who did not love me and those who abandoned me. I was never wrapped in cotton wool and treated with care. I never had a safety net to fall back on. If I had, I would have never discovered my abilities.

Humans are meant to survive. We are the most adaptable of all species. When we lose our sight, we find our way with our ears and our touch. When our hands are cut off, we write with our feet. I entered 2018 as an able-bodied, healthy, energetic woman. How could I say that I have had a bad life? I feel like I have had a terrific journey. There was never a boring moment. It was constantly learning. I never needed to go bungee jumping or skydiving. I never needed to look for adventure. My life was always pretty damn exciting as it was. I began to see my whole life as a holiday, with new sights and sounds to be taken in. I deeply inhaled every scent of life so that I wouldn't miss even the tail-note. I knew to throw myself into every challenge with all my heart. Every problem is simply an opportunity to find a solution.

For the time being, my problems were all financial and career-based. But what I was doing was working. As I settled into my first TV job, the finances improved. Soon, I was making more than one hundred pounds an hour, whilst picking up additional corporate events that paid even better. I travelled the length and breadth of the country, presenting at a variety of events from policing conferences in London to the Business Federation Awards in the Reebok Stadium. Those years of reading books and following Open University programs were bearing fruit. My own legal battle through divorce, domestic violence, home repossession and eviction, and child custody, helped to a great degree. People actually thought I was a solicitor myself. I had plenty of energy in that first year, despite the on-going legal cases I was fighting.

This job was a game-changer. It gave myself and my kids a decent lifestyle, and allowed us to get onto the property ladder. It also gave me a huge insight into the plight of refugees and asylum seekers in detention centres. My growing interest in the shambolic state of affairs at the Home Office laid the foundation of my understanding of conflicts and refugee issues, which I would remain deeply committed to for the rest of my life. I would become heavily involved in the stories I was covering. Asylum seekers arriving in the UK with their families endured months of detention. The number of children detained had risen to an alarming level between the years of 2005 to 2008. As the numbers touched two thousand per year the plight of these children at the detention centres was too disturbing. Also, I couldn't understand why some asylum cases were taking longer than nine years to resolve. It appeared that the Home Office was immune to all the harsh criticism that programs like mine were heaping onto their failing system. It was a clear case of abominable management, with a backlog of cases going back 20 years. The utter incompetence and apathy of the Government irritated me to no end. I got involved in a lot of refugee movements and followed up the judicial reviews of bigger cases, like the Home Office's sudden and unlawful Highly Skilled Migrant Program (HSMP) rule changes of 2006. My show also helped the campaign for a judicial review against the Home Office's decision to change the requirement for Indefinite Leave to Remain in the UK from 4 to 5 years in 2006. They had changed the goalposts for migrants overnight and it was something that needed to be challenged.

My constant highlighting of refugee issues led to me becoming the poster girl for the Congolese community too. I would stand with Congolese protestors outside detention centres in the West Midlands, covering their demands for the resolution of asylum cases. The cold detachment of the government to these immigration issues was an eye-opener. The politicians did not know or care about the black market operating thanks to the exploitation of illegal immigrants. In the absence of regularised status many would work illegally for a pittance. And the children suffered. There was the obvious question. How could a child be illegal? No one had an answer.

There were asylum seekers with three to four children, surviving on food vouchers of forty-five pounds a week. They had no right to work. Many had been in the country for ten years or more. I wondered why they could not be given a right to work and contribute to the economy while their claims were being heard. As I covered the issue, I crossed over from a journalist covering events to a social activist advocating the better treatment of refugees. As I joined protest walks I came across Tim Finch of the Refugee Council, who advocated a pathway to citizenship. I learnt that many people were effectively in bonded slavery as they worked in the shadow economy for as little as £1 an hour in jobs that no one else wanted to do. It became clear that London was one of the cities that mainly relied on this black market; the Government couldn't possibly be unaware of it. Thousands of asylum seekers were forced into a life of deception. They had no choice but to survive like this. Some were educated professionals who were keen to put their skills to work. I was able to meet one: a photo editor who was using his skills to document the unjust system of immigration, but couldn't make a career out of his talent. These people were being exploited, and most were living in utter destitution. Most had nothing to return to; their families were being killed back home. They faced jail and possibly death if they returned.

The open racism taught by the propagandists to local white youngsters viewing these protests was depressing. These kids were taught to hate without knowing what they were even hating immigrants for. I became very involved in work towards the prevention of radicalisation in all communities. I interacted with the youth and simply asked them where they would flee if they were persecuted in their homeland. Some would say they would go to warmer places like the Caribbean. When I explained that everyone would want a good place to go to, they would understand. Of course, I'd explained it to them in a language they understood, as I had no reason to exploit the issue of immigration for politics.

Immigration should not be seen as a marginal hard-left issue. All sections of the community, including the church, the mosque, the synagogue and civic society, should come together on human rights issues. Before worrying about rogue states in the Middle East and their repression of people, one should have the insight to realise what we are doing in our own backyard. This was my gateway into the abuse of power and disregard of basic human rights that I would also discover was happening in my country of origin. I would later be deeply involved in the fight for the rights of the unrepresented Baluch and Pashtun people back home.

There were some people trying to bring attention to these issues. The Home Secretary at that time, John Reid, would describe the Home Office as 'not fit for purpose' only to be rewarded by Tony Blair then splitting Home Office into two departments. John Reid would end up being replaced by the first female Home Secretary, the rather disappointing Jacqui Smith. I was disgusted by what I saw back then. Imagine my horror when the United Kingdom became even more immigrant-unfriendly with the regressive Brexit referendum of 2016. Large groups of people had actually voted to leave a trading bloc that gave the UK a huge number of benefits, only because they thought it would mean fewer immigrants. It was depressing.

Back in 2006-07, I was interested in my own Pakistani community too. I had witnessed reverse-racism first hand in conversations at Pakistani social gatherings. I had been revolted by the racist attitudes towards people of other races and colours. It came from a deep fear of losing our own culture to the overriding influence of the host culture. I also understood why younger boys in any community were easy prey for the politics of hate and could easily become disillusioned. They were constantly being told that they were different by their families, and this notion was only reinforced by everything they saw. Even simple forms have 'diversity' sections that ask people to clarify whether they are British, British Pakistani or 'Other'.

This was the time of Guantanamo Bay and the Anti-Terrorism Bill. It led to an official crackdown on the spread of radical literature, and areas like

Sparkhill in Birmingham came under the spotlight for the first time. I had been moderating conferences for the National Association of Muslim Policing at the time, which had helped me delve deeper into these issues. As a result, my name was even suggested for the 'Friends of the Manchester Police', a panel proposed to prevent radicalisation of the Muslim youth. This was because I had inadvertently started developing the image of a good, sensible role model for the Pakistani community. There were other, similar offers but there was a reason I stayed away: I was averse to being a part of any project which I felt was only paying lip-service to a cause. This attitude would not change in later years. I was always a woman of action, and would find most conferences and seminars to be time-wasting exercises. Nothing is more frustrating than seeing people pretending to make a difference. I did what I could through the content on my shows and with how I raised my kids. They would certainly be well-informed about why and how racism and immigration was used to cement personal politics.

When I moved to the West Midlands, I was secure in the knowledge that the kids would be taken care of, and I could devote more time to my work. We'd moved to a small, friendly village that was close to all the big city amenities. The kids loved the small three-bed semi-detached home. They were older now, and we worked as a team. They never let me down. I'd done the research and put Inaya in the same school as Ridha; a great Catholic primary school in Henley-in-Arden, Warwickshire, with good results, incredibly small class sizes and a caring family environment. It was one of the top 25 schools in the country. Inaya could be a bit of a handful in the mornings as Ridha took her to the school bus but Ridha managed it beautifully, jumping into the disciplinarian role. It was a complex arrangement but she made it work. She was an absolute star, although she would complain about Inaya's dramatics for years to come. In any case, at Legal TV I had a constant supply of caring and conscientious Czech and Polish babysitters if I ever needed extra help with the kids.

Sahir was at an even better school in Stratford-upon-Avon, the King Edward VI Grammar School for Boys. He loved the independence of making his way to school himself, and it was great to see him thrive. Having said that, he says he found a lot of the school crowd to be a bunch of empty-headed, pretentious, insufferable posh toffs. Some were born with silver spoons and were classist, while others from more average families also got sucked into this pseudo-elite atmosphere. Stratford-upon-Avon was Shakespeare's town, so it had a certain reputation, but the desperate efforts of the people to match that air of grandiosity were unsuccessful. Sahir had been to Caistor Grammar before this school, and would later go to Burnham Grammar near Slough. According to him, none of the kids in these schools thought they were anything special, despite passing the same selective entrance exams.

Having missed the children all day, I would look forward to spending some time with them in the evenings. They would groan as I would nag them out of their games and into my room for a bedtime chat. They would bake me my favourite pizza and put me to bed. We had developed something of a tradition: the kids would press my feet and I would read to them at bedtime. They had learned that all they had to do was rub my feet for a few seconds and I would fall asleep. Sure enough, the mum who had started her day at 4:30am would be gone within a few minutes. I had talked in my sleep since I was a child. During my first marriage, I was plagued with nightmares, and would wake up with my nails digging into my palms. I'd be tired and my neck muscles would be tense. Now that I was on my own and there were fewer sleep hours, it was restful sleep. But on the outside, I was like a child fighting off sleep, and continued chatting and making weird comments largely because of the sleep deprivation. My kids would giggle uncontrollably and record my sleepy babbling on occasion.

Things were better overall. So much better. But the finances became an issue again. I realised that my job would not be enough to cover the mortgage payments. I needed an extra £1200 a month. I didn't even have enough money to buy a gas hob and a fridge for the first three months, so I shopped daily and became a microwave/convection oven expert. One morning, I picked up the Yellow Pages and started calling all the radio stations for possible jobs. The second one on my list pretty much gave me a job over the phone. Apparently, they needed a breakfast newsreader and producer urgently, and I'd somehow managed to ring them before they'd even put the advert out. The station manager himself happened to take the call. "I hear a smile in your voice," he said. "Come and meet us." I did, and that was that.

Sunshine Radio was owned by the Laser Broadcasting Group when I joined. The output covered North Worcestershire, South Shropshire, North Hertfordshire, and Monmouthshire from our studios in Hereford. It was the best training in radio I could get; a masterclass in everything from voice projection and articulation to scriptwriting in simple language. I started producing and presenting news and sport on their breakfast show, and learned how to edit. The most challenging thing was grappling with football names and fixtures; it was like a new language to me. The shift was non-stop from 6am to lunchtime. On some days, it would be 2pm before I could leave for my main TV job at Legal TV in Birmingham. It would take an hour and a half via the Kidderminster Road (A456) to reach the A38. I was basically on autopilot until I saw the Aston/Birchfield/Perry Bar exit. I was coming home earlier though. It was my second year at Legal TV by then, and I had a larger team.

Looking back, I don't know how I did it; this was a gruesome schedule. But the cold, frosty starts did not bother me. I woke up just before sunrise. I would set off at 5am from Astwood Bank, and take the B4090 to Ludlow. It would take just over an hour if there was no ice on the roads. My drive in the darkness was lovely in its own way. During the drive to Ludlow Hill in scenic Shropshire, one has to frequently stop for herds of sheep or the occasional deer on the road. I managed to literally enjoy every step of the journey to my destination.

I'd needed to pay a mortgage and it had led to Radio, something I had always wanted to do, but that wasn't the point. I had to remember what was important. I made sure I always drove cheerfully to work, just like my Daddy. I made sure my breakfast was interesting and different every day. With a tub of cold rice pudding and perhaps a slice of coffee cake, I made the start of my day sweet in all manner of speaking. My car was my home and I was prepared for every eventuality, from a surprise job interview to being stuck in a flood. Looking back, I don't know how I managed to shop, cook, help with homework, and take the kids ice-skating. It seems that the more there is on the schedule, the more competent one becomes. The only secret ingredient for this extra energy was freedom. I wasn't in a prison anymore. I did everything with a happy vigour. We were eating better and looking healthier.

I remembered how a £30 grocery bill would cause an earthquake at home on my husband's salary. The children and I had been well-drilled: we wouldn't take the grocery bags from the boot of the car if Ijaz was home, but would smuggle them in while he was not looking. We wouldn't dare unpack them while he was around for fear of being shouted at. The bags would go straight into cupboards until the coast was clear. We'd then set about putting everything in the right places. It was strange. We were always made to hide and tiptoe like this, but if I did not shop I would also get into trouble. Ijaz would complain endlessly that there was never stuff in the house, that I'd never made any dessert, and that other people came home to a great spread. But I was also not allowed to go over the £30 mark. If I did, there was hell to pay. It was a strange dichotomy and an impossible situation. As I started making everything from scratch, another woman in our social circle sniggered that I might as well get a cow and start milking at home too. Funnily enough, if I'd had a way to obtain one and knew that it would help, then maybe I'd have done exactly that. Feeding a family on £30 a week was ludicrous.

As a single earner, I was surprised that I had a higher grocery bill and could afford it. All of us had more responsibility but we also had so much more rest. We were sleeping better even though we had earlier starts. Sahir was now having to commute from Redditch to Stratford-upon-Avon. It wasn't until I'd be part of an anti-narcotics campaign later in life that I would realise how proud I should have been. That young teenager was commuting across counties and coming across people on all kinds of substances, but he never touched any form of drugs. What he took away from his long journeys was not a drug habit, but an understanding of how to look after himself and how to figure out the best and safest ways to travel. He developed maturity and independence. This would be useful when we would move again and he would find himself with another obstacle course to tackle just to get to his new school.

Ridha also evolved, transforming from a little girl into a responsible mother figure, always making sure Inaya behaved on the way to school. I feel she is a far firmer a parent than I am. Inaya thought of her older sister as the parent she must not disappoint. Inaya's constant crying when I was with her father slowly disappeared too. She had not lost a parent. It was as if she had three parents now. When I brought up the idea of remarriage, she was the only one who actively resisted the idea. The logical explanation she gave was that we were a complete family already. A perfect unit. A new person would have no role, and would not fit in.

For years their school teachers had no idea that they were from a 'broken' home. It wasn't that we hid the fact, but it wasn't obvious from their behaviour in school or their grades. When I mentioned in passing how I was a single parent to one of their teachers, he was genuinely shocked. Our journeys to school and work were earlier and longer, but we look back at them fondly. I remember singing at the top of my voice as I drove in the early hours through the sleepy villages. After my daily two-hour commute from North Kelsey to Aston, Birmingham, my new, shorter drive was nothing. I would start the day with Radio 4, to catch the World Service, and then switch to Chris Moyles on Radio 1 to keep me alert and the drive interesting. This made me realise why professional drivers around the world are more informed and aware than the rest of the population: They learn everything first-hand, not from books. Geography, history and culture really can be learned while driving from one area to another, absorbing everything including language, scenery, and the attitudes of local people. Anyone driving that much is bound to end up listening to a lot of radio.

I listened to entire lectures on everything from economics to political history. The power of radio is simply huge: in today's world, it has a far greater reach than TV. Many people are commuting longer hours and simply do not have the time to read or watch videos if they are driving or stood on a train. But we can hear while we iron or wash dishes. Everyone wants to be in their own bubble. For some reason, we would much rather listen to a voice in our ear than connect with the real person sitting next to us.

I understood for the first time how my late grandmother had countered her lonely existence after my grandfather passed away. Radio became her partner. She didn't wait for us to give her attention. She was ahead of the times. She found company in the radio the same way new generations would find companionship in their lonely lives by surfing the internet and following the daily lives of YouTubers.

§

It was a bitterly cold afternoon in March. I was in beautiful Herefordshire, the county considered the fair land and gift of God. I had taken the kids for a day out. It was too cold to sit outside with the picnic we had prepared. I loved sitting in the car with my kids with hot food; it was always a great way to connect. With a tasty treat in the privacy of a car, I found children would open up. I have had long discussions about life, relationships, ethics, and politics over sumptuous pizza and warm doughnuts. Parents who constantly worry about perfectly clean cars and spotless clothes miss out on the laughs they can have with their kids. People often ask me how I've raised my kids to be so upright and moral. All I did was talk to them and listen. I simply showed them that I loved their company and they never had any urge to stray.

Great food must be accompanied by a roaring conversation. As we took in the scenery and enjoyed French baguettes with cheese and meat, I thanked God. I thanked God for my great kids, for the food, and for the warm car we could use to come this far and enjoy the beautiful views. My father had taught us to recite '*Al-hamdu lillah rabbil 'alamin'* (Thank the Lord of all the Universe) three times to count our blessings. To this day, every time I stand under a hot shower (which isn't always possible because of my adventures), I am thankful for the luxury.

We often forget how much we have around us that we should be thankful for. We never value the limited time we have with our loved ones, especially our families. We often hear people say that kids grow up very quickly, but it is more than just a cliché. Parenting is a fascinating experience. In order to make our children perfect for the rest of the world to see, we miss out on the funny, tender and memorable moments we could be having with them. Children are often used as showpieces, like cars and homes are. We protect commodities, thinking they are precious. A scratch on our car will upset us to no end. But we generally think nothing of scarring a human's body and soul: A human that is unique; a human only we have the privilege to behold.

I dusted the breadcrumbs off their sweatshirts and thanked God for the comfort. We drove off and had probably travelled for less than five minutes when the car suddenly died on us. The car had broken down right there, in the middle of nowhere, with three kids in the back, after I had just been thankful for it. I looked up at the heavens quizzically. "Are you serious?!"

I quickly arranged for a recovery, but all the way back I was worried sick, thinking I would lose my job. Doing two jobs in two different counties wouldn't be possible without a car. The old Mercedes was a headache to maintain. Electronic keys cost an arm and a leg, and even small parts were costly to repair. The car was rusted in places and would frequently get punctured tyres thanks to my mileage.

I spent a week without a car. I wondered why God would punish me for being grateful. Then, on the ninth day, as a brand-new BMW stared back at me, I understood how my gratitude had been rewarded. There were no more huge fuel bills and flat tyres. It was a sign of good things to come. In less than two months, the job insecurity would be gone too, and I would be given what I wanted more than anything: The chance to have even more quality time with my children. In life, we will often think we have been treated unfairly if someone or something is snatched from us. But in time, the reason for it is revealed. Thanksgiving dinners bring big fat turkeys.

I have always been the one who will be called for help, whether it's advice or to pick up and drop off something or someone. For job interviews, exam preparation, or even morale support, I was usually on speed dial for those who knew me. As I dropped a friend for a job interview near Newbury, I explored the town and fell in love with it immediately. On the motorway, I read a sign for Southampton. I had an interview myself at the BBC later in the day, which I was doing only to gain some experience. I was feeling great about coming far enough to make it to the final interview. At the time, I was applying for Broadcast Assistant and Radio Producer positions.

Two of the three interviewers gave me a very tough time. They kept asking me technical questions. I thanked God that Physics had been a strong subject at school. Towards the end, the interviewers asked if I would consider a possibility in Southampton since the Birmingham position was not open anymore. Had I not spent the day doing a favour to a friend, I would have probably not known what to say. But in that split-second, I decided Newbury would be the perfect semi-rural setting for the kids, and that Southampton was commutable. However, I came out convinced that I would not be selected.

I lost the friend but I got the BBC job. When I got the call, I couldn't believe how keen they were to have me. I had only been in my first house for a year. My small, brave step had taken me from an unknown village in North East Lincolnshire, 20 miles away from the nearest town, to the Midlands. Now, it was taking me to the South of England, straight to a Weather Presenter position for the biggest region the BBC had. I remembered how my ex had felt he could not compete with his professional medical degree in the South of the country. He took up jobs in the North where there was less competition. And here I was, a Pakistani housewife with three young children, literally moving to the bright lights and the big city.

If you think you can't do something or can't have something, remember that perhaps it's just because you haven't given it a go yet.

Chapter 9

It was July 2008 when I was offered a position at BBC South. I accepted the early morning weather presenter position because it meant I could spend more time in the evenings with the children. It was also because I had been talked into the prospect of remarriage.

My sister thought it was time for me to settle down, and was enthusiastic about a young man who had proposed to me. I had briefly met him through work in Pakistan, and he had kept in touch via email. He had popped the question after months of only watching me on TV shows. One evening as I left work, he called me and announced that he wanted to marry me. I did not take it seriously, thinking it was just an infatuation, but we maintained contact over the phone for over a year. This was to be the only offer of marriage (or even romance) I would get in the entire period of my life post-divorce in the UK (a good 7 years). I agreed on the condition that he move to the UK and get settled, so I could see how well he interacted with my kids. Any place for a man in my life would now depend on whether he could accept my children as his own. But the minute this gentleman arrived, I realised that I was not the woman even I thought I was. This was not the unsure young girl who had never stepped out of the home. This was not the housewife you could walk all over and not even say 'thank you' to. This was a woman who worked in a corporate setting and took crap from no man.

And yet...I was to make more mistakes when it came to men. Professionals often spend so much time involved in research related to their career that they have no time or ability left to work on carrying out due diligence on any relationship prospects. It's understandable that people would never believe that I did not consult anyone or investigate the relationship histories of the men in my life, but it is the truth. Of course, hindsight is 6/6, so I can kick myself for the rest of my life for not seeking out advice or doing any research.

My feeble argument for my utter stupidity is the fact that I led a very isolated, sheltered life. I grew up with no siblings or cousins around. I was a day scholar at a strict single-sex Catholic school, and quite a tomboy besides, I had no interest in romance. And then one fine day, I got married to a cousin who was sixteen years older than me, and who I had only spoken to on two occasions, one of them being our engagement. For over twelve years, I was a housebound housewife, and an over involved mother to three children. I secretly did think that, once I was out of my first marriage, I would be able to reclaim my lost years, but doing two jobs a day with three kids and no family or friends around to support left me with no time to even get a facial or any real sleep whatsoever, let alone a chance to date men. My rather demanding lifestyle meant I could not afford to spend time making friends. As a result, I developed a closer relationship with my children, and enjoyed their company far more than most parents ever do.

From the time of the proposal to the time when this gentleman actually moved to the UK from Pakistan, I had transformed from a housewife to a rather focused, busy professional, and the children were enjoying a lifestyle that involved no drama at all. I explained to this young man that my decision would be based on my children's welfare, and that it would be a Herculean task for him. He insisted I give him a chance. Despite his repeated efforts to connect, we were just too different to develop any common ground. I also would not see or hear from this man for months on end. But even though things never took off, I never dated anyone else in that seven years. In the end, I had to put my foot down and just say no to this offer too. I decided that I was too old to settle down, and that it was too much to expect someone else to adapt to such a dynamic, particularly someone who was single and had no children of his own. It was the best decision for all concerned. Despite my decision to walk away, he always maintained his silence about us, which increased my respect for him. I elected to do the same. I had abandoned all romantic ideas of finding love or ever settling down by 2011. The only reminder I kept of the man who got closest was the dog he bought for me.

Since the death of Brutus when I was fourteen, I had maintained a distance with any new dogs introduced into the household. I did not want to love and loose again. It was so cruel that I had not had the chance of saying a proper goodbye to Brutus. That day, I'd been about to miss the bus (as usual), so I had not gone over to check why Brutus had not bounded up to greet me. He was lying still in the far end of the garden. I returned home only to be told that Brutus was no more. There was no send off. I had missed him so much for years afterwards.

As a single parent juggling two jobs with three kids, I couldn't give in to the thought of a pet. I loved the vibe of the new house, especially as I stood in front of the symmetrical lawns at the front of the property in Wash Common, Newbury. The purple wisteria on the porch was the stuff of dreams. I took in the view of the rather large garden at the back of the house. With its tall, mature trees, it was ideal for reading books, building tree houses, and having smoky barbecues.

It was our first day in the house. I had not even unpacked a box. I was thinking about all this, and imagining myself lazing in the sun and what books I might read in the comfort of my nice garden, when I suddenly heard yelps of glee. As I walked to the front of the house, I saw a pickup truck parked outside. The next thing I saw was the most beautiful puppy imaginable bounding out of it. The children were trying to cradle it. I think I fell in love with him at first sight. I was totally confused but soon it became clear: someone had just put another huge responsibility on my already aching shoulders.

I had made up my mind to return the Belgian Shepherd puppy. But that night, the little darling grabbed my ankle with both its paws and refused to let go. Like Inaya, he clung onto me for dear life and finally fell asleep. The minute I moved, he would start to whine. I sat all night in the kitchen with his small head on my foot. From that day on, he and I were inseparable. I had to rush home because he would start to cry if left alone. He would sit in my lap when I drove. My T-shirts and socks were his comfort blankets. For the first of couple of days, he refused to eat, so I fed him with a fork. In time, I learned to cook dog food and treats, and his shiny coat was the envy of all. Only the best dog food was bought. He was simply gorgeous and adorable but we knew he would grow up to be fierce and strong, so we ended up naming him Maximus, after Russell Crowe's character in *Gladiator*. Sahir suggested it once, somewhat tongue-in-cheek, and it just stuck. And just like that, we had a new member of the family.

My home was complete.

§

The four and a half years at the BBC from July 2008 to Nov 2012 started off on a rather bumpy note. A couple of years before, while on placement at BBC Look North, I had decided I hated the atmosphere. Yet there I was, at the oldest broadcasting house in the biggest of the corporation's England regions. I had left the job I loved for a safe job with a reputable institution. It would earn me a name, status and acceptability with the family.

The first year at the BBC was characterized by workplace bullying and office politics. And yet I stayed there far longer than any other job I'd ever have. The first few months were an odd mix of extremely positive reception from the very loyal and loving audience in the sunny South, and painful backstabbing and blunt rudeness from my immediate colleagues and a few seniors in the newsroom. While my bosses were happy with my rapid progress, I faced considerable opposition from many others within the organization. I was new to office politics, and took the comments personally.

It was a tough first year, with frequent jabs at trivial matters like the size of the car I drove combined with downright naked jealousy. Sadly, most of this came from female colleagues.

The girl who started the job with me was a much younger pretty girl and had no children. She came from a background in media and was married to a BBC anchor. I tried to help her with legal advice as she went through a divorce. She seemed benign enough. But I would soon discover that she had been going around spreading hateful things about me. I overheard her myself one day in the dressing room, talking to a fellow presenter. I ignored it. A few weeks later, I turned on the computer we both used, and on the screen was an email about me to a fellow sports journalist. It amazes me to this day to think about women in the workplace who spend more time trying to damage other women's images or opportunities than they do on improving their own abilities. There was one senior woman in News-Planning who found it hard to hide her obvious dislike for me. She left no stone unturned when it came to snubbing me and was not at all keen to help me in my career progression. I looked much younger than her, but she didn't know that I was her age, and could understand her insecurities. The minute she got engaged, her whole personality changed. Overnight, her scowl turned into a smile.

The problem with women in this day and age is they want everything, but they put unrealistic demands on themselves. Multi-tasking is a myth in my experience. We try to do everything at the cost of our health, our mental peace, and our relationships. Women who work in a corporate setting need to give themselves a break. You cannot be a domestic goddess while handling a stressful 24/7 job. Women who work in high-pressure work environments are constantly putting even more pressure on themselves, with the feeling that they are falling behind in areas that they need to excel in to gain social acceptance. That ring on the finger, a man's last name, the babies, the perfectly folded towels in the powder room: these define us when it comes to 'the perfect woman'. Not the degrees, the research, or the six figure salaries. And we make it harder for ourselves, both at home and in the workplace.

Professional women need to change their attitudes and work more collaboratively to strengthen their numbers and positions in the corporate world. Women who choose to stay at home must also be allowed to make that choice, and be supported when and if they choose to return to work. I frequently saw women returning to work after years of investing in the home, and being treated harshly. Equally, housewives can make rather unforgiving and disparaging remarks about career women. In a world where women are still trying to close the pay gap and struggling to crack the glass ceiling, the gender disparity is not helped by petty jealousy toward other females. We need to increase our numbers in the workplace to gain enough influence to bring positive change for women.

§

In my first marriage, all I wanted to do was get to bed early to escape him. I hated waking up in the mornings. There were a few days when I wished I would never wake up. My first husband came from a family that operated on strict military-style rules. Although my father-in-law had been retired from the army after serving as a prisoner of war in the 1970s, he had maintained an army discipline at home with his wife and kids. I, on the other hand, came from a family where there were never ending breakfasts, and mealtimes were full of laughter and discussions. We were not bound by restrictions of time and fear. Ijaz imposed the same restrictions on his own family. Even on weekends we were expected to be up at 7am, with timed showers and breakfasts served up with no variation or relaxation. I remember fantasising of a time when I would spend Sunday mornings in bed with the man of my dreams and do simple things like read the Sunday newspapers. That never happened, not least because of that man never turning up, but also because I had no time left...and perhaps no inclination left either.

After moving to Worcestershire in 2007, and doing an early radio shift as well as an afternoon shift Legal TV, my sleep schedule had taken a hit. With even earlier breakfast shifts on the BBC in 2008, my sleeping pattern was set to four hours. This pattern continued, and eventually I would be left with no ability to sleep for longer than four hours in one go. Even on a really relaxed lazy day; it would usually be about two and a half hours. At the BBC, I would feel sorry for myself for maybe a minute at most, and then jump to my feet. I began to love the dark morning drive from Newbury to Southampton. I had chosen the racecourse town to settle down in because of the semi-rural setting and good schools. The neighbourhood was safe. Established professionals and landowners made up the demographic. The girls could safely walk to school with their friends. Sahir could commute to his school easily too. Burnham Grammar was not nearby, but with the regional trains, we made it work.

I had timed my journey to precisely 26 minutes in the morning. I would sneak out in my pajamas with my coffee cake and Snack-a-Jacks, and not a trace of makeup. I would quietly drive away from my wisteria-laden neighbourhood with the informative BBC World Service keeping me company as I went through the town. By the time it finished, I would be on the A34 with my loud music ready. I loved my alone-time. My only fear was that the very glamorous Reham Khan, known for her stilettos and designer outfits, would be caught in her pajamas one day. It did happen, but I think I looked so different I wasn't recognized. As someone with that added pressure to look perfect all the time, I must confess that I always wanted to get into my shabby slouch-wear and comfy trainers.

During my Legal TV days, I could get away with old trainers under the suit. Even at a ceremony almost a decade later, I would be wearing my trusted Nike Airs under a wedding gown. On the BBC however, it was a full reveal. The ladylike look was maintained only for the few minutes of screen time. As one of only two people in the office at 4:30am, it was easy to slip in and not change till much later.

First on the hectic list was the detailed radio broadcast for Radio Berkshire at 5:30am. Since I lived in the county, I could give a very personal touch to those commuting a little later than myself. I loved doing radio, and really worked on my delivery, my scripting and even my banter. It helped to have great radio presenters to work with at BBC Berkshire. The jump from legal issues to weather was sudden, and with me being the perfectionist my mum made me, I had to make sure I knew everything. I sat in libraries learning everything about weather before I was sent off for Met Office training in London and at Exeter. We were told that we had been hired to replace the meteorologists as times had changed. The older men in suits were not needed, whereas a journalist's more story-telling approach was. But to explain complex weather systems in simple language, I had to make sure I completely understood it myself first. Fortunately, Physics had been one of my strongest subjects at school so I picked it up quickly. For the BBC South region, I was petrified that my accent (which was a mix of Northern with a Welsh tinge) might be a problem, so I worked hard to speak clearer, and slower than I was used to.

On my first lunchtime broadcast I got such a positive response that I was called into the editor's office and told that I would be doing the evening shift next. A stylist was assigned and from there my look was perfected. The stylist was keen to spend the entire dress allowance in one go by kitting me out in the full designer get-up. We clicked immediately and I applied her advice to the T, using her years of styling BBC greats like Terry Wogan coupled with endless audience research statistics. I worked on every aspect of my appearance and presentation with a clinical approach. My boss would wonder why the others were not using the stylist's advice. In no time at all, South Today audiences were tuning in to see my parting wave and a shot of my shoes. There was even a golf trophy named after me in Hampshire, fashioned in the shape of my high heels.

After three years of a gruelling schedule and financial uncertainty, I was finally stable and settled into my new beautiful home in Conifer Crest. Gone were the days of driving up and down the country with a tiny toddler while having to pay heating bills over the phone. Back in the early days, I had no time to stop to make a phone call and pay my bills. Luckily, I knew my card number off by heart, and could complete transactions over the phone while keeping my eye on the road. It was a nifty trick that came in handy for a busy single mum. Far more difficult was making sure I could make enough money to pay the tanker. You would pay up-front before they delivered the oil. Eventually, as I started getting a stable income, it wouldn't be the heating or the groceries that would worry me. Looking back, I wonder how I paid the child-care fees of nearly £900 a month.

I strongly feel that hardworking members of the community are not rewarded for their contributions. Instead, middle-class parents, and single mums particularly, are penalised for not taking handouts from the state. There should be more of an incentive, especially for single parents, to stay in work. I'm sure other hard-working mums and dads look longingly at those non-working parents leisurely walking their children to school. How I longed to have just a bit of a cushion to spend some time with the kids in the morning. But jobs are hard to come by, and even harder to retain once employers find out you are a single parent.

I once turned up ten minutes later than expected to the BBC newsroom. Even though there are set shift times in newsrooms, ambition drives journalists to arrive long before their shifts, and stay back late for post-production meetings and general gossip. For some of us, there is no choice but to work. But we have young families, and registered childminders who charge by the second. Employers are not sensitive to this in Britain. When turning up late, I was happy to pretend to Martin in Planning that I'd had a bimbo moment and locked my keys in the car, but did not want to admit that I was late because my child had a fever and I'd had difficulty finding emergency childcare for her. I had lost an opportunity before, and was not willing to jeopardise my new job.

I also saw how, despite anti-discriminatory laws, there was bias against women who are about to get married. Bosses immediately think, 'pregnancy risk' and 'maternity leave'. During my time at the BBC, one potential anchor deliberately hid her pregnancy at the time of her interview because she knew the system all too well. Ironically, I was seen as the ideal candidate, and least likely to have babies; a go-getting, ambitious, fiercely committed career woman. No one could have imagined I had three children at home, and did a job I didn't particularly care for only for their financial security.

There were so many women who'd worked alongside me who had to give up on the careers they had built because there were no crèches at work. The childcare bills for an individual trying to complete an education while working should be treated sympathetically. In some cases, the extortionate childcare fees force women to abandon their careers altogether. The salaries on offer are nowhere near enough to cover these exorbitant additional costs. Not everyone is mad enough to live and work across three different counties. I might have been, but it's not for everyone.

I remember struggling to understand the tax credit system in the UK. In the end, I decided I had no time to fill in long forms, and opted to work longer hours. There were, of course, people who were experts at living off the state. I was shocked when I learned an acquaintance of mine was living comfortably in a nice area of London without having to work, only because the family knew how to work the benefit system. Three perfectly healthy adults in the house were choosing not to work because they felt the job opportunities were beneath them. I found the attitude unforgivable, and still do. Although this acquaintance was married, the couple chose to show themselves as separated. The husband actually worked abroad at a very good post, but the wife got single parent benefits. I was a single parent raising three kids on my own, working nonstop only because I didn't have the time to understand how the benefit system worked, or more specifically, how to 'work the system'. And I didn't want to know.

The tax credits system was a particularly long and tedious process. I had no time to fill in forms, stay on hold on the phone, or stand in offices. I could not find a registered child-minder in my area, so I had to opt for an expensive day-care nursery far away from the home. If I used trustworthy next-door neighbours for childcare, I could not claim it back since they were not registered. At one point, I felt as if I was only making enough to cover the childcare expenses. I was lucky that I started making really good money, but not many do. It was extortion. The child would be there for an hour or two at most, but I would have to pay for the full session. Class timings meant I had to frequently pay for both the day and evening sessions, even though Inaya was not there all day.

Similarly, the primary school allotted to us when we moved to Newbury was very far away, so I needed a complex system of child-minders to drop Inaya to school. I could pick her up when my morning shift ended but mornings were a problem. In the end, I convinced the council to give her a space at a primary school near Ridha's school, so the girls could walk to school together. Had it not been for my convincing writing and mitigating skills, we would have had to put up with the ludicrous situation.

Not everyone would be as driven or committed as I was about my children's education. I believe the state should support those who are working very hard, as well as be supportive when people need a helping hand because of a sudden change in circumstances. However, it should not be a continuous drain on the community and hardworking taxpayers. While I agree with a welfare state concept, I do not believe that one should have a free ride indefinitely. There should always be that safety net, so that we do not abandon our fellow humans, but every person is capable of pulling themselves out of a dire situation and bouncing back, if they have the drive and the will to work hard.

§

2011 was a turning point in my life. I finally realized that I did not need a man, love, or a companion to be happy. The kids were older. I could afford to hang out with work colleagues a bit more. I had finally settled into the BBC job. I had been promoted to a senior broadcast journalist position. I had found time to decorate, and I had painted the walls of my home with the colours I liked (warm chocolate and a vibrant grey). There was wisteria on the porch and a dog in the beautiful garden. The girls walked to school happily with their friends and neighbours. Sahir was finally at a grammar school he loved. Life was perfect, but I needed more than perfect. I have always envied people who can sit for hours poring over magazines or lazing in the sun, but my loved ones know that a life too comfortable would kill me.

When men were trying to chat me up, they would make the cardinal mistake of suggesting that I needed to slow down, and that I could do with some relaxing time off. A man attempting to change me is going to be shown the door before he even turns up at the doorstep. I liked the pace of my life. I liked the hours of my work. My rest IS my work. There is nothing more exhausting to me than a holiday where one is doing nothing. I live life in a mode of "You only stop when you die!"

I have been surrounded by exceptionally lazy people throughout my life. The men in my life had no work ethic or interest in their jobs. They were on perpetual holidays. Some of the violence in my first marriage was centred around phone calls from the hospital in the middle of the night to the doctor on call. The rage following a call that you are being paid extra to attend was ludicrous. If the doctor happened to be called after he had dozed off, the whole Rehman household was forced into a literally rude awakening. Stripping the covers off the wife and sleeping child, and throwing them on the floor was familiar practice. Turning on all the lights while shouting the favourite Punjabi expletives was also part of the routine. We knew to lie very still while the circus played out. Soon, he would be gone, and we could get a couple of hours of peace.

My children and I were desperate to stay out of my husband's big, cold house, but we never wanted to leave our own warm, much smaller home. To think I had wondered if my kids would blame me after the divorce. After all, they had lost financial security and that big house. They'd been deprived of a parent. It was strange to have these thoughts only for them to inform me years later that they had hated the bigger house. And the announcement later that I wanted to sell the first home I had bought, which was a much smaller 3 bedroomed semi-detached house, brought tears to their eyes.

With Ijaz, we had learned that the only way to avoid loud shouting and abuse was to be around other people. Ijaz would often say, "You seem so happy around other people". On weekends when we went with his friends to watch Bollywood films, or went to their houses for dinner, we would never feel like coming home. He would not shout in front of strangers. Cinema offered not only physical safety, but mental escape too. The Bollywood film scripts seemed so tame in comparison to my melodramatic life. They offered the romance and the laughter missing from it.

When driving back from school one day, I remarked angrily to my older daughter that she would never have dared to throw a tantrum in front of her own father. She quipped back wittily with, "Well you should be proud of the fact that I feel safe enough to voice my opinion. I'm not scared anymore. I'm blossoming". I couldn't hide my smile. It was true: they were blossoming into confident young people who knew their worth. Big houses and luxury vehicles cannot build character or self-esteem. Only the knowledge that you are loved unconditionally can do that. Although having two parents would be ideal, sometimes just one person who realises the privilege of being a parent can do a decent job. The only condition for success in anything you do, whether it's a professional career or being a mother, is that you must love what you do.

The trouble with the men in my life was that they were living unhappy lives. Not being true to themselves meant they couldn't be true to anyone around them, be it colleagues, friends, or partners. I was taught the value of freedom, and given the dream of flying. I passed this much-cherished freedom to my children. Their souls are not trapped, so they are bound by love not by force. They can go wherever they want to go but despite this, I find that they always stay close to home.

After the first year at the BBC, when I would frequently have to fight my tears on the way back home, I settled into the environment so well that the people who had given me a tough time completely warmed to me. I learnt to give witty retorts to sarcasm and immediately had a better response. I stopped taking myself and the jabs seriously, and I was treated much better immediately. My family life had become settled too. I had abandoned any romantic idea of a 'knight in shining armour' and of me settling down as a housewife. I had settled into the new identity of an independent professional woman. I had moved into a beautiful property and the kids had made good friends in the neighbourhood.

Money was enough to cover our outgoings, but our expenses were increasing. Sahir and I were traveling out of the area every day. Ridha was in secondary school. We had a bigger house and a huge, rather demanding dog. Maximus was certainly a handful, and would eat literally anything he could sink his teeth into. From sofas to fences to doors, Maximus chewed into everything, and that was just the tip of the iceberg when it came to him. Belgian shepherds are hard work, but I realised that they were still easier than most grown men.

My corporate event earnings had gone down because of my growing profile at the BBC, and I really needed to improve my income. One day, out of the blue, I got a call on my mobile phone from a man who said that he was looking to hire someone for the weather presenter position for Sky Breakfast. I thought this was rather bizarre and unprofessional, and was convinced it was a hoax call. I had not applied for a job with them. I discussed it with a male colleague and we agreed that it was very odd. I made some enquiries and found out that this was indeed the boss at Sky. I was one of just two ladies he'd called.

Rather excited and nervous, I went in for the interview. The salary was more than double my pay at the BBC. Not only was the Sky package mouth-watering, but it was not even a regional position. It was the main breakfast weather presenter position for the whole of the UK on Sky. I walked in and was taken to the weather office where I was enlightened on software they used. The older lady there was warm and friendly. I played around with the graphics to get accustomed, and found it much simpler than our BBC set-up. I was then taken to meet the boss. The grey-haired gentleman received me, and took me around the impressive newsrooms, studios, and galleries. We then walked to the cafeteria. I asked for an Americano and he watched closely as I heaped in the sugar. He commented with shock at my sugar intake.

"I can understand why I like my sugar," he said, "because I'm a post war kid and sugar was rationed. What's your excuse?"

I raised both eyebrows, shrugged, and replied simply, "I like it!"

We walked back to his office. He seemed very intrigued by me. I wasn't sure where to place him. Was he a down-to-earth boss? Or was it something else? The conversation was not about my MET office training or knowledge about our audiences. He was mainly talking at me. Telling me what he did. How he had improved the show. Then suddenly he asked if I was single.

"No, I am not. I have a lovely man in my life," I fired back. It was a convincing lie, and did the trick. He wasn't interested in details of my lovely phantom man. He moved on. With the next thing he said, the reason he was so friendly finally became clear.

"You see I have two blondes on the sofa already," he stated. "I needed a brunette."

I shot up in my seat. To say that I was furious would be an understatement. I made no effort to hide my distaste at his sexism. This man had so much authority that he seemed to believe he could say whatever he wanted. His misogynistic remarks were not appreciated and I made it clear.

"Well I am sorry to disappoint you," I replied. "I am not what you are looking for. I am not a real brunette. My hair colour is out of a bottle. It changes when I want it to". And with that, I turned on my heel and walked out.

Ridha saw the look on my face as I got home. I told her that I wasn't going to get the job. When she pestered me about it, I told her what I had said to him. The 15-year-old held her head in her hands and cried, "Mum! Why did you say you are not single? You should have ignored his silly comments. We needed this job!"

I looked her in the eye and said, "Listen to me Ridha, this is not who I am and this is not who I want you to be. I will get something bigger and much better than this, and I will not have to compromise my integrity for it. We need to earn respect more than a higher salary".

The job eventually went to another woman of Asian origin by the name of Nazaneen Ghaffar, the other shortlisted candidate. I like to think that she got the job based on merit, and that this guy did not use the same sleazy approach with her. Although at the time the Sky News weather presenter position on its Sunrise programme was a very tempting offer, I knew that being principled and uncompromising brings only momentary disappointment. Though not very worldly or cunning, my decisions have taken me to greater heights. I have been on non-talking terms with employers at times, but they couldn't fire me even then, not with the business I was bringing in.

Getting involved with bosses is not the way up for a smart woman.

Chapter 10

I was never an anti-social person, but it's fair to say that I went out of my way to avoid certain encounters and social circles. Despite this, I would often end up meeting a wide variety of strange and interesting people. In one instance, I met the ex-Chief of the Army Staff and former President, General (retired) Pervez Musharraf, at a large gathering for Pakistanis near Slough.

My newly made friend, the drama producer Laila, was a social butterfly, and her bubbly requests were hard to refuse. I found her lively exuberance endearing. She suggested I drop in to this party for a while. She knew I avoided Pakistani community events. I had successfully avoided the Pakistani social circles since I'd become single. A divorcee is easy prey for our 'society uncles', and I was also thinking about protecting my children from their biological father, and preventing him from finding out where we lived. I asked the gentleman whose marriage proposal I was still considering to accompany us to this occasion.

The gathering was in the house of a rather strange drunkard. Everyone addressed him simply by his initials rather than a proper name. He had apparently been a first-class cricketer in the 70s and 80s but I had never heard of him before. I was told that he was a presenter on an Asian channel. He was so sloshed that he couldn't pronounce my name, continually referring to me as Rehab and laughing at his own 'joke'. The walls of the small house (even the tiny bathroom) were covered with pictures of him with every Pakistani politician I knew.

That evening was extra special as the gathering was in honour of the former President Musharraf and the man he had hand-picked to be PM, Shaukat Aziz. It was an odd mix of people, from the ultra-rich to the ultra-sleazy. I was immediately recognised from 'off the telly'. I maintained a safe distance from the men as I sensed that this gathering was in large part just a collection of eye candy for the former General. I sat with the wives of the retired General and the former banker-turned PM. Both ladies were very friendly, and warmed to me immediately. Mrs Shaukat Aziz was an incredibly humble woman, while the rather well-dressed Mrs Sahiba Musharraf had a regal air to her.

A few minutes into the gathering I signalled to both my friend and my suitor that I wanted to leave. This was not the sort of place I was comfortable with but it took me a good thirty minutes to finally get them to go. Everyone wanted to get close to the former President, who was enjoying the music and red wine. I spotted the journalist and author Christina Lamb sat with him. I had enjoyed reading her book *Waiting for Allah,* which revolved around the blunders of Benazir Bhutto and the political engineering at the time. Her argument stuck with me: that it was ironic that the country formed on the basis of the two-nation theory was still searching for a collective identity.

Musharraf would grab the mic and break into his favourite songs. The one I remember is the famous Bollywood number *Tu meri ashiqui hai* (You are my love). His bald bouncer, Jimmy Chauhdry, stayed close to him and made sure no one photographed or recorded the intoxicated General singing away with the professional musicians, entertaining everyone. It was the maestro Hamid Ali Khan and his son who had been called in to sing that evening for the man who still thought he was king. It was a small drawing room, but the *mehfil* (intimate concert) atmosphere was maintained by the owners of local TV channels flinging £20 and £50 notes at the performers.

At the time, Pakistanis like myself had been given the impression that this General was different: an upright, no-nonsense guy. I watched the scene in quiet disappointment. Here I saw the reality of those in the corridors of power, and it disgusted me. The atmosphere would be disturbing for any self-respecting female. I recalled how a young devout Muslim boy from Bradford had sought me out at a policing conference that year to pick my brains on who was the best leader for Pakistan. He wanted me to tell him who was better: Pervez Musharraf or Imran Khan. I had given the young lad some sisterly advice: to pay more attention to the politics of Bradford than Pakistan. This was a bright kid who'd won a scholarship to Oxford, but there was clearly much he had to learn and understand about the realities of the world. It would become apparent years later that I had given him some extremely good advice

My friend nudged me and pointed to the heavily made up *peshkash* (production) introduced to the President. One of these voluptuous *sari*-clad women had apparently been flown in from America. I did not know who to feel sorry for: the young ladies paraded in front of this powerful man, the men facilitating this, or the country these men ruled. No one else seemed bothered by the shenanigans. Stunning Polish bartenders served the guests, ensuring that the alcohol kept flowing, and everyone was merry.

I stood up to help myself to some food, and was just making up another plate for my friend when two men came up to me and said, "*Kubhi hummay bhi serve ker dein*" (You could serve us sometimes as well). I immediately put the dish down and called out to my friend, "I am leaving. You are welcome to stay".

I walked out with the host's live-in girlfriend pleading for me to stay. As I made my way towards my car, my suitor and friend followed me rather reluctantly, giggling at my 'childishness'. I realised in that moment that this man wouldn't be able to defend my honour if it came to that. He wasn't the only one of course: There were countless who would never measure up to what I was looking for in a man. Life would teach me that only I could protect myself.

Following that sour experience, the host sent us all another invitation for a quiet private dinner with no riffraff. My suitor's family had a military background, and he felt that he had made an impression on the chief guest and the host, but I told him clearly that he was mistaken. I suspected it was more to do with them trying to befriend me. After several further invitations, I finally accepted one. It was, indeed, a quiet affair this time, with only four or five couples invited. The General, the PM, and their wives treated me with a lot of respect. Sahiba Pervez greeted me warmly and appreciated my traditional ensemble. She had a sharp sartorial sense.

Hafiz Pirzada had also been invited. The ageing advocate was admired for his legal prowess, and had been a witness to many historic moments. I discovered that his old age had not dimmed his passions. He lived up to his romantic image, spouting couplets here and there, and even singing the famous *Kabhi Kabhi* Bollywood number, smiling appreciatively as I helped him with a few verses when his memory failed him. I was amused, and reminded of the famous verse by Ghalib: "*Go haath ko jumbish nahi ankhon mein tu dum hai*" (I may have lost mobility but my eyes still function). Pirzada *Sahab* also came across as a die-hard romantic rather than a sleazy lecher. He invited me warmly to his hunting lodge in Hermitage, a stone's throw away from my own home near Highclere; a similar invitation to many others that I did not accept. But after avoiding even a dip in the frying pan, I was about to jump straight into hellfire.

§

My mother always said that she had premonitions, and that she recognised that same ability in me.

The first time I remember such a thing was the night my grandmother passed away. My own mother was very disturbed as she put me to bed. This was unusual as she would always tell me stories. I went to sleep almost immediately. In my dream, I saw my mother's funeral. I had never seen a Pakistani Islamic funeral. In fact, I had never seen any funeral of any sort. I saw my mother's body wrapped in the white shroud, laid out on the traditional wooden divan bed. A close view of her face showed a thick black thread on her eyelashes.

My older brother recalls me telling him about my dream. I was only eight at the time. When I woke up, I was in a car going up to my grandfather's house in the hills of Abbottabad. On our arrival at the familiar tall ochre house, the kids were kept in the staff kitchen. Outside, I could hear sounds of women crying. A little later, one of the adults must have realised how absurd this idea of keeping the children away from the funeral was and led us back out. As the time for burial approached, there was a last-minute panic. After a few minutes of scrambling, they found what they were looking for. It was a black thread from the covering of the holy *Kaaba* in Makkah. It was laid on my grandmother's eyelashes before she was taken to her final resting place.

Then, decades later, there came that cold November morning in 2010. I was more reluctant to get up for my 4am shift than usual. I dragged myself out of my bed and into the car. Nothing was lifting my spirits. I would normally be ready well before the first TV broadcast, but I was taking my time that day. I had just straightened one side of my hair when I got a call on my mobile. It was my brother's son, Hamza. As soon as he said, "Here, talk to Barimummy,"

I knew something was wrong. Ridha had apparently had a premonition of it. And just as she had been forewarned only the night before, he was gone. It was my father.

Nothing can prepare you for that shock. Even if you'd worried about the death of a parent all your life, and imagined what it would be like, you could never be ready. I had so many conversations left in my head: conversations we were meant to have, things we needed to say. How could he leave without answering the millions of questions I still had for him? How could he go without keeping his promise of coming over for summer to stay with me? With floods of tears, I immediately called my travel agent to book my flight, and then my told my son. I walked out to find my producer. He saw it on my face immediately, knew that something dreadful had happened and told me to go home. The irony of it hit me quite suddenly. When someone is no more, we take off immediately to find them, but while a person is alive and is desperate to see us, we have no time to visit.

I don't know how I drove back home. Sahir had called a friend over, who drove me to the airport. On the way, my cousins told me that they were going ahead with the burial. They could not wait for me to arrive. It was an eight-hour direct flight and it was freezing in our ancestral village of Baffa, but still they decided to bury Daddy without me. I wouldn't even see his face one last time.

It was early afternoon as I arrived at the village home. I had put a *burqa* on over my top and trousers. The place was empty. The funeral guests had gone. My mother rushed to hug me. Amid her tears she whispered, "Why is your skin looking so bad?" That was typical Mummy. Four days after the birth of my first baby, she had asked me why my tummy was sticking out. My mother, bless her soul, wanted us to always look perfect. Of course, we did not understand her loving concern. We saw it as criticism. As I was led to the small mound of earth, where my daddy was buried alongside his parents in our family cemetery, I lifted my hands in prayer. But to me that didn't feel like bidding him a final farewell. To me, this was not where my Daddy was. Coming all this way just for this had given me no satisfaction at all.

I watched how everyone comfortably moved on. But I couldn't. I come from a religious family who believe in Allah's will, but at that point in time I couldn't just snap out of my grief like I was expected to. I went back to our home in Peshawar to search for a final letter, or a few words; something from him to me. There was nothing of the sort. Instead, the inside of his cupboard looked like a scrapbook about me and the kids. Every little thing I had ever sent him, like cards, letters, and gifts. My pictures adorned the shelves like a small religious shrine. He loved me so much but kept it quiet all his life. If only I had known that someone loved me this much. If you love your kids, you should say it to them often. Hug them even when they push you away. That is all they want from you: Just your time and your smile. My kids are better than me. As I rush around giving instructions right, left and centre at breakneck speed they often grab me for a hug or randomly say, 'Mum you look beautiful' just to make me stop long enough to look at them and smile.

Even though I was lucky enough to have the best dad anyone could ask for, I regret that I could not spend as much time with him as I would have liked. It took me a good two weeks of compassionate leave before I could see or talk to anyone. To this day little things remind me of Daddy. I stop to notice his favourite perfume in a busy store, an elderly man's socks on the train, and of course the sight and smell of rotisserie roasted chicken.

My father passing away changed something in my head. I decided that I wanted to be as near my mother and sister as I could be. I had to be there for them now that he was gone.

§

Ghullam Yahya Khan emerged from his red and white double-storey brick house in the early hours of the morning at the sound of the prayer call. It was still dark. His tall, imposing figure and flowing snowy white beard were recognisable from a distance. For the beautiful village of Baffa, a valley surrounded by picturesque snow-capped mountains, my grandad was known as Haji *Sahab* (or Master *Sahab*). To us, he was just Abbajee. His day would start with a brisk walk from his home to the mosque for *Fajr* prayers. Like most Swatis, Abbajee was bound by a strict *Deobandi* Sunni faith and would return home only after performing *Ishraq* (an additional supplementary prayer after sunrise), a tradition followed by my Daddy and then by my brother.

Some days after prayers, Abbajee would put on his wellies, and with his rifle in hand, walk all the way to the nearby town of Dumbara, for *shikar* (hunting) in the marshes. Hunting is second nature to Pashtun families. Haji *Sahab* (although an academic, progressive man) was very much true to his pure Lughmani Swati roots. As a crack shot with the gun, he encouraged even his granddaughters to accompany him occasionally on the morning hunt. I personally do not like killing living things, but am very fond of target shooting as a sport. Many wild hares and local pheasants were brought back from these morning expeditions, while all the while a walking lesson in science and nature would be given.

For the former principal, the day started with Quran teaching to the boys in the neighbourhood. Mohammad Ali Mian (now a businessman in New York) was one of these kids, and recalls those early morning lessons fondly. His own father, Shamsuddha *Sahab*, was part of that enlightened community, and was the first one to publish a magazine from Baffa. In fact, Baffa was the only town in Hazara Division with an intermediate level institution as early as 1934. Breakfast was freshly cooked crisp *parathas* (Danish pastry-style bread) cooked in *desi ghee* (unclarified organic butter) and served with *makhi* (honey), double cream and fried eggs. My own father would eat fresh double cream mixed with honey for breakfast well into his old age, and despite this obvious disregard for calorific content, he stayed slim until his death. Sometimes traditional pancakes called *manian* were also cooked. Unlike traditional *parathas* in the subcontinent, rice flour was used for the *parathas* in our household.

The local milkman, known as Gujjar Baba, used to bring the milk in a black urn to the *bangla*. The locals called it 'The Bangla' because it was the first brick house in the area. He would drop the delivery in the smaller of the two kitchens at the back of the house. Ammajee, my grandma, would check with a lactometer when he was not looking, and shock him by telling him accurately how many parts of water he had mixed in the milk. He believed she had magical powers to detect his deception, and was terrified of her. My grandma wasn't the sort of woman you could pull a fast one on. Her small eyes were sharp and piercing. She could sense what was going on. Even in her late age when she was immobile, she controlled the entire household from her bed. As a younger woman, she was not only a decisive woman, but a decidedly courageous one. She was not much for hysterical emotions and had no patience for teary outbursts or tantrums.

She would love telling us how the serious Master *Sahab* had been bedazzled by the sunshine falling on her auburn hair. That one glimpse had resulted in a proposal and an extremely loving union for the very young Zohra Jaan. My grandmother would have been hardly 14 at the time of her marriage but was already over 5' 7", exceptionally tall for a Pakistani woman. The strikingly attractive redhead had lost her mother at a very young age. The stepmother had intentionally taught her no housekeeping skills and refused to give her any sort of education. The idea was that the young girl would be rejected by her future husband and would return to the father's home to a subservient life. But her educationist husband loved her dearly and immediately set about teaching her at home.

He was known for his rather flowery, literary Urdu. Once, he wrote a letter to his niece to inform her of her father's death. The words used were so difficult that the girl only discovered what they meant a day later. He had used the complicated term *Saniha-i-Irtisaal* to describe the death. As soon as his young wife learnt to write in Urdu, the young couple started writing to each other whenever they were apart. One of these letters was intercepted by my grandfather's grandmother. The young girl was reprimanded for writing to her husband, but it did not stop their romance.

When Zohra Jaan fell pregnant after a few years of marriage, her husband would smuggle in her cravings in his pocket. Child deaths and infant mortality were high at the time. The couple lost their firstborn (a girl) when the child was only two years old. Their first son was born a couple of years after, and my grandma fasted one day every month for the rest of her days for his health and life. The couple loved to take evening strolls but it wasn't in step with cultural norms of the time. My Abbajee would cover his face as a simple disguise on these walks so the couple could maintain their privacy. One evening, the local police officer approached him and pulled off the scarf. He was shocked to see the young local Master. He immediately apologised and explained that he had mistaken it for a kidnapping. The young couple were adventurous, too, and occasionally slipped out for a late evening swim in the river Sirin after dark.

As the young teacher made rapid progress in his career, his salary was raised to 100 Rupees, which was a lot of money in the days before the Partition. The loving husband decided to buy his wife shoes decorated with pure silver for 90 rupees. The family were landowners so did not really live off the salary, but nevertheless my grandmother didn't appreciate such extravagance. In any case, she told us that they were ridiculously heavy to walk in (perhaps he was trying to slow his hyperactive wife), but, ever the practical one, she kept them in a safe and sold them years later to help build her dream home, Nayyar Manzil, named after my Daddy.

It is tradition in Pashtun families to spend a lot on gold jewellery. My grandma was always laden with it. When the Partition riots started however, she thought ahead, buried all of it in the *Tandoor* clay oven, and sealed it. Perhaps this squirreling ingenuity was hereditary: I always used to hide my jewellery in the baby's disposable nappies carton. The house below Nayyar Manzil belonged to her friend Guladamay, and a tall jojoba tree grew in her courtyard. The top had branches reaching into our house. *Sinjli,* or jojoba berries, were popular with the kids. My grandma, being a fair one, was in the habit of buying the berries off her friend. After breakfast adolescent girls would be taught *Naazra* (Quran pronunciation) with translation by my Ammajee. To maintain *purdah* for the girls, Abbajee would keep an ear out from the balcony above. A variation of a dumbwaiter was used to send snacks and teas up during the day. Abbajee would otherwise spend his time tending to the grapes up on his beautiful wooden balcony. He was also fond of mending *shaheed* (damaged) Quranic scriptures, which people would bring to him.

An afternoon siesta was a must for my grandma, but was occasionally interrupted by a young, mentally-disturbed man who insisted she keep his money for safe-keeping. This destitute man would saunter in and touch her feet to ask for money he had left with her previously. Zohra Jaan had the reputation of being brutally honest and utterly trustworthy. By the time afternoon tea was laid out, young girls would drop by to learn cutting and embroidery from my grandma. Even garments like coats and trousers were taught. My grandma mused that, in her youth, they were so accomplished at needlework that they would measure threads before starting a piece to see who would finish fastest. In fact, back in the day men were taught everything too. My cousin told me that even Abbajee could darn his own socks beautifully.

Sections from the *Bahisti Zewar* (a book written specifically for women by Maulana Thanvi) would be taught alongside the vocational training. In the evening, the *tandoor* (clay oven) would become the gossip point for the villagers. We were rice-growers as a family, so fragrant basmati rice from our own fields was cooked in the evening. Ammajee boasted that her *katchi* basmati would reach seven homes. Orange and pink blossoms framed the well under the tall pomegranate tree. The *oghra* (rice water) would also be given to all the family to drink, and be used as a facial toner.

We were the only Muslim family with a hand pump. It was placed outside the house so the whole village could use it. Providing water is the duty of a good Muslim. There was only one other hand pump belonging to a Hindu family in the area. My Daddy recalls pleasant, harmonious times growing up with Hindus and Sikhs pre-Partition. There was never even a trace of racism or bigotry.

Evening supper was always after *Maghrib* (evening prayers), and there would always be meat cooked with vegetables on the menu served with white rice (e.g. *palak gosht* (meat and spinach), *shuljum gosht* (meat and turnips), or *aloo gosht* (meat and potatoes)). Abbajee would have his dinner after his return from *Isha* prayers in the mosque. For him, Ammajee would make *karori* (a thin crispy rice cake) by coating the rice with extra butter and flattening it down with a dish. I remember her making us crispy squares of puffed wheat called *murunday*, sweetened with dark molasses syrup. Even for supper, Abbajee liked double cream served separately with the curry.

Ammajee had a low wooden carved *takhta* to pray on, resembling a Japanese table, instead of a fabric *jaye namaz* (prayer mat). And whilst sat on it, the maid would bring a silver urn for her to wash her feet and complete her ablutions before prayers. My cousins remember how, in the dark stillness of the evening, the only sound echoing in the courtyard would be Ammajee reciting her intention of prayer, the *Niyyah*. "*Salor rakat Namaz Masputam*" (I make the intent to pray four *Isha rakat farz* prayers) would be heard as they waited impatiently for her to put them to bed and tell them stories.

Baffa is on the Northern edge of the Pakhal valley of the Mansehra district. Beyond the valley lie the majestic Himalayas. It gets very cold in the winters. Ammajee would use a Kashmiri style *kangri* (a straw basket with a clay urn inside it, filled with glowing embers) to warm the beds. The glowing embers were covered with ash on top to prevent burns, but a quilt or two was frequently burnt by my multi-tasking grandma.

Night-time care was incomplete without putting *surma* in her eyes, and tying her long red hair (by now turning a silvery-grey) up neatly in a *kasava* (bandana). Kids would fight over who would get to sleep in Ammajee's wooden *palang* (bed). In the end, an additional bed would be placed near the bed to accommodate all the kids. Just before bed, both the husband and wife had a habit of reciting *Surah al-Mulk* aloud from memory. Although a deeply religious family, they had a progressive attitude too. A big radio was placed on the veranda and played international news and current affairs. This became a habit Ammajee continued with after she lost her husband in 1979. In the long and lonely eleven years that followed, she continued to regale us with folk tales and scientific news she had heard on the radio, a ritual hated by my college-going sister, as she would have to sleep in Ammajee's room when grandma stayed over with us.

Abbajee's storytelling was mainly of an academic nature. Even his glow-in-the-dark *tasbeeh* (rosary) was used to amuse the little ones. However, he had a fun, hands-on approach to teaching science. He even once brought an industrial Ice cream machine home to teach the kids the practical uses of chemical changes. The older ones would learn geography as he carved out country maps on the skin of an orange. The one with the most correct answers would win the first orange.

Our parents had extremely strong geography and maths skills. Highly-educated people from Baffa often surprise me by informing me that my grandfather had taught them after he retired. Free maths and science support was offered throughout the afternoon by the retired educationist. However, my Daddy did not appreciate the academic instruction as a child, and preferred sports. He was a naughty child, with a fondness for truancy and playing practical jokes. Once, to get out of a lesson, Daddy put Abbajee's hat on a wasp nest. It had the desired effect: The unsuspecting victim picked up his hat, got stung by the wasps, and lessons were cancelled.

For the kids of the family, my older aunt Zaitoon *bibi* was a great tutor for A-levels on all curriculums, including American and Cambridge systems. Zaitoon *bibi* was much older than my dad and uncle. They loved her like a mother. She would get the confessions out easily. She was very keen on personal hygiene so the little grubby brothers were made to scrub their feet before getting into bed. My dad, being very pale, didn't have to scrub for long, but Sultan Unca, the slightly darker one in the family, would always be spending hours scrubbing away to get his feet as white as my father's. Surprisingly, despite being darker and the skinniest, he was Ammajee's favourite, and was also considered quite debonair as a young man. To this day, the younger ones in the family see him as the epitome of a macho, good-looking man. The favourite son would get a freshly-baked cake nearly every day. Ammajee left her handwritten recipe book of clay-oven cake-baking to Zaitoon.

Zaitoon *bibi* was the pillar that held the family together. In the last ten years of her life, Ammajee preferred to stay at their place. Most of the grown-up grandchildren had become doctors, and they reciprocated the love they had received as kids. I found my Ammajee adorable, and the clash of personalities between my mother and grandma was entertaining. My mother was a bit of a slow, wise turtle, while my grandma was impatience and energy personified.

My father ended up with four siblings. The eldest son was initially named Ghullam Farid, but Maulana Thanvi suggested that it was better to be the servant of the All-Wise (one of the names of Allah) than the slave of Farid (the Sufi saint). And so, the boy was named Abdul Hakeem Khan. He lived up to his name and went on to become the Chief Justice of Peshawar High Court, and later the Governor of the NWFP (now the province of KP).

The younger daughter, Zubeida *bibi*, would later become my mother-in-law. Zubeida was studying in Lahore College at the time of the Partition. This college became famous as one of the symbols of the independence struggle when a 14-year-old girl, Fatima Sughra, planted Pakistan's flag atop it. When the riots started, the girls were evacuated from the boarding school and sought refuge in a local advocate's home. My mother-in-law was a funny, pleasant woman. She told us how difficult it was to spend that night hidden away; there wasn't even any water to wash hands and face. She found one of her *dupattas* outside. It was damp, and she wiped her face with it. In the morning, the Advocate's wife came and told the girls that the cat had peed on a *dupatta* lying outside.

With great difficulty, my aunt and her cousin were brought back home. Despite the taunts from the locals, Abbajee defiantly sent his girls to study at the best institutions of the time. He was committed to the education of the women in the family. So much emphasis was placed on learning that my grandma would use mules laden with wheat as a barter arrangement to buy all of the huge volumes of *Maulana Thanvi's Tafseer* (Exegesis).

Haji *Sahab* was respected across the town. All he had to do was lay his shawl across the seats of a public transport bus if he wished to reserve it for his visitors or family. Everyone would recognise it. The seats would remain unclaimed. My cousin recalls that Khaista Khan, the driver of the Government Transport Bus, would deliver a basket full of organic chickens to the grandchildren of Haji *Sahab* in Mansehra every so often. Their family driver would collect it from the bus stop near the Ziarat point in Mansehra.

This was the Pakistan I had heard about from my family. This was my background and my culture. With my Daddy's passing, one more link to this family was broken. But now, it was time for me to rediscover all of this on my own. It was time for me to go home.

Chapter 11

Following my beloved father's death, my mother shuttled between Saudi Arabia (where my brother lived), Pakistan (where my sister lived), and my own home in the UK. She loved being at home with my girls, as she could watch all the soaps to her heart's content, a luxury denied in the rather strict households of my siblings. My kids valued her presence too. Sahir told me how she had walked past him as he studied one day and amazed him by casually pointing out a complicated solution using her expertise in Further Mathematics from decades before. We were genuinely upset when she headed back to Pakistan.

My sister had recently remarried and, since her previous marriage had been far from a fairy tale, I wanted to take the pressure of looking after mum off her. I thought my kids could have a brief cultural immersion too. My CV could also benefit from working in a conflict zone but, above all, I wanted to spend time with my mum. This was something I regretted not doing with Daddy. After seeing her rather rapid deterioration after Daddy's death, I knew I didn't want to leave it too late. I figured that, even if I got only a few days of work covering an election tipped to bring 'the big Tsunami', I would at least see history being made. I had planned to stay only for one academic year but my plans were about to change dramatically.

I was one of the few anchors who managed to retain their jobs following the BBC's Delivering Quality First cuts (DFQ). I was working as a senior broadcast journalist at the BBC when I was offered a position at News One in Pakistan. I had spent a week in Pakistan visiting all the major channels in August 2012. The first stop was 'Hum TV' where the rather adorable and blunt Sultana *appa* introduced me to Pakistani TV by saying, "*Bhi yahan tu batmeezi chulti hai. Mere channel pe aakay log makool kyun ho jatay hain?*"

She had said that on Pakistani television, only indecent and loud behaviour sold, but people expected to come to her channel and behave in decent, sober fashion. She sent me off to view her breakfast show the following morning and give some feedback. Fahd Mustafa, the morning host, and KD, the producer, both came across as educated and progressive. However, the content in the show and script did not reflect their intellect. The producer explained that their core audience was not very educated, and lived off salaries well below Rs15,000 a month (approximately £100). They were here to make money, not responsible programming. Fantasy and escape was the surest way of capturing the audience. I spoke to the owner and suggested they try a late-night news show, very much like the newer cult programmes such as *The Daily Show*.

After a few other stops, I met Daniyal Ali Khan, a friend of the family who was desperately trying to teach filmmaking to Pakistanis. He suggested Seema Tahir as the perfect match for me. So I marched off to News One and quickly found that he was right. I immediately hit it off with Seema. I also managed to completely blank the CEO, Tahir A Khan, who'd been in the office too. I somehow managed not to make the connection that they were husband and wife.

One of the reasons I thought this would be a good match for me was because Seema had been praying when I was led into the office. The lady had a hard shell but a soft centre. She started telling me about her daughters, and how they found it difficult to settle in Pakistan.

"You girls come all enthusiastic to work here but run away as fast as you can too". I looked in her eye and said, "Seema, I don't give up that easily". I had made up my mind that I was going to work with this woman.

The next stop was GEO, but it took me less than five minutes to get fed up with the folks at the biggest television network in Pakistan. The amount of time it took at GEO, going from one office to another, factored into my decision-making process. At GEO, I was led from one floor to another and given forms to fill out about existing salary scales and previous wage slips. When I insisted I was only there for an informal meeting, I was then led into a boardroom for an interview with a 20-something man with a Mohican-inspired spiked gel coiffure. He introduced himself as Mag. I later found out that he was the famous religious scholar Ghamidi *Sahab*'s son. He proceeded to quiz me condescendingly about how much I knew about Pakistan and politics. I felt tempted to tell him my age, but controlled myself and answered his questions with fake politeness and inward irritation. Sensing this, he suggested I meet his editor, but by then I had already had enough. I endured for only a little longer before telling them that I had a flight to catch and leaving. I was ready to go home, but told my mother and my sister that it looked promising and that I could well be returning in less than two months to start a new job at News One. The money offered initially was disappointing, but it was the 10pm slot.

The decision to resign from the BBC was daunting but I was always a risk-taker. The day I handed in my notice, I picked up the phone to tell my mum that I would be with her in a matter of weeks. I didn't know exactly how she would react, but I was obviously excited to tell her, and to hear how pleased she would be. I could practically hear the warm, vibrant tone of her voice when she would tell me how happy she was that I was coming back.

Except she didn't. There was no whoop of joy. Instead, after a pause, my mother announced to me that her daughter-in-law and grandsons would be moving in with her in a matter of a week or two. My kids were sitting across the dining table and saw me frown in disbelief in a way I have frowned many a time in life.

"What?" I asked

"Well...you could look for a house near me," she responded.

"Why would I want to rent a place near you? Sweety lives near you already, and that arrangement wasn't working. I have resigned Mummy! And you're telling me this now?"

I didn't know what to think. I didn't know what to say next. I was just amazed. After urging me to come back and upend my entire life, my mother now told me that there was no room in her house for me.

§

Those early days of my career seemed a long way away now. I remember taking morning classes at the East Coast Media Centre for Media Broadcast Journalism. Then Inaya and I would make the long journey to Birmingham together so I could do my show on Legal TV. We would sing nursery rhymes most of the way, and while she slept I would listen religiously to Radio 4 and audio lectures produced by the Open University. They were happy times. I loved my job, which had mostly centred on detention centres, refugees, the Counter-Terrorism Bill and radicalisation. The social activist in me was very much visible in the content of my program.

Then I'd moved on to the BBC. I had a beautiful home that I had lovingly decorated, and a settled, permanent staff position, which came complete with maternity, pension and further benefits as a senior broadcast journalist. I shared the red sofa with Sally Taylor, the main news anchor and a living legend, who had been presenting the main 6:30pm bulletin on *South Today*, in the biggest region after Scotland. Sally was one-of-a-kind: a female anchor ruling the roost for over fourteen years. Not only was she an inspiring female icon, but as time went by I found her to be far more helpful than most women around me. She wasn't a sugar-coated pill, but rather a soft-centred gold toffee. The senior sport presenter was the effervescent Tony Husband. I loved our on-screen team, and the adoring fans of Southern England. My job was good and my children were well settled in a lovely area. My 4.30am start was rough at times, but was nothing compared to my gruelling earlier commutes from Lincolnshire to Birmingham. In general, life was good. And I left it all behind when I landed in Pakistan on the 12th of December 2012.

When I did finally land in Pakistan, the first sight that greeted me was the looped TV news footage of the dead body of veteran and respected politician Bashir Ahmed Bilour. I was horrified at the lack of basic principles of dignity in death. The Bilour family had an unbeatable record in the main constituency of NA-1 at the heart of Peshawar. Even Benazir Bhutto, who was much loved by KP voters, had not been able to dislodge him. He had beaten her by over twelve thousand votes. I watched in despair as the bare torso of this brave son of the soil, who had stuck with the principles of Bacha Khani, was shown covered in splinters on live TV. I tweeted angrily in protest, only to get the reply, "You are new in Pakistan. You will get used to this lack of ethics". But I knew I would never get used to things that were wrong. Of course, this resolve would soon be challenged an innumerable number of times.

Bilour's death meant that the NA-1 seat was, conveniently, up for grabs. There were many out there who would never have defeated him. A few months later, in the subsequent general elections, the NA-1 seat would be won by none other than Imran Khan, although he would be defeated in his own home town of Lahore. But that was the future. For the moment, I had far more pressing concerns than the future happenings in Pakistani politics. I began setting up my new headquarters. With the help of my dear friend Maria, I found a beautiful six-bedroomed house in F11, Islamabad, within a week.

The house was opposite her friend Lubna, and as her husband happened to hold a senior position in the police, it was considered a safe choice. With the amount of space we had, and the layout of the place, I had many ideas. The plan was to give the ground floor rooms to my mother and my brother's sons, and keep the upper portion for myself and my kids. I employed a guard, a driver, a cook and a housemaid to make sure everyone would be well looked after. I planned to do all that I could for my mother while reconnecting with my school friends. I had basically envisioned the leisurely lifestyle of a typical 40-year-old auntie-type in Pakistan. I was determined to make this work for everyone, one way or another.

I thought I would only work a few days a week and that it would not be too punishing since I was now an anchor. I had been given a large team and a company car to use. All I had to do was worry about my appearance, as was the trend in Islamabad. I set about finding myself a stylist. Saleha took me to her designer and school-friend Bina Sultan. I was trying to find out if she was interested in doing my TV wardrobe but she didn't seem too interested in talking shop at first. She just wanted to know personal details about me, which I evaded. She then interrogated me about my drug of choice. I pretended to be cool and laughed it off. But this woman was clearly in too relaxed a mood for it to have been naturally induced. She persisted, and when I declared that I had never touched drugs, she announced emphatically, "Well then, let's jump straight into cocaine!" Then the subject turned abruptly to the cricketer-turned-politician Imran Khan, and a strange devotion poured out. He was clearly a regular at the house parties. The culture shock continued as a very tall, bald man with a big booming voice sauntered in. He was a TV presenter of Baluch-Pashtun origin. We chatted briefly about news channels and politics. As he interrogated me about where I'd come from, I looked at my friend and, sensing my unease, we left the Pakistan we never grew up in.

About a month later, Bina gave me a call and said there were a couple of jackets I could borrow for the TV show. I dropped by in the early afternoon and found the woman slightly less loud, though she did keep referring to me as 'baby'. As I tried on a coat, I found something bulging from one of the pockets. I put my hand in and pulled out a large brown fudgy substance wrapped in polythene. Bina jumped to her feet and immediately grabbed it back. "Oh *Bhen*..." she swore. "I think one of the models must have left it in there". I left in a bit of a daze at this world that I had no knowledge about.

Maria later took me for a pampering session to a local salon. We lounged on huge comfy armchairs with footstools while our feet were scrubbed and acrylic toenails applied. Arms were coated in creams and wrapped in cling film. All we were expected to do was bitch about everyone and everything around us. I took a picture and sent it to Ridha, who was already looking forward to moving to Pakistan.

'I could live like this,' I thought to myself. I recalled the words of a friend of mine from years ago. "Reham has never liked to give herself a rest. You are burning the candle at both ends. Slow down". I make people around me dizzy with my pace and they tend to think I'm stressed out. What they don't realise is that some people find relaxing lifestyles boring. If I didn't have constant challenges in life, I would not know what to do with myself. I just like being busy without any motivation of money or fame. There are people who can literally be bored to death, and I'm one of them.

I was about to be reminded that not everyone lived a pampered lifestyle. As I set about starting my job, I also found that no one would turn up to the office at 8am, and that the Internet would not work in my grand office. Half of the first floor was given to me as my personal office with a built-in make-up and dressing area. I was being kept very sweet. Perhaps it was thought that I would be entertaining political guests in my spacious office, as is commonly practiced by Pakistani political anchors.

The problem was that I looked much younger than I was but was not prepared to entertain guests and forge personal contacts, as is the trend for Pakistani anchors dominating current affairs. I introduced new rules. No one was allowed in my office except for my female make-up artist. Instead of alcohol hidden away in cabinets, for the special guests, there were now clean prayer mats stacked up. The crew was treated with respect, and a culture of writing scripts and emails was introduced.

I was told I didn't look or behave like a Pakistani woman. Turning up to work at 8am is not the norm in many offices, particularly TV channels. Initially I was met with resistance by the inner lobbies. The first two programs were intentionally sabotaged. But I was never one to sit down and cry in despair. I was a woman built for resistance and very quickly won them over.

§

It was a cold January afternoon when I first met the man who promised the tsunami of change. Before leaving for Pakistan, I had been invited to overseas PTI events after receiving a random email from a taxi driver in Birmingham. He had become very disillusioned with Imran Khan but still supported PTI, and asked me to attend an event to help the party. I had no idea about the party, so I checked out a few videos and looked up Rabia Zia, a woman most PTI men were desperate to delete. I remember attending one of these events and seeing nothing but chaos and disorganization. Unimpressed, I left after fifteen minutes. Yet here I was, a year later, back in Pakistan, and with an interview request accepted by the celebrity politician.

I had briefed my guard before going to Bani Gala. He knew to stay with me at all times. So off we went, first to the secretariat in Islamabad, where I met Naeem ul Haq for the first time, the Chief of Staff and main spokesperson for the big man himself. He interviewed me in a cold, messy boardroom. It smelt musty and dusty. He then jumped into my car and we drove on to Bani Gala, the mountaintop residence of the PTI leader.

As Naeem walked ahead of us, my goofy guard whispered in my ear, "This guy is dodgy".

I nodded in agreement as Naeem led us into the property, which sprawled over many acres and boasted views of Rawal Lake and the city of Islamabad. The place had an old feel, and smelt like my grandfather's house in Abbottabad. I was led into a room where I saw an older man dressed in black from head to toe, stood with his back to us, trying to start a fire and failing. It was the legend himself.

I wore a black high-neck jumper under a long blue full-sleeved ankle-length printed *kameez* (tunic) and blue trousers. I had worn a very dull outfit on purpose, to project a serious look. I sat down in a red armchair as the man in black sat down on the settee opposite. From across the coffee table, he stared at me. I noticed that his cornea was ageing and had that grey look. My first thought was that he might need a cataract operation. He stared at me unblinkingly, while Naeem introduced me as an anchor who'd recently joined Tahir Khan's News One.

"So where have you come from?"

"The UK," I said

"No, where in the UK?"

"Berkshire."

"Where in Berkshire?"

"West of Reading?"

"Where? I know all of Berkshire".

"Newbury...you know Newbury?"

"No, where is it?"

I resisted the urge to roll my eyes. This barrage of questions was direct and unsettling but I met it coolly, making clear that it was his interview I was here for. He persisted with queries about my age, which I also dodged, prompting him to follow up with, "What are you, like 30? Well, you're a baby compared to me. Do you exercise?"

'No," I replied, slightly perplexed. "I am allergic to gyms and fitness".

"You should exercise," he continued. "As we grow older we need to maintain our fitness".

The talk of this man was odd; blunt to the point of rudeness. I got up and asked to use the bathroom. When I came out of the bathroom, an Alsatian was sat outside the door. I knelt to stroke him and started talking to him.

"He doesn't respond to English, only Urdu," grunted The Man in Black.

I desperately wanted to reply that I didn't think dogs spoke any language but resisted, not wanting to jeopardise the interview. This beautiful Alsatian was called Sheru (meaning 'lion') and had belonged to the former President and dictator of Pakistan, General Musharraf. Imran got the dog after Musharraf went into self-imposed exile.

I sat down again and the celebrity gobbled a plate of fried eggs and bread. The rest of us just sat there, looking on at him demolishing his food. I wondered if he might be diabetic. I got up to leave. As we moved outside, the dog followed me, and I noticed he was hobbling in pain. I mumbled something along the lines of, "I think there is something in his paw," but it was met by another unconcerned grunt and shrug. "It's just a thorn," the Man in Black muttered. I debated silently whether to take the risk of taking the thorn out myself. I decided against it but hoped The Man in Black would later tend to the dog.

Some men just do not listen to sincere, sound advice. Over a year later, I would discover that it had been a poisonous porcupine needle in that paw, and it had caused an infection. Within a few weeks, the beautiful dog that I had met was dead.

§

The first two months at work were not the easiest. I would overhear a few of the boys making plans to dislodge me, but even they became loyal supporters as the months went by. I rallied with the owners for their salaries, and ultimately left in protest. There was something very concerning when it came to the treatment of staff within the media institutions. The technical crew had not been paid in months, yet as a newcomer, I was being paid handsomely. I also learned that from that moment on, my salary would come to me through a media partner instead of directly from the owners.

In an outburst, I made it clear that it was unacceptable to work in such conditions; where no money was being spent on production and crew. The owner and his media partner took me along to show me three other premises which I could use instead. Later that evening, the owner said that another media partner had arranged a dinner in his honour and I should be introduced to the fraternity.

As I entered the rather artistically decorated home of Ali Qadir Gillani (who I later discovered would facilitate this sort of social mingling on a regular basis), I immediately felt uncomfortable. There were other columnists there, like Cyril Almeida, who I met for the first time, and who later become infamous for his controversial Dawn Leaks story. There were politicians too, with sleazy arrogance on their faces and scotch in their hands. One such chap, with tousled hair and a bored look that comes from too much privilege and very little to do, was a minister called Khusro Bakhtiar. He strolled over, but an experienced eye made a quick assessment and he didn't even try his luck. A few other young, privileged and bored brats were also around, along with some old uncle-types, desperately trying to hang onto their fading virility. I caught sight of one I had met just a few weeks before. I immediately squirmed at the sight of him. To my horror, the man began edging his way towards me. This was the PTI leader and spokesperson of the party, Naeem ul Haq.

Naeem ul Haq was not alone. He was with an exaggerated version of himself, apparently some party financier from the U.S. I saw whiskers and sleaze on the left, and more whiskers and more sleaze on the right. I sat down on a sofa well away from both of them, while their whiskers twitched away at the sight of this young, Western journalist in a blue tailored suit. I turned in my seat to face the guest to my right and tried to avoid the ghastly gaze of the two balding lechers. Suddenly, I felt a hand touch my knee. I felt a cold shiver of disgust and turned to give the owner of the offending hand a glare that promised to cut it straight off. He started to mutter something, but I immediately got up to make my way to the far end of the room, to try and make idle chit-chat with the younger media men.

One of them was Sheryar Taseer, the blue-eyed younger son of the assassinated Governor of Punjab, Salman Taseer. I vaguely followed his conversation and planned my getaway from this party. It was evident that I was being paraded as the new eye-candy in town. The prowling, sleazy figure of the Chief of Staff to the PTI chairman was relentless in his chase. I saw him approaching us from the corner of my eye and backed away until I hit the glass cabinet behind me. I muttered something to Shehryar Taseer along the lines of, "Save me from this sleaze-ball," and the young men tried their best to ward off the creepy man. Cyril mentioned his son and I immediately took the opportunity and said, "Oh, you are Ahmed's dad". The bluff worked and Naeem ul Haq backed off.

I decided in that minute that I would make any possible excuse to leave not only the party, but the channel, too. I mumbled something about a football match that I couldn't miss and got out of there. I declined as many invitations from the host as necessary until everyone, including Ali Gillani, recognised that I was not a young plaything. From that moment on, Ali and I forged a friendship based on respect. He didn't bother to invite me to any more parties but kept me updated on all the gossip, something I later regretted not paying more attention to. I had found myself at least one friend in this unfamiliar, chaotic world.

The dinner parties and gossip were of no interest to me. I was more interested in the real Pakistan. I had consciously tailored my show's content around rediscovering my homeland and heritage. Within the confines of the pre-election frenzy, I focused on real people and not high-profile politicians. I have always been a proponent of the attitude that representatives in Parliament should be those who can best speak for their constituency. I loved the idea that in the UK, an unknown person who best represented the community, or had some particular ability, could rise from the bottom to the top in politics. The rise of the son of a Pakistani-origin bus-driver to the post of the Mayor of London was a great example for the rest of the world to follow. Despite being relatively new to the scene, it was clear that many of the elected Members of the National and Provincial Assemblies (MNAs and MPAs) were unsuitable for public office (although in fairness, this is true no matter where you go). I wanted to find those people who would genuinely be great representatives.

In 2012, while I was at the BBC, I'd received a message from a few Conservative members in Southampton and Portsmouth, asking to meet. Over lunch, the three gentlemen explained why they needed new representatives. Although I had devoted all my free time to work with ethnic or deprived communities, and particularly with disabled children and youth, I had no idea it had been followed so closely. So much of my time went into supporting charities that my editor suggested I should learn to say no a bit more, and that

I would soon get exhausted if I continued running around helping everyone. Over lunch, I was told that a female MP in a very safe seat was getting a lot of complaints. Apparently, on a Sunday, a veteran party worker had called her up and was miffed at the response. The lady had not been keen to entertain a constituent on a Sunday.

I was flattered that I was being considered a potential future Conservative candidate, but I excused myself. I kept getting calls from the chap who had introduced me to the circle. I explained to him that I would have to leave my BBC job and that this was impossible as I had no other means of earning. He told me that the campaign would be funded. In the end I had to confess to them that I had children and needed an income to survive on. They still insisted I go for an initial interview to Cambridge, which I did. It was snowing that day and I struggled with the little one in the back of the car on sleet-covered roads to make it for the appointment on time. The interview turned out to be more of a confidence building exercise. I kept saying, "I don't know how I can commit to a political career," and the interviewer kept suggesting ways in which people coped. I told him that I was planning to go away to Pakistan for a year. The response was: "Just make sure you come back in time for the September conference".

I thought moving to Pakistan would improve my CV and maybe make it possible for me to pursue a different career, and perhaps even make room for politics too. I also fancied the idea of starting a business in Pakistan and importing goods to sell in the UK. The idea of changing my career from showbiz to business, and possibly working from home, was at the forefront of my mind: I wanted to spend more time at home with the children, and found the BBC job unchallenging. But in Pakistan, I got sucked into an even busier work schedule than ever. Not only was I working on TV, but I was travelling a lot more too. And as I travelled, I saw with dismay that all those sitting in Parliament were out of touch with the common folk. The elite were snooty as well as incompetent.

After only a few programmes with these celebrity politicians, I was bored. I set about finding real people with real issues. As I had roots in the tribes of KP and Baluchistan, and could speak the language, I naturally focused on these two provinces. I belonged to a family that had been part of local politics and had played their part in the struggle for Pakistan, so I had more inside info about this region. I also felt a natural empathy with my own people. As I took the opportunity to explore the region, I started to fall in love with the rustic simplicity and hospitality of the people. My shows began to get noticed for including a lot of Pashtun voices. Three shows on primetime were aired in Pashto with subtitles. The American embassy watched these closely, and I was immediately asked for full transcripts of the shows. General Asad Durrani, the former Director General of the ISI (Pakistan's intelligence agency), also kept a hawk-like eye on my interests and program content. He invited me to a dinner at Saddle Lounge. The purpose was to sway me gently towards their narrative, which was in stark contrast to mine. I was discussing on my shows how Ashraf Ghani was a clear winner because of his Pashtun origins, his prolific career, and his impressive abilities as an orator. Durrani and his other dinner guests insisted that Ghani was not as popular as I was suggesting. I was unconvinced at the time, but when the national unity government was announced, I understood the motive of the meeting. The Afghan refugee vote in Pakistan had been withheld for the first time in these elections. I clearly was not privy to this or other information Durrani had.

To my surprise, Pakistani TV shows were not in the habit of discussing Afghan or Iran policy on primetime. News from the areas bordering Afghanistan and Iran were not given any coverage on mainstream TV. It was mainly India-bashing when relations with neighbouring countries were ever discussed. The leading parties also seemed disinterested in addressing the concerns of the peoples of these areas. The focus for politicians and media heads alike was North Punjab and Karachi.

I decided to change this, primarily because I had more knowledge of the area, geographically and historically. Additionally, a story was developing here so it made perfect sense to me, logically and geo-strategically. The interviewees and subjects were intentionally selected to give audiences something radically different from the preferred set formula of three main topics: the cricketer-turned-politician, the Chairman of the MQM, and the head of a one-man party known only for his crassness. In the relatively young, ratings-mad media machine of Pakistan, transmissions were dominated by ugly catfights between attention-hungry politicians, and even hungrier channel owners.

My shows were noticed for featuring unusual and informative content presented in an interesting style. I was genuinely enjoying the exploration of a new world, and apparently it shone through in the presenting style. There was once a stop in the city of Kohat, to spend the day with a small-town tailor who was elected as a District President of the party. The exuberant character who showed me into his home and life was adorable. At one point, he innocently showed he how he was cultivating cannabis at home (which we had to edit out). I heard everyone erupt into laughter around me. I hadn't really understood what he was describing to me in the local language.

Right from the start, I put my foot in it by calling a spade a spade. Most of my shows were appreciated by ideological supporters of PTI, the party of change, as they contained honest criticism of their failings. Like every patriotic Pakistani, and like a typical expat, I was frustrated by the fact that we were lagging decades behind other countries. The shows were mostly from exotic and remote locations considered largely unsafe to travel to. I would be invited into the homes of everyday people whenever hotels were fully booked or considered improper for my stay, and I fell more and more in love with the people and the land.

Charmed by the local *chadars*, I adopted the traditional look. I was travelling to remote places like Nok Kundi in Baluchistan and Bajaur in the tribal areas of the country. As I was going back to my roots, I started observing the *purdah* as per requirements of the culture, and to blend in. The locals loved how I adopted their cultural look and enjoyed sampling their food. To me, it felt natural to sit on the floors with them. It was like a reincarnation. It felt like returning to something I was very familiar and comfortable with.

I had been so lonely all my life. I had been taught to be polite and smile through everything, but the heart was restless. Out there in the rough rugged terrain, from the Chaghi Mountains of Baluchistan to the Khigana Mountains of Kohat, I experienced peace. After years of night terrors, I smiled in my sleep too. The concept of *Sukoon-i-Qalb*, as described by Maulana Thanvi, seeped into my consciousness. I abandoned my expensive designer stilettos. I sold all my remaining jewellery. I travelled lighter. TV work and posing for cameras became tiresome. All trappings of my class-consciousness and pretension evaporated.

§

Election season was in full swing. The much-hyped Tsunami was looking pretty mediocre to me (on the ground at least). But initially, every show I watched had an overconfident take on the *tabdeeli* (change) that was about to sweep the country. The analysts on my shows shared these sentiments. The slogan of change, colourful flags, and concert-style campaigning may have been borrowed from the Barack Obama campaign, but PTI lacked organisational skills. However, even after a rather lacklustre rally on March 23rd, PMLN leaders looked nervous. I couldn't understand why they felt so threatened by this new party. I saw PTI as no threat to PMLN.

However, the analysts would puzzle me with their use of phrases like 'unpredictable result' and 'could swing any way'. In an off-air chat during an interview with the Chief Minister Punjab's son, his team asked me for my take on the 23rd March event. Did I think PTI was gaining strength in Punjab? I remember categorically telling them that there seemed to be no threat to them in Punjab. In KP however, key seats would be picked up, and they looked like a growing force. The smug attitude of PTI leaders and the over-cautious approach of PMLN leaders would all make sense to me much later. I had focused on the young, new faces of PTI, and irritated a few senior journalists by accurately predicting which seats PTI would win. My only source was my ear-to-the-ground, and analysis of the mood of the constituency. I was regularly ridiculed for my lack of knowledge during the breaks of live shows, merely for saying what was clearly against the paid agenda that everyone else was on.

By the time of the election itself, I was at AAJ TV. During the live transmission of the elections, I was surprised when my guests were suddenly replaced by the new bureau chief of AAJ. My new guests were two journalists I wasn't familiar with. As I opened the discussion, one of the men, Amir Mateen, rather condescendingly suggested I sit like a prop and let them set the theme. Clearly he mistook me for the young girls who would merely complement the older, silver-haired analysts. I ignored him. As I continued my line of questioning, he rather rudely rebuked me in the break, calling for me to be replaced. I couldn't believe he was saying it right in front of me. "This young girl has no clue how to run the show," he called out. I said nothing, and sent a message to the Managing Director, Ahmed Zuberi, asking to remove the guests immediately, or I would walk away. The gentlemen were both removed and replaced by my pre-booked guests. This was my first taste of what it was like to stick to the script handed over by higher authorities. A year later, at PMLN leader Daniyal Aziz's house, the same man would apologise profusely to me in public for his rudeness.

I was able to get some pretty high-profile interviews in this period. My interview with Hamza Shehbaz, the son of Shehbaz Sharif, was certainly interesting. I found him to be an extremely polite individual. Not only was he courteous to me, but he also braved the blunt attacks of my makeup lady, Sitara. She was very direct and informed him that they had chosen a couple of unpopular candidates. He listened to her calmly and assured her that it was now too close to the elections, but he would bear her comments in mind for the future. His pleasant response charmed her, and she was raving about him the whole way back. He left after the interview but insisted that our team should stay back for a lunch prepared for us. I wanted to milk the opportunity, so rather cheekily asked his coordinator to try to get me an interview with Maryam Nawaz Sharif. It worked. They squeezed me into her busy schedule, and soon enough, I was being pleasantly surprised by her mannerisms as well.

I was expecting a lady with all the airs and graces you'd imagine of the heir apparent of a powerful dynasty. But unlike the princess label she had been given by PTI, she came across as a focused, time-conscious woman. She would get up and open the door herself to call her next appointment in, rather than ringing a bell, and stuck to the allotted time. Interestingly, we all thought that Hamza had the mannerisms of his uncle Nawaz, while Maryam had strong administrative skills like her uncle, Shehbaz Sharif. She was operating the office with the discipline an army officer maintains. While Hamza came across as a more laid-back and diplomatic politician who could connect because of his *awami* (everyday and relatable) appeal, Maryam was very direct and to-the-point, unlike most Pakistanis one would meet. She was certainly not a stereotypical, pampered, *desi*-elite woman, but very independent and competent.

None of us would really know how independent she would prove to be until the post-Panama crisis that hit that family in 2017. But I felt the visceral hatred for this woman was undeserved. She was not the 'Pharoah' that she had been labelled by people who had not met her. She simply did not waste time with idle chit-chat and pleasantries more typical of the subcontinent. Women are expected to be more docile and sweet. A taskmaster man is admired, but a no-nonsense woman is intolerable in our society.

In my quest to find out more about the grassroots issues, I started looking for election-related stories from the mostly-ignored, federally administered areas, and Baluchistan too.

One of my favourites was the first woman candidate ever to contest in the smallest tribal agency in FATA. As we made our way from Peshawar to Bajaur (which borders the Kunar province of Afghanistan), our host (an MNA from PPP) informed us that he was leaving as there had been a suicide bombing. My producer, Ali Akbar, told me that it was a female suicide bomber who had blown herself up in front of the main hospital in the town centre. I was undeterred, and told him to just keep on driving.

We had to change the venue but managed a very lively interview with the first female candidate from the tribal agencies. The whole interview was in Pashto but was a huge hit with the audiences. Sitting on traditional *charpoys* (woven beds), with rose bushes all around us, we chatted happily about her aspirations. She had her face covered throughout the interview but her enthusiastic personality was still obvious, thanks to her hand gestures and tone. It was so nice to meet the supportive husband and the bubbly female candidate in person.

On the way back, I decided to give my dedicated team a nice dinner. The local fish was very popular, and as I sat with my crew in a straw shack, eating tons of fried and barbecued fish, it started to pour. By the time I had finished, there was knee-deep water outside. I had so quickly formed a good bond with my crew that they put *charpoys* and chairs together, before allowing me to step out of the shack. They would not let me get my feet wet. I smiled to myself at this twist of fate. These men were not highly-educated from overseas but they had the chivalry of Sir Walter Raleigh. I was neither a queen nor a romantic interest. Care and respect may not always come from those relationships we expect it from, but from unexpected quarters that we hadn't considered.

The next stop was Baluchistan. I had long-been fascinated by the land of my origin. It is said that Qais Abdur Rashid returned from Medina to Zhob, and his final resting place is in Koh-i-Suleiman in Baluchistan. Additionally, the few remaining from my mother's Pannee tribe are settled in Naushki and Sibi. I'd made a contact following a row on a live show over the issue of Baluchistan. One of the lesser-known guests called my producer, complaining that we had given more time to a corrupt politician than a genuine, struggling politician like himself. I immediately called back to apologise and the man urged me to come see how bad it was for myself. He promised to provide security and arrange meetings with local women. The offer was too interesting to refuse. I was mentally prepared for all eventualities in this adventure of a lifetime. I booked a couple of interviews with the Pashtunkhwa Milli Awami Party and the persecuted Hazaras community leaders. On landing, I was escorted by a heavily-armed private militia, sat in a tinted Land Crusier, and driven to a home full of excited Baluch women. I heaved a sigh of relief.

My host, Mir Mukkarram Zehri., looked rather menacing with the typical Baluch Sardar ensemble. After a few minutes, I discovered that the rather scary exterior was a cover-up for an American-accented man in his thirties with strong feminist views, who had returned to fight it out. When he found out that I had lined up interviews with all his rivals, he was annoyed, but also concerned for my safety. I kept flouting their security measures but after a while, he and his family could barely stop the smiles at my brazen attitude. It was a complicated security procedure, which involved changing vehicles and drivers to safely conduct all the interviews with rival factions. It was like *West Side Story*. I didn't realise how dangerous or tactless it was to go from a Baluch tribe to a Pashtun household and then to the Hazaras area. Soon enough, I'd realise how dangerous it could be.

As I travelled from Quetta, through the mineral-rich Baluch belt to the literal pot of gold that was Reko Diq, two things stood out. The first was that the bravado of the Pashtun chiefs and Baluch Sardars would vanish the moment a call came in from the Inspector General Frontier Corps (IGFC). On one occasion, a scary-looking Sardar, who would pull out a gun at the slightest provocation, literally jumped off his divan sofa and nearly saluted when the IGFC made contact. It became clear who was calling the shots in this province.

The second thing that tore at my heart was the sight of educated yet jobless Baluch youngsters addicted to drugs. The landscape changed non-stop, but the story of deprivation and misery remained the same throughout the belt. NA-260 (Quetta-cum-Chagai-cum-Mastung) was considered the largest electoral constituency of Pakistan, spread over 700 kilometres and bordering Iran and Afghanistan. It was not only an administrative impossibility to govern, but had the additional challenges of stretching from a Pashtun stronghold in Quetta into a mainly Baluch belt. Cross-border smuggling and infiltration was a huge additional complication.

The military *jawans* (soldiers) deployed here stand no chance in front of the sniper fire from the dark mountains outside Quetta. Cross-border smuggling of crude oil and drugs is out of control. From Hilux pick-ups to camels, everything is used on a nightly basis to drive across the sands from Iran to Pakistan. The border with Afghanistan is porous and never ending. As I covered the constituency in 2013, I found that 60 candidates from 73 tribes were participating. Analysts were way off the mark with their absurd predictions that a Baluch candidate would win. Outside of Quetta, no one even dared to hold a rally. Only the Jamiat Ulema-e Islam (a party with a Sunni Deobandi identity) appeared everywhere, but I could tell that the elderly Pashtun man sitting in Quetta would win NA-260 hands down.

My first interview was with that very same man, Abdul Raheem Khan Mandokhail, from the Pashtunkhwa Milli Awami Party (PKMAP) in Quetta City. The entire interview revolved around his irrational separatist arguments. I was still reeling from the shock of his openly bigoted views when I saw my cameraman whispering to someone on a bike, explaining who I was. I immediately alerted my host and told my cameraman that I would be taking the next flight back. The cameraman in question was from the TV channel I was working for. I knew that local crew would often have connections with both kidnappers and the intelligence agencies.

AAJ TV ran on a shoestring budget. The manager told me that I would have to make do with the small bureau office in Quetta, and that there was no need to take my crew. Something definitely wasn't right. I asked the host to hire a reliable local cameraman instead, which turned out to be a great decision; the cameraman was amazing. Khair Mohammad was as daring as I was, and could speak all the local languages. Our reckless attitude got us into trouble with our host family a couple of times but it was worth it. His photographs of me holding an AK47 in the desert would not only form my national identity later, but I found that (unknown to me) I was the pin-up girl of the Kurdish movement too.

After the first interview, I filmed the Baluch ladies who sat waiting for me. They were full of life despite their rather tough lives. On-air, they gave me their brave stories of fighting it out alone as widows or political activists. Off-air, we talked chocolates, face-washes, and boys. From there, I went on to visit the Hazaras community. The Hazaras Shias are immediately recognisable because of their oriental features. As a result, they are easy to gun down. The Hazaras community had seen horrific attacks and ethnic cleansing since 2001. The year 2013 began with over 120 people killed in twin blasts. The following month, 84 more were killed.

Over 350 of the 518 polling stations in the constituency were considered highly sensitive. Rockets would land in the homes and vehicle convoys of those not favoured. Political offices were targeted with bomb blasts, particularly the PPP's. To ensure safety, most candidates chose to stand as independent candidates and not use party flags. It was an eye-opener. Reality sank in slowly as I witnessed the security risks the people faced first-hand. On the way back to Quetta, our own vehicle narrowly avoided a bomb blast on the infamous Sariaab Road by mere minutes.

The ethnically Mongolian Hazaras are distinct because of their quiet grace as a community. The women showed me the endless graveyard where their husbands and sons could be found. Most families had lost four or five males. I interviewed them, trying to hold back my tears as young children told me stories of how they were orphaned before their eyes. The widows described how they'd seen their husbands shredded to pieces. Though a Sunni Muslim myself,

I could not understand why a Shia population would be brutally murdered like this. We were taught that the Holy Prophet (PBUH) marched into Makkah with an army of ten thousand soldiers but declared an amnesty. All those who had attacked him and his family were also pardoned. There could not be a greater example to follow.

My hosts had very moderate views, perhaps because of an educated family background, or perhaps inter-racial marriages had broadened their minds. The father of the candidate had married an educated Urdu-speaking lady who was an active member of the MQM, while the candidate himself, Mir Mukkarram Zehri, had a Bosnian wife. Most of the family had married into Pashtuns so it was a healthy cultural mix. The following morning, we set off for their hometown of Dalbandin, close to the border with Iran. My spirits lifted because of the stunning landscape. To the left were the awe-inspiring black mountains of Chagie (famous for the nuclear tests), and on the right were the undulating white sands. The long journey was an eye-opener, as I saw the Western-inspired politician trying to convince locals to vote for him. But Zehri would be left frustrated, as every village had already sold its votes. In some places, they had been given as much as thirty thousand rupees for the votes of a small family.

Although new to the country, I could understand why the poor would do that. Democracy is a luxury that only the elites can afford. For a poor parent, the priority is where he or she gets the next meal. At the time, a bag of 20kg flour cost less than a thousand rupees in Islamabad, but was double that in the Baluch belt. Besides, the choices given to them weren't exactly radically different from each other. The poor learned that everyone made empty promises, and just wanted to rule over them. Elections were the only time to make a quick buck.

It was dark as we entered Dalbandin, a good nine hours later. There was no electricity. Battery-operated lights hung from shops. A feast of stuffed lamb awaited me. In my room, two young teenage girls slept on the floor to keep me company, and giggled away most of the night. We connected, even though I could not speak the language. One of the girls had recently acquired an unexplained disability: her leg muscles were wasting away. She was the spitting image of the famous Indian film star Kareena Kapoor, but could not be married off because of her affliction. There was no medical facility for miles. A taxi to the nearest town cost over two hundred rupees. Every young couple I met told me that their firstborns had been stillborn. I made a mental note to return to provide them with some sort of local medical facility as soon as I could.

I tried to raise the issue of Baluchistan repeatedly with political leaders I got access to but failed to get a listening ear. The following morning, as I was taken to visit Nok Kundi (famous for its copper reserves), Zehri expressed his anger at the political leaders for their lack of understanding of issues. He had briefed the leader of the PTI too, but had been disappointed. At Nok Kundi, I discovered that the copper mines were owned by a Chinese company, and that there were no employment opportunities for the locals. It was easier to get crystal meth than jobs here. As I had suspected, the seat was once again won by the bigoted leader of PKMAP. The independent candidate, like many others, left the country utterly disillusioned.

I continued to return to Baluchistan after the elections to cover the relentless attacks on the Hazaras through the summer. The room in Quetta where I'd stayed was hit by a rocket just three days after my departure. I escaped the rockets, the firing and the bomb blasts, not to mention the rampant abductions of Baluchistan. But only weeks later, on a fine sunny day minutes away from home, I was not going to be so lucky.

Chapter 12

I've never been particularly superstitious, but the 8th seems to be a bad date for me. A coincidental catalogue of painful incidents would fall on that day. And one of the most significant was on the 8th of August 2013.

I was doing a 7pm slot on AAJ TV, and bringing in a lot of sponsorship. I was getting attention for doing exceptionally well while still on a small channel. The salary was improving but it was still not that impressive, and I wanted to move to the 8pm slot. I was working harder and longer than most people I knew because a large chunk of my time was being spent teaching production techniques and scriptwriting to existing crew and college students.

The channel owners were noticing, and increments were coming in without me asking. My opinions on content direction of the channel as a whole were being valued. In an effort to improve my penetration into the market, I proposed an ambitious two-hour program for *Eid*. This would be telecast as our festive period offering. We planned celebrity guests, and the Royal Palm, Lahore, was decided as the perfect venue. I took on the stress of producing an ambitious outdoor broadcast with staff who were unfamiliar and inexperienced with such events. The measly budget given to me was far from sufficient to put this together, but I used some Pakistani *jugar* (crude ingenuity) to achieve what I wanted.

Everything that could go wrong, went wrong: from guests turning up four hours late, to other guests leaving early because of other commitments. To make matters worse, the Governor of Punjab, Chaudhry Sarwar (who would later join PTI), suddenly arrived, and his security protocol wouldn't allow our electricity generator in. We had all been fasting and working round the clock. When we finally finished at around 1am, I decided to treat the crew to a lavish Ramadan *Sehr* in the city's famous food street. We feasted on the reigning family's alleged favourite dishes of *paye* (trotters) and *nihari* (beef stew).

There seemed to be something wrong with the driver. I discussed it with my producer as I suspected he was on weed, and asked the boys to check. I also told them that he should not eat too much so he wouldn't get sleepy. Both Sitara and I had questioned his driving but neither of us had been assertive. My regular producer, Ali (who usually took care of travel arrangements) was off getting married, and the substitute was not nearly as experienced or obsessional when it came to safety precautions. Against my better judgement, and persuaded by the thought of getting everyone home for *Eid*, I decided to travel back to Islamabad from Lahore.

At 8am, we were about forty-five minutes from Islamabad. A few minutes after I had nodded off, the vehicle drifted from the fast lane to the extreme left lane of the motorway and crashed into the concrete barrier. We were lucky the MPV did not fall into the Sawan River. But I was not lucky. I'd been sat directly behind the driver and was launched across the vehicle into the sliding door. The sliding door flew open on impact and I fell from the still-speeding vehicle onto the middle lane of the motorway, about a hundred yards away from the site of the crash and directly into oncoming traffic.

In those first few minutes I lay paralysed on the road, I mentally assessed the damage to my body. My mind raced as I realised I could not feel my right arm. My eyes searched for it but I couldn't see it. As I looked up, I spotted my hand with the red perfectly painted nails lying lifeless away from me. My world collapsed. It looked like my arm was detached from my body. My content producer, Waseem, came running to me and sat hunched over my helpless body. The look on his face didn't match his reassuring words. One look at him had me certain that I had been badly injured. I lay there, not even feeling the pain as I thought desperately how I would support my children. I had never told anyone that I was a divorcee and had three children. None of my crew members knew. I could hear my makeup lady wailing from the hard shoulder of the road. She had also fallen out behind me and was crying out loudly in pain.

I was totally conscious and coherent so I assured myself I had no head injuries. I could feel that I could move my body so I deduced that my spine must be fine, but the arm had probably been cut off as it lay lifeless at my 11 o' clock. I saw the rather dazed-looking driver looking down at me. He was a tall, odd-looking man, and had been driving carelessly throughout. In fact, the motorway police had pulled him over and cautioned him twice. I'd been getting irritated by his driving but had so much else on my mind - and a lady who is assertive quickly develops a reputation of being a bitch, whereas a man is admired for not taking any crap.

I recalled how my mother would kick up such a fuss when taking me for recordings to the TV station. She would demand good vehicles, food promptly served on the set, better lighting, and better scripting. Everyone saw her as a difficult woman. I would get embarrassed too. Society gives such clear and unfair gender roles, and these messages are subliminally yet effectively transmitted to young children. To think that I suffered accidents, small and big, through fear of being perceived as a horrible woman for pointing out the obvious.

I wasn't going to take any chances now. As I lay on the road and people from other vehicles ran over to help, I fired off instructions at everyone. A nice old man rushed over with a refilled 7-Up bottle of water and I refused to drink from it, knowing it was not bottled mineral water. Instead, I asked him to check my clothes. The bearded man had a Hindko accent from Mansehra which was familiar to me. He took the scarf from his neck and covered me with it, then took charge by telling my much younger crew, "She is our own daughter. You don't have to worry".

I told them loudly not to move or lift me, even an inch. I insisted on waiting for an ambulance with an orthopaedic stretcher. It took 40 minutes for a Rescue 1122 ambulance to get to us. I got my orthopaedic stretcher but the car was a basic Suzuki van. Each time the driver braked, the stretcher would slide up and down. I stayed calm and recited Quran verses while poor Sitara cried uncontrollably and asked for her husband. I had no one to call out for, and was more worried about upsetting my mother and my kids. As Waseem pestered me for my next of kin, I told him to call Saleha, the same lady Sahir had called years ago when I burned my hand. Waseem knew my nephew and had already called him, but I told him to make sure the rest of the family were not told.

It took another painful 45 minutes to reach the Pakistan Institute of Medical Sciences, the huge government medical complex in Islamabad. The doctors attended and referred me for MRIs, X-rays, and ultrasounds. But then I was left on a hospital trolley for 30 minutes. They were busy, and there were no female nurses to attend to me. However, things changed when Saleha arrived on the scene. Immediately she began bossing everyone around and getting things done. I caught a brief glimpse of my nephew, Yousaf, looking ashen-faced and devastated. Saleha had also brought a dentist, who quickly and expertly stitched my chin. As soon as the fractures were plastered and my wounds stitched up, Saleha, appalled by the lack of hygiene and the general condition of the hospital, said she was taking me to her home.

The right side of my body, from my shoulder to my ankle, had bone fractures, while the left side had soft tissue and surface abrasions. I looked a fright. But I wasn't bothered about the fractures. I knew that there was something horribly wrong with my right arm, and it seemed to have been overlooked among all the obvious injuries. The arm had swollen to three times its size and I had no sensation in much of it. There was excruciating pain emanating from my neck to the bicep. And I could not move. One of my biggest fears in life has been getting a disability that would leave me with a loss of dignity. I always had an obsession with privacy, and found it uncomfortable to change, even in front of family females and friends. The thought of needing someone to bathe me and take me to the toilet was terrifying.

There I lay in Saleha's guest bedroom, unable to move and in unimaginable pain, but the worry of my financial responsibilities prevented me from crying. By the evening, my family was finally told. My children were brought under the pretext of visiting someone, and were not mentally prepared to see me battered and bruised. They were told literally just before they walked into the room. Sahir entered, took one look at me and passed out. He fell to the floor, flat on his face. It was almost funny. Ridha was shivering in fear and crying uncontrollably. The little one was in shock. I had no choice but to joke and make light of my situation, just to make them feel better about the ugly state I was in.

A few minutes later, my sister and my elderly mother came over. As I hugged my sister, I finally cried as she told me my brother was going to arrive from Saudi Arabia and wanted to speak to me over the phone. I had loved and hero-worshipped my brother all my life, but had become distant with him after he had hidden the fact that they were expecting a fourth child. We had not seen or spoken to each other much. I had realised that they did not need me in their lives anymore and decided I would no longer wait for phone calls or visits from them, heartbroken.

As night fell and the painful minutes ticked away, I started realising that there was no one near enough to hear my cries of pain. Saleha had retired to her bedroom upstairs. She had changed. She wasn't there to hold my hand all night like she had done before. I could hear family and friends talking noisily in the living room. The sedation was not working. I couldn't sleep, I couldn't cry out, and I couldn't move.

The next couple of days were spent deliberating where I would be taken for surgery. The problem with Pakistan is that, although we have the best surgeons in the world, hospital care and hygiene is among the worst in the world. Nursing staff are poorly trained, and pain management is not well understood. Many families prefer to avoid hospitals and choose to stay at home, hiring private nursing staff. I experienced these problems first-hand, seeing extremely unclean surfaces everywhere and even rats chewing on expensive machinery in the hospitals. On one occasion, I nearly died when the home nurse made me stand up briefly to take me to the toilet. I was clearly not well enough to stand up and my blood pressure plummeted to a life threatening 40/60.

I was eventually taken to Quaid-i-Azam Hospital, Rawalpindi, because of its reputation for hygiene and the legendary surgical expertise of Dr Khalid Aslam. However, the pain in my arm still went unnoticed and unattended. The orthopaedic surgeon did his job exceptionally well but it was not the fractures and the obvious wounds that kept me awake all night. The cold morphine that swept through my body would leave me helpless but not give me enough respite to sleep. My nephews did what the adults could not. From feeding me lovingly to putting my eyeliner on, these boys looked after me like a mother would. My brother had been over during this time and it was wonderful to get a hug from him. For a while, it was just like old times. But then, as soon as he flew out, it was back to square one.

Yousaf and Umer (my adopted nephew) spent the night by my side. They had me laughing and giggling, despite the fact that I couldn't open my mouth and was on soft foods. Tears rolled down my eyes at their antics. My own children were finding it difficult to cope with it all, and my home staff kept them away on my instructions. Sahir's initial shock turned into anger. He became outspoken and disillusioned, particularly with faith, actively questioning why a God would repeatedly put a woman through this much pain. He had always been quite strong and resolute in this regard, but this incident changed his perspective. He told me it was the biggest factor in causing him to question everything he had ever believed in. Ridha was also deeply affected, and withdrew into her shell again.

On August 24th, the day of the key surgery, my eldest nephew, Abubakr, was there for me. I could see him hiding his fears in his smile as he rolled me into the theatre. Some people disappeared on the day and others did so in the next week. As I was wheeled back into the room after the operation (still under the effects of anaesthesia), I vaguely registered the presence of Saleha and her husband, waiting for me. It was the last time I was to see them. I slipped back into unconsciousness and Saleha slipped out of my life as inexplicably as she had entered it. She wasn't the only person who would suddenly vanish. Just before the accident, a gentleman had shown interest in me for marriage but I was unconvinced by his efforts. Against my judgment, he was informed of the situation, but he chose not to come and see me.

I returned home to recover alone. Even personal requests over the phone to take me for tests were ignored. By the 8th of September, exactly one month after the crash, I had decided to send my kids back to England. The sight of me lying helpless in bed wasn't something I wanted them to see. With my right foot plastered and my right arm in a sling, life at home was challenging. In the first few days, I fell twice in the bathroom as I struggled to wash myself, insisting on independence. My right hand was weak, and I couldn't hold a pen. The right arm was lifeless, and I couldn't reach behind to do the strap on my bra. The hyperactive woman who made people dizzy could do nothing but be helplessly immobile for the first time in her life. I remembered how getting up from my bed to go to the bathroom for *Sehr* during Ramadan had seemed like such an effort just a month ago. Now I looked wistfully at the door, unable to even take the few steps towards it.

On the plus side, being forced to rest did help my skin and my overall health. My crew members kept bringing me *desi murghi yakhni* (organic chicken broth) and my first cousin (the only friend who stuck around) would lovingly feed me homemade pumpkin soup and make onion seed oil for the swelling on my arm. I began reading all the books I'd never had time for, and started writing.

My love for my iPhone grew during this time as it was the only thing I could write on. As I wrote lengthy articles, I slowly fixed my feeble hand. In fact, I now find it hard to write on anything else. I wrote this book on my iPhone.

I saw the accident as a liberating experience. Everyone left me. The interest of gentlemen declined due to my injuries. But I also made friends, for the first time in years. I felt more comfortable in socialising now. No one wanted to hit on a crippled woman. For a woman who is considered attractive, making friends is not easy. Women will hate her and men will want to have her. It's a lonely existence. My crutches became my wings.

After the first 24 hours, when I had been worried about my employment prospects, I never again saw the crash as a dreadful thing. Not once did I feel depressed or angry at God for putting me through this. I was surprisingly upbeat and positive throughout. I understood that it was my fault for not being more careful during travel, and chose not to press charges against the driver either.

I survived a near fatal crash but a much bigger accident was only a few months away.

§

I returned to work exactly a month after the crash, in a wheelchair and with my arm in a sling. I had managed to convince my bosses to let me return to the coveted 8pm slot. We had to change the set around so only my left profile would show as the right side was still slightly scarred. My right arm had to be strapped to the chair, so it would not fall off. Each day, my loving crew would carry my wheelchair up two floors because the lift was broken. For the show, I would be transferred onto my black presenter's chair. For the intro, my makeup lady would hold me up, so I could stand briefly to give the opening headlines. My stylist, Naureen, got a range of outfits in stretchy fabric to slide over my swollen arm and boot. Months passed by and my confidence and grip on Pakistani politics grew. I had developed a strong Pashtun identity and voice on TV. It was difficult, but we had made it work. My no-nonsense approach and grassroots reporting style of program was gaining the attention and irk of the leading anchors. I was sitting on a smaller budget and channel, yet denting their established ratings.

As I became more confident, I decided to attend a few tame dinner parties here and there. Ali Gillani's smaller dinner parties were very educational on the bizarre lifestyles of the pseudo-elites. At one of these, I noticed everyone bullying a young-looking British-Asian girl in Ugg boots. She described herself as an educationist but didn't seem to have any knowledge of the education policy in Pakistan or UK. She was openly being teased for sleeping with the boss and tweeting for him.

I paid little attention to her, but it struck me as very odd to be unashamedly bragging about the sexual nature of her job. She kept smiling at the jabs. What did catch my attention was her absurd plan to introduce sugary cereals to schools in KP. Amused by her daftness, I recall suggesting to her to get some information about our Pashtun culture and some practical ideas for the province. She came across as very strange. Her vacant expression would almost instantly be replaced by hysterical reactions. However, time would tell me that she was a lot smarter than I gave her credit for.

That was Anila Khawaja, who'd arrived in Pakistan soon after the October 2011 *jalsa* (rally) and was appointed International Media coordinator of PTI in April 2012. Looking back, much of the cast in my soap opera was introduced to me via Ali Gillani (also known as Ali G). He was the local Mr Gatsby, and he would host a circus of politicians, media darlings, and boys from the establishment almost daily. The man was a walking encyclopaedia on the secrets of the morally and financially corrupt self-proclaimed elites. I avoided the parties, but Ali G would be my first point of research on issues and personalities that I was featuring on the show. Somehow, it never occurred to me to get a rundown on men who were interested in me romantically. However, the first time I was introduced to the wife of Jahangir Khan Tareen, Ali's words rang through my head.

Ali and I were both into art and décor, so much of the gossip would be inside info on the wives of the politicians, and their sense of style. Ali had described how, on the first visit of Mrs. Musharraf to JKT's house, she had appreciated the decor wholeheartedly. On their departure, Mrs JKT had branded the First Lady an upstart. Meanwhile, established elites like Ali G described JKT as an opportunist who from his humble beginnings as the son of a police officer had climbed right to the top. His rapid rise from middle-class teacher to Imran Khan's personal cash machine was ridiculed by many.

Jahangir Khan Tareen was the General Secretary for PTI, and one of the wealthiest people in Pakistan. JKT had been a private tutor to the young Moni. The charm of the good-looking tutor not only succeeded in wooing the snobby heiress, but also resulted in the taking over of the entire family estate. After 'inheriting' the first of his sugar mills from his father-in-law, he was introduced to politics (ironically by PMLN's Shehbaz Sharif), before joining PMLQ and being elected in 2002. Part of his success, though, lay in his ability to charm General Musharraf. Along with Aleem Khan, he had been one of the lucky few candidates who formed President Musharraf's cabinet. He served as special adviser on agriculture and social sector initiatives to the CM of Punjab, Chaudhry Pervez Elahi, before becoming the Federal Minister for Industries and Production from 2004 to 2007 in Musharraf's cabinet. His business grew phenomenally during the Musharraf years, which was unsurprising given his position as Federal Minister for Industries and Production. During this period, he was given water reservoir projects and mining contracts from which he made a lot of money, and several bank loans were waived as well. In 2011, he along with other PMLQ politicians jumped onto the PTI bandwagon after IK's overnight success in October 2011.

Similarly, Aleem Khan went from (in his own words) washing dishes in Canada with his future brother-in-law, Faraz, to being one of the biggest land developers in Pakistan. Aleem Khan's success was even more miraculous than JKT's, as he had no inherited lands of a spouse to nudge him forward. In fact, he somehow went from a 25-year-old late-stage cancer sufferer to a billionaire in less than a decade. In his constituency of NA-122, no secret was made about the campaign budget. A modest estimate suggested at least 1 billion PKR.

I never paid much attention to the personal lives of politicians, and I would regret that. I didn't absorb much of what I thought was gossip rooted in jealousy. However, I would find out only a year later that Ali had described JKT accurately. As early as 2013, Ali had given me a detailed account of how JKT was the epitome of white collar crime. Jahangir made sure he paid more tax than anyone else and his paper trail was perfect, but the extent of his white-collar manipulation was extraordinary. It was rather shocking information but I dismissed it. It wasn't anything I would ever have to act on after all...

§

By the following January, I was back in my normal shoes, albeit in a lot of pain. It was a remarkable recovery, but I was about to crash into something a lot more damaging and scarring than I had ever faced. By the winter of 2014, I had established myself as an influential anchor with a following. I had a growing Insafian (PTI youth) following, partly because of my connections with PTI workers at a grassroots level. The friends I had made were PTI workers too. I started receiving invites to PTI gatherings and briefings.

One such occasion was a briefing for anchors at Dr Waseem Shazad's tastefully decorated home in Chak Shahzad. I arrived wearing heels, but was struggling as I entered. Shah Mehmood Qureshi saw me at the door and remarked, "You have recovered miraculously".

Hobbling in pain, I stupidly spluttered, "No, I am just faking it".

To this, the rather smooth gentleman replied, "I must say, you are very good at faking it then".

Red-faced, I followed him inside. I was ushered into the sitting room and sat down on a chair beside the party leader, Imran Khan. Imran jumped to his feet and went off to sit further away. I thought it was odd. At no point did Imran look or speak directly to me during the briefing. The briefing itself was unconventional since, unlike other briefings I had attended, here it was the anchors who were giving it to the party leaders. In a few months, it would all make sense to me. I suggested setting up a think-tank that would give factual information to party heads using grassroots connections.

There seemed to be only one other anchor there with any sense. Kashif Abbaisi seemed unimpressed by The Leader, and appeared as exasperated as myself with the lack of knowledge and political acumen on display. Shireen Mazari, the rather loud and brash Information Secretary (known more for her rudeness than her communication skills) bulldozed all our suggestions by giving us the standard response of most political top-tier leaders: "We are doing this sort of stuff already".

As we moved outdoors to the high tea spread out for us, Kashif Abbasi whispered, "I am not prepared to be ruled by a daft leader".

As I nodded, I caught sight of Imran taking interest in our interaction. As soon as I caught his eye, he averted his gaze. We were then called for a group photo. I managed a smile, despite Naeem ul Haq standing in close proximity to me.

As we all left, and our cars drove up one-by-one, Shireen Mazari caught sight of a bearded Pashtun driver, and loudly exclaimed, "And who is being driven by the Taliban?!".

"It could only be me," I coldly replied.

I meant it as a joke and a put down, but those words were to cost me dearly later that very year. The perception that I had hard-core Pashtun values and was from an orthodox Sunni Deobandi background was already deeply disturbing for the top-tier leadership of PTI. My careless sarcastic comment had laid the foundations of deep resentment in the future.

I maintained a regular social contact with a group of women in PTI who preferred to call themselves 'the JKT girls'. This group of women in their late 30s worked voluntarily and simultaneously with all three top-tier leaders: Shah Mehmood Qureshi, Asad Umar and Jahangir Tareen. I was used to their breathless gushing about these three older men, and chose to tolerate it. Through these people, I would get to know how undemocratic the party actually was as they vented their frustrations to me. A few of them were women who had left their careers in London to come and work for PTI.

I became quite close to one of them during this time. In between her moaning about how she was getting nowhere in PTI, she would try to hook me up with men, much to my annoyance. Her first attempt to introduce me to a young, upcoming anchor in 2013 had been met with raw anger. She nevertheless kept on trying, and in 2014 started with her efforts to hook me up with an industrialist, and then to a close friend of hers. But, through a strange twist of fate, it was her romantic aspirations that led to a huge moment for me. One morning, she heard that a man she was interested in was arriving for the session of the National Assembly. She had two passes and asked me to go with her. While she drooled over the man she was dreaming about, I was about to run into the biggest and most unfortunate accident of my life.

The session was important as it was about a cash injection from the Saudis to the tune of 1.6 billion USD. During the break, I stood with this JKT girl and a couple of her media friends. A senior journalist, Ijaz Haider, was slagging off Imran Khan. All sorts of names were being thrown at him, from 'arrogant fool', to 'an utter failure' in KP. As I stood listening to them while writing on my phone, the arrogant celebrity in question walked by. Immediately, the same journalist stubbed out his cigarette, ran to the leader, and grabbed him by the arm. I stood in the doorway with a faint smile on my face at this sudden volte-face. I could hear the anchor begging IK for an interview.

Imran talked down to the much smaller man, saying, "Ijaz, you do anti-PTI programs!"

The journalist responded, pleadingly, "No sir, you have to see how we covered your non-politicised police force so positively only last week. And your polio efforts too!"

The grovelling was intolerable but it worked in the end. As I sniggered to myself, Imran spotted me, and his annoyed expression was suddenly replaced with a beaming smile. He nodded to acknowledge me, and I responded with a sardonic smile.

"Is this the way to get interviews with Mr Khan?"

He immediately turned to Naeem and said, "Naeem, have we not responded to her request? Attend to it!"

Naeem did his 'Yes Sir's, then called out to me, "Reham, I will call you later to arrange".

And that was it. The entourage left. I glanced over and saw Ijaz Haider and his producer looking very pleased with themselves.

That very night, I started getting text messages from Naeem. Eighteen months before, I had ignored his sleazy messaging, but as an established anchor liberated by her injuries, I wasn't feeling particularly forgiving. He had sent me a message in early 2013 which read: "Gloria is waiting in her Jeans for you!"

It was a comment based on the popular coffee chain Gloria Jeans. Clearly, he thought he was being witty. I had shuddered but chosen to ignore it. Now, as I read the nonstop messages asking for a romantic candlelit dinner, and suggesting that there was no harm in sharing a simple dinner of *daal chawal* since both he and I were single, I decided to expose this sleazy man for what he was. I forwarded all the messages to my friend from PTI, and when I received no satisfactory response, I decided to make a formal complaint. I was told to complain to the top man himself. So I did.

The response from the chairman was very friendly but not the professional, serious one I expected. In fact, his text suggested that it was my stunning smile that was to blame, and that it was the same across the world. On reading this irresponsible response, I just lost it. I was so outraged that I sent him a long text detailing the reasons he and his party were failing in KP and at large. In extremely harsh terms, I told him that this was not the way professional women should be spoken to by his Chief of Staff, and that it was perhaps this casual attitude to harassment that allowed such lewd behaviour to continue unchecked. I remembered all the sarcastic hints made by foreign journalists as to Mr Khan's own inappropriate behaviour, and reminded him that this was why decent women did not join PTI, before telling him this irresponsible attitude was perhaps the reason for their poor politics and governance. I was, after all, a journalist and could go public with the evidence.

To this barrage of criticism, he replied, "I have never had anyone speak to me like that, not even my grandmother". I responded that perhaps if someone had spoken to him like that when he'd been younger, he would have learned a few basic rules. He replied, "I am too old to hear a lecture about me, my party and KP. I apologise categorically and assure you it will not happen again".

With that, not only did the texts stop, but my producer informed me that the interview had also been promptly cancelled. I stood there, fuming and texting away in the home of PTI leader Gulzar Khan, while his daughter was watching excitedly. I sat there openly disparaging and cursing her leader. The girl only registered that I was talking to Imran Khan. Everything unacceptable about the situation was ignored. I found it strange that the rules and principles that should have applied to everyone were compromised for 'The Hero'. He could literally get away with murder.

FBI research suggests that our first impressions are correct about people. We instinctively make a judgement that is very accurate. If you get the impression that someone is an arrogant, rude, ignorant, callous human being in the first meeting, you are most likely right in your reading.

§

My first text to Imran read, "You are being used. You will start off on these protests, be used like tissue paper, and be flushed down the toilet. This is an exercise to control you and Nawaz, and nothing more".

I was speaking as a PTI voter and an informed journalist. He responded with his typical, irritable arrogance: "I am not someone who can be used or directed to do anything".

On the 11th of May 2014, after his first *jalsa* preceding the *dharna* (sit-in) on Jinnah Avenue, I met a young Pashtun woman. I had decided to drop in to the *jalsa* as it was right outside my office. This woman had fought with her family and was alone in the rowdy crowds. She told me about her mission to see Imran Khan in person. She had a serious obsession with him, as many did. I related this incident on TV, and sent Imran a brief text about how committed his followers were.

He replied immediately, "But what did Miss Critical think of the speech?"

I responded that it could have been a bit better and added, "You failed to mention electricity issues etc".

He replied, "You didn't listen to all of it". To be fair, that was true. I never did pay much attention to his speeches. They were never particularly intellectual.

On the 5th of May, just before this protest, I'd done a program on why it was wrong for a political party to boycott a media channel. I had shown evidence on the show that what IK was saying was incorrect, and that GEO had not been the first channel to show the PM speech on Election Day. Just before the show, I received a call from Asif Zuberi, one of the bosses at my channel, questioning my subject matter. He asked why I was supporting GEO when its owner was a thoroughly despicable man. I replied that the idea was not to support any channel but to point out that it was wrong for IK to boycott one. If anything, it was an anti-IK show. I decided to run it anyway. I got a text after the show from the same gentleman informing me that he was very disappointed.

On the 15th of May, we finally got the wave of approval from IK himself that the interview was back on. However, the confirmation came only the day before it was due to take place. After my recent argument with The Leader, I wasn't expecting it to go through. My producer was on tenterhooks. The night before the interview, I was at Tuscany Courtyard, an Italian restaurant popular with PTI. I was with a couple of PTI activist friends. As we sat down, my friend Malaika pointed out the long table to the left of us where the chairman of PTI and the top-tier leadership was sat. I hadn't noticed and chose not to pay any attention. I was more interested in our little discussion.

A few minutes later, PTI's international media coordinator, Anila Khawaja, entered with Ali Zaidi, a PTI leader from Karachi who had been on my show earlier that same day. She noticed us and walked up to our table. She was a thin, attractive British woman who had been in the country for 8 years now and worked voluntarily for the party. I found it rather strange that a woman who had no family or paying job in the country could afford to live in a posh F-sector and travel everywhere. I'd never really paid much attention to her. As I rose to give her the customary peck on the cheek, I noticed Imran from the corner of my eye. He was sat with his back to me but turned fully in his chair to stare at us in obvious surprise. It was clear to virtually everyone in the restaurant.

As we left the premises, Malaika and her friend stopped to greet The Leader. I said my *salaams* to all the guests too. Naeem ul Haq piped up, "Chairman, Reham has been given an interview slot tomorrow evening". Imran nodded and asked what time. Naeem turned and repeated the question to me. I internally rolled my eyes again and dryly responded, "I believe it's 5:30pm". To the right of Imran sat Shah Mehmood Qureshi. I turned to him and I said, "It's about time. I have some deep reservations about how the party is functioning". SMQ, known for his polite, flirtatious charm with women, responded, "Well, we must put your concerns to rest". I managed a smile and left.

The day of the interview came and my producer Ali Akbar, his usual stress levels doubled, looked as if he would faint.

"Ma'am, I even got up to pray this morning. They have cancelled on us so many times, I am worried they may do it again".

"Relax Ali," I said. "It's not such a big deal".

At this point, I had completely lost interest in interviewing big personalities and was more interested in on-ground reporting in KP. We reached the Chairman Secretariat and Malaika was already there. The first thing she said to me was very odd. "Why did you wear this blue? It's not so flattering. Should have worn red, or even black," she complained.

"Malaika, I've come for an interview, not for a date!" I responded, quite shocked by her questions.

The chairman walked in with a beaming smile on his face, to the amazement of the crew. They were used to his usual rude and aloof behaviour. I was cold and distant. I'd not forgiven or forgotten the Naeem incident and our conversation following it. I started the show with a stinging taunt at the fact that they had kept cancelling or rejecting our interview requests. That opening clip would later be used everywhere as evidence of romance between us. But nothing was going on. If there was interest, I was unaware of it. I would become very aware of it later, and would be rather amused at this one-sided silliness. It wouldn't be until mid-June when he'd next ask to meet, saying he had something of high importance to discuss.

Throughout the interview, despite my taunts and blunt accusations, he responded with a calm, polite, smiling demeanour, accepting his many failures of governance in KP. My team and I were shocked but took full advantage and recorded a two-hour show with him. The chairman seemed to be very available. In breaks, I would go back to my unsmiling face, reserved for men at work. In one break, I ordered a crew-member to get his act together using the word *beta* (Urdu for son) in condescending fashion.

Imran remarked, "You just called him *beta*. Surely, he must be older than you? Can't be too soft. But why so unpleasant?"

I looked at him straight in the eye and said, "One has to be unpleasant in Pakistan to make sure men don't get any ideas".

I looked away and we started recording again. Meanwhile, he seemed to enjoy torturing me with his pleasantness. A rather excited Malaika kept prompting me in my ear. The interview finished, and Imran went and met the crew. I introduced Ali Akbar and taunted Imran again. "This man even prayed *Fajr* today, so the interview would not be cancelled".

Imran turned to him and said, "You should pray all the time. It works I guess".

The crew couldn't get over his sweetness. As we were packing up, we heard crying from the lawns. My PA whispered in my ear, 'Ma'am, your friend is crying outside".

I poked my head out to see what was happening. Malaika was indeed crying audibly, and the chairman was trying to make her stop by patting her on the back. I knew what this was about. Shireen Mazari had refused to give Malaika a human rights advisor role she had been coveting. Naeem spotted me and called out: "Reham, please join us for a cup of tea". A group of ten people were sat in a circle, with a few others standing behind them. There were some-higher-ups and a couple of MPAs. Malaika came over to get me. My makeup lady got all excited and said, "You should sit for a while. They are asking so nicely". I was wearing very high heels and was tired. I went reluctantly to join them. Jahangir Tareen and Inam Akbar and were among those I met there for the first time.

The first thing Imran said to me was, "Don't be awful like that Talat Hussain. Stop criticising the party. Why don't you join the party? We could do with people like you".

I turned to him and said, "Why, do you want to do what you did with Fauzia Kasuri? Have me leave my nationality and then abandon me?"

He didn't respond and changed the subject. Somebody mentioned Fayaz ul Hassan Chohan, and one of the guests chipped in that it was I who had put him in his place in a program a few weeks before, which had caused the party much embarrassment. It had been a show about the Islamic Ideology Council, and a possible ruling on second marriages. Fayaz was an ex-JI politician with strong right-wing ideas. I told this group that Fayaz had been misquoting from the Quran, and had merely corrected him.

Imran looked at me. "What do you know about the Quran?"

"Yes, how could I know? I'm just a baby. Only people in Pakistan can be authorities!" I replied sardonically.

Imran, in conciliatory tone, replied, "You could just say that you have read the Quran".

I found his response very strange. 'Everyone is meant to have read the Quran' I thought. Months later, I would find out that he hadn't and couldn't. The gulf between our family backgrounds and lifestyles would be made very clear.

Imran then decided it was the moment to flaunt his 'meritocracy'. He got up from his chair and walked over to a rather unimpressive man, putting his hand on the meek man's shoulder. "This, Reham, is my MNA from my hometown of Mianwali. So much do I cherish merit that I did not give the ticket to my own cousin, but chose to give it to this man instead".

I believed him at the time. Years later, I would meet the brother of the overlooked cousin in a very different frame of mind, and with a very different understanding of the kind of man Imran was.

Chapter 13

My first memory of my first husband was just his voice, singing "*Oh parosan kee larki tujhay dekh tabiat pharki*." (Oi my neighbour's daughter! A glimpse of you turns me on).

It sounded like a lazy drawl. Ijaz was living in our house in Peshawar along with our other cousins, struggling with a medical career. Oddly enough, I never actually saw him. The other cousins were all very studious and hardworking. He had been forced into a medical career he did not want to pursue. In turn, he made his younger brother go for the civil engineering career he had wanted for himself. Ijaz would probably have been slightly happier if he had been allowed the freedom to choose his career path. He was the product of a disturbing, oppressive childhood and carried the guilt of a mother left behind to suffer at the hands of an abusive father.

I had no idea of any of this until I got married to him. I don't remember ever seeing him until I was 18, but I'd heard the bad press from his own mother and the rest of the family. It was mainly innocent stuff like bunking class and loitering. He was described as a boy who spent his time flunking exams and chasing after girls on his motorbike. Ijaz never hid his lack of interest in academics from anyone. In fact, he would gleefully tell me all his naughty stories himself. One of his favourite stories was of how he scarred his face. He had stopped getting into fights early on in middle school because he feared disfiguring his face. But stalking girls in the afternoons was also not so safe, as he was to find out.

Once, while following a group of girls on his motorbike, he had had his eye too much on his target and not enough on the road in front of him. He slammed the bike straight into a lamppost on the side of the road. He hit the pole twice because of the force of the impact. Along with the rest of the injuries he sustained, Ijaz also ended up with tiny shards of glass digging into his face. Even before his young adult stories started circulating, Ijaz already had the reputation of being a little terror when they were all younger. My older sister had suffered at his hands too. Because of the rocky relationship of the parents, Ijaz and his mother frequently stayed with my parents when he was young. My sister described him as a disturbed child who had become a bit of a bully towards his other cousins. He would enjoy making her cry by snatching her dolls from her and hanging them on tree branches out of her reach.

Through our marriage, I saw a man who harboured deep resentment of his unhappy childhood and meaningless jealousies towards others. He wanted to impress all these cousins, but he couldn't find anything nice to say about any of them. I found his disparaging comments upsetting since I had been the loved and pampered baby cousin. It wasn't only my much older siblings, but also my first cousins who doted on me. I was closest to my Daddy's older sister's family. To this day, her children and I have retained a close bond. I love them all to bits, but since most of them live in the U.S., I have never been able to see them as often as I would like. Only three of her children lived in Pakistan, and I managed to maintain regular contact with them. Throughout my time in Pakistan, her daughters were a huge support to me. Whether it was setting up the home, or babysitting my little one, or my accidents (physical and emotional), they were always there with their warm hugs and sound advice. The older one, Shaheen *baji*, (although heavily committed to her medical profession and family) was always the quickest person to give sound health advice.

My firmest buddy through all my adventures, though, has been the younger daughter, Samina *baji*. Since she lived in Islamabad, it was possible for us to have long breakfasts together and bargain with Pashtun fabric shopkeepers on an almost weekly basis. Her warm exuberance made her a woman one could never stop falling in love with. She and I share a history. Throughout my time in Pakistan as a child (and then later when I returned), Samina *baji* and I enjoyed a close, communicative relationship. It all started when I put her on a strict diet and exercise regime before her own wedding back in 1983. I was just a 10-year-old but she credits me with making sure she got the 28" waist for her wedding. She reciprocated this love and attention in countless ways. After my crash in 2013, she would attend to me and prepare my favourite pumpkin soup. She was ever ready with her Urdu poetry gems to keep me entertained, or to help me through my grief (quickly followed by heavy complex carbohydrates).

Their brother, Zahid *bhai*, was a senior advocate like his father, Mufti *Sahab*. His sharp wit and intellect made him one of my favourites. His rather Western taste in music echoed in our home when I was a little girl. 'That's the Way (I Like It)' by KC and the Sunshine Band was always played in his car. His wedding was the first Pakistani wedding I attended, and I immediately fell in love with his wife. Their older two boys, Imran and Shoaib, grew up around me, and became as dear to me as my own nephews. Shoaib grew up to inherit the best qualities of both sides of his family. Honest and honourable to the core. He has always treated me with as much respect as his own mother. After moving back to Pakistan, I also became very fond of the youngest son, Hassan. On his engagement in 2014, the whole family came together. It was wonderful to see our third generation so closely bonded, as we had all been. Of course, the times were very different now, and this would raise a new series of problems. The youngsters would naturally be very active on social media, and this would give rise to fresh attacks. This time however, I was not the sole target.

As the kids had grown older, I had tried suggesting to them that they could meet their biological father in the safety of the homes of family friends. They reacted negatively to this suggestion but I persisted for a while, seeing no reason to deprive them of a safe opportunity to reconnect with a parent. Soon however, I would be shown exactly why my kids were probably correct not to go near this man. For years after the divorce, I had to put up with harassment and cyber bullying by my ex. I lived in terror that Ijaz would find out where we lived, and had taken several measures to ensure the safety of the girls for the walk to school. I also made sure that my children would not put too much info on their social-media profiles. But one day, I discovered a message on my Facebook that stated clearly that he knew we lived in Newbury. I immediately alerted the police.

An officer took a detailed account from me. He explained that the law hadn't progressed enough to protect us in this regard, but gave me a hint that someone could unofficially have a word with the suspected offender. The attacks ceased overnight. In Pakistan however, there was no British Police or judiciary to help us out. Right after that engagement of my young nephew, Hassan, the attacks started again. They targeted my daughters and didn't stop there. My cousins and their daughters were also targeted. The campaign was particularly good at capitalizing on certain negative sentiment, as well as general misogyny, so it would focus on the girls. It would succeed in unsettling many of them, as girls of a marriageable age in the family started deleting my kids off their Facebook and Instagram pages without warning, to protect their own privacy. This was not the first time my children and I had suffered at the hands of these tactics. They'd been affected at first, but would soon become accustomed to it. All they could really do was tighten security and be more careful about what they shared, while grinning and bearing whatever would appear online, twisted to make them look bad.

We had always been secure in the knowledge that we lived on the straight and narrow, and could not be blackmailed or embarrassed as a result. Because of this, we all lived proudly and unapologetically, with nothing to hide. With this rationale, we all made the mistake of thinking that we could not be slandered, and our image could not be tarnished. Just how much hate and abuse could be levelled at someone who is completely clean? I was about to find out the hard way. The truth, it turns out, is often almost completely immaterial.

As the attacks started again in 2014, Ijaz left no doubt in anyone's mind. He began posting material no one else could possibly have access to, such as my first passport, old family photographs, and even the children's original birth certificates. My 16-year-old showed me a fake Twitter handle @RidhaPornstar with pictures taken from her friend's Facebook accounts. Even so, my kids were able to shrug off a lot of what went on online. Ridha was naturally dismayed that she couldn't so much as appear in a picture at a friend's house while holding a glass of water without it being found, edited, and thrown online with some caption labelling her an alcoholic, or something else equally horrendous and defamatory. The most aggressive posts about Sahir would centre on his long hair and love of guitar, trying to paint him as some sort of Satanist. But in general, Ijaz's campaign of hate centred on my family, and anyone who had ever tried to build a positive relationship with us.

Sadly, Ijaz's sick allegations had extended to Zahid *bhai*'s son too. Just before my divorce, the 21-year-old Shoaib (Hassan's older brother) had visited us. Ijaz stooped to another level of low by declaring on Facebook that Inaya was Shoaib's daughter (complete with Photoshopped images of the two for comparison), even though Inaya had been two years old when Shoaib had first come to visit us.

As I filed for divorce, Shoaib had pleaded with me to reconsider and give his uncle a second chance. Unknown to me, Ijaz had already started the sick rumour of an affair between me and my nephew. Shoaib respected me like a mother so, instead of telling me of this gossip, he completely cut off from me. For eight years my kids were deprived of an older, loving family member who lived in the same country, just because of their father's lies.

After seeing the ugly campaign, Ridha commented rather philosophically that she had thought she may have attended her biological father's funeral someday, but this unfortunate man had now deprived himself of that courtesy too. What I found amazing was her strength in the face of such a vicious campaign. If my father had done that, I would have probably broken down completely, but there was no demonstration of reactionary anger from her. There was quiet restraint and understanding. This man had a problem. We did not.

§

While the cyber bullying continued, a certain exceedingly famous politician was doing research on me. Since I kept to myself and was not active in Islamabad's social scene, not much was known about me. But it didn't matter; he had launched his pursuit.

A couple of weeks after the second interview in May, he asked to see me again. I declined politely. I had already got the interview I wanted. But the tiger continued. The texts were very business-like this time. The post-interview chat had not ended on a pleasant note, and his brief complimentary text about my smile had not been entertained favourably. He had bluntly requested to see me alone, emphasising that he wanted to discuss something very serious and important with me. I made my excuses.

He persisted and asked to see me again, in a public place. A dinner at Tuscany Courtyard was suggested. He said that a couple of other anchors and PTI leaders were invited, along with a musician, Salman Ahmed. It sounded acceptable. Reluctantly, I joined them for dinner after my evening show. As soon as he saw me, his eyes lit up. I, on the other hand, took one look at the long table and saw no news anchors whatsoever, only women of notorious repute in Islamabad, sitting alongside Asad Umar, Naeem ul Haq and Salman Ahmed. My displeasure was evident to all from my expression. I chose to sit next to Salman Ahmed, and deliberately ignored Imran. To make it clear that I did not want to be near Naeem, I made a point of picking up my chair and placing it as far from and his bad breath as I could. The man sitting on Imran's right kept staring at me. He was the owner of the Hyatt Tower on Constitution Avenue. Next to him sat Bina Sultan, a fashion designer by day but also the lady-of-the-evening for many, including Imran (according to the man himself).

I pretended to be deep in conversation about polio to Salman, while texting my nephew to come and pick me up as soon as he could. I remember Asad Umar looking at me as if he was disappointed. I worried about what the rest of the restaurant might think. I did not want to be labelled as one of IK's girls. Meanwhile Salman flooded me with info about the work he wanted to do and how he needed Imran's backing to ensure further funding from the Bill Gates Foundation. He was trying to get me excited about a DVD of his polio work. I controlled my comments about what I really thought of the polio campaign in Pakistan.

Imran suddenly reached out from his place at the head of the table and touched my arm to get my attention. I jumped, rather alarmed. He was like a little boy desperate for my acknowledgement. Not long after I was served, my nephew arrived. On seeing who I was having dinner with, he was immediately starstruck. Imran looked sad as I introduced my nephew to him and got up to leave. He met my nephew warmly and volunteered to take a selfie with him. Then he texted me immediately, asking why I had left. I texted back saying that I had been given the clear impression it would be a briefing for anchors and did not appreciate being deceived. He apologised, saying that it was the owner of the restaurant who had brought the other two women to sit at the table. He praised my nephew, and I thanked him for taking the selfie, saying that Yousaf liked his gesture and his jawline.

Imran replied, "But what did the *khala* think?"

I didn't bother to respond.

A couple of weeks later a serious and urgent request to see me again was made. He suggested a short meeting and made it clear that it was of an official nature.

When I asked what it was, he merely said, "Don't be afraid, it isn't fun and games. And please don't bring your guard with you. You have nothing to fear. I want to discuss something of high importance". It stirred the journalist in me, but his reputation was a concern. I guess it's true: curiosity kills the cat.

I was shivering with fear on the inside but, as always, I pretended to be confident. I kept reminding myself that I had a phone on me with a friend on standby, ready to help. The chauffeur-cum-valet led me into a huge dimly lit room with a high ceiling. There were no staff around and I became even more nervous. What the fuck was I doing here? The man quietly pointed beyond the large drawing room and directed me to the veranda. The celebrity was walking on the lawn with his dogs. He spotted me and called me over. Sensing my nervousness, he blurted out, "What did you think? I would pounce on you like an animal?"

Rather embarrassed by his directness, I blushed and looked down at my Brazilian handmade high heels. He followed my gaze.

"Oh, you can't walk in those," he said, disappointed.

"Well, I had not thought that I would be going for a walk," I replied. I turned to my large bag and said, "But luckily, I have flat shoes".

The BBC had taught me never to go anywhere without a flat pair in the bag. I sat down, took my shoes off, and slipped on traditional Pakistani leather slippers while Imran watched with interest. He smiled as I stood up, impressed by my efficiency. As I walked towards the beautiful garden, I noticed him pick my heels up carefully and put them in the middle of the coffee table, away from the dogs. As we started walking, he said, "You are pretty tall".

We walked up and down the long garden, and Imran seemed impressed with my energy level. He looked approvingly at me a few times, as if he was pleased I could keep up with him. He talked and talked, and we walked and walked, until it was time to eat. All the while he was figuring me out. I maintained a safe distance. He kept switching gears. He would talk about the frustrations of his politics before jumping to a compliment. There were a few questions about why I was in Pakistan, and a few comments about where I should place myself. I couldn't figure out what he wanted. He mentioned how his media image was being tarnished by 'the bastards at GEO', the leading media group. He appreciated the role of overseas Pakistanis.

He then checked me out like a coach and asked once again, "Do you work out?"

I gave him the same answer I had given him over a year ago. "No. I told you, I hate exercise and I hate gyms".

"But you must!" he cried, like a concerned skipper. "How old are you, 30-35? After 30, decline sets in very quickly". I made a face and ignored the question for the umpteenth time. "You know what you remind me of?" he added. He stood facing the house in his signature style with his hands on his hips. "When I was building this house, there was an Afghan labourer who I used to watch, working all day in the blistering heat. He was so hardworking that one day I thought to reward him. I went over to him and offered him some money. The man looked at me and asked what it was for. I explained that I admired how he worked so hard, and wanted to give him a prize. The man pushed my hand away and said, 'I get paid for the job'. You, Reham, remind me of that Afghan. You are proud. You have no price. You can't be bought. That's what I like about you".

The cook called us over for food. Imran marched off to the white patio table and signalled for me to follow. There was a Pakistani style salad, *chappatis*, and a sloppy curry of *desi murghi* (country chicken). Imran, rather embarrassed at the service, quickly explained that the food might not be to my liking since the guy wasn't really a proper cook and was incredibly useless. I smiled politely, assuring him that it looked fine. As I ate, I noticed Imran kept gently offering me warm *chappatis*. He was being a very good host. I was a little surprised by this since his lack of hospitality (verging on rudeness) was well-known. I had witnessed it first-hand when we first met back in 2013.

It was beginning to get dark. Imran had been rather quiet and melancholic during the meal, talking about Suleiman, his son. He disappeared to the bathroom. I presumed he had gone to wash his hands. I'd noticed his table manners were far from acceptable. Ironically, he'd watched my movements closely as I ate and commented, "You eat so nicely! So ladylike. Jemima was such a sloppy eater". He was hardly the epitome of good etiquette himself, so it struck me as rather odd.

While he was gone, I was attacked by huge mosquitoes, like locusts at a crop. I was scratching my feet when he emerged from the bedroom. He pulled a chair close to me and sat down. He looked different than before, when he had been sitting across the table from me. He now had a glint in the eyes as he looked straight into mine. Flustered by his penetrating gaze, I looked away and explained that I was covered in mosquito bites. The next thing I knew, his huge hands had grabbed my ankles protectively but gently, as if to sooth the insect bites. I jumped in my chair at this unexpected, yet tender gesture from him.

He leant forward as if to kiss me, then groaned and got to his feet. He pulled me up with him, taking my hand in his hand, and almost dragged me away from the patio, down the stairs into the darkness of the garden. With my free hand, I held onto to my *dupatta* as it got caught in my feet. He walked slightly ahead of me, holding my hand tightly, and led me away from the house to the swimming pool. He briefly let go of me, then swung me around to stand facing him. It was as if he feared being watched near the house. He started to say something, and as I looked up expectantly, he instead closed the distance between us and leant down to kiss me. It was a light brush initially. I froze in fright. As he proceeded to kiss me more ardently, I put both my hands on his chest and pushed him away. I was shivering. He seemed shocked.

Guilt swept over me. "I can't do this," I announced. In a daze, I fell to the ground beside the swimming pool. Under my breath, I cursed myself for putting myself in this situation. 'What was I thinking? Coming out to meet this playboy. I deserve this'. I looked up to see that Imran had not moved from his place.

"What can't you do? I don't want to sleep with you," he said. "I knew right from the start that there was no possibility of anything else with you".

I stared back, puzzled. He continued.

"I am looking to get married. I don't want anything else with you. I want to marry you".

"Are you mad? Are you totally insane?" I said, standing up in shock. "You don't even know me! How can you think of marrying me just like that?"

Imran responded with irritating calmness.

"I know enough. I have asked my *pir* [spiritual advisor]. I am just waiting for the green signal. As soon as I get it, we are getting married".

To say I was surprised would be the understatement of the century. This was totally insane. It was also possibly the least romantic way that anyone had ever tried to propose. But the ludicrous nature of the situation didn't seem to register with this man, and he continued unflappably.

"Look, I need to get married and I think you could be the one. I just need your parents' names to check something".

I stared at him in disbelief, slightly outraged but mostly amused at his arrogance. I gave him a lopsided, sarcastic look and quizzed him: "Did it occur to you to ask if I had a say in the matter, or is that not something you think about?"

"Look, ideally I would love to take you out to Tuscany and places, but I am Imran Khan. You are Reham Khan. We clearly can't do that so we will just have to skip a few steps". He shrugged his shoulders in matter-of-fact fashion.

I shook my head incredulously, smiling at the temerity of the man. His arrogance and disregard for the workings of society was almost adorable. I explained gently, as if to a child.

"Imran, I don't know why you think that I would be happy to go along with that. I have a wonderful life. Why would I want to compromise my freedom and independence after fighting to get it?"

He gave me a winning smile.

"For *Naya Pakistan* [New Pakistan] of course. You can really help me in my mission. We can be a great team".

"You have this IK status! You are a celeb! Your life is scrutinised. I don't want to be a part of that," I replied.

"Oh now, that's not very brave is it? I have done enough already for this country. I can't marry to please the public!"

"Look, you are not even a normal person. You are like...Rapunzel!" I replied in exasperation.

"What's Rapunzel?" he asked.

"What?" I spun around. "You don't know what Rapunzel is? Are you serious?"

He looked back, completely blank.

'Oh, this man does need me,' I thought to myself, before proceeding to explain the fairy tale.

"Rapunzel was a princess who was kept in a tower, away from everyone else. She was cut off from the world. A prince came and took her away to show her the world. It's just like you are".

"Oh...but I want to be the prince," he answered, goofily.

"No Imran, you are Rapunzel! You are up in a tower all by yourself, with no idea about the real world. And I don't want to be the prince who saves you".

He just threw his head back and laughed.

"Come here, walk with me".

And so we walked again. This time, when he tried to get close, I said, "Touch me and I will kick you in the balls".

He laughed, amused. He seemed to enjoy my prudishness, but he did at least behave.

"I am 42, you should know," I said.

He threw his head back and heaved a sigh of relief which seemed feigned.

"Great, so I won't look like a cradle snatcher".

We walked a few more steps and suddenly Imran asked: "What was it? Was he abusive?"

I looked up at his abrupt question.

"Your husband, I mean. Was he an alcoholic?"

I didn't confirm or deny.

"So was my father," Imran replied to my silence. He stopped walking and continued.

"Night after night, he would come in drunk after partying with his mistresses, and then hit my mother. I spent my childhood watching her cry and beat herself. I waited desperately to grow up so I could kill him. I had planned to drive a dagger into him when I turned 15. I hated him so much. He gave my mother unimaginable pain. He would just flaunt the mistresses in her face. *bechari* [poor woman]".

He shook his head at the painful memory. I immediately melted. In that moment, he reminded me of Sahir and all he had witnessed. Imran then went back into thinking mode and we walked a bit more. "You know, these Sharifs are such bastards. They do these constant attacks on my personal life only because I am single. I have wanted to settle down for a long time but I can't find a woman who would fit the bill. I miss my boys but they can never come back. Suleiman still believes his mother and I will get back together one day. You know, one day when he was little he asked me, 'Will we be together as a family in *Jannat* [heaven]?' It broke my heart". Imran shook his head again, as if to shake the painful memory out.

I was moved by the declaration of loneliness and love for Suleiman. I wanted to reach out and give him a hug when he abruptly and loudly called out to the driver.

"Safeer, *bibi* has to be dropped back home". And just like that the evening ended. The driver came running and I walked away, leaving a rather depressed and forlorn-looking man in the garden. I wasn't sure what to make of this bizarre evening. I put it to the back of my mind.

At the start of the following week, I got a text. Imran explained how he was busy that evening with a female friend of his. He described it as 'dinner followed by fun and games' with a woman in her forties who wanted some light entertainment like himself. I was shocked at this admission. I responded that he should not text me again as we clearly had two very different sets of values; that in my world, you couldn't kiss someone on a Saturday, propose marriage to her, and then sleep with another woman on the Tuesday. I was shocked and puzzled but decided that he had clearly been using marriage as a cover story, and thanked my lucky stars that I had not fallen for it. I put him and the incident out of my mind. The words of my colleague from the BBC rang in my ears. "Darling," Sam Fraser had said in her typical theatrical style: "Whatever you do, don't sleep with Imran Khan".

A few days later, I was sitting in a formal meeting in an office in F10 with potential financiers for the film *Janaan* when my pitch was interrupted by a phone call from an unknown number. No one but my crew had my number, but sometimes calls from the UK came up with no caller ID. I picked up, heard the deep, well-broadcasted voice with its signature "Hullo", and literally jumped out of my skin. I quickly said, "I'm in a meeting," before he could say anything else. He chuckled softly and said, "OK, call when you are finished".

Barely hiding my flustered condition, I continued with my presentation, trembling on the inside. He seemed to have enjoyed catching me off guard. My mind was racing. 'Why was he calling me? Why? Did I not make it clear?' Then the typical RK guilt kicked in. Cursing myself silently for my impulsiveness, and terrified to the core, I texted him back when I left the meeting. He called back. All I remember was my anger. I could virtually see him smiling to himself on the other end of the line.

"You got jealous," he kept saying. "I like that".

"I did not get jealous. I don't understand your types, and do not wish to understand either".

"I want to see you again," he said

"Well, you can't have everything you want. You might be used to it but I'm not used to giving men what they want!"

"Baby, you are so fiery, like a true tigress".

"I'm neither your baby, nor one of your tigresses".

The cricketer then changed his fast delivery to a spin, and explained in a rather lengthy text why he did what he did. He was used to women who wanted no-strings-attached sex, and that was his lifestyle. But he wanted to change because he was unhappy. He wanted a woman who would take him out of all of this; a woman who was different. He wasn't looking to sleep with me. He wanted to get married and I was the only one he had come across who he thought fitted the bill. I repeated that he had no idea what I was like, and he repeated that he was only waiting for a green signal (the *Istikhara* that his *pir* was doing), and that he was not interested in anything beyond marriage.

I was unconvinced, so I didn't even point out that he should be doing the prayer himself. And then he started a charm offensive that I was in no way prepared for. There were no celebrity airs and graces. There was a genuine effort to get to know me, frank confessions of how and what went wrong with Jemima, why he had fallen into this depraved lifestyle, how he hated the Lahori circle, how morally corrupt they were, and how he missed his children and wished they had a mother like my kids had. He repeatedly painted an image of Jemima as a typical hysterical woman who would cry in front of the kids and emotionally blackmail them into sending him messages. Slowly but surely, he chipped away at my tough exterior. After all, Imran was a skipper who had perfected his attritional game. He kept changing the field to catch me out at my weakest. It would only be another few months before I threw the match away in reckless fashion typical of Pashtun players.

Chapter 14

In June 2014, my attention quickly turned to a new and distressing issue in the north of Pakistan. After the U.S. War on terror in Afghanistan, there had been a steady rise in violent terrorist attacks across Pakistan. We lost thousands of civilians to suicide bomb attacks and the military had also suffered heavy losses. After several failed attempts at dialogue with the militants, a massive joint military operation was launched in North Waziristan. The operation involved the Air Force, Navy, artillery, and ground troops. Around 30,000 troops were deployed for this operation.

The operation started from the towns of Mirali and Miranshah in North Wazirstan. The idea was to flush out terrorist elements from their sanctuaries in the tribal belt bordering Afghanistan and Pakistan. Social activists like myself (few as we were) worried about the indiscriminate bombing of settled areas in North Wazirstan. I was the lone voice on TV, saying that innocent women and children would be harmed along with the militants. I was also pleading for appropriate arrangements to be made to house the internally displaced persons (IDPs). I could foresee the problems. There did not appear to be any coordination between the military and the politicians. The provincial and the federal government appeared to be unprepared to deal with the influx of IDPs I was mainly concerned with the schooling and health issues of the IDPs. As operation Zarb-i-Azab was imminent, I tried to raise awareness through my shows about how unprepared we were for the consequences.

As I feared, over 800,000 IDPs suddenly found themselves living under open skies in extreme poverty and hunger, in the scorching heat of June. The camps had inadequate facilities. For these proud Pashtun tribes, the *purdah* of their women being violated is very disturbing. Overnight, scores of women were out in the open among strangers. I watched their despair at how the supporters of the operation, all political parties, and seemingly every other faction of our society had shrugged off the responsibility for this war and those affected. As the IDPs poured into KP, other provinces were already shutting their borders to them. These proud tribals had sacrificed their homes for the peace and prosperity of the nation, and no one wanted to help rehouse them. At the start of the operation, no one had even arranged drinking water for these displaced people. I tweeted about it and Nestle immediately responded by delivering thirty-eight tons of water to the main relief camp in Bannu Sports Complex, which they would then continue to do every week. But hardly anyone else was doing anything. No one cared.

I saw women who had never stepped out of the home stand for hours in lines for rations. In their thick *burqas*, they queued for hours and were herded like sheep with sticks by the soldiers on duty. The rations were of poor quality - cheap *ghee* (clarified butter) and old bags of flour. But the desperate women waited to get what they could. I watched as the pregnant fainted in the searing heat while others with small children struggled desperately. Most of these families lived alone in their villages with the males having gone to find work as far away as Saudi or UAE (and most probably ending up languishing in the prisons because of petty visa violations). I saw poor women cheated out of the little money they had by local crooks charging as much as 600 rupees for a wheelbarrow to transport the rations for them.

Only a couple of NGOs were allowed to operate in the area due to the sensitive nature of the operation. Over 85,000 children arrived in Bannu, and I worried about their safety and education. I ran from pillar to post trying to get any sort of help from the provincial and federal governments. From the KP Education Minister and the PTI Higher Education minister to the FDMA and PDMA, I knocked on all the doors. But everyone was too busy with the big upcoming PTI protest, the *dharna*. No government ministry helped. I tried everything I could. But even a few months later, when I would find myself in a position where I thought I could persuade people to help, no one would listen to me.

However, throughout the year, with the help of local social activists like Mohsin Dawar (a lawyer who became my main contact in Bannu), we managed to put around 950 children back in school. Initially, the tall Waziri boys were squeezed into any small room we could find for them. The boys and their teachers surprised me with their eagerness to continue education. I would initially go wrapped up in a huge *chadar* to respect local customs, especially while meeting the *masharaan* (tribal elders), but within a few minutes they would put me at ease. However, the typical Pashtun white *chadar* became my signature look by the summer of 2014. It was this white *chadar* that would help Imran spot me in the crowd at his rallies. He would scan the crowd from atop the container for it, and send me a disappointed text if I had not dropped by.

On the 9th day of the operation, a group of journalists, including myself, were flown into Miranshah courtesy of the ISPR (the media wing of the army). We were given a rather funny, ill-prepared briefing in Tochi Mess by the Major-general in charge. He claimed that 80% of the area had been cleared within only nine days. When we questioned how many terrorists he had eliminated and whether he could reveal their identities, he answered that he could not be expected to put heads on the table in modern warfare. When the Reuters reporter pressed further, he gave a bizarre statement of how the terrorists, having 'smelt' the operation, had 'fled and dispersed'. The briefing reinforced the idea that aerial bombing wasn't really the ideal method to eliminate terror networks, and caused more long-term damage to communities than good. As we were taken for a guided tour through the Adam Khor bazaar (which was less than 1.5 km away), I wondered why a terror network right under their nose, which had allegedly been cleared in nine days, had been allowed to fester for over nine years. The rather unconvincing response was that the civilian government had not given the green signal until then. I walked through the bunkers and ignored the ammunition laid out for display. What intrigued me was the neat handwriting in notebooks, with sedatives, hallucinatory drugs, vials of Valium, in every drawer I opened.

One officer would say that the flattened shops in the market were a result of an aerial surgical strike while another would say it was because of the IEDs laid out by the terrorists. As I walked through the destroyed shops and damaged houses of Miranshah, I wondered how the people would rebuild their lives when they were allowed to return.

My heart bled for those who had been bearing the brunt of militants and conflict for decades through no fault of their own. Their tribal pride and heritage was now reduced to rubble. How does one prevent anger and resentment when a people are stripped of dignity?

§

"I will do macro. You will do micro".

Those were the words he spoke; the man that I, and many other British Asians, had voted for in 2013. That was what he said as he tried to persuade me that we were a perfect match.

"You see, I have to focus on the big stuff: The vision, the target. I can't read all this stuff. Your keen sense of attention-to-detail is what I need. You focus on how we achieve the target. Handle the media image. Suggest the changes. Develop policy. You will be my Roxelana..."

His words would trail off and he would hold his hands in a grandiose gesture visualising the glorious future. This would become a familiar persuasive technique.

"You are just the woman I need. You will keep me on the straight and narrow. You have no idea of the life I've led. It was so depraved. These women around me..."

He would shake his head in revulsion as he said this.

"I have never met a woman like you. So upright, so courageous. Only you can guide me. I will be up there doing the victory speech and I will look down at you smiling up at me. Baby, I love your smile".

He would go back into the fantasy.

Was I going to be so easily convinced to marry someone of his reputation? No. But was I intrigued by what he said, and falling for the way he was charming me? Possibly. "For *Naya Pakistan*," he had said to me at Bani Gala. We would make a difference, together. With the IDP situation, I'd already seen how one voice on TV, trying to raise awareness, could get drowned out by the white noise. Perhaps the wife of the nation's hero would have more sway than a journalist? However, even exploring the notion meant that I needed to bring the most important part of my life into the equation: my children.

Summer arrived and so did my kids. We had planned to tour Kashmir in their break. It was early July. I had quit my job, so had no 8pm pressures to attend to for a change. Imran insisted on meeting them as soon as possible. And so, the very day they landed, a car was sent to pick us up.

A meeting was going on in the living room, so we were ushered into his bedroom. Sahir was impressed by the books in the sportsman's bedroom. He was particularly surprised to see books in French lining the shelves. I didn't volunteer information about who left these books behind. My kids didn't know much about him, and didn't know what to expect. I had my back to the door when it suddenly burst open. Imran popped his head through the door, apologized for being late, and said that he would be right back.

The kids were taken aback by this casual attitude. The politeness of Pakistan's biggest celebrity had certainly come as a surprise. All I had told my kids was that I had been offered a position by him: to take charge of his PR and Media. But as he came in and sat down in the chair next to me, his high level of interest in their mother became apparent. His charming and attentive behaviour had alerted the girls at least. Sahir was never the type to notice such things unless he was looking for them, and he remained oblivious. But the females in the room quickly realized that this was about more than a mere job offer.

Imran insisted that the girls go and have a swim, and dived into a deep discussion on politics with Sahir. The discussion centred on *The Prince* by Machiavelli. Sahir spoke earnestly about the often-concerning writings, including one story involving Renaissance noble Cesare Borgia. According to the story, Borgia once dealt with the troublesome region of Cesena in Romagna by deliberately putting a violent, cruel man in a position of power. This brutally efficient noble, Ramiro d'Orco, would control the population and carry out most of Borgia's dirty work. Eventually Borgia would have this same man publicly executed for his crimes. On seeing the despised noble's head on a pike in the *piazza*, the people suddenly looked to Borgia as their saviour, rather than the source of their problems. Borgia had used strategy and empty spectacle to consolidate his power, carry out several unpleasant tasks, rid himself of a loose cannon, contain an unruly people, and paint himself in a better light, all in a single move. Machiavelli's book used this story to comment on the effectiveness of duplicitous strategy: simultaneously commending and condemning Cesare Borgia. The anecdote raises interesting questions of whether morality has any place in effective governance, and whether Cesare Borgia should be admired or reviled for his cunning.

This naturally incited significant discussion between the two in that room in Bani Gala. Imran insisted that such strategies were ingenious, and such attitudes spot on, whereas Sahir argued that Machiavellian methods were immoral and callous by definition, and that the book was clever satire. Imran however, continued in his praise of these techniques. Sahir had attempted to underline the importance of compassion in politics, thinking that it would strike a chord with Imran. After all, his party's message centred on change, justice and decency. But Imran ended the discussion by saying "Machiavelli's ideas work".

The night ended with a lovely dinner. Imran declared that my little one was adorable, and nicknamed her *Piddu* (meaning 'tiny'). Ridha picked up on the signs of this strange evening straight away. Sahir did not, and was bowled over by his friendliness (no pun intended). But little Inu remained unimpressed. That would not change. Young kids are the best judge of character. They don't hear the words but they listen with their heart. A young child can sense danger even if you repeatedly say "I love you". There are those who can console a baby with their first touch and there are those who can make a baby scream, no matter what they try. Our basic animal instincts are suppressed by the subliminal messages fed to us by society. This leads to some surprising truths, such as this one: If the first kiss doesn't convince you, then nothing ever will.

The following day, I had planned to take my kids to Neelum Valley in Kashmir, to escape the heat. Imran started texting me early in the morning and wouldn't stop. It was as if he were having a meltdown. He wanted to know where I was going and how long I would be gone. He worked himself into such a frenzy over why I wasn't answering his questions. He was leaving for the UK, where he would meet his kids, and displayed a particularly random and erratic thought process. It became clear that he was stressed because of his sisters. I certainly hadn't been expecting the Spanish Inquisition.

The constant back and forth messaging was giving me a headache and after a few hours I finally decided to leave the never-ending conversation, much to his annoyance. I was about to find out that such nonstop messaging was very much his style. I could only access Blackberry Messenger on my iPhone if it was connected to the Wi-Fi at home. I finally decided that we were getting too late, and left him texting away. It wasn't something that I was used to. But I would soon learn to get used to a lot of his disruptive tendencies, and realize that his life was characterized by far worse habits than this.

On his return from London, Imran asked me about my plans for *Eid-ul-Fitr*. I replied that I had promised to spend *Eid* in Bannu with the IDPs to show solidarity. The night before *Eid*, Naeem Ul-Haq called me up and surprised me by asking if I would like to accompany the rest of the anchors being flown in with Imran to cover the celebration. Imran had suddenly arranged for his *Eid* to be with the IDPs too. I explained that I had not started my new post at PTV, so couldn't cover the event. Naeem informed me that another female host was also accompanying them without a camera crew.

I had originally planned to go with Al-Khidmat, a charity that worked extensively with IDPs in Bannu, but agreed to travel by helicopter with Imran, instead of by road with them. Imran behaved like a teenager on a school trip during the journey, occasionally touching my shoe with his, which was something the hawk-eyed anti-IK anchor Javed Chaudhry did not miss. Throughout the trip, I was shocked at the mismanagement of the party. We left so late and then the helicopter had to make an emergency landing in Kohat. We had already missed the *Eid* prayers. In the lounge, while we waited for replacement vehicles to be arranged, I was shocked to learn that none of the ministers knew where the main camp was. They also couldn't find their way to the Bannu sports complex. I wondered why the local female MNA, Ayesha Gulalai, was not being particularly helpful on the day.

I chose to sit in a non-bulletproof vehicle, and Imran followed me to the car. I was sat in the back with IK's two favourite and most inefficient ministers, Shah Farman and Atif Khan, while Imran sat in the front. The conversation centred on the crushing defeat of their candidate in Peshawar. The party had lost the prestigious NA-1 seat that Imran had won. The poor choice of an unknown Afghan-origin candidate had not gone down well with the largely Hindko-speaking, inner-city Peshawar constituency. I heard Imran cursing his Chief Minister, Pervez Khattak, clearly not for the first time.

"That bastard made me do it!" he roared at Atif Khan.

I was busy on the phone ordering food for *Eid,* but still added to the conversation.

"Mr Chairman, you are the boss. You have to take the blame, not Pervez Khattak, for wrong decisions".

He turned in his seat and sniggered at me

"Reham *bibi*, it is because clean people like you don't like to get their hands dirty in politics".

I had been hushed.

Inside the hall in Bannu sports complex, there was more mismanagement. I worried about Imran as the security seemed pretty relaxed. There was a heavy senior army presence there though. They sat with us as if they were all part of the political party. Imran was whisked away somewhere inside to eat. I carried on giving live analysis on several TV channels. His Chief of Staff sent a special car for me and the other female host, and we caught up with the others. Imran had remembered the rural health centre that needed support that I'd told him about. It seemed that the whole day was planned around my suggestions. I was touched that he had been listening. 'This man is really into me,' I thought to myself. 'He's not so bad after all'.

The following day, he pulled at my heartstrings even more. He had sent his staff back home for *Eid*. I had told him that I would spend the day with my family. He asked me to spend the day with him, and drove himself all the way to F11 to pick up my kids, with only his personal guard. Someone saw him at the traffic signal and tweeted about his simplicity. This was very convincing, persistent courtship.

My children, unaware that Imran had come to pick them up, took their sweet time in coming outside. Imran sat happily in the car, waiting patiently. I had asked my makeup lady to cook *haleem* and sheer *khorma*, which I took to Bani Gala. We all sat down to a pleasant family dinner, just Imran, myself and the kids. There were no celebrity airs and graces. He was being normal, sweet, down-to-earth, and charming. His efforts had worked. Imran had won me over.

By the end of June, Imran had made two announcements. He had announced to the public that a big Azadi Freedom March would take place on the 14th of August, Pakistan's Independence Day. And he had also announced privately that he wanted to marry me. On the marriage front, the next step was my introduction to his sister, Aleema. She was clearly prepared for it, but pretended to be taken by surprise as Imran called her in from the garden. She walked into the room slightly annoyed by Imran shouting out to her so loudly. As soon as she entered, he announced, "I want you to meet the woman I want to marry". The rather blunt introduction caught both of us off guard. After his friend Moby, she was the first person I was introduced to, and I had to endure a two-hour meeting with her. Later in the year, she would deny she knew anything of the marriage plan.

The two siblings decided that the 8th of August was best for the *nikkah (marriage)*. It could be announced after two weeks. Imran added emphatically that it must be announced within the month of August. Aleema and Imran exchanged knowing glances at each other: clearly there was a reason that it needed to be in this date range. She even remarked tauntingly, "I know why you are keen to announce so soon".

I assumed they did not want it to clash with the Azadi March. The impression I got was that it would be only a four-day event. Another fleeting thought I had was that perhaps the unwanted pregnancy reported earlier in the year had not been aborted after all. I did not interrupt their discussion. It was as if I wasn't even sitting there. I only found out later what Imran had been promised: If he walked into the capital, Nawaz would go, and the crown would be his to take. I would spend all of September consoling a broken man who felt cheated.

After this meeting, our children were introduced to each other at a formal family dinner. Suleiman and Sahir sat on either side of Imran while Qasim sat near my girls and I. Aleema's family was there, and so was Rani's lovely daughter, Hajra, and her daughters. Aleema's daughter-in-law had prepared a lavish spread. We picked up pizzas for the boys on the way. A rather weird individual from Birmingham called Max was there too. He had the look of the *desi* folk one would avoid on *Chand Raat* (eve of *Eid-ul-Fitr*) in Rusholme. Zakir Khan, his wife and kid, as well as his in-laws were also invited. And just like Aleema, most of those invited would later profess to have had no knowledge of our wedding plans.

They were being hospitable but the vibe, particularly from Aleema's daughter-in-law, was not very welcoming. It was mainly a quizzing exercise. Zakir's rather loud Brazilian mother-in-law enquired where my daughter went clubbing in London. Ridha found it odd but politely ignored the rude assumptions of the woman.

Aleema's older son, Shershah, and her husband were pleasant enough, but quizzed me on my religious beliefs. They came across as quite secular. I took to Qasim immediately as he was happy to chat. Suleiman looked nervous and unsure of himself. I had never seen such a sad looking boy. I didn't see him smile once the entire evening. Sahir talked confidently in contrast. Suleiman kept looking for his father to turn to him for attention. He hardly spoke. I wanted to get up and give the poor boy a hug. On the way back, Ridha and I discussed how withdrawn the kid looked. He'd clearly had a very different upbringing to any of mine. It wouldn't be long before I began to realise how messed up his world really was.

§

By the end of July, as I seriously started to consider Imran's marriage proposal, Ijaz's cyber bullying jumped up a notch. It had gone from a lone Facebook account to my videos going viral on portals associated with PTI. But I shrugged it off. That was the best he had, which was still nothing.

Meanwhile, I still did not know how to broach the Imran situation openly with my kids. We were sitting in one of our favourite rooftop restaurants in Islamabad when I confirmed to my kids that something more was on the table with Imran. All three reacted differently. Sahir didn't react negatively, but didn't react positively either, thinking for a second before suddenly then jumping to, "Wait, you haven't already said yes, have you?" Perhaps he thought I was impulsive. He was largely worried about me having to deal with another psychopath, so his opinion would vary wildly as he tried to assess Imran's behaviour. Eventually, he would say that it was my decision, having seen some positive signs from Imran.

Ridha also didn't seem to have too many objections to the marriage. She was excited about the prospect of a wedding reception rather than the marriage itself, and immediately jumped to what type of wedding dresses I should try. Inaya's take, however, was very interesting. Inaya was a typical British 11-year-old. She had no familiarity with Pakistan and could not speak a word of Urdu when I arrived. Since the divorce, we had made fewer trips. But then I'd moved to the country, and Inaya had to quickly adapt to a scary new atmosphere. Inaya was enrolled in a posh school in Islamabad. She had not only picked up Urdu within weeks, but she coped well with this sudden new cultural immersion. Instead of familiar surroundings and an older sister, little Inu was now surrounded by maids, drivers, and guards.

I threw myself into work. Inaya never made any demands of me, which was something I didn't appreciate immediately. She was much younger than other kids in her class and was bullied at school for her accent, but she showed the fighting spirit of her Swati blood and soldiered on. She kept all this from me until much later. She felt I had bigger problems to deal with.

After just a couple of months in our new set-up, Inaya had mastered the language and was a confident shopper. Unknown to me, she also enrolled herself into easy-Urdu classes at school. I had not planned to stay for longer than one academic year and did not want to put extra pressure on her. But her argument was that she should learn to be fluent in Urdu if she was to pursue that Bollywood film career.

I had strict instructions to be back for 9pm to watch the Turkish drama *Mera Sultan* with Inaya. It was a historical epic on the Ottoman Sultan Suleiman the Magnificent. Inaya is perhaps most like me out of my children. She sings and dances around in the house, and has an amazing photographic memory. I remember her coming back from school as a tiny four-year-old and retelling the story of Guy Fawkes, word-for-word, as it was in the book the teacher had read from. She is also independent like me, and finds it annoying to be treated like a child.

It was Inaya's emotional intelligence that shocked us right from the start. Her profound statements about life and relationships would be remarkably mature and helpful. The other two kids had mixed feelings but were generally a lot more open to the idea that it could work. Inaya was the only one of my three kids who was not keen on the idea of me remarrying. She was also vehemently against marriage to IK in particular. Sadly, she would be bullied at school for the next few years from all sides, thanks to her 'political connections'. She would also be targeted outside of school, by Imran's older sisters. Social media accounts that didn't even belong to her would be used as evidence against the child.

One day, Inaya suddenly asked me at the dinner table if I understood the value of my hard-earned freedom. She then questioned if my marriage would mean a stepdad who would be nasty to her. When I assured her that he wouldn't be nasty to her, she pondered for a minute, and then asked, "What if he is too nice to me and expects me to reciprocate?"

Her advice was sound. Her concerns were unfounded however. Imran was neither nasty nor overly nice. He had hardly any interaction with her at all, never even talking to her, other than to criticise her for speaking in English if he overheard her talking to me.

As it became clear to her that I might accept a proposal, she quizzed me further.

"Are you marrying him for money?"

"He doesn't have any money," I replied, laughing.

"Well that's even more concerning," she said, with a disapproving auntie look in her eyes.

I now believe that kids should be consulted on all matters. Those untainted by society's whispers have the best judgement.

Chapter 15

Sometimes, the biggest issues come from nothing. Something that seems absolutely innocent and harmless can come back to harm you in ways you could never have imagined. One of these things, which caused a significant number of problems for me, was a video of me participating in a Strictly Come Dancing style competition for the BBC's Children in Need in 2011.

Naturally, I had been perfectly fine with such an easy way of contributing to the cause. It was not unlike me to jump at any chance to help. I had also walked across the Spinnaker Tower in Portsmouth for Comic Relief in 2011. This time, all I had to do was display some fancy footwork. 'Why not?' I thought. Imagine my surprise when I'd see this develop into a major 'scandal' for me many years later. The video was found and made viral via online portals allegedly controlled by the son of a senior PTI leader. Supposedly, this was proof of my shameful ways and despicable character.

The day after I'd discussed the proposal with my children, I got a long, hateful message from the man who had been wooing me for over two months. Imran said that his sisters had sat him down and showed him a hate website, 'Truth about Reham Khan', which had clearly been set up by my first husband and his new wife. Imran's reaction was surprising and inexplicable. I'd told Imran about Ijaz's relentless cyber bullying in our first conversation. He had been so sympathetic, cursing at the man and repeatedly asking how someone could do that to their own kids. He'd said all the right things, and said them convincingly. There had been no cheesy chat-up lines, but compassion and understanding. He'd even said, "You do have amazing legs in those photos from your BBC days". Apparently, Zakir had introduced 'the BBC beauty' to him. I remember him asking me if I still had great legs, and me snubbing him by saying they were destroyed in my accident.

Yet here he was, sending me A4-size texts, expressing his anger at why I had not told him this. I tried to remind him that I did, before realising it was a one-sided conversation. I sent him a short, stern message that he had no right to question me or talk to me like that. Compared to him, I was an angel. What I had done had been in public, and not something to be hidden or ashamed of. I told him not to contact me again and that I was glad this had happened. I now had a sense of the unreasonable man he was.

Following the military operation in North Wazirstan, I had been spending most of my time with IDPs in Bannu. The situation had worsened following the Zarb-i-Azab operation. This meant that I was struggling with my live 8pm slot. Channel owners across Pakistan never had much interest in Pashtun stories, especially Tribal areas stories. There was no positive story about the armed forces or PTI to be found here, and no Government was paying attention to their plight. All they wanted were stories of the PTI boycotts and rallies. I found it boring and tedious. To make matters worse, one night my content boss called me up and suggested that I let another anchor do my 8pm slot the next day, as he had the Finance minister, Ishaq Dar, lined up to discuss the budget that was being announced. He suggested I do the 11pm slot instead for that day.

I had been getting impressive ratings and did not appreciate this misogynistic ordering. I politely replied that the chosen anchor could deal with my slot as well as his own while I took the week off, and slammed the phone down. The following day, as I had anticipated, I learned that the anchor in question had failed to get the finance minister for the channel. The minister had instead chosen to sit with my former colleague Nadeem Malik on the rival channel, Samaa TV.

I then sent an email to my CEO, voicing my irritation at this unprofessional behaviour, and told him I could not continue with this sort of offensive interference. Ahmed, the CEO, had always been very accommodating, but had too much on his plate to attend to these issues, even though they had been raised before. I was surrounded by offers double my current salary, so I decided to take a much-needed break. The channel decided to withhold my last salary, something which is commonly practiced in Pakistan. Contracts are frequently breached and there isn't much one can do in terms of taking people to court. It is far more common to use these practices against women, as they rarely have backing behind them, as well as technical staff, who are considered dispensable.

I had told Imran that I was between jobs, and also mentioned my salary issue. Gallantly, he picked up the phone and asked Naeem to instruct the channel to release my payments, which they did at his bidding immediately, without asking any questions. In Pakistan media, no one refused the *Kaptaan*. Imran also offered to send money for my children's rent in London till I got the payment, before insisting that it would only be a few weeks before we'd be married, and that I wouldn't be working on TV when I was his wife. I hadn't agreed to the marriage or to not working on TV, and I'd reminded him of both these facts. But he'd smiled victoriously.

Now, just a few weeks later, he'd deleted me off Blackberry Messenger after this fight. I also received a text asking for the return of the money he had sent. I had already called his driver and made out a cheque, but receiving a text like that struck me as very cheap. It wasn't a lot of money (about £450) and I thought he would have some grace, and not stoop so low as to ask me for it.

This was far from the end of course. He would be back before long, begging me to take him back and pleading for me to handle his doubts gently. Throughout our time together, an often-repeated phrase was, "Doubt is the beginning of faith".

And every time I heard it, I would reply, "No, Imran. Love is a leap of faith. There is no question of doubt".

What I should have said and known was 'doubt is the beginning of more doubt'.

§

Was I in love? The short answer is a no. I wasn't in love with Imran, at this point at least. It would be insane for me to have already been in love with him. It can take years for true love to develop in many of the strongest relationships. I had been erratically pursued for a couple of months by a man who confused me, and displayed many concerning tendencies and incongruous patterns of behaviour. The man had countless adoring fans that might have killed to be in my position, but I was not like them. After his behaviour, it seemed that he was not the right man for me. But I was definitely becoming attached to him, and I would be lying if I said it didn't affect me.

With my eyes looking like huge tennis balls, I sat with the crew and set off for Lahore at the crack of dawn. I had joined the state TV channel in mid-July but had not started my show yet. The Managing Director of PTV, Mohammad Malik, had organised an interview with the Chief Minister of Punjab. The man was the backbone of the ruling party, PMLN, and the younger brother of the PM. Anyone else would have given their right arm and a leg for this opportunity. Yet here I was, with my head full of molten lead and my eyes stinging from the tears of the night before. I felt more angry and insulted than heartbroken. Instead of catching up on my sleep, I channelled my anger into researching the CM. My brother used to joke that "when Reham gets angry, give her a task to do. She works like a woman possessed". I think he may have had a point. I find it therapeutic to focus on work, and it helps get the anger out of my system. I was looking for something interesting that others may have missed but, try as I might, I struggled to find much wrong with the almost android-like, hardworking qualities of the CM. Nevertheless, in the five-hour journey, I'd gone through all his projects in detail.

Malik was a close ally of Shehbaz Sharif, and was incredibly keen to get everything arranged perfectly. He was very nervous about what I would ask the CM. Malik even arranged makeup at his own wife's salon, instead of trusting the PTV makeup artists. I heaved a huge sigh of relief as the accomplished makeup girls at the salon completely covered my puffiness and other signs of my childish sobbing of the night before. I switched into professional-mode and insisted on interviewing in the opulent withdrawing room.

I headed towards the Model Town residence, fully brainwashed by the propaganda of how stuck up the Sharifs were. Their attitudes were often compared to Marie Antoinette's behaviour. PTI had labelled them as the *badshahs* (kings). Shehbaz Sharif was portrayed in media as a man who was prone to getting married every so often to any attractive woman he laid his eyes on. With all that negativity, I marched into a tasteful parlour. As I looked around, I saw a penchant for Faberge eggs and an obsessional attention-to-detail in the decor. It all looked familiar. I went into the powder room and did a double take at the painted basin. It seemed like someone had been consulting my decorating notes.

As we sat waiting for the CM to arrive, several people dropped in to greet the team. I was still in a bit of a daze, and slow to register that some were his close family members. Their attitude was pleasant and down to earth. A man introduced himself as 'the one who was not in politics'. He joked that he was the businessman who kept earning while the family kept spending it all on politics. I was later told that it was the younger, Oxford-educated entrepreneur son of the CM.

The atmosphere was casual and relaxed until the CM walked in. I had my back to the entrance, but the immediate pin-drop silence suggested that the taskmaster had arrived. It was as if everyone in the room had stopped breathing. I noticed that the room suddenly emptied as everyone presumably scampered to their duties. The CM walked in with military precision. I half-expected him to snap his feet together in attention. He greeted me in a very brisk, professional manner. We sat down. The makeup artist attempted to take the shine off the CM's face, but this man, with his silvery grey hair and unusually long fingers, dismissed him. He had no time to waste. We jumped straight into the interview with no chit-chat and no deliberation.

The older man kept meticulously rearranging the pen and notepad in front of him. I had discovered who my obsessional replica in the house was. Besides short water breaks, the CM answered my questions for 60 straight minutes. After the intense grilling which clearly showed my PTI tilt, we stood up. Before I could thank him, the CM surprised me by saying in a rather fatherly fashion, "Thank you. Very tough interview young lady but I appreciate it".

With that, he was gone. No sleazy overtures. No arrogance. He was just brisk, clinical and professional to the core. This was clearly a no-nonsense type who with many other pressing work engagements. As soon as he left, I heard people breathing again. And that was it. Lunch and refreshments had been arranged for us but I left immediately after the interview. My boss stayed back to edit out a few bits, presumably to try and soften the interview. But I had been on fire and it wasn't possible to soften the relentless 60-minute onslaught. Besides, I thought the CM had an answer for all my questions. The interview was a huge hit with both PMLN and PTI viewers. Ironically, I got compliments for looking beautiful. No one had noticed my swollen eyes. Everyone liked my cover up.

I was sitting in Street One Cafe in F6 (a popular PTI haunt) with my kids one night. The cricket celebrity was forgotten, and single mum mode was in full swing. Then, as I sat there enjoying chocolate fudge cake with my family, my bliss was suddenly disturbed by the following stinging text message: "Well you seem to be back to your cool, composed competent look while interviewing SS I see".

I wasn't expecting this at all. I had firmly shut the door on this rude man. I stared at the message in a confused state of mind while two other messages quickly followed along the lines of, 'I have been a total mess for days and it has had no effect on you at all. So it meant nothing to you while I have been miserable'.

"Well what was I supposed to do exactly? I replied. "Maybe you failed to notice my puffy face, and the layers of makeup needed to cover my eye bags?"

Replying was the wrong thing to do. The frequency and length of the messages kept increasing. I should have known what to do; I had recently blocked a female relative for sending me long, toxic messages. Eventually, he told me he wanted me back on Blackberry Messenger. "I can't get you out of my head," he kept saying. "You have driven me mad. I was so miserable that day that Aleema said, 'Imran, I was so pleased to see you look so happy. It's such a shame'. She was so concerned that she called Salli over to cheer me up".

I almost laughed. That would certainly have done the trick. Everyone in Pakistan knew that Yousaf Salahuddin could provide entertainment alright. I had heard stories of 'Salli kee Haveli' (Salli's mansion) since my childhood. My sister's husband had been taken there by his media mogul business partner, and had told her of the colourful events at Yousaf Salahuddin's. And now I knew that Yousaf Salahuddin was Imran's best friend. Imran confirmed all the rumours I had heard from everyone in the media industry. Male, female, shemale, or all of them together, he was allegedly a one-stop late shop.

After a couple of days, the conversation turned to, "Why didn't you tell me?" I would repeatedly respond: "I showed you the whole Facebook account and pleaded with you to have it shut down. You never looked. You were always busy or didn't know how to use Facebook yourself". At first, he was adamant that I'd never mentioned the website. Then his stance switched to 'But you should have forced me to sit down and pay attention'. Of course, I would soon find out that making him sit down to look at something required a Herculean effort, and resulted in several new frown lines. His concept of listening was walking away. Where smokers and the unfit failed, I succeeded, by matching his pace and being able to talk nonstop at the same time. In fact, I could sprint as fast as he could, which he would compliment me on. But as with all his compliments, it would be used to feed his paranoia.

After a few weeks of discussing the dance, he said to me, "But it's not a private video. How could you do that in public?" I was stunned. "I did it in public, Imran, because I don't have anything to hide. I don't get up to anything behind closed doors. I'm not ashamed of it". That started a fresh argument on why I was not embarrassed.

A couple of weeks went by. He changed his tone to a level of softness that only a few might have heard from him.

"But darling, when I have doubts, don't fight with me. Just take my doubts away. Don't fire back at me. Answer my queries. That's all".

The next thing I heard was: "I have to see you".

"But how can you see me? You are up on that stupid container".

"So come to the container".

"What? How and why? I don't want to have this argument in front of the whole party and fans," I exclaimed.

"I just want to see you," he pleaded. "Just for a few minutes, come with a friend. I'm stuck in this hellhole. Need some air".

The hellhole he referred to was the parade of his own creation: the *dharna*. On Pakistan's Independence Day, the 14th of August, PTI had decided to launch the *Azadi* March (Freedom March), in order to protest against the systematic election rigging that they were accusing PMLN of executing. Together with another group, the Pakistan Awami Tehreek (party of the people) led by Canadian cleric Tahir ul-Qadri, a large group would travel from Lahore to Zero Point in Islamabad (near the PM House) and cause disruption in the capital. It was kind of like an extended version their usual rallies and *jalsas.* The stated aims were to secure the dismissal of the government and the resignation of Prime Minister Nawaz Sharif, electoral reform, the elimination of corruption, and a snap election. IK and the leadership travelled in the large 'Azadi Bus', followed closely by party supporters on cars and bikes.

I was reluctant to forgive him but did support the party. As I waited, along with many other journalists and reporters, for the Million March to arrive on the 14th of August, I was disappointed to learn that it had not even left Lahore. The following morning, a skirmish at Gujranwala was reported between PTI and PMLN supporters. My concern for Imran's safety grew. The cavalcade finally arrived in the early hours of the 16th of August. The delays and heavy rain had already affected the ground support. I saw the President of PTI, Javed Hashmi, give an unconvincing speech in the rain. He was later rushed to hospital for pneumonia. Imran addressed the few left behind after 4am. He had texted me on the way to say his bladder was bursting and he had asked to stop at a house in F8.

Imran was as unhappy with the numbers as his planners. Both had been relying on each other to deliver the promised one hundred thousand motorbikes. The 'Million March' looked more like a few hundred. Imran returned to Bani Gala in a huff. The move shocked all of us watching, and he was rightly condemned for abandoning his loyal supporters after promising to stay with them until their objectives had been achieved. The number of supporters present dropped significantly. Though he would return the next day and insist on spending the night with his supporters, and actually follow through by setting up a makeshift bed on top of the Azadi Bus, the damage had been done. The sit-in would limp on though, and would morph from the initial march into what would be known as the *dharna*.

As the days went by I kept hearing reports of the chances of imminent violence erupting. Eventually, a lot would be written about me, and a 'compromising video' of the goings-on in the container. It would be insinuated that I had been with Imran, even though I only ever went inside the container three times, and these were not private meetings. The first was on the 19th of August when I finally found a friend who could go to the *dharna* with me. As we entered, the whole of the KP cabinet was sat around a slightly tipsy-looking Imran. The guy who went with me took a few photos, but was so nervous on meeting the big man (who was in a very friendly mood) that he picked up IK's phone instead of his own. Both the phones were identical and it was an honest mistake, but Aleema's younger son (who had been giving us dirty looks already) grabbed the young man by the collar. Imran very gallantly broke up the fight but the young man was still thrown out. Imran kept trying to talk to me. I described the threat of violence and he embarrassed me in front of everyone by loudly proclaiming, "Reham thinks there is a threat". I gathered only later that this was exactly what they wanted.

It was the first time I had seen him since the family dinner. I was concerned about his safety and wanted to warn him. He just laughed it off, but then unexpectedly touched my knee in front of everyone else. I nearly jumped out of my skin with embarrassment but he didn't care. He made it very clear to everyone what he was thinking. Aleema arrived with her female cousins and sat with us as we continued the political discussion. Imran and I weren't alone at any point. A little later, I was led upstairs to the container's rooftop stage. I listened with a couple of other anchors as he made his speech. When he finished, he found me sitting on a bench at the corner of the stage. He came and sat next to me. "Do you know how badly I want to kiss you?"

"Do you know how badly your nephews want to kill me?" I replied. He just shrugged like he didn't care. He looked so old, haggard and worn out. My anger was replaced with sympathy and I forgot what had happened. Right then, he needed support. I gently suggested that he rest a bit. He responded, "I can't sleep in this fucking prison. It's noisy all night here".

I advised him not to tire himself out while speaking, and perhaps not use too much power. I suggested that the stage secretary, Faisal Javed, could teach him voice exercises and techniques so he could speak for longer without straining his vocal cords. He signalled to Faisal to come over. "Am I looking tired and exhausted?"

Faisal immediately responded, "No, no, not at all Khan *Sahab*!"

It was my first taste of how you never told the Supreme Leader the truth.

The second time I went was at the request of fellow anchor Waseem Badami, who had been getting warnings from PTI for asking too many pertinent questions. He was under a lot of stress as his boss at ARY, Salman Iqbal, kept sending him texts during live shows, telling him to control his ciriticism of PTI. He had been told that a list of blacklisted journalists had been sent to the Leader and his name was on it. He asked me to get me a meeting. I called Ali Zaidi, who was more than happy to accommodate the request. I waited for Badami in the Azadi Bus where Ali Zaidi gave me a long lecture on how he believed his Leader should stay single; why marriage was not for Imran. At the time, I wasn't sure whether it was because Ali fancied me himself or whether he was panicking about IK's marriage.

The final time was in the first week of October, as I interviewed Imran for my new job at Dawn News. While Imran greeted us with warmth, the environment in the container was icy, with very hostile glares from Shireen Mazari and Aleema's husband directed at me. Unknown to them, Imran was still wooing me, despite my pleas that I could not cope with his set up.

§

The human cost is irrelevant to those who have grandiosity on their mind. From Louis XIV to present day megalomaniacs, nothing has changed.

I was not part of the *dharna* plan. My ardent suitor never disclosed any details. However, I, like a few others (I stress, a few others), had warned him as early as May of what the purpose of it would be. I repeatedly cautioned him in June and July. My exact words were: "You do realise that you will be used and discarded like toilet paper? Nawaz will be controlled and so will you". I received an angry and proud response along the lines of 'No one can dictate to me, and I'm not on anyone's script!' I never criticised it again.

It was well after the sit-in started that we were communicating again, and by then I felt too sorry for him to tell him the truth. He was already demoralised, and perhaps that's why he would claim he needed me 'for inspiration'. He was losing and knew it, but was too proud to accept it. Those who had led him into it had no plans, and people were criticising him. Everyone knew he had failed, and he knew he had failed. He wasn't becoming PM. The government was not going anywhere, and he was trapped in that container. His circle didn't do pep talks. He had lived a life where he had been judged only on winning. I had never been interested in medals and trophies myself. I remember playing a pretty decent game of table tennis at school but my sports teacher found it exasperating that I wasn't at all motivated to crush an opponent. I never understood the thirst to be a winner.

Imran turned to me when everyone turned their back on him. He would call me from the container and plead with me to come to the *dharna*. But this was a scary place, not least because of the glares I would receive from his two nephews atop the container, but also the lecherous, fixed looks of some other PTI leaders. I needed a few people to take me there, and a few more to get me out. At no point did anyone from PTI or his personal staff help me. But his face would light up with a broad smile when he would spot me in the crowd in my signature white *chadar*.

On the 28th of August, Imran and Qadri were called for a meeting with Chaudhry Nisar by the Chief of the Army Staff. Imran was seen sporting a smile in the television footage. But the meeting did not have the desired result. Soon after, Javed Hashmi revealed that Imran had told him that the *dharna* had been planned with the establishment to facilitate a technocratic set up. I realised that the main PTI mouthpieces had put in good money to secure a place in that expected caretaker set up. They were all fed a dream. It also became clear why Imran wanted a Mrs by the end of the month. Imran actually expected to become PM. Javed Hashmi also revealed the plan in a press conference: Imran had told him that, under pressure from the protest, the new Chief Justice would dissolve Parliament, and elections would be held in September.

However, the plan for causing disruption didn't take shape until August 30th 2014, when PAT and PTI supporters attempted to attack Parliament. The protestors were effectively dispersed by heavy-handed police action and gas shelling. Out of the 4000 arrests made, 99% were PTI workers. In the days leading up to this, Imran was desperately hoping to be arrested and made a martyr in some manner. He was so confident that he went home to flush some special stuff down the toilet too. But Imran wasn't arrested. I however lost my PTV job criticising the heavy-handed approach of the government on TV. Javed Hashmi left PTI, and I heard Imran curse him and Chaudhry Nisar daily. Until then, Imran had been repeatedly saying that Chaudhry Nisar would bring 60 Parliament members with him to PTI. It never happened. All his hopes were dashed. Imran turned to me for solace as any chance of the government toppling disappeared, with no sight of re-elections. The new Chief Justice did nothing and neither did the COAS. PMLN had survived the attack. I never once said

'I told you so', but I secretly hoped he would have learned from this experience and would focus on governance now.

The sit-in dragged on in some shape or form for a few months, quickly becoming more of a nightly entertainment. The government relaxed too. This seemed to work better for supporters and leaders alike. Imran had the freedom to go home as he liked and only occasionally show his face in the evening. Nevertheless, he felt trapped by the whole affair, which was failing to bear fruit. This long and ultimately futile series of demonstrations would eventually be called off after 126 days. A national tragedy in Peshawar would provide PTI with a convenient excuse to call time on the whole, drawn-out affair.

As time went on, both of my older children would be baffled by Imran's conduct. Sahir had been brutal in his assessment on the very first night of the *dharna*, when Imran had said he would stay with his loyal supporters until the PM resigned (even if that meant days of camping), only to arrive, look at the disappointing numbers, and go home almost immediately. After our break-up in early August, Sahir had commented on his fickle nature, and said, "Look at it this way mum: I think you just dodged a bullet".

Similarly, Ridha would hold her head in grief at Imran's frequent, disastrous steps. Fully believing in Imran's message, she (like the rest of us) couldn't understand his bizarre spree of mistakes. I would smile and say, "It's OK darling, he will be forgiven," to which she emphatically declared: "Mum, I know that Allah keeps saving him over and over again, but one of these days he may run out of patience with this man".

None of us knew quite how true her words would prove to be. When I would try to reason with him about his lack of interest or his faulty decisions he would shut me up by saying, "You know, even my mum thought I was a duffer, but I became successful didn't I? You are so arrogant to think you can offer a suggestion to me. What have you ever run? A crew of 4 people? Do you know how big my party is? What the hell do you know about leadership and how to manage people?"

I knew nothing about managing a party, but I had learned that only good consistent performance can guarantee success. I knew he could not become Prime Minister but I did want him to leave a legacy. I wanted him never to lose his hero status in the hearts and minds of millions of people.

Chapter 16

The *nikkah* was pronounced on October 31st, 2014 in Imran's bedroom, away from prying eyes.

Like many of my generation, I was fed a culture of Bollywood, where the practice of *Karwa Chauth* (fasting and praying for the long life of your husband) was presented so romantically. The concept of the husband being like a god is promoted in both Hindu and Urdu literature, with terms like *Pati Parmeshwar* and *Mazaji Khuda* liberally sprinkled on both sides of the border. The husband is referred to as the *Sartaj* (crown); the sanctity of marriage symbolised by the *Mangalsutra* (sacred thread) and the central parting coloured with red *sindoor* (powder). Widows in the subcontinent traditionally wear only white, to show that all colour in their lives is gone when the husband is no more. These were concepts we had seen a million times over. The woman as a *dasi* (devotee) is glorified in our culture regardless of our religion. Young, progressive men across the country would be bowled over by my spontaneous declaration in the famous press conference in the constituency of NA-246 (Karachi) in April 2015, only a few months from this moment, where I would refer to my husband as the only jewellery I needed to enhance me. "*Mera shohar hee mera zewar hai*", I would cry out.

Here I was, a woman who had earned her independence, worked in the cutthroat media industry, and actively worked to spread awareness of legal rights in marriage and divorce. People sought advice from me on a regular basis. Yet at 42, I was no better than an 18-year-old die-hard romantic. I put my brain to the side at the time of the *nikkah*. When the *Moulvi* (Islamic scholar) asked me what my demand was for *mehr* (dower money), a right given to women under Islam, I responded that I did not have any demand. I have never wanted material guarantees. But in my romantic idealism, I chose to forgo my basic rights under law, and Sharia too.

I wore a pure white organza *shlawar kameez* by Monica Couture, which had a huge silk rose embroidered on the front. I had less than thirty minutes to prepare.

I stood in the bathroom thinking, 'This is too ostentatious for a simple *nikkah*'. In the end, I covered the offending rose with a huge organza *dupatta*. Zakir and Awn sat on the long sofa at the foot of Imran's large bed. Imran sat next to me on the red armchairs, facing the *Moulvi* across the coffee table.

It happened so suddenly and quickly. We had been arguing via text only the day before about how Moby had told Imran that I used to dance topless in a bar in London. Imran told me that Moby had found out that we were about to tie the knot, and had said that he would be bringing an ISI officer with him the next day to reveal sordid details of my connections and racy past. I had told Imran that I was fed up with their dirty accusations, and that I had had enough of his texts too, asking if he could leave me alone as I found all of this behaviour bizarre. I spoke sternly to him, saying, "I think it's best if you stop bothering me". Imran had kept texting me for a few hours after that, apologising and saying that he was only discussing information with me, not accusing me. He insisted that we tie the knot the following morning as planned and that he would never mention Moby ever again. And in less than 24 hours, I was sitting there, actually getting married for the second time.

I was overwhelmed with fear. There was no confidence in my voice as I whispered my 'I do's. Awn, by contrast, couldn't contain his excitement. Immediately after the *nikkah*, Imran behaved as if I had been his wife for ages. We all moved outside to have a cup of green tea as if nothing had happened. Once they left, I walked back into the bedroom. I was still shivering on the inside. As I tried to calm myself with a cool drink of water, Imran walked in. From across the room he said, "Well...Mrs Imran Niazi".

I managed a weak smile. The distance between us was rather un-romantic. The next thing he said was perhaps slightly more disconcerting, had I understood at the time.

"I don't know what I was so worried about. A huge weight has been lifted from my shoulders it seems. It feels fine. I feel fine. I had all these silly doubts and they have all gone away".

I nodded slowly, trying to decide how to react to that statement. As would be the case for months to come, I decided to let it go. He looked happy, almost jubilant.

"This *Moulvi* chap...he is...well...umm...different," I said.

"Yes," Imran replied. "He is very learned. We needed someone to respond to all the Islamic questions, so we decided to put him in the core committee. By the way, he wants you to visit his madrassa and library".

"Oh, does he?" I said.

Later that evening, he reiterated his thoughts as he held me close. "This is such a relief. It feels so right. I don't know why I had any doubts. I knew after meeting you that you were the right woman for me. And all through August while you tortured me, I could not bear to think of being with another woman".

I didn't interrupt him. I should have reminded him that the August drama and subsequent delay had been his own fault, but I didn't want to ruin the moment. He seemed to be in such a joyful mood.

"You know, I cried on the night of our wedding reception when I got married to Jemima," he suddenly added

"You cried?" I said. "Why?"

"Because it became clear to me that it was so wrong. Jemima had a few drinks at the reception, and passed out. I cried myself to sleep. You see, even before the formal announcement, I had begun to see the change in her. And when we went for our official honeymoon, it was the most depressing time for me. Things went downhill as time went by. She was so young and became insecure about my past experiences".

"But Imran, why did you tell her about your past experiences?" I exclaimed.

According to Imran, her confidence levels improved only during the last few months of their marriage. They had been separated for quite some time. She had been living in London. She flew in for a few weeks to give the marriage one last go, even though Imran's *pir* had told him to finish it. She had been told that Imran had been seeing another woman who lived close by, in Bani Gala. "I think it made her jealous," Imran chuckled. But she was soon back in London, socialising again. And when, finally, the picture of her and Hugh Grant came out in a tabloid, Imran was left with no option but to divorce her. Imran told me that he had seen the same image in a dream a few weeks prior to that. When the picture came out, he discussed it with Annabelle. The family were not in favour of the divorce. After three weeks, Imran finally gave her a divorce.

I didn't really know how to respond to this account of his first marriage on our wedding night. Despite not really wanting to know much of his past (and not asking), this would not be the last I heard of Jemima or other exes. I felt awful that a young girl had been made to listen to past stories, and could completely relate to her. Imran, ironically, described Jemima as a woman who had awful taste in men. In the first weeks of our time together, he kept discussing and ridiculing Jemima for her choices: from Hugh Grant, who had been caught with a prostitute in Hollywood, to Russell Brand, who had been very open about his drug abuse and sex addiction. Imran insisted that she went for men who behaved badly. Imran disapproved of her choices but the fact that he seemed very similar to these other men flew over his head. Interestingly, Imran was all praise for her father, who had always been unapologetic and open about his string of mistresses.

It seemed Jemima had worse luck with men than me, but Imran blamed her volatile temperament for her many failed attempts. He told me that her ex-boyfriends had asked him for advice on how to deal with her temper-tantrums. I remembered reading somewhere and almost cheering that her first boyfriend, Joel, who was from the Cadbury dynasty, was dumped on the hard shoulder of a motorway after a heated argument. No one questions men when they lose their temper, but women are defamed for it. Imran was dismissive of her obsession with hanging out with celebrities too. He said he couldn't reconcile himself to the fact that his young wife loved parties and hung out with young celebrities. He first saw a glimpse of the fangirl in her when they met Hugh Grant at a party. Imran said he could see how starry-eyed she was, and it filled him with disgust. Once again, Imran failed to recognise that he was also a celebrity who had been known for his partying. I pointed out that she was free to do what she wanted, but Imran simply continued by saying that her family regretted the fact she had left Imran, and worried about her as she moved from one bad egg to another. The way he put it, it seemed less like Imran and Jemima, and more like Imran and the Goldsmiths.

I hadn't asked to be told any of this but it taught me a lot about Imran. While he could not shake off his past, I was thinking of the present. Late that evening I said, "I really need to go home now. Inaya must be wondering where I am".

"Where do you think you are going? You are my wife, madam. Not going anywhere for the rest of the weekend".

"But Imran, I haven't made any arrangements for her and I can't just disappear. The older two are not here either".

"Oh, come on baby, we just got married. You are not seriously going to leave me".

"But you have to go to the *dharna* anyway".

"Oh, it's such a bore. Don't worry about that. I will show my face for fifteen minutes and be back before you know it. You are not going anywhere".

And that was the way with Imran. He always got his own way. There was never a question of accepting a no. He didn't use domineering tactics. He would simply opt for the adorable pleading tactics that kids use on their parents. And I loved seeing him happy. For the first few days, he kept asking me, "Do you love me as much as I love you, Reham?"

I gave him the honest response: "Imran, I love you more with every passing day".

It may have started with his relentless pursuit, but I grew to love him as I loved my children. When alone with me, the arrogant angry man on TV that I had always disliked had the vulnerability of a child; a child who had grown up feeling he had to bring in medals to be loved. It seemed he was not used to unconditional love. In those first months before the announcement, Imran was keen to learn how to be a caring partner. I had never been in a proper relationship. I had been married before, but the togetherness that I had been deprived of all my life was now a reality.

For weeks, I had been discussing with Sahir how Imran was pressurising me and how my brother had refused to get involved in the marriage. When I had broached the subject with Munir, he had been struck by grief. Over a period of 24 hours, my brother tried to gently suggest that Imran was not a Muslim. He ultimately said, "Marry anyone but him". I was shocked and hurt at this response and completely misunderstood the well-meaning advice. Sahir consoled me by saying, "Mum, you do what you want". And then, after weeks of cold feet, I finally did it. I dropped Sahir a text simply saying, 'Done'. He immediately knew what I meant and sent me a quick 'congratulations' and a sheepish selfie from his lecture hall.

In the week that followed, I set about organising my move into Bani Gala. The packing of stuff from my F11 home was taken out of my hands. I was told to return with Inaya and my clothes. The rest of it would be taken care of by Safeer, the Man-Friday. The Bani Gala property was designed like an old barracks, with the rooms arranged in rows opening into a central courtyard. Imran's wing could be bolted from the inside and consisted of a main hall with three bedrooms and a gym. Imran's large bedroom had great views of the huge garden and on a clear day Faisal Mosque could be seen from the patio. The bedrooms to the front of the property were known as the Suleiman and Qasim bedrooms. Imran knew that I shared a bedroom with my daughter in my own home, and suggested Inaya have Suleiman's room, which was directly opposite his master bedroom. But just a few days before the marriage, he called me to say that he had changed his mind, and that the room outside the private wing was airier and had better views. I was touched that he wanted to give the better room with a view to my daughter. Later, I understood that it was perhaps not a suggestion based on consideration.

I found Inaya's room to be too far from me but she liked the newfound independence. It did mean I would check on her several times a night, and tell her to keep her room locked at all times. My older two were studying in the UK but visited frequently, and all three shared her bedroom. Imran suggested I use the wardrobes in Suleiman's room for my clothes. Suleiman never used this room when he stayed, even though I left the décor untouched, down to the framed doodles of his childhood on the walls. Qasim's room was also left unused and untouched.

As my stuff arrived, I was horrified to find that nothing had been properly packed. The furniture, mirrors and paintings were all horribly scratched. It had all been dumped in a Shehzore truck and brought to Bani Gala. I didn't say anything, but the horror was visible on my face, and Imran shouted at the driver for ruining everything. I said nothing, thinking that it was a bachelor pad so they obviously wouldn't understand, and simply ordered re-varnishing and repairs. It was obvious to all visitors that someone had moved in, and it was also being discussed on social media and national TV.

One of the biggest issues in moving to Pakistan had been my dog Maximus. Elaborate arrangements were made and customs clearance arranged. I only ever used my personal contacts for influence once, and it was to make sure Maximus would be released and reunited with me as soon he landed. After so many grazed knees, chewed-up fences, and angry neighbours, Maximus was very much part of the family, and I was going to ensure that he was in Pakistan with me. He was frequently used by my nephews and their friends to get the attention of the girls in the neighbourhood. Surprisingly, Maximus had adjusted very well to Pakistan even though there weren't any grassy areas in my urban, six-bedroomed house where the 60kg beast could run around.

Bani Gala seemed like a dog's paradise. Maxi's new residence certainly allowed him more space and freedom to run. And much like his owner, he slowly fell in love with the man of the house. Imran would return this affection. Sadly, there would come a day when the love for this canine would be turned off as suddenly and abruptly as the love for its owner.

After the initial arrangements were sorted, I immediately set myself the task of making life as comfortable as I could, and improving the house so it would befit a world-famous celebrity. I was told that we would announce the marriage within a week. The possibility of a *valima* on the container was discussed, but we both quickly dismissed the idea. That would be exceptionally cringeworthy, particularly at our age. The announcement would be made right there, from Bani Gala. I was acutely aware of my nephew Shoaib's wedding reception on the following Saturday, and didn't want to ruin it.

Being a house-proud woman, I wanted to make sure the house was presentable in time for the announcement. The house was literally and metaphorically falling apart. I threw away all the threadbare and torn towels and stocked the bathroom with shampoos, deodorants and face creams specifically for his needs. As I would breeze in and out of the bathroom, handing him his perfectly pressed shirt or deodorant, he would turn and say in a rather pensive tone, "I never knew the *sukh* [bliss] of marriage before".

"Why, did Jemima never look after the house?" I asked.

He would make a face and say, "Baby, she wasn't interested in much. Most of the day was spent sleeping. She missed the London parties. She hated the weather and the house too. The first two years were very difficult. She was initially happier when we moved into the house in E7, Islamabad, but not for very long. She had this dreadful temper, throwing things at me when she would get angry. Once, she tried to trip me over with her leg. Another time, she threw a phone at me. Once, she wouldn't stop swearing at me and I slapped her across the face. She went crying to her brother, who in turn told her to apologise to me. I wanted to divorce her right there and then but Annabelle talked me out of it. Another time, as she became aggressive with me, I lifted my hand in self-defence and broke her arm. She was walking around with her arm in a plaster after that". He laughed as he said that, as if it were a hilarious memory.

I listened to his rant quite shocked. It was understandable that a young girl from high society could not be expected to live happily in a domineering joint family system. Being married to a much older man who expected a traditional stay-at-home wife was bad enough, but to be slapped and have bones broken was unforgivable.

"Imran, it's not funny. That's abuse! You broke her bone!"

"No, it was an accident. I merely lifted my hand and it broke".

"Imran, I've been hit too. But to break a bone requires a lot of force and aggression".

"But what could I do? She was very rude and insulting, especially after she inherited the money, she would not listen and was condescending all the time".

"Imran, that's not building my confidence in you. Abuse is abuse. The other person provoking you is no excuse. It's not right or normal to hit others".

"Yes, but I was a very angry young man. I used to chase after people with bats in my cricketing years. I've mellowed down with the years. Learned to control my temper".

"*Ahaan* [sure]," I said, unconvinced.

"But you have nothing to worry about my *thabro* [chubby face] ...you smile and make everything OK. You know, on days that I was so fed up of that fucking *dharna*, I would scan the crowd and then I would see your face. It shone in the crowd like a 100-watt bulb. I remembered what my grandmother said after returning from the wedding event of my *mamoon* [uncle] with my Bengali *mumani* [aunt]. She said among their dark-skinned women, our women were shining like light bulbs. And that's what you were, in your white *chadar* with your face shining bright with your beautiful smile".

"Yes, and you made it so obvious to all watching. Everyone knew that you were looking at me," I replied to this rather disturbing racist comment.

"I never thought I would find love like this. You've got me addicted to you. I can't go back to my harem now. This is what love feels like. I just want to be alone with you. The last *Eid* we spent together was the best *Eid* I've ever had, with just you, me and your kids around. I want to have a son with you straight away, but you must promise only to speak in Urdu and Pashto to him".

"Imran, I am 42, it's a bit old for having a baby. I don't think it's safe at this age".

"Of course you can. I even discussed it with Annabelle. She says she had all hers after she turned 40".

And that was very much the Imran I knew. Romantic, complimentary and dreamy-eyed. He not only appreciated each and every detail of the changes I was bringing into the house, but also reciprocated my care. He started out by putting a dry towel for me outside the shower cubicle. I had told Imran how my father after his *Fajr* prayers would always bring fragrant *motiya* flowers for my mum and put them on her bedside. Imran listened, and as I would step out of the bathroom in the morning, I would be greeted by hand-picked roses and fragrant magnolias on my bedside and my pillow, laid out by Imran. It brought tears to my eyes. Even now, it brings a smile to my face, despite all that followed. He made me love him when I thought it wasn't possible for me to love anymore.

I would wake up for *Fajr* and read the news on my phone till 7am, when Inu would get up for school. Imran would wake up well after nine. He was a creature of habit. Every morning, he would pick up the intercom and order tea and carrot juice for himself, and I would wait for him to ask me. "Baby, chai for you?" It set the tone for the rest of the day. If he didn't ask me, it meant he was upset with me. He could stay sulking for days on end. But for the most part, our marital life was the picture of togetherness. At night, even when I had been awake up for hours, I wouldn't move so that his sleep would not be disturbed. Most nights, he clung to me like a child holds a mother. Initially, I couldn't believe how loving his tone and words were. It was hard to believe that this was the same man who had a reputation of being arrogant and aggressive in public. The love in his voice never failed to amaze me.

§

From October to December, there were very few times where Imran lost his temper with me. These were the days when he made an effort to stay clean too. It resulted in long, unexplained depressive episodes, but most mornings were fun. Everyone knew we were married. It had been discussed in the Cabinet on the Monday after the ceremony. I had moved in. Imran was happy. But some others were clearly not.

As soon as the *nikkah* was pronounced, the favourite anchor of the nation, Dr Shahid Masood, started conducting hour-long programmes on my marriage. He described me as Delilah, a honey trap, even Monica Lewinsky. Privately, he would quiz my content producer about the marriage. I was naturally outraged that there was no respect being shown to Imran's wife. When I asked Imran to address the issue, he made a feeble call to his friend in Dubai, Imran Chaudhry, describing me as a decent woman who should not be attacked this way. But the attacks continued.

I got so angry at these rude programs that I labelled the anchor 'a fly waiting to be swatted', but he didn't understand the insult or stop. Imran laughed it off in private, saying that the anchor had come to him in the container and told him a bizarre story that I was a spy for MI6 who had infiltrated the Taliban in Quetta, and that the British High Commissioner, Phil Barton, had come to my rescue. Imran would call him a man who had a habit of lying. Apparently, exactly a month after the Taliban story, Dr Shahid announced to Imran that my first husband and he had been colleagues in Dublin, and he'd known me as a housewife since then. I simply said, "Imran, tell your friends to stick to one story. Either I was a housewife or a secret agent. Besides, I have never even been to Dublin". Imran just laughed at the mad stories.

Imran wasn't interested in quashing the rumour-mongers. He was more focused on trying to get me to eat everything he liked. Like a doting parent, he would insist that I have fruit like he did at breakfast. Before long, I was having an identical breakfast to him: tea mixed with psyllium and honey to sweeten; fresh fruit and homemade yoghurt with two half-boiled eggs. I introduced freshly baked croissants on Sundays, and wholemeal bread on alternate days, as he would have hardly any carbs. I also changed the milk from buffalo to goat milk to bring his cholesterol down. When I married him, his LDL was 171 (which is quite unhealthy). By the following summer, it had come down to 138.

To prevent heart disease and cholesterol issues, Samina *baji* had suggested a teaspoon of homemade almond cordial, and I would also ensure he had a teaspoon of ground *Ajwa* (date seed powder) in the morning, according to *Sunnah* (practices of the Holy Prophet, PBUH).

Many have attributed the decline of civility in the political landscape to Imran. He had set the trend for rude name-calling of political opponents. He would refer to the Sharifs as *gunjas*, a derogatory term for baldness. One day, I walked into the bedroom to catch him massaging his head methodically. Immediately concerned, I asked if he had a headache, and volunteered to massage his head for him. He casually said that he was just doing exercises his osteopath had suggested after his fall. Imran could always come up with stories to hide the facts. Absurd as this explanation sounds, I believed him. In fact, I got more concerned. As I was cleaning the drawers one day for leftover offensive items, I discovered post-hair implant care leaflets. Imran had been following the post-care advice of massaging follicles according to The Hair Institute. I never told him that I discovered this, but began to massage fresh aloe vera pulp from plant leaves into his scalp every morning as he read his messages, to stimulate hair growth and shine. I would apply it on his nose too, to avoid his skin peeling, as he loved sunbathing.

Imran would impatiently wait for me to get ready for the morning walk. He would stick to the same routine every day and was repetitive with his stories too. Every morning for almost a year I heard the same stories, jokes and clichés.

"There was nothing here when I first arrived. NOTHING. I chose and planted every tree myself".

It was an impressive monologue he had crafted. The kids also memorised the narrative of the morning walk, and would do very good impressions of him. Sahir and Inaya picked up on his claim to have built his political party from nothing, and would regularly imitate his low drawl, and suddenly burst out with 'FOR TWENTY YEARS, I STRUGGLED,' with unnerving accuracy.

The morning walk would start from the edge of the swimming pool at the foot of the garden area. He would curse at the view that had been 'destroyed' by the houses of poor people who had moved into the area at the bottom of the hills. He called them 'the matchboxes'. We would go down the steps and he would complement my gorgeous dog, while belittling the local ones that people had gifted him. He hated one of them in particular; the one we had rescued with his ears cut off. We would then walk down to the fruit trees to pick guavas. It was a vast expanse where, every so often, hundreds of fruit trees were sent for plantation. This was mainly down to Amir Kiyani, the man behind the debacle of the PTI's Rawalpindi local body results.

Imran was warned by several people (including me) of the mishandling tickets, and of money changing hands in Rawalpindi. But he paid no attention until the day PTI was wiped out in the area. They had suffered a humiliating defeat only because of the tickets being sold locally for peanuts. Imran noticed the disappointment on my face, and picked up the phone to shout his head off at Amir Kiyani. But by then it was just spilt milk. Amir never lost his position in the party. These people had no regard for the way things should be, or the responsibilities they were ignoring. They had no time to cater to anyone but themselves. This man ended up getting a road paved to his plot in the Margalla Mountains. A year later, a local estate agent would show me this road, and I would sit down and weep. I'd just been to see village right next to this place where women died in labour every day because there was no road.

Our walk would continue down into the overgrown jungle all around the property. Imran would stop at the same three spots every day and repeat the same phrases. He would have made one hell of a tour guide. On the first stop, he would turn back to look at the house, and the record would begin playing: "You know, I did this all by myself. There was nothing here when I first arrived. Suleiman used to call it a pile of dirt but I turned it around to this paradise it is today..."

We would work our way through the overgrown areas at the extremities of the estate, and then stop at the rocks on the cliff-edge. There was a large, central rock that was dubbed 'Conference Rock', where he would sit with his arms around me, enjoying the sun. I would constantly worry about the little dogs slipping from the cliff-edge but he would hold me back and say, "If a dog is stupid enough to fall, it deserves to die".

Besides my worry for the dogs, these were beautiful moments and I cherished them. He would often talk about his future as Prime Minister. During the *dharna*, whenever he had renewed hope, he would paint a scene of him standing up there, giving the victory speech.

"Baby, you will be down there smiling up at me, with your beautiful face lit up like a bulb".

I knew it wasn't happening. It was all over as we had predicted, but I didn't have the heart to ever say that after we got married. I assured him that I would have a green silk suit ready, which I did later pull out for his NA-246 (Karachi) campaigning. I would gently and repeatedly give the example of Modi, the Indian Prime Minister, who was Chief Minister of Gujarat for a decade, and then elected to the top job because his seemingly strong governance record, despite all the other negative baggage.

As the months progressed, and the complaints against his CM, Pervez Khattak, piled up by the minute, we all tried to warn Imran that this would be disastrous for the party and KP. The ideological supporters, including myself, couldn't understand why Imran had chosen this man. I suggested we move to my mother's house in Peshawar and Imran take more interest in the running of the province. Many like myself felt that a team of conscientious people could get work done very quickly in KP if Imran wanted it to happen. But Imran could see no wrong in Pervez. Imran had a grovelling attitude to the Chief Minister. Pervez behaved like the boss even in our home. He would saunter in and light a cigarette like he owned the place. Imran was totally in awe of him. This hero-worship had begun at Aitchison School, where Pervez Khattak was a 'full blazer' (a big deal at Aitchison) because of his sporting talents and (according to Imran) an extremely good-looking man. The most common rumour in PTI circles was of the Chief Minister's fondness for weed; the reason for his physique and lazy 'don't give a fuck' attitude. I only saw that the Chief Minister wouldn't eat much, but couldn't stop heaping sugar into his tea. When I shared the gossip of the '*Charsi*' nickname the CM had earned and asked if it was true, Imran merely giggled in agreement.

The morning walk would end with Imran climbing onto a square raised platform from where one could see for miles. He would admire his home again and start the verbal bashing of his sisters. This daily vitriol would increase after the announcement of our marriage, when he found out that Rubina had started building her own home right outside his gate to display her annoyance at the marriage. He would stand there, look at it, and start off about how unreasonable and insane his two older sisters were. He would recall how they drove Jemima mad, and he eventually moved to Islamabad to give his young wife some relief from the joint family system.

Imran described Rubina as a bitter spinster who hadn't been married because of the manipulation of a close relative. She had apparently suffered because of his arrival. The birth of a son was the only way a woman would gain respect in the Niazi family, so Imran's mother had finally 'succeeded' when he was born, to the detriment of his sisters. That favouritism meant a lifelong bitter relationship with the older sisters. Rubina bullied Imran for much of his life, ironically, for his looks and lack of intellect. Apparently the family had worried about him because he was a bit of dunce. Rubina may have forgiven him for stealing the family's attention but Imran had harboured a resentment, and had labelled her a mad woman.

The words the siblings used for each other were simply shocking. Imran would often make fun of Aleema and her political aspirations. "*Waddi ayi Fatima Jinnah* [She thinks she is bloody Fatima Jinnah]". It may have been true but it sounded cruel coming from a brother. In front of Imran, Aleema had said quite clearly to me, "He is not a brother to me. He is a commodity. We have to get where we want with him. So I don't think of him like a sister would".

The older two spent their time travelling and socializing. Even though Aleema was married, she chose not to live in the hut her husband had made at the foot of Imran's winding drive. She lived at her brother's home. Her children were also in Imran's house. I thought it was what Imran liked. It seemed quite a nice and natural arrangement. Imran would chuckle at what he believed was the biggest blessing of our marriage: that he had his home back. He said that the house had been completely taken over by friends and family. He loved finally being left alone to enjoy his piece of paradise.

The youngest, Uzma, was the one he liked best. Of all the people that he talked about, she escaped with the least criticism. He thought that she was an irresponsible mother for abandoning her young boys to go off on endless religious preaching expeditions. But he didn't mind her much as a person. He didn't mention Rani much, except that she had no mind of her own. Apparently, Rani did what Aleema dictated. I already knew this to be true. The driver, Safeer, had handed me a phone during the *dharna* in September and asked me to change the settings. I didn't know whose phone it was. It was open on a text from Aleema with the highest font setting, and read, "*Haram* Khan is here looking victorious, and the PTI girls have sat her in the front row".

It was certainly no accident that I was given the phone. As I returned it, Safeer informed me that it was Rani's. When I told Imran about Aleema's text, he laughed loudly, exclaiming, "I don't call her Hitler for nothing". It shocked me because my brother was such a gentle being who had no ability to say anything nasty about any woman, especially his own sister. Even when we disagreed, we wouldn't resort to such distasteful comments, so it was certainly a shock to hear them from Imran. Imran went onto tell me that Aleema felt it was her duty to dictate to everyone. She would not let Imran give his home, Zaman Park, legally to Rani. She had been living in it since her separation from her husband, Hafizullah Niazi. Rani had made Zaman Park her home following Imran and Hafizullah's dispute, which was over the NA72-Mianwali ticket not being given to Hafizullah's brother, Inamullah Niazi. Inamullah Niazi had left PMLN to join PTI in 2011 on the promise of this ticket. Imran broke this promise.

With his daily rant over, Imran would end our walk near the front gate and then turn back. He would make fun of my lack of knowledge of the local trees the entire way. He took pleasure in educating me on their names and the flowers they bore. He had promised to take me to the plains of Deosai for a romantic getaway when the flowers bloomed in August. He would remind me daily of how much he wanted to take me there. But we never did reach that promised land together.

On these walks, we would talk in detail about our future together, and his plans for the property. Imran wanted to build a little chateau-style summerhouse facing Rawal Lake, just above the strawberry and lavender fields I had planned. On the top of the main home, he wanted a new bedroom for us, with full-length glass windows giving a 360° view of the landscape. On almost a daily basis, I would hear the same words from him: "Now this is your home baby. Do what you want to it". But as he slept at night, I would look up at the ceiling with the uneasy feeling that it was not my home. I was the outsider, and the real owner of the home was thousands of miles away, but watching every breath I took.

Meanwhile the campaign against me on social media was gathering strength. To my surprise, following my own complaints my Facebook account was shut down. I contacted the head of Federal Investigation Agency. Despite formal complaints, no action was taken. Pakistan Telecom Authority also appeared to be powerless. A journalist, Gul Bukhari, stepped forward to help me, but I was already Imran's wife and this journalist was said to have PMLN loyalties. I didn't accept her help, instead turning to my husband, who asked me to meet one of his star hackers. His party was famous for its expertise and dominance of social media, but the fact that they had a team of hackers was news to me. While Imran was at a *jalsa* in Multan, I met up with this rather shifty young man in a coffee shop. But instead of helping me, he asked for more details about myself, and showed me a complete file created on me.

He followed the children and I to the car, and his prying style made us very uncomfortable. As I walked down the stairs, with him following behind, I heard another boy whisper to him, "So, has the *nikkah* happened?" I turned around sharply and questioned him. He shrugged it off by saying, "Oh, just a friend asking about my marriage". I put two and two together. I made some enquiries and found out that this chap seemed to be working on the direction of Aleema's sons. But crucially, he was going to be of no help to me. I could do nothing but bear the brunt of the many social media attacks that were to come.

One of the most disgusting rumours started when we first got married; that I had become pregnant and was blackmailing Imran into marriage. Of course, there was no truth in this malicious rumour whatsoever. Imran had already expressed a deep desire to have a child with me, but the age factor terrified me.

God knows what is best for us, even if we can't see it clearly.

§

I ended up learning a lot of concerning things through Imran. The more I learned about his past and his acquaintances, the more out of place I felt. Between rich, cunning operatives like Arif Naqvi and JKT, feudal lords like Shah Mehmood, powerful and influential families like the Goldsmiths, and a whole host of depraved people from Imran's cricketing past, I struggled to find my role. It's difficult to fit in amongst that kind of crowd when your origins are so different. I was just a committed journalist who also wanted to be a good mother and partner. At the core of it, that's all I was. For all the talk of me being a very ambitious person, I was just trying to do the best I possibly could, and, in time, possibly do something for my homeland and for KP. What I would learn about Imran and the people in his life would make me realise just how small my thinking was, and how naïve I was.

Imran told me that he'd actually been interested in Jemima's older half-sister, and was friendly with the father. The young Jemima, however, was apparently so besotted with him that she came down for a holiday in the Salt Lake Region on his invitation. Zak, his partner-in-crime, accompanied them with another woman. The two couples went on an expedition to explore the area. Imran would laugh about how he was fooled by her earnestness. He described how they walked until they reached a poor man's hut and Jemima had emphatically declared that she would be happy in a hut like that if she was with him.

I thought it was a bit cruel; a girl that young could have meant it sincerely without realising what she was promising. According to Imran, she'd only had one boyfriend before him. I didn't understand why he was so keen on talking about his ex-wife or his conquests all the time. It had nothing to do with me and certainly did not interest me. He, however, would frequently compare. From her sloppy table manners to her lack of interest in housekeeping, it was a constant badmouthing of her and praising of me. It was ironic, as I wondered how somebody could possibly eat worse than him. It reminded me of my first husband. Both Imran and Ijaz would tell me in great detail of the unhygienic habits of their previous partners, as well as taking great pleasure in torturing me with their own sloppiness. Both also had very unhygienic toilet habits. For a hygiene freak like me, it meant cleaning up after every use. Both loved my attention to personal hygiene and, like Mowgli from the *Jungle Book*, were in awe of how I never smelled bad. Imran was completely unaware of basic hygiene as prescribed for Muslims. No amount of coaxing could get him to follow basic principles, such as hair removal, method of ablutions, etc, according to *Sunnah*. Ijaz had better personal hygiene than Imran, but the bathroom still needed heavy disinfecting after use.

I gently tried to introduce forks for salad, and urged Imran not to spit back in his plate. He didn't mind me gently laying a napkin on his knee. I suppose he enjoyed the mothering. Some days, I would stand in front of the door and not let him leave until he shampooed his hair properly before letting him go for an interview. He would always listen. From my young nephew who adored him to the lady who did my hair, everyone volunteered advice and took an interest in his appearance. He would ask adorably for advice on how to use the face creams and eye gels that I would get for him.

Imran's spirits rapidly started evaporating after November 30th. He must have been given renewed hope, but as December drew in, depression did too. Imran was already fed up of the *dharna*, and the cold nights didn't help. There were only a handful of people left. He wanted out so badly. It was getting very difficult for his people to even get him to go every evening. He would leave very late and come home early. My program would finish at 11pm and his texts would start pouring in, asking where I was and how long it would take me to get there. Every night, it was the same routine.

On the morning of the 16th, the Army Public School Peshawar Massacre happened: 49 killed, including 132 children, some as young as eight, mown down by six gunmen. I got the call just as I was about to give a lecture on media and ethics in the Islamic University. My contact in Peshawar told me that the incident was so horrific that they were only releasing the news bit by bit. As I made my way to the rostrum the hostility was clear on the faces of the journalists from GEO at the event. They were against what they saw as my husband's extremely undemocratic stance. But I didn't care about them. I was literally shaking, and instead of making a speech I merely said, "Please let's pray for the departed souls". My mind was whirling. I kept thinking, 'Why now? And how could something this dreadful happen inside a cantonment area?' The students and guests were not yet fully aware of the scale of the tragedy.

I couldn't bring myself to look at the images of the dead bodies or the bloody scene of the school auditorium, so much like the Russian school incident at Beslan. In fact, not only did this brutality appear to be inspired by that previous horror, but the way the footage was subsequently shared was almost identical. I remembered how every image of Beslan was imprinted in our memory. It was not only the killing itself, but the shared images of the tragedy that spread terror. The children were all I could think about. I couldn't even imagine what the parents must be going through. I was asked to do a live transmission in the afternoon and could barely keep myself together. I flew to Karachi in the evening instead of going to APS. I had always been one to be the first to rush to the scene, but I bailed out on this one. Most journalists who covered the event were traumatised for months afterwards. My correspondent gave me a very disturbing minute-to-minute picture off-camera. But when we cut to him in the live transmission, the bosses would not allow him to give us the full picture and he was quickly pulled off-air. He was clearly saying something no one wanted to risk giving air time to.

As I reached the airport for my flight to Karachi, Imran texted me that he was flying out to Peshawar. The army had arranged for all politicians to fly out to the incident. That night, I did a live show with guests from Karachi. The shiny faces, taken from the Facebook accounts of those young boys killed in the auditorium, were enough to rip my heart into pieces. The stress on my face couldn't be covered by makeup. I may not sit and cry in private or shed tears in public but my face becomes visibly puffy. When unhappy, I immediately look much older. I sat up all night in my hotel bedroom unable to sleep. The following morning, I interviewed Pervez Musharraf. It was yet another pointless political interview of a heavyweight personality. I decided I did not want to do this anymore. It was to be my last political show for a long time.

As I returned to Bani Gala, the last thing I wanted was to host a wedding celebration. My children had come over for the winter holidays and we'd been planning a small wedding party. I'd asked my nephew and a close friend to come over to Pakistan for Christmas, hinting that there could be a surprise they may not want to miss. But with this horrific APS news, I decided to abandon all plans. My immediate thought, like that of every other parent in Pakistan, was not to send my own little one to school.

My head was heavy. I had not slept at all. I had spent the night looking at the selfies of the young boys who had died. As I returned home and carried my dead weight into the bedroom, I saw Imran walking outside. He seemed relaxed and happy.

"Baby, the *dharna* is over. Thank God!"

I will never forget the look on his face. In that split second, I wondered, 'Have I married a man who thinks of people as collateral?' I quickly suppressed the thought. "But Imran, it's the most dreadful news ever!"

In a flash, his expression changed to a serious one. "Oh yes, it's dreadful! They showed it to us all, the bodies all piled up on top of each other".

And that was pretty much it. Imran's attention quickly turned back to the more important things in his mind, like our wedding announcement. Just before APS, the news of our marriage had been picking up steam. It had become difficult for me to face colleagues and staff at work. Imran, Awn and I were discussing how to announce the marriage. A *valima* ceremony on the container was suggested again, which we both dismissed. We discussed guest lists. Imran wanted it very small. He was keen not to invite anyone from PTI but we counted all his immediate family. It was still sixty people. He seemed excited about the prospect of a garden party. He seemed so in love. These were also happy times for Awn, who was buzzing with excitement like an old aunt.

The dogs in our house had other priorities. The two big alpha males would always fight, and I ended up being bit one morning in December as I tried to keep them apart. Imran quickly called the head of SKMT to ask how many injections I should have. This might seem trivial, but for Imran to do that for someone was extremely out of character. You could be bleeding out in front of him and he still might walk straight past (as he would later do with Sahir). Empathy was never his strong suit, but I saw him genuinely worry about me. There were moments where it seemed like my wellbeing mattered more than anything else in the world to him.

Imran wouldn't allow me to travel too far, deeming it unsafe. Since the marriage hadn't been declared, security cover had to be covertly provided. His personal driver, Safeer, and guard, Ayub, were on duty to pick me up and drop me, but I carried on driving myself out of work to avoid raising suspicion. I later found that I'd been followed on bikes by intelligence agents, and the car had been photographed going in and out of Bani Gala. Post-APS, the marriage hum became an unavoidable noise.

The marriage news was finally confirmed because of a leak by a girl who was an employee of the ISPR. She had suddenly arrived to work for me as a volunteer researcher while I was at PTV in August. Post-APS in December she tweeted the news of our wedding and, within a few minutes, I received a congratulatory text from the assistant to the Director General of the ISPR, Colonel Shafiq. I showed it to Imran, who said nothing. I sent a curt reply to the Colonel suggesting that he should wait for an official announcement from me.

The *Daily Mail* also announced on the 31st of December that the marriage had already taken place. I kept quiet on Twitter following my husband's instructions. Imran, on the other hand, decided to make a grand move, and tweeted: "The reports of my marriage are greatly exaggerated!". He had discussed it with my kids and I. We'd all insisted it was a bad idea, but he did it anyway. At the time, I thought it was just something he thought was funny or cool and rolled my eyes at the Mark Twain inspired idea. It did not occur to me at the time that Imran was not a particularly literary guy. In retrospect, I am convinced he was told to get out of the marriage in December, and was delaying owning up to having already gone through with it because of this pressure. He had travelled to London one final time to talk to his sons. He told me he was going to break the news to them face-to-face. It was obvious he'd been lying to his kids and Jemima about the marriage so far. His sisters were also not entirely sure whether I had just moved in or a *nikkah* had actually happened.

The truth would come out soon though. I wasn't used to living under such pretences but had hope that everything would soon change for the better. I was in for one hell of a shock.

Chapter 17

'Your wedding day is the most special day of your life'. It's a statement that is often repeated, and it is certainly ingrained in the minds of many young women all over the world. Millions of women ruin the intimate moment of the pledging of their love because they are under such pressure to create a perfect (looking) day. The designing of this perfect dream wedding centres around expensive dresses, big functions and elaborate flower displays.

Not only was I not given any time to plan the most anticipated wedding of the year, but I was also clear in my mind that I must lead by example. The tradition of investing huge amounts of time, energy, or money in the planning of the wedding day must be broken. As luck would have it, despite technically having plenty of time available (and more than one window of opportunity) with which to plan a wedding look, I was never able to prepare for an actual day. I wasn't even told when our 'public' wedding day would be. It was almost an elopement of sorts, or a court marriage, when, after months of his pursuit, we finally tied the knot on the 31st of October 2014. The next step would be a very delayed public announcement on the 8th of January, which was little more than a rushed photo shoot.

My kids had literally just flown back to the UK for studies and exams, under the impression that the façade would continue for some time yet. But just one week after tweeting that reports of his marriage had been greatly exaggerated and making me an accessory to his lie, Imran made the move. He gave me less than two days to get ready for the announcement. On the way back from work, I stopped in Blue Area with Awn to select a brocade for Imran's *sherwani* (Pakistani tailcoat). In the florescent light, it appeared more beige than golden. I'm useless with colour recognition. The tailor followed and nervously took the measurements of the groom. Yousaf and Awn, in true hero-worshipping fashion, suggested a slim contemporary fitting to the tailor to make Imran look 'fit'.

I picked up an off-the-rack outfit from Karma and asked for minor alterations. There wasn't time to get a *dupatta* to match the dress. If anyone were to look closely, they'd see it wasn't the same as the fabric of the *achkan* (dress). It was a look that is associated with old Muslim Turkish heritage. I intentionally chose not to wear red.

A makeup artist and a hairstylist were brought to me by Awn. We had just met, and it was a nerve-wracking experience for them. I gently guided them through a fresh and very simple look. The jewellery was loaned for the day as I didn't have any time to buy any. I never really cared to spend money on jewellery anyway, which was ideal since I would never receive anything of the sort from Imran. He kept saying that his mother had kept gold on the condition that his bride was a Muslim Pakistani, but his first wife had been Jewish and white. He never gave it to Jemima. The thought was sweet but I knew his sisters better than him by then. I assured him that I was past the age of wearing gold. But I did make it clear what I really wanted. With Allah as my witness, I asked him to work towards making KP a model province.

The day came. There was media everywhere. I had not invited anyone from my family. Contrary to media reports, my mother and sister were not present at the *nikkah*. The only ones there from my family were Inaya and Yousaf. I told my sister on the day and she arrived later that evening to congratulate us. My personal assistant, my makeup lady and two of my crew members arrived to help with the arrangements. My dear, supportive friend Maria was also there, along with her friend Lubna, who had arranged the jewellery. And from Imran's side, the original two witnesses, Zakir and Awn, were both present.

The media had been camped outside since the early hours, just for a glimpse of us. Imran got ready and popped his head in through the door.

"*Challo* [Come on], let's do this".

He mingled happily with everyone. He seemed fine, but between then and the time that I arrived in the drawing room for the official photos his mood had changed. The young photographer (who only found out what he was doing when he arrived at the house) was at his wit's end trying to get a decent photograph. I had warned him that it would be hard as I would not pose, but it was Imran who wanted to get it over and done with as soon as possible. He wasn't smiling, and was complaining about the collar being too tight.

The *Moulvi* did a rather Western-inspired ritual, and had even brought gold rings for us to exchange. That made Imran smile. The initial pictures that were released to media were not actually from the photographer, but were candid shots taken on Awn's phone and sent to his man on the outside, who had been promised the first photo. It was of me holding my hands up, asking Awn to give me a minute to adjust my dress that was too loose for me. And the iconic happy picture of the beaming bride was actually me looking up at balloons entangled in the candelabra. Imran wanted to get it done quickly so he could get out of the tight sherwani. Pictures do lie. Pictures can be used to perpetuate lies, too. And we all lie for pictures.

The whole process took less than fifteen minutes from start to finish. The actual photographer, Bilal, had managed to get only a couple of useable shots, which were later released. We both pleaded with Imran to give us a few more minutes, just for a few private photos. He was in no mood. I took him aside and whispered, "Imran, I want one of us together, for me". I had never had a romantic picture of myself with any man all my life. I wanted a special memory. He rebuked me harshly and tears welled up in my eyes. He saw, turned on his heel, and left.

A few minutes later, he re-emerged in shabby bottoms and a sports shirt. He sat and ate the Pashtun-style lunch with the guests, happy again. I posed alone for the photographer for two more pictures before joining the guests. I could see he felt guilty but it was too late. Embarrassed, he went down to the secretariat. Awn suggested we both go down to give the crowd a glimpse. I was in no mood. I could sense Imran had external pressures. He was being made to feel guilty. I spent the rest of the evening alone with my guests.

Imran came back much later in the evening. My sister and her husband had arrived to wish us well. He sat with them and started praising me: "It was so well received. You know, this was all because of Reham. Everyone loved it. The whole country is in celebration. If it had been me, I would have just put out a selfie. Baby, well done! Huge response. The supporters loved it". It was a Bollywood-like coverage of the new love story.

He was thrilled with the response. The media had been hungry for content and the audience needed something to smile about. Despite the awful timing of the announcement, the followers and the general public were happy. There were celebrations across Pakistan. In a country where there is so much bloodshed and bad news, there are few reasons to celebrate. Pakistanis fell in love with us. It was a story of hope for so many: the simple look, the simple ceremony, the second marriage; the whole package just sent a message of positive change. For months, the look would be copied. It set a healthy example that people were happy to follow.

I left the guests for a few minutes to go to the bedroom to pray and he followed. "Why are you so quiet?" he asked

"Imran, all I wanted was one keepsake for myself. I wanted a memory and you couldn't give that to me. Was it too much to ask?"

"Oh fuck off!!!"

I was thunderstruck. Imran had never spoken to me like that before. He disappeared into the bathroom. I was acutely aware of the guests next-door in Inaya's room. I left the room in shock.

In the days that followed, he would flip between very sweet and extremely cold. Pictures of the wedding had not been well-received in London, he told me. A dirty campaign had started on social media, with my stomach circled to suggest that the reason for the marriage was an unplanned pregnancy. I knew his family was behind it but I said nothing to him. I never mentioned Jemima or Aleema.

Soon after the wedding was announced, there was a day when I noticed Imran in a particularly quiet and withdrawn mood. At first, he mentioned casually that his older sister Rubina had once again sent him her signature long email. This time, the target was my 11-year-old daughter and her alleged Twitter account. Rubina found it objectionable, and questioned the parenting of the woman Imran had married. When I responded that it was not only a fake account, but that targeting a child was rather petty, he agreed. But then he started on my choice of clothing in the UK, and that even his white ex-girlfriends found it un-Islamic. He said that he had been receiving emails demanding to know how he could have accepted a woman like me.

When I tried to discuss this bizarre list of silly accusations, he just walked out in a rage. He had a habit of going off into a non-verbal sort of frustration and then storming out. It would be followed by days of cold silence. No matter how I tried, he would close up and not respond to any attempts at conversation. Only days later would I finally be told what the trigger had been and who had prompted him to behave in such a way. I ignored it all. There were bigger problems facing our people than such petty family issues. After all, this was not a cheap soap opera about in-laws torturing the new wife...or was it? I assumed that they would all settle down.

My brother was only twenty-four years old when he got married, and the girl was hardly twenty. As he was the only son, we expected my mother to be too possessive and worried about the new addition to the family. My sister sat me down and made me promise that we would always take my sister-in-law's side, and never encourage my mother (or anyone) to indulge in backbiting. Not only did we keep our promise but my mother ended up being as fond of her daughter-law as she was of her own daughters.

In my first marriage, although things were very difficult with my husband, I was given hardly any trouble by my in-laws. Despite having the reputation of an angry man and an awful husband, my father-in-law was never harsh with me. In fact, the family advised my husband to change *his* behaviour. The marriage to Imran was, of course, a completely different story. He was not a brother or a father, but a commodity to be used. I had unknowingly disrupted the moneymaking and the fundraising misappropriations carried on in his name, not to mention the political inheritance. They were worried about the possibility of my presence being further cemented by the arrival of a child. Their brother's happiness was irrelevant; they could not risk a new child.

When Imran had returned from his trip to London at Christmas, he looked as if he had aged a few years. He sat down and told me bluntly that the news of our marriage had not been welcomed. Suleiman had threatened Imran, saying that if he ever had a child with me, he would never see his father again. It didn't matter to me what they said to him as I wasn't mentally prepared to have another baby at forty-two anyway, but it hurt me that Imran was telling me this without remotely caring how it would make me feel.

I said nothing. He went on to say that Qasim had clearly been brainwashed by Aleema, and had blurted out, "*Abba, phupho* says she will ruin your politics". Imran said Jemima had also screamed at him, blaming him for not caring that Suleiman had A2 exams in the summer, and saying that he was a selfish parent for disturbing the child. I said nothing. I was too disheartened to even ask what Imran had said in response. It's not what others think of you that hurts. It's when those you think are your own can sit and hear it being said without putting up any kind of defence. To me, it didn't matter what his ex thought, or what the world thought. I only needed him to be mine.

On the morning of the *valima* however, Imran was bouncy and happy as could be. He had been getting a lot of media publicity, and the country seemed to love the new National *Bhabhi*. A few critics picked on him for not smiling enough. To be fair, we had been married for two months now and it was hard to keep pretending we'd just got married. For the *valima*, he insisted on driving to the venue himself, and my sister was amazed that my new celebrity husband was so funny and charming. I had no idea where the lunch would be. All I had said was that I would prefer it to be with the poor. On the morning, I found out it was at Mufti Saeed's *madrasa*. I had no idea who Mufti Saeed was or why Imran had chosen him to pronounce the marriage. The choice of host and venue was attributed to me, even though I had no part in the decision-making. I also learned that Mufti Saeed's name had been put on the list of possible additions to the core committee of the party since March. I was blamed for this too. The troublemakers had already started.

The misinformation was everywhere. Even foreign publications used suggestive language like 'Reham wore a purple *abaya* [Saudi *burqa*] to the madrassa', implying I had Saudi loyalties. It had actually been a rather revealing number from Monica Couture, made for Lahori high society. I had wrapped a huge *dupatta* around me to stay covered. It had been a last-minute selection, as I hadn't been given any time to plan anything (again). In true Bollywood fashion, I only wore one earring. No one noticed.

It was mad when we got there. An utter mob. The crowd and media were desperate to get a glimpse of the new couple. They had been lining up outside the home and venue for hours to see us together for the first time. It was calmer inside as only an official photographer was allowed entry. As we emerged from the school after the lunch, the journalists forced their way in, desperate to get a soundbite. It was a scary experience for my youngest. In the frenzy, my daughter got pushed, and hit her head on an iron handrail. Her new stepdad simply told her that she would have to get used to it. Imran was in a happy mood all day; cracking jokes, driving very recklessly, and watching whether I was eating properly or not. This pattern continued throughout the marriage: we would have four good days, and then he would do something so inexplicable that it was hard to smile.

Before the news was made public, he had decided (without consulting me) that I would handle his media image. Although I was from the media, the idea wasn't particularly appealing to me. However, I did what I was told. I immediately started making sure he would read newspapers in the morning, and had summaries of news programs from the previous night delivered to the breakfast table. I discovered that, until the 30th of December, the tickers and program descriptions were edited in such a way that there were no mentions of me, even though they were constantly mentioning me in the news. I found this omission very odd.

I also discovered that no one was briefing Imran on the main issues of the day before his almost-daily TV interviews, which was why he frequently made foolish remarks. I once heard him accuse PMLN of rigging, claiming 43 presiding officers had been assigned to the constituency of PTI leader Hamid Khan. I texted him to inform him that the 43 presiding officers were in fact appointed by Hamid Khan, and criticised the idiot who had misinformed him. To this, he had simply replied, "See, this is why I need you". He admired my political sense, and made the fatal mistake of saying it aloud to many in his close circle, including Moby, Aleema and Jahangir Tareen. When surrounded by the intrigues, backstabbing and manipulative games of Bani Gala, it suddenly dawned on me how lucky I was to have a loyal bunch of people around me. I may not have a huge party apparatus, but those who worked for me demonstrated exemplary loyalty and support.

After the news of our marriage was out, I didn't have to hide away in the bedroom anymore. We would be sitting in the garden and Jahangir would walk in. I would leave them alone generally, but sometimes Imran and Jahangir would bitch about something or other with me. Jahangir and Awn used me like an errand boy to carry messages back and forth, or to convince Imran into attending an event. There were several distinct 'lobbies' within PTI itself, all wrestling for a measure of power and influence. The JKT lobby had access to the home, and the key figures were Pervez Khattak, Inam Akbar, Aleem Khan, Faraz Ahmed Chaudhry, and Awn. Chaudhry Sarwar was later added to this group, but found it difficult to cope with their lack of organisation and constant bickering.

The opposing lobby of Shah Mehmood Qureshi was weak, and had no access to Imran's home. Imran disliked Shah Mehmood and his wife immensely. His addition was only on the insistence of Aleema Khan. The Aleema, Moby and Shah Mehmood lobby was something Imran was forced to tolerate but the frictions were obvious to all. Of course, I had to bear the brunt of the daily rants. And there was another lobby which Imran was seemingly not conscious of. It was covertly and remotely led by Asad Umar, and the operatives on the ground were Shireen Mazari and Naeem ul Haq. Aneel Mussarat was also very close to this lobby. This lobby was not accorded the same respect JKT's was. The media community was well aware of Ms Mazari's impolite attitude, but once inside the home, I was stunned to discover the awful language used by my husband for and at this lady. It was beyond shocking. I tried my best to make him behave more appropriately towards her, but Imran was just too set in his ways.

Ironically, the woman and her daughter rewarded my efforts on their behalf with open attacks on me. Nevertheless, I just felt strongly that my husband should not demean or speak in a derogatory fashion to any woman, whether they liked me or not. But Imran simply responded with, "Oh come on! Shireen is hardly a woman".

§

Imran claimed that he made up his mind when he met my kids.

That was what he reiterated in our first TV interview together as Mr and Mrs Khan. We had just returned from the *valima* and I was still in my bridal outfit when I saw the anchor who would conduct this important interview. It was the man who had been exposed for hosting engineered shows years ago. I had been sent a video clip by a concerned overseas Pakistani PTI supporter. It showed leaked footage of a program by this anchor and another female presenter, which was meant to show Malik Riaz, the notorious land tycoon, in a positive light. This had become a huge scandal at the time but it appeared that Pakistani audiences had very short-term memories. Here he was, smoking away in the *gol kamra* (round room). He said hello in a familiar tone, as if we were friends, although I had never maintained a social contact with this anchor of notorious repute. I had appeared as a guest in two of his shows to the utter shock of my crew. They'd thought I had better sense than that. One of them was around the time I married Imran. All dinner invitations from the anchor had been declined before I got married to Imran. This anchor and I were not on a first-name basis as he claimed during the interview, much to my annoyance.

The host insisted I sit in on the show. I explained that Imran was reluctant but the man shrugged it off, saying, "Don't you worry about him. I will handle him". Sure enough, Imran was convinced and I was told that I would be on the show too. I had no idea what the questions would be but I did ask him to mention the designer who had sent the dress. In the interview, Imran praised me for my *Iman* (faith) and explained that he meant freedom from fear, and freedom from ego. He might have meant to win over voters as he jokingly added that he didn't think my *Iman* was as strong as his own, but he was about to find how uncompromising I could be over principles. My strong *Iman* would set us apart.

I was reluctant to sit in on this interview, but I couldn't have imagined what it would cause. I never would have thought that it had been arranged just to frame me. Imran was reluctant to have me join in but, on the insistence of the PTI mouthpiece, he relented. The first question was about who would be banned and shut out by me now that I had arrived in Bani Gala. I replied that the traditional, welcome approach at Bani Gala would continue. The second question was about IK's children, and the third was about the possibility of starting a family. I simply said that I now had two more sons, so we had no plans of expanding the family further.

The next question was about my political ambitions. I explained that I was offered a seat with the Conservatives in the UK but declined because I did not want to give up my job, and that nothing had changed. I felt that if I kept a normal job, it would mean we had an honest income, as well as serving as a good role model. The anchor asked IK what kind of public image he would expect from his wife, to which Imran responded, "I expect my wife to be how she is". Imran went onto justify his choice by saying, "I don't need to ask anyone. I'm 62 years old. I didn't need advice. Public opinion doesn't matter to me. I'm free to choose". It was pretty convincing.

The anchor then turned to me and probed further on how I would change myself or Imran. I responded that I knew who I was and that it would be immature to dictate to each other. The anchor continued, "Reham, you will be criticised at every juncture. How will you cope?"

It would seem like an open threat when I would see it again later on. But at the time, I was confident. "I don't care about criticism. It's not in my nature to get nervous," I replied. "However, I take my position very seriously, and since what unites us is that we both want the best for Pakistan, I do not foresee any major problems".

I said this and believed it. But time would tell that my husband and I were on two radically different paths. I thought my role was to serve Pakistan and those who had voted for him. He thought his role was to rule even those who were not prepared to vote for him. I wanted to offer personal sacrifice and Imran considered it his birthright to be made a leader. And to that end, he believed that whatever needed to be sacrificed should be sacrificed.

Imran continued giving his reasons for marrying me. He described me as an amazing mother and declared that he made up his mind to marry me after he met my children. He continued to heap praise on us, saying that was it difficult to raise three children single-handedly, and bringing up their excellent academic records and strong values. Imran went on to announce that he would never be unfaithful to me as the hurt caused by being unfaithful was a grave sin. He preached that one should not marry if one cannot carry it through. There were many grand, sweeping statements made throughout this bizarre interview.

The anchor pressed further to ask if I would help with the fundraising for his charities. Imran declared emphatically that I HAD to help, especially in SKMT Peshawar, his new project. I tactfully excused myself, saying that I had my own causes that I was passionate about and felt that there was already a competent team in place who did not need any help. I would always maintain a distance from all the charities. I never had so much as a guided tour of any of his SKMT hospitals or anything to do with the Imran Khan Foundation, let alone any real involvement or oversight.

Imran mentioned his first marriage and kids throughout the show. In the break, the host pointed out that Jemima had been mentioned by name four times. I dismissed this observation of the anchor as a father trying to appease the kids and the ex to maintain cordial relations. In any case, my husband's ex was far from the most surprising and concerning thing this anchor brought up.

The interview took a dark turn when the anchor then asked me about my experiences of domestic violence. I had never spoken about this or mentioned it in public. I wondered how he had learned about this. I said that after one dreadful experience, I was apprehensive when it came to my second marriage but had never spoken about domestic violence publicly as the other person was not in the public domain.

The following day, I would find an article published in the *Daily Mail.* My ex-husband was accusing me of maligning him. I immediately understood: the question about domestic violence had been meant to entrap me. There was no way Ijaz could have done this without some organised backing. I was a journalist and even I wouldn't have been able to get anything published in a newspaper that quickly.

All I wanted was to move forward. This creature was my past. Yet here he was again, interfering with my present. None of this was going to simply go away.

§

In the Willows, my first husband would attempt to 'correct' much of my 'corrupting' and supposedly Western behaviour. In Bani Gala, my 'Western' beliefs would be corrected again, in a different way. Settling into my new environment was complicated enough on the public front, but there was a layer to the personal side of things that I was completely unprepared for. I had heard the stories of Imran and his ways, and was certainly wary of the potential issues that might be carried forward from Imran's playboy past. But I certainly didn't expect to enter Hogwarts.

On a day in November, I'd walk into the bedroom to find my new husband lying naked on a white sheet, rubbing *kaali daal* (black lentils) all over himself. He laughed in embarrassment as he rubbed them on his genitalia. He then stood up and shook the lentils onto the sheet for Anwarzeb, the home help, to take away. I stood there in shock. Imran explained that Ahad, his brother-in-law, had brought a man with him who had recommended the treatment because he believed someone had done some black magic on Imran. I tried to explain to him that this was pretty ridiculous, but since we had been married only a few days, I didn't voice my opinions too strongly at this bizarre practice.

One day, soon after the public announcement, I reached the front door to find a penetrating, disgusting smell emanating from the depths of Bani Gala. I made my way to the garden where Imran was walking, and asked him about the smell. He said he couldn't smell anything and that I was imagining things. I started investigating and soon traced it to the kitchen. The kitchen staff sniggered and pointed to the back of the kitchen. Two pots were on the hob. The *kaali daal* episode had clearly been repeated. Like last time, the lentils were slow-cooked for 72 hours in two separate pots. Then they'd be thrown into the river. I marched back to find my husband and told him how the staff were making fun of these strange practices.

"Look, you are a leader. You talk about Islam in your speeches. Do you realise that this is un-Islamic and prohibited? It is *shirk* [taking someone as equivalent in power to Allah]".

He shrugged his shoulders. "It's just to make Ahad happy. He says once it's thrown in the river, I will throw up or bleed and the curse will go".

"What curse?!" I exclaimed. He shrugged, offering no explanation.

I thought it was a cover story initially. But as the months went by and I saw him reading silly self-help books, it gradually sunk in. Imran's superstitions lay deep. It was a way of life so far removed from the sort of family I belonged to. We were a family that would frown at palmistry and laugh at horoscopes, but here I was, married a man who literally dabbled in the occult. This was a man who'd blamed his confusion and mood swings on the *pir* while trying to woo me a year earlier. Imran had begged me for forgiveness, explaining that the *pir* had told him not to marry me. There had apparently been a mix up of my parents' names with the names of another woman (the *pir* had told him I was a woman who'd had a string of sexual partners, and, more shockingly, that these partners had been white). I didn't know what I found more bizarre, the reliance on a spiritual guide or the fact that these accusations were coming from a man with an utterly dreadful past himself. Of course the racism was another level entirely.

Apparently there was not only one *pir*, but a revolving door of them. A new female *pir* was introduced to him by Awn in 2014. This allegiance was about to take Imran to another level of absurdity. It didn't stop at black lentil magic and *Taweez*. I was about to find out that my husband believed in a whole host of crazy things that were beyond any logical or rational human.

While my husband went about dabbling in the occult, I tried to focus on true spirituality. Imran had promised to take me to Makkah after the marriage but didn't seem too keen when the time came to make good on that promise. Then one day, he suddenly announced: "Baby, we are going for Umra [pilgrimage], just as you asked". Awn confirmed it, adding that a chartered private plane would take us there.

"Awn, that's a dreadful idea!" I exclaimed. "We should not be taking favours. You guys keep talking about the protocol of the Sharifs".

"*Bhabi*, Khan *Sahab* will back out. It was so difficult to convince him. The flight times are not ideal. Zulqarnain *bhai* has made arrangements."

"Awn, why can't we take the Emirates flight? He sleeps late anyway. He can sleep on the way."

Booking the 3am Emirates flight to Jeddah did not go down well. The fact that there were no meetings arranged for him in Saudi just worsened his mood. On the flight, I coached Yousaf and Inaya on the rites and rituals. Yousaf had come along on Imran's suggestion, to look after Inaya. Inaya didn't seem to need much looking after though; she was well-prepared for this trip. Inaya had researched how to perform an Umra on YouTube. For the pilgrimage, there are certain acts that must be performed, but above everything is the intention. This is why *Tauheed* (the solemn belief that there is only one God) is the first step of our religion. This belief must be pronounced so we accept it with our heart and say it aloud: '*La ilaha illulhau Mohammad dur Rasool Allah*'. Only after this can one proceed to the next four steps: the pillars of Islam. Making the intention in your heart and then performing the ritual to reaffirm is the core principle of our faith. It's like saying I love you; it is worthless until you believe it to be true.

On the approach to the holy Makkah, there is a point called the *Miqat* where men enter a sacred state known as *Ihram*. Here, the intention to perform the pilgrimage is made by pronouncing a special prayer. Men must have changed into unstitched fabric to prepare for the spiritual journey ahead. It is an important component of Hajj or Umra. Just before the pilot announced that we had reached *Miqat*, I directed my nephew to get up, change, and make the intention (*Niyyah*) for Umra. At this point, Imran interjected. "There is no need. We will do it when we reach Jeddah". I protested that it was mandatory and couldn't be done in Jeddah, but he told me to zip it and went back to sleep. Both Awn and Yousaf ended up listening to him, not me.

When we landed, Inaya and I were let through immigration but Imran was kept waiting, even though it was a VIP area. They didn't give him preferential treatment. His anger was palpable, clearly arising from this disregard for his celebrity 'leader' status. This was something I failed horribly at: treating my husband the way he expected, like a hero and celebrity. I treated him like a husband and partner. I kept saying, "I don't want to be the wife of a celebrity. I don't care about being Mrs Imran Khan. I love you because you are my husband, not because of your status. You as a person is all that matters to me". I never realised that this was the wrong thing to say. I'd come from a family that always kept me grounded, and being a mother was also a very sobering experience. You may be waited on hand-and-foot in public, but the diva attitude must be left at the doorstep. At home, you'll find toenails to be clipped, hair to be braided, and favourite dishes to be cooked. With

Imran, the biggest tragedy was that he was all alone. No friends, no children, no siblings, and no real relationships. There are two types of people that surround celebrities: sycophants and spongers. There was no place for a real person around Imran.

We were received by Zulqarnain Ali Khan, CEO of Zultec, and his wife Rabia, and taken to the hotel in Jeddah. It was typically gaudily decorated to suit Arab taste, with everything in bright gold. The balcony had a nice view of the seafront. I threw open the French doors and asked if we could go for a walk later. I noticed that he wasn't in the same euphoric mood as I was.

He was in no rush to leave for Umra, and getting quieter by the minute. We finally left late at night. On our arrival, we were immediately recognised by Pashtuns and surrounded. For a while, Imran and I got separated. Yousaf grabbed Inaya's hand and followed me as we were taken to a nearby hotel. The people were keen to offer hospitality.

The crowd was ecstatic. They carried us on a wave into the Haram Shareef, the holy Kaaba.

Imran was finally smiling. This was a reception befitting a celebrity. He saw how the young Pashtuns were overjoyed to see their *Bhabhi*, and tried to keep me close to him. There was constant commentary in Pashto to guide me. The continuous directions were so distracting that I couldn't focus on the prayers I was reciting, nor keep count of how many times we had circled the Kaaba. For me, prayer is a very private affair, and I had been waiting for this moment for so long. It was embarrassing to be videoed while praying. I couldn't even look at the Kaaba properly. Once the seven *tawafs* (orbits) were completed, we started off on the *Sa'I* (walking seven times between the hills of Safa and Marwah). Imran got extremely tired. He complained that walking barefoot was painful. Meanwhile, my 11-year-old carried on without a whimper. I could barely perform two *rakat nafal* (prayers) before being rushed along.

He was briefly euphoric on the way back, and commented that he had never received such a reception. He had been for Umra before, and wondered if something like the *dharna* was the reason for this warm reception. Mrs Zulqarnain commented that it was perhaps because of a Pashtun *bhabhi*. I made a face and complained that it wasn't really Umra with the non-stop intrusions from people telling me to lift my hands now, or to look this way, or that way, and then videoing it all. "I have to come again to pray properly," I declared. Imran turned around and said: "*Bus hogaya Umra. Koi zarorat nahi hai Maulana jee*". (Enough, Umra is done. There is no need, *Maulana*).

He would often taunt me for my religious beliefs, and for being rigid like a religious scholar. *Maulana* was his pet name for me. He had rather relaxed religious beliefs compared to most Pakistanis. He had only received religious guidance via a *pir* or spiritual teacher. Our belief as Muslims is to read the book *ourselves* in Arabic, and to understand its meaning first-hand. Rituals cannot be relaxed or modified according to personal taste. There is only one kind of Islam. It is not a religion that comes in many shades, as is sometimes propagated. Islam cannot be diluted. Some of us might not be practicing Muslims, but Islam is clear about what is permitted or forbidden.

On reaching the hotel, he slipped back into a depressed mode. Uncharacteristically, he went to bed early each night and wasn't in the mood to chat at all. I was puzzled by his behaviour. He said he was depressed because the last time he had been there it was with Suleiman. I bought the story at the time and was very sympathetic. I would understand the real reasons much later. One was obviously the fact that he could not carry 'mood enhancers' on foreign travels. Additionally, every moment we were appreciated in public as a couple meant several nasty texts and emails from all the women he had unfinished business with, not least his ex-wife. But the most important reason behind this sullen reticence was the mutual resentment between him and the Saudis.

We woke up one morning to the news that King Abdullah had passed away.

"Baby, the King is dead! Oh no, the King lives!!! Bastards! They should all be killed". He continued his cursing in Punjabi. "May they all be destroyed. May they all be ruined!"

I looked at him and said, "Imran, this room must be bugged. Shouldn't you be a bit careful?" Then I asked, "Are you going to the funeral?"

"Of course not!" he protested loudly. "I don't want to see those bastards".

"So why is Dunya TV claiming you are?"

"That bugger Zulqarnain must have said I am".

He turned the TV off and walked over to his lavish breakfast spread. During hotel stays Imran would order literally everything he could think of, and go through everything too. He always insisted I eat more too. I found it adorable that a man who was infamous for eating alone, not caring if he had offered to others or not, would always share with me. Over breakfast, he told me that we'd been invited to lunch by an influential local journalist, and that Zulqarnain was hosting a dinner for SKMT in the evening. I pulled out an Arabic-inspired blue and green outfit designed by the Chief Minister of KP's daughter-in-law. The lunch was actually a quiet family affair at Waleed's house, the owner of Jeddah United Sports Company. I immediately hit it off with the ladies. They were keen to know our love story. For the first and last time with Imran, I felt I was being treated as a woman who had married a man. They were interested in us as anyone would be in a normal, ordinary couple who had found love late in life. There were no judgemental looks or suppositions that I was a plant, agent, or gold-digger. The ladies teased Imran on what a catch I was. Inaya had made firm friends with the family too. But Imran didn't look happy nor did he smile proudly as I expected him to. He was uneasy as pictures were taken, and didn't seem to like me or Inaya being appreciated.

The two of us headed to Zulqarnain's dinner alone. Imran suggested the kids go amuse themselves elsewhere, and they happily went shopping. The stage was set for SKMT fundraising in the gardens of Zulqarnain's house. Imran was barely looking at me. Zulqarnain made a speech and again mentioned that IK would attend the funeral of King Abdullah. Imran then gave a speech, and announcements for generous donations were made. As soon as Imran's speech was over, the selfie hopefuls attacked us. The new *Bhabhi* was getting swamped.

To make matters worse, Inaya arrived, and was shuttled straight to the stage by the family and Awn. Imran was visibly irritated. I took Inaya by the arm and headed into the house via the kitchen. At the time I thought it had been her hat and jeans that had bothered Imran. But months later I would understand that Imran feared Suleiman and the rest. My child wasn't supposed to be seen in public with him. Inaya kept herself well away from Imran right from the start, and he was too busy to make an effort anyway. In Bani Gala, her life was either in school or in her room. The two exchanged customary greetings but would never build any real relationship.

The following day, I went with Awn and the kids to buy jackets for my husband from the local mall. None of his old stuff fit well as most had been presents. I used Awn as a model to get the best fit. With the shop owner barely even entertaining my demands, I took my face covering off. He recognised me, smiled, and immediately got the jacket with the exact buttons I wanted. It was important for me that my husband looked his best. I broke my 'Don't buy designer' rule for him. Awn was surprised that I was not buying anything for myself, and told me about his ex-wife who had kicked up a full-blown public fight over Louis Vuitton bags in Selfridges.

Despite my requests to Awn to not use chartered planes, they had arranged a private plane to take us to Madina the following morning. Zulqarnain kept reminding me that it had cost him a lot but Awn suggested it was not from his own pocket. We reached Madina and were given an exclusive entry to Rawdah Mubarak (sacred chamber), the place where the Holy Prophet (PBUH) passed away, and is buried. I could pray to my heart's content. I was grateful for the privacy, and the privilege of close access to Riadhul Jannah. Inaya had fully thrown herself into the experience, and was busy making video logs for Ridha. From Masjid Nabvi, we went for lunch at the hotel overlooking it. Imran was chatting to everyone and enjoying the lavish array of food. He loved eating out and holding court. He would entertain everyone with his politically incorrect jokes, and anecdotes from his cricketing life.

We then went to Masjid Quba, the first mosque that the Prophet Mohammad (PBUH) built. Inaya and I were left alone. I prayed with other women, unnoticed and uninterrupted. It remains my best memory of the whole trip. Like the countless people who had visited Madina before me, I felt inexplicable inner peace. I prayed for the safety of my immediate family and all Pakistanis. These are the only things on my wish list. Allah has always looked after me, so I have never needed to ask for anything more.

Finally, we visited the historical site of the Battle of Uhud. I was once again surrounded by adoring Pashtun fans. Talking to the National Bhabhi in Pashto seemed to renew their hope of a prosperous future for KP, so they could return to their families who they hadn't seen for years. I promised to do all I could to get them out of the jails where they languished, and to keep pressurising my husband to create job opportunities in KP.

Unfortunately, not only did my requests fall on deaf ears, but I would be repeatedly reprimanded for not understanding politics and being too idealistic. Imran would frequently complain to me, in public and in private. "Reham *bibi*, the problem with you is your idealism is up here," he would say, gesturing above his head. "Bring it down to reality".

I would respond pointing to the floor.

"Imran, idealism can't be down here. It always has to be up there, otherwise it's not idealism. It's compromise".

Chapter 18

In the first 'official' month of marriage, I happily entertained the PTI leaders and their wives to small, home-cooked dinners. To my surprise, these would become open political discussions and decision-making exercises. The obvious chaos and the lack of decorum shocked me. I never got involved or went down to the secretariat to sit in on any PTI meetings, although I would later be accused of doing exactly that. I never personally tried to make contact or build a relationship with any position holder or donor to the party.

At the first dinner, the topic of discussion was GEO, the broadcaster Imran and PTI had boycotted. It was interesting to see how their viewpoints would change as they moved from the withdrawing room to the dining room, and sat next to different people. It was decided that the boycott was to be ended, and that I would be sent to talk. Imran asked me to meet Ibrahim Mir, the CEO, for a one-on-one to break the ice. He was entertained to an elaborate lunch at JKT's house. For over three hours, Ibrahim lamented how Imran had betrayed his trust and embarrassed him in front of his own father, Mir Shakil. He sounded heartbroken. I told Ibrahim that I was not PTI, and nor was I Imran. I had certain rules. If he violated them, I wouldn't help facilitate communication. I explained the first one: that Ibrahim would only talk to me, and I would convey directly to Imran. "If you involve anyone else, I will back off," I told him. Ibrahim met with Shireen Mazari that same evening. I sent him a simple text saying that I would not now get involved.

Imran and Ibrahim were both desperate to patch up their differences. Ibrahim had suggested a good way of saving face for both parties: Imran and I could do a telethon for SKMT fundraising as a couple. It was a great marketing ploy. It would be seen as a goodwill gesture by PTI supporters who had been made to hate GEO. Imran agreed, but then, without consulting or informing me, gave the telethon to the rival channel ARY. The fundraising telethon was broadcast live from the secretariat in Bani Gala. Imran had conveniently thrown a tantrum over something the night before, so never spoke to me in the morning about this either. He made sure I would not find out (perhaps because he'd been so admonished for the interview we had done together after the marriage). I was also aware that Aleema wanted me to stay well clear of SKMT and IKF, which I did. Celebrities arrived from all over the country but I only found out about the telethon once it had actually started. I stayed in our bedroom the entire evening.

At the time, I understood that there was pressure from the stepchildren and the ex, and I thought it would be sensible to stay out of sight for a while. I also knew that the kids were threatening not to visit. I could sense Imran's unease at broaching the subject directly, so I suggested taking Inaya to London for half-term, even though my children did not have half-term. Imran was relieved, and kissed me on the forehead in gratitude. We had a quiet understanding. Nobody needed to know our reasons, but the news was leaked.

As Inaya settled on the plane, she asked, "Mama are we leaving because Suleiman and Qasim don't want to see us?" I could see that she felt insulted and hurt. I'd raised my children to feel proud and secure of who they were. I covered up with those useless mummy lies that kids see right through. I was, however, happy to take a break as I had not been back to England since I'd moved to Pakistan in December 2012, though since I had not been working for much of the year, I was stressed about finances. It never occurred to Imran to ask if I needed a place to stay, spending money, or a pick-up from the airport. In fact, an old friend came to pick me up and I stayed in her two-bedroom bungalow. It was a tight squeeze, but we managed. I didn't want to take any PTI favours. The worst part of the stay was having to pretend to my friend that my loving husband was calling to check on me. Imran never did.

Awn kept contact to instruct me to meet a Mr Zulfi Bukhari and also a Mr Aneel Mussarat. Zulfi's Bentley, with his Indian chauffeur Sudhir, arrived. We had a nice chat about his time with the family, and IK's visits. Sudhir drove to an office in Mayfair where a young man in a purple suit received me. He looked like he spent a lot of time in the gym and salons. I remembered him from a visit to Bani Gala. In the boardroom upstairs, Zulfi introduced me to one of the leading marketing companies in London, London One Marketing. I couldn't fail to notice how sycophantic they were. He was obviously a cherished client. I asked for some guidance with the launch of a jewellery line that I trying to establish on the FairTrade model to create job opportunities for women in KP. Nothing ever came of it.

Zulfi's behaviour during the meeting was curious. He had the same bored mannerisms of his leader. Imran had quite a poor opinion of Zulfi's political intelligence, and would frequently be irritated by his persistent questioning on why things were not being done in KP. But Imran was all praise for the way Zulfi had acquired money at such a young age, almost overnight. Looking across at this rather young, bored man, I too wondered how he had come so far. A quick check and I found that he was the son of the politician Wajid Bukhari, who made a lot of money during the Zia years by transporting Pashtun labourers to Libya and Chad. I remembered reading about how one particular trip had resulted in over 400 labourers drowning at sea.

As I sat in the meeting, I suddenly developed a sharp, piercing headache. I asked for a coffee and then some paracetamol, but as the minutes ticked away, the headache got so bad that I asked for a break and went to the restroom. It was puzzling. People who knew and worked with me knew that I never got headaches. Even with the occasional flu, I never needed to take a break. I was generally a very healthy individual with no medical complaints. But I had been getting these unexplained headaches ever since I'd got married. Imran had worried about it in the first week, and thought it was related to my nerve injury from my car accident. He had called an osteopath who was visiting, who treated me. Imran had sat outside the room, keeping an eye on the proceedings. He had this extremely suspicious possessive streak in him, and it amazed me that he could be so jealous.

I returned from the restroom but the headache just got worse. I finally asked to leave as I found it difficult to focus. I sat in the car but the headache continued to worsen. We were stuck in traffic, and Sudhir was giving me all the gossip on Bollywood stars. I had to ask him to stop the car. I barely had the time to open the door before I threw up violently. It was uncontrollable and unexplained vomiting. Sudhir was like a mother hen, and I immediately panicked that he may think I was pregnant, which could cause problems with

Imran and his kids. My friend was in a state of panic on my return, thinking it might have been her food that had made me ill, but I assured her that my stomach was fine.

The headache wouldn't go away. She put me in bed, now convinced it was high blood pressure. She called a doctor friend over who only confirmed that my blood pressure was as low as it normally was. She then thought it must be a pregnancy, but I assured her I had just had my period so knew it wasn't. I managed to get up to perform ablution and started to pray. The headache miraculously went away.

For years, long before I got married, my friend Maria had insisted that her illnesses were due to black magic. I had laughed it off. But there was one night when my cousin, Samina *baji*, had begged me to stay over, and shown me her shirts with mystery cuts in the back, near the hemline. I had sat there making fun of how the designers she was wearing were using cheap fabric. She would insist that these were top-of-the-line outfits from the best designers and that she did shopping for everyone but no one else had this problem. I had told her to walk like a lady to avoid ripping her clothes. I was an educated, Westernised woman who believed that everything had a logical, scientific explanation. I thought she was losing her mind and told her to stop being silly. She kept insisting that it was mentioned in the Quran, and had happened to the Prophet (PBUH) himself. How could I deny it?

Now that all these strange things were happening to me, I was less sure. Of course, I had been living in Bani Gala, so this was hardly my first exposure to all things 'black magic'. I soldiered on. The next meeting in London was with another benefactor of Imran Khan, Aneel Mussarat. This time it was a cab with ripped seats that was sent for me, rather than a calf-leathered Bentley. I met this small, bald, shifty man in a Mayfair hotel. He seemed uncomfortable with table etiquette, and as I sat down to breakfast he man peered at me through round glasses with piercing eyes. He was tense throughout the meeting. I could tell there was something this man wanted me to commit to, but he was using the typical Pakistani method of beating around the bush, fluctuating between bragging about how he owned so much property in Mayfair and Manchester, and professing his love for Imran *bhai*.

After several years in Pakistan, I had learned a lot. When people appear to be really interested in helping you, they are really looking for a way to help themselves. I developed a great skill in annoying such people by pretending not to understand what they wanted till they left me alone. That look of frustration amuses me to this day. Eventually, this school dropout blurted that he was concerned about the new couple's expenses, now that his beloved Imran *bhai* was married. He wanted to offer me kitchen money. I nearly choked on my Danish. "Kitchen money?" I gasped. Had this been said to me a few months before, the man would have had to run for his life after hearing my response. No one would have dared to offer me kitchen money. I decided to contain my anger, and smiled back coldly.

"Why would you think we need kitchen money?"

"Well *Bhabhi*, he is not alone now, and I just want to help. You will have expenses that I want to help with".

"And how much exactly do you have in mind?" I enquired.

Aneel replied, "One crore initially, with a 10% increase steadily".

I raised my trademark eyebrow, and gave him a sarcastic smile. "And for this, what will Imran have to do?"

"Nothing *Bhabhi*, nothing. He can just join our board as an honorary member if he wants to".

Sensing that I was unconvinced, he added that this was obviously not a figure set in stone. He was willing to do anything to express his complete devotion to Imran *bhai*. I wanted desperately to tell him that I knew exactly how much he loved Imran: he had confessed himself that Shehbaz Sharif and his wife, Tehmina Durrani, were his frequent guests at one of his flats.

I decided I had done my duty as Mrs. Imran Khan and asked to leave, fuming at the temerity of this man on the way back. He wanted to buy me off with ten million rupees and an increase based on my performance. I was naturally insulted that he thought he could buy my loyalties. But in time, I would learn that the easiest way into Imran's ear was via money. He would always describe people with money with great admiration. For people with money, Imran had the most patience and charm.

A few weeks later, Aneel visited us in Bani Gala with Chiku Jahangir (the brother of PTI's Fauzia Kasuri). The purpose of the meeting was to dislodge

Jahangir Tareen and his group. This was clearly a Naeem ul-Haq faction. I watched the two men convince Imran over a cup of coffee that he had to get rid of Jahangir. Aneel went as far as telling him that Awn Chaudry had been bragging in London that he would be the next candidate for Chief Minister of Punjab. Imran couldn't tolerate their campaign against JKT, and blurted out in front of them, "I didn't know Naeem could be so vicious. Jahangir told me that he was going to do this".

I did not disagree with their concern about Jahangir's influence over IK but they probably got the impression, like most others, that I was in Jahangir's camp. Since Jahangir was happy to pour money into the media, with anchors regularly coming in and out of his home in F6, he had perhaps created this myth himself. They preyed on Shah Mehmood's insecurities, and, since he did not enjoy the access to the house that Jahangir had, he had no way of finding out that I was not his opponent.

Aleema's visceral hatred for me didn't help either. Over a year later, I would be sent screenshots of Shah Mehmood's wife's Facebook page, where she was calling me a bitch. I had never met the lady, and found their lack of knowledge of their real opposition baffling. I wasn't part of anyone's lobby but I was everybody's messenger. I could not see how Jahangir added value, and saw his appointment as undemocratic. But Imran would not hear a word against him.

§

Imran's boys hadn't stayed for long. The minute they left, Imran started sending me messages to come back via Awn. I was busy collecting plants and fine china for my new home. I wanted to plant a field of lavender in Bani Gala and make home-made lavender oil products. The day before I flew back, I got a call from Awn who said a dreadful incident had occurred. He wanted to know if I had seen or heard of a photo on Facebook when all Imran's old buddies had met up in my absence. Apparently one of IK's closest gang members had been visiting and had died the following day. I proceeded to look it up and found the photo of a group of ten men having a late-night dinner with IK and Zakir.

I didn't pay much attention to this until I arrived back home. Imran was pacing up and down in the bedroom as usual. He seemed pleased to see me but also very disturbed and nervous. He told me how it was upsetting that his friend had suddenly died. I had forgotten the incident. The man, Vikki, had been the owner of the large brand Mobile Zone, and was only in his early fifties. He had been wanting to meet up with Imran for a long time. Finally, while I'd been away, Zakir had driven him all the way from Lahore to Islamabad. According to Imran they arrived at 10 pm, had dinner with him and returned to Lahore that very night. At 7am the next day, Vikki had complained of a headache and asked his wife for a cup of tea. When she returned, she found him dead.

"He even brought a present for you," Imran said, and pointed to it. I looked at the silver present. ''Was he an alcoholic?" I asked.

Imran stared at me. "How do you know?"

"Well, that's an ice bucket for a magnum. It's massive. I've never seen a bucket this big".

At my response, Imran relaxed, threw his head back, and laughed. He told me that Vikki had heroin dependence issues. I thought it was odd that Vikki had not stayed over after coming all the way from Lahore, especially since I was not at home, but I was so happy to see Imran that I didn't probe any further. A couple of days later, I saw a tweet by senior journalist Umar Cheema, in which he had hinted that a friend of Imran's had died of an overdose in Bani Gala, although he got the name wrong. In typical style, the journalist was trolled by PTI social media specialists and made to apologise, as well as delete the tweets. His editor apologised on his behalf too.

I was too distracted by my new domestic role, designing matching tablemats and setting up home with my Wedgewood china, to investigate the causes or circumstances of the death. The house desperately needed repair work. There were so many structural problems and incorrectly-fixed roof tiles. Imran didn't pay much attention to the death either, despite claiming that he'd found it deeply upsetting. True to his tradition, Imran did not attend Vikki's funeral. Of course, Imran had a habit of avoiding funerals. He had made a lot of enemies with this heartless behaviour. Salim Safi, the Pashtun anchor and activist, never forgave him for not paying his last respects to his mentor, the founding member of PTI, Dr Farooq. That man had launched Imran into politics and drafted the first manifesto. He was killed in a targeted attack on his clinic for his strong anti-Taliban stance. Similarly, the anchor and comedian who worked tirelessly for SKMT fundraising, Dildar Pervaiz Bhatti, died while on tour in the U.S. in October 1994, but Imran was allegedly too occupied with Jemima to attend his funeral either. Another time, during their courtship, Imran and Jemima were allegedly in the guesthouse of a gentleman in Kalabagh who happened to pass away in the night. Imran left hurriedly, without attending the funeral.

I considered such things to be of paramount importance. Attending funerals and offering condolences is basic courtesy, even for those we are not particularly close to. It was always more difficult with Imran though. While I was in London, the mother of the Chief of the Army Staff, Raheel Sharif, passed away. I spoke to Awn and texted Imran to ask if he had attended the funeral. I didn't see why that would be an issue; in our culture, it is considered a moral obligation to offer sympathies. Imran was reluctant to go, but I had heard that he had been less than polite in their earlier meeting during the *dharna*. I felt this was a good way to build bridges.

On my return from London, I insisted that Imran and I go to Raheel Sharif's home to offer condolences. We were driven by Awn to the residence of the COAS. To my surprise, as we drove up to the house, the Chief was standing on the porch with his wife and son, ready to receive us. I thought that this warm and friendly welcome by the Chief of the Armed Forces was very unusual for a politician. Their welcoming attitude and down-to-earth demeanour was met by a rather awkward response from Imran. It was as if he was upset with them. I appreciated their hospitality; the conversation was genuine and normal. The Chief and his wife seemed really into Imran. The wife was warm and chatty. She confessed to be a fan of the cricketing hero. We discussed diets, clothes and children. The Chief was in no hurry to end the meeting but Imran kept rushing me to finish my coffee. His rudeness was shocking and embarrassing. I didn't understand why he was not comfortable with this interaction.

§

In Bani Gala, I continued my efforts to highlight our areas, especially Swat positively. With the film script for *Janaan* in development, I turned my attention to skills-training in these areas. Swat is renowned for its emerald mines and other stones. As a kid, I had seen gemstone dealers come to our house to sell precious stones to my mother. She had a well-trained eye, and could easily spot a good stone from a poor one. She would often tell me that stones were smuggled out by the sackful from the mines, and it was such a shame that our stones were bought dirt-cheap then set in designer jewellery overseas and sold for exorbitant prices. Neither Pakistan nor Swat were ever mentioned in the end-credits of the product.

For overseas Pakistanis, one of the most gratifying feelings is to see something with the 'Made in Pakistan' label. I remember when Harrods would sell cotton sheets and hosiery proudly labelled as Pakistani products. But in recent years, our exports have diminished, and some products are intentionally not labelled. I want it to change. I want the likes of Tiffany and Cartier to say that what they have is a Swati emerald.

Before my marriage, I had started meeting many local gemstone dealers, who had told me how hard it was to get the Chamber of Commerce to support the local gemstone industry. I figured that if we started training our young girls in gemstone cutting and 3D jewellery design, we could make international-standard jewellery from Pakistan. My friends and I had planned a trip to Bangkok to learn about jewellery design and methods. But after the wedding was announced, Imran would not let me go anywhere. It took a lot of effort and persuasion before he allowed me to go for two nights.

The night that I arrived, he called me to ask when I was coming back. I said, "After two nights," to which he responded, "Well after one night now because you said two nights in total". I laughed. "I just got here Imran". He whined that he was missing me, didn't know what to do without me, and that I should come back as soon as possible. I thought it was cute, and agreed. It didn't feel like he was controlling me because he was so sweet about it. I loved how he loved me. I couldn't turn him down.

During my short visit I spoke to many designers and jewellery makers who expressed the desire to collaborate. The President of the Gemstones Dealers association was impressed by my enthusiasm, and subtly mentioned how a Minister from the Musharraf cabinet had once come over for an expo. Despite this, no progress was made in extending bilateral co-operation in the mines and minerals ministry. On my return, I discovered that the Minister in question happened to be Jahangir Tareen. It was interesting to note that Jahangir had not done anything towards improving the opportunities for the gemstone industry, but had always been blamed for acquiring granite mines during this era.

Imran greeted me on my return with a wide grin on his face.

"So, how is Ms Entrepreneur?"

He was clearly happy to see me. We sat in the big red armchair. He held me tight like he always did. It seemed he had really missed me. He always seemed interested in what I was trying to do. He loved how I would passionately go on and on about whatever I was working on. He seemed to be watching more than listening to the content. At the end, he would always say, "My baby is such an eccentric".

I started off by giving him every detail of the trip, especially raving about the Italian designer who would design my jewellery collection for me. I showed him the catalogue, and he saw Alessio's rather good-looking face. I mentioned that he was gay. Imran immediately sniggered and said, "Darling you don't have to tell me he is gay. I'm not insecure". I was a little confused. "But he is, Imran!" I exclaimed. Imran seemed unconvinced. I went on to tell him that I had to make a day trip to Dubai to register my firm, and he immediately protested. "But you just came back! No way am I letting you go again!"

He said that he would ask the KP Government to arrange an investor's road show in Dubai on the same dates I had lined up my appointments. To my surprise, on the 24th of February, a chartered private jet had been arranged by Mohsin Aziz, the alleged economic genius heading the Board of Investment and Trade of KP. Suddenly, we were heading to Dubai together. Also on board were Asad Umar and Atif Khan, as well as Mohsin Aziz, his wife, and others. Like Zulqarnain, Mohsin Aziz tried hard to impress upon me how much the trip had cost him. This time I was better prepared. I turned around and asked, "Is it not coming out of the 12 crore of Asian Development Bank funding?"

He mumbled something and quickly moved away. Had I caught him off guard? I was quite shocked that this man had managed to get a Senate seat. Local journalists hinted that my husband had set the bar very low. They jeered that Khan's standard was way lower than the other parties and that it was possible to get a seat the KP government for a paltry four crores (40 million rupees). One thing was for sure: the standard of intellect had really sunk.

While I was still reeling from the shock of meeting the brains of the BOI, the conversation onboard the plane became even more bizarre. It was clear that the projects the KP team had planned for the expo were poorly thought-out and hastily prepared. It was laughable. One of the projects was a chairlift over the unspoiled Lake Saiful Muluk, one of the most serene and scenic areas in KP. I looked at them, shocked at the shoddiness of the scheme. Imran laughed hysterically at both their ludicrous ideas and my alarmed expressions.

The other talking point during the short journey was the potential arrival of the infamous Khossa family into the party. Asad Umar and I were the only two who seemed to be upset by Imran's justifications in including these electables. After about fifteen minutes, I realised no one was interested in our arguments against the joining, so I instead focused on making sure Imran was served properly and ate properly. Looking after Imran was something I enjoyed a lot. At some unknown point, our dynamic flipped from him being interested in me to me trying to give him everything. As the days went by, I was getting more and more attached to him. I was slowly slipping into a deep descent, and losing myself and my identity completely in my utter devotion to my husband.

We arrived at the Armani Hotel in Dubai. I was surprised at the choice and the standard of the hotel, as it did not seem to match the figure they claimed they had spent, but didn't say anything. In the evening, we were taken to Imran's usual hangout in Dubai, Imran Chaudhry's house, for a dinner. I was a bit wary of him. I remembered my content producer Waseem Abbasi telling me that he was the source of information for the anchor and irritant Dr Shahid Masood at the time of the marriage. We entered and were greeted by several people. The air was full of Botox and Louboutins, not to mention that pseudo-friendliness only the nouveau-riche of the subcontinent can manage.

I was thankful to find Rabia *bhabhi*, who I had first met during Umra, and her sweet daughter-in-law. I voiced my discomfort under my breath and she told me that they were a tad uncomfortable too. I met all the ladies as warmly as I could. Then suddenly a man shoved his hand out and said, "Hi Reham," which I ignored in favour of a polite *salaam*. He looked at me and awkwardly and said, "Oh, you don't shake hands". It turned out to be the host of the dinner, Mr Imran Chaudhry, Imran's rather 'benevolent' host whenever he stopped in Dubai. He pointed to a large bedroom and said, "That is Imran's bedroom. Why don't you stay over?" I smiled. Imran was familiar with my expressions by then, and politely declined the invitation.

I kept myself busy with the sushi as the plastic guest list was suffocating me. I looked away as familiar female 'friends' draped themselves over Imran. Imran seemed to be enjoying the atmosphere and mingling with his old crew. Another benevolent friend, Sadruddin Hashwani, came over. The Pakistani actress Veena Malik also appeared with her new baby. As I stood up to meet the family, Imran called me over to come and say hello to the Galadaris, an eminent Emirati business family. They had money, so naturally Imran was impressed and willing to engage.

The ladies he was stood talking to had married into the Galadari family. I remembered the two sisters from school. A lot of eyebrows in our circle were raised at the time at these arranged marriages. I said hello to them just like I would say hello to anyone, but noticed that Imran was giving them special attention, and wanted me to do the same. For me, money had always been at the bottom of the list of attractive traits in people I meet. I sat down wearily again at my dinner table. After what seemed like a decade, Imran leant over and smiled.

"Baby, you breathing?"

"Just barely," I whispered back.

We left after a few pictures. Imran was in a very romantic mood when we returned to the hotel. He also asked me casually how committed I was the following day, as there was a tea in my honour. I remembered why I had come to Dubai in the first place, and said that my meeting to register my firm would probably take less than an hour. The next day, the expo Imran had talked about for foreign investment into KP began. Imran left early for it. Awn arranged a rather expensive hairstylist who ruined my hair. Awn then escorted me to my appointment and Aleem Khan joined us too.

The meeting took barely thirty minutes. It was a straightforward procedure but couldn't be done on this trip as my proposed company director wasn't with me. In any case, the meeting was constantly interrupted by people coming to talk to me. These were not selfie hopefuls, but people who had been denied an audience with the great leader. I would become familiar with this routine over the next few months. People would hunt me down, start off with complaints about how and where Imran's government was going wrong then, in most cases, offer their voluntary services to help. They all had one thing in common. They, like the rest of us, all thought that Imran was being misguided by the likes of JKT, Pervez Khattak and Aleem Khan.

I remember one gentleman, who introduced himself as Raza Jaffer and was representing an Australian firm called Fortescue, who had a great idea for waste management solutions and the improvement of the mining sector in KP. He spotted me in the hotel and begged me to get an appointment. I directed him to Awn, who assured him that he would make the meeting happen. Imran and I discussed it later and he said that the man who headed the company, Andrew Forrest, had indeed tried to help the mining sector in the past but no one had followed up. In Imran's words there was no one 'of capacity'. The meeting never happened. It turned out that, as Awn had hinted, Imran Chaudhry hadn't want the meeting to go ahead, so it didn't. Contrary to popular belief, I had no influence or sway over Imran. He would show enthusiasm at my suggestion and then go and do the opposite.

I slipped quietly to the KP investment road show to see how my husband was doing. The first thing I noticed was that there were no investors there, only young PTI folk with their Facebook pages open, hoping to get a selfie with the celebrity. The couple of finance journalists who had attended were asking questions which the unimpressive and unprepared KP Ministers had no answers to. On each question, Asad Umar would step up from the front row to go to the rostrum and give a corporate, smart answer to satisfy the audience. I looked down in horror at the poor-quality content of the brochures on the desks. The pictures and content had simply been copied-and-pasted from the internet. There were faces of American children and German goats.

The conference broke up for lunch. Imran and I had a pleasant lunch with a nice man called Ghalib and a couple of other people. Ghalib was from Hazara and was extremely concerned about JKT's overbearing influence on Imran. He took advantage of Imran being away from JKT for once, and tried to persuade him about how he needed to sort things out before it was too late. Ghalib even went as far as offering another plane so that the dependence on Jahangir would finish. Imran seemed more interested in the cheese board and bread, but he entertained Ghalib politely. The same gentleman would pay us a visit later in the year in one last-ditch effort to pull Imran out of JKT's clenches. Imran had this knack of listening to people intently, pretending to be shocked by the information, and getting really convinced by their arguments, while remaining unmoved. His stance would be unchanged. As we returned to the room, Imran reminded me of the event he had mentioned the day before. I discovered I would be going by myself to a ladies-only gathering. I groaned at the prospect of spending my afternoon with more silicone dolls. Imran chuckled at my discomfort, and lovingly asked me to do this for him. I got up like a complaining teenager and freshened up, but didn't bother to change into anything flashy.

The car arrived with Mrs Imran Chaudhry. I was told we were going to Mrs Arif Naqvi's house. I arrived at Emirates Hill, the exclusive, luxurious, gated residential area of the rich expats. The car pulled into the drive and the door was opened by a white butler. We were made to sit in a lounge and wait for Faiza Naqvi to arrive. There was no gathering arranged in my honour. This was meant to be Mrs Imran Khan paying her respects to a very busy lady who had been left very disappointed by Imran's dismal performance in the 2013 elections. "We had such high hopes," the lady lamented. What followed was an intense interrogation about Pashtuns and Talibanisation, and a debate on dialogue versus action. The lady wanted my view about extremism in KP. I was my passionate best, defending Pashtuns and insisting that we should not be labelled extremists simply for practising our religion. I said all the things that I believe in, and (at the time) thought my husband believed in. After all, this was his public stance. She argued over each point and I provided logical, grassroots evidence to the contrary. Mrs Imran Chaudhry hardly uttered two words in the entire meeting, looking from one lady to another desperately trying to follow the conversation. Mrs Naqvi had a flight to catch so we bid her goodbye. I was confused about the interaction but confident that I had satisfied all her queries, and asked her to stay in touch.

Mrs Imran Chaudhry didn't say much on the way back either. I returned to the hotel room. Imran was waiting and immediately asked how it went. I exclaimed sarcastically, "I had no idea I would be called in for a private audience with the Queen".

He smiled patiently and said rather seriously, "Baby, they are very important. Arif Naqvi funded 66% of my campaign in 2013 himself".

"Oh!" I gasped. "Well, I think I made a good impression and answered all her questions. Mrs Naqvi said she had such high hopes from you, and was so shattered by the results".

We didn't discuss it any further but I was to find out much later how my answers were all wrong and perhaps helped put me on a slippery slope in this marriage.

Chapter 19

As the Senate elections approached in March, the gifts started to pour in. There were of course the regular suppliers, but in times like these when candidates were being chosen, we had a lot more crates of dates and bottles of honey, arriving to sweeten *Khan Sahab*. In Pakistan it is traditional to send presents to newlyweds and a lot is spent on wedding gifts by close friends and family. However, there weren't many presents received at the wedding announcement. One of the reasons was that I had made it clear that we would prefer donations to SKMT instead, since Imran had set a huge target for the opening of the Peshawar branch of his cancer hospital. The other reason, I suspected, was that his family and friends were still sulking.

This was the wedding of a high-profile couple. There would be so many media reports later of the expensive diamond rings, flats and cash that I received. In reality, I only received two or three gifts in total. And of those, the only one of note was from Dr Javed Asghar, who was just an Imran well-wisher who believed in his vision. Dr Asghar had crafted a diamond bracelet for me himself, while also commissioning an artist from New York to paint a huge portrait of our iconic wedding picture. Imran, rather ungraciously, called it a monstrosity in front of the dear doctor. My husband could not tolerate it at all. To make matters worse, this life-sized picture also appeared in an interview of his, behind his head in the mirror. I had not placed it there, nor was the setting done on my instruction, but Imran reprimanded me severely after the interview. He had clearly received an earful from someone. I had the disturbingly huge reminder of our marriage moved to the back of Suleiman's room, out of sight, so it wouldn't offend anyone again.

There were a couple of other presents from unknown PTI supporters. One was a gold chain and the other was a pendant with Quranic inscriptions. They were received by the staff and I wore them with pride. Only two or three PTI leaders gave wedding presents but they were not noteworthy. This was exactly what I wanted since I didn't want to be under any kind of obligation. Perhaps some already thought I was not a good investment. Conversely, my family showered us with presents. Since all of them were overseas doctors with no political ambition whatsoever, I had no problem accepting these gifts. But as the Senate approached, I suddenly realised that many new relatives might appear out of nowhere. I stood in front of Imran, took my SIM card out, and threw it in the bin. I didn't want to be contacted by these 'relatives' or anyone else. I could contact my children through other means.

I told Imran not to ask for my opinion about any of the possible candidates as I did not want to influence the decisions in any way. I told my nephew to say to everyone that I would be unavailable for any meetings until after the Senate elections. As the time approached, Imran sneakily asked me about a female candidate. I replied that I didn't know her personally, which was true. I later regretted this as I knew *about* her. She was the only highly-educated and competent candidate. She was a Cornell post-graduate and a self-made single-parent who had lost her husband, a senior police officer, in the war against terror. Apparently she'd had no chance, as Pervez Khattak had made all the decisions already. These were still early days for me and I was an ideological supporter who trusted The Leader. In private, I spoke passionately about how I supported justice and equality. Imran knew how fierce an idealist I was. When he asked me for guidance on the Senate, all I said was, "Imran, make me proud".

The final list was shocking. More shocking was the fact that the media chose not to discuss how awful the representation was. The list did nothing to build my confidence in the man I had married. All those who'd sent gifts during the Senate nominations had been rewarded.

Before I moved in, there had been no concept of buying groceries for the house. There was plenty of food but it was never bought. It was sent by various benevolent benefactors. The problem with all free things is that beggars can't be choosers, so it wasn't exactly the sort of food which was healthy or to our taste. The buffaloes, goats and chickens arrived as frequently as Navaad, the farmhand, managed to kill them. Flour and grain was sent mainly by Jahangir Tareen. The regular delivery of tinned, bottled and groceries (from Tetra Pak) thanks to Mohsin Aziz, was rewarded duly in the senate too. Fresh fruit and vegetables were delivered regularly from the farm of PMLN senior minister Tariq Fazal Chaudhry. Imran's love for delicacies like partridges and teetar was handled by several suppliers, mainly from Mianwali. Crates of game and poultry were delivered by other political hopefuls from all over Punjab.

Politicians were exploited by Imran's staff too. If anyone charged, they would be the butt of jokes forever. Shah Farman had not been forgiven for charging Imran five thousand rupees for a bottle of honey once. Amin Gundapur had once been caught delivering bottles of Black Label honey to The Leader, and had also been generous to Imran's love interests in the past, especially Ayla Malik. He continued his generosity towards Khan's kitchen with various regular cooked and uncooked supplies. I remembered how my brother had resigned from government service because contractors would bring him crates of mangoes on *Eid* (as bribes). He never accepted these gifts since he knew what they were for.

Just after we got married, I saw alcohol in Imran's bathroom. I was putting my jewellery in a safe place and suddenly had two bottles staring me in the face. One was a bottle of Sherry and the other was Absolut Vodka. I asked Imran and he said that they belonged to Moby. Supposedly, he had left in a huff, so they were still there. I wasn't entirely convinced but let it go. A few weeks after the marriage, my little curious 11-year-old walked into our bathroom and accusingly asked if my new husband drank. I told her that the bottles were not his and poured them into the toilet in front of her. It was embarrassing; my kids were brought up in a house where alcohol was never served or allowed. I couldn't tell them that I had stumbled into a marriage where drinking was a very minor thing.

Moby was the first person Imran introduced me to while proposing to me. I was invited to have tea with his best friend one afternoon in the summer of 2014. To avoid being noticed, we would use complex methods and odd timings to meet. I didn't want anyone to find out just yet. I walked in a bit earlier than expected and saw a rather large man with a bulldog appearance on the sofa opposite Imran. Imran jumped to his feet. I noticed he had a golden credit card and a rolled-up note in the palm of his hand. He quickly and smoothly put them in a wooden jar on the mantelpiece. I didn't at the time know what

Imran was using the credit card or note for. I sat down on an armchair. Imran began to introduce me. The man looked unaffected and unimpressed by the praise Imran heaped on me.

Moby didn't ask me any questions. He seemed disinterested. His friend and leader was animatedly telling him how he had found the perfect woman, and how she even knew about the pregnancy story, the abortion and his other problems. Imran continued to describe how stable and mature his choice was, but his friend still seemed unmoved. Imran then embarrassed me further by sitting next to me and announcing, "I want to have a baby with this woman. A boy who she will only speak in Urdu and Pashto with".

I went red, not at all prepared for this announcement, but the man in front of me finally reacted. His face could not conceal his shock and distaste at the announcement. He made his thoughts clear almost immediately. "There is no need to rush into these decisions. There are already too many children in this world".

I was puzzled by his reaction. When I voiced this to Imran, he dismissed it and said it was because, despite several marriages, Moby had no children. I accepted this explanation sceptically. The vibes I was getting were pretty loud and clear.

Moby moved onto the next topic, and discussed security risks to the property. I agreed with him, and insisted that it was unsafe without a boundary wall or barbed wire. There could be an infiltration. He was happy to talk about these issues. Imran suggested we exchange numbers and emails. He impressed upon me that everything I felt needed to be done should be communicated to Moby, which I started doing regularly. But Moby wasn't the sort of person who got things done, although this was true for most people around Imran. He was surrounded by incompetent people who mainly liked complaining about each other. They were all so busy backstabbing that nothing ever got done. Imran quite enjoyed these non-stop emotionally draining conversations, and much of the day was spent texting back and forth over such petty turf issues.

Imran had nicknamed his friend 'the serial divorcee' because of Moby's experiments with marriage. Imran described his relationship with Moby as just like that of a husband and wife. Specifically, Moby was the nagging wife; a pessimistic character. It was clearly an arrangement that worked well for Moby, as he didn't like to live with his 'rather awful' wife, as Imran put it. But my husband insisted that it was so depressing to live with Moby because he would always be the bearer of bad news. With Moby, it was apparently always doom and gloom. But I felt that Imran secretly wanted every one of his friends to remain single and available so as not to break the merry party. When Zulfi was thinking of going ahead with a divorce, Imran actively encouraged him to do it as soon as he could, while I pleaded with the young man to not destroy his home.

I felt that Moby never forgave me for his loss of influence over Imran. Moby's room was given to Inaya, which probably also didn't go down well with him, or the rest of his friends. During this time there was an ongoing serious property dispute between Moby and Aleem Khan over some money still owed to Aleem. The perception that I was close to Aleem Khan further compounded the problem. The inside story was actually that Imran loved Aleem's lavish lifestyle and asked me specifically to support his rich friend. I genuinely got on well with his domesticated, simple wife, but our connection was limited to choosing fabrics from Lahore and exchanging recipes.

Moby and Aleema saw Aleem Khan as my main support, which didn't help matters. During the NA-122 (Lahore V) election, they actively campaigned against him. I could understand as Moby had been with IK since the 70s. He was one of the original musketeers. They had so many fond memories together, which Imran often shared with me. Imran often mourned Moby's massive weight gain and loss of good looks and blamed his unhappy indulgent lifestyle. In his younger, fitter days, 'Mobster', as Imran fondly called him, had a crush on Dimple Kapadia, the Bollywood babe of the film *Bobby*, known for her beautiful mane of hair and hazel eyes. Imran arranged a meeting for his best friend with his crush, and took great delight in recounting this comical story. The friends had all been sitting with the actress, waiting for Moby to make his entrance. Moby was in a state of panic and couldn't decide what to wear. After several changes, he finally emerged wearing a sleeveless leather jacket. Imran said he looked ridiculous in the sweltering heat. Poor Moby failed to say a single word to the gorgeous actress through the entire meeting. Essentially, Moby had managed to provide plenty of material for his friends, who could now tease him for the rest of his life.

§

We were on our morning walk. I was blissfully unaware of what was on his mind. We sat on Conference Rock and he suddenly opened up. "I want the boys to come for their Easter break. But I am not sure how to do this. They will find it awkward". I suggested we take everyone to Nathiagali. That way, they would be on neutral ground, and we could subtly break the ice. I could take my kids there first, and Imran could bring the boys over after spending a couple of days with them at Bani Gala. Imran smiled and said, "What a clever baby I have. That's a great idea".

However, for Imran, it was pressure from all-quarters, which was bad news. If there was ever a man who could not deal with pressure, it was Mr Imran Khan. I was shocked at how easily he would crumble. It would take almost nothing for him to fall apart. I wondered how he had captained the team for Pakistan. His abusive tirades were perhaps the worst kept secret in Pakistani cricket. Imran had never even understood why he was criticised for his World Cup speech in which he forgot to mention the effort of the team. He would remember their behaviour at the time and curse at the team members, describing them as 'ungrateful sons of bitches' who made such a fuss over the fact that he wanted them to give their winnings to Shaukat Khanum Memorial Trust. He used particularly disparaging remarks for Javed Miandad and Salim Malik. Apparently one of them had alerted the rest of the players that all the gold and cash gifts arranged by local traders after their win were to be directed to SKMT. Imran made all the decisions about which charity matches to play in India too. How much each player received in appearance money for these charity matches was also down to him.

With Jemima and his kids, it was clear he could not exercise this control. Imran was always anxious about Suleiman. This anxiety was voiced to me almost every other day by Imran. He would worry about Suleiman's reactions and said that the young boy would break down crying at the slightest stress, even at 19. Apparently, the kid had never recovered from the divorce. Imran had told me that Jemima kept him on his toes with either direct phone calls to him or messages via the children. The kids called Imran a few times while I was in Bani Gala, asking him why he had made 'Amma' upset. Just before the start of the *dharna* in July, Jemima was particularly sensitive. Imran told me she had just miscarried and was devastated. She had been dating Russell Brand at the time. I was very touched by how supportive Imran was during this time. He knew the relationship with Russell was going through a very tough patch as the comedian had consulted Imran for advice. In Imran's words, her repeated disastrous relationships and dreadful taste in men were taking a toll on her. He described Jemima's relationship with her mother and brothers as pretty 'fractured'. Apparently, they all turned to him to communicate with each other.

His concern for his ex appeared to be charming before we got married. I saw him as an understanding ex capable of remaining good friends. Unfortunately, I would discover the level of control his ex-wife and her family had over him when I started to live with him. Despite his supportive behaviour, Jemima had expected Imran to entertain the kids while she went on holiday with Russell, even though Imran's *dharna* was about to start. At the time, Qasim was suffering from a serious tendon injury. Imran simply told me that he could not say no, despite the stress of the *dharna*. It appeared that Imran had no say in anything, and could not stand up for his rights as a father. It was still early days for us, so I didn't feel I could comment. I did think it was odd that she could seemingly have whatever relationships she wanted but Imran had to seek permission from her for his. After all, the kids didn't even live with him. He only saw them for a few days in the summer, or on Christmas and Easter. From the minute Imran proposed, till December, when we were all over the news, I heard Imran repeatedly say that he needed to go see the kids and get their approval.

After the *nikkah*, Imran told me that Aleema had also played on his children's insecurities. She had brainwashed the kids into believing that I would be bad for his politics. Qasim had later blurted all of this out in front of him. Imran claimed that Aleema laid the agenda for all the sisters, while she openly campaigned against me throughout the marriage. A famous film star, Atiqa Odho, married to one of the few genuine hardworking PTI-ans, visited us soon after our marriage. The lady wanted to warn me what problems could be expected with stepchildren but I was confident that I would win them over. After all, I was the cool auntie. Everyone called me *khala*, even those who were not related.

All the kids loved me wherever I went, and this was Suleiman. My life at the time revolved around my husband's happiness, and Imran's joy was Suleiman. I would love him like my own, and build up his confidence. I'd show him this was his home. Kids just need love...right? I was so wrong.

Despite my best efforts, the visit did not go well. I made sure they had their favourite dishes ready for them. I tried to chat to Qasim, who at least responded, but Suleiman stayed detached throughout. Just before the boys were about to arrive, my kids arrived. A friend of mine also arrived from England with her own kids. I headed to Nathiagali and opted to stay in holiday flats instead of the official residence of the KP Government. The snow covered walk between Doonga Gali and Ayubia was a challenge but we attempted this rather risky trek anyway. Nathiagali was quieter than normal so we had a great time. My friend pointed out that I looked exhausted. But for those two nights in that rented room, I actually slept. We walked, we danced, we laughed.

Everywhere I went, people complained about education and healthcare issues. They felt there was finally hope, now that I could deliver their messages directly to the main man. I did so diligently, which contributed to a rapid decline in my popularity in my husband's eyes. On the third day, when I enquired about the boys, Imran announced in a sad voice that they had missed their flight. I questioned it and he agreed that Jemima was being difficult, and that she must have done it on purpose.

"The bloody Jew asks me to pay for their tickets. She is an heiress. Imagine... her asking me to pay for their airfare," he snarled.

"It's OK Imran. You don't contribute to their upkeep at all. PIA Tickets twice a year are hardly worth mentioning," I replied.

What I found odd was that in public, he kept saying that she was unfairly targeted for being Jewish, but in private, this was how he would refer to her. He held resentment towards her for sending lawyers to him immediately after the divorce, to ensure a final financial settlement so that he could not claim anything later. I interjected that it was pretty standard. Since he was a dependent with no income and she was the one with the money, she would be expected to do this. But he shook his head at her attitude and insisted it was just her meanness.

Imran said that he noticed Jemima had stopped following his prescribed lifestyle after she received her inheritance; splashing money on socialising and herself. Even her stylist coming to blow dry her hair before she went out was something he had disliked. I couldn't understand why a young woman spending her own money to get her hair done was an issue. He liked how I was low maintenance. Most days, I would be doing my hair and makeup in the car. He got very jealous if I wore lip-gloss, so forbade me from that. I changed my look because he would make snide remarks for days. "Baby do you want to go into modelling?" he would snigger at me. I didn't have an income or TV wardrobe anymore, so I didn't really have much to look glamorous with.

After the boys finally arrived, I asked when they would be joining us. Imran said the kids wanted to stay in Bani Gala because Qasim was down with flu. I guided Imran over the phone to where the medicine was, and what the correct dosage was. He was very careless with medication. He had once given them an anti-spasmodic by mistake. On one occasion, he couldn't figure out why he couldn't sleep, only for me to inform him he had taken Imodium instead of a sedative. He laughed hysterically.

On the 1st of April, I decided we would come back. I called Imran to tell him that it was my birthday on the 3rd. He asked me what I would like. "Don't ask me. Surprise me." No gift ever appeared. However, on my return I was informed that Maximus had been attacked by Motu again, and had lost his eye. Shock and fear hit me, and I rushed into the bedroom. Imran was watching a film with the boys. I gave a vague hello, then asked, "Where is Maximus?"

Imran said that Maxi was not back from the vet's yet, but assured me that the dog was fine. I walked out of the bedroom and saw the dog being led into the hall, still a bit drugged, with my children walking dolefully behind him. Maxi's eye was barely visible through the swelling, and the whole right side of his face had been shaved. The area was covered in stitches. He looked a mess. My tears started to fall over him. I could do nothing but weep silently. Imran and his boys had followed me, and I heard the voice of my husband saying, "He is OK. Don't worry".

Maximus didn't look OK in the slightest, but I couldn't speak and didn't want to let anyone see my tears. I went into my room and stood over the wash basin, crying. Saima came over and gave me a hug. My husband never came to console me.

I collected myself and joined everyone in Inaya's room. They were trying to cheer me up so I decided to put a smile on my face. I make sure never to disappoint those who try to put a smile on my face. You can't hurt those who can't see you hurt. From the open door in the distance, I could see Imran and the boys walking in the garden. He saw me and headed towards the room.

The men who owned Bani Gala joined us in the room and sat down. Imran tried to make small conversation with the kids and my Saima. Ridha and I exchanged glances over the effort Sahir and Inaya were making with the boys. They were failing. There was no warmth. It was awkward, especially since I knew my friend was observing all of this. They left after barely ten minutes. It was late, so I retired to my room, locking the door of the wing behind me so my kids and Saima could not see that I was in the spare bedroom. I sat there and waited for ages. Finally, I slipped under the bedcovers. In the early hours of the night, Imran finally slipped into the room quietly. It was as if I wasn't his legal wife. It was as if he was hiding from his parents, not his children.

He asked me if his decision to not go into Parliament for the joint session was a good idea. He had vowed to stay out of Parliament until his rigging claims were investigated. A joint session of the Parliament was called on the issue of Pakistani forces joining the Saudis in their war in Yemen. A few weeks earlier, I had tweeted about the humanitarian aspect of the new war. We were sitting down for breakfast. Normally Imran would be engrossed in texting while I read articles and scanned Twitter trends. I would occasionally interject with snippets of info, which I felt he should be aware of. He wouldn't pay much attention. That day, immediately after my tweet, he asked what I was tweeting about. I read him my tweet and he said that it was very good and that he would tweet the same. Through our entire time together, other than this tweet, I cannot recall a single instance of him doing something I suggested, or taking inspiration from me. That day I had felt rather pleased with myself, thinking he and I had similar values after all.

So now, weeks later, he asked for my advice on this issue, stating, "I've decided not to go to Parliament. I'm right aren't I?"

I nodded. "Yes, if you don't want to go, don't!"

"Shireen, Shah Mahmood, and these other wannabees are desperate to sit in Parliament. Makes them feel important," Imran added with disgust.

"Well this is not the best time to return," I replied. "Besides, they should invite you back with respect. Perhaps not until after NA-246. Because you can't give them a chance to humiliate you".

He hugged me and stayed until I dozed off. I woke up as he left but didn't protest.

The following day passed with me mainly being busy with the guests and Imran with the boys. That night, as midnight approached, Saima kept nudging me to go to my husband. I knew he was busy with the boys but went anyway so she wouldn't think my husband had forgotten to wish me Happy Birthday. I waited all night in the spare bedroom but Imran never came. I could hear the very loud action-thriller on in his bedroom.

Hours went by and morning came, but he did not. I listened to the loud soundtrack of the film for the first half of the night, and to the scrambling of mice in my bedroom for the second. Eventually I got up to pray. My time at Bani Gala led me to pray extra *nawafil* and *Tahajjud*. I moved more and more towards praying to calm my troubled heart. I firmly believe that it was these prayers that protected me and my children.

Morning came. I made the bed, unlocked the door of our wing, and went outside so no one would find out that we had been sleeping separately. I sensed that for my birthday my kids and friends had planned a surprise. I walked into the garden. There was no sign of my husband, but Ridha was up already and asked me to go for a walk to Conference Rock. As we approached it, I saw a big white gingham hamper, full of all my favourite things: my favourite sweets, my favourite tea, my favourite pictures in pretty frames, and even my favourite storybook as a child. She had put a lot of thought into it. The year before, she had received a beautiful hamper from us. We had all contributed with our ideas and love.

It's simple really: Children who are loved and raised with honesty will learn to love honestly. Children who are brought up on fears and lies will only learn to fear everything and be dishonest. The difference between these two sets of children was so obvious. Suleiman and Qasim were never rude to me. But they seemed to fear being nice to me. Soon after they left, Imran showed me his text in which Suleiman had warned him to make sure he was being careful as I could get pregnant. It was clear that Imran had assured him that it would not happen. Funnily enough, I discovered I was late as soon as they left. Imran was overjoyed, but it turned out to be a false alarm.

In the evening, I finally saw my husband walk into the room with the boys where we had gathered to cut the cake. Saima had decorated the table with red rose petals. As I cut the cake, Imran managed a barely audible 'Happy Birthday', before walking away with his boys to the main dining room. During dinner, I caught one of the staff trying to take a picture of all of us sitting down together and I stopped him. We didn't realise that Saima had taken a photograph of Imran and I with the cake. Suleiman asked why Imran was not going back to Parliament, and Sahir, in the capacity of an older brother, explained the abuse Imran could face because of the extreme position he had taken on rigging.

The night before the session I found out from a female anchor that my husband was going to the Assembly. On the day, as the nation watched my husband shamed by the Defence Minister, I chose to watch an interview of the film star Meera. However, when I heard my husband had been shredded to pieces, I jumped to defend him on Twitter. Meanwhile, my friend had posted the birthday picture of Imran and I on Facebook. I'd later find out that this had also not gone down well. Unknown to me, Imran's arrangement with Jemima had been for me to not be in the house when the kids came to visit. But Imran would never tell me the truth. Perhaps Imran never told anyone the truth, not even himself.

April had started on the worst possible note. Unknown to me, a concerted effort to dislodge me had been launched. It had started before the marriage announcement, and now I was walking blindly into the traps set for me.

§

I came home one day to find Imran looking very worried. This was usually the case whenever his ex-wife or his sisters had sent complaints about me.

Surprisingly, on this occasion, I was not the trigger. He was concerned about his kids being exposed to cannabis in England.

I was pleased to see him behave like a concerned parent and spent a good hour giving my signature lecture on parenting. I suggested that Imran gently start off by giving personal examples of how he had seen cannabis abuse ruin cricketing careers, and how the drug remained in the system for years afterwards. Imran interrupted me by telling me that he worried more because of Jemima's brother. I was confused. I thought he had meant the risks associated with school playgrounds or with friends at parties. Imran told me that Jemima was concerned that the boys could be exposed to cannabis in the company of one of their uncles. I was dumbfounded. I remembered the story of their uncle, Zac Goldsmith, the Conservative MP, being expelled from Eton for marijuana use when he was only 16. What could I say? I couldn't understand the world they lived in. If the grown-ups around them, their role models, were doing drugs, what hope did the kids have?

Imran was anxious about Suleiman's slipping grades also, but here too the problem was that none of the Goldsmith men, despite being sent to Eton, had gone to university. Zac's divorce was pronounced four days after he became MP for Richmond, on grounds of adultery. James Goldsmith was known to have flaunted a string of mistresses and wives. But of course, I couldn't say to Imran that the boys were surrounded by poor male role models who cheated on their wives and dabbled in drugs. Whenever I've needed to refer to a role model, I have presented my squeaky-clean brother, who won a full scholarship to MIT for his post-graduation. All the boys in our family adore his company and look up to him.

Jemima was only 21 when she married a 43-year-old Imran. For Jemima, marrying a much older man from another culture couldn't have been much fun. Imran always said that he had connected better with his in-laws than his very young wife. Friends would tell me how the cultural restrictions weren't the ideal start for the very young London socialite. Her time with Imran is described by most as a very suffocating experience for her. I could very much relate to a very young girl separated from all of her friends and surrounded by much older people in an oppressive atmosphere. Her two brothers also got married in their early twenties. However, the Rothschilds and Goldsmiths shared a strong historical and religious bond. Both were Jewish banking families, with a history of political posts and influence in the Conservative party. In fact, Sir James Goldsmith was a protégé of Edmonde de Rothschild, long before his two sons married into this even richer Jewish family.

Ben had only been 22-years-old when he tied the knot with Kate Rothschild. And after that nine-year marriage fell apart, Zac then married her much younger sister, Alice, who he had been having an affair with. Kate was rumoured to have been having an affair with the American rapper Jay Electronica and their divorce was labelled the very first 'Twitter divorce' after an ugly lashing out on Twitter between them. Despite Ben being arrested after slapping his wife during an argument over the alleged affair, the historical bond between these two Jewish banking families was still visibly extant when, within a year, Zac had divorced his wife and married his mistress Alice Rothschild. Between the two Jewish banking dynasties, this connection is understandable.

The bond between Imran and both the Goldsmiths and the Rothschilds was harder to understand for me. Imran said that he was the emotional coach for not only his own ex-wife's man problems, but also for Kate Rothschild's. According to Imran, Kate was devastated when the rapper she fell in love with converted to Islam and refused to continue an affair with her. The rapper was affiliated to the Nation of Islam, which is described as an anti-Semitic organization by its critics. Since the Rothschilds were not only known for their banking supremacy but also for being active Zionists, I piped in that perhaps it was the surname that caused conflict in Kate's relationship, and pointed out that one of their ancestors, Walter Rothschild, was responsible for drafting the declaration for a Jewish homeland in Palestine in 1917, which came to be known as the Balfour declaration.

I found it strange that Imran made a point of extreme public rhetoric against the Americans and Zionism, while sharing close ties with those who had a clear interest in furthering Israel's cause. Imran was also very close to his brothers-in-law, particularly Zac. Imran maintained that in a violent argument once where Imran slapped Jemima, it was Zac who urged Imran not to divorce his sister. Imran had impressed upon me that it was not his ex-wife but her family he was good friends with. He was especially indebted to 'Jimmy' as he had not only left more than enough money for his eight offspring to live off in luxury, but had also designed Imran's future.

As time progressed, my gut instinct told me that Imran had to do their bidding, not because of any good-ex-husband responsibilities, but for his own political wellbeing. Less than a year later, my worst fears would be confirmed: A seasoned politician swore to me that a meeting had taken place, confirming Imran's U.S support. To cross-check the story, I cornered the former Director General of the ISI, General Ehsan ul Haq, in Sadruddin Hashwani's home, who confirmed Imran's connections to the Americans. According to him, at a meeting in 1996 between the late Foreign Minister Sahabzada Yaqub Khan and Henry Kissinger, a third party was also present. That third party was Sir James Goldsmith. The Pakistani foreign minister was then categorically told by Kissinger to "Look after our boy". When Sahabzada asked who their boy was, the answer he received was "Imran Khan".

I had started reading up about James Goldsmith during my marriage, and stumbled on an article by David Goldman in the October issue of Executive Intelligence Review (EIR) in 1984. In volume 11 of EIR, he wrote, 'Sir Goldsmith created an elaborate network of puppets in Britain and the US to create an elaborate cash laundering network in the United States between 1981 and 1983'. The EIR staff investigation also raised questions concerning the finances of the political network broadly linked with Kissinger Associates Inc. According to it, General Vernon Walters of the State Department (the chief protégé of Henry Kissinger) was, for a long time, employed by Goldsmith.

Everything made complete sense when I realised that James Goldsmith had always been politically active, and had even founded his own party in the 90s called the Referendum party. It was a single issue Eurosceptic party which laid the foundations for Brexit. Before him, his father, Frank Goldsmith, a hotelier of German Jewish descent, had been a conservative MP. Besides his portfolio of 48 hotels, he was known for being one of the founders of the King David Hotel in East Jerusalem, over 46% of which was funded by notable Jews. Following the decisive six-day war, East Jerusalem was successfully annexed and the hotel was extended.

Through the early months of marriage, I had struggled to understand Jemima's hold on IK. He clearly hated her phone calls, and cursed her after each one, but could not say no to her. Initially, I thought he was just a doormat because of his kids, but it began to dawn on me around September that it was a much stronger hold than that. It was too much information that I should have looked into long before I got married. All I had listened to was Imran's speeches and his constant rhetoric against the Americans. Not only do we venture into personal relationships with our eyes wide shut but when we go to the voting booths, even the journalists in us have no real idea what we are voting for. The information is all out there but we choose to follow the propaganda we are fed.

§

One day, Sahir walked into my room and confronted me about Tyrian White (universally accepted as Imran's love child). I was unprepared for his questioning. Sahir had thought it was a malicious rumour. He'd been defending his stepfather on social media.

I mumbled something like, "I thought you knew already!"

"No Mum, how could I know? So, it's true! You married a man who has a child out of marriage? Doesn't he say he's 'a strong Muslim'? I thought that wasn't allowed!"

I had feeble answers. The hypocrisy of talking about Islam and then leading a life away from its principles was clear. But Sahir was more shocked that Imran did not take responsibility for her, especially if it was true and everyone knew it. I tried to explain that he had been young and all over the place; that it was all in the past and he had embraced spirituality.

Sahir remained unconvinced. I had raised my kids to be responsible and never lie. We were a family unimpressed and unaffected by his fame, so our knowledge on him was limited. All Sahir knew was that this man was famous for cricket and talked about Islam in his speeches. He had grimaced at his cricketing references but appreciated the moral lectures Imran was always giving. Sahir had been kept away from the Pakistani social circle in his adolescence, so he hadn't yet understood the hypocrisy of it. I sat down and thought 'I must love this man to have compromised on so much for him'.

Imran actually spoke about Tyrian very proudly. Apparently, she was the spitting image of his own mother, Shaukat Khanum. He appreciated her for getting her life together despite all she had been through, especially her mother's passing. Imran used to curse the Sharifs, blaming them for creating the issue. Tyrian could not visit because he feared the Sharifs. He would dream of when he would come into power and it would all be possible. Since that didn't look likely, I suggested he not wait and just do it discreetly, but he said he couldn't risk it.

More than the Sharifs, it was Jemima who was damaging Imran's politics. She was posting images of herself with Tyrian on Instagram. In one post, she called the youngster her stepdaughter, leaving no doubt in anyone's mind that Imran was her father. The timing was curious. I realised that my growing image in Pakistan had motivated this subtle blackmailing. I felt sorry for the poor girl who was now, through no fault of her own, always at the centre of her parent and guardian's issues, and a political tug-of-war.

During Imran's repeated emotional issues with Suleiman, he said to me that he would communicate more with Tyrian. He showed me some of her texts. It seemed she gave the most sensible advice in the family. She told Imran repeatedly to ignore Suleiman's childish demands, and to not be emotionally blackmailed by them. She would say, "He will grow out of it soon". But Imran told me that it had taken Suleiman ten years to accept Tyrian. Imran would stay in contact over the phone and meet Tyrian in Jemima's house when in London.

After a few weeks of our marriage, as we discussed Tyrian, Imran casually added, "You know she isn't the only one I have". He grinned mischievously. "There are 5 in total, that I know of".

"Five what?!" I gasped.

"Kids," he laughed

"What? You have five illegitimate children! How do you know?" I asked.

"Well, the mothers told me," he said.

"All White's?"

"No, some are Indians. The eldest is 34 now".

"How Imran? Why did the mother not come out with it?"

"Because she was over the moon! She had been married for ages and couldn't get pregnant. She was overjoyed, promised to keep it a secret, and begged to keep it. So I said OK ".

"And the rest? Why did they never speak?" I fired at him. There were so many questions in my head.

"Well, because they were all married and they didn't want their marriages to be destroyed," he said.

"Does anyone else know?" I asked, still reeling.

"Only Jemima does. I told her," he replied nonchalantly.

I didn't know what to say. It was done. I was his wife and he was what he was. His lifestyle was so different to that of my social circle. I didn't know anyone like him or his friends. It was a bizarre life. It was all sex, drugs and rock n' roll. I had grown up in a time and a culture where it was not cool to be irresponsible. I didn't want him to tell me more.

His frequent stories (even of other people's antics) had a terrifying effect on me. I realised that these were not merely stories, but suggestions. He was testing my boundaries and seeing how open-minded I could be. Even before the marriage, I had reprimanded him when he'd joked that Pashtuns were famous for their bisexuality. I had made it clear that these jokes and suggestions were unacceptable to me.

However, the scandalous sex stories continued. Imran would even boast of a threesome with Grace Jones that he really wanted to replicate with me. He enjoyed torturing me with constant reminders. He went as far as suggesting going to a discreet place like Hong Kong where no one would recognise him. I would look at him in horror as he'd throw his head back and laugh. He would revisit these fantasies, describing his alleged threesomes with the black singer and a famous model-wife of a rock star back in the eighties. He thought I was uptight as apparently other Pakistani women had no issues enacting their husband's fantasies. He would quote extreme examples from his close friends. I would put it down to him being under the influence.

When these hints did not work, Imran explained how having an occasional 'service' while overseas was pretty standard for those friends of his who were stuck in a situation where the wives had 'retired hurt'. On the one hand he would say infidelity caused problems, while on the other he exonerated his inner circle from this burden by citing health issues of their wives, saying it made it inevitable that the husbands would go elsewhere. Imran educated me on the sexual habits and alliances of all his social circle and had the habit of renaming all his friends and party people with, to his mind, more suitable and appropriate names. He was especially proud of the nickname 'Fundo Fucker' for one of his close friends.

I thought about these naming conventions. My sister Salma was known as Sweety. Ridha was always known as 'The Princess' of our family. Out of my friends, the most imaginative was Maria, whose affectionate terms for me would usually involve some sort of creative profanity. She loved the term 'shitface'. But even she didn't live in a way where she would ever use those names to genuinely describe her friends.

Chapter 20

Islamabad looks beautiful in February and March.

It was nice to see Imran enjoy all the colours of his garden. He asked me to design his secretariat, and build an additional bedroom upstairs in the house for us. The architect was Ali Asghar, the son of Air Marshal Asghar Khan, the man IK was frequently compared to. He had started Tehreek-i-Istiqlal, a secular, centrist party back in the 70s. It was a failed movement, believed to have had the support of the establishment. Ali Asghar was desperate to win favour with IK. He had lost his seat in the by-elections. By now, I knew that Imran liked two kinds of people in his party: those who had money and would spend money on him (like Aleem Khan), and those with a gangster appeal, such as Amin Gundapur, who also happened to be generous when it came to extravagant gifts. Ali Asghar was neither. IK only tolerated him because of the strong, liberal lobby behind the party. Ali had rather secular views. But as a man, IK didn't think much of him.

Ali was hoping to be considered for the Senate. Many of us thought his soft-spoken, educated ideas were best suited to the upper house but Imran was unimpressed. To make matters worse, Ali had tied the knot with a girl called Maliha, a stunning PTI MPA, just a few months before. Not only was this lady beautiful, but this fiery politician wasn't going to stand for the depraved behaviour of some in the party. I was genuinely fond of the lady as I appreciated how she had stood up to the sleazy public advances of Shah Farman, a KP Cabinet Minister. That confrontation had made the rounds and reached my ears too. Shah Farman was known to unashamedly brag about the perks of his job. In one instance, he spent thirty minutes on the phone trying to win favour with the new *Bhabhi*, assuring me I had nothing to worry about as he was making sure all women were intercepted on the way to Imran. He was keeping himself busy to protect my marriage. I was so disgusted that I immediately told my husband that a sexual harassment board needed to be created. There were so many women who complained about the sleaze-net that stood in their way.

Maliha appeared to be hardworking and passionate about her constituency. She braved the inevitable attacks for being twice divorced. I could relate to her. Imran however, would listen to our reasoning but refuse to give any role to the modern couple. He spoke disparagingly about Ali and thought the man had no backbone. He believed that Maliha wasn't as innocent as I thought. The problem with good-looking women is everyone wants them, and it's common and easy to start malicious rumours against them when one realizes that they are out of reach.

In the Islamic Republic of Pakistan (in direct violation of Sharia law), it is somehow permissible to have several illicit encounters, but the Sharia-prescribed route of women staying in wedlock through remarriage raises a lot of eyebrows. I often heard other women speak disparagingly of women who had been married more than once, like Maliha. Ali Asghar and his wife persevered through the injustice, and he volunteered his services for the new secretariat building, as did his wife for interior design. I was assigned the job of helping with and approving the design.

Imran would fantasize about us working together, in a manner akin to Albert and Victoria. He would frequently mention how the couple had changed the face of Britain. Inspired by history, I designed the room with a removable partition, so our offices could be separated during his party meetings but opened up when needed. Our desks would face each other when the partition was withdrawn. To our right would be a full-length window and a balcony to take in the view. I kept a staircase at the back, so we could discreetly reach the office after our morning walk, without being seen from the front of the building. He would hand me all the files of complaints and tedious reads daily. My job was to make bullet points and brief him. This pile of 'tedious reads' was often added to by people from all over the province with evidence of corruption and political interference.

One big file I had to go through detailed claims of nepotism in over 500 appointments at Hazara University. The PTI leader Azam Swati had been directly accused of it. Along with the dossier of information provided, Imran's own home staff urged me to pursue this with the boss, as they had on-the-ground knowledge of it. But as always, my words fell on deaf ears. The issue was quashed effectively and never made it to the news. Like almost all complaints of misappropriation of funds and political appointments, it was never resolved.

Protesting teachers camped outside Bani Gala through the spring. I was not overly shocked to find the openly sleazy and foul-mouthed Shah Farman at the centre of this controversy too. Imran merrily stayed indoors as they had blocked the main entrance, and of course he could always escape on the helicopter. For me and Inaya, it meant missing appointments and tuition classes. There was only one dark, muddy and rather dangerous path at the back of the property that we could use. I would be frequently stopped by the protesters outside that back gate too. They would show me their certifications. Most of them were post-graduates and well-spoken. They begged me to convey their genuine grievances, which I did repeatedly. Initially, Imran promised to look into it, but he was disinterested and left it to the Minister. Imran was now looking towards the Judicial Commission, banking on a good result from the judiciary to force a re-election, or some other manner of political victory. He had no time for petty affairs like running the provincial government of a province which did not have enough votes to get him into power.

After the *dharna*, when I'd pleaded with him to take an interest, he had entertained my idea of living part of the week in Peshawar. My family home was in a leafy suburb in Peshawar, so I suggested that we use that instead of taking any favours or using a government house. I felt it would be enough for Imran to just be seen to be spending time in Peshawar to motivate people into getting work done. However, motivating my own husband wasn't the easiest task. When I would plead with him to attend to an issue by visiting the location, he would literally wail, "Do you have any idea how long I have been doing this for? I am so fed up of this crap. It's been twenty fucking years! I can't do this anymore!" It was clear that Imran felt it was high time he was 'given the prize'. I would reason with him by saying, "But Imran, Nelson Mandela spent 27 years in a cell with no end in sight. Narendra Modi was a Chief Minister for 10 years before he became PM. He was voted in despite his radical views because of a good governance track record. Prove yourself in KP then look to the centre".

"Do you know how old I am?" he would angrily snarl back at me.

"But Hilary Clinton is 67 too. Does that mean she will just give up?"

I should really have saved my breath. Imran was like an impatient toddler at heart. I was mistaken in thinking he wanted my advice or encouragement. He wasn't looking for motivation to work harder. He just wanted his throne.

In my first meeting with Aleema (which lasted a good two hours), three names were brought up repeatedly. She boasted proudly how she had effectively eliminated one of them. It sounded more like a threatening message to me. It was the PTI UK leader Rabia Zia, who Aleema had publicly fought with over funding issues.

The other current annoyance was Saifullah Niazi, a poor young boy who was mysteriously deposited by his mother at the PTI office. Incidentally, his father's name was also Imran Khan Niazi. Before Aleema, the driver, Safeer, had also been brainwashing me against this man. They described him as a penniless man who had made a lot of money off PTI. Safeer even claimed that Saifullah had taken one lakh off him to start his business. Aleema couldn't tolerate his hold on Imran. She couldn't understand why he was second-in-command in Imran's absence. There was a hint of some other kind of close connection. I wasn't sure what she meant but also noticed that Imran appeared very fatherly towards him. My mind flashed back to what he had said to me about fathering more than just Tyrian.

The rather aloof Saifullah seemed to reciprocate Imran's love. He knew his position was secure, so never bothered to even say *Salaam* to me. Imran simply told me he was shy. There seemed to be an inexplicable bond that everyone was very jealous of. In between shocking, abusive words for her brother, Aleema tried to gauge my loyalties towards Saifullah. "I had never met him," I told her simply. Satisfied that I could be on her side, she exclaimed excitedly, "I want you to move in as soon as possible so I can throw that man out!"

She then moved onto the next obstacle in Bani Gala: the chief of the harem, Anila Khawaja. Aleema, like many others, suspected that this woman was not from an innocent background, and explained how Anila had arrived at the home of a Lahori elite, and through that connection had rather rapidly infiltrated PTI to reach Imran. Her influence on Imran was unquestionable. They all believed she was a plant. Aleema wanted her eliminated. Ironically, a year later, she would team up with Anila to combat a newer enemy: me.

Anila was neither shy nor aloof. Imran was terrified of her. Through the courtship she kept approaching me, over the phone, via DM, and in person. She was direct. She wanted to know what was going on, and her eyes would follow me unblinkingly throughout my visits to *dharna*. Imran used to call her 'Fatal Attraction' and suggested that she could be very psychotic. The minute Imran would see her near me from up on the container, he would message, asking what she was saying to me. His fear of Anila suggested that she had some incriminating evidence on him. He would become feverish and anxious about what she would do if news of our marriage came out. Through the marriage, she was constantly messaging him, begging for meet ups. During the marriage I also found that Imran had rather heartlessly asked her to do a background check on me six months before we tied the knot.

She first arranged a tryst at her brother's wedding in Dubai. Awn told me, and I confronted Imran, who then insisted on taking me with him. I asked him how she got in touch with him, and he said that he had accepted an invite on Blackberry Messenger. When I asked him why he had done this he had no answer. I deleted her from it, but in April, as I handed him his stuff as he left, there were messages from her, explaining how and where they would meet in Karachi for the sex she was craving. Imran, in embarrassment, took the phone I handed him and left quickly. He sent me a loving message from the helicopter. I messaged back saying that he didn't need to play these games with me. Awn must have told him that I looked very distressed as they left. As I handed Imran's bullet vest to Awn, he asked why I was looking like I had seen death. I had no words.

In my confusion, I went to my friend's house but couldn't speak. I had been invited to the next day's Hum TV awards in Dubai. I was hoping to sign a contract with them for my new film, *Janaan*. Everything was ready. As I watched the news, I heard Altaf Hussain make jeering remarks about the National *Bhabhi*, taunting me with an invitation to visit Karachi and not to be afraid. All my pent-up anger was taken out on him instead. The Samaa TV lead anchor asked for a beeper over the phone and I lashed out at the MQM chairman. I returned his taunt with a stinging reply, making it clear that he did not own Karachi; we, the people who lived here, did. "How dare he invite me to Karachi while sitting in fear in London? I can come and will come whenever I want. Tell your people to prepare *haleem* and *kulfi* for me!"

The words were met with a roar of approval from supporters and media across the board. Imran called me from Karachi. He was overjoyed by my crushing response.

"I am coming," I said quietly. He understood why and agreed that I should. I decided to make an excuse to Hum TV, saying that they hadn't booked me a business class seat, and instead got a PIA ticket myself for the morning flight to Karachi. I couldn't sleep all night. I could only think of what must be going on in Karachi. This was not a woman out to carve a political career for herself but a woman desperate to keep her man away from other women. I wanted to show everyone that Imran had a wife now, and she would be with him from here on. It was to put a stop to any thought of sexual antics on political tours.

To please Imran, I took out the green raw silk I had bought for his victory speech in November that never happened. To my dismay, as they viewed this green outfit with obvious suspicion, simply standing by my husband resulted in much discussion by the planted mouthpieces about my 'designed entry' into politics. They even viewed my green outfit with suspicion. On my arrival, I had no idea who was who. I recognised Naz Baluch off the television but had no idea what her designation was. At the airport, I was pulled like a chicken by rival lobbies in PTI. Unknown to me, Nazia Rabbani, the women's wing Sindh President, had been ignored at the airport. She was rightly annoyed but it was clear that she was not the inner circle. I promised her that I would visit her home as soon as I was done with my commitments. Paying attention to ordinary party workers was not the trend the party followed. In the car I was handed half a dozen phones. Every PTI worker wanted me to speak to their pet reporters.

I arrived at the hotel. Imran looked very pleased to see me. Later that evening, instead of spending time with me, he sat and watched the full Altaf speech on TV. I didn't interrupt as he rarely took an interest in news or other people speaking. After the speech, I gently coached him on a few points, and he encouraged me to write more, not only for his speech, but also JKT's. He thought Jahangir did not have any people skills, and that his speeches were particularly bad. I promised to take care of it. In the car the following day, I simply pushed a sheet with bullet points towards JKT as I knew he was too egotistical to take direction from me. In the late afternoon, I asked Awn to invite everyone to the suite for a brainstorming session to add to the speech.

I retired to the bedroom leaving them alone to approve the speech points I had written. I did not want them to know I had contributed. As the time approached for the *jalsa*, Imran seemed uneasy, and kept saying he was worried about my safety. It wasn't until I arrived at the *jalsa* with Faisal Vawda that it dawned on me: Imran had insisted I would not be seen on the stage at all. I was meant to be down in the crowd. I looked at the tiny, cramped venue. They didn't have enough people, so they had selected a narrow road to pack people in, so the turnout would look more impressive. Arrangements were poor so it was mixed and unruly. I said I would brave it but Faisal Vawda refused to let me stand in the wild crowd. It was inconceivable for any woman to stand there, let alone Imran's new wife.

I understood my husband's predicament, and explained to security that I would put my head down and make a dash for the stage when the light went, and that's exactly what I did. The crowd never saw me. Only a drone camera noticed me, with a 3-sec shot of me climbing the steps. There were three rows of seats. I was made to sit in the extreme end of the stage in the back row. But the crowd was getting bored of the speeches and started chanting *"Bhabhi! Bhabhi!"*

Ali Zaidi came up to me and pretended to be apologetic but announced rather loudly, "Your husband's instructions were to put you here. He didn't want to compete with you".

I thought his comment was in bad taste but said nothing. The chanting continued, and Munazza Hussan a senior PTI leader finally asked me to join her in the front row with the party workers. The crowd still could not see me as there was no electricity, but word of my arrival had spread. There was a lot of Pashtun community participation. As Imran started his speech, I was asked to leave. The reason given was that my husband had concerns about my security. I left immediately, disappointed and angry that I couldn't listen to the speech I had helped write. As I sat in the car, news cameras ran live footage of me, painting a picture along the lines of, 'Even his wife doesn't want to hear his speech! She prefers to sit in an air-conditioned car'.

We couldn't leave until the Great Khan left so we waited in the car and followed his convoy. He was already in the hotel bedroom when I arrived. He wanted to celebrate but I was in no mood to smile at a man who could not even own up to my being his wife. It was not a political role I craved, as the schemers suggested. I just wanted everyone to know he was my husband and off-limits to other women. I was trying to save my marriage by accompanying him but he was just too fearful of annoying his benefactors. I told him that I had a headache and wanted to sleep. I tried to get some sleep as he left for dinner without me.

The following morning, the media was granted a press conference at the airport. As Imran finished, they turned to me and asked if I had received the gold jewellery Altaf Hussain had promised me. Imran Ismail, the candidate for NA246, whispered in my ear to take the question and to thank the women for their bravery, which was the whole point of my appearance. We were asking women to step out to vote, so it was seen as a symbolic step that Imran's family women were also facing the threats and taking the risk to step out onto MQM territory. I answered: "*Mera shohar he mera zewar hai*". (My greatest adornment is my husband.)

The answer made many men across Pakistan fall in love with me, but it led to my own man hating me.

Awn needed me for the first few months of the marriage as I facilitated his position in the household. The world saw him as my right-hand man. Even Imran branded him as my spy among his friends, but I was always irritated by his constant presence. I wanted to be in direct contact with my husband, but Awn would also shower my daughter and nephew with presents. I had to reprimand him a few times as I was uncomfortable with people trying to buy their loyalty.

Awn kept informing me of the women trying to get cosy with my husband, and of the sisters and nephews maligning me. I was later told that he was batting for everyone. He was asked to plant these seeds of doubt in IK's mind too. Awn would encourage me to attend PTI functions. Since he was the go-between, I assumed these had been approved by my husband. The events were arranged by PTI while the media was set upon me. I never asked to attend any event or arranged any interview. I had always tried to go with the flow and do whatever was needed in support of my husband. This attitude would cost me.

It was being discussed on the news how my appearance in Karachi was an indication of a planned entry into politics. My presence was being used by JKT and his handsomely paid social media team to create the idea that we were very close. The opposing lobby of Shah Mehmood Qureshi was weaker, and existed in a constant state of panic. My appearances at all PTI events were arranged by Aleem Khan and Usman Dar with Awn Chaudry, (who had assumed the role of personal secretary to IK). Dinners for female workers and families were arranged to introduce me to the party supporters and increase vote banks. Nothing was arranged without Imran's consent or approval. On these dinners, workers who were against Shah Mehmood and Aleema Khan Niazi were photographed sitting next to me, and the pictures would be leaked on social media.

On the way back from one such dinner in Sialkot, organised by Usman Dar (or UD as everyone called him), I got a call from a rather irate Shah Mehmood. He was shouting down at the phone in frustration. He was outraged that I had been sitting next to a young boy called Hafiz Farhat, whose leaked tape exposing Shah Mehmood's failings had been circulated widely. The boy had been served a disciplinary letter.

I tried to explain to Shah Mehmood that I was unaware, and that I couldn't stop people from taking photographs with me, especially those I didn't even know. But he wasn't listening. I was amused at his silliness and later repeated his words back to Imran. Imran swore at Shah Mehmood, saying that he would sort him out for speaking to his wife like that. Back then, I didn't know that what Imran said he would do and what he would actually do were two very different things. I did try to find out about this boy later. As it happened, Hafiz Farhat could not be disciplined much: when we met he told me he had bundles of evidence for misappropriation of funds by Aleema Khan in the Imran Khan Foundation, and that he had shown these to IK. At Imran's request, the boy had not released this info to the media.

Shah Mehmood was seen by the majority of *Insafians* and locals in his home constituency of Multan as useless, but he was adored by his female followers. He was not seen as someone who had much influence, which was fairly accurate, as Imran hated him and ridiculed him in private. Imran enjoyed Dunya TV comedy sketches against Shah Mehmood and would laugh hysterically with his core group. Jahangir

Tareen, on the other hand, had serious influence. He was seen as a dangerous overriding influence on Imran. Everyone knew that Imran would violate every rule in the book for him. However, Jahangir remained unhappy about the extent of Imran's defence of him. He wanted more, and I was roped into reinforcing messages on behalf of JKT to Imran. These were early days, so I couldn't understand why Imran would not put his foot down. He would give much of his time to the attention-seeking behaviour of the top tier but not to governance of KP. I had put my faith in this man, as had millions of others. "Make KP a model province for me," I had said to him when we had our public ceremony. But Imran had no time for that. There was no reason to repay anyone's faith in him.

§

What's even more annoying than an individual who always keeps an eye on their money? An individual who always keeps an eye on the money of others.

To only associate with people simply because of the size of their bank balance is quite a repulsive trait in my eyes. Both Ijaz and Imran hated spending a penny of their own money. But even more pathetic was their cringeworthy sucking up to people with money. When I would ask Ijaz for money for spare uniforms for the kids, he would scream his head off at me, but when around rich cousins or friends, he would become the sweetest person on the planet. I once picked him up from the airport in Pakistan only to have him shout all the way from Rawalpindi to F7 at my alleged lavish spending on daily necessities like water and milk. He shouted so much that, as I parked the car in Gol Market, F7 Centre, all my make-up had come off. My eyes looked puffy. As we entered the jewellery shop to pick up a bracelet his niece's mother-in-law had ordered for her engagement, I was mortified to see my cousins sitting there already. They had also arrived from the U.S. to attend the wedding.

I had to fit outfits for myself, my husband and my kids on a budget of just £100 for the reception. As soon as Ijaz saw my cousin's wife trying on a bracelet, he asked me loudly in front of them if I had also selected a bracelet for myself. Seeing the older husband of a young client, the jeweller immediately produced the bracelet I had initially tried on when choosing the bracelet for the bride to be.

I signalled to my husband to leave the shop for a minute. As we stepped out I said, "This is too expensive, and it doesn't match my outfit either. If you want to buy something, buy me semi-precious amethyst strings as they match the outfit and are far cheaper". I pointed to the shop next door and took him there with me. But Ijaz turned on his heel and returned to the same shop where the cousins were sat. He announced to the jeweller that he should pack the bracelet he had initially shown, and to charge it to his credit card.

My outfit was a pink lilac. I had no earrings or necklace to go with it. Ijaz bought the heavy gold bracelet, set with turquoise, without looking at me. The bracelet was too big for my tiny wrist, but I couldn't stop him. The cousins were impressed by this generous husband, and as we sat in the car I looked down at my sister-in-law's loose hand-me-downs which I was wearing, and wondered if my life would ever change.

It did change, but for the worse with Imran. As an older woman with my own money, I did not need Imran to buy me or my children any basic necessities. In fact, I paid the grocery bills for Bani Gala. But here was a man who was not only impressed by wealthy people, but lived off them. By providing small favours, they could dictate to him in whichever way they wanted. It was embarrassing and frustrating. He encouraged me to associate only with the rich ones. When I would come and protest about their upstart snobbery, he would laugh it off and tell me to persevere. I just avoided them as I have a low tolerance level for people with a lot of money and no sense.

After a horrendous introductory meeting with Jahangir Tareen's wife, Imran continued to introduce me to his rich benefactors. Moni Tareen, although pleasant towards me, was extremely rude and domineering with my husband, which I found hard to tolerate. Her own husband's subservience was understandable, but my husband's utter lack of self-respect annoyed me no end. When I came back, rather cheesed off, after Mrs Arif Naqvi had summoned and then cross-examined me, he laughed it off. When the invitation by the Naqvis was withdrawn, I wondered what could have happened. I researched the financier. A quick browse revealed the surprising rags to riches story of Arif Naqvi. This man went from being an American Express credit card salesperson to becoming friends with Gaddafi's son. His almost overnight success had him quickly rubbing shoulders with dignitaries at Davos. Arif Naqvi was the head of the Abraaj group, an equity company in the UAE. I tried to discover a bit more about his success story on the internet but instead found out that Abraaj is partly owned by the family of Saddam Hussein's nuclear weapons mastermind.

The infamous "father of Saddam's nuclear weapons program", Dr Jafa Dhia Jafar, and his brother Hamid Jafar, are executives at the Iraqi company Crescent, which is the founding general partner shareholder and limited partner of the Abraaj Group. It donated between $500,000 and $1 million to the Clinton Global Initiative annual meeting. Weeks before co-sponsoring this meeting, the Abraaj Group was awarded the first of hundreds of millions of dollars in loans. They were also given investment management contracts through the U.S state department's overseas private investment corporation (Opic), a federal agency overseen by then-Secretary of State, Hillary Clinton. In addition to the Clinton Global Initiative, the Abraaj Group sponsorship also coincided with Gulftainer's initial efforts to take over a Florida port. The Abraaj Group paid the Clinton foundation, and the Jafars were rewarded with Port Canaveral Gulftainer Deal.

Enquiries within the financial circles of UAE uncovered another rumour connected to Benazir Bhutto and her husband. The financial sector gossip suggested that Abraaj had Benazir Bhutto to thank for the start-up finance, the private equity firm itself and the supermarket. I wasn't sure what to believe and it made no sense to me. Why would someone close to Benazir Bhutto be financing Imran? But then again, the *dharna* was financed by staunch PPP supporters, like the property tycoon Malik Riaz. There was a lot of shady stuff going on and I was struggling to piece it all together.

I had a flashback to the 2013 election, when PPP supporters were told to vote tactically in Punjab for the PTI. Imran was not willing to discuss or listen to anything regarding the source of anyone's money or their affiliations. He was like a kid, all googly-eyed in a candy store. Imran wasn't the best PR for his rich financiers either. In an effort to get me to share his adoration, he boasted that his main financier had paid $1,500 for one of the most beautiful actresses in Bollywood. At the time, she had been an escort in Dubai. It was meant to slag the particular actress off, but I just rolled my eyes and replied, "I think no less of her for selling her own body. But your friend, a married man, doesn't go up in my esteem with that bit of info".

§

May came, and the invitations that had initially come pouring in, stopped. Nothing ever came of them. In the meeting with the Naqvis back in February (the investors and benefactors of the 2013 election campaign), their deep disappointment with the result had been made clear to me. Everybody was keen to keep them sweet. It was understood that as soon as Mr Naqvi had time to spare from his foreign travels, he would invite Imran over for a weekend. His private plane was to be sent, and only Imran, myself and JKT would go for this trip. I was looking at it as time away with my husband.

Since Imran was so keen for me to have a child but I had not conceived in our time together I met a fertility expert. She couldn't find anything wrong with me but finally suggested IVF-C injections to boost conception. My gynaecologist had advised I have the IVF-C right before some time off. I told her that there was a weekend getaway planned. The doctor told me that it sounded like just the thing we needed as a couple. She could sense my stress. She understood the sleepless nights, the headaches, and the story behind the ready smile without me having to confide in her. I took the IVF-C shot in the arm but was told rather last-minute that there was no trip after all. So upset was Imran that he never even touched me on the cancelled weekend, and the shot went to waste.

At the time, I thought JKT was upset with Imran, and even said to him, "I think he is not facilitating this trip because of this Wajih mess". I thought Jahangir might be sulking. I had recently downloaded Whatsapp so people could contact me. Unlike Imran, I'd always hated endless messaging and phone calls. My rule of thumb is that a text longer than a single line must be of an emotional nature, and not worthy of my time. I never usually carried a phone that year, and would continue to dislike being constantly contactable. I mainly used the device for reading or writing articles, or e-mails. Nothing irritates me more than people bombarding me with messages. I have a habit of blocking people who don't respect my sense of space.

As soon as I got the app, messages flooded in, mainly by Jahangir about how he felt Imran was not doing enough to protect him. Contrary to what was assumed in the media, I did not particularly trust Jahangir, and did not appreciate his wife bossing my husband around. In April, when Justice Wajih (the head of the tribunal looking into the allegations of nepotism in the 2013 intra-party elections of PTI) had pursued his case and investigated, Jahangir had thrown tantrums right, left and centre. I would turn to find Imran also busy texting Jahangir on the same issue. Imran would write loving, big-brother emails to pacify him.

Imran shared most of his correspondence with me, even complaints about me by his sisters, his hussies, and the planted social media teams. One day, he asked me to read an email which he claimed was a tough message to Jahangir advising him to swallow his ego and learn to get on with people. I read it and smiled at him. "Darling, that's not a harsh email at all".

"I can't believe he is being so fucking greedy," Imran said in exasperation. "What more does he want?"

"Imran why are you surprised he is being greedy? You think he is with you to support your cause? That's a bit naive".

Imran was very disturbed at Justice Wajih's deadlines and media talks. One day, while we were all sitting on the veranda, Imran made a sudden announcement. "I think I'm going to take this opportunity and get rid of everyone, dissolve everything. This is a golden chance to remove that bastard Ejaz Chaudhary and that fucker Mehmood ur-Rasheed. Then I'll reinstate only the people I want, slowly, with new rules".

Even though Imran wanted to protect Jahangir at all costs, his sudden announcement scared everyone. Jahangir went a bit pale. He enjoyed his position of General Secretary more than his money. His humble background had left him with a chip on his shoulder. He was very aware of the town gossip that his current wealth was all because of his very rich wife and his use of her family lands. I would frequently sit him down and say, "Slow down. This stress is costing you your health". He was a cancer patient. I couldn't comprehend why he was not enjoying his life with his family. Some days, he would look like death.

Our trip to Dubai would not happen though. It had probably been cancelled because of me. Clearly, I had not made a great impression on the Naqvis. My biggest flaw is that I cannot be a hypocrite. If I love you, you will know. If I dislike you, I will make no effort to hide it. Similarly, I am an activist through and through. If I feel that a people are being persecuted I will stand up for them. To me it makes no difference if they are children in Yemen or children in India or indeed in my own hometown. I will raise my voice for the underprivileged and the tormented. I stood by the Hazaras when they were persecuted in Baluchistan. I also spoke up for the Waziri tribes. When I speak passionately about Pashtun culture and my own religious beliefs, I am often misunderstood. I possibly gave the Naqvis the impression of a very rigid Sunni Muslim, who was intolerant of other faiths or races. I merely stated that I did not equate removing a *burqa* as being liberated, and that I certainly didn't view every bearded man as a terrorist. I like to believe that I have a better understanding of ground realities than those who live in air-conditioned elite areas in Dubai and Karachi.

Not only was the invitation withdrawn but I was told that the funding had also dried up. At the time, I didn't know why, nor would I have cared. I would have said 'good riddance to those who do not understand that I talk of tolerance and equal opportunities for all regardless of their religious beliefs or race', but I was to find out in just a couple of months that my beliefs were not the same as my husband's.

This painted a rather confusing picture, as Imran himself was the creation of seemingly pro-Saudi extreme-right elements of the General Hamid Gul type. It was Imran who talked publicly about the rights of the Taliban, not me. So why were educated, enlightened Shias investing in him secretly? Was Imran lying to the public or was he lying to his investors? Perhaps he was lying to both. He was certainly lying to me.

It wasn't only the Naqvis who withdrew invitations. The official invitation to visit Iran came in early June. There was a lot of fanfare about this. Everyone was so excited at this news that Imran's old hairdresser, Dar, got outfits off one of the best-known designers in Pakistan for me to wear on these visits. Two outfits were sent. I chose a high-collar full-length coat-style *Sherwani* dress to fit in with the strict Iranian female dress code and reflect both cultures at the same time. I also wanted to create the best possible impression and promote Pakistani haute couture. I knew it would draw a lot of media attention from across the world. After a month of delays, I was then told the trip would not be happening after all. Apparently, the Minister was not available for all of May or June.

The cancellation clearly angered a few people, and started another round of baseless accusations on social media. I was accused of stealing from the designer. But I never even wore the outfit. It remained packed in the box. The man responsible for returning it simply did not do so immediately. The designer heard about this, and quickly sent back a handwritten confirmation that he had indeed received the clothes, and I had not kept any of the outfits. But I couldn't help but despair at the fact that these accusations kept cropping up.

A very strong impression of my Deobandi Sunni family background was being deliberately created by my opposition. As Sunnis in Pakistan, one must concede that we have never felt threatened or insecure, and have enjoyed privileges that come with being a part of the majority. However, it also meant that I was brought up in a household where I was never made conscious of these differences. I never asked my friends or staff or colleagues what their faith or sect was. My ears never pricked upon hearing certain surnames. I differentiated based only on 'Is this person likeable or not?' I couldn't have ever imagined that my sect would be an issue in Bani Gala.

I did think it was odd that my outfits were described as *Abayas*. I'd gone to great lengths to make sure that for travel (like Umra in Saudi Arabia), I would not wear the signature Saudi-black style of covering. Instead, I'd opted for my traditional trademark white to reflect my Pakistani identity as I boarded the plane. And for the Umra itself, I'd asked for a green outfit; for Medina, a light tea-rose pink.

Representation of our unique Pakistani culture was always at the forefront of my mind. Much of what has gone wrong in Pakistan has been because of our inability to balance our relationships. Extreme tilts have caused much bloodshed and mistrust. Sadly, my efforts were not appreciated, and the suspicion grew. Silly scandals were invented daily. But of course, I was no stranger to silly scandals.

Chapter 21

After getting married to Imran, I had to give up a career I had worked so hard to build. I was suffering financially. I'd had to forfeit my primetime current affairs show. It had been a well-paid job with a leading media organisation, Dawn News, and I was on 15 lakh rupees per month (approximately £9,750). I had a son at university who could not get any significant student loans because his mother had remarried, and the student loans company refused to believe that my partner could have no income. My costs went up as I had no free make-up or wardrobe anymore. My husband never once offered financial help, nor did I want to burden him.

By May, I had decided that I needed to do something. I needed another job. Of course, I couldn't go back to current affairs and politics, given my new situation. Perhaps it would have been interesting to try, and be an openly biased anchor in modern media - though in truth, of course, all publications and media outlets are biased in one way or another. In fact, those extremely biased anchors would continue to blame me for even carrying on in my role for the two months I was told not to disclose my marriage. One journalist who had been around for years had ridiculed me for working while being courted by Imran, when the truth was he had desperately wanted the PTI Information Secretary position for himself. But since he was as egotistical a man as my husband, they had parted ways around the 2013 elections. My boss thought differently, reiterating that he was impressed at how I maintained my neutrality. It hadn't been difficult for me. I saw all the problems in PTI. In fact, I had been always very critical of their lack of performance in Parliament and KP. I wanted them to be addressed and let my sense of justice do the talking. And this was not to the taste of the chairman.

Hosting a show related to politics wasn't an option now. So in the end I decided on a lighter kind of chat show, to celebrate those in Pakistan who had really achieved something and should be regarded as 'heroes'. My bosses were not in favour of an entertainment show, and certainly did not want to take me on at my old salary. We finally agreed to get a sponsor, but most reputable businesses did not want to give the PTI leader's wife an endorsement. I finally got a three-month contract and a weekend slot, and began compiling a list of celebrity guests. I had some heroes to find. Of course, at the time I thought my husband would top that list in a heartbeat. It was only later that I would really question the legitimacy of his status as a Pakistani hero. For my bosses, the biggest celebrity in Pakistan was naturally ideal for the launch of a show that they were not too keen to air. Imran ticked the boxes for them.

That interview didn't go quite as I'd expected. Several critics were vocal about it. Imran had slipped back into his public persona. I had tried desperately to reveal his lighter side, but he'd stuck to his buzzwords and well-rehearsed script. As we walked back into the bedroom, he asked, "How did I do, baby?"

I sighed. "It was perhaps the most boring interview I have ever done, darling".

He spun around and shouted, "Well you should have coached me beforehand then!"

I was stunned and didn't say anything. After all, it had been a wife interviewing her husband about life, food, and music. I'd expected him to be natural. I'd expected him to be like he was in private with me: loving, romantic and funny. Why would I coach him for that? It would take me three hours of editing to make the interview marginally less boring. Ironically, he had been a lot more flirty and friendly in our interview the previous year, when I did not even know him. Later, I would be copied into emails sent to him from experts in the U.S, teaching him how to use certain words like 'mafia' and 'change' repeatedly in speeches and interviews. He had perfected the repetitive technique typically employed in the advertising industry. Clearly, even I had failed to break this programming.

The other, lesser-known celebrities were a lot more fun to chat to. Through this show, I got to know a few truly extraordinary people. I heard the inspiring story of the paraplegic artist and model Muniba Mazari, marvelled at the tenacity of the first woman to climb Everest, Samina, and her supportive gem of a brother Mirza Ali Baig, and was in hysterics with the giggly music maestro Rahat Fateh Ali Khan. There were requests by my husband to include people like Ali Zafar, a singer-turned-actor, and some other third-rate performers. The Zafar interview was not a particularly memorable but there was nonstop off-air moaning about my husband. Although I had become used to everyone getting my listening ear just to criticise the performance of the PTI leadership, this time it went on and on and was of a far more personal nature. The singer was heartbroken. He and Imran seemed to have a strange connection. Later in August, Imran would share a horribly self-indulgent half-parody song by Ali Zafar on Twitter. I wasn't sure if the singer even realised that he was actually taking the piss out of people exactly like himself and his beloved hero when he sang '*I am a rock star and I fall in love on a daily basis*.' My son walked in to my room to show me the tweet in utter disbelief. When I asked my husband why he had tweeted about a ridiculous song, he replied, "Baby, I didn't hear it. It was only to sweeten him". I wasn't sure if I preferred this over him tweeting an endorsement of the song because he *had* heard and liked it.

The most endearing interview was of another singer who had committed more time to his passion for education than his singing career. The incredibly shy Shehzad Roy opened up slowly during the show, and I couldn't help but be inspired by this real and rather underappreciated hero of our time. The audience reaction was similarly positive. This man's quiet personality was so impressive that many of us had failed to notice that he had only three fingers on one hand. In that interview, we forged a friendship.

Good values taught at home from an early age are reflected in good behaviour throughout an individual's life. Not only had he excelled in his chosen career, but he was also a supportive husband, a doting father, and on top of that, he had devoted his life to ensuring quality education for Pakistani children. After the interview, I pleaded with him to join the board of governors of my child refuge centre for street children, 'Zamong Kor'. He assured me of his full support but declined a position of any sort, which increased my respect for him further. Here was a young man who wanted no position of authority or political aspirations, but just wanted to contribute back to the community.

In the end, The Reham Khan Show was an important and worthwhile platform when we stuck to its purpose and told the stories of the nation's pride. But in truth, a fair few of the interviews turned into typical run-of-the-mill PR exercises, like the one with my husband. I wasn't in it for that. As clichéd as it sounds, I was only ever in it to make a difference. My goals had not changed, and never would. My priority had always been to ensure the safety and security of my family. Once I could provide for my children, I aimed to provide for everyone I could and do something worthwhile. It was ironic that so many assumed that I was eager to enter politics at the time, even though I had built my career on criticising those in power and pointing out their failures. I intended to serve my country and help my people, and I didn't need a fancy office and a lofty title to do it. The Reham Khan Show introduced me to the kinds of capable and talented Pakistanis that brought me joy and pride, and I sorely wish I could have focused more on them. That would have been a show that I would have been happy to make for years with no salary. Eventually, I would do just that. It would be only a couple of years before I would start travelling around Pakistan with a camera crew to try and bring out the beauty and wonder that I knew existed in my homeland. In one of my travels, I would find a talented singer with real emotion in his raw voice, and would wonder how he had lived his simple life with this amazing hidden talent, while people far less talented than him sat in high castles and decided his fate.

I wanted to change all of this so desperately. The crucial moment for me had been in 2014, when the IDP situation had flared up in North Waziristan. But then, I had simply been an anchor trying to make her way in the messy world of political media. Now, a year later, I was the wife of the chairperson of a popular party in the country. He was the symbol of change. So surely it was a different story now...wasn't it?

Sadly, it wasn't. Even after Imran proposed, he could not help my cause. No one in PTI would listen. I wasn't bothered if I got the credit, but I wanted my husband to be praised for positive steps. At times, I tried to underline that even if the welfare of our people was not a priority, his ministers should realise that a lack of effort would be bad for their political futures. But still no one listened. In fact, by May 2015, IKF (run by Aleema Khan) pulled out of the only rural health centre that was at least providing some relief in Ghoriwala, Bannu. It only required 2 million rupees per month to keep the services running (approx. $18,060). I begged IK to intervene. It was such a small amount that so many could have paid it out of their own pockets. I reminded him that the local body elections were only a month away. I reasoned that Shehram Tarakai, the Health Minister, should at least keep the centre running during the critical months of May, June and July, when child health illnesses are at a peak. No one listened, and PTI were wiped out from Bannu, and Shehram's hometown of Swabi.

I felt deeply that I needed to be doing something to help my people. Not only would my husband not help any of these people, but he would also get in the way of any activity I would undertake that may have helped some situation. He would feel deeply uneasy at the thought of letting me interact with any politicians or diplomats. I was surprised when my husband, a politician with a self-professed Islamic identity, would ask me not to wear my *dupatta* in front of foreigners, especially the U.S. Ambassador. I did not follow orders. I told Imran that I did not wear the *dupatta* to please my husband, nor would I take it off if it offended the Ambassador.

Richard Olson appeared to be a close friend and ally of Imran and perhaps didn't take very kindly to me after that initial meeting. Imran tried desperately not to let me speak much at all in front of the ambassador. If I were to play devil's advocate, perhaps I could say that my husband was just trying to protect me from exposing my real views to this very important ally. Maybe he wanted to keep me in his life but my dreams for Pakistan clashed with the agenda he was told to stay on. However, Richard Olson seemed very keen to pick my brains on political issues, particularly India. I could sense my husband's nervousness from across the dinner table as the ambassador chose to sit next to me. I said what I believed in and what I thought at the time was the ideology of PTI.

I cannot be sure if Imran was trying to protect his idealist wife from speaking her mind or was feeling insecure at the attention she was getting. Nevertheless, he abruptly insisted we left the dinner party and did not even leave me enough time to politely wish everyone goodnight. He was very quiet on the way back. It reminded me of when I had heard that the Afghan Ambassador wanted to drop by some months prior. Since I was a Pashtun, I had suggested that we receive the Afghan Ambassador and his wife and kids for a casual meet up. But Imran told me to not come and say hello when His Excellency dropped by. Instead, the Chief Minister would meet him. I did not appreciate the harsh Afghan policy of the Chief Minister and thought that we should perhaps have been a bit more welcoming as a couple. But Imran did not approve of me meeting any diplomats, while some party members would put me in an awkward situation by arranging Ramadan dinners specifically for the ambassadors.

I could sense that Imran did not really want me to speak at all, so I would avoid conversation with them and take a friend to these occasions. However, he never sat me down and briefed me on what he wanted. I realized that he was not capable of being honest, and instead took a policy of creating situations and pitting people against one another. He was a master of creating misunderstandings.

§

June was marked by Ramadan. Religion had become more important to me as the years had gone by, and this was the first Ramadan I'd had as a married woman in years. In the first week however, I felt very ill once again, with frequent vomiting and headaches. Imran had to go and visit his boys, so I took the kids to Nathiagali. We stayed in the holiday home of Javed Asghar, the owner of Doctors Hospital, Lahore. It was a lovely small property and since there were no staff, I could cook myself. We had the house to ourselves. I was still feeling ill on our first evening there, but literally overnight I got better. I took a selfie in the morning and was shocked to see myself looking so fresh and well without any makeup.

We spent a couple of days completely alone. It was just long conversations about life, love, and friendship with Sara and the kids over mugs of hot chocolate and board games. I never heard from my husband. On the third day, as locals found out I was there, staff at KP House, the provincial government's official guesthouse, asked me to drop in for an *Iftar* dinner. I wasn't very fond of the cold KP House but still went for a couple of hours. As we sat down for *Iftar,* I finally got a message from my husband. There was no 'I love you, I miss you, how are you, what's up?' Instead it read, "You can't imagine how embarrassed I was in front of my kids. They saw your tweet and were shocked. Why would you tweet about our intimate relationship?"

I responded: "I am missing you too. I find it extremely sickening that a 19-year-old boy is monitoring my timeline and entire message threads. FYI, the tweet is about true love so don't flatter yourself. I did not mean you". I was so hurt that I couldn't even eat. I asked to leave KP House and went to bed. I recalled Suleiman's earlier April message: "Be careful. I hope you know that she can get pregnant if she wants to". I had been shocked that the young man could say something like that to his father.

That kid almost had nothing to worry about. Barely a week or two after this, on the 29th of June, we left for Lahore together. We set off in the afternoon from Bani Gala. I had been feeling nauseous again but struggled on. There were already strong winds as I approached the helipad. As we sat inside, I casually commented on the weather not being that brilliant for flying but was ignored. Not long afterwards, the weather turned rather nasty. I saw the alarm erupt on Awn's face. Imran and I would never put the headphones on. Imran would usually get some shuteye, and I would read or ready myself for our arrival. When the helicopter lurched the first time, Imran sat up and leant forward to inquire. Awn was sitting on the edge of his seat, clutching the headrest in front of him. His big eyes had become unusually large. Yousaf described it best: toad-eyes of anger or fear. "*Dadoo* expression [toad expression]," he remarked.

I tried to ask Awn what was being said, but he was so tense that he just lifted his finger, signalling to me to be quiet. In his ear, he could hear the pilot being told to make an emergency landing. I felt a bit sick as the helicopter dipped and lurched but I stayed calm and detached. Jahangir was pretending to be unperturbed but wasn't doing a very good job at hiding his obvious nervousness. He tried at least. Imran was positively freaking out. He clasped my hand, and put the other hand on my knee protectively. I stroked his hand reassuringly and noted that I was wearing my rings. I remember thinking that if the helicopter crashed, my kids wouldn't get them.

Even as I thought this, the windows became covered with a thick layer of dust. There was zero visibility. Everyone's panic and fear was further compounded by the pilot suddenly looking around to see if anyone else could see anything. You know it's bad when the pilot starts looking around for help! Miraculously (and it was certainly a miracle we came out of it) we survived that one, only for the pilot to carry on and send the helicopter spinning into another dust-storm. When we went into it a second time, I wondered why he was doing this. Why not just make an emergency landing?

The fear on the faces of these men was very telling. I said a prayer under my breath and relaxed into my seat with my head back. Imran couldn't get over the fact that I didn't appear scared at all. He kept repeating it over the next few days, both privately and publicly. The incident really exposed him. His vulnerability was clear. It always amused me when I stopped to think about it: some people fear death so much that they can't enjoy living. The most liberating feature of faith is the freedom from fear, especially the fear of death. People who want to live long, or can't face the idea of death, tend to run after material things and live out unhappy lives. It's a bottomless pit: material needs can never be satisfied. The more one gives in to temptation, the harder it is to be gratified.

It would puzzle me later though: Did he admire my strength, or hate me for it? Complementing me for TV appearances and my physical and mental strength was not unusual, but he may still have resented me for all that I stood for.

§

After we'd tied the knot, I had been told to move into Bani Gala that very weekend. I was told not to worry about my house. Everything would be packed up and delivered across. When it arrived, the furniture was horribly scratched and the mirrors were broken. Imran shouted at the staff for being so careless. I was surprised that he recognised it was nice, imported furniture. I was surprised that he cared at all. I told him not to worry about it, and that I would get it fixed.

The more worrying part was moving Maxi in, given all the dogs there. To complicate matters, on the day I brought the dog over, Imran was upset with me. I had been babbling and had told him how I had met General Musharraf at a dinner in England. With nothing to hide, I joked about how Musharraf loved to sing. To humour the General, the professional musicians had started a karaoke for a few minutes and as the mic had been passed around, we'd all joined in. I had sung a couple of lines of a song too.

Imran went ballistic and stormed out, shouting, "How could you sing for that bastard!" I explained that I had not sung for him, and that he and his wife had treated me with a lot of respect. It had been a small dinner gathering with the General and the former PM Shaukat Aziz. Both of their wives were sitting with us. I explained that I had set my own boundaries and it had been a familial sort of gathering. But Imran was not prepared to listen, and wouldn't speak to me the following morning.

I had arranged to bring my dog over that day. As I headed out to the patio with Maxi on a leash, Imran didn't even look at me. I called out to him but he didn't budge. Unknown to me, his dog Motu had been released. The dog was a mix of the Alsatian gifted by Musharraf (who was called Sheru, meaning Lion) and a Kochi sheepdog called Sherni (meaning Lioness). The name Motu literally translates to 'Fatty'. I had to marvel at how unimaginative the names were. Although they'd found it amusing, my kids did wonder how someone could name their dog so callously. Sahir had given us the idea for our dog's name. He hadn't been totally serious when he had launched into Russell Crowe's famous speech from Gladiator years before, but we had all agreed that the name Maximus, and the gladiatorial context, certainly seemed to fit with the Belgian Shepherd that had just entered our lives. By contrast, Imran had seemingly not even bothered to put this basic level of thought into naming his dogs.

On this day, Motu happened to be out and about. Like a flash of lightening, he charged towards Maximus. I screamed as Motu leapt up several feet and pounced on Maximus's ear. The helper, Sajjawal, came running, but Motu would not let go of the rather shell-shocked Maximus. Imran came over rather slowly. By then, Motu had been restrained and the damage had been done. All I could do was hug Maxi and cry.

Later Imran said to me, "I was so mad at you but you looked adorable as you hugged the dog and repeated, 'I'm so sorry Maximus'. I felt so much love for you. You sounded just like a little child. So cute. All my anger vanished".

In December, the dogs would accidentally come face-to-face once again, and this time I would get injured. Imran followed me to the bathroom and insisted I go to the doctor's, even though it wasn't a proper bite as such. He made a phone call to the head of Shaukat Khanum Memorial Trust immediately for advice.

He also insisted that I have a pregnancy test before having the medication. I told him I wasn't pregnant but he kept saying how he'd managed to get the girl related to Mansha's family pregnant with just a drop. So, I had the test, and it came out negative. After the marriage he would ask me to get a pregnancy test even if I was just a few days late.

The many dogs in the house resulted in a series of extra problems throughout the year. Both Motu and Maximus fought over me. It didn't help that Imran soon began to only give attention to my imported Belgian Shepherd, and would ignore his own, local dogs. We had several incidents. In April, Maxi's eye was gouged. The dog situation was to be mishandled by the staff repeatedly and never really resolved over the course of an entire year. I was against the idea of chaining up one of the dogs for half the day, so a new system was devised. In the evenings at sunset, the staff were meant to shut the wooden louvre doors from outside before letting the dogs loose. The two dogs would immediately shift into attack mode at the sight of each other, even through windows and transparent doors. The shutter-like louvre doors would serve as a barrier between the two dogs, and allow them both to roam freely in shifts, one outside and one inside. They could both wander as they liked and there would be no issues, provided someone remembered to close the outer doors.

By the end of June, Ramadan was in full swing. We would all stay up until *Sehr* in the early hours of the morning. My nephew Yousaf would occasionally stay till breakfast before heading home. Embarrassingly, Imran would refuse to turn down the music in his room during *Taraweeh* (extra night time prayers). Club music would be blaring out continuously throughout the night until *Sehr* was served. I couldn't hear what the kids were up to so I would pop my head in every so often just to check on them.

One night as I entered the room, the kids were hyper. That evening, Sajjawal, in his laziness, had forgotten to shut the doors. Maximus had been outside the children's room as usual in the main hall. As Yousaf had entered, Maximus had followed him into the bedroom, laid down and fallen asleep. Sometime later, while Yousaf and Sahir were in the middle of a heated game of FIFA, Sahir had noticed the doors on the far side of the room. He could see out of them, and from the corner of his eye, had seen Motu quietly walk by and sit on the other side of the glass.

Sahir and Yousaf had both immediately panicked, and tried to silently work out a plan. Sahir had looked at the dog lying fast asleep by his foot and tried to get out of his seat to somehow get the outer doors shut (despite being on the inside). But the second he tried to move, Maxi woke up, turned, and flew to the door, ready for a fight. He ran straight into the door, cracking the square glass pane near the floor with his head, while the room erupted in mass panic. Inaya and Ridha started screaming while Yousaf and Sahir leaped to their feet, pushed furniture out of the way, and sprinted to the doors. Sahir grabbed Maxi by the collar and dragged him away before he could force his way through the small hole in the door, while Yousaf (unsure of what to do) decided to heroically squat in front of the broken glass, putting his ass between Motu and the inside of the house. Sahir got Maxi outside the room, thinking they'd had a narrow escape, only to see Maxi bleeding from the head thanks to a shard of glass. But it could have been much worse. Motu had, thankfully, not moved, perhaps somehow sensing that the battle had already been won.

I arrived right after the incident. The children were shivering with relief and adrenaline as they told me what had just happened. We walked together to the dining room, laughing nervously, relieved that everything was OK. Imran joined us as we sat down for *Sehr*. I turned to Sajjawal and told him that his negligence had almost resulted in another accident, but in the very next moment the 'almost' in my sentence became redundant.

Sajjawal had gone into the kitchen to bring in food for *Sehr*. I glanced around the room and saw immediately that the outer doors in this room had also been left open, and Motu was once again on the patio, gazing in. I suddenly realised that the door to the kitchen had also been left open and Maxi was now sitting on the floor in there. As soon as the swing door between the kitchen and dining room was opened by Sajjawal, I shrieked that the dog would come in behind him, only to watch in vain as Maximus shot into the room.

Ferocious barking erupted. It was an exact repeat of what had just happened. Sahir again reacted immediately, quickly and confidently getting up to stop Maximus from reaching the glass panelled door separating the two dogs. Maximus had been raised with a lot of love by us. His repeated injuries were hard to bear. Sahir grabbed his collar, but this time in reckless abandon, the dog had turned his head and planted his huge teeth in the palm of Sahir's hand. The young boy was stood right beside Imran's chair at the head of the table. Sahir hardly made a sound as blood gushed out everywhere. He turned to the side where the basin was and ran his hand under the water casually, seemingly not registering the massive hole in his hand. I screamed and rushed to help him. Imran did not move from his chair as the boy bled in front of him. He paused for a minute to look as I held Sahir's hand under the running water, before turning back to his meal.

I began shouting at Sahir for being stupid. Tears started streaming down my face. The inside of the young boy's palm was outside, staring back at me. Imran continued with his food. I dragged Sahir back into Imran's bedroom. The new Chitrali cook rushed in behind me and tried to help by bringing over the medicine box. I told him to get the car ready and bundled Sahir in. My driver, Wajid, came running up from the servant quarters to help. Yousaf and I took Sahir to the Accident and Emergency of Kulsoom International Hospital. An emergency bandage was applied but we were referred to the bigger facility of Shifa Hospital towards the other end of Islamabad.

We waited for more than an hour to be attended to. Contrary to popular belief, moving to Bani Gala meant I no longer had any support staff around me. As a high-profile anchor, I'd had an entourage with me at all times. Other than the standard makeup lady and stylist, I had a TV crew of four people, and personal home staff of four more at my beck and call. Now as Imran's wife I stood there alone until dawn, with only a devoted driver to help find doctors and go through the complicated private hospital procedures of Pakistan, I realised how unsupported I was.

I watched my son try and make jokes to calm everyone down, despite the blood dripping from his hand. I watched him try to suppress sounds of pain as he was injected with thick fluid around the wound again and again. I finally understood how much I had compromised for a callous man.

I entered the bedroom at around 6:30 in the morning to find Imran sleeping peacefully. It had not occurred to him to call me once in the past four hours. I got into bed as far as I could from him. With his sleep disturbed, he enquired if everything was OK. I responded coldly that it was. And that was that.

Only a few weeks earlier, I had found Imran worrying about a small lump in Suleiman's jaw. I suspected it was just an inflammation of the gums because of the kid's excessive sugar intake. Even so, I was as worried as Imran until the day we found out that it was nothing to be worried about. But Imran had no ability to sympathise, and he was not the type to even pretend to care if he had no immediate interest attached. It explained a lot of things: whenever someone by his side fell ill or died, he was not inclined to give them any time. He was ruthless to the core.

By June, he knew he wanted nothing to do with me. This was well before any political campaigning in Haripur was even planned. It was, however, following his trip to the UK. Not long after, Zulfi would tell me that there had been clear hints during that trip that Imran was tiring of the marriage.

§

The vultures of PTI were desperate to tear me to pieces but couldn't find anything to hang me with. And so, in July 2015, they had a story published about Mrs IK in the *Daily Mail*. Apparently I had lied about a course I'd taken to get a job at the BBC. The local media had turned that story into one alleging that my degree was fake. Fake degree stories were definitely making headlines as General Musharraf had insisted that all parliamentarians be at least graduates and, consequently, lots of candidates had been caught producing fake qualifications. The Information Secretary and JKT media team pressured me to react immediately, and, in uncharacteristic fashion, I did so.

Initially, neither Sahir nor I could figure out the issue. Sahir woke up yet again to see his Twitter feed blowing up over another controversy involving his family. He came to me in a confused but determined state, and we both sat for a second, completely nonplussed. The story was obviously false but unlike most stories, this one had been quite specific in its claims: that North Lindsay College did not offer the course I had attended. It wasn't until Sahir asked me where the college was, so he could call and ask them for my details, that it suddenly hit me that the story had been technically correct. North Lindsay College did not offer a course in Broadcast Media, and even if they did, I wouldn't know, for I had gone to the Grimsby Institute. Clearly there was a typo out there somewhere.

Sahir had been sat next to me with a laptop open on my official website. When he had created it, he hadn't bothered writing the early biography pages. The site had been developed to promote my recent shows and journalistic work, so Sahir had written content for that, and then simply ripped details of previous education and work straight from the official websites of other places I'd worked. As I read those few paragraphs, I finally found the problem.

"Do they have the right college?" Sahir asked.

I didn't even have to respond. Sahir saw the look on my face as it suddenly dawned on me, and let out the most humourless and resigned laugh I'd ever heard.

I had not proofread the information on the website. The college named had been popular among the local Asian community for study support courses. We had lived near North Lindsay College and I had been looking at some courses for Sahir there. We had muddled the names. It was just a careless mistake of a busy working mum. After all the so-called 'controversies' that had hit us, this was almost inconsequential. Sahir had been the type to always take it to heart and challenge anyone who dared to slander his mother, but it had simply happened too often. Both of us were becoming immune to this drama.

We weren't entirely sure what to do. It was a simple mistake that had been blown out of proportion. And it had been turned into huge propaganda. A juicy story of a high-profile former journalist with faked credentials. The *Daily Mail* had facilitated an attack on a woman who had not only worked hard to earn an honest living, but had fought for her own educational rights and tried her best to ensure other girls would not have to face horrible abuse. This woman was abused via a campaign on national TV because of the two men she had married and supported. These were the same British tabloids that would cheer Malala.

With the correct information to hand, Sahir immediately fixed the information on my website, and that only served to make the situation worse. He then called the institution and retrieved a huge number of details, including my course code, start and end date, and even an attendance record. He compiled this all into a statement and urged me to release it immediately. But the damage had already been done. It was just another way in which a completely concrete part of my life was deconstructed and somehow made into a scandal. It would be a while before this story died down.

In Pakistan, as with most developing countries, any stories that come from the West are believed far more readily than local news. The general perception is 'The West cannot lie like we can'. The narrative is strong, and those who suggest an alternative are literally and metaphorically shot down. The Pushto poet Ghani Khan was right: war must be won with the pen.

When I figured it out, I had to smile to myself at the pettiness of those involved. A woman whose spirit cannot be broken down by punches can only become stronger because of petty attacks. In any case, my website stated that I was halfway through my postgraduate training when I got my first job, clearly implying that I had never needed it to get an anchor position. In fact, I had never needed to give a CV for any of my three UK jobs, nor had this short course been a requirement.

While the Chairman of PTI himself did nothing, the Information Secretary of the party, Shireen Mazari, tweeted against the Chairman's wife. Yet still no one batted an eyelid.

Chapter 22

July was the month of change. That was what came to be understood, as anticipation for the major ruling by the judiciary in favour of PTI and the expected gains for Imran reverberated through the house. The Judicial Commission had been formed under a Presidential Ordinance on April 3rd on PTI's request, to investigate allegations of rigging during the 2013 general elections. Months of investigation, countless testimonies, and endless back and forth between PTI and PMLN had led to this moment. There was an air of something like positivity around the house, although it could have just been entitlement and delusion. Sahir told me about one of the most in-depth conversations he and Imran had ever had. They'd been sat for breakfast one day, and Imran had been upbeat and confident of victory. "He told me that there is a 95% chance that there will be overwhelming evidence of rigging, and fresh elections will be called," Sahir recounted incredulously. "He was that confident". Imran put the other 5% down to other positive outcomes, like Nawaz Sharif being forced to resign through a judicial action. Imran was confident that he'd finally be given his rightful place. The conversation did not make any sense to Sahir. When Sahir asked what made him so sure, he had just gestured up at the ceiling and said Allah had given him strong signs, as if that would clear everything up. I don't think any of us were expecting elections, or for anyone in the house to suddenly be handed power the next day. But we certainly were eager to see what would happen, and whether Imran's desires would be fulfilled.

While all this was going on, I was worried about Pirzada *Sahab,* the chief petitioner for PTI. He looked particularly frail and ill. When I asked why Pirzada *Sahab* looked off colour, my husband quipped, "Because he is lovesick". My mind flew back to when I'd been looking for my first job back in 2005, and meeting people in the ARY offices in London. While there, I'd met an attractive older woman who bore a striking resemblance to the British Pakistani singer of the 70s, the late Nazia Hassan. We started chatting, and she'd told me that funnily enough she and Nazia had actually been close friends. Anyway, this very lady would later turn out to be none other than the beauty the rather charming Mr Hafiz Pirzada had fallen so desperately in love with. Indeed, he apparently died of heartbreak later that year (in September 2015) because she'd married someone else. Naturally, I heard this story from the gossip queen of the capital: my husband.

Imran and I had flown into Chitral the day before the Judicial Commission result to attend to those affected by flooding. The Chief Minister, his lackey the Education Minister, the speaker of the Assembly, and (of course) JKT went with us. The army had received us, and Imran, the Chief Minister and I were led into the base for a cup of tea. Pictures would later be released by PTI's social media team to suggest that I was part of an official meeting.

We stayed in the beautiful Hindu Kush Heights hotel, which belonged to the family of the former Prince of Chitral. I briefly visited the garden and dining room, but stayed in my room for the rest of the trip, reading up about the area and the history. Imran flew around locally doing *jalsas* since the relief operations were being handled mainly by the armed forces. He looked slightly disturbed as we unpacked on the first day. I would never ask him about his family, but he would occasionally rant about whatever it was they had done.

Sat across from me, he let loose this time with an hour-long tirade against Aleema. Apparently, her son was getting engaged and our trip coincided with his visit. He went on about how Aleema had said he was humiliating her by turning up right at the time of the engagement. This nephew was getting engaged to the hotel owner's niece. Imran claimed he had no knowledge of it, and had not been invited to the ceremony. Instead of being apologetic, his sister had blamed him for his lack of understanding by turning up in Chitral that very day. Of course it was humiliating for Imran that he had not been invited. Everyone knew him and naturally, the media would comment. I didn't even bother to offer my comments. I listened quietly, not knowing what to say.

I joined Imran, JKT and Awn for dinner in the evening. I kept getting phone calls from work, so didn't notice what Jahangir was saying. I was puzzled at his remarks. He kept saying, "Look Reham, no one knows Barack Obama's sisters!

People only know Michelle Obama". I was befuddled and didn't respond to this random remark. When I returned to the room, Imran said to me laughingly, "You realise Jahangir was tipsy?"

"Oh! I was wondering what he was rambling about".

Of course, tipsy or not, Jahangir was trying to talk sense into me because someone had given him the impression that I had banned the sisters, or prevented any contact with them. I remained oblivious to how Imran was playing us all. I wouldn't understand his modus operandi until much later.

Imran disappeared early the following day. All I was told was that he was going to Kalash valley and the flood-affected areas. When he came back that evening, he looked pale. He staggered into the room a man broken and beaten. It was the 23rd of July 2015. The Judicial Commission had released their report, stating that their investigation had found that the polls were in large part 'organised and conducted fairly and in accordance with the law'. The result left Imran completely shattered. It broke my heart to see him like that. He couldn't speak. He had been defeated. He looked like he had lost everything. He looked at me with helplessness in his eyes. All I could do was quietly comfort him. I knew nothing could console him. His public aura of defiance was nowhere in sight. The commission's report had finally laid to rest PTI's allegations that there had been massive manipulation in the 2013 elections. It stated that there was a lack of substantial evidence.

I had seen it coming. The legal case had been poorly prepared and presented. But Imran's hopes had been high. He was up on time every morning, ready to attend the court. My heart sank every day as I thought of the inevitable disappointment he would face. I had tried to suggest more evidence or a better team, and even that he should not be so optimistic. But Imran, true to his character, put all his eggs in one basket, and 'dreamt like a milkmaid'. But when the result came, there was no one there for him in his grief and misery. No family member, friend or ex-wife to be seen. Not even his groupies were there for him. And then there were the other senior members: the way Chief Minister Pervez Khattak and Atif Khan laughed mercilessly through dinner was unforgivable.

Back at the house, Sahir had been going through the 237-page report and had already written an excellent article on the faults in it. The document was contradictory in many ways, and Sahir had been quick to isolate all the contentious elements. He explained how the report detailed many irregularities, which it would later ignore as it concluded that there was still no reason to invalidate or doubt the results of the election. As he finished his summary, Sahir simply reiterated to me that as controversial and pathetic as this document was, it was probably not wrong. There probably hadn't been a massive amount of rigging, just the usual irregularities. "This is probably a poorly-written report," he added modestly, handing it across to me. "But at least Imran can use what I've written to save face".

Imran needed all the help he could get here, although he would never really appreciate Sahir's effort or offer a thank you. He sat on the balcony of JKT's room in that hotel in Chitral, sad and quiet while the mirth continued at the dinner table inside. I noticed a Qaumi Watan Party female MPA constantly sending memos with a phone number to the Chief Minister, asking him to return her call. Clearly the CM was making future local political deals with his old party while Imran mourned alone.

We returned to our room. I don't know what I had said to Imran on hearing the news and later that night, but he thanked me for how supportive I had been.

"Reham, no one else could have handled me like you did. You know, normally I want to be alone when I lose, but you were simply amazing with how you supported me. I can't imagine anyone else standing by me like this".

I was surprised and thought he meant it. He sounded earnest and sincere. This was only the second time that he had ever appreciated my understanding. The first time had been in September, when the *dharna* had well and truly failed. He had insisted then that we would be together. As I hugged him this time he seemed even more genuine. But perhaps he was already wondering, now that it was clear he wouldn't be leader any time soon, if there was any real point even having a wife, cramping his lifestyle. He rolled over and slept.

My attempt to be completely at my husband's side during this time came at the cost of my immediate family turning against me. When we returned, I was greeted by a mother who was none too happy about me missing her birthday. I also got a rather hurtful message by my first cousin whose son's wedding I had missed. Meanwhile, my husband had already started opening the doors to all those he'd been keeping at a distance. The first example came in the form of Anila Khawaja being given the freedom to come and go as she liked, as before. We had just returned from Chitral and a PTI worker's convention was being held. She had something planned for them again. I questioned him and he didn't even bother to be polite. He basically told me to shut up and put up. He wouldn't be entertaining any dramatics from me he said. And I did shut up. I was helpless in keeping the chief of the harem out.

The security was replaced too. The Pashtun Anti-Terror Squad guards were replaced by Aleema's men, who were distant relatives. Imran started meeting his sisters again and kept it from me. He did not allow me to join the NA-150 celebrations in Zaman Park in Lahore, where he met his old friends again. Moby returned to the scene too. I found out about these meetings a month later, and that too from a TV show. I never asked where Imran went or who he met. I had never told him to sever ties with anyone except his bed partners. Even then, I tried to curtail it only by asking for a list of people coming in through the gate. I suggested that only people on a select list would be let in. But to my anguish, Anila Khawaja now showed me how I had no rights as a wife. When stopped at the gate, she began screaming at the Political Secretary in full sight of all guards and guests, telling them that she would tell Imran to fuck all of them if they stopped her. I was helpless. All I could do was to question the secretariat manager.

"Who am I?" I asked angrily. "Am I his wife or not?"

He hung his head and replied, "Yes, you are".

But it was a losing battle. Everyone knew that I was a nobody. I just had to accept it. Imran had probably had enough of pretending to be a husband. He wanted his old life back. He wasn't given the Promised Land, so he was going to stop the praying. Anila Khawaja and the others were more influential than the legally wedded wife. My children, who were brought up to believe in the sanctity of marriage, would be left to question whether there was any point of a religious legal binding. It seems mistresses have more rights than wives.

§

Immediately after the result of the JC, another critic of Imran would be kicked out of the party. Imran would privately curse the senior retired judge Wajihuddin Ahmed, but could not afford a public confrontation with the very respected judge so had been using delaying tactics to keep things civil. The party had held intra-party elections before the general elections in 2013, and, unhappy with the obvious nepotism, anchors like myself had done programs about it. Internally, a tribunal had been set up to investigate the intra-party elections, headed by Justice Wajihuddin Ahmed. The judge had recommended that Jahangir Tareen, Aleem Khan, Pervez Khattak and Nadir Leghari's party membership be suspended based on the tribunal's decision. But since the findings were not to the taste of the leader and his right-hand man, the tribunal was dissolved that March. Justice Wajih had defiantly continued with the tribunal only to be issued a show cause notice following a defeat in NA-246 (Karachi) in April.

As discussions continued through the months preceding the JC, no resolution could be reached. By July, Justice Wajih's frustration boiled over, and he and Hamid Khan visited Bani Gala. Imran sat with the two gentlemen he despised for over three hours, with only obedience and sweetness dripping out of him. I kept popping my head into remind him that a gentleman was waiting for him and noticed how Imran was using the soft, pleading charm that he had used on me the previous year. I was impressed by the performance. Contrary to popular belief, Imran can control his anger and hide his irritation extremely well when he wants to. As the elderly judge finally stood up to leave, I chimed in by asking him not to go to the media, reiterating what my husband had said. I assured him that we would keep trying together to get Imran to review past mistakes and set democratic norms within the party. Both gentlemen were polite to me but they knew that this man would not change. They had decided it was time for them to change their stance.

By the 5th of August, Imran had not only cancelled Justice Wajih's basic membership, but also openly threatened anyone who followed in the ideological footsteps of the senior judge and dared to challenge his decisions in the future. Imran made it very clear with an emphatic declaration: HE was the ideology.

My nephews and their friends have grown up in front of us. We see them as family. Yousaf's childhood friend, Shahab, was particularly dear to us.

Unknown to me, his uncle was the PTI candidate in NA-19 (Haripur), the largest constituency in Pakistan by population. The seat happens to be where my mother's family hail from and there had been a lot of speculation in the media that I would contest it. Of course, I had no such plans.

I was invited to drop by during the campaign. My main interest was seeing the ancestral home of the candidate's family as a possible location for my upcoming film *Janaan*. Shahab's father had an interest in filmmaking, and their family home was a beautiful traditional estate dating back from pre-Partition days. Sir George Sikander, their father, was a well-known political and historical figure in our region. The large, round pond with a traditional *hujra* (outdoor reception area for men) and the orange orchards surrounding the historical property were perfect for my Pashtun romantic comedy. As I left Bani Gala on the morning of the 7th of August, I had no idea that it would turn into a high-profile election campaign and be described as my formal entry into politics. I took my kids along. We were looking at it as a mini-break in the hilltop town of Abbottabad.

The local PTI leadership of Yousaf Ayub, Ali Asghar and his wife Maliha were family friends of ours. Yousaf Bhai had promised me a visit to my mother's village of Paniah, which I had never seen. Maliha promised me her legendary home cooking. Growing up around political figures, I was expecting the typical tame lunch for the ladies in the candidate's family home and mingling with the female voters. As I approached Haripur, Yousaf Ayub came to my car and said that I would be expected to make a brief speech, before running me through a few bullet points. I panicked. A couple of days ago, I had asked Maliha to write me a couple of Hindko phrases for my visit, but we started discussing set décor for my film and never got around to the Hindko. Now, being confronted with the prospect of addressing a crowd in Hindko was not something I was prepared for. We got to the venue, which I saw was not a home but a large public ground. The crowd started gathering, hearing that I had arrived. Soon, it was much larger than a corner meeting. I had to leave my daughters in the car as there was no nearby home they could go to. I tried to look calm and walked to the stage. I heaved a sigh of relief as it was quite dark by then, and there was no arrangement for lights on the stage. Nevertheless, as I got up to speak, an emergency light was used, and there was the blinding flash of TV cameras. But it didn't go too badly. I said something that people liked. In fact, it was a big hit. I used a mixture of Urdu, Pashto and Hindko to deliver an extempore speech. Late that night, as we sat down to a sumptuous spread in Maliha's home and joked about my funny Hindko, I got a call from my husband.

"*Bari dhooandaar speech ker dee hai sunna hai tumney*" (Heard you did a very powerful speech today), he said approvingly. Embarrassed, I said, "I have written your first article for *The Express Tribune*, and they will run it as a regular feature from now on". I'd always found it hard to accept compliments. A little while later, we got another call. It was Yousaf Ayub, who said that the lacklustre campaign could benefit from a few more appearances from me. Everyone seemed to now be taking an interest in what had clearly been a dull campaign so far. The Deputy Inspector General called, saying that they were expecting retaliation from the opposing camp, so extra security would be deployed from the next day. My main concern was that I had not brought extra clothes for these appearances. The following morning, I went door-to-door and spoke at several small gatherings. From Haripur to Tarbela and back again, I worked hard at this unexpected campaigning, visiting 14 union councils in 48 hours. My daughters sulked; it was very hot and they strongly disliked being surrounded by unfamiliar people or photographed.

Imran was supposed to address a grand *jalsa* on the third day. We stayed over at Ghazi, in the rather ostentatious home of a new rich coalition partner locally nicknamed the *jahazon wala* (shipping man). In the morning, we all took out the outfits we had saved for Imran's *jalsa*. Dressed in our best whites, we travelled back from Ghazi to Haripur. I was looking forward to seeing Imran address the crowds in my hometown of Haripur, where people had been giving me so much warmth and love. The city and I waited in anticipation. We made a short stop for lunch and a corner meeting at a party worker's home. I sat down after making an emotional speech about what a wonderful husband and leader Imran was, when Yousaf Ayub held out his phone to me. He showed me a text from my husband. Yousaf Ayub looked confused and, with a smile on his face, said, "I don't know why your husband has sent me these instructions. Apparently, he thinks seeing a woman in public in a conservative place like Haripur is not acceptable".

The text was an instruction to Yousaf Ayub to make sure that I was kept away from the Haripur *jalsa*. I went red in the face while he just shook his head, rather bemused by my husband's sudden declaration that women should not be seen campaigning in Haripur. As I turned my head to hide my embarrassment, my nephew showed me a text from IK on his phone, saying the same thing but putting it differently. There I sat on the sofa, with people feverishly photographing me. The mouthpieces of PTI on Pakistani media were equating me with the late Fatima Jinnah and Shaheed Benazir Bhutto for my bold confident speeches, even as my husband was telling others to make me disappear.

I decided to leave for Islamabad rather than wait for him in someone's home. As we drove back, I realised how tired I was. I bought the kids ice cream and headed to the house of a friend I had long ignored. In the evening, Awn called me up and said it was his birthday. I had come to regard Awn as a brother, so immediately went to buy helium balloons and met him for dinner. Imran had gone back home but Awn had stayed in the town centre for his birthday dinner. He'd also invited Fauzia Kasuri, who met me rather coldly. I was taken aback since I had been her only advocate in Bani gala. She had now been recruited back, as a strategy to support JKT's defence against Justice Wajih's principled stance. She did not realise she was just being used as a temporary fix to appease ideological supporters.

Later that evening, as I entered our bedroom back home, Imran was pacing up and down yet again. He said a bright hello to me and I responded coldly. I walked briskly towards the bathroom to get the cufflinks I had saved for Awn's birthday. Imran piped up, "Ayub says you lifted the dead campaign in two days!" I was gobsmacked at this man's temerity. I didn't even bother to respond. Days later, we had a discussion in which he put forward a silly excuse about his relatives in Mianwali, who were questioning why his wife had been seen in public. I didn't even bother to argue the point. He went on to emphasise his point. "Why doesn't Yousaf Ayub use his own wife for campaigning if it's OK for women to be in politics?" I informed him that his wife was very much in the field and would contest in the next elections. The couple were involved in each other's politics.

I understood he was getting insecure. I didn't want to embarrass him further. I could see the real reasons for the poor excuses. Did he really think anyone could take his celeb status away from him? How could Imran Khan, of all people, be insecure?

§

August brought to light something that would shock and disturb the nation immensely: the Kasur sex scandal. I had been following the story long before it was officially announced. Up to 300 children (mostly male) were filmed while being forced to perform sexual acts in the village of Hussain Khanwala in Kasur District, Punjab. The scandal involved an organized crime ring that sold child pornography and blackmailed victims and their relatives. On the 10th of August, a couple of days after the Haripur campaign, I took a flight to Lahore. It was a rather last-minute decision, so Aleem Khan's brother-in-law, Faraz, came to receive me. It was a rather impractical choice of vehicle for the roads we would drive on. The two of us drove all the way to the small village of Hasan Pur in Kasur District. We thought we were going to just drop in to the homes of the victims. Nothing could have prepared us for the crowds and heavy media presence there. There were so many people surrounding the vehicle that we could not open the car door for me to get out. Faraz panicked, as we had not arranged any security. But the people had been waiting in the sweltering heat for hours, so I just got out, waded through the crowd, and went into one of the homes to meet the victims. I remember the sweat of the cameramen dripping on to me as I pleaded with them not to follow me into the home and film the young boys. After several polite requests, they agreed not to broadcast the faces of the boys they had filmed. No other political figure had visited yet. The media seemed to have found a new darling in me.

After speaking to the media, I left the place to seek sanctuary in the home of a local PTI leader named Qazi Hassan. He and his family had themselves lovingly cooked for me. I had not met a more genuine family in all my time at Bani Gala. Even their 10-year-old daughter had made a dish for me. Their warm hospitality touched me. Over lunch, we discussed in detail how we could start an advocacy program, provide a trauma counselling service, and give full legal support to the victims. This scandal was a huge embarrassment for the reigning PMLN as one of their MPAs had allegedly been involved in the cover-up. I urged local and top-tier leaders to pursue this. Yet again, no one had the time to help or the sense to take the political space. However, PMLN were pushed into passing a bill in the Senate to criminalise child pornography for the first time in Pakistan. Continued pressure, by a small section of media and social activists produced this new law.

It was a positive step. However, real justice to the victims of Kasur has yet to be delivered. I couldn't forget about APS, and I would never forget this either. My mission was becoming clear.

§

Karachi, jet skiing and scuba diving. That was what was on my agenda as I prepared to fly out to join my kids for a few days of fun. I had promised them. Awn told me that Imran had just told him he was taking his boys for dinner at Tuscany Courtyard. I immediately called Imran and reminded him about how the owner had been extremely rude to me. The team of *Janaan* and I had met him for the film a couple of times. One day, he sent me a rather odd message and told me to fuck off via text. He'd been upset that a meeting had been arranged with his business partner by us. It was quite random since I did not know him in any personal capacity. I never stepped foot in the place again, and neither did Sahir. I showed Imran the texts but I suppose he couldn't say no to free food.

I also reminded Imran that the papers would report negatively on how he was entertaining his boys in my absence. Imran laughed and said, "But Qasim likes the thin crust pizza". I volunteered to order in the pizza and Suleiman's favourite burgers. Imran laughed again and said, "OK then" but still took the kids out. Sure enough, stories of me being kicked out of the home circulated for the next few weeks. Pictures of them were being shared and my conspicuous absence was being highlighted by PTI themselves.

As I landed in Karachi, the local PTI media coordinator (Faisal Vawda's man) had organised a media talk. As we stood there before going live, I joked with the media coordinator, who was very dear to me. He had been pushed into the background because of the turf war between the three PTI leaders in Karachi. I asked him if he had chased up information on a local shelter for destitute children and he said that it had slipped his mind. We carried on with friendly banter and I very innocently said to him, "Don't you '*Bhabhi! Bhabhi!*' me!".

This interaction was filmed. This clip was taken out of context and played on PTI social media platforms. That very night, Imran forwarded me an email by a keyboard warrior from the Naeem ul Haq camp named Tabinda Samar, in which she expressed her annoyance at my attitude with party workers. This single social media team member's emails were apparently enough for my husband to be convinced that his wife must be put away. Ironically, I'd praised my husband in that very media talk and professed my undying commitment to him, reiterating that I was a wife who was supporting her husband. If he were still playing cricket, I would cheer him on, and if he were to become a mountaineer, I would support that too.

On the way, Faisal Vawda told me that Asad Umar had organised an Independence Day rally which he wanted to invite me to. Knowing Asad Umar, I was surprised. Before landing in Karachi, I had only accepted one invitation, as the chief guest at an empowerment conference for women in media. This had been arranged by a PTI anchor very close to JKT's wife. I did not want to go to a rally in the heat of August. I was looking forward to a glamorous event with models and actresses. My motive was to lock the casting for my film, *Janaan*, on this trip, and to relax with the kids on the beach.

We arrived at Faisal's house to find it already full of PTI leaders and workers like Arif Alvi, Imran Ismail, and PTI sweetheart Shahzeb Khanzada. Shahzeb, a popular young anchor, was to fall from favour the minute he started asking questions of an ideological PTI supporter. As we sat in the withdrawing room, Faisal came over with his phone to say that Asad Umar was on the phone. I took the call. Asad asked me how the kids were. I replied politely. He then said, "Apparently there is a rally of some sort today. I'm not sure if I will be going either".

"I am already committed this evening, it's a prior engagement," I replied apologetically.

The phone call ended. Faisal looked at me expectantly and I repeated the conversation. Faisal was befuddled. I turned my attention to the more important discussion of why the PTI Chairman should come to Karachi and visit Sukkur. Shahzeb and I were insisting that it was the need of the hour while Arif Alvi seemed indecisive. The president of PTI Karachi, Ali Zaidi, was against the idea. He spent most of his time in Dubai, where his family lived. Over the phone, Ali argued that it was inadvisable for Imran to visit. Ali clearly couldn't come back in time for Imran's expected arrival on the 19th of August.

I retired to my room to take a shower and get my hair and makeup done. After nearly a year of personal neglect, I was now being treated to professional makeup and a gorgeous outfit for the evening (sent by Nomi Ansari). Oblivious to the politics in the party top-tier, I got ready. As we left for the hotel, I noticed Yousaf looking rather tense. He said he had overheard Imran Ismail say to Faisal Vawda over the phone, "Conjure up an excuse but make sure Reham does not attend the rally". I dismissed the comment, saying, "But Yousaf, I am going to the other event".

At the event, the PTI-loyal anchor (who insisted he was a medical doctor) shocked the audience with his blatant gender insensitive language. His non-PC comments had me groaning. I did notice how Fauzia Kasuri left just before my speech with her faithful groupies. I then caught sight of Sahir leaning dejectedly against the entrance door to the hall. He wouldn't come in. His eyes looked sad. I was familiar with this expression. Sahir's casual attitude can be deceptive; he is an extremely perceptive person. I could see something had happened. Regardless, I carried on. As we left the premises, Sahir whispered to me, "What the hell is going on?"

"What do you mean", I enquired.

"Imran was on the phone shouting at Awn about you attending the PTI rally. He went on and on about how you must not attend it".

"But I am here, Sahir," I replied.

I could see how Sahir felt humiliated and upset at my husband's devious methods. I did what most mothers do: I covered up and pretended that I was fine with it. As we returned that night, Faisal had a similar stunned expression to my son. Faisal went onto tell me that on Imran's last visit to Karachi, Faisal had conveyed to him how my political role was wanted by both PTI supporters and the kingmakers alike. I threw my head into my hands and wailed. "Faisal *bhai*, no wonder he is being weird. Why would you say that to him?"

He responded: "Because *Bhabhi*, I have been told this. You would be great for PTI".

I went to bed feeling very queasy. The following day, I woke up to pictures of Imran hoisting the national flag in Bani Gala with his sons and Yousaf Sallahuddin. As I had predicted, the news in three major Urdu dailies added how Mrs Khan had been kicked out of Bani Gala for the boys' visit.

The day went by relatively peacefully. I met a few actors for auditions and visited a couple of media buying houses to pitch for my film. The following morning, on the 16th of Aug, I woke up to eight tweets from my husband. The tweets categorically stated how Reham would not be given a PTI ticket and would not be attending any future PTI events. I stared in horror. I knew what media would say even before I read the reaction. I put together a diplomatically-worded tweet endorsing what my husband had said. I then messaged the man I had married, the one who had promised to give me honour.

"How could you do this? Why would you embarrass me on social media?"

His feeble response was, "I am only trying to protect you. People hate you and are jealous of you".

I didn't bother engaging in any further discussion and instead called a friend to distract myself. Later that afternoon, I was interviewing the leading actress, Mahira Khan, for my show. Even though I did not cry, the makeup artist struggled to hide the puffiness on my face. It was to be my last assignment for Dawn TV.

§

Over August, the signs of voodoo were everywhere.

The years of mocking my family and friends over their fear of black magic came back to haunt me. I started finding the same mysterious cuts in the back of my night-shirts that Samina *baji* had described. Every so often, *taweez* (amulets) would appear in bedside drawers. They would typically have Imran's full name written in the centre in Urdu, with strange figures drawn in a grid around it. They would be folded tightly, and resembled chewing gum sticks. I'd developed a habit of cleaning the drawers out to get rid of the snacks being regularly smuggled into Bani Gala, and hence would stumble across these. When I asked Imran where they had come from, he would tell me that Uzma's (the youngest sister) husband, Ahad, had brought them. The amulets would typically appear every time I was away for a few days, and usually when the boys were over for the holidays.

The last *Taweez* I found came with a baby photo of Suleiman, in-between two pieces of paper. My young, rather anglicised assistant laughed at me as he took it to throw into the river, saying I was losing my mind. But when he came back, he was shaking, and confessed that as he touched the *Taweez* and put it in the water, he'd been blinded for a minute with a severe headache. He had to sit for a while as he did not feel well enough to drive. I'd asked him because the staff wouldn't dispose of the items for me when I would ask. I was told by guards at Bani Gala that Aleema's husband would come and bury amulets in the flowerpots near the front door, and strange spells were cooked in pots in the room of Navaad, the man who looked after the buffaloes. I called the same friends and cousins I had previously jeered to ask for help. Their recommendations were reciting certain Quranic verses.

I was totally at a loss. Black lentils, spiritual advisors, magic amulets? Just what the hell had I gotten myself into here? My family had always adhered to a strict code of simplicity, as prescribed by *Sharia*. No practices falling in the sphere of *Biddah* (heresy) are practiced. Even the concept of 40 days of mourning after a death is frowned upon. Superstitious practices or magic is strictly forbidden. So for me, this was a huge culture shock. I developed a habit of constantly reciting the four *Qul* (verses from the Quran) and *Ayat-ul-Kursi* to ward off the evil eye.

I asked Imran to make sure he would recite the *Ayat-ul-Kursi* if and when I was not around. To my surprise, he informed me that he did not know it. I sent it to him in a text, only for him to tell me he could not read Arabic. And so I decided to send it to him bit by bit in Roman English so he could learn it. Much of his knowledge about Islam had come via people who had become his spiritual teachers. I explained to him that the beauty of Islam was that every individual must read the Quran themselves to eliminate the middle-man. This would take away any misinterpretation or misinformation.

I had always had a strong unshaken belief that there is only one power in the world: that of Allah. I had only ever asked him for help. But there were a couple of times where people had hurt me and betrayed me without reason and I had drifted away. I was sulking at my creator like an angry teenager. These were very brief periods in my life. I would come back to find solace in prayer again. The most wonderful outcome of my marriage to Imran and everything that came after, was that, despite all that was done to me and all that was planned against me, my faith became stronger. Every attack strengthened my faith. There is no other explanation for how I survived so much. There was so much time, effort and money poured into campaigns to destroy my image and career. But every time I stood on the prayer mat, I would be protected from all kinds of attacks, human and supernatural. I owe my deep spirituality to those who wanted to destroy me.

You will go through these periods in life when you sit alone with tears stinging your cheeks, questioning God. Why is this happening to me? Why, when I have done nothing wrong? Why am I being punished? Why would you give me so much pain? You will not understand while you are suffering. You won't understand why you are alone. But a few months later, you will see how much better off you are because of that horrible injustice done to you.

I had only wanted a small home where I could bake cupcakes with my children and look after my husband. I wasn't expecting to get married to a romantic hero from a Bollywood film. But I ended up marrying men who made me wonder if being with the villains of stories could possibly be less agonising. My first husband would mock me by saying that I was so incompetent that, I if I left him, the only way I could survive would be to be a Page 3 girl (glamour models who are featured topless in British tabloid *The Sun*). The insult was absurd, not least because I was never a woman with the right kind of 'assets' for that.

Had my first husband been a kind, quiet man, I would have never left him. But then I would not be who I am today. My life was not intended to be ordinary. The quiet life wasn't what I was born for. We simply don't know our strengths until we are put to the test.

§

It was a balmy evening in August. Like most evenings, I joined my husband as he walked up and down the long garden at the back of the property. He would get upset if I was late to join him. I saw this possessive attitude as flattering rather than suffocating. As I reached him, he extended his right hand towards me in a familiar gesture. My thin fingers were crushed in his large hand, with his rather thick fingers an awkward fit for mine. He greeted me with a pleasant smile as always, and asked, "How's my baby today?"

In my typical style, I would start babbling excitedly about my day. He had labelled me as an eccentric, and I got the impression he found eccentricities adorable. He would shake his head, amused by my passionate descriptions, and laugh wholeheartedly at my exasperations.

As we walked he suddenly said, "Baby, why don't you have a glass of red wine once in a while?"

I rolled my eyes and responded, "Darling, I'm not a forty-plus man at risk of heart disease".

"It's good to have a glass of red wine occasionally," he persisted.

I gave him a quizzical look and he changed the subject.

Later that night as I sat down for my evening meal, unusually he sat down with me. Imran would avoid eating in the evening. He again asked me, "So you have never had any red wine?"

I stopped and looked at him suspiciously.

"Why do you want me to drink red wine so desperately? What is this about?"

"Oh, nothing. It's just that Nomi Shah brought me some stuff and brought a bottle of red wine too. When I said to him, 'You know I don't drink red wine,' he replied, 'Oh, it's for Reham. I said, 'Reham doesn't drink'. Nomi was surprised and said, 'Oh really! Did she say that to you Imran? Daniyal Aziz, the PMLN MNA, told me he helped a rather drunk Reham into her car after a party!'"

As Imran said all this, he got up from his chair to my right and walked to the bathroom. I followed his movement with my eyes wide open, and then I whispered angrily, "Imran, you see this!" I lifted my clenched fist up from my side: "If someone had dared to say that about my wife to me, this punch would have found his nose!"

Imran laughed nervously and said, "Oh, he just repeated what Daniyal had said to him. You know what bastards these PMLN are!"

"No Imran, I know who the bastards are, and they are not in PMLN," I replied through gritted teeth. "Daniyal would never say a thing like that about me. I know the family. They have always treated me with utmost respect. His father once came to stand by my side when he saw I was uncomfortable with a tipsy man who was trying to talk to me at a reception in their home for the diplomat Robyn Raphael".

"OK relax, no need to get worked up!" said Imran.

"I am disappointed that anyone can walk up to my husband and say stuff about me. People do not dare to say anything about a girlfriend. I'm your wife for God's sake!"

That night, as my husband held me close, he threw a couple of British place names at me and asked if I had ever lived in those towns or cities. I said, "No, why do you want to know?"

"Nothing," he replied. "I've played for these counties so was asking if you were familiar".

"Of course I am familiar," I said. "I was doing weather for the South of England!".

We fell asleep. In the middle of the night, I suddenly woke up with a start. My body clock is set to *Fajr* so I'd always wake up before *Azaan*. But I was surprised to see it was not yet time. Since I was wide awake and felt uneasy, I decided to pray *Tahujjud* (special night prayers). As I returned from the bathroom and walked towards the prayer mat, I noticed the cushions on the sofa at the foot of the bed were disturbed. I pulled one of them up to fit it back in the seat of the sofa, and discovered Imran's Blackberry hidden underneath it. He had never hidden his phone before. I picked it up and stopped dead in my tracks. The first message on the screen was from Max, a weird man from Birmingham I had met at the big Bani Gala family dinner the year before. As I looked at the thread, it became clear why my husband had been asking about living in Maidenhead, and his sudden interest in red wine. Just after I had nodded off, Imran had messaged him back that he could not find out if his wife had ever lived in Maidenhead. Max had asked him to confirm where I had lived, and had insisted Imran meet Nomi Shah again for further details of my fondness for red wine.

I stared at the bizarre juvenile messages with my head spinning. What was my husband doing? Why was he trying to find out where I had lived and if I had a penchant for red wine? I walked over to him, woke him up, and demanded to know what this was all about. He cooked up a silly story about how the *News of The World* journalist, Mazhar Mehmood, was about to do a story on my past. The infamous reporter often referred to as the 'fake sheikh' had done stories on Tulisa and Pakistani match fixing. Imran said that the journalist was a cousin of Max, and so he felt he should warn Imran. I wasn't prepared to believe all this bullshit.

The following morning, I wrote him a long email explaining the sanctity of marriage. Many months later, I had to re-read my own email and it stabbed my heart again. It sounds like a young girl, earnestly trying to keep her marriage intact. But that marriage was only sacred for me. It was simply an 'arrangement' for the man I was married to. And the arrangement was inconvenient now.

Was he trying to find dirt on his wife to justify getting rid of her? From the day his sons visited in August, the campaign to get rid of me had been accelerated. In print media, both in Pakistan and the UK, and electronic media in Pakistan, the maligning campaign had been re-invigorated. Stories of us sleeping in separate rooms, eating separately, and having violent arguments were circulated. I was described as a woman who was physically abusive, out to kill her own husband and take over the party. When I would express my anxiety at this ugly campaign, Imran would shrug it off by saying, "Oh, don't pay attention to these. Arif Nizami is a drunk prostitute. That other one is an arrogant asshole. This type of news used to circulate about me and Jemima too".

I quietly responded, "But then you guys did get divorced ".

Chapter 23

"He lies and uses everyone, and everyone lies and uses him".

That was what I heard from everyone who knew him in a personal capacity. I would in time sympathise with this completely. I never knew what to believe. Initially, one of the biggest issues between us was his constant questioning of my past. It was a Spanish Inquisition every other day. He had huge trust issues. Before we married, I threatened to ditch him because of his accusations on two occasions. My forgiveness and tolerance was to give me more headaches now.

I had reason to believe that Aleema and Moby had initiated the poisonous campaign against me in August 2014, and every so often there would be top-up doses. Imran's obsession with my past did not cease. He specifically wanted to know if I had ever had a white boyfriend. Photoshopped images with radio host, Alex Dyke, were circulated on social media. The interrogation didn't stop after the marriage. It was constant suspicion and questioning. In intimate moments, he would ask for details, and would insist that he would enjoy it because it would make him jealous. Maybe it was his kink, but it had the opposite effect on me. It was very off-putting.

While I had no interest in delving into any of that, he would not stop bragging about his past conquests. Imran was keen to tell me everything right from the start. I thought it was a daily confessional moment; perhaps he wanted to get it all off his chest. I tried to listen like a counsellor. But his list was endless. I was overwhelmed by the mass of unwanted sordid details, from the French stunning beauty who he had dated but couldn't kiss because of her bad breath, to weird encounters with wives of famous local and foreign politicians and position hungry female parliamentarians. He had seemingly slept with everyone on the planet, and would even share sickening details of the sexual preferences of other friends and their wives.

My mum had raised us with extreme prudish values. I come from the sort of family where sex is not linked with lust. For our older generation to our youngsters in their early twenties, the idea of sex is only associated with falling in love, and always in the context of a committed relationship. As the family is deeply rooted in religious beliefs, the idea of an open relationship is unthinkable. Imran initially wouldn't believe that I had not had a colourful past. He would just shake his head in disbelief. His lifestyle was so out of the ordinary that no one could compete with his hall of fame. He had effectively been a bachelor all his life with no pressing responsibilities of providing for a family. He found it hard to comprehend the life of us ordinary mortals. Life after parenthood revolves around children, for most of us at least. For a busy mum of three, it's hard to find time to sleep, let alone sleep around. He also couldn't understand that living in a Western society didn't mean everyone was immoral or an alcoholic. I know many people of all ethnicities who choose to drink responsibly, or not at all, and remain committed to the same partner for their entire lives.

Immorality is not restricted to a race or a religious identity. I feel morality comes from being raised in a loving and secure home. My children have the freedom to choose where they live, and the freedom to go where they want to go. They are not pestered with questions or treated with suspicion. As a result, they never leave home. They choose to spend all their spare time in Pakistan. They were never told not to drink or do drugs, but the effects and the way they could destroy lives were discussed. And that was all. More importantly, they grew up with only my influence. I never smoked, drank, or did drugs. It is very possible to live, socialise and work in the West, have white friends, and work in music and media without doing any of those things. Many of my colleagues in media were either teetotalers or had the occasional glass of wine on festive occasions. But Imran would insist that it was not possible, that he knew more than me about life in the UK and it was inconceivable that I had managed to avoid drunken orgies.

He would then start off about his experiences. When he had proposed to me, he had appeared to want to shake off the depraved lifestyle he owned up to having led. According to him, he had been very depressed after the result of the 2013 general elections and his nasty accident. He had gone on the rave. According to Imran, in this period, a young girl (who happened to be Mian Mansha's nephew's wife's relative, the most influential industrialist in Pakistan) had become pregnant. We had all seen a journalist's tweet, hinting at Imran getting a young 21-year-old pregnant in May 2014. Umar Cheema's story was accurate about the pregnancy, but he had been accused of lying, and trolled horribly. Imran had publicly reacted with anger to the accusation, and had maintained that GEO was a media group out to malign him.

The story had in fact come to me first. In the winter of 2014, I was sat in Zaffranos Cafe in F11 when someone who worked for General Hamid Gul's thinktank asked to meet me. He, along with my content producer, had come to convince me to do a piece on this very story. They told me that there were recordings of phone calls of Imran threatening this young woman and telling her to abort the child. I had scolded them and sent them packing, saying I wasn't a tabloid journalist who'd be interested in the bedroom antics of politicians. It was barely even a secret; the girl's own cousins confirmed it to me. PTI women like Fauzia Kasuri showed pictures of the girl openly. Anchors talked about the intercepted calls of an irate Imran calling the girl to get the pregnancy aborted. The girl's close friend told me that the abortion was quite late in the fifth month and there was a designated doctor in London who had been performing these duties for a decade. He also told me that Imran had a friend in London who looked after him, and also cleaned up any mess created by The Leader. I never believed any of these stories.

Months later, however, I was being told by Imran Khan himself that it had actually happened. He described the girl as a bit of a nerd. He'd been surprised at her getting pregnant, but insisted it had scared him. It was a watershed moment for him (a phrase he used liberally to explain his frequent change of heart). He said he was so scared that he had decided to end his wicked ways and settle down. He claimed he wanted no more of that disgusting life. I was convinced.

Seemingly intelligent women all over the world fall prey to the arrogant belief that they can cure a man. In reality, nothing and no one can change you for better or worse, besides your own inner suggestibility. I also kept telling myself that he was perhaps bragging, and that it never happened. After all, he could not impregnate his own wife. But the months went by, and as he revelled in telling each sordid detail, I became less convinced that I could bring about any change. He later revealed that it hadn't been just a one-off threesome in a state of depression after his dreadful fall and injuries, as he had initially described it to me. It had in fact been just another night of sexual depravity, virtually indistinguishable from all the other orgies that were very much the norm in his life. It would be a while, but I would hear a lot more about this story, and I'd learn where the girl was living. At the time, she'd been advised not to go public for fear of *Sharia* punishment in Pakistan. And as per Pakistani culture, the pressure of brushing this under the carpet and getting married off instead was a priority. I was told that she'd been scarred by the experience, and the constant threats and bullying had been too much to cope with. And I would receive confirmation that DNA evidence of that aborted pregnancy of January 2014 was still in existence.

There was so much to take in, and this was just one story. He was obsessed with talking about sex and sexual gossip. I was apparently boring as I didn't have anything to contribute, even gossip-wise. He would bring up Ayla Malik, a PTI politician he had been involved with, and say that she always had lots of gossip on everyone. Apparently, the only reason he'd had to stop seeing Ayla Malik was because her boyfriend of eight years had come to confront Imran. The gentleman was a media mogul, desperately in love with the woman. He basically came to Imran and said, "Look, if you are not serious about this woman, please leave her alone as I want to marry her".

Imran recalled the interaction and said it was an embarrassing moment for him, but he assured the boyfriend that he would stop meeting her. And yet, throughout the marriage, there were phone calls between Imran and Ayla. Ayla Malik remained a constant presence in Imran's life, and was openly referred to as chief consort up until the 2013 elections, even when rumours of a secret marriage were rife. Later, while proposing to me and trying to comfort me about the ugly campaign his sister had started, Imran confided in me that Aleema had started a similar campaign for Ayla and her young daughter. They were maligned, threatened with severe consequences, and forced to back off. At the time, I couldn't understand why the sister would have a problem with him settling down, especially if the lady in question had a lot in common with Imran.

Then there were the Bollywood stories, which were also laced with prejudice. It was the attitude of the women in the family towards other women which was most shocking. Bollywood and cricket have always had a long-standing romance, but the good thing is that now we have stories of legitimate relationships being openly accepted, with happy endings. Imran was keen to confirm all the stories I had thought were just rumours. The most famous story, of course, was that of a Bollywood superstar of the 70s. Considered to be one of the sexiest heroines of all time, there had been rumours of Imran and her. We had heard these whilst we were growing up. Imran confirmed to me that they were true. Though Imran was happy to sexually engage with actresses, he and the family clearly thought little of them. He recalled with a smile how his mother had been called by the newspapers, asking about the actress. She had replied, "My son would never marry a prostitute!" and slammed the phone down.

Imran's stories always painted the women in an unflattering light. He told me how he met her in Bombay, had his fill, and moved on. But, according to Imran, the lady followed him to London and became clingy. Imran said she scared him because she would ask to be slapped around during sex. Apparently, she was used to this kind of violence. Her boyfriend at the time had reportedly hit her in front of his guests at a party in a hotel, and so badly that her eye was left with permanent damage. I would check both these stories with a film producer friend of hers months later, who told me that it was actually Imran who had chased her, and that she had been very financially benevolent towards him. The sexy bombshell of the 70s had described the interaction with our mutual friend rather disparagingly (in her filmy words) as, "*Naam baray aur darshan chotay*" (the hype was bigger than the rather small package on offer)". Perhaps that was the root of the insecurity complex Imran had. I suppose many women are misled by the utter myth of big hands and feet suggesting a bigger package elsewhere too.

Many of Imran's stories left my childhood memories of well-loved stars utterly tainted. He went on to tell me how one of the most beautiful icons of our time, a young singer, was the most boring fuck he had ever had. He found it odd that she not only chose to get involved with him, but that her own brother would bring her to meet Imran. He described his distaste for the family and their value system, and at how she was constantly trying to get Imran to set up a business with her father. I found his comments quite hypocritical since it takes two to tango, and pointed it out to him, but his logic was, 'I am a man, and a demi-god at that. The same rules do not apply'. As always, I would later be told an entirely conflicting version by others. A friend of the family in question explained that it was actually Imran getting involved, using their cars and wanting to be a part of the business while romancing the young star. The father put his foot down and the relationship was nipped in the bud. After hearing all these stories, I didn't know what the truth was, but I certainly didn't accept my husband's skewed version of events.

Then of course, there were female politicians, like the one who, according to Imran, in her desperation for the Information Secretary position in PTI, had suddenly asked to meet him at midnight. He had naturally made himself available immediately. According to him, she seduced him but as he dropped his trousers, she suddenly demanded exclusivity, which dampened his libido. He says he walked away, and the promised Information Secretary position walked with him. She, of course, told a very different story. According to her it all started when she received photos of the celebrity cricketer's crown jewels one day, like many other women had before her. When she messaged back saying, 'How can I be sure it's of yours?" he sent another picture, this time with his wristwatch in frame, saying, "I am sure you recognise this watch, don't you?" So hurt was the lady that the television makeup rooms across the country were told a different story by a very distraught woman for years to come.

I'd also been noticing the constant sexting ever since the *nikkah*. It was hard not to. A couple of times, I caught him responding to a woman who was constantly attacking me with vicious misogynistic comments from her Twitter account. She called herself one of 'Daddy's lil girls', and Imran had told her that she would always be his 'special one'. Privately, he made fun of this girl's big nose and called her 'Sindhi Maria' for some reason. He gave me the same explanation he had for most women in his circulating harem: that she was filler, with the worst possible bad breath. Halitosis was a talking point for Imran. He would comment on my great teeth several times a day, and how my breath was so fresh. He was extremely good with dental hygiene himself. He complained how he was surrounded by people with bad breath. It became a code word whenever he was travelling with Faisal Javed and Naeem ul Huq (or Naeem ul

Fuck as Imran liked to call him). These two were on the top of his 'bad breath cheating husbands' list.

Imran loved sharing other people's cheating stories. Apparently Naeem's whiskers would start twitching in the presence of women. Imran told me how Naeem's wife had once caught him cheating on her with the TV actress Faryal Gauher, and had bitten him in the shoulder. Imran and Awn also constantly referred to Shah Mehmood's (apparently rather open) association with his assistant, who served on the JC legal team. Awn would bring Imran and I gossip of how a KP President had also been awarded the post because of Shah Mehmood's appreciation of the local beauty. No one in the party batted an eyelid at this nepotism. They openly flaunted it. Besides Jahangir, PTI leaders made no effort to hide their 'extra-curricular activities'. According to Imran, Jahangir had been caught once by Moni and hadn't dared to cross her again. But he clearly had his female admirers, the 'JKT girls'. I found the thought nauseating.

Imran insisted he used to tell all young men never to cheat on their wives because it would break the women. Infidelity, he said, destroys homes, causing pain and irreparable damage. In our first meeting (and repeatedly through the marriage), he confided in me how he hated his father for constantly cheating on his mother. He would go back to those memories, and recount a young Imran who had been left traumatised by the sight of his mother crying hysterically and attempting self-harm because of his father parading his mistresses around with no regard for her. He described a father who would arrive home drunk night after night, leading to violent confrontations between the parents. He had clearly been left deeply disturbed because of the turbulent relationship of his parents. If he caught me looking sad or not smiling, he would fly into a rage and storm out. He would later come and explain his behaviour: "Baby you have such a beautiful smile. When you have that look of disappointment on your face, it reminds me of my mother and how she looked at my father's many failings". It would drive him mad the minute I would be quiet, or had a disappointed expression on my face. "Baby, why do you stop smiling?" he would enquire.

I would reply, "Imran, has it ever occurred to you to do something to put a smile on my face? There is deprivation and misery. You promised to bring change and you are doing nothing about it".

§

Imran would mutter something and blow over me every night before going to sleep. When I asked what he was doing, he told me, "I am doing the same prayer my mother used to say for me, for my protection".

He would hold me close to him; so close that I would sometimes not move so as not to disturb his sleep, but I slept a bit better when he held me. On days when he was angry, I frequently lay awake looking up at the unfriendly ceiling and counting the downlighters. I couldn't sleep at all. It wasn't only his unexplained anger and sudden mood swings. When angry, he would make a fortress of pillows around him, and was inaccessible. It was impossible to reach him in that mood. He would not give me a reason or an opportunity to make things right. No reasoning or apologising would work. The words of an Arab friend (who had lost his beautiful Irish wife to cancer) rang in my ears: Never go to bed without making up. That had been his wife's rule, and he had not known she would die so suddenly, with so many regrets.

Something else felt wrong too. It didn't feel like home. It was like I was in a hotel room, or in someone else's home. I couldn't get myself to sleep. One night in August, I woke up suddenly from a nightmare. I had dreamt that Imran and I were swimming in the pool in the dark of the night. In the pool behind us was a white woman, swimming up towards the surface. I noticed her, and, as Imran hadn't spotted her yet, I tried to push her head down so he wouldn't see her. I was trying to get rid of her in my dream.

In reality, I could never really get rid of any of the exes, but I didn't initially see Jemima as any threat to our relationship. Besides, she was the mother of his children so it was understandable that contact had to be maintained. I had never even brought up the subject of Jemima in the house. She was his past. I was his present, and I was confident of Imran loving me. She was mentioned only by Imran, and frequently. In private, it was far from complimentary. In public, she was mentioned in all interviews, and very favourably. I understood it was good for his image to be seen as a good ex-husband, and I used it myself in speeches. He may not have told me he liked her, but he was a very accommodating ex-husband so I wasn't really lying. Other people brought this up. During our first interview together on the evening of the *valima,* the interviewer had asked if I was disturbed by the presence of 'Rebecca' in the house, referring to the Daphne Du Maurier novel. I was puzzled at why he would say so.

When I would look after Imran back then, he would comment on the *sukh* (bliss) of marriage and how Jemima had never provided him with that, saying, 'Reham, not every woman is like you". But only a few months later, insulting articles were sprouting everywhere and social media sites owned by PTI started putting up romantic photos of Jemima and my husband. It was noted that he looked more in love with Jemima, and seemed distant in photos with me. I got fed up of her constant phone calls and demands, so I didn't want to discuss her in private even when Imran brought her up. One evening as I entered the room, Imran was pacing up and down. He looked up and had just started his sentence with, "Jemima just called..."

I put my hand up and said, "Don't want to hear it," and backed out of the room.

A couple of days later, on the 3rd of September, we were sitting for breakfast when I noticed a link to a *Daily Mail* article on Twitter with the headline 'Reham Khan claims Jemima is behind the smear campaign'. The article quoted a cousin of mine in the UK, who had apparently claimed that I had said that Jemima had been driving the hate campaign against me.

"Have you seen this?" I asked Imran. He replied that it was what he wanted to tell me the other day. I casually muttered something on the lines of, "Well, what goes around comes around," and moved onto the next article. He was getting ready to leave for Sindh, and I was getting ready for a conference on education hosed by the NGO Alif Ailaan. I used to put on makeup in his bedroom as he got ready in the bathroom, so we could talk. He didn't like me disappearing while he was around. I would use the hour he was in the gym to take a shower or sort my wardrobe out. Besides that, we were inseparable while in the house. He had perhaps received calls from her or the kids. I guessed this because, even after a couple of hours, he was very tense and asked me why this article had been printed.

I turned around and said, "How would I know?"

"But it says your cousin said this".

"Imran, I don't have any cousins in the UK unless you count my ex-husband. You think I had something to do with it?"

"Qasim says mum is so upset because of this article".

I replied, "Well, she should deal with it, just like my kids and I have dealt with it on your advice. 'Well left', isn't that what you say?"

I was honestly not at all sympathetic because of all the rubbish that had been thrown my way, but not for a minute did I think that Imran did not believe me. I got ready and went to my conference. It was a long affair and Baber, JKT's social media head, had lined up an interview with Shahzad Iqbal, which I was running late for. I got back and we immediately started the interview. I had not checked Twitter all day. In the interview, I gave assurances that I had no problem with Imran announcing on Twitter that I would not be allowed to contest from a PTI platform, as I could not give up my nationality and had no intention of contesting in elections. The interviewer than stumped me by asking me about the day's tweet by Imran about Jemima. I had no idea about the tweet. I answered the question, and as the interviewer took a break, I signalled to Baber and asked him what it was about. He hadn't seen it either. Apparently this was the big news of the day, but my husband, who had promised me repeatedly that he would never tweet again without discussing it with me first, had left at 2pm without informing me that he had tweeted about me once again. I was embarrassed, and wished I had cancelled the interview.

In my anger I sent out an email to Imran. "I see who you see as family and who you don't". I also called Awn and angrily told him that they should all watch the interview. If they chose to not defend me, I would have the ability to defend myself and I would also speak now. It was an empty threat driven by helplessness. I realised that it was pointless to expect this man to defend me as his actions were tied to purse strings in London. I was alone that night, so I prayed and forgot about it easily. Imran was apparently up all night. He came back and we didn't even fight about it.

A few days later, the night before his flight, he casually mentioned he was flying out to London to meet the kids the next day, and staying the whole week there. I had heard whispers from the staff down at the secretariat, and was waiting for my husband to tell me he was going. It was odd since he had just seen the kids and he never stayed there that long. He passionately kissed me over and over again and I asked why he didn't tell me earlier. He got angry and said, "Awn should have told you". I replied that Awn was not my husband, and that informing someone that one was going away was a courtesy even a mistress would be afforded. He got rather angry at this.

I fell asleep. He woke me up again and was extremely loving towards me. As I clung to him with tears in my eyes, I explained how embarrassing it was for me to find out from the staff. He left in the morning and I was renewed with hope that he did actually still care about me. But as the days went by, pictures of him with Qasim from Jemima's social media were included in news stories that suggested that he was back with his ex-wife. Through the entire week, he never once called or texted me. Instead, I got a call from Awn, begging to see me. I saw Awn as a member of staff and did not appreciate him warning me that my marriage was in danger. He came over and said he had been literally crying on the way in to meet me, and that even if my husband hit me, I must not leave the property. He said that Imran had confided in him on the night of the 3rd of September in Sindh, and had said he saw no light, but only darkness for the two of us. Awn begged me to cancel the trip to London on the 20th of September. He also gave me a message which was apparently from his own mother: to sacrifice a black goat and spill the blood around the property to protect my marriage. I laughed off his bizarre suggestions and reassured him that we had patched things up. It had just been a couple of angry emails. I said that we had made up on his return, and that Awn had nothing to worry about. He seemed unconvinced, which puzzled me.

A couple of days later, Awn called me and conveyed Imran's message that I should not fly out to India. I had been invited to attend a conference for female journalists organised by India Today in September. Apparently, Imran Choudhary from Dubai had told Imran that my visit was being advertised in Delhi and getting a lot of attention. Awn asked me not to attend the conference as a sign of goodwill towards my husband. My husband couldn't even say it to me directly. I was pissed off but decided not to make a fuss, and cancelled it. I sent a curt message to IK saying, "India trip cancelled as per your instruction".

I wasn't informed of his arrival, just as I wasn't informed of his departure, but I had a feeling it was early on Sunday. I couldn't wait to see him. Although he made me mad with his aloof behaviour, I had missed him. At exactly 7:30am, I sensed he was back and woke up. I looked out of the window and he was walking in the garden. I quickly opened the door, walked towards him, and tried to kiss him, but he avoided it. I thought he was upset about leaving his kids as usual, so I let it go. He remained polite for the rest of the day but distant. I waited for the evening, but he didn't so much as look at me.

Later, when I unpacked his overnight bag, I discovered that a blister pack of Viagra had clearly been used. He carried the pills in the overnight bag. I couldn't understand why he would do it if I wasn't travelling with him. Besides, on any of our travels except Dubai, he would never even touch me. Why was it used on this trip? I didn't know what to do or what to say, so I didn't say anything. I had been severely ill while he was away. These were typical signs of voodoo magic but since I didn't really believe in magic, I put it down to menstruation-related complaints. However, yet again, the minute I would re-establish prayer after my periods, I would feel much better. To be on the safe side, I started organising regular Quran recitals in the home. As I read, I finally understood the meaning of Chapter 68 (*Surah Al-Qalam*) in which God recommends patience and perseverance to the Holy Prophet (PBUH) in the face of challenges. We can only choose our own actions, not those of others. Sometimes, no matter how hard we may try, if there is no receptive ear, the message will not be heard and we will be accused of madness.

The stream of concerning September incidents quickly became a flood. On the 20th of September, a TV channel had announced that I was leaving Pakistan that very day. Then, on the 22nd, Ali Ghumman, the Facebook Lead of the PTI social media team, wrote to the chairman to ask for clear direction about my defence, saying, "In the past, we were specifically asked NOT TO defend RK or touch her subject on social media at all". When I questioned Imran about these rumours, he suggested that someone might have read the email exchange of our row. He then wrote an email to me, expressing relief that everything was sorted between the two of us. This was done as a ploy, for the benefit of those phantom people who were apparently reading our e-mails and leaking inside information. I wasn't satisfied with his explanation but let it go.

On the 23rd of September, Arif Nizami did an entire show on my marriage, claiming that we were divorced already. We woke up late as Imran and I had been watching a Bollywood flick *Humari Adhoori Kahani*. Ironically, the film is about undying, unselfish love. Imran taunted me that I had turned him into a soppy romantic. The following morning, Imran told me not to worry as the social media team would release a clip of all of us happily playing cricket together, and that would sort everything. I reminded Imran that Arif was quoting him when he said things like 'Nightmare on Elm Street', but Imran insisted that it was because Awn or someone else must have read our emails from the 3rd of September, in which I had threatened to leave him by the 20th of September if he did not keep the sanctity of the marriage intact.

On the 24th, Imran drove me and the kids to Nathiagali for *Eid*, and insisted that Yousaf accompany us. He knew that I'd taken another painful shot of IVF-C the night before. Just before leaving Bani Gala, Imran was asked to pose with the sacrificial goats sent by a worker. Imran never arranged a sacrifice of his own at Bani Gala. As always, I had to make my own arrangements to offer the mandatory sacrifice in my village. It is required by Islamic tradition for the man of the house to initiate the sacrifice. Most just hold the knife as a token gesture before the professional butchers complete the task. Imran was handed the knife and a picture was taken.

As we set off for Nathiagali, I saw that Imran was angry at me for the photo. Since I had not arranged the photo, I initially thought it was because I was also in it, so I emphasised that I was only in the background. I understood that he would get lots of angry emails from his female supporters if his wife was seen with him. But this time, it was more to do with the mandatory *Sunnah-i-Ibrahimi* (a religious practice linked to the Prophet Abraham). He had clearly received an email chiding him for taking part in this standard Muslim practice. His mood improved as we neared Nathiagali. He got on the phone to invite Zak, and encouraged my sister and her husband to come over too. I thought we would get some time alone but just as I got the sentence out of my mouth, Imran started shouting at me. The rest of the holiday was spent arranging food for the rather large party at KP House.

Imran spent his mornings walking with Zak and my brother-in-law, and his evenings on the phone with someone from England. He would hang up as I entered the room. When we were finally alone, he seemed keen not to let the

IVF-C go to waste. I told him I had a bit of lower abdominal pain because of the injection, and Imran got very angry at me for expressing my discomfort. I went to the lounge of the suite after he fell asleep and quietly burst into tears.

As I returned to bed, he hugged me and whispered, "It will all be OK". All did turn out to be OK for me in the long run but not for my marriage. It was a sad and distressing moment when I realised how I kept thinking of it as just 'my marriage'. For Imran, it seemed like it wasn't *his* marriage at all.

In our first TV interview together, Imran had proclaimed that the one thing Reham could be certain of was that Imran Khan would never cheat on her. Publicly, he promised his fidelity. Privately, he lived in fear that I would be unfaithful to him, and voiced his jealousy openly. He would often say, "I will never leave you... only if you are unfaithful to me. Well I wouldn't leave you...I would shoot you then". He believed women couldn't be faithful to him. He recalled how Emma Sergeant had been very keen on marriage. He had reluctantly agreed but while he was on tour in Australia he found out that she had cheated on him. That was his lucky escape from a relationship he was not interested in but had felt obliged to go through with as she had looked after him so well after his injury. As soon as we got married, his suspicious nature got even more exhausting. He asked me to stop wearing glossy lip colour. To make him more secure, I changed my look so that I appeared older, and toned the makeup down after frequent taunts of, "Darling, you are not a model on a ramp".

Meanwhile, though I had eyes only for my husband, Imran was getting quite bored by the matrimony. It wasn't just his old harem; I'd feel uncomfortable when my friend's rather young and attractive daughter would also be sized up. I remembered how I'd been sat next to a rather rotund older man in a live transmission once, before the marriage. Imran was texting away to me, professing his undying love and commitment. Suddenly this gentleman sat next to me announced, "We were very close to Jemima you know". I looked up, startled, as he continued, "Imran Khan isn't husband material. We saw Jemima suffer. He tried. But the contractual bindings were too much for him". I texted the entire conversation to Imran. He dismissed it with his signature expletives.

That gentleman's name was Humayun Gohar, and he had apparently been a close friend of Imran's. Imran later told me how part of the problem had been

Jemima's social circle in Islamabad. It was mainly Asma and Rashid, a couple who had been the main support system for Jemima when the family moved to Islamabad. In Imran's words, these two were like personal servants for her. He used particularly derogatory language for the wife. The cook, Sajjawal, suggested that there were occasions where wives of his friends were found in Imran's bedroom. The servants had witnessed many such encounters when called into the room to kill house lizards. Imran was terrified of lizards and would jump up on tables on spotting them. A very close friend and confidante of Imran's confirmed that this list of benevolent friends included Rashid and Zakir. I was praising both the ladies for being so lovely when Imran's friend sniggered that they were quite lovely to Khan *Sahab* too, and swore that he had witnessed it himself.

Imran accused Heidi particularly (who was married to the golfer Taimur Hassan) of destroying his marriage with Jemima. He said Heidi planted seeds of doubt and corrupted her mind while he was away. When I questioned further, he told me that Taimur was caught by his wife, and she told Jemima that both her husband and Imran were at it. The woman linked to Imran was Zainab, and later, devotees of the leader insisted that it was this woman who introduced him to alcohol. I found that hard to believe as he was in his 40s by then, and I had heard from my friends before our marriage of how he was always seen with a glass of tipple in his hand at parties.

After a few months, Imran forgot what he had initially said to me, and it emerged that Jemima had not been misinformed about his infidelity. She was outraged and gave him an ultimatum. Even before then, there had been many hysterical fits where his phones and diaries of contacts had been sent flying across the room. After the affair with Zainab, Jemima decided to get her own back at Imran, and that's when people began to hear rumours of her and Hugh Grant in England. Imran told me that it was actually years earlier at a party in London. He was disappointed to see his wife drooling over the stars, especially Hugh Grant. He described her as someone who was easily impressed by celebrity. The final blow came when the infamous picture of his wife and Hugh Grant was printed in a tabloid. Imran was travelling in the Goldsmith aircraft, and opened the paper that morning only to be greeted by his wife's indiscretion plastered across the paper. He still took three weeks to pronounce the divorce. He did not want to but there was no choice left for him, as it was now public knowledge. But he also told me that he had been told to get out of the marriage by his spiritual advisor months earlier.

Through these two years, the couple had visited marriage counsellors on Jemima's insistence. One interaction that Imran described to me was quite insightful. He said, "I was sex deprived, and she took me to this counsellor with huge breasts. I can't recall anything except that Jemima kept on droning about my flaws, and I couldn't keep my eyes off the woman's breasts". Needless to say, counselling did not work. Imran said that the last time Jemima came over to Pakistan just before their divorce, he was surprised to find a rather different, responsive wife. He described it as the best sex they had ever had in all their time together, but as soon as she returned, she was back with Hugh Grant.

Apparently the marriage had been difficult right from the start. The sex was a big issue. I could understand, as she was a very young girl and had only had one boyfriend. But Imran insisted it was awkward because there was no chemistry. I thought to myself that if that very young girl had been told half of what I was told, it was no surprise she was turned off. Imran said the sex was non-existent, especially after the children. His goofiness did not help either. On one occasion, in response to Jemima in an argument, he'd blurted out something about a prostitute. She immediately packed her bags and marched off to Asma and Rashid.

Surprisingly, Akbar S Baber of all people (one of the founding members of PTI who left and become a major critic of Imran's) claimed that it was Imran who tried his best to salvage the marriage. He recalls how Jemima would call him for hour-long telephone conversations, complaining about Imran, and he would try to be the big brother as much as possible. He describes a rather subservient IK who lived in constant terror of displeasing his wife, especially after she became an heiress. He claims Imran really tried to follow the rules. When receiving a phone call from a rather loud irate wife, he would respond gently, "I'm on my way Jem". Akbar described a self-disciplining Imran, who would physically slap his thighs on occasion, whenever he failed in pleasing her, or when he forgot an important date, etc.

Apparently, Jemima would demand that her husband put the kids to bed and make time for her. IK would be terrified if he was back later than 6pm from work. It was the reverse in our relationship. If I was a minute later than 7pm, I would start getting his texts, as well as Awn's. He would get extremely annoyed if I took the kids out for dinner. A few weeks after our wedding announcement, I went to Rawalpindi to see my family, and took my nephew and his cousin to dinner at the Pearl Continental. Imran's own driver and guard were both with me, and kept Imran posted of my location throughout the evening, but when I returned at 10:30pm, Imran was pacing up and down waiting for me. No sooner had I entered the bedroom, he started shouting at me, so loudly that even the guards outside the house could hear. He started off by saying that if I did not want to behave like a married woman, maybe I should have stayed single, because this was no time to be getting home. He went on and on. I was shocked at this outburst but did not utter a single word. He turned off the lights and went to sleep sulking. I genuinely did not class it as controlling behaviour at the time. In fact, it felt good that he wanted me to be around constantly. I only went out to see my family one other time, on *Eid*. I obeyed the rules and was always back in time for his return.

Looking back, it may not have been possessiveness, but perhaps an early attempt to create an environment for divorce. In the years with Jemima, apparently the day started very late and finished early, so party matters were not getting much attention either. This short work schedule was also an issue in our relationship, but here I was, insisting he pay more attention to his work duties. His typical work day was only three hours long. Sometimes it would be only a press conference or an interview, so essentially it was a photo-op. No time was given to governance issues or policy-making. Exasperated individuals would contact me but Imran was in no mood to talk politics in the evenings. He would say, "Baby I'm fed up of all of this". He would roll his eyes in exaggerated exasperation, using his typical phrase, "Such a bore". The man I married had started deteriorating while married to Jemima, but by the time I reached him, he wasn't even a man anymore. He was not a cricket celebrity. He was a supreme leader, surrounded by sycophants and suppliers. As his political career touched new heights, his rapid downward spiral as a human being was accelerated.

His sexual adventures had started even earlier than his cricketing career, but the delving into drugs started later he claimed. Imran said that he first started on cocaine when Jemima took the kids away. According to a close friend at that time, it was a habit Imran picked up with a new woman in his life. He was an elected as an MNA from NA-71, and a beauty from his neighbourhood was to catch his eye in the assembly. It was of course, Ayla Malik, the wife of Baluch *Sardar* Mohammad Rind, who had come in on a reserve seat. PTI founding members also corroborate the timing of his coke addiction. The infamous *Sardar* Rind later joined the party in September 2015. As usual, I found out via Twitter. I looked up at my anti-status quo husband from my phone, and said, "Imran, is this not the guy you said was slamming Ayla's head into the wall? Is he not the guy infamous for his violence, and with countless FIRs to his name?"

Imran shrugged his shoulders. "So? Every Baluch *Sardar* is like that".

Tactful answers were one of many things that were beyond the leader of change.

§

There are signs all around us, but we either choose to ignore them or have trouble guessing at their true meaning. Even pictures that we are drawn to are linked to our sixth sense or intuition. I found one sign in the home of Rashid and Asma. Though long-ignored by Imran, Rashid's stock would soon rise again when the question over payments for Bani Gala would arise in 2017. We would sit on Conference Rock daily and Imran would point out the land directly below that belonged to Rashid. He then would repeat that he didn't like the couple at all.

This couple had tried repeatedly through the year to connect with me. I quite liked Asma and her passion for supporting local art. Imran had said awful things about them, so I was slow to entertain them. When the boys came over for Easter, Asma hosted a tea for all of us but Imran didn't tell anyone, so in the evening they came over to us with all the food she had cooked earlier. She had remembered all the boys' favourite dishes and they ate it all happily. Imran's opinion of them, however, did not change, and he had thrown them out of the inner circle. According to Imran, Rashid had sent him an angry text saying that he should not have forgotten how they supported Imran through everything. Imran texted him back saying, "I didn't know there was a price for being a friend". When I tried to advocate for them, Imran told me that Rashid had been thrown out of Bank Al Faysal for fraud, but the story had been quashed for the sake of the reputation of the bank. In the last week of our marriage, however, Imran started becoming close to them again, and suggested that I put Rashid's name on the board of governors of Zamong Kor, the home for street children.

'Zamong Kor' means 'My home' in Pashto. Since the operation in North Wazirstan, I had been trying to put together a facility for orphaned or destitute children where they could be safe and could flourish. Imran had suggested in March that the flats of Khazana Sugar Mill, on the outskirts of Peshawar, would be ideal for this purpose. I wanted a solution which wouldn't isolate the children from the community but agreed after some persuasion. Together with the Assistant Chief Secretary of the KPK provincial government, Dr Hammad Agha, I helped develop a proposal to ensure that over 800 children could be accommodated, with each individual flat housing ten children and two female guardians. I was told it was the first PC1 (Planning Commission Form) completed by the provincial government. Clearly, there wasn't much will to work. The main features included a football ground in the centre, and badminton and basketball courts around the flats. The idea was to encourage children to pursue their innate talents and create high achievers. A competent family friend, Ayub Zakori, personally supervised the renovations and donated all the furniture from his factory. We had asked for seed money of PKR 50 million ($450,000) but had devised a self-generating revenue model. It all looked very promising.

I turned around and questioned Imran. "I thought you said Rashid is unscrupulous with money? Why would I keep a person like that?"

Imran had clearly forgotten what he had told me earlier, and mumbled, "You don't have to let him handle the finances".

"But that is his area of expertise. What else can he do in an education project?" I asked.

I would later find out that Rashid was put on the board of directors after all. In fact, two years later, I would see a picture of Rashid sitting next to Imran at an official dinner, laughing away like they were old close friends. Rashid had come to the rescue in the case of the dubious Bani Gala transactions from Jemima to Imran.

In late October, Asma had invited us for dinner. My husband had accepted, and then surprised me by driving himself to the dinner. It was just the two of us in the car. As we struggled to find the house that he used to visit regularly, he held my hand on the way and kissed it tenderly. It was lovely to be alone as a couple. At dinner, the four of us sat together to a friendly chat. My eyes were drawn to a picture on the wall. I mumbled something about it being fascinating. The following day, Asma appeared with it gift-wrapped for me. I was so pleased, but Imran remarked, "Oh don't tell me it's that awful picture. It's so dreadful".

I disagreed. Very soon, the reason I was drawn to it would make much more sense. Everyone who visits my home asks if it is a portrait of me. The painting shows a girl sleeping peacefully on a couch, oblivious to the fact that the sofa is out in the open with snarling wolves all around her, and darkening skies above. She has no idea she is not in her own home.

Imran was very close to a chap called Pasha. His wife, although the daughter of the owner of Sitara Mills, was a rather simple down-to--earth woman. Towards the start of the marriage, Imran had asked me to make plans with Zulfi to sell his agricultural lands and invest the money somewhere. He seemed to be keen to provide some sort of financial stability for the new family he wanted to start. One day, he told me excitedly that he had sold his Clara apartment in Diplomatic Enclave and bought the penthouse flat from Pasha in the Grand Hyatt Tower. He encouraged me to do the same, but I have never been into asset building. In October, I enquired to see if I could also buy one for my nephew for the same amount Imran had paid (just over one crore rupees, approximately 70k GBP). Pasha (in Imran's presence) laughed and said, "*Bhabhi*, it's not for one crore. That was just for Imran *Bhai*. Khursheed Shah sent me five-and-a-half crores in cash and I declined. The fifth-floor flats are going for over eleven-and-a-half".

For Imran's birthday on the 5th of October, I had arranged a small surprise dinner for him. The night before Ridha and I were asked to join Imran on Aleem Khan's campaign. We flew together on JKT's plane. Inaya had stayed behind to organise the beautiful cake and arrangements. The barbecue dinner was arranged by Pasha. I had invited my family, Imran's cousin Samina and his close friends. My mother, despite her illness, travelled to Bani Gala to join us. In the morning, I had organised a Quran reading. This time in his bedroom, to ward off the evil eye or any black magic. Usman Dar's social media team followed us all day, filming everything - the several cakes arriving, the general preparations, as well as the recitation of the Quran. The girls and their friends had decorated the swimming pool area with fairy lights and candles. In the afternoon, Imran and I were sitting down to a quiet, pleasant lunch in the dining room when his guard, Ayub, stormed in. His face was red with anger. He glared at me and announced that he was a guard and was not there for menial duties. My driver and PA were all chipping in to help take chairs to the swimming pool. I was keeping Imran distracted while they arranged everything.

When I first came to Bani Gala, Ayub would be cooking and ironing clothes too. He was always treated as family, but now he thought he was talking to a soon-to-be ex. I was amazed as Ayub spoke so loudly and rudely, and Imran said nothing except, "OK ". I turned to Imran and said, "How could you let him be rude like that? He can't speak like that. He was glaring at me. Did you not see that?" Imran merely said, "It's not right for you to get angry at the staff". I wanted to remind him about his expletive laden-language used routinely on them but instead I got up and carried the chairs to the garden myself. A little later, I bumped into Ayub and sarcastically apologised for asking him to help out. It was not even me who had asked him to help, but my driver. Imran's staff had been given a clear idea of the plan being hatched.

The guests arrived and we appeared every bit a couple in love, with banter borne out of familiarity. I invited everyone into the dining room for the cake cutting. Imran initially refused to cut the cake or blow out the candles. Goldie, his old friend, grabbed his hand and had him cut the cake. I cut a piece and held it out to Imran, but he refused and turned to the social media team immediately, warning them not to take any pictures and to delete what they had. I was embarrassed and turned away quickly but everyone saw. My mother nudged him to have the cake but he left the room, ignoring her request. He headed out to the swimming pool, encouraging guests to follow him for the barbecue. He was angry at me for the pictures of the Quranic reading put on social media by the cameramen earlier. He had received an email and phone call complaining about the Islamic tilt of the pic. I stayed behind with my mother, who could not walk and needed help in feeding. She asked, "Why was Imran so rude?" We as a family are used to men with immaculate manners, and birthdays were always celebrated with a lot of love and effort. The only two men behaving rudely in company, or harshly with women, have, sadly, been my husbands.

There was an icy silence between us that night. I understood that Imran was helpless because of where these directions were coming from, but nevertheless, his refusal to own his wife was hurtful. I had to forgive him and not make a huge fuss. The following day, he was even more angry and cold.

Anger and coldness. It seemed like those two words went hand in hand with the word 'marriage'. All I could do was try to convince myself that there were men out there who never allowed their women to feel so insignificant.

Chapter 24

It is simultaneously comic and tragic to think of how well I had my husband's back, even as he was busy scheming behind mine.

Blissfully unaware of what was being planned, I continued to support him and to work on building his image. Once again, I was told in the afternoon that there was a wedding we must attend: the son of Haroon ur-Rashid (an elderly journalist, well-known for his angry outbursts) was getting married. Imran hated the man but was always petrified of what Haroon might say about him in media, so always treated him with a lot of respect.

As we were driving back from a dinner a few weeks before, I heard my husband in the front seat put on an extremely respectful tone and address someone on the phone as *Qibla* (a title of extreme respect). I asked who it had been as Imran had been so uncharacteristically deferential. He cursed softly, and informed me that it was 'the SOB Haroon ur-Rashid'. He described him as an emotionally demanding person who was easily offended. That afternoon, I had invited over a couple of Indian producers who had shown an interest in making a film on Imran. I wanted to meet one filmmaker since he'd built a reputation for portraying parent-child relationships very well in his stories. I received them and gave them an idea of the aspects of Imran's life we would like to see on screen. Imran had promised to turn up for a brief meeting but turned up very late. I left them to chat on the veranda and went off to get ready for the wedding reception, making an extra effort as Haroon ur-Rashid *Sahab* had been exceptionally kind about me on TV all year. All I had done was serve him food myself once.

I would normally get ready in Inaya's room as there was no mirror in the spare room. As I emerged, I saw the lights on in Qasim's room and went to turn them off. Imran would get very upset if things were left on, particularly air conditioners (even in the hot summers). Even though my three kids shared one room, I would run in to turn the AC off before he made a fuss. I walked into Qasim's dark, dusty room and was shocked to find Aleem Khan with his wife. On the settee beside them was a pile of dirty clothes, and the couple were staring down at the threadbare rugs. Qasim's room was never used, and never cleaned either. The furniture and the furnishings were worn out and the décor was an eclectic mix of leftovers. The lady who did my hair had recently seen the room, and had blurted out, "This place is a shambles compared to your immaculate house". I tried to find out why the guests were sitting in the filthy room but the staff just shrugged their shoulders and smiled.

"Why does no one tell me there are guests in the house?" I complained later.

"No one could find you," Imran replied.

"There are only three bedrooms," I continued. "Where could I be? Don't you see that it matters to me that guests are greeted properly and there is a clean place to invite them into? How come everyone is here for a wedding and I have no clue!"

"Awn should have told you. It's not my job to tell you," Imran replied

"Imran, you have to understand my background. We don't keep our houses dirty. We treat guests with respect. The servants ignore me. You won't let me keep a maid".

Everyone's attitude had changed. I should have realised why. Later as we left the wedding, Haroon ur-Rashid came over to my side with the snide remark, "You can ask for a handbag for 7/8 lakhs....as long as it is under ten". I didn't immediately register the meaning. In a recent interview with Awn's ex-wife, my husband had announced that he would divorce me if I asked for a handbag with a ten-lakh price tag. It became clear that the comment had been taken seriously by others, as I myself should perhaps have taken it. As we were about to leave the wedding, I noticed the leader of PMLQ, Chaudhry Shujaat Hussain, standing at the entrance, and said my *salaams.* He and I might not have agreed on politics but I respected him, for he was a very chivalrous man. He'd had the decency to speak up during the degree scandal fabricated about me earlier in the year. He was also the only person who would contact Imran in November to try and reverse the damage done.

After the wedding reception, Imran and I discussed the possible film about him in detail. Imran loved my idea and told me to lock it with the producers.

However, he said that it should only cover as far as SKMT and his first marriage. I didn't see at the time why he wanted a film about him to stop at his first marriage, but agreed with his idea. We then discussed in detail how obviously upset Aleem looked. He had spent so much time and over a billion rupees trying to win this constituency. In the end, the 5000 votes painstakingly collected by a young PTI worker, Sania Kamran - still waiting to be registered! - could have come in handy. There was also the Christian community they had overlooked, despite me pointing them out. PTI had lost by 2500 votes only because of intra-party lobbies.

Two more nights of marital bliss then passed. JKT and Awn had been conspicuous because of their absence, but did mean we had more time to ourselves. I turned my attention to the house. Thanks to my brother, I'd developed a keen interest and understanding of buildings and structures. I'd practically applied my knowledge a few times in my first marriage. So when I noticed water seeping into the walls from the roof of Bani Gala, I climbed up to the roof and identified that the tiles had been placed in the wrong direction. Instead of the water sliding off, it was getting trapped. Those same roof tiles were hard to source. It had taken six months and constant nagging for them to finally arrive in October. The internal arches of the courtyard had severe water damage. I scratched the surface with my nail and huge bits came off. The plastering had been done on unprepared surfaces. Water had been seeping into the cracks. I had it all removed and finished properly.

In the centre of the main courtyard was a fountain area which had been left unfinished. On the day of my flight to England later that year, I had sent my driver to pick up the fountain from the masons. The woodwork of the house was termite-ridden and rotting away. The doors had gaps, so snakes were often slipping in and hiding under the beds. Of course, rats were also a huge issue, and I spent much of the year cleaning the house and setting up rat traps. But the rodents I was so intent on killing were not the filthiest secret in Bani Gala, and later in the year they would lead me to all those things I so badly wanted to ignore. Imran had also wanted the whole driveway paved. I didn't want to use those contractors only after party tickets for their families to oblige us, so kept delaying. But in the end, the decision was taken out of my hands.

I threw myself fully into decorating the house. It's something I love, but life has never really allowed me much time for it. My time in Lahore (supposedly campaigning for Aleem Khan) was actually spent poring over fabric books with his wife and decorator. Imran would happily be dragged into discussing every element, from the paint choices on the wall, to the fabric and its upholstery. To the delight of the upholsterers, we looked very much like a new couple setting up a home. The décor was coming together bit by bit. The grey and black colour scheme looked great. The sofas were finally finished. The hours of selecting the right colours and fabrics had paid off. I paid 3 lakh rupees (approx. £2000) for the sofa fabric myself, instead of taking money from the bundles of cash which kept pouring in. I was told it was mainly from Aneel Mussarat. Imran asked me to use it for staff salaries and general expenditure. I felt uncomfortable using it for personal spending. For construction work and general repairs to the property, there was a rather handsome fund from another benefactor. I had always paid my personal driver and PA myself, not only because PTI did not want to accept them as staff but because I was brought up that way. But by now, I was somewhat aware that the way things were done in Bani Gala was very different to the way I used to.

The doors were a huge expense, with the panels costing about 75,000-plus rupees each (approx. 575 GBP). Since both of us had no income, I decided to make one door at a time. The ones to the back of the property were not visible so I had them made in metal since it was more durable and cheaper. Imran was keen for me to finish all the work quickly. One day, he enquired why the doors were not all finished. I lamented how costly wood was. I had already bought two rather expensive carpets out of my own money. But he insisted that I should order them all right away, and if I needed solid wood, he could just get it from the timber they had confiscated. I stopped dead in my tracks. Was my husband and leader saying that his wife could get illegal, confiscated timber by sending her own people for the bidding?

The PTI Government had announced a crackdown on the timber mafia the previous year, which had been well-publicised. It involved the removal of a minister from their coalition partners, the QWP. Imran had trashed the party publicly and sacked two ministers on corruption charges. This year, they had not only welcomed both of them back, but had given key ministries to each of them, including Irrigation, the only ministry performing well under PTI. Control of Mining had been agreed in the deal too, as well as the most important one: The Home Ministry. I had confronted Imran about this. I stood there with an audio recording of my inside source in QWP. The audio confirmed the deal between the CM of KP and the head of QWP, who was an old benefactor of the CM. Imran had shouted at me, saying it was impossible; he would never allow it. He did not even want to listen to the recording in my hand. A couple of weeks later, on the 8th of October 2015, the news was confirmed in the media. Imran did not even offer an explanation. I did not ask for one.

On the 20th of October, I learned via the news that Home and Irrigation had gone to the QWP leader's son, Sikander Sherpao. Mining and Labour had been given to the lady who was constantly sending post-it notes to the CM's hotel room in Chitral at the time of the JC announcement in July. It was all becoming clear to me: Imran was not willing to listen to anything against his CM Pervez Khattak. And here he was, suggesting that Mrs IK should get all the timber her heart desired from their confiscated stock. They would send someone to bid for it of course, but it would still be comparatively dirt cheap this way. I just stood there, staring at what I had married.

Was it all just a farce? I refused to take my husband's suggestion and continued slowly on my budget. I shouldn't have been surprised. Everything in the house was paid for by others: the dates, cows, goats, cars, petrol, salaries, hundreds of trees, and even the construction work. Back in March, both Yousaf and I had pleaded with Imran for weeks to take the issue of the local bodies cantonment seats seriously. We had wondered why he did not notice Rawalpindi being wiped out in the local bodies, until I discovered that Bani Gala was kept green by the likes of Amir Kiyani: Over 500 trees were delivered regularly to the property by the Senior Vice President of PTI, the man in charge of giving out the tickets. A brief spell of abuse at Amir over the phone and the matter was forgotten. Imran's paradise was far more important than the hell Rawalpindi's people were living in, and even that he owed to Jemima.

I had heard of film sirens being sent gifts by admirers. An infamous Pakistani beauty was frequently mentioned in gossip circles. She would apparently ask for bulk supplies of her favourite perfumes in exchange for time with the sender. Everyone criticised her for being a mistress of all the industrialists. But here was the head of a political party claiming to be bringing in new democratic practices. How could he not see it was dangerous to accept such favours? I was not accustomed to accepting gifts. My mother had taught me that there was no such thing as a free supper. I had once received a limited edition gold-plated Dolce and Gabbana phone by post from a male admirer in my Legal TV days. The gentleman had sent me a text earlier to keep an eye out for it. Not only did he receive a blunt warning but I also sent the gift back, unopened, angry at having to pay the recorded delivery for it.

In all my time as an anchor in Pakistan, I never once got the proverbial *lifafa* (bribe) by any individual or an institution. As I started working in Pakistani media, I slowly realised that pretty much everyone on TV had a financial feed beside their salary. Most of the well-known anchors were romanced by the media wing of the intelligence services. A few feeble attempts were made to contact me but my blunt approach quickly crushed these efforts. Since I did not entertain men in the office, a lady was sent for an initial assessment of me. She then asked me to meet her senior. A Mercedes was sent for me and I met a Colonel with a rather arrogant air about him. He was clearly used to people sucking up to him but as I cut him down to size, he became rather friendly. He offered me a tour of Gilgit Baltistan with full protocol and elite security. I declined, saying that other female anchors who had taken up this invitation had faced rather offensive insinuations from colleagues. The Colonel was shocked by my refusal to toe the line. A couple of weeks later, he tried a softer approach. He invited me to visit a think tank of a lady friend of his. Over a lovely spread for tea, we had a frank discussion. He explained why he wanted well-spoken women like me. I responded, "Colonel *Sahab*, you have so many already. The properties and land you have aren't big enough to tempt me. You have given all the good ones to our top anchor," I finished mischievously.

At my cheekiness, he burst out laughing. Later, he told a mutual friend that this woman was brutal with her honesty. I assured him that, although I didn't allow for interference with creative direction, I was always loyal to national interest, so he did not have to offer any help, material or creative. I'd had a similar meeting with General Bajwa, the Director General of the ISPR, in 2014, to discuss filmmaking. It ended with my polite refusal to work under their direction but we did continue to share ideas on film topics. He was the one who encouraged me to make a film that would revive Pashtun pride.

It was interesting that the agencies tried to contact me but no political party ever approached me with a bribe or instruction on content. My crew would comment on their lack of extra earnings because of my principled stance. I had initially believed that there were some people in media who did genuine unbiased factual journalism. But it slowly became obvious that the majority of TV shows were pro-PTI, while the other two parties had only a couple of TV channels that had a slight tilt towards them. I realised that the channel salaries could not possibly buy the expensive Mercedes convertibles of the anchors. Those sports cars and planes of pro-PTI TV anchors had another source.

At the other end of the spectrum was me, and I was seemingly on my own. Perhaps it was because I'd come in from abroad, an outsider, or perhaps it was because I'd started in media later in life. Perhaps I was the only one with parents who had taught the need for integrity. Perhaps I was just a fool. But I never capitalised on any opportunity that came my way. I survived on my monthly TV salary alone. Perhaps I had not been offered a bribe because I was seen as pro-PTI and was doing the job for free. Even as Mrs IK, I amassed no wealth, and never used my position to set up a business or acquire assets. This may have been one of the reasons I became unpopular with those who wanted to make money under my cover. Many people came to me for project suggestions. There were some who wanted me to stay in the kitchen and went as far as saying it. The head of Pakistan's only media ratings agency Medialogic, Salman Danish, was a permanent fixture at Bani Gala, as were heads of mega advertising agencies, like Inam Akbar. He famously once said to me, "I want you to just stay at home and make *chappatis*". Considering how much time the man spent in Bani Gala, he could have been my kitchen helper.

The leading channel owners were all Imran's 'friends', from Tahir A Khan of News One to Zafar Siddiqui of Samaa. Even Ibrahim at Geo seemed very much emotionally attached to the cricketing hero despite the boycott initiated by Imran. Senior anchors and journalists were like party workers. During the JC I saw prime time hosts offer suggestions in the legal aspect too. I can only think of a couple of anchors who were not part of the core circle of Bani Gala. In fact, it would be much easier to name these than to read out the list of those that were on PTI agenda. They played together, partied together, and worked together. Even the channel Imran had boycotted had placements like Yousaf Beg Mirza, who behaved like a senior advisor to Imran. It was a classic example of Professor Sheldon S. Wolin's inverted totalitarianism. It was a new kind of fascism where the corporate power is a collaborator. This was the skipper's team; the media as propaganda arm of PTI, meant to further its agenda and cover up its failings. And the receivers lapped it all up. Why wouldn't they?

I was very far from that kind of life. I found that those who took a genuine interest in me never had any inclination to spend money on me anyway. Though I would I frequently complain about that, I was actually glad for it. It allowed me to honestly say that everything I had was the result of my honest earning, and that I didn't owe anyone anything in coming this far and giving my kids a decent upbringing. The reason I had no one interfering in my life since my first divorce was because I was earning my own and spending my own. I took no favours from family, friends, or benefactors. I did not even touch my inheritance. Friends would point out that I didn't have to work that hard. "You could live off your inheritance," they would say. But my father died without using a dime of *his* inheritance, and that was what I admired about him.

My father worked hard, and was a happier person than any man I have come across in life. A simple man with no complications who was a joy to be around; no drama and no hassle. A quiet man who didn't have to shout to make his point or swear to shut the other person up. All three of his children shared a lot of his traits, even though we had such different personalities. We would work tirelessly like him, be progressive like he was, read a lot, and barely ever watch TV. We picked up his religious beliefs too. But most importantly, we picked up his attitude of being supportive of our children, with little expectation of any return. We also inherited a refusal to be part of anything illegal to further our careers. My father left Pakistan in the late sixties because he could not conform. My brother left a government position after just a few years as he could not function in an environment of rampant corruption. My sister would work in the development sector for over a decade on a pittance because she liked what she did.

But Imran was a different beast altogether. His lifestyle was nothing but alien to someone from my background. And that lifestyle and its habits were supported and reinforced by constant free supplies. He said he admired who I was but I suppose he couldn't change his habits or his reliance on benefactors. No one likes to be told the harsh truth. I made the fatal error of telling him that the people around him were using him as a commodity and spending on him to further their own ends. He would defend himself by saying he didn't care.

In the first few weeks of us being together, I voiced my view. "I think you could have been different if someone had genuinely cared for you". When one becomes a celebrity at 21, is surrounded by sex and drugs, and has no strong figure to keep them grounded, they are bound to be destroyed. When I compared him to my own 21-year-old, who had been brought up in the West by a single mother, was perceived as Westernised, and had no family support, I felt sorry for Imran.

§

It was a warm, muggy sort of morning.

Imran and I had a late, lazy start. Late starts were normal for Imran though. He didn't like making himself available for meetings before 3 or 4pm. Of course, Jahangir could just saunter in, and would never be made to wait. This would annoy the likes of Asad Umar and Shah Mehmood. Shah Mahmood lived in a perpetual state of frustrated insecurity. Imran avoided him as much as he could.

Imran was in a very romantic mood. I loved these times together and I would wait until he would go for some exercise before getting ready. That morning, I felt what novelists describe as 'that warm glow'. Just before stepping into the shower, I asked Anwar to open up all the glass doors and clean the space between the wooden and the glass double doors. I had been trying to get the rat population under control; there were rat droppings everywhere. It was quite difficult to eradicate them. The only thing that worked were the glue traps.

After my shower I went to Inaya's room to check if Anwar had cleaned properly. The doors were open. The sun was streaming in. I was about to step out but heard voices nearby, so stepped back inside. I wasn't dressed appropriately and my hair was still wet. I went over to Ridha, who was on a bed next to the door to the veranda, deeply engrossed in a book by Osama bin Laden's wife. Imran was sitting on the other side of the door, talking to someone outside. I had barely sat down to give Ridha a hug when I heard clearly what Imran was saying; and this from a man who had told me how beautiful I looked without makeup that very morning, and whose scent had been on my skin just moments ago. My broad smile froze on my face.

The other man was quiet as Imran reeled off a list of allegations. He started with his sisters' complaints about me, then moved on to concerns about my 'shady' past. He alleged that I had connections to everyone, including Malik Riaz and the ISI, and ended by saying that "Reham suspects us all of being corrupt". The man interjected a few times, and then finally said: "Whatever you have to do, you must do it now. Don't delay it".

I went to Suleiman's room in a daze and put a *shalwar-kameez* on. I returned to Inaya's room. I'll remember the puzzled look on Ridha's face for the rest of my life. Filled with anger, I advanced to the patio door. The character assassination continued. The last thing I heard my husband say was, "I can't have this conversation with her..."

I stepped out and didn't even bother to look towards the man who was sitting with him.

"I need to have a word with you. Can you step in for a few minutes please?"

The tone was nothing short of anger. With those two sentences, I turned on my heel and went back inside. I waited for fifteen minutes in his bedroom but he didn't show up. I went out to the garden and the driveway but there was no sign of him. I saw Awn and JKT walking down to the office, talking to each other. I went back to his bedroom, trembling all over. A few minutes later, he came in from the garden door. I picked up the Quran and went up to him.

"End it now. This minute".

He took the Quran from my hand, put it down on the table, and said nothing. I repeated myself: "You want to divorce me, do it!! Do it now but please don't insult me".

He looked as if he was in pain. He shook his head and seemed to mumble some sort of denial.

"Imran, I heard with my own ears! Don't strip me in front of other people. Let me go".

He kept staring at me. There seemed to be genuine regret on his face. My hands went to the neckline of my *kurta*. I felt as if I couldn't breathe. I tugged at the hooks and it ripped open. "This is what you have done, Imran! Stripped me naked! How could you? Imran, how could you! Why couldn't you come to me?"

He held my wrists in his hands and said, "No, I didn't mean it". I freed my wrists.

"I can't face the world". With tears streaming down my face, I stumbled into the bathroom, opened the drawers, and took a bottle of my nerve relaxants out. He came in behind me, took my wrists in his hands again, and wouldn't let go. The contents of the bottle spilled all over the floor. I backed to the end of the bathroom crying, and slid down to the floor. He left me there.

I don't know how long I sat there. My mind was not working or thinking. I just cried quietly. It became dark. I moved into the bedroom. I couldn't sit anywhere we had sat together so I sat on the floor near the foot of the bed. He had gone down for an interview with Waseem Badami. I wondered how he could just go and give an interview. I couldn't even step out of the room to face Ridha. She finally knocked on the door, so I had to wash my face and go to her room. I don't make a habit of shedding my tears in front of my kids so I tried to be normal.

It was rather late when I went back to his bedroom. He wasn't there but the used tissues had been picked up from where I had left them on the floor. He emerged from the bathroom and asked me to sit down. I sat down. From across the coffee table, he spoke clearly. "Reham, I am not divorcing you. I'm not planning to divorce you. Please believe me. What you heard was not right. I'm apologising. It will never happen again. Give me one more chance, please".

I didn't believe him. "I heard, Imran. Ridha heard. Stop this. What day are you waiting for? Local bodies? Say the date. I will sign an affidavit promising not to reveal it. Let me go. Look at me. I have earned nothing except my pride. All I have is integrity. *Mujhay zaleel mut kero* [Let me go with decency]. You want to wait till the 30th of November? The 30th of December? The 30th of March? I won't say a word until you want. Just end it now".

He rushed over to me, touched my feet, and said, "Reham, *mein bohat bara chutiya hoon* [I am a huge cunt]. Today was a watershed moment for me. I draw the line here. I have had doubts put in my mind but I needed this. Never again will I think like this. Give me one last chance, please. I don't know what came over me. Please forgive me".

I spent that night awake, like I had many others. I went to Inaya's room. The following morning, I left early for the only thing that gave me joy: The Street Children project. My friend, Ayub, and Shakeel, the project manager for the street children shelter, were with me. Ayub was as supportive of me as he was for his own family. He put his heart and soul in Zamong Kor for me. For months, we had been going over details, painstakingly planning the kitchens, dorms, and playing fields. But that day, my mind kept wandering.

Shakeel came over and suggested we go pay a visit to the workers of Zamong Kor who had been injured in the recent earthquake. I nodded. I was walking around in a daze. My head was hurting but my soul was numb. Ayub sensed something was wrong and insisted we have lunch. Since I had no home to go to, I stayed at the local Pearl Continental hotel with them for hours. The whole team had lunch, with desserts, followed by more desserts. They could all see I looked like death. Awn called a few times, asking when I would return. It was the all-important gathering of the SKMT in Islamabad. I realised that I could not smile and pretend to be a happily married Mrs IK. I told Umer (who had assumed the role of my personal assistant) to tell him I was busy in meetings. I also kept receiving emails from Imran, asking for forgiveness. It was as if it wasn't a serious issue.

People kept coming up to me as they always did, complaining about the failures of governance in KP by the PTI. A police officer came over and told me that everything was a mess, and that I should ask IK to pay a surprise visit to the local 1122 service. I took their numbers and noted their complaints as I always did, but my reassurance was weak that day. I'd lost the will to defend him. But since was I in no hurry to return, I listened patiently. There were lots of issues, from the controversial Health Act 2015 (drawn up by Imran's cousin

Nausherwan Burki) to the corruption of Pervez Khattak's family. The list was endless and exhausting. And I was beginning to get very exhausted too.

§

General Hamid Gul, the rather colourful and flamboyant ex-Director General of the ISI, died with many secrets in his chest. He was responsible for giving the nation a lot of rude surprises, but his own creations gave him frequent mini-cardiac arrests too. He was credited for playing an active role in creating the Mujahideen and supporting Kashmiri jihadists like Hafiz Saeed. His association with Imran started back when Imran was toying with the idea of politics. The General encouraged him and thereafter supported his political career. Since my arrival in Pakistan, I had been frequently invited to events hosted by the General and his son, Abdullah Gul. It seemed that they had quickly become very fond of me. They would proudly introduce me to their select ambassadors, and ask me to speak at their events. General Hamid Gul even tried to convince me to take an active role in his Mesaq think tank, which I politely declined.

This generous attention was perhaps not viewed favourably by their old favourite, Dr Shahid Masood. He was an anchor with a reputation for spreading doom and gloom. Although not one to socialise, the General was the only interviewee whose home I had visited, as I had wanted to enquire about his ailing wife. I thought the family respected and liked me; I thought I was considered a daughter and a sister, but my misunderstanding was to be rudely corrected.

In the middle of the big *dharna*, the General's creation had shouted from atop the container that he wanted to get married as soon as possible. Soon after that, I interviewed the former DG ISI in October 2014, about two weeks before my marriage to IK. The General asked to see me in the office alone afterwards. The conversation that followed was bizarre. In a split-second, his usual affectionate and fatherly tone had changed to that of an interrogator. As soon as I sat down, he said rather bluntly, "So, tell me what's going on exactly!"

I looked back, puzzled at his tone. "What do you mean?"

"I know what's going on. Young lady, you are being monitored. Your activities are being followed".

"Who's monitoring me? The ISI?"

"No, there are other agencies who report to me. I know everything, so why don't you tell me straight up".

I think he expected me to be scared but I wasn't one to be bullied. He almost jumped right out of his skin as I coolly responded, "Well if you know everything already, why should I tell you?" I looked back defiantly into his eyes and he got flustered.

"This cannot be allowed," he grumbled

"What cannot be allowed?" I continued defiantly

"This marriage. What is happening".

"Well I thought you were a deeply religious man. What objection could you have to marriage? What is happening? There is a proposal, families have met, and marriage is being discussed. Pretty standard Pakistani stuff".

"You cannot marry him?" he almost shouted.

"Why not?"

"Because he is a national leader".

"So?"

"And you, you..." he trailed off in frustration.

"And I what?" I responded in an irritable tone.

"You have a foreign element attached to you. I will not allow it!" he said, quite flustered by my brazenness.

"Really! Well, we will see about that". I got to my feet and added dryly, "Perhaps Pakistan needs to brush up its intelligence-gathering skills General since I am not the one with a foreign element attached to me!" before marching out of the office. I immediately told Imran about the unpleasant encounter. He showed me an earlier text from the General which read: "Abort the marriage!!!"

I couldn't understand why the General would be so against the marriage. Imran laughed away and said, "Ignore the man, baby. He is a lunatic. He talks about world domination".

General Hamid Gul's frustration could have been because he was constantly being given these shocks by his protégé. He was also one of the few who got to meet the first ever candidate to be Mrs Imran Khan Niazi. He retold the story to his close confidantes of the white woman brought to his home. Although they didn't like the idea of their protégé marrying a foreigner, they said nothing. A few months later, Imran's secret marriage made headlines, but to their surprise, it was not the lady who had accompanied him. The woman in question wrote about Imran and this betrayal in her own book, but said that she had forgiven him as he had brought her closer to God in the process. Just before our marriage, a few people would mention her name frequently in front of me, and say that she was making a fool of herself as she was constantly chasing him, while Imran tried his best to shake her off.

I discovered why this particular woman had a huge issue with me soon enough: she had dreamed of becoming the new Mrs IK for years. This was Kristiane Backer, an MTV DJ who had converted to Sufism because of her then-boyfriend Imran Khan. Imran had promised her marriage, like many before her. The German-origin Brit dated Imran from 1992 to 1995. The couple had a very open, live-in relationship. She is remembered as the one who famously set fire to his apartment. Even though she visited Pakistan a few times and spent a lot of time with Imran, he unceremoniously ditched her in the spring of 1995. First, he accused her of cheating on him, and then later said that one of his spiritual advisors had said the union was not recommended. In reality, he had been secretly planning his marriage to Jemima Goldsmith since September 1994. I genuinely felt very sorry for this poor woman whose love story Imran had ruined.

Imran on the other hand, had a very poor opinion of Kristiane in general. While he was proposing to me, he was seen with her in restaurants in Islamabad. In June 2014, she was very much around, and was seen leaving with him late at night from Tuscany Courtyard. Awn confirmed how she had continued to chase Imran through the summer of 2014. They all spoke in disparaging terms about her, even suggesting that she was a woman available for use when needed. When I confronted Imran, he made it sound like she was a very damaged woman, and he was being kind to her by not deleting her completely. They remained in contact through our entire marriage. Kristiane was a woman scorned twice so, predictably, insisted in long emails that Imran should divorce me. The vitriol in her emails was heavily contradicted her public image of Sufism. When I tried to discuss her bizarre list of silly accusations, Imran would just walk out in a rage. He had a habit of going off into a non-verbal sort of frustration and then storming out. Sometimes I would not even know what had triggered it. It would be followed by days of cold silence from him. No matter how I tried, he would close up and not respond to attempts at conversation. Days later, I would be told who had prompted him to behave this way.

Clearly Imran had clearly led Kristiane on again in 2014, and she wasn't going to let it slide this time. Revenge is a dish best served cold. It seemed that the woman scorned twice was very much in the driving seat to destroy my marriage in 2015.

Chapter 25

"I must have been through about a million girls... but then I fooled around and fell in love"

Imran sang a couple of lyrics to me and insisted I find that song for him. When I found the single 'Fooled Around and Fell in Love' by Elvin Bishop, he looked at me, held my hand, and said, "This is what has happened to me. Fooled around and fell in love". The song did seem to fit him. It became an evening ritual. He would play it every night and listen to it on repeat for a good hour. He loved dancing to music too. When we got married, he would constantly remind me how jealous he was of me dancing with anyone else. This would be followed by, "Teach me how you do that *bhangra* step with your shoulders". I tried my best but the shoulder movement wasn't one he could master.

His second favourite track was 'When You're in Love with a Beautiful Woman' by Dr Hook. Thankfully, I happened to know and like the song. I was quite taken aback by this side of him, which only wanted to dance the night away and be merry. It was quite amusing at first but I had no idea then that it was not a naturally brought-on mood. Listening to music for hours was something we did a lot of. I introduced him to my favourite Arjit Singh music, and he made me dig out all the old U2 numbers and Nusrat Fateh Ali *qawwalis*. Ironically, his all-time favourite was *Jinhoon Karna Ae Yaad Dila – Os naion aana* (The one you remember and miss is never going to come back). The last film we watched together was *Humari Adhoori Kahani* and he loved the music. Only a few weeks before we parted he smiled and said, 'You, my *thabro*, have turned me into a soppy romantic'.

My first husband always used to complain about us always turning on too many lights on in the house. *"Tere yaar Kee shadi hai kya?"* (Is it your boyfriend's wedding?) he would cry crudely in Punjabi. I took after my Grandma who used to say, "Turn all the lights on. I'm getting fretful". I inherited this love of brightness, as it were. I get depressed with dark rooms. I even sleep with curtains drawn back to look at the trees as I sleep, and to be woken by the sunrise. My first husband preferred dark curtains to create a complete blackout. It was a rather suffocating feel with the smaller rooms in England. When I first visited Bani Gala in daylight, it was a crisp bright winter's afternoon. But after I married Imran, I found the house to be rather dark and gloomy in the evenings. Imran would keep turning the lights off, making it look cold, grey and eerie.

As soon as he would disappear into the bathroom, I would turn a couple of dimmers on, but as soon as he emerged, he would immediately turn them back off. I initially thought it was because of him being rather frugal, but I noticed he was very sensitive to light and sound. He couldn't bear bright light, and would sometimes sit with sunglasses indoors too. I had always made fun of celebrities who wore sunglasses inside, and thought it was a fashion statement, or just a day off from eye makeup. Here, I discovered it was sensitivity to light; not only because of the late nights, but also because of the nightly abuse his body took. I started educating myself about his habits and soon it became clear that it was his drug abuse that had made light so intolerable. He loved sunbathing but couldn't tolerate the sun on his eyes, and would have washed out eyes. He had a heightened sense of sound, too, at certain times of the day. I have very sharp hearing, but he could hear even the slightest movement outside the door. On a few occasions, he surprised me by accurately identifying someone outside. And then at other moments, he would essentially be deaf. Initially, I put it down to what my mother used to say: that men have selective hearing. My demi-god certainly had no ears for criticism.

I was used to young, musical teenagers. I was never the sort of parent who would ask for music to be turned down, but the decibel level that Imran preferred in the evenings was outrageous. At first, I thought it was to cover our conversation or any romantic activity, which is customary for new couples in Pakistan. Music is used for modesty. But it soon became obvious that he really enjoyed the music at deafening levels. Even my kids commented on it, but the reason for it didn't occur to any of us. It was one of his friends who clued us in by hinting that certain substances affected the sound of music. Imran would turn up the speakers from 7pm till 2am. No conversation was possible. It was embarrassing in Ramadan: *Taraweeh* prayers are said in the evening, and no music is played in our homes in the first ten days of *Muharram*. But Imran had no regard for this. He would tell me to hurry up if I turned the music off to pray in the bedroom. I liked to recite and pray in the bedroom to counter the black magic, but I would frequently have to go to my daughter's room to focus on my evening *Isha* prayer.

Imran had strict instructions: no guests after 7pm. I wasn't allowed to stay out with the kids either. Even if I went to cook in the kitchen for a little while, he would come looking for me. I found this constant attention flattering, and not in the least bit irritating. The more he asked, the more I gave. It was physically exhausting to be up most of the night, only then to have to rise for *Fajr* and for Inaya's school. I used to join him back in bed after sending Inaya off, but couldn't really fall asleep. Sometimes if I would doze off on these all-nighters while Imran enjoyed music or a film, he would forcefully wake me up. My friends quickly noticed that I was looking very tired and puffy. I would say "He kept me up all night" and they would tease me about my husband's virility. When it came to that however, it was actually the opposite. Imran would disappear to the bathroom several times a night. He would then suddenly appear to be very energetic and interested in initiating romance. But there would be very little...'success', for want of a better word.

I was suspicious, and started keeping a tab on his disappearances. He would make at least three trips to the bathroom every night, and return more hyper than before. He would notice my sudden quietness, and the puzzled look, and would become even more doting. When questioned, he would either deny outright or be dismissive. He would typically go to the bathroom every hour, and eventually I started noticing the tell-tale traces of powder on his nostrils, and the cotton swabs with Vaseline in the drawers.

He must have hated his time with me. He was obviously used to much more lively companions. Imran would frequently say that I shouldn't worry about his addiction because he needed a partner to do the drug. The fact that I would not be that partner meant it wasn't fun for him to do it either. Whenever I would find traces and look disappointed, or panic about his health, he would gently say, "Baby, what do you know about drugs? You have never done it. A line of coke is just like half a glass of wine". This line was repeated often and was each time received with the same rolling of the eyes. He quite enjoyed my reaction. I would sit and show him articles of the extensive side-effects, and how it would stay in the system for years. I tried to explain to him that his impotence could be due to the drug. It would scare him for a day at best, but try as he did, he couldn't stop. With repeated disappointments in his political career, he was increasingly becoming demoralised. As the months went by, I saw that the amounts being delivered increased. I could do nothing but parrot on about the dangers of what he was doing and hope that he would eventually see sense. Instead, the consumption increased.

I developed a habit of going in before the servants to wipe away all surfaces with antiseptic wipes so they would not see any trace of the powder. It was everywhere: the side of the bath tub, in the window sills, and, occasionally, on the glass coffee table. I don't know what I was thinking because they must have seen much worse over the years. I guess I wanted to let them believe that he was a changed man. I firmly believed that this was the task he had given me, and that I would support him out of all his dependencies. Maybe there are women out there who can relate to behaving illogically when you love someone. Now that I look back, I have the same reaction most of you will have: 'What were you thinking woman?' But this is a detached, outsider point-of-view. When you are in there, some really smart women lose their brains. I have never pretended to be intelligent when it comes to personal relationships. I can, however, give great advice to others.

The man who would be so quiet and dull all morning would become like an energised bunny, bounding across the room and dancing the night away. He would insist on me getting up to dance with him, and even teach him the dance steps from the video on Facebook that he had been so irritated by. Initially, I was a bit embarrassed but thought it funny, but as the months passed by, so I began to realise that it was just an artificially-induced pleasure. It was not love for me in his heart, as he claimed, but something else running through his veins. Accepting the reality of his tragic existence, a wave of sadness would sweep over me. He knew that I knew. He would look into my eyes and ask gently, "What is troubling you?" I would shake my head silently. He knew that we were both powerless: he because of the years of residue in his system, and I because of his political position. Who could I ask for help?

I became obsessed about reading up on signs, symptoms and methods of regular users. I started making the connections. Imran had a well-prepared lie for everything. On our first night together, he had slipped something under his pillow after turning off the lamp, and couldn't talk much after that. I presumed it was a denture because of his age. I discovered later that it was a mouth guard. When I asked him what it was for, he said it was because he ground his teeth, but I had never noticed him grinding his teeth when he slept without it. In Saudi Arabia, he did not use it, and spent most of the time sleeping, but was also very depressed and angry.

I realised much later that it was because of jaw-clenching typical of cocaine users. In the first few weeks of marriage, I had cleaned out the drawers, very innocently thinking that my husband was using too many sedatives. There were all sorts of tranquillisers, mainly benzodiazepines like Xanax and Lexotanil. Bobby, his cousin, delivered the banned drug Rohypnol right in front of me (also known to me as the date-rape drug). What I did not know was that the drug was not used as an aid to sleep, but as a way of assisting the comedown after the last line of coke. It helped to prevent the jaw-clenching, and calm a person down so that they may get some sleep.

After he would go to sleep, I would start looking through chat threads of drug users and began learning about how drugs are mixed to prolong the high, or to bring the high down. I remember reading from medical websites as well as chat groups of those who had been out for raves. I had never seen an ecstasy pill in my life, although I hadn't seen much else either. When I discovered the playbunny-shaped tablets in a paracetamol dispenser, I genuinely had no idea what they were. I searched for images online and when I found a match I felt as if someone had punched me.

It was considerably upsetting for me to read about this and to recognize what was actually happening around me. I had joked with Bobby that I would ban his entry if he didn't stop his delivery rounds of Rohypnol. At the time, I had not known what I was saying, and slowly it dawned on me that everyone was constantly and intentionally maintaining Imran's lifestyle to further their ends. Rohypnol would make him completely unaware of what he was saying or doing. He was often left with no recollection of entire days that had just gone by. His loud gestures and frequently rude insinuations in his political speeches would often be while he was still heavily intoxicated. He didn't remember any of them.

I remembered how one night back in Ramadan, as we joined the kids for *Sehr* in the early hours of the morning, Imran had sat down with Sahir, who had already been there, preparing for the fast.

"You are a confused atheist," Imran blurted out suddenly.

Sahir looked up in surprise, and then looked to me in confusion. There had been no conversation before that comment. It had come very much out of nowhere. I signalled to Sahir to ignore the comment, and the kids just smiled at the obviously delirious and random comments of their stepfather. The next day, Sahir teased his stepfather for what he had assumed was a harmless gaffe the previous night. His remarks caught Imran off-guard.

"I don't understand, what did I say?" Imran asked.

The smile on Sahir's face immediately vanished. He repeated the comment. In a loud, booming tone, Imran vehemently denied ever saying such a thing. The conviction in his voice was such that Sahir turned to me with an incredulous look, as if he was asking me to confirm that he hadn't imagined the whole encounter. Sahir was not aware of Imran's habits, and didn't understand why Imran had no memory of the previous night.

I became accustomed to checking his yellow cylindrical pill container several times a day to see what he was taking. The typical day's cocktail would generally consist of half an ecstasy tablet and one or two lumps of coke, followed by two to three sedatives at night. It wasn't until the last month that he started hiding the dispenser in his jacket pockets. I didn't know how much was too much, so I took a picture of the drugs and asked a British friend who moved in particular fashion industry circles. In his typical overtly camp style, he trilled back, "Darling, that's not one line! Whoever is telling you that is fucking with you".

It appeared that Imran was doing about six grams a night. Around Aleem Khan's campaign and right after it the cocaine use shot up to a ridiculous level. Three bags of the magic stuff were consumed in one night. He was sinking right in front of my eyes and I watched helplessly. I thought it was repeated disappointments in politics. But perhaps even the secret maligning plan he had drawn up for his own wife tortured him on some level. He needed to bury that inner voice of conscience in more white stuff. He would avoid my questioning eyes as I discovered the empty plastic bags in the bin wrapped in torn scraps of newspapers.

Just after we tied the knot, while I was in the middle of filmmaking, I had been thinking that my film crew must be dabbling in drugs. I decided to ask them to explain what I had found. A large plastic sandwich bag full of mystery capsules had been delivered by Zakir. One of the production crew opened it in my office and tasted it in front of four other crew members. He exclaimed that it was speed, but of some lethal variety. I went back home and flushed them down the toilet, but the candy just kept coming back, from various sources and in different varieties.

I'd faced severe mood swings and depressive attacks in the first two months, but I didn't know enough to understand that it was him crashing. He was either hiding it rather well, or trying to cut down. He would openly light a roll-up cigarette in front of me, filling it with a substance broken off from a round flat black mixture. He would heat it and add it to cigarette, and sometimes smoke in the afternoons. He gave me the impression that it was marijuana but it did not smell like weed. I would stumble across it several months later when making a documentary for an anti-narcotics campaign and discover it was black tar (heroin).

The odd thing was that Imran would appreciate me a lot throughout the marriage for being such a clean woman with no vices. Once after a visit from Zakir, Imran said, "I said to Zak 'I have found the woman who is unbelievably amazing. We've been together over eight months and she doesn't do anything'".

I replied, "Imran, there are many people like me who don't do anything. It's not that amazing".

He would say repeatedly; "You've made me give up cocaine. It's no fun when your partner doesn't do it". And he would say it as if there was nothing else good about the marriage. I realised later that he wanted me to think he was not doing it anymore, so I would never talk about it after he carried out his plan. However, the drug use had increased so much by October that it couldn't really be hidden. The day of the NA-122 (Lahore-V) result was a major moment. We had been watching the results on TV. Aleem Khan had lost.

I was trying to be my supportive best, insisting that he had done really well and that it was a victory of sorts. I was totally engrossed, and didn't notice that Imran had left the sofa. Eventually I got up to check on him, worried he might be really upset. The door of the bathroom was open, and on the window sill was a huge heap of white dust. Imran was lining it up with a nail brush. I stood frozen to the spot. Imran spotted me and saw the shell-shocked expression on my face. I turned on my foot and walked back to sit on the sofa like a robot.

Imran rushed towards me immediately. He grabbed my feet pleading for forgiveness and then pulled me into his arms.

"Baby, I'm sorry. It's just that...today, with this result".

He begged me for forgiveness over and over again. I had never wanted to catch him in the act but it wasn't just that. Seeing the amount being used in one go hit me hard, like I'd been struck by lightning.

We all deceive ourselves constantly. Some do not want to confront their own reality and some cannot bear to confront the reality of their loved ones. We don't want to know their secrets because the truth is painful. I knew that this was who he was but I wanted to turn a blind eye to his weaknesses. We exaggerate their qualities. We are economical with the truth. The sight of my man... my leader... reduced to that of a helpless addict burnt my eyes... and my soul. I didn't know what to say or do. I didn't know who to ask for help. Who could I ask for help? My mind raced through the options. There was no one I trusted. There was no friend he had I could approach. How exactly do you take Mr Imran Khan to rehab? The fact was he was slipping back more and more, and the cold realization that my love couldn't cure him was sinking in.

When my first husband would get drunk every night, I would get very angry about it, especially when he would collapse in public and I'd have to put him in the car and drive him home. My attitude was not the least bit understanding, but with Imran, I was gentle. Not once did I show anger or accuse him of being a drug addict. Instead, I adopted a quieter approach. Every morning, I would find his saucer hidden in a new spot, with a credit card and residual coke. I would move it so Imran would know that I knew. He had asked me right at the start to support him in getting out of his bad habits. I made gentle suggestions, and he made endless promises to quit.

I never even made a direct or insulting comment about his addiction. I only ever mentioned the E-pill once. I could see a growing campaign against me, with images of his sister, ex-wife, and sons being promoted on PTI social media. It was deliberately being painted that his ex-wife and sisters were his family, and that I was an outsider who had no place. After he returned from one of the Lahore *jalsas*, I asked him why his nephew was telling the Information Secretary to put up old pictures of Yousaf Salli and Aleema to hype his upcoming birthday on his Facebook page. He reacted with a lot of anger, and said that his nephew was not doing anything of the sort, and that I was hallucinating. At his shouting, I blurted out indignantly that I wasn't hallucinating as I wasn't the one who was dependant on popping a pill before making a speech. He went white with rage and, with a threatening glare, said, "Why, you fucking bitch!" Then he repeated it. I looked at him, stunned and embarrassed. The following morning, as I was stood in the bathroom, he came up to the window outside and muttered, "I am sorry about last night". I was more stunned at the apology. At the time, I took it as genuine remorse.

And then the night came when I would fall for it yet again. Those promises of change and of cleaning up his act that I so desperately wanted to believe would appear again. He held me close to him all night and kept saying, "I'm cross with you that you are going". In the morning, as he hugged me tight, I said to him firmly, "Look, this hanky-panky has to stop. You need to clean up your act".

"So take my phone and delete everyone off it".

"But you have a new phone all ready to use. Don't give your number to the world. I'm gonna download Viber for you. Yousaf will show you how to use it. Let's stay in touch this time".

He complained about the phone being heavy and I said, "Use it for today. We can replace it with a lighter model tomorrow". He told me to get the phone from his overnight bag, which I did. I pottered around slowly, packing. I felt so renewed with love that I didn't feel like leaving him. Finally, I came to say goodbye and he hugged me tenderly. He had a certain quietness about him. He looked troubled. I hugged him again. He walked over slowly to the bathroom as if he were carrying a great weight.

"Why are you going now?" he grumbled.

I responded, "Why not come over on Saturday? It's our anniversary. Surprise me".

"How can I see you there. The boys are there".

"We can have dinner together and you can go to the boys afterwards for the night".

He just stared at the sink without responding. I went out of the room and then remembered I had no UK SIM card, so came back and asked if there was any money around. I needed a few pounds for a SIM at the airport. He surprised me by being overly helpful and took out money from his toilet bag, giving me all of it. It was about £40 in total. Unsurprisingly, one or two of the notes were tightly rolled up.

I left with a content smile on my face, and love reignited in my heart. I sat in the car with Yousaf in the back seat, already busy downloading Viber. I decided to leave the kids in London with Sara, and to return in a week if Imran didn't show up. As we reached the airport Yousaf handed me the phone. As soon as I looked at it, the mailbox opened up.

If I had the choice to wipe out one incident in my life...

§

I don't know how I walked into the airport or how I ended up sitting on the sofa in the VIP Lounge at Benazir Bhutto International Airport, Islamabad. I must have been visibly shaking as I read the content on the phone over and over again. I was staring at the emails that would leave me with no excuse to stay with the man I thought I was married to. The illusion of love and holy matrimony shattered forever into a million pieces, piercing my heart, my soul and my entire existence.

There are no words to describe the pain...the pure physical pain I felt as I read the headings and names. It was almost more painful to see the dates and times of the email exchanges. I remembered what the two of us had shared a few moments before the emails were sent. I sat there with my world crashing down on me. If my upbringing had allowed me to scream, I probably would have shattered the glass with my cries. What I was looking at was sickening. There was one email thread over a 24-hour period between Imran and a hairdresser from Lahore. In another, he was telling a woman how he should have married her instead. Another email thread was between him and a woman he had never met, as he asked her for information about my past. And one conversation, that had continued for several weeks, between him and the ex-girlfriend Kristiane Backer was informing him of arrangements made with my first husband: to attack me as soon as divorce was announced and to use a lawyer's advice to gag me. My husband had conspired with my lifelong tormentor.

With trembling fingers, I sat there and forwarded the emails to my own account, as well as Sahir's for safekeeping. Then I texted my husband. It was now impossible for anything to damage my shattered mind, but the response had me stunned yet again.

IK: Just when things look good something comes up. We are jinxed... Safe flight

RK: You should ask for forgiveness from Allah. Im coming back to bannigala to show u it all

IK: One day I will tell u what I have been going through these last 10months. The messages ,emails texts forwarded by people about your past. How confused I've been. How torn I've been. Loving u and yet doubting everything u had told me about your past. Have seeked guidance from spiritual people which made me even more confused. Am going mad !

What the fuck!

It took me 43 years to finally realise that men can lie with conviction even when caught red-handed. I returned to the cold house that could not be a home for me. I entered the courtyard and his bedroom. Anwarzeb was vacuuming the bedroom. I signalled for him to leave. Imran stood in the doorway and asked me to come outside to talk.

"I have nothing to ask you anymore. No more questions left," I said

"Come outside," he insisted.

I followed him blindly to the same rock he had stood on just a year ago, when he had held my hand and promised me the world. But here, there was no tall confident man standing proudly, showing me the paradise that he wanted me to be a part of. In that moment, it dawned on me who he really was, as he sat squatting with his head in his hands, looking like a kid who'd been caught with his hands in the cookie jar, the big, loud man nowhere in sight. He finally looked up as I stood towering above him. He stammered, "I was confused. You don't know what I've been going through these last 10 months".

I said nothing.

"Who is Shahzad?" he said suddenly

"What?"

"Who is Shahzad?"

"Shahzad is my brother-in-law".

"No, the other one you had an affair with..."

"You bastard," I said, almost in a whisper. It was the first and the last time I would swear at him. "This is not about me! Tell me what this is!"

I shook my phone in front of him in anger. My right arm was so stiff with pain that my phone fell on the edge of the rock. I rescued it, then calmly turned around.

"You know why I am like this?" I said. "Because my mother is like this. My sister is like this. My brother is like this. My friends are like this. You know why your sisters are like this? Because you are like this! Your father was like this!

"There must be some good left in Pakistanis that this country has been saved from you. My people have been saved. And Allah has saved me. Imran, all this year I kept wondering why Allah would deprive you of your wish. And today, I realise how he protected me. The last thing I would want is your blood in any child of mine.

"I don't know...Nawaz might be a criminal...he might be a murderer. But you know why Allah has given him his place? Because he knows how to respect his wife and daughter.

"Imran, *jao, tum azaad ho* [Go, you are free now]"

And I walked away from him, away from that rock, and away from the false promises forever.

I went to Suleiman's room, stepped into the shower, and scrubbed myself. I felt violated. I collapsed to my knees and sat there, crying uncontrollably. I felt unclean. I had been defeated. I could not help this man. It was no duffer I had been dealing with. I had been dealing with a player. I washed myself repeatedly. I felt like a woman who had been raped in public.

Twenty-three years of my life had been spent in a battle with one man. The words I had blocked away for years now rang in my ears. My children and I were still being abused and tortured, even though I had managed to get us away from that abuser. But the man I had supported with every ounce of my energy had collaborated with that monster. There was no refuge or respite.

I wrapped a towel around me and stepped out. He was standing outside.

"Give me one more chance. Forgive me," Imran pleaded

"Get out. Get out!!"

I got dressed and tried to calm myself. In a state of confusion, I sat down to write Umer a reference for his university. I waited in Imran's bedroom near the phone for the car to arrive to take me to Coffee Republic, a hangout where my sister wanted us to celebrate her husband's birthday. Imran walked in again and muttered something to the effect of 'Why is this happening?' I stared at him, almost laughing in disbelief.

"All of this is happening because of you! You are a part of it. If you had any shame, if you had the fear of God touch you in the slightest, you would have died of embarrassment right here at being caught, not asking questions about me. I'm not guilty! It's you!"

He muttered something about fearing God and not being able to kill himself. I looked at him coldly and said, "You want me to stay? Prove it! Write an email back to this woman saying 'These venomous lies against my wife must stop. I'm a married man and it is immoral to communicate with me and to break my marriage' ".

All I ever wanted was for my husband to actually defend me. He should have done that even if I had the filthiest past imaginable, as I had done for him! I had spent a year being an accessory to his lies and finding myself covering for his depravity. And this was what I got for it. He sat down in front of me and said, "I'm writing an email. This is what I will say". He then read out a polite email of how the allegations were not based on evidence. I stood up and said, "No, you have to say that you should stop spreading and sending me venomous lies about my wife. And stop writing to me. I'm a married man'. Then make a public statement against Dr Ijaz Rehman saying, 'Targeting of my wife has to stop. I stand by her, and this man should stop talking about my wife' ".

"I can't do that," he said. "They will attack you more. Why open yourself up to more attacks? I am just protecting you".

"Thank you very much. I love how you've been 'protecting' me so far," I said. "Please don't protect me anymore. I have had enough of your protection. Keep everyone sweet, and watch quietly as people shred me to bits".

I walked out. A few minutes later, as I walked into the bathroom to get the money from the safe for a bill that needed clearing, Imran called out again from the garden.

"*Saath rehna hai ke nahin*?" (Do you want to stay with me or not?)

I approached the patio door and this time responded calmly.

"Don't tell me to give you another chance when you don't mean it. Don't tell me to stop. Tell these filthy women to stop! Put a stop to what you are doing. Put a stop to this campaign against me. Can you do that? Will you do it? Will you tell everyone to butt out of our marriage?

"You want me to get rid of the party people?" he asked.

"No, I want to know why a woman who has done no wrong is being maligned? Why do they want me out so badly? Is it because I am patriotic? Is it because they can't tolerate a woman who knows how corrupt they are? Is it because they see this woman could be a hurdle in the way of them taking kickbacks? Or is it because you are a part of this nexus of evil and you can't tolerate a conscience sitting in your bedroom? Will you put a stop to Jahangir Tareen's and Pervez Khattak's corrupt ways? Will you?"

"No, I won't! Fuck off!"

I'm not sure what I should have expected. In my state of blindness, I walked out. Umer stood in the courtyard. He could see something was very wrong. He had asked me for the payment for the electrician. I went back to the bathroom, opened the safe, and took out the money. I counted exactly 18,000 out of the 5-lakh bundle. I left the rest of the roll of banknotes on his toilet bag and walked out of the paradise I had been promised, from the cold house that had never been my home. All I had with me was my phone, which had the words that had shattered my illusion; the words that would haunt me for months to come. As I stared out of the car window, I couldn't even cry.

I remembered how outraged I had been at some sexting I'd discovered only two days before. But now, I was staring at emails from even earlier. My mind went back to late September. When Imran had gone to Lahore for campaigning, I'd fallen ill again, vomiting violently. Awn told Imran, who, uncharacteristically, called me himself a couple of times. Imran insisted I go to the doctors but there was no driver at home. My driver was with Inaya at the school. There was no sign of Safeer. Imran returned later that night and shocked me by putting his hand on my forehead and gently asking how I was. Now, I would discover why he had been so considerate. He had been chatting to a hairdresser called Aimen Shah at the same time. Clearly, she would pay my husband regular visits to tidy up more than just his hair. In the long, detailed chat thread, they had discussed the best discreet meeting places they knew, from the notorious *Salli kee Haveli* (Salli's mansion) to his own home in Zaman Park. Zak had facilitated these clandestine meetings for years. They had been so easily arranged. It was incredible: not only was my husband cheating on me, but a leader in the middle of an important rally had the time to message back and forth like a young, jobless boy. His perfect performance with me – the truly caring husband - could have won him an Oscar.

The day after this, Imran had questioned Safeer intensely about his whereabouts. Safeer hadn't offered an explanation. He'd been assigned to Imran's sister Rubina, as I found out later. She had recently suffered from a stroke and needed physiotherapy sessions. Imran clearly knew this too, but was using the driver to cover up for him. A couple of weeks later, I'd overheard Safeer ask my driver to get some money off me for petrol. I opened the kitchen door, gave Safeer the money myself and told him to use my car to take Rubina to the doctors, adding that the Hilux was inappropriate for her as it was not comfortable. I wanted to make it clear to the staff that Imran's sisters were not to be disrespected. No games would be played between us. Later, I would feel a stab to my heart as I was accused on a TV show of not giving my cars to the sisters for use. But the sisters had never been keen on their sister-in-law. And

I could deal with that, because I was not married to them. All I needed was the loyalty and love of my husband. And here I was, staring at every form of betrayal I could have possibly imagined, and several that I never could have.

Backer had got her revenge. She was the go-between, designing the divorce and seeking assurances from my first husband for continued support afterwards. My 'decent' politician husband would play the role of a bruised and the battered soul, but maintain a dignified silence while Ijaz would do his dirty work for him. Ayesha Jamil, the solicitor, inisisted they get a gagging order on me. Of course, Backer would be there with spiritual support, ready to tell my husband why it was best to get rid of me.

I looked at the email to the married women from my husband. 'Should have married you instead. You would have been ideal'. He was flirting gleefully while carefully plotting against me. He was displaying uncharacteristic compassion to me to mask his dirty deeds. But the Andaleebs, Aimens, Aylas, and Anilas seemed insignificant. This was much greater deceit than mere physical cheating on a wife. This was not manslaughter. This was cold, calculated murder.

The ease with which I forgave him every time makes no sense. My children aside, I genuinely cared for him more than I have cared about anyone in my life, and I know it doesn't make any sense. Even after the divorce, when he would make some silly comment (and they became increasingly bizarre), I still felt for him. How can you hate someone and cringe for them at the same time? People would come up to me and say, "You still care, Reham". And I would respond, "You have no idea what this man has done to me. How could I care about him?" He had betrayed my trust beyond forgiveness. My lone fight spanning 23 years ... my battle to rebuild a life for myself and my children ... my struggle to reconstruct my confidence and that of my children from scratch. I had erased all the harsh words, expletives, and jabs from our minds. Ten years of blood and sweat to wipe away the tears, and finally I'd found a man so big so strong so brave so loud; a man larger than life. It was the best nest. My little ones would be safe. I would be safe in those big hands. Those hands had held my hand for hours. Those hands had held me all night so close. Those hands had fed me lovingly. Those hands had tried to iron my frowns. Was it an act? Was I an amusement? A woman to be used and disposed of? Was I just a new flavour?

I had married a single man because to me, no other arrangement was acceptable. I didn't believe people could be together except in marriage. I believed in monogamy and fidelity, in love and in loyalty. I had accepted him with my heart and with God as my witness, in sickness and in health until death. I couldn't even think of him falling ill. And here I was, exposed by him to the whole world. How could he hurt someone who had done him no harm? How could he negate the very thing I stood for? How could the man I loved so dearly join forces with the very man who had abused me and my children for 12 long years? It had been now over 23 years of unrelenting, inescapable abuse and Imran was complicit in crime. How could anyone do this? Without a trace of guilt or a drop of remorse? I wondered how much would he score in a psychopathic test. To him, I was not even worth the courtesy of a one-night stand.

Chapter 26

As a child, I would hide my injuries from my faint-hearted mother, no matter how much it hurt. That's what I'd always done. 'Never let them see you cry, never let them see you bleed'. Even when people thought they saw it, they would never know just how much was happening to me on the inside.

I walked out quietly to the car and asked Umer to drive me to Coffee Republic. I sat with my children as the family cut the cake and sang Happy Birthday. My face told the story but I never had anyone close enough to me who would care to pick up on the turmoil inside me. My film producer brought the second lead and scriptwriter Anwar Maqsood with him to meet me. From the corner of the eye, I saw Naeem ul Haq walk in with guests and sit at a nearby table. We exchanged brief hostile looks. In the noise and laughter of the busy café, only the two of us knew the truth.

Umer sensed there was something wrong as I sent the kids to Sara's house and asked him to drive me here and there. I did not go to Sara's home till very late in the evening. She was flying around as I headed to bed, pampering me and making sure I was comfortable. All I wanted was to be left alone. I spent all night tossing and turning. My mind was blank. After months of confusion, there was too much clarity. The first thing I saw early next morning was a text from my husband. He said he would send me a text from a safe phone in 30 minutes. I responded.

"You have violated my trust, my love and my unquestionable loyalty. Don't humiliate me publicly. I ask for nothing else".

Despite learning of his true nature, there was still a part of me hoping he would apologise and promise to become an honest man. Fortunately for me, he finally broke the facade. He suggested I go away quietly. The divorce would be announced in a week. I instead boarded the flight to Birmingham. The girls were so excited about the holiday; I did not have the heart to break the news to them. Sara was bubbling away. I pretended everything was OK. I met the airline crew and pilots as if everything was normal. As usual, I didn't open up. I didn't want to ruin other people's day with my tears. I always knew I would cope with everything better myself. Confiding in others is not ideal, as the little I say seems always to be thrown back at me. After Imran, I could never trust anyone with even a small part of me.

I landed at Birmingham Airport and was received by the organiser of the media conference, the PTI head in London, and female party workers. During the drive to London, I listened to the familiar complaints and criticisms of about Imran and his policies. As I reached my room at the London Hilton, I received two emails, one from my husband and the other from a worried Zulfi. On the morning of the 30th, Naeem ul Haq announced to the world that everything had been decided mutually and amicably by Reham and the leader of the PTI. Imran followed with a tweet praising my moral character and describing divorce as a painful time. I simply tweeted that we would be filing for divorce. I was playing blind yet again. By the following morning, a divorce paper had been signed by my husband and my belongings had been packed by a removal company belonging to someone called Samad, the same man Imran had used to do research on me when he was proposing. The whirlwind pursuit had ended with a dark twister.

All I was worried about was my frail old mother. Would a second divorce kill her? Such a high-profile divorce was not something I should have put her through. I avoided talking or texting completely. I didn't want to respond to anyone. My sister called and volunteered to go talk some sense into Imran. Sara insisted on calling him. I told them both that they did not understand who he was. They'd only seen his public face. Both now got to see a glimpse of his madness but I felt that these two women, like so many others, still blamed me for the outcome. But I no longer cared what anyone thought. I was trying to piece it together and it physically hurt. There was a part of me that loved him, or at least the man I had married. But it wasn't real. This was his real face, and I despised it.

He had replied to my message the day before with an A4-size text, starting with how the previous day had been the most humiliating day for him. He accused me of several pre-marriage affairs before ranting on about a major in the ISI who I apparently used to meet in a flat in F10. This was all new to me. It had never been brought up before. I sat there in disgust and informed him that I knew these were lies and that he was looking for an excuse. I was incredulous. I had confronted him with evidence of his cheating character with Aimen Shah just the day before, and here he was, accusing me of having affairs before our marriage. He jumped from one name to another. He sounded crazy. Then he texted: "I propose we immediately seek divorce. You or I could say that your British-born kids can't adjust to Pak and you are going back to the UK and we are sadly parting". What could someone say to that? Even after all he had done, he expected me to lie for him and make life easy.

I did try to set the record straight but I was talking to man who had spent a lifetime believing his own lies.

"Imran, it's you who has a past, not me," I had replied. He had been disloyal to me in our marriage in every possible way, from cheating to planning a campaign to malign me involving my ex-husband. He had given an abuser the satisfaction that he could still hurt me and my kids, even after 23 years. And that was it. That is how an 'honest and brave' man behaves when he gets caught: he accuses the aggrieved innocent party of corrupt ways and gets away with it.

His army of anchors were prepared for the assault. Some had stakes in the caretaker technocrat system expected after the removal of Sharifs. Some had enjoyed evenings of drug induced orgies, doing lines on the naked bodies of female anchors with their Leader. They all jumped in with such extreme attacks on my character that no one could believe them.

I sat in my room in London. I didn't know what to think. We emailed back and forth until the day the divorce papers were given to me. He had signed the divorce on the same date as the date he insisted we get married. Never again did I ever respond to the man who had not deserved my loyalty.

§

"Imran *bhai* feels that he doesn't owe you anything for an eight-month relationship".

Zulfi sat in front of me with the divorce paper. I had sat quietly and listened to the whole rigmarole. But on hearing this, I couldn't help myself. "Zulfi, both you and I know the reality of the 'eight-month relationship'. He doesn't owe me anything because he cannot give anyone anything, but at least don't insult me by telling me what it was."

And that was it. I had asked my husband to surprise me on our wedding anniversary and he did. I finally got something out of him: His autograph on a divorce deed, worth 100 rupees and signed on the day he had signed the *nikkah* papers. I sat there in the dimly lit Italian restaurant, watching Sahir struggle to control his anger as Zulfi continued to speak. Sahir demanded that Imran not be in the house when I came to collect my things, only to be told that my stuff had already been packed and would be removed in two days, and that I could never return to Bani Gala. I had boarded a plane to England as a married woman and former journalist, going for a media conference and perhaps a short holiday. Suddenly, I was unmarried, homeless and directionless; effectively stranded on a different continent while strangers rooted through my personal belongings.

My friends described him as sheer evil for doing it like this. I think it was the biggest gift he could give to a woman who had been prepared to give him everything; who would have taken a bullet for him; who would have sacrificed anything and everything for his happiness. If he had sat me down and said, "Reham, my children want you out", I would have quietly left. If he had said to me "The only way I can become PM is if you leave", I would have left. If he had said to me "I have fallen in love with someone else", I would have left. I am not one to cling to people or places where I am unwelcome. For me, distancing has always been easy. All I had requested of him was to treat me with decency and respect. I never asked him for anything, but he could not be honest to me.

The man whose claim to fame was honesty. The man who was the last hope for a nation that had been treated unjustly. The man who led the movement for justice. The man who stood for the rights of the people. This man couldn't be honest, couldn't be fair, and couldn't be brave enough to face a woman. A woman who he had pursued. A woman who was unwilling to get involved. A woman who had done him no harm.

In the end it took so many people, so many plans, and so many conspiracies to get rid of that woman. I was an unprepared, unarmed woman, battling it out alone. It was painful. No...it IS painful to be deceived by your husband.

§

How do you talk to someone who has only learned to talk *at* people? Especially after the *dharna*, this habit was reinforced. You could be trying to say something about Burma for an hour, but one word would distract him, and he would start off on a tangent. Phone conversations weren't possible; he would talk for a few minutes and then hang up.

Following the announcement, my friend Sara, who had been by my side throughout the marriage, desperately wanted us to stay together, saying, "It's not too late to patch things up". Umer happened to be on speakerphone at the time, and heard this comment, interjecting, "Over my dead body!", echoing Sahir's earlier stance. Sara asked me if she could talk to him anyway. I told her that it was pointless and warned her that he would talk and talk and talk and then hang up.

I saw her nodding silently while he was on the phone, trying to get a word in edgewise. Despite the agony I was going through thanks to my husband shredding me to pieces publicly and privately, I couldn't help but smile at her incredulous expression as the call suddenly ended.

"Reham, he was talking and talking and talking and then he just hung up!" she exclaimed

"He said all he had to say," I replied

"But I didn't get to respond to anything. He didn't stop for me to even reply".

"Why do you think I told you there is no point," I responded. "He is judge, jury, and executioner. Evidence, analysis, or research is immaterial in front of his judgement".

His texts were long and sent her in a daze. "How could you be so many things? An MI6 agent and on the ISI's payroll? Does he not have the ability to think rationally? And if he had so many contacts, why could he not check this out beforehand?" she said.

My memory shot back to a scene on our first meeting when I had joked, "What if I'm an MI6 agent?" And he, in his trademark flamboyant style, had scoffed, "Do I care?" When Hamid Gul had tried to stop the marriage, Imran had instead chosen to tie the knot immediately. And now, he had chosen to cut that knot just as quickly. In no time at all, he was back in public, business as usual. He was back to repeating the same phrases in his constant press conferences, like he had just gone through a minor blip, rather than a divorce. The same gestures, the same words. I looked for care or compassion and saw only cold and dead eyes. There was nothing there. If that was how it was then...why? Why marry me? What was this? Did it happen? It was as if none of this had ever happened....

I remembered how I'd taken IVF-C and we'd gone to Nathiagali for *Eid*. This was a man who had been planning to have a baby with me while he was also planning to ditch me. A divorce was being planned and TV anchors knew about it before I did. Understanding this mentality was beyond me. This was an unimaginable level of sociopath.

People asked me why I didn't hit the bottle. Why did I not fall to pieces? Why did I not feel suicidal?

It was simple. I would utter a single line before I opened my eyes in the morning: "Allah, please help me" And he did.

§

To provoke controversy, I frequently say, 'All men are bastards. Some are obvious bastards. Some are covert bastards. The ones who appear to be bastards are safer as you know what you are dealing with. The men who hide behind a facade of manners and politeness are the coldest of bastards'. I could never have predicted just how true my provocative and politically incorrect remarks would prove to be.

I was 42 when I discovered a horrible truth: a man who pays you compliments and holds you close all night can brutally drive a blade in your back and frame you for the crime too. But my little princess was only 18 when she had to confront this truth.

Ridha was the first girl in our family. The long, curly perfect ringlets framed an angelic face. She was the perfect girly-girl who would play for hours with her Barbies and Bratz dolls. She was the quiet and careful one who everyone would compliment. She never did anything wrong. It was always poor Sahir who would break things or step out of line somehow. I loved the fact that I had a girl who dreamt of white weddings and swooned over people like Chris Pine. I had never been like that as a young girl. Love, boys, clothes, and all such things were never on my mind. I never really knew any gossip either. But my little girl dreamed of love, family, and pretty hampers. I indulged her and enjoyed her different personality.

Unlike me, she was shy in public and chose to let the other two do the talking. This lack of independence worried me, and we had nicknamed her the 'Islamabadi auntie' who would get her minions to do her work while she rests, but we all indulged her too. Ridha was a girl who dreamt of joint family set-ups like in the Bollywood classic *Hum Saath Saath Hain*, a title which quite literally translates as 'We are Together'. She couldn't think of a holiday without her siblings and her cousins. Having to live away from Ridha so that she could continue her education in England was one of the hardest things I've ever had to do. I missed her dearly but never once cried in front of her. I was adamant that Ridha would get the British university education that I was deprived of, and that she would learn to be an independent woman for her own good. She pleaded with me to let her go to a University in Pakistan but I stood my ground.

No one was happier for me to be finally married than my older two. Ridha was relieved to see me with a man who would grab my hand while talking to me on the dining table, and feed me lovingly with his own fork. She could only see what Imran showed her: A doting husband who would tease his wife for being an eccentric. He appeared to be goofy and forgetful at times like most old dads. She never saw us fighting. She was oblivious to what he was planning.

After the divorce, Ridha showed me pictures she'd taken of us holding hands and smiling at each other on our morning walk. She had captured these intimate moments from the porch. When the news of the divorce came, she crumbled before our eyes. The pain of the deceit was unbearable for the young girl who liked mugs of hot chocolate topped with marshmallows and Cath Kidston prints. I saw the sweet, smiley girl change into a hardened woman who did not believe in love anymore. She had seen all sorts of bastards: the good ones, the bad ones, and the absolutely horrific ones.

All I could feel was guilt for how I'd put a young girl through so much pain because of my marriage. My friend consoled me and said, "But isn't it better for her to not be naive? Yes, it is painful, but it will make her stronger. She is now better prepared for life". But parents like me want our kids to believe in Santa and the tooth fairy for as long as possible.

I saved Imran as a liar on my phone after his texts to my friend Sara. To justify the divorce, Imran was accusing me of ridiculously far-fetched things. I looked silently at the lengthy texts of my husband... my pride, messaging my childhood friend and telling her what a loose-charactered woman I was. This was the friend who had seen me in the UK and had been with me throughout my time in Islamabad, who loved and admired me for how I had struggled in life. She had been by my side through my entire time in Bani Gala, and had seen me constantly working for my husband. This friend was also one of the thousands of fans he had; one who had idolised him since childhood and thought he was above the rest. She was one of those who thought he wasn't an ordinary man. She looked at me dejectedly and said quietly, "So basically there are no good men out there". I made a weak attempt at a smile and said, "See, your hubby is an angel compared to the men in my life".

She wasn't the only one who reacted this way. Sahir had done his best throughout the year to get on with Imran but had eventually accepted that there would be no substantial or warm stepfather relationship there. But the revelations shocked him to the core. Like me, he could never have imagined Imran would be so far gone. It simply wasn't within the realm of his understanding, especially when this person claimed to be at the pinnacle of human decency. Imran would often lecture to Sahir about the importance of *Iman*, the Islamic combination of faith and righteousness. Sahir had often wondered if he received these lectures because Imran thought he lacked decency. It was almost impossible to reconcile all that with these new revelations, and try to comprehend the extent of Imran's hypocrisy.

The truth also hit Yousaf, who looked up to Imran. Yousaf, a sensitive child, was shocked that his hero had turned out to be a scarecrow. He took Imran as family, but his *khalu* used his presence tactically, to try and make it seem like I was promoting and overly-involving my family. Yousaf was only following Imran's orders when he accompanied us to Umra or Gilgit Baltistan, but photos of him with us were used in a propaganda campaign. It hurt him to realise that he'd been used as a scapegoat through the marriage. Eventually, the nasty experience would help him carve out a career in law for himself.

And of course, there was me. I would stay awake all night and think 'How could he say all those things about me?' Was it extreme paranoia and jealousy? Was it that he was easily brainwashed? Was it drug-induced? Or was it that he was simply a weak man who was desperately looking to justify his unjust act?

He could have just said "I don't love you anymore".

Or "I never loved you".

Or "I needed to get married".

"I needed a distraction".

"I'm bored of you".

"I love someone else".

"Jemima won't let Suleiman visit if you are here".

But saying anything like that requires honesty and courage. And these are traits that a lot of men do not have, even when they happen to be the loudest in the land.

To think that I had never even contemplated having so much as a boyfriend, let alone illicit affairs of any kind, and that I was probably hated by the ISI for not sucking up to them. What a waste of a single life. What was the point of being 'oh so pious'?

After Imran had been so rude at his birthday celebrations, my mother, a far more intelligent woman than I, had left with a heavy heart but did not say a word to me. She had always disapproved of his personality (even before the marriage), particularly his rude speeches. I remember when she used to see him on TV and declare in disgust, "He is completely mad, this man".

I was least bothered about the abuse directed at me through the media at Imran's direction. I was only concerned about what my mother would say. I avoided talking to her for weeks because I was worried about the emotional attack I would get for another divorce. I remembered her reaction to my first. This was something else, and so public. I had caused so much embarrassment to the family. I felt extremely guilty for not listening to them. But when I finally met this proud, elegant woman, she never said a word. She just hugged me.

She asked no questions. This would be her last year with us. We connected like we never had. She was proud of me it seemed. She understood who I was and what I stood for. She respected me for the woman I had become. And to me like many of us, the approval of a parent is what we strive for all our lives.

The year was spent laughing together. She even made fun of her own inability to speak, clearly because of her debilitating Parkinson's. In her last days, I got the mother I'd always wanted: the one who did not want a perfect smile or perfect life. She valued me being around her enough to not criticise me for my worldly failings. She appreciated me for living and loving dangerously. She appreciated my honest approach to life, and my refusal to conform to superficial values of society. Maybe she even wished she had lived a life like mine.

§

I had borne a lot of attacks while I had been married. No one who should have defended me did so. When the attacks failed to cease, it became too much for Sahir to tolerate. I had been married to men who said they had to have me, and vowed to protect me, but when I needed them they never delivered. Yet here was a young boy who had no money or power, but had the courage to defend my honour. By August 2015, there were planted shows on mainstream TV with my first husband. Despite the advice I was receiving from my husband to not respond to attacks (which I passed onto my son), Sahir wrote a passionate and heartrending article to defend me and posted it online.

Sahir had become used to the lack of privacy, even though he never would have wanted it that way. He wasn't the type to write about anything like that, preferring to write about something he considered interesting. His other blog posts were film reviews, suggestions of music, and political commentary. He would happily see if he could make sense of contemporary British politics, or the Israel-Palestine conflict, but he would never write anything personal if he could help it. Yet here, he did. We would regularly clash on this matter, and he would openly mock my insistence on keeping a dignified silence in the face of such abuse. According to him, people needed strong examples, and responded far better to brutal put-downs and powerful retorts than they did to dignified silence. So, he began writing, and threw a passionate defence of me out into the world, when my husband and everyone around me failed to do so.

A couple of years later, someone told me how that blog had blown them away. People wanted to know more about me and how I had single-handedly raised such wonderful children. The fact is that the biggest privilege I have been given is that I am mother to Sahir, Ridha and Inaya. All mothers will naturally be biased but I am probably in the minority when I say that parenting was a breeze. I read somewhere that you have 18 years before your child becomes an adult, so there is no need to rush through all the lessons in the first few years. It's sad to see parents constantly correcting their children rather than enjoying time with them.

When Sahir was four years old, I lived next door to a writer named Horace Dobbs (who also happened to be an authority on dolphins). I complained to Horace about how slowly Sahir did things. It took ages to get him ready in the mornings. I censored the bit about my husband screaming and shouting at us in the mornings. Horace smiled gently. With his fifty-year-old wisdom, he said, "And why do you want him to match your speed? Let him do it in his own time".

As soon as I left Ijaz, that was what I did. I gave the children the freedom to flourish at their own pace. I took the pressure off. I stood back and appreciated them for how different they were from me. Sahir appeared to be laid back but there was a lot of thinking going on behind that careless exterior. His core strength lay in objective evaluation; he was a 'big-picture' kind of person. Ridha's hardworking and cautious approach in handling work, studies and money perfectly complemented Sahir's relaxed attitude. Sahir never really concerned himself with what he deemed trivial matters, like punctuality and organization, but Ridha's sharp focus made her the only one who could get him to address issues immediately, through persistent reminders. And Inaya was always the deeply analytical one. She gave profound advice like a wise sage. Right from the start, I had handed my kids responsibilities according to their abilities. Ridha first helped me book a trip Disneyland Paris when she was only 11 years old. From that moment on, every holiday has been booked by her. Initially we had a surprise when we found that instead of Southern Italy, she had booked a villa in Cyprus. But it ended up giving her a life-long lesson in geography.

My unconventional style of parenting did not negatively affect my children. Their behaviour and academic results were never a cause of anxiety for me. The only time schooling was affected was following my marriage to a celebrity cricketer. Inaya had to miss months off school amid security threats to us, both fake and real. But now we had to deal with an extremely sudden, public divorce. Besides being as disruptive as anything can really be, it also meant the family was once again left homeless.

It was like the winter of 2005 again. This time, I had around £1400 in Pakistani rupees but had no one around me who could go and change the money. I had no job and no house. I spent a week at a Hilton Hotel on Edgeware Road in London, courtesy of Zulfi Bukhari. I went to a friend who kicked me out after four days along with all my suitcases. Another friend took me home and we stayed in her attic bedroom. I slept on a duvet on the floor and gave the double bed to the girls. A few days in the hotels of two other friends helped me through the month of November. All of this happened while the Pakistani media claimed that I had taken millions in cash from PTI financiers, and that a huge financial settlement had been given for me to keep my mouth shut. Nothing could have been further from the truth. I was in a state of shock.

Inaya ended up missing months of school. She was a strong girl and kept a brave face in front of everyone, but her health suffered. She became anaemic and fainted a couple of times in school. This meant more time off. Most tried to be sweet, but seeing people whispering around her when she returned to school wasn't easy for the young adolescent. A select school for children of the super-rich and politicians offered better security, but the other pupils had inside information on her former stepdad, which was disturbing at first. They all knew about his addiction and habits, and Inaya would be bullied relentlessly as a result.

At the start of 2017, the school's principal invited me in for a chat, and told me that the school's administration had unknowingly admitted my first husband's children. Inaya was never curious enough to find out to try and identify her half-siblings or her biological dad, but they were now apparently in close proximity. The school did not make the connection as to why my first husband, who had no job in Pakistan, had suspiciously arrived back in the country. Of course, I knew why, and who had facilitated this move. The tactics were different and yet still the same. So many machinations had been used when I defiantly returned to Pakistan a few weeks after my divorce from Imran. And now he was trying this.

It's funny how neither of my partners could see what I was made of. They not only failed at crushing my spirit, but their obsessive stalking following the divorces meant they had little time to focus on their respective careers. By contrast, I believe in swiftly moving on. Being immediately thrown into extreme financial hardship after both divorces left me little time to dwell over the past and what they were doing with their lives.

The moves to disturb me were petty beyond belief. I decided to let them suffer by going super silent on Imran. This time, I knew my enemy. This time I was no one's wife. I knew both of the men who had colluded to attack me. And I wasn't going to let them win.

Chapter 27

Every interview and personal interaction reminded me of a man I never wanted to hear of again. I believe in freedom of speech, but even when I would ask for a list of questions beforehand, all appearances and interviews turned into 'What happened? Who did it?' Friends and well-wishers would bombard me with news and pictures of him. I started deleting people from my timelines and messaging apps for sending me memes with his face in it. If I would accidentally come across his picture, I would put a hand on his face. I couldn't bear to see the face of the man who had betrayed me beyond belief. Not only did I feel like an utter fool for failing to realise what was happening around me, but I found the elite class (even acquaintances of mine who despised him) to be unsympathetic. The most common response was, "But he is like that. Everybody knows what he's like! What were you thinking?" Some put it quite harshly. "You got swept away by the fame and celebrity status of the man". I smiled, but their words stabbed my heart.

How do you explain it to someone? How do you describe what he said to me, and how he said it? How do you explain that a 40+ year-old woman, who had lived in the West for most of her life, could be as naive as an 18-year-old when it came to men and relationships? No one would believe that a woman who could be so confident in public would actually be an introvert. No one would believe that a woman who worked in media had never socialised with colleagues. No one would believe that Imran had been the only man to ever pursue me relentlessly.

And when I could finally bear to look at a picture of him, I looked at those vacant eyes. Did he miss me? Did he have the courage to repent in private? Did he remember me making him midnight snacks? And then I realised: of course he didn't. I was just another woman to him. How many must have catered to his every command, perhaps far better than I had? They must have treated him like the celebrity he was. They must have fussed over him a lot more than

I did. How silly of me to think he would remember things like my homemade pizzas and Mushroom steak sauce. That wasn't what he wanted. I couldn't give him the excitement he was used to. Why would he miss the same boring wife who sat waiting at home every day, when he could have more than one at the same time? Why would he want anything like that when he could have companions who shared his interests and wouldn't give disapproving looks at the mere mention of certain activities? Why would you put up with a woman who couldn't join in the fun? Why would you live in your own home like a criminal who was hiding traces of evidence all the time?

As a biography on Benazir Bhutto once suggested, Imran slept with everyone, and it was something he felt no shame in. In fact, the way he boasted about it suggested that he wanted to impress on me (and everyone else) just how sexually active he was. The sexual escapades of his cricketing friends were just as depraved. I was certain I was only told these stories to open my mind to similar possibilities. It had the opposite effect. To me, sex is not a basic need. One does not need to be satisfied like a dog or a donkey, with anyone and everyone that can be gotten hold of. It's only something one would progress to and enjoy with one person in a loving, long-term relationship. It's also not something one cannot happily live without or (if not entirely perfect in a relationship) compromise on.

I understood I was marrying a much older man, so I had no unrealistic expectations, but Imran was too obsessed with the idea that I could be disappointed. To me, him holding me close to him with my head resting on his chest was enough to last a lifetime, but he had lived a life of superficial performances and accolades. He neither understood nor could accept that I had lived a pretty dull life compared to his circle and was very happy with being inexperienced, with no feelings of being less fortunate.

The fact is that people who have a sense of self-worth do not need medals or marks on the bed post to feel good about themselves. I came from a family who always made me feel like I was the most intelligent, beautiful being that had walked the earth. I found it annoying that my mother couldn't stop praising me. In fact, I remember cringing every time she said something complimentary in front of people. The choices I made in life had a lot to do with me reacting against or rebelling against the mindset that I deserved better. I swung to the other extreme and consciously became non-demanding in life. Imran on the other hand, said that he had been bullied all his life by his older sister Rubina. His surroundings had undoubtedly played an important role in shaping him, as had mine.

The following summer, I sat with an old friend who had no idea about what had happened. I said, "I can't get over the fact that I didn't see through his lies. What hurt more than anything was the fact that I could be this stupid?"

My friend replied, "Reham, if you are not a murderer, you cannot think like one. It's not that you were stupid. It's because you couldn't possibly imagine someone could behave like that...because you can't behave like that".

And as the weeks went by, like a detective slowly solving a murder, piece by piece, I put the motive, the plan, and the incident together in my head. The more rationally I analysed it, and the more people I interviewed, the more I realised that the whole of that very public ten months had been a farce. The compliments had been warnings. The jokes had been jibes. The unexplained fits of anger had been frustration because of the delay in the divorce. I was used like many before, and deleted when not needed.

The answers were all there in front of me, but it was still so difficult to understand. It would be a while before I was able to deal with the weight of this betrayal, and it would take even longer for me to put the pieces together and make sense of all the chaos.

§

A couple of nights before my departure for England, I had discovered texts on his phone from several PTI women position holders. A couple of minutes before, he had held me close and wailed about how he did not feel up to going to Lahore for the local body elections. I had motivated him by saying, "It's only two days. It will be over before you know it". I didn't know that the spoilt leader was being motivated in far more enticing ways by the women waiting for him in Lahore.

Andaleeb Abbas's text read, "Oh come on, I will ride you so hard over and over again". This woman was PTI's 'President of Punjab' at the time. Uzma Kardar of the media team went a step further, saying, "Why are you depriving the dick now that wifey is not going to be an issue either". I demanded to know what the hell these texts meant. He told me that Andaleeb was an alcoholic. Supposedly, she would hit the bottle at that time of the night, and it meant nothing. "Baby, please don't make an issue and come back to bed," he said casually, and rolled back to sleep.

"Come back to bed?!"

In my frustration at his response, I walked over to the bed and slammed the TV remote down on the side table so hard that it cracked. He sat up in bed again with a weary face. He just didn't seem to care.

"Imran, why don't you just kill me instead," I suggested jeeringly at him. "It would be more respectful than this callousness. Here, take this right here," I said offering him a dagger from the side table. "Drive it through my heart. I would prefer dying to this insult. Uzma Kardar, that mad woman, is texting you that your wifey is not an issue anymore? You are telling me not to make an issue? What does she mean? Tell me what the hell is going on!" But not even an excuse was offered. He didn't care that I was in tears. He simply shrugged and went back to sleep, saying, "They are texting, what can I do?"

In my entire time with Imran, I never once hit or abused him in any way. Shouting and hurling expletives was never my way with him. There was only ever that one time when I softly whispered a swear word before I walked away from him forever. Throughout the marriage, I was just a helpless wife with tears in her eyes, continually pleading with him to stop destroying everything: his life, his politics, and us.

I sat up all night. These women were regular offenders. Uzma Kardar was not only in the habit of regularly sending him images of her genitalia but would force her way in to stand or sit next to him, even in my presence. I dismissed her as a disturbed woman. She had warned me in person at Aleem Khan's house, right at the start of the year, that I should put up with it since they were not going to back off. Back then, I had too much faith in my husband, and I suppose arrogance too. How could he possibly be interested in women like her and Andaleeb? Post-divorce, much to my embarrassment, a Pashtun journalist advised me that the service offered by Andaleeb was comparable to that found in Amsterdam. I clearly could not compete with their varied talents.

The sexting was a bizarre mix of images being exchanged and bragging about sleeping with other men. One particularly shocking text was from a younger woman saved as 'Maha Khan PTI Chakwal', who would regularly inform him of the number of cocks she had enjoyed the night before. In the past, Imran had apologised and blamed it on his drug-induced depravity. He kept promising that he was changing, and that friends were already saying he was a changed man. I used to go quiet and pale-faced for hours during the early part of the marriage but that night I demanded that it stop. I did what most wives would do: kick up a fuss. But instead of apologizing, he just went back to sleep.

One of the things that amazed me was how and why our intelligence agencies did not expose this man, despite knowing the full extent of his lustful antics, drug abuse, and general immorality. Imran's penchant for sexting was apparently well known in Lahori circles. Most female anchors had excitedly reported receiving images of his genitalia. When my film producer told me this, I dismissed it as a vicious rumour, wondering why someone of his stature would take a risk like that. But Imran was indeed that reckless. I would soon learn that a cameraman at a press conference had once accidentally managed to record Imran's simultaneous conversations to three women, begging them to meet. One was busy with her husband, and another said that it wasn't possible as it was Ramadan. When the channel owner was given this evidence, he refused to make it public. Imran went over personally to thank this channel owner. However, I was told that two copies were kept: one with the channel owner and the other with a friend. Perhaps they foresaw a day when this would be required.

The morning after the confrontation, I had to visit Zamong Kor to oversee the building work and last touches to the refurbishment. The sight of the progress made me so happy. By the time I came back I was in a far more forgiving mood towards my husband. However, instead of being apologetic, Imran was in a bit of an aggressive mode. He told me that he was not happy about my tantrum the previous night, and that he wanted to sleep in peace so I was not to disturb him. I returned to a locked bedroom door. I wasn't about to give up on him and asked him to open up. We talked for an hour. His mood suddenly changed. He became loving, and complained like a child as to why I was abandoning him when he was feeling so miserable about going to Lahore. I said, ''Look it's only for two days. I must go with Ridha. Besides, I can't be seen with you anyway".

He held me close all night like a clingy baby. In the morning, as I hugged him goodbye with a cheerful big smile, he looked very sad. In less than an hour, I was to discover how my husband, who had been labelled 'Im the Dim', had fooled us all so convincingly.

So many baseless accusations had come my way. I hadn't been desperate to marry Imran. I hadn't blackmailed him into marriage using pregnancy. I didn't try to poison him to take over his godforsaken party. I didn't have links with Malik Riaz, or anyone else. And I wasn't an MI6 agent, or any other kind of agent for that matter. I think I would have proved to be a very poor one; clearly my character analysis and decision-making were far from infallible. The truth is that there was no plan to put me into Bani Gala but there was a very strong one to dislodge me. It took a team of concerned advisors sitting in London, who would advise my husband on how to execute the plan. There was an exit strategy team too. Kristiane Backer was part of it, finally getting her revenge for Imran betraying her all her life. There was a solicitor called Ayesha Jamil, who provided legal advice on how to gag me. And there was Fauzia Kasuri's brother, Chicku Jahangir, whose claim to fame was 'the guy seen in airport pictures with Imran in London'. They were all seen openly socialising with my first husband and his wife in Facebook posts after my divorce. People who loved me would send me these pictures and weep tears of anger for me. But I knew a secret much worse than this.

Throughout the marriage, anchors, like the man whose house I had met Musharraf in, would contact anyone who claimed they knew me from England and try to dig up dirt on me. They would feature my first husband's interviews on primetime TV. Imran told me himself that these anchors had been in touch with him directly. As soon as the divorce was announced, the anchors who had led the campaign against me were seen being received by Imran as honoured guests for the grand opening of SKMT Peshawar.

The author Khalid Hosseini says, "And that's the thing about people who mean everything they say. They think everyone else does too". I believed he wanted to change. I believed he wanted my support. I believed everything he said. But he never meant a thing. The same man who, as he was pursuing me, had said that he had never met a woman like me, now insisted that I was just pretending to be virtuous, after a year together. His hussies like Bina Sultan had labelled me as 'pious pussy' early on in the marriage. But the conversations of my husband about me following the divorce were full of bizarre accusations.

All the things Imran said to my friend Sara were repeated word-for-word by Arif Nizami on national television just hours later. Several TV anchors, huge social media teams, and PTI leaders were assigned the job of maligning me. Imran played the saint and never uttered a bad word against me in public. But in private, I was told of how he felt, and even heard him on speakerphone. I listened as my former husband swore at people for interviewing me or giving me coverage.

And of course, it didn't stop there. Imran had been emailing random women he had never met (and who I had only met once or twice) at embassy events. He had been pleading for incriminating evidence of any sort against me. There was one woman called Faz Zia that I had met at a musical concert in a restaurant in Southall once. The performer was a lady called Tarranum Naz. As I enjoyed her performance, she pointed to me and announced to a hall full of people, "We are not only performers, we are *faqirs* [mystics]. See this sweet-faced girl here? Remember my words. This girl will be very famous one day. She will make history particularly in our part of the world".

I dismissed the comment as a simple compliment and thought she'd confused me for someone from Bollywood or something. As we left the venue, my friend asked to be dropped home. With her was the other woman, Faz Zia. All I knew about her was that she was a makeup artist. In the car, she told me her sad story. Apparently, she had been the main earner in her marriage but one day, while she was doing a bridal makeup session, she discovered that her husband was getting married to another woman on the same street. I provided a listening ear and dropped her home, since I was the only sober driver around. This woman was not an acquaintance of mine and had never been to my home. And Imran Khan used her as an authority on my character.

My husband had even called the 'friend' I had entertained in Bani Gala and Nathiagali to ask about my past. This was on the 11th of October, but that 'friend' did not tell me until after the divorce. This was a friend that I had helped through a troubled marriage with legal advice and emotional support. After my divorce was announced, I made the mistake of staying with her for a couple of days, and she was very quick to ask me to leave her home. Her change in behaviour was obvious and contemptuous, after she had insisted I stay only with her during my last trip earlier that year, while I was still Mrs IK. The same friend who was worried sick that I had a headache and cooked endless elaborate dishes to entertain Mrs. Khan now made it clear that I must take all my bags with me as I left so that I wouldn't return. It's ironic that those who we have cared for and never hurt feel the need to be disloyal to us, and those we have never met might be sitting somewhere far away praying for our safety all night.

I saw friends and family members who had been around me during the Bani Gala period disappear quicker than you could write 'opportunists'. But I saw my kids not only stand by me but never blame me once for the huge mistake on my part that had caused them pain and violated their privacy. True love never deserts you. It wants your happiness at any cost.

§

While I was married to Imran, I faced countless accusations on everything from interfering in party politics to trying to poison my husband. In reality, there was no one around Bani Gala that I thought was competent or bearable, and certainly no one that I would have considered working with. Throughout my time at Bani Gala, I only ever encountered one sensible man in the secretariat. He seemed not to have any direct political affiliation but seemed to be vaguely connected to the establishment. Salman Aftab had a loose role of being the focal person for KP. He kept a hawkeye on everything that happened in the KP Government. He re-endorsed my idea of good governance in KP and over my time at Bani Gala, I was used as a messenger by him to convey to Imran what needed to be done, as well as detailed information on what was being done incorrectly. I was not sure where he got his information, but when I checked it with my sources on the ground, it seemed like the best advice, and in the interests of KP.

One of the biggest claims made during the campaign was the promise to eliminate corruption within ninety days. An accountability commission had been formed under the undisputed and competent General Hamid. The gentleman took his job more seriously than he was expected to, and kept uncovering the shady deals of ministers. They were all linked to the Chief Secretary and Chief Minister. He had tried to reach Imran several times. Now, through Salman Aftab, he sent me a message saying that he would like to see us two alone, without the presence of JKT or Awn Chaudry. Imran agreed to the meeting. As I entered the room the gentleman stood up to greet me, clearly pleased to see me there. I looked across at my husband and it was obvious that he wanted me to leave. I responded pleasantly to the guest and left the room, saying if they needed anything, I would be next door. Imran clearly wanted me not to hear what General Hamid had to say.

Later, Salman Aftab asked why I had not sat in on the meeting. These were early days and I trusted my husband. I thought that if they met alone, Imran would take the right steps against the Chief Minister. Everyone knew he was corrupt but my husband did nothing. It was a torturous sight to see the Chief Minister just saunter in as if he owned the place. Imran was totally subservient to him. Not even JKT spoke the way Pervez Khattak chose to talk to Imran.

Months would go by, and the desperation of General Hamid would increase. He insisted on seeing me again. This time, he was brought through the gates whilst lying flat in the backseat of a car. It was timed so that there would be no Awn or JKT in the house. They were all busy in a core committee meeting in the secretariat downstairs. This was towards the end of the marriage, and I had lost much of my faith in the promise of '*tabdeeli*'. Nevertheless, I listened to General Hamid. He was an earnest man who took a good hour to explain in detail what was being carried out under the watch of the Chief Minister. He begged me to get my husband to intervene. He asked me to use my influence on Imran when he was in a good mood.

Like a wife who doesn't want to expose her husband's weaknesses or admit her lack of influence, I suggested politely that he should write a strongly-worded letter to Imran himself. I don't know why people assumed I had any influence over Imran. The fact was that through our entire marriage, he never listened to my advice, although he did consult me on everything. He would ask and agree with my opinion, but then choose to do exactly the opposite.

On one occasion towards the end of the year, he kept pestering me for advice on who to give the ticket to in the by-election of Mandi Bahauddin. I refused to give an answer for days. I knew he would not listen to me. We had gone through this exercise so many times. Besides, there were no brilliant options to choose from. Finally, he forced me to give him an answer. With a sour expression I took out a sheet of paper with the statistics and pushed it towards him on the coffee table. The year before, I had watched in shock as Imran could be seen on TV going to an infamous electable's house to congratulate him on joining PTI. I sat there and spelt it out for him wearily.

"If you give it to this fake-degree electable, who is accused of immigration fraud, you will win the seat. He is assured 67000 votes. Your factor added will give you an extra 10 -15k vote. He is a winner. If you give it to Shah Mehmood's man Tarar, you will lose and be disgraced. You could give it to your young PTI youth leader, who is the face of clean politics. You will still lose but will retain your integrity".

Imran heard my rationale and then gave the ticket to Shah Mehmood's man. PTI lost the seat by a huge margin.

§

The biggest name in property business in Pakistan was Malik Riaz, the founder of the Bahria Townships. Before moving to Pakistan, I had seen him in a leaked clip with two Pakistani anchors in an allegedly planted show. I had a vague idea that he was very rich, influential, and that everyone from anchors to the politicians lived off his handouts. I had either successfully avoided all offers to do agenda-driven content or was not considered ideal for such tasks. Somehow, throughout my time as an anchor in Pakistan (before, during, and after my marriage), that proverbial *lifafa* never came. The media wing of the ISI made brief contact but I showed a clear disinterest, and was never pursued actively by them either. I was possibly the only high-profile anchor and politically-linked individual in Pakistan who never met or spoke to Malik Riaz, which remains true to this day.

Soon after I got married to Imran, I threw my phone SIM away, and the only route to me was via Awn Chaudry, my nephew Yousaf, and the boy who I wanted to make Pakistan's Karan Johar. Through Awn and this struggling filmmaker I had taken under my wing, I heard that Malik Riaz wanted to meet me. In my foolish idealism and lack of understanding of quite who of I had just married, I made it clear that I would not entertain any such request. At the time, the Bahria Peshawar Project was being discussed and I did not want to have any link to it or the gentleman behind the investment. The Additional Chief Secretary (ACS) Dr Hammad Agha, an upstanding and competent bureaucrat, was also adamantly sticking to the principle that if any property development was to take place in KP, the area must be identified before it could be given a green signal from the Government. Dr Hammad told me that Malik Riaz wanted to establish an office and circulate pro formas for his scheme. Prior to this, his teams were scouring Nowshera for land. Malik Riaz had employed a retired colonel who had met the Chief Secretary and Secretary of Local Government. They were going all out for Riaz.

Rather naively, the ACS just stated the law as per Local Government and Peshawar Development Authority's processes for development of such a housing colony. Investors were required to submit an application that included a declaration of assets, capabilities, site plans and full details of the site area. Hammad Agha declared that whoever wanted to start such a process was welcome to, but the law was to be followed to the letter, and sent these recommendations to the Chief Secretary and Chief Minister. Hammad Agha was removed as ACS soon after our divorce. Apparently, Imran had been overheard in Bani Gala categorically stating: "Get rid of the *mochar*" (moustached one).

Imran held a grudge against the ACS as he felt Hammad *Sahab* was communicating with me about the misdemeanours of the KP government, which was accurate. However, Hammad was not the only one. I was inundated via post and email with complaints and files of evidence from ideological workers who saw me as the only route to IK. Stupidly, I conveyed every complaint. It's clear in retrospect that Imran had not wanted that from the women in his life.

With the Malik Riaz issue, Imran, true to his personality, would call him a murderer in front of us, and vow that he would not let the fraudster into KP.

But by September, when I found him regularly hiding his phone under sofa cushions and in old jackets, I noticed at least two phone calls to Malik Riaz on IK's phone for each day.

Ironically, the man I had never had any contact with had told a mutual friend about how much he respected my integrity, but my own husband could lie blatantly about me. Soon after the divorce (true to his style), the property tycoon exposed IK by publishing flight details along with pictures of his own private aircraft. Imran had asked for it to fly to India for a cricket match in March 2016. I happened to meet Riaz's brother in a property office in Bahria once, to discuss the possibility of setting up refuge centre for women and children. The property tycoon's brother had completed projects focusing on the elderly, and I wanted him to set up a similar project focusing on children. He was more interested in giving me details about my ex, informing me of how Malik Riaz had been asked to financially support the *dharna* of 2014. Even though Imran was no longer my husband, I felt embarrassed when the chap jeered at my ex for living off his brother in front of everyone. All the people in the room laughed. I silently cried.

One of the other accusations that IK levelled at me to my friend (and a cousin who tried to get us back together) was that I had been on the ISI payroll, as well as having been openly in an affair with an ISI major. He would shout out accusations on the phone to her, not prepared to listen to sense. A few months after the divorce, Imran went as far as asking a former Director General of the ISI about this alleged affair. That man, Zaheer ul-Islam, apparently walked out of the meeting in disgust, saying later to someone, "This man is a raving lunatic!" and refused to meet IK again.

§

My first solo interview after the marriage was given to Moeed Pirzada, after the Karachi trip on 7th May 2015. It was a safe choice as he was one of the more committed supporters of the PTI. He had always treated me with respect. At the time I gave him the interview, I didn't think much of it. I'd had a couple of reservations about his line of questioning and the way his program had been edited but I dismissed them. For example, over the interview he had put a picture of Cinderella and her prince fitting the shoe on her foot, which I thought was odd. He opened the show with some surprising questions: "Where has she come from? What is she up to?" How many other politicians' wives or potential First Ladies have ever been asked about their intentions in getting married to their husband?

One of the most difficult aspects of writing about my experiences for this book was to sit down and watch all I had said through that period, as well as all Imran had said. I had to try and understand how the game had been played. I had been played. Well and truly played. I was an unsuspecting, unarmed woman at the mercy of wolves. I realised this as I sat there, trying to piece it all together: how I had been little more than a gladiator in a sick spectator sport.

In his interview, Moeed had asked me seemingly innocent questions but it was all there: the hints of the future planned for me. He described Imran as a Greek hero who was meant to be alone. And now I had arrived, as a wall between him and his fans. I answered to the best of my ability, emphasizing that I was in fact a facilitator, to reach the hero. The ordinary man on the street now had direct access to him via me, as I would read all the letters which had previously gone straight to the trash: I would stop and talk to people when I was out and about, shopping with the kids. But I was being a simpleton. I was perceived as an obstacle to those who had invested time and money in their protégé with the intention of making more money. But I had lived my entire life without making any money immorally, or accepting money or favours to compromise my integrity. It doesn't take more than a few minutes for people to figure this out. This was clearly why I was never made any offers either. It also meant that on occasion, I was overlooked for some jobs and opportunities. In the Bani Gala house, I was naturally a huge source of irritation when people realised that I would not fall for bribery or let others profit.

I did myself no favours by putting my cards on the table and making my thoughts very clear to Imran and his close confidants. I was trying to be the facilitator but my messages went into the void. I would even have people like Shahid Afridi raising concerns with me. When I'd met him back at Legal TV, I could never have imagined I'd one day be sat with him in the *gol kamra* (round room) of Bani Gala, and that we'd be holding our heads in our hands in grief at the blindness of the *Kaptaan* and the failings of the KP Government. Lala (as he was known) didn't profess to be an intellectual, and made fun of his own inability to pronounce big words. But I realised in Bani Gala that his heart was in the right place when it came to KP and Pashtun welfare. He would pop over with his chef to make Imran's favourite dishes and, like many other Pashtun brothers, would plead to me to make my husband aware of where his provincial government was failing. I made excuses for my husband's inexcusable, unconcerned behaviour. In private of course, I voiced my unhappiness daily, but Imran had wanted a wife to tick a box. He expected me to be grateful for being Mrs IK and look the other way. He did not appreciate a conscience in his bedroom.

Our finest qualities are our biggest flaws too. If you are a great orator in public, you can too easily carry this into your personal life. And my biggest flaw has always been that I talk too much. I leave nothing to the imagination. I'm an open book. Time and time again, good friends would plead with me to be careful, and to not say much. But I have lived my life with my heart on my sleeve. And as Imran would say to me when I would try to offer suggestions to reform his behaviour, "Baby, you cannot teach an old dog new tricks".

One other famous Pakistani anchor, Salim Safi, put it to me quite bluntly after the divorce: "I am unsure if you are a very smart woman or a very stupid woman. My gut feeling is that it's the latter". To the frustration of those who care about me, I realise my failings. I know I'm wrong to trust. I know I'm too open. I know I should be more cunning and I suppose I could be a tad more careful but frankly, I don't want to change! Those who love me do so because I'm not cunning and devious. I don't admire shrewd and manipulative people. I might have materially suffered because of my nature but to be honest, it has saved me too. And at the end of the day, I have genuine people around me. I would eventually ask the only friend I've had in the last three years (a person who bore the brunt of my post-divorce mood swings) whether my utter lack of regard for worldly matters (like moneymaking, asset building, protecting my financial interests etc.) was ultimately my biggest weakness.

"No," replied Suhela. "This is your biggest strength".

"Should I not attempt to change?" I asked.

"No!" she replied passionately "Never change. You do as you please and then the world has to adjust to you. It always does".

The first and only interview given to GEO was to Salim Safi. He had not asked for it. I was told by JKT and Awn that I was being used to break the icy relationship with Safi, who was the only Pashtun voice in mainstream media. PTI desperately needed him to stop exposing the poor governance in KP. He was the only one with grassroots knowledge about KP, and was vocal with his criticism. Safi was nicknamed 'Safi *Kameena*' by Imran, a fact known to Safi (*kameena* is a word which is far from complimentary). Both men were stubborn in their stance and would not back down, but Jahangir persuaded Imran to patch up with Safi. The plan was to see if Salim treated me with respect. If so, Imran would also give him an interview. Jahangir and Pervez Khattak had already given interviews.

On the day of the interview, the whole team of GEO stepped out to receive me along with Safi. According to tradition, a shawl was placed on my head to signify respect, and the new bride was given a gold gift from Mrs Safi. The interview was much softer compared to his trademark style. It shifted all blame to Chief Minister of KP, with no criticism of IK. There were tough questions for me, but I did not mind as long as Imran came out looking good. Only after the divorce would I realize what direction this interview was hinting at, where the questions had come from, and what the plan was.

When we were off-air, Safi gave me files of research on Asad Umar. Asad was one of three sons born to General Umar, the right-hand man of General Yahya. General Yahya is largely credited for the breakup of East Pakistan. Asad came from the ruthless corporate background of Engro Corporation. He was sold to PTI followers as the highest paid CEO in Pakistan, who gave up his salary to join the political struggle of '*Naya Pakistan*'. He was considered the brains of PTI. But Sahir and I discovered he wasn't the financial genius he was made out to be when we dissected a 'shadow budget' put forward by PTI in 2015. They tried to show how they would do things differently with their 'Grand Plan for *Naya* Pakistan'. But the numbers simply did not add up.

Insiders at Engro also told a very different story to what was being pitched. Apparently, Asad was let off quietly as he was running the company into losses.

I found him to be a polite but rather observant man, quick to notice a woman, but rather subtle with his advances, unlike Naeem ul-Haq. I wasn't sure whether PTI gave Asad Umar their signature snobbery or genuine frustration, but he never seemed happy with anything or anyone in the party. He chose a rather passive aggressive route. He seemed to have a covert role in events pertaining to my divorce and the ideological movement to dislodge JKT; he was the one who was arranging the pawns to carry out the execution, a dark horse who never confronted anyone outright.

Immediately after the divorce, a girl from PTI UK started sharing screenshots of conversations she'd had with him. According to her, he had been cheating on his wife with her and she wanted him to leave this wife. When he didn't, she leaked it on social media and he ended up with a brain haemorrhage. The story was covered by Aftab Iqbal in a skit on his show too. My mind immediately flew back to when I'd seen his adoring wife passionately making videos of his speeches during the *dharna*. I remembered her looking up at him with pride. I could feel nothing but pain for this poor woman. I was amazed and disappointed. This man was part of the PTI culture in every way. He was also the focal person in charge of KP, and a whole host of concerning new initiatives for the region. Asad Umar was the man behind the newly-renamed energy organisation, PEDO. It was appropriately named, as it was going to fuck KP's future if it went ahead.

The predecessor to PEDO was called SHDO, and had been originally set up in 1986 for small hydroelectric projects. The changes to the organisation by the former Engro man had some deeply concerning elements. Hydropower projects would be run through public, private and public-private partnerships in KP. It sent alarm bells ringing in my head as it sounded more like projects described in *Confessions of an Economic Hit Man*. The private sector had always been unsuccessful in KP because of the lack of sovereign guarantee, which only the Federal Government can give. That was why the organisation had been developing projects like Malakand rather successfully with its own resources. The gross revenue stood at 2.5 billion per annum from the Malakand project alone. Now it was being proposed that this earning would be used to fund high salaries for the new appointees under PEDO. These were jobs that bureaucrats had previously carried out on much lower salaries. Privatising this also meant projects could be awarded to investors of their choice. When transferred to the private sector, the province would only get revenue through nominal water use charges.

PEDO involved the privatisation of these new hydel projects to PTI cronies at unknown but presumably low prices. Thereafter, the government would be deprived of all revenue from the projects they had started, besides the small benefit from the water usage charges. And PTI were free to run them as they liked, and potentially even sell them back to the government at a loss after leeching the businesses of all profit. In one case, 6 billion rupees were spent on approximately 200 small-scale 5KW to 50KW projects, which is the equivalent of spending $54 million on the distribution of a few hundred simple solar panels. So, the pertinent question was simply this: Where did all that money go?

In other words, PTI appeared to be abusing their power as a provincial government by fast-tracking projects with 'potential' and subtly privatising them. In doing so, they were effectively handing themselves significant investment and capital, and stealing streams of present and future income from existing government budgets.

The immediate issue at the time was the appointment of the CEO Akbar Ayub Khan in clear violation of the rules set out. Akbar had served as a CFO in Engro under Asad Umar. It seemed clear to me that he was changing institutions into companies and employing his own people, which could lead to a hold on resources in the long run. The CM of KP wanted the brother of his favoured MPA for the General Manager position in PEDO, even though the position was several bands above his pay grade.

Not only was PEDO appointing people on mouth-watering salaries, the Lowie hydropower project in Chitral was approved despite being in clear violation of the rules. Everyone piled the pressure on the chairman, Shakil Durrani, to meet the preferred Chinese company, including Asad Umar, Pervez Khattak, local politicians, contractors, and the CEO himself. Durrani insisted on verifying the eligibility of the Chinese company, and discovered it was too small to carry out the contract. He faced opposition, and despite his protests, the company was given an acceptance letter without fulfilling the legal requirement of visiting the company's facility in China. He, like many others, had to resign in protest, and was maligned in trademark PTI-style.

So, in conclusion, PEDO was a farce, with no highly qualified engineers, no organisational structure, and rules that were blatantly broken. The Machai and Ranolia power plants were completed in July 2015 but the transmission lines remained incomplete, leading to a loss of 40 million rupees per month. An extension was granted to Ranolia power plant at an additional cost of 700 million rupees. Like General Hamid of the Ihtesaab Commission, Shakil Durrani tried his best, but Imran would not listen to anyone showing him evidence (including his wife). The technical experts in the Board of Directors were kept in the dark while outsiders took decisions relating to PEDO.

I took the file back to Imran and briefed him in detail, but he was more interested in how Safi had conducted himself during the interview. I pleaded with him to look into the energy deals and the appointment of Akbar Ayub Khan. He promised he would do so, but promises were only a way of avoiding further discussion for Imran. Two years down the line, I was reading that the party faced further embarrassment after going through lengthy and expensive legal battles to maintain the appointment. The CEO was ultimately removed following court cases, only to be replaced by another one from the 'old boys network'. It amuses me when people think that Imran and I ever had any arguments that an average couple have. It was always corruption. It was always abuse of power. It was always Imran's reluctance to fix things.

When the Salim Safi interview was aired on the 5th of August 2015, Imran called me up and said, "JKT's family were all praise for you. You handled it extremely well". I had protected both Imran and his best friend Jahangir. I never saw these interviews until it was too late. I had no idea what was planned for me in August. I walked straight into it. On the 7th of August, I was thrust onto the stage in the Haripur NA-19 by-elections, and my shaky Hindko was put to the test. As I left the Bani Gala property, I saw the gate lined with DSNGs. They were waiting for me to make a comment. Baber Ata, the chief of JKT's social media team, called me and said, "I have leaked the headings: 'Reham Khan formally enters politics today'. Let's give PMLN sleepless nights". I chuckled, not knowing that it was only going to give me and my husband sleepless nights apart.

The interviews framing me were all recorded and aired well before the Haripur campaign. The image of me taking over party politics was created even before I set foot in the political arena, and well before any speech was given. In the interviews, I gave soft, friendly answers, in keeping with the role of a proud and loyal wife. I thought I was helping my husband, but I was helping a malicious plan for a divorce.

After the divorce, Safi was given another interview. I saw how his line had changed completely. This time, the tough questions were met by a woman who defended all those women who had loved blindly according to our tradition. After the interview, an older Pashtun woman, who had been betrayed by a husband she had been faithful to, called me and heaped praise on me. This time, I knew the praise was genuine.

§

"Imran had been told to get rid of you. He agreed but just asked for some time".

Those were Hafizullah Niazi's words, when I met him for the first time in December 2015. I bumped into Imran's sister's estranged husband at the Avari Hotel, Lahore. I'd been invited to meet Bollywood actors visiting Pakistan at a film event. Hafizullah Niazi was a well-spoken columnist and analyst, one of the ideological founding members of PTI, and the husband of Imran's sister, Rani. His brother, Inamullah Niazi, was the one I had been told about when Imran had met me for our May 2014 interview. He'd been promised the seat of NA-72 (Mianwali) if he left PMLN. He did so, only to be betrayed.

I could see immediately why IK had deleted these brothers from his life. The man had an impressive personality and an instinct for politics. He never said a bad word about his wife. He also appreciated that I had not said anything derogatory about Imran. However, he reconfirmed my suspicion that my fate had been sealed after the April visit of IK's sons. Apparently, my birthday photo had caused quite a stir in the Goldsmith household. Similarly, this chance meeting with Hafizullah did not go unnoticed by Imran. He unfollowed me on Twitter within fifteen minutes.

Hafizullah appeared to be more shaken by Imran's betrayal than I was. He explained how he had given his all to him. He was not the only cousin who had suffered at Imran's hands. His other cousin, Majid Burki, had been a victim of Imran's insecurities and complexes. Majid was a first-class Pakistani cricketer, and a huge star. He was the darling of the crowds long before Imran arrived on the scene. He had this elitist air about him and was quite the heartthrob. Not only was he recognised as a very graceful batsman, but Imran told me how Majid had managed to marry the most beautiful woman in the family. It seemed that it was jealousy more than meritorious efforts at play when Imran kicked him out of the team.

Imran's relationship with the Burkis was curious. Immediately after proposing to me, Imran had handed me his autobiography and specifically asked me to read a couple of chapters. I am the sort of a person who reads from cover to cover. I never got to the end of the book, a fact Imran kept making me feel guilty for. But after our breakdown, there was no interest left in him at all, so I never got around to finishing the book. Sahir was then handed the book, and also didn't get very far. He found the tone egotistical and boring, and gave up. In the first couple of chapters, one of the most noticeable features was that he hardly mentioned his father or his rather middle-class family. It was all about the Burki clan. As I got to know him, his inferiority complex and hate for Mianwali became obvious. It was déjà vu: my first husband had an identical complex of being the poorer, backward cousin to very rich, rather well-connected cousins. It's a complex that drives people to run after material success at the cost of personal relationships. With both Ijaz and Imran, hatred towards their fathers compounded the situation. Imran had been on non-speaking terms with his father for much of his life. Imran despised his father and his lifestyle, but had become much worse himself. The uncomfortable relationship meant that Imran had often been the subject of ridicule by his father. Imran narrated an incident when both of them were travelling to Mianwali. His father, irritated by his son's diva airs and graces, chastised him a couple of times. Imran recalled how they emerged out of a local restaurant; Imran was overjoyed that the people there recognised the celebrity. He felt vindicated.

The Burkis (his mother's side) were reputed to be sophisticated. I met the very knowledgeable Jamshed Burki and his adorable wife Abida *baji* after I got married. They were both the epitome of grace. I immediately took to them, and encouraged them to spend Sunday mornings with us. Jamshed *bhai* knew my family and tribe well. He would sit for hours, explaining our history with references. I believe Abida *baji* and her recommended prayers kept me safe while I was in Bani Gala. She gave me a copy of the *Manzil* (Quranic Verses), which I read while I travelled. The other cousin was the ageing Dr Nausherwan Burki, who oversaw the KP Health Act, 2015. I got on well with him and his kids but could see how his controversial appointment and style of work would not go down well with the doctors and professors in KP. I also met Shahid Burki, who had served as Vice President of the World Bank, and as the de facto Finance Minister in a caretaker setting in 1996.

I started noticing how Imran had copied the Burki mannerisms, but (as all parodies are) he was more exaggerated, so it didn't look right. The Burkis have a quiet masculinity about them that commands respect. They are neither loud nor overly expressive. Imran copied to an abnormal extent, which is why his gestures, laugh, and conduct appeared fake at times. In private, his demeanour and mannerisms were completely different and far more effeminate, even childlike. He would sometimes break down under pressure and cling to me, howling loudly. I would wonder how this man, who could not handle so much as a single email from a random party worker, could possibly handle the pressure of any public office, let alone that of a Prime Minister.

§

Pretty much everywhere you looked in Bani Gala, there were pictures of Imran addressing crowds at major *jalsas*. Most people would focus on the great Khan in these pictures as he made his forceful speech, but my gaze was always drawn first to the thousands of pairs of shining eyes, unblinking in their devotion as they looked up at their Khan with hope. They loved him and trusted him blindly, just like I did. He revealed little of his real character in public. It was this reserved and aloof attitude that kept me from discovering the real Khan until after we got married, and even then, he kept up the pretence to the best of his ability. I tried to bridge this gap between his adoring followers and him by relaying messages to and fro. Until then, there had never been a link between the Leader and his followers. As a journalist, I saw other party leaders reinforcing the negative narrative about him, perhaps eyeing the Chairman's seat. In the passing months, I saw how his family, friends and senior party members exploited his celebrity nature. I was naturally prompted to defend and protect him. As any big strong man in our society, he would protest that he didn't need protecting, but any wife would understand how we nurture our families, despite their protests.

When Imran described his childhood, it was clear he had been left at the mercy of servants. He described how he had been subjected to nudity by older maids and cousins. Imran joked about a maid who would forcefully nurse him when he was about 4-5 years old. It became such a habit that Imran once grabbed her breasts in front of his mother, much to her horror. He told me how an older female cousin would force him to touch her when he was not even ten. As Imran joined Aitchison, this sexual curiosity got the better off him and he had a couple of interactions with a boy in his class. He spoke of a time when a boy signalled to him to follow him into the garden of the school property and performed a sexual act on him. Later, in Worcestershire, while he was doing his A-Levels, he described an incident in the showers where a 12-year-old boy came and forced himself on an 18-year-old Imran.

In later years as a celebrity, he was never short of suppliers. Part of the tragedy with celebrities, especially those in politics, is that there are many who are keen to keep them entertained. Sexual entertainment is the most frequently used tool to control politicians. Imran had no shortage of such men and women, who provided him with varied entertainment. There was a man in every port (so to speak) to cater to all the celebrity's dependencies. All were rewarded with top PTI positions. This was the sad truth that awaited the countless ideological followers who may have been thinking 'Why has this person not been removed for their repeated political failures?' The answer, regrettably, was that these people were integral to the entire messed-up state of affairs. They were the entertainment themselves.

From his confessions to me, it was clear that Imran was not the sort to say no to any opportunity. He once recounted in detail one such story. Apparently, one night he had spotted an absolutely beautiful woman. He had never seen anyone so stunning. They got down to the business, only for Imran to find that the encounter was not with a woman. I asked him what he did next and he simply replied, "It was too late to stop". I put this as a hypothetical story to my male friends. Their responses were dramatically different. One said, "I would have run a mile," while the other said, "I am not blind". The most common response was, "Well, if you are a hetero male, nothing could possibly happen."

Over a year later, a rather excited female journalist would one day try very hard to reach me. I was busy in a meeting at the time but eventually managed to squeeze a few minutes out for the urgent information that she had to share. This rather breathless journalist told me that the film actress Resham had just called her and told her how the new transgender dancer Rimal was over the moon because she had just provided her services to the great Khan. My lack of surprise shocked the journalist relaying the story. She proceeded to swear at me in Sindhi, saying, "*Zaleel aurat*! I can't believe what an idiotic woman you are! You knew all this?"

A few months later, in the summer of 2016, a new male acquaintance asked if he could speak to me as he was quite disturbed. He clearly sounded very angry and emotional. I was friends with his older sister and we had a respectful distance between us, so he couldn't come out clearly with the story he had just heard. With great difficulty and pain in his voice, he said, "I had no idea how much you have suffered at the hands of this person. It's so cruel for you to have gone through this awful marriage".

It turned out that he had been told by a PTI leader from Punjab how the Chairman of PTI had disappeared with the transgender dancer at an event he had been invited to. The PTI leader knew I was friends with this family, so called them and said, "We can't follow him anymore. This chap has been misleading all of us. Now that we know his true nature we feel even sorrier for his ex-wife. After she visited us, we were convinced that she was the best thing that happened to him". It is strange that so many of the compliments I've received in my life have come packaged with such negativity.

After the divorce, the stories kept pouring in of who had supplied what, where, and when. They thought I had no idea. A part of me wishes that I'd had no idea. But I knew, not because I was looking but because the great man told me himself. The evidence is all around us. Sometimes, we blind ourselves to the truth. I remembered how I had once deduced that a friend of mine was married to a gay man on my first meeting with him. My friend couldn't see that her husband was gay, even as he felt another man's biceps in the kitchen while exclaiming in rather camp fashion, "Oh my god, you are so strong". Instead, my friend simply believed she was not attractive.

I missed a lot of similar signs during my marriage. I also saw how Imran would quickly notice and appreciate attractive men. Money and good-looking men appeared to be the two things that impressed him the most. He raved about the past beauty of people like Pervez Khattak, Zakir Khan and Murad Saeed. The way Imran spoke fondly of Saqlain Mushtaq, the Pakistani spinner known for his cute boyish smile, disturbed me. His admiration for the rather macho Minister from DIK, Amin Gundapur, and his undying love for the youngest MNA from PTI, Murad Saeed, was even more shocking. Before my marriage, I noticed how everyone in Islamabad café shops would burst into giggles every time the young Murad entered with Amin Gundapur. There were hostel caretakers in Peshawar who told us details of the young boy's hostel life. But the affection that Imran and Murad shared was unmistakable, and a shock to my system. Murad could do no wrong. Whether it was faking his degree or misbehaving with media, Imran had given strict instructions to his media cell to protect the boy at all costs. The pretty boy from Swat, returned Imran's appreciation with unblinking devotion for all to see, even from atop the Azadi container. Other than Murad's looks, I couldn't see what his qualifications or credentials were for his National Assembly seat. I also supposed Ali Amin Gundapur qualified purely on the grounds of his rakish appeal, with his long hair and threatening moustache.

Then there was Zak, who had an unmistakable bond with his skipper; Imran always kept Zak by his side. Zakir and Imran had been inseparable since their cricketing days. On every little holiday that Imran took, Zak would be a fixture. I could clearly see Zak was as popular for his looks with the ladies as he was with Imran. The long-term, live-in relationship with Moby was odd too. Imran would refer to him as his wife. Moby, while married for a third time, chose to live with Imran and not his own wife. I found these connections hard to understand but chose to dismiss them, deeming it paranoia. However, while cleaning the bottom-left drawer of my husband's side table, I found empty cigar cases and huge tubes of KY jelly. When I asked what they were for, Imran explained that the lubricant and the metal cases were used together. His 'preferences' became clear. My look of horror produced peals of laughter from my sexually liberated husband.

I had caught my husband 'admiring' male genitalia through his impressive DVD collection several times. It was embarrassing to walk into the bedroom of a husband who was pleasuring himself to images of male bodies while his wife was busy cooking in the kitchen. Initially, he would cover it very well by saying that he was seriously thinking of having surgical enhancement as he felt he could do with another two inches. This was a recurring conversation. Apparently, he had also done some research on it. I didn't quite know how to respond to such a delicate matter in diplomatic fashion. I was genuinely shocked at his obsession, particularly at his age, and dismissed it as silly nonsense. But his insecurities lay deep. I found it sad and depressing. If Imran Khan, the much-loved, much-imitated, and much-idolised icon for several generations, could be so insecure then what hope did an ordinary man have?

The fact is that it's not what you achieve or what you possess, but how loved you have been as a child that determines how confident you are. People often said to me that they felt threatened by me. They felt that I was better than them; that I would take over. But 'they' were not my concern. What was depressing was that Imran thought he was replaceable. To me and many political analysts, PTI meant Imran. With no Imran, there would be no party. There was not a single person who could pull a crowd on their own. Some thought that I brought that crowd-pulling factor but it was ludicrous to imagine that I could overtake Imran. Now that I look back, I remember how I gave an interview during a comedy show in July 2015, which was reputed to give a hard grilling to its guests. Awn Chaudry and a girl from Lahore had arranged it. Surprisingly, Imran sat through the whole show, listening intently to every word. In the end he said, "Baby, you did very well. That's a difficult show. Wouldn't it be great if you become more popular than me?"

I'd been embarrassed at what I thought was lavish praise from him. I had no idea how uncomfortable he was getting. His insecurity was illogical. Even if I were to get any position, it would be after Imran. It was the same for Nusrat Bhutto and Nasim Wali Khan. Once they lost their husbands, they had to keep going with the mission. But perhaps that was their fear. After the divorce, I heard the worst possible accusation: that I had been trying to kill him.

On the 2nd day of *Eid-ul-Fitr* in July 2015, I had left in the morning to visit my mother. Imran had been sitting in the dining room with Naeem, Awn, Faisal Javed, and another PTI guy. I returned home at 10:30pm, worried that Imran would shout at me for coming home so late. I found him lying quietly on the bed. This was unlike him. As I touched his forehead, I felt the cold sweat. He said he felt queasy. He panicked me further by saying that he had been getting a tingling sensation in his arms and feet. I had been worried about us being so far from any medical facility since I'd heard of Rubina's recent stroke. I checked Imran's smart watch. His heart rate was down to 44. I immediately shouted for Awn who checked his blood pressure and it was very low. Amid protests from Imran, we packed him into the car and rushed him to Kulsoom International.

At the hospital, while Yousaf, Sahir and I worried, Imran behaved like a baby. I told him to let the staff check everything but he made a huge scene over the nurse inserting a cannula in his vein. He insisted she had done it incorrectly and pulled it out. The doctors said that it wasn't a stroke and his heart was fine. Imran refused a blood test. He kept saying he had eaten some *mithai* sent by his cousin, and it had perhaps not agreed with him. Imran hadn't eaten anything else. This would often happen; without me in the house, the servants wouldn't even prepare anything for him. When I was out, no one would feed him.

After the divorce, my caring and covering up was rewarded as several news outlets began reporting that he'd been in that hospital because I'd poisoned him. Apparently, this was step one of my master plan to take over the party. And what had really happened? I had rushed him to hospital because he had been doing drugs on an empty stomach. The media was accusing me of poisoning my ex-husband and all I could do was stay silent. Mansoor Ali Khan, a leading anchor, dug out the original report from the hospital to clarify my position and immediately received a call from Aleema, reprimanding him.

I forced myself to smile in public while these accusations were made. I wasn't even interested in denying the rumours. People did not matter. These accusations came from none other than the man whose life and wellbeing I had been praying for. I would frequently plead with him to stop with his habits because I couldn't see life beyond him. I knew if anything happened to him, his family would not even let me be near him for a minute to grieve. I spent over 12 months fearing for his life. There I was, trying to make sure he wouldn't collapse, making sure his LDL would come down and that he would eat on time, trying to get tall, towering security guards so that his head would be protected, trying desperately to keep him off the drugs. And he was spreading a rumour that I was poisoning him?

It didn't matter what his mouthpieces said. It didn't matter what the world thought. But I wondered how he could not see how much I cared for him. He surely couldn't be so deluded? I stopped cooking the Thai dishes I used to make for him because it reminded me of how I had wasted my energy. I stopped eating his favourite cheese because it reminded me of how he enjoyed it. In the end, no one believed their stories and they couldn't damage my image but it hurt beyond anything that words can explain. I hated myself for feeling hurt by a man who was clearly callous, but the heart doesn't listen to rationale.

Chapter 28

It took me over four months to heal. Initially, it felt like physical pain; a tightening in my chest like an angina attack. I would lie awake all night and all morning, finding it difficult to jump out of bed like I used to. I couldn't remember a time in life that I had felt this hurt. It was an insult for a proud woman who thought she was reasonably intelligent and morally upright to be betrayed by a man who was financially and morally bereft of any principles. The term 'projection' came to mind from psychology lessons. These individuals attribute their own failings to another individual. A liar will label another a liar.

I tried to focus on my work, but doing a current affairs show meant having to go through news of my ex constantly. I could not bear to hear his voice or see any image of him. I escaped to Turkey for a couple of days but everything, from the historical references to the cheese and honey served to me, reminded me of how I had invested so much of my time on him. I also had so much inside information on everyone that it became difficult for me (and embarrassing for my guests) to carry on with the hypocritical nature of our current affairs shows. But I soldiered on. NEO was a newly launched channel and offered an impressive salary. I had taken a major financial hit because of the marriage and needed a cushion to get myself back on my feet.

I also tried to focus on the filmmaking. Since I had not been working on a news show in Bani Gala, I had devoted my time to my first film, *Janaan*. Since I had no office of my own anymore, the dining room was used as the film office. From casting to scripting to wardrobe planning, everything was done in that room. From March to August 2015, we locked the venues and cast. I spent countless hours correcting and improving the script with Sahir and my nephew Behram. It was exchanged backwards and forwards between myself and the scriptwriter until it was finally ready in early July. We proceeded to start the shoot at the end of August. Despite my efforts, we had only managed to source 10 million rupees (approx. £66,400) before the first shoot started.

Several allegations were thrown at me (as they always were), claiming that I had taken crazy amounts from various people to fund the film. In actual fact, I merely introduced my young filmmaking partner to investors, and never directly took a penny from anyone. Miraculously, we managed to shoot the bulk of the film on a shoe-string budget of 12.5 million rupees. I had to give 1.2 million rupees of my own to clear some bills. I even instructed the crew to take furniture and tapestries from me to use for the sets I had designed. I wanted this film to be perfect.

Post-divorce, a little more money was added by a British Asian fast food chain to complete the song numbers and the more elaborate wedding scenes. *Janaan* was released in September 2016 and became the first Pakistani film to be included in the UK top ten. The female character was loosely based on me and was a huge hit with audiences. However, after using my name to sell the film, the young filmmaker conveniently forgot my endless hours of commitment. He not only never shared the profits, but did not even have the decency to thank me for my efforts. Some find it unbelievable that I have allowed people to exploit me like this. But I have never helped anyone for personal gain. After seeing those that I loved so much be deceitful with me, the deceit of a greedy little boy was not that hurtful. Besides, I could take comfort in the fact that the story and characterization was well-received. The reception was eerily positive toward my specific contributions; the weak points of the film were said to be mainly things to do with post-production and execution, which I had been excluded from. And that was enough for me to feel that my effort had been compensated. I could take comfort in the fact that my story had been appreciated and the young talent I had hand-picked would flourish.

The film was one aspect of my life at the time. But for now, I was back to what I was good at, although my heart was drifting away from it. My office at NEO had become a bit of a political campaign office as people poured in with their grievances throughout the day. Exhausting as it was, it took my mind off my divorce and helped to channel my energies. I loved to listen and I wanted to help. I used my pain to relieve the pain of others. When I put things into perspective, I found my grief was trivial compared to the suffering of many. This realisation set the stage for the next, and arguably most important, phase of my life and work. Charity and social activism would soon take over my life.

Home life had completely changed though, for the third time in as many years. I was back to being a professional and my free time was centred around the most important thing in my life: my children. It was also the first time I could even consider developing or following any of my interests. People often think that I was always focused on my career, and there could be no room for romance in my life. But it was life that never allowed me a window to explore my romantic side. Perhaps now it is too late. It is not my age, but the burden of responsibility that restricts me from pursuing personal happiness yet again.

It began with love for my mother when I persisted in an unhappy and abusive marriage. Then came life as a struggling single parent. With the passing of my father and my sister's new-found happiness, I packed away the dreams that I had always had as a young girl. Marrying a man over twenty years older than me was a conscious decision. Marrying a cause was the biggest romance of all. Now, after all I have seen and endured, I am more committed to my view of taking responsibility for those you love. I took responsibility for my family, my children, and my husband. I moved to a much bigger responsibility very happily. Perhaps I always knew that personal happiness was a wild goose chase.

Some people say that people like me have the appearance of being devoid of all human emotions. Maybe they have a point. But being this way means being so deeply romantic and idealistic that we realise it's difficult to attain that perfection. I remember watching Leonardo DiCaprio in *The Great Gatsby* with friend. She seemed unimpressed. She was a realist with a different outlook on life: her preferences were attainable pleasures like diamonds and Jimmy Choo shoes. Disappointed at her unenthusiastic response, I turned to my even more unromantic, career-orientated daughter, Ridha, who was reading the book for her English Literature A-level. She also thought it a pretty silly tale. But when I repeated the dialogues passionately, she started absorbing the message. I explained to the cynical teenager how love should always be unselfish, and that it has more to do with an image of the beloved that perhaps bears no resemblance to the reality. By the end of the hour-long lecture, I'd managed to get her interested in the novel, if not in the concept of love.

I could easily relate to Gatsby. When you love someone, you want to give them everything. It's not a business deal. There are no returns and no dividends to wait for. Daisy was perhaps not lovable to the reader, but to Jay Gatsby, everything in his world was built around her idea. My view was similar, but now I can see that it was just a figment of my idealism. It had very little to do with the person. I was in love with the idea of love. I was alone in my devotion and my idealism. Like Gatsby, in my blind love, I'd entered the world of the very people I always despised.

Coincidentally, the other novel Ridha was reading at the time was perhaps a much stronger resemblance to my life experiences. *The Age of Innocence* has always been my favourite book and film. Everyone around the main characters, Newland Archer and the alluring Ellen, knew what was going on, but the lovers were unaware. In their earnestness to protect their families, they end up depriving themselves of true love. Archer admired Ellen's quest for freedom but remained chained to what was expected of him. I related to both characters; Archer for sacrificing his love for his duty, but more to Ellen, who chose freedom for herself and from guilt. Very few films are as true to the books they adapt as these two. I grew to love the films as much as I did the novels.

Coming from a family of avid readers, I had a wide reading selection to choose from. My love of British historical romances came from my older sister, while my uncles left behind the work of the philosophers. My philosophy on life and models of politics is inspired by Confucius. My childhood favourite was *What Katy Did*. It's the story of a young, impatient, irrepressible girl who becomes paralysed. It shapes her character as she battles with her disability and comes out on the other side with flying colours. *Little Women* was another of my favourites, one I became fascinated with as a teenager. I identified with Jo's wild spirit. I wanted to grow up to be her, to have that fierceness to protect your family, no matter what it takes. She even chops her hair off in defiance of the social norms of the time and is happy to sacrifice her crowning glory to provide for her family. My heroine would grow up, and the readers could follow her journey into *Jo's Boys*, which must have subconsciously inspired me since I would also start looking after homeless children one day. That became my role in life. The only difference is that a Professor Bhaer-type is still very much missing from the scene.

The more books we read, people we meet, conversations we have, and cultures we are exposed to, shape our personal growth. They define the role we play in society. As F. Scott Fitzgerald put it, "I'm not sure what I'll do but – Well, I want to go places and see people. I want my mind to grow. I want to live where things happen on a big scale". I would be given the opportunity to go places and see people a lot sooner than I thought.

On the 8th of June, NEO told my producer out of the blue that there would be no show from the next week. No termination letter was sent. Not even the courtesy of a phone call was made to me. They'd offered me a contract with a two-month notice period or equivalent salary in lieu of notice. But all I could do was look on as they suddenly withheld that salary, then spread the news that I had been terminated. For the first time in my short career, I had lost my job, and I was reading all about the unethical termination via social media.

Initially, they had been very keen to pay me upfront for the first three months but by March their attitude changed. The rumour was that Imran had been threatening the channel owners to get rid of me. He hadn't allowed any PTI member to be on my show and then he was apparently trying to have me removed. And the channel owners were getting frustrated with my content. They had wanted me to come out and expose Imran openly on the show. Instead, I was being me. I was an expensive but useless commodity for them. The last show I did for them was on IDPs.

I flew out to England for my son's graduation, only to find myself effectively stranded once again. I again saw the attitudes of people around me change on hearing I'd lost my job. Friends turned their backs on me rudely and abruptly. Once again, I was short on cash with no roof over my head. I had no money in my British account and no efficient mechanism to get money over from Pakistan. Funnily enough, I had been feeling pretty low until that moment. But when I hit rock-bottom, I suddenly felt completely cured. I drove around Hampshire and Berkshire and sang along with the kids to all our old favourites. In an instant, the old Reham was back, but this was an even stronger version of myself. It was a rebirth. I had discovered my power was that I had always been carefree. As Freddie Mercury had sung, 'Nothing really matters. Anyone can see. Nothing really matters to me. Any way the wind blows'.

§

"*Haramzadi, khati tu mera hai!!*" (Bastard woman, I am the one feeding you!)

And with that, he slammed the double doors of the big American fridge on my hand.

I did not react. He turned to look at the 11-year-old waiting for his breakfast at the unpolished pine kitchen table. It was a familiar morning dose of abuse, sarcasm and glares. But this morning was special. It was the boy's first day at Caistor Grammar School. He was dressed in his brand new dark blazer and grey slacks. He had passed the difficult entrance exam with flying colours. But his father was still not happy with him or his mother. His mother had been doing Bond assessment practice papers with him for years, preparing him for not only these tests, but for the rest of his life. But this man was still screaming that she was a lazy, incompetent mother. Ijaz turned to the boy and said something to him in Urdu littered with Punjabi expletives. To make sure the little boy understood every word, the man translated.

"You know what your mother was? A maggot!! The maggot that is in faeces! I extracted her, and brought her to this level".

As his angry father turned his back, the boy looked at his mother and mouthed the words 'Get me out of here'. The memory of the little helpless 11-year-old pleading silently to me will remain forever etched in my mind.

I walked my son out the front door and to the bottom of our drive so he could take the school bus for the very first time. I knelt and hugged him tightly. All I could feel was pride: my handsome son was all grown up and going to senior school. We suddenly heard a grating voice from the door of the house. "Stop your drama". This sad old man could not even come and share a moment of pride with his wife and son. It wasn't the only memorable moment of my life spoiled by another man's insecurities. It would happen again years later, as I flew to the UK for Sahir's graduation. On the morning of the most important day in Sahir's life, I was driving myself to the courts in London. Someone had filed a trivial suit in an attempt to malign me and disrupt my charitable work. It wasn't even going to achieve anything. It was done only to inconvenience me. And it had worked. This was definitely going to cost me.

As I struggled with a rental car and the awful rush hour traffic, tears were streaming down my face. I was alone again. My employers had suddenly terminated my employment. They hadn't paid me for over two months and now they had breached contract. My friends' smiles had hardened into coldness and hostility. Everyone had abandoned me. I was never going to be a part of my son's graduation ceremony. As I finally found the courtroom I was meant to be in, I learned that the hearing had been adjourned. I was late, but the taxi driver who had been used to file a case against me had also not turned up. I had written my statement myself and handed it to the usher. The judge called me in with the other party, and I explained who I was and why this was being done to me. All this wise man said to me was, "I believe you are getting late for a graduation ceremony".

A tear slipped out. Here was the kindness of a stranger who could see the truth staring him in the face. This man believed me and understood what was dear to me. But those who claimed to be friends or lovers would try to ruin the one special day I had worked for all my life. And it finally sunk in: the hundreds of times I had heard 'I love you' were repetitions of the easiest lie of all. Humans, like pet dogs, have learned the tricks that get them the treats they want. Words, and particularly those three, makeup the laziest trick of all. The main difference is that pet dogs are far more faithful than humans.

It took another long commute out of London and back to Camberley to pick my girls up. We sped to Southampton just in time for the ceremony. I don't know how we did it but the four of us pulled together and made it happen, again. It was these young kids who helped me; who had always helped me. The designer-laden women trying so hard to impress upon me that they were my friends had disappeared. The love-professing men were also mysteriously unavailable when needed. It was only an unseen force that helped me overcome all obstacles. I never had any explanation besides divine intervention.

We parked the car and ran together. The mum was in her high heels and the girls were trying to keep up. I reached the grounds outside the graduation hall. I was seriously out-of-breath and my hair was all over the place. The pictures of the special occasion show a mum with a smile of relief on her face. But the signs of puffiness from stress and tears at the sheer selfishness of small people are also there.

As I slipped my hand into the crook of my son's arm, he smiled broadly.

"So...you made it!"

And I smiled back. "Yes!"

I had made it.

§

Being unlawfully terminated by NEO and being backstabbed by my *Janaan* co-producer was strangely liberating. It allowed me to turn my attention to what my heart had set itself on. Perhaps it's clichéd to say that I wanted to help 'make a difference', but that has always been who I am. I was simply making the step up from providing for my children to providing for all the children I could. I had seen the negative image of my homeland that had been developed and spread, particularly abroad. I knew of the contempt that the elite held for the common people, and their complete lack of effort in solving the issues plaguing the country. All I had seen was people claiming to want to make a difference but wanting power solely for the sake of their own wealth. There was a void that needed to be filled. And so, the work of RKF jumped up another gear.

I had been campaigning to protect children through every avenue available to me for years. I'd done it initially as a TV presenter but now I could be a fully-fledged social activist. I resolved to make sure that every project I undertook would have an element of subliminal advocacy against sexual abuse. I tried to raise the issue over and over again, in every interview I gave, and in my first commercial film venture, *Janaan*. My motivation to protect our children came from an understanding of how damaging this abuse is, and how it is everywhere. My own early experiences with odious men had certainly opened my eyes too. The understanding of this abuse is woefully inadequate, and it is generally left under-reported and unattended. The Mashoom initiative of my organisation, RKF, was built on hyper advocacy, and a push for severe legislation to be proposed and implemented.

While I was doing this in Pakistan, Sahir had started working in Parliament with my good friend Khalid Mahmood, one of the better men in politics that we had encountered over the years. Sahir would tell me excitedly of his projects with the Shadow Cabinet and Shadow Foreign Office, but it was his view on Jeremy Corbyn which I found particularly interesting. The man stood for something that resonated with me and my son. But both of us were now apprehensive about big men who would claim to be fighting the good fight. It reminded me of my own flirtation with British politics, and my early experiences in the UK.

As it is, I am one of the few journalists who has truly *seen* political leadership very closely. I smiled to myself when Jeremy Corbyn was picked on for not being charismatic enough. I could see how he was different, and also exactly what we needed. A perfect look doesn't make a perfect leader. Give me a crooked tie any day to a crook in power. His hand-knitted shabby sweaters spoke volumes for a life led honestly. He didn't need a classy lifestyle or riverside schooling to attract the voters. The British public had finally seen through the Eton Mess. My smile turned to disgust when Corbyn was accused of lying. Of course, I would never be arrogant enough to assume that I would always be right about anything. I think by now, I had realised that I was not as good a judge of character as I thought. But unlike someone else who had promised change, I saw more genuine effort from Corbyn right from the start, and certainly more consistent stances on global issues and policy. Sahir confirmed this, and would often tell me of how he had seen Corbyn listening attentively for hours in meetings with citizens and advocacy groups. The media onslaught against him was disgusting. I remembered how another Labour leader who had blatantly lied to us had never been so maligned by the media.

Like many in the community, I had raised my voice against the implicit British involvement in the Iraq war. Like many, I had not forgiven nor forgotten the indiscriminate bombing of the innocent in Baghdad by the U.S. employing their familiar shock-and-awe tactics. The resentment ran so deep that years later, when the BBC Radio Berkshire presenter Andrew Peach asked me on his breakfast show if I had read Tony Blair's autobiography, I reflexively responded with a dry, "I don't read fiction anymore". This caused more of a reaction than I thought, as the head of regions called me into his office for a gentle reprimand. It seems the outspoken social activist in me had always been stronger than the journalist. Of course, journalism was my bread and butter so I had to restrain myself.

The Liberal Democrats had attracted me when I was younger, as they had for many students. But David Cameron had exposed their empty rhetoric. The monumental failing seemed almost designed. Their U-turn on student fees shattered any belief that they were different. The only thing that became clear through the coalition was that Nick Clegg seemed to be good at survival politics. His claim to fame is possibly only that it was a rather rapid personal trajectory for him as a leader.

As a voter, I had traditionally opted for the Conservatives. Perhaps it was the colonial influence clouding my decisions. I had lived in rural Yorkshire before moving to semi-rural Berkshire. Perhaps the geography influenced my voting preference: it was dominated by blue. My upbringing and social status dictated my choices too. As I touched my late twenties, it was only the anger at Tony Blair that prevented me from supporting Labour. However, as I started working as a single parent, I slowly realised how wrong the Tories were. The transition took a while. The anti-Blair feeling persisted through the BBC years. My classist upbringing, public persona, and Newbury environment perhaps suited the Tories, but my reality matched Labour. The only problem was the leadership, which had no Tony Benns anymore. In fact, Labour under Blair appeared more conservative than the Conservatives. I didn't even realise how I had always been ideologically centre-left. Yet my kids and I were members of the Tory Party all the way up until 2014.

Many of us vote without thinking carefully of who we really are and what we truly support. This lack of self-awareness and knowledge of how politics affects us is true in the UK, and was certainly the case as I cast my vote in Pakistan in 2013. We are fed a story so charming that we never understand the subliminal meaning of it. It wasn't until I moved to Pakistan that I started paying serious attention to politics. Even then, it was just a TV show for me until the elections. I was busy preparing the best and most balanced content. I had not yet seen the propaganda machinery at work. I was very much a victim of it. What strikes me as obvious now, particularly after my misguided romance with PTI, is that there is no escaping the propaganda. I ended up voting for parties and candidates without engaging my own brain. I was fed a narrative and happily gobbled it up. Our voting behaviour is much like ordering at a fast food outlet. It is served hot so we eat plastic happily, thinking it is real meat. We give in to the temptation of upsizing our meal without really wanting it.

After the elections, I realised that politics was not something only politicians should concern themselves with. It wasn't just a position or a seat in Parliament. We, the electorate, need to demand effectively. The impression that only a few people are really suited to politics, or that politicians know better than us, arises out of laziness, or perhaps a lack of confidence in our own abilities. Political decisions are mostly made by people who do not accurately represent their constituents. Nowhere is this truer than in Pakistan, where elected representatives drink imported Perrier water while 80% of the population lives with either contaminated water or no water at all. These politicians can't possibly know how their decisions actually affect the public.

§

For more than five years, I'd lived in a country blamed for nurturing terror while being ravaged by it more than almost anywhere else. The country flipped between labels like 'our special friend', 'a close ally' or 'an Islamist state' as and when it suited the Western powers. Like so many in the West, I read the same books, watched the same films, and followed the same soaps as most Westerners. I discovered that the reality on the ground contrasted heavily with the narrative reinforced by the West. This was not a land of extremists. People of different faiths, sects and races lived in harmony except when paid militants from opposing lobbies created situations and then used respective community heads or clerics to incite violence.

Politicians across the world thrive on peoples' fears. Using race and religion is the oldest trick in the book. Since time immemorial it has been used to secure personal empires. In 2016, America, the world's biggest melting pot, would see it being used successfully by a Presidential candidate. Such occurrences would leave me uneasy at the thought of what may await me if I did something as simple as change the location on my Twitter feed. I shudder inside at the thought of the world that we have created for our children. We live in a world of increasingly divisive political landscapes. Our children must choose between two extremes: Trumps and the Trudeaus. It's a radical shift in how politicians are behaving.

Both these types are intriguing. Both use media effectively. One is a darling and the other is abhorred, but they both occupy the space. It can be viewed both negatively and positively. At times, both types take it too far. While Trudeau seemed the type who saw everything as a photo opportunity and was less likely to pay attention to serious governance, his diplomacy faux-pas' were milder compared to someone like Trump, who forced many Americans to be apologetic for their President's language. As a parent, what would I want my son to become? A man who poses casually with his family in front of the Taj Mahal, or a man who proudly wears his misogyny on his sleeve?

Having said that, I was perhaps one of the few who was not that surprised (or depressed) that Trump won the election. Immigration talk and racial hatred have always won elections; he just did it openly. He was a business man who did the maths: which states had the most votes and what did they want to hear? Say it and win comfortably. Who cares what the rest of modern America wants? I felt that, because he was not the establishment's favourite, he might end up unintentionally playing a positive role internationally. He had business interests in Russia and China; he would not want to destroy these relationships. The Henry Kissinger strategy of world domination might have just been disrupted. If Trump had not derailed the train completely, he had at least put an emergency brake on. The slight disruption to normal service might just be enough for the rest of the world to close the gap. We can see that the language of diplomacy has changed, from small fingers threatening to press the biggest nuke button to large hands cradling the tiniest of refugee babies. The world we live in is full of fear but there is still hope. It's just dancing away to a different beat.

Fear is not something limited to electorates. When one considers how dramatically different our political landscape now looks, it isn't surprising to see the nervousness of Western powers at the emerging authorities of Turkey and China. When Erdogan rose to power, I could sense that his strong Islamic identity would continue to cause problems for him. His early speeches containing religious poetry were not just a cause for concern in a secular Turkey. Although the political ban at home was finally lifted, it had raised alarm bells even in this, the West. I could see his shift towards liberalism as a short-term measure to allay fears and ensure European Union status. As the years went by, his stance on world issues and style of governance intrigued me. I started following Erdogan's political journey with more interest after the 2013 election win of the Sharifs. The reigning family in Pakistan had close ties with Turkey. The Turkish leadership and the Sharifs shared a strong, practising Sunni Islam background. The emphasis by the Sharifs on infrastructure seemed to be directly inspired by (and even implemented in the city of Lahore) Turkish companies. Bilateral intelligence and security support had been discussed. I wondered if the strong relationship with Turkey and support for Erdogan was causing the family's persistent problems.

Some of Erdogan's own political decisions would puzzle me, particularly his changing stance on Syria. I could not understand if it was a U-turn or a bargaining chip for him. As the years went by, I realised that Nawaz Sharif's regional alignment strategy with Turkey and Central Asian countries was making him stronger, but was making him a threat to certain other powers. Was the West getting nervous about the Sharifs' growing bond with Turkey and the Central Asian states? And why were the powers-that-be in Pakistan favouring those who were mimicking the Arab spring model of protests and sit-ins?

The networking of the Sharifs had made them stronger than the planners at home. Over the course of 2015, I was to witness first-hand how much of an irritation Nawaz had become. He had to be removed by hook or by crook. When I landed in 2013, I'd heard various academic debates on my own news channel about the Bangladesh model being brought in. These shows were neither primetime, nor presented well enough to be noticed like the output of the propagandists. Even I did not register the message at first. But eventually I understood how the Bangladesh model had been effectively utilised to control the Sharifs.

In 2015, I saw how Nawaz was cornered over the Yemen issue and left with no option but to bow to pressure at home, mainly created by PTI. The Saudis demanded that Pakistan support them in their war in Yemen. As a long-term benefactor and ally, Pakistan's involvement was expected. Many of us believed that the decision to send boots-on-the-ground had been made behind-the-scenes at the beginning of the year. But Nawaz had to take the decision to Parliament, and suffered an embarrassing defeat as they voted against military involvement. The Saudis probably never forgave Nawaz for this.

When the Nawaz family were thrown into the Panama crisis in July 2017, they were to irritate their Saudi hosts further by keeping the Qataris close. Nawaz ended up annoying both. As a budding journalist I had craved for such inside information. Not in a million years would I have imagined that the stories would come to me via a marital relationship. No one could have foreseen how I would be caught up in the middle of it all.

In the last months of 2017, an observant Muslim family would end up being attacked for being blasphemous on the wording of an oath issue. Electoral law dictates that every candidate must take an oath declaring the finality of the Prophet. This had allegedly been reworded from 'I solemnly swear' to 'I believe'. Even though all the parties were onboard with the proposed changes in Parliament, PTI supported the anti-blasphemy protests that the governing party had to face. Even though the words were swiftly changed back, a minister had to step down. I didn't know whether to laugh or cry at the hypocrisy and the drama being played out on TV and the streets of the country. This was the same PTI leadership that sat with extremists and militants, and insisted that terrorists were abandoned and misguided brothers. Anti-Arab lobbies like the Mehdi Foundation UK (led by the openly blasphemous Ali Gauhar) and other proponents of a modern softer Islam like the Quillim Foundation were strong backers of PTI. The people behind PTI advocated a diluted version of Islam but would take action on something silly like this. Conversely, the Nawaz family had always had a strong Sunni religious identity. Their association with the Tableeghi Ijtimah at Raiwind and their close ties with Saudi Arabia and other Arabic nations (which were further cemented because of their exile) were well known.

This movement seemed clearly motivated to break the traditional right-wing vote, as the post-Panama Nawaz Sharif was actually getting more popular. Now abandoned by friends and the old guard, he and his daughter had decided to behave like their party symbol. The lions were roaring back, louder than ever before. The internal party fragmentation never happened. The maligning tactics had failed. In fact, the political engineering by the establishment had ended up giving Nawaz's daughter the best possible launch pad into politics. These were unintended consequences, but the public were rallying with their cause. Nawaz

Sharif was free to say whatever he wanted now that he was banned for life from holding political office. Unshackled, he became more volatile than ever. He had been an elected PM thrice but he gained even more respect and admiration for his resistance. The real winner however was Maryam Nawaz Sharif, as she made history by becoming the first political leader to start her career opposing the military establishment. Not even her father could boast those credentials.

Not everyone has been this lucky in Pakistani politics for taking a moral stance. Malala was painted as a CIA agent, like many others who had fled into exile because they were powerless to fight the propagandists. I would wonder how many other myths had been conjured up about other individuals and issues; how many lies had we been fed? I thought that if people could lie about me, why would they not lie about issues where there was a lot more at stake?

Night after night, the primetime hosts would tell lies about my family. I shudder to think of how many lies we may have been told on India, Afghanistan, Syria, and Iran. The corruption claims were not new either. Every government in our 70-year history was dismissed on the basis of corruption. No PM has been allowed to complete a term. Benazir Bhutto wasn't even allowed to return as PM for a third term. She was considered too dangerous and risky to keep alive. She was killed in front of the whole world and the killer was never caught. The masterminds will never be found.

I eventually realised how the media was utilised and fed information by external forces, and rewarded handsomely for it. The role of hyper-aggressive advocacy in this manner filled me with grief and anxiety. A few weeks before the Arab Spring, I'd been listening to the radio while driving to work and heard a journalist describe how an uprising could hit the Middle East in the coming weeks; an uprising that would change the political landscape. He then went onto explain how and which countries it would hit. A couple of months later, my television revealed that the movement had occurred. The events had been described with chilling accuracy by this journalist weeks earlier. How had he known?

This answer was blindingly obvious when I thought about it. This had been conceived, planned, and financed very carefully. After the Arab Spring, I feared Pakistan might be the next target. My son had recently completed his thesis on the bottom-up approach of the U.S. that sparked uprisings across the Middle

East. This heavy-investment approach was being used here too, although I was initially slow to realise it. It was a well-scattered, thousand-piece, 3D jigsaw, and I was too inexperienced (or too lazy) to piece the ugly picture together quicker.

The terrorist attacks in the towns and cities were horrific, but the terror spread into the hearts of the people by the narrative on media was even more disturbing. To separate fact from fiction, I embarked on a journey to every corner of Pakistan after my divorce. People saw it as political campaigning but it was actually to see for myself what people really wanted. As I had guessed, it was basic needs like water and health that the majority have to live without. 80% of the population does not have clean drinking water. I was using my charity to bore for water and install hand pumps in areas that were just off the motorways or next to dams. I had never understood the point of all the money invested on things like polio-eradication programs when it was simpler and cheaper to just provide clean water. Diarrohea is the biggest killer in Pakistan. But now, I understood clearly. There is no mega-kickback in water projects.

As I travelled via Dera Ismail Khan in KP to Zhob in Baluchistan, and Talagang and Mianwali in Punjab, I saw some of the most deprived and ignored areas of Pakistan. It was a journey on what should have been the route of the much-hyped China-Pak Economic Corridor. This Western route had been dropped in favour of the Eastern corridor, which further benefitted the rich, developed province of Punjab. My travels reinforced my beliefs that this repeated injustice with the poorest provinces and areas would result in growing disillusionment. As time went by I pieced together a simpler cruel reason which was that creating equal opportunities doesn't suit local politicians as empowered informed voters would not choose them as leaders anymore. But also because where there is equality and justice there is nothing to rise up against. There would be no cause for creating chaos. Chaos results in collateral and creates opportunities to invade, divide and control.

The role of a social activist is tricky. I'd naturally wanted people to stand up for their rights but always had to tread carefully to make sure that I did not support any separatist agenda. I was always a strong advocate for the provision of better opportunities for neglected provinces like KP and Baluchistan. But there was little or no interest to improve job opportunities and living standards for these areas across all parties. The reason is simple: the majority of the voting power lies in Punjab. The foreign policy regarding Afghanistan was far from helpful: both provinces shared an impossible-to-regulate porous border with Afghanistan.

The poverty of those living in these areas was exploited by those who sought to spread militancy. The locals in Pashtun and Baluchistan were used by both internal and external forces to fight their proxy wars. When death is near certain because of lack of income, militancy seems like quite a tempting proposition. It was the only career option offered in these areas. Young boys were paid handsomely, and, in the event of their death in the line of duty, their large families were supported thereafter. In my observation, it has little to do with strong religious convictions, and more to do with financial gain and the glamour of gun-brandishing. The religious label helps to remove any residual guilt. Boys learn that crime literally pays.

While I saw much deprivation and poverty, my hope was restored on meeting the more sensible people in the most remote areas of Pakistan. I was welcomed without a trace of misogyny or sexism. I would initially go to these areas covered in thick long *chadars* but they would within minutes treat me as if I was one of the lads. I was seeing all I could. I stopped over in the Malakand to meet the family of my security guard, and check potential sites for a refuge centre for women and children. I also managed to visit the area of a local who had bumped into me at *Sehr* in a restaurant during Ramadan.

Malakand division (previously an agency, then a provincially administered tribal area), is bounded on the West by Mohmand and Bajaur agencies, and classed as an insecure area. As I arrived at the venue, my staff panicked on seeing the crowds gathered. According to the military intelligence report, nearly 7000 people had turned up. We had no idea, and were completely unprepared. The boys wanted me to make a short speech and a quick exit, but the crowd was not having it. They were all keen to meet me in person and convey their concerns to me. As the frenzy increased, one of the boys in my team pleaded with one of the men, saying, "Please maintain a distance. She is a woman!"

"She is not a woman!" the man roared back at him. "She is my leader! She is my elder".

This was the reality of these people. They were neither blind nor barbaric, and certainly not sexist, but they have been misrepresented in Western media and literature. Even our Pakistani media would simply echo what was said in the West. But local news coverage of these areas on mainstream television was non-existent, and still is. They rely on their cue from the Western media outlets, which almost always means that the only elements highlighted are the negative news items related to terrorism or extremism.

Local journalists never seem to get space for their articles or TV packages when it's a story from KP or Baluchistan. The internet and phone signals are very poor in most of these areas. In fact, the 2017 census placed our population at 220 million, and only around 18% (approximately 35 million) of the population are said to have access to internet. Out of these, only 15 million have smartphones, of which an estimated 67% are male and between 21 and 30 years old. All of which means that only an extremely small proportion of the population have any access to the misinformation and agendas of the corrupt media machine. This general lack of internet and TV might have saved my people from the sinister plans to divide and destabilise.

Chapter 29

I returned to Pakistan in August 2016. My son had graduated and I was not burdened by a job. In a way, this was a fresh start. Since Bani Gala, I had been living in a smaller place in sector F7 of Islamabad (which was fine, since it was just Inaya and me). But when I returned from England, I decided to change this too. My driver from Bani Gala, Wajid, helped me move into my new home in a highly sought-after area of the city, with beautiful views of the Margalla Hills from my roof. My origins in KP were just over those hills. For the first time, I could wake up as I liked, and sit in the mornings watching the sun rise and thinking of the next step in my mission to help this country via RKF. Wajid lovingly unpacked each piece of Wedgewood and forced me to order curtains. He helped me reclaim the person I was. I decorated my new home as I liked, and filled it with light.

Before long, I would have more lovely, upbeat staff in the home: the emotional Saeeda *baji,* who cried or laughed hysterically at the drop of a hat, and Tariq *bhai,* the man extraordinaire. Tariq was 28 and had three sons. He became the man I trusted with my home and money. I would listen to his in-depth political analysis as he drove me around the country. I looked forward to waking up for my morning coffee; each one of the home staff and my RKF volunteers would compete to make it for me. Life was different now, and I was trying to enjoy it.

This new lifestyle allowed me more time for family too. I could spend more time with the one person who had the most influence in shaping my personality, my ideas and the way I articulate them; my mother. People who spend some time with me often are surprised to discover the real me. My interests have always been extremely varied, but I always turn around and say, "I can't do even 10% of what my mother could do". That woman was a walking encyclopaedia, a specialist in everything. From changing sockets to gardening, from writing poetry to solving maths problems, the woman was a genius. But as with all geniuses, being ahead of her time meant leading a rather lonely and misunderstood existence. She did not know or care much about gossip and wasn't obsessed with shopping like the other women of her socio-economic status. Her husband was in awe of her intelligence but society, particularly the women (her daughters included), judged her unfairly. She did not fit into the stereotypical image of a housewife. In turn, she lived in perpetual fear of her environment. Her life was dictated by what people would say. There was only one thing I had that she didn't: courage. The courage to be herself. The courage to refuse to fit in. Sadly, she could never share her ability with the world because of this fear. So suppressed was her creativity because of her social status that the world would never get to learn from this wonderfully intelligent being.

After my divorce to Imran, we really bonded. Sadly, during this time she largely lost the ability to speak as Parkinson's took over her frail body. The elegant lady who could speak several languages fluently and gave the best speeches I had ever heard was reduced to a state where she could hardly speak, and used her index finger to communicate. The proud perfectionist, who would refuse to entertain guests if the marble floors were not gleaming and insisted on cream white curtains and sofas even in the heat and dust of Pakistan, had accepted her deteriorating health. She would even laugh and poke fun at her disability.

I jumped in with pet phrases that I had picked up from her. I would run through the list and she would be in visible hysterics at my cheeky mimicry, even though her laugh was soundless by now. She had finally accepted the simple reality that she was never loved for being a domestic goddess or for her immaculate appearance. She was loved for who she was inside. I, in turn, started becoming more accommodating and would dress up just for her. I would change from my normal dull and loose clothing to wear bright coloured clothes, slap on the makeup and put on jewellery when visiting her. It was my date with her and sure enough she would notice every little effort I had made. She would comment on the quality of fabric and the cut. I would take her favourite treats for her and would show her all the funny videos that were circulating, and also the Bollywood songs which she was denied in the rather strict atmosphere of my brother's household (he would turn a blind eye to this). I had finally converted my mother to my ideology of freedom and this was my biggest win.

Gone were the questions and the guilt trips of 'Is this right to do or not?' There was just acceptance.

She had been asking for me for two weeks but I had been over in the UK to visit my children in the Christmas holidays. On one cold January morning in 2017, right after my return, I woke up and felt an urge to go see her immediately. Normally I would go on a weekend, but that day I got out of bed and called the driver to get the car ready. I left before breakfast. Bahria Town was so far, and weekdays were such long days for me, that visits were not always possible. But that morning I decided to go visit her just like that, wearing the deep shade of purple that she loved so much

She had her back to me as I walked in. She was sat in her wheelchair with her breakfast lying untouched in front of her and her two medical attendants arguing over her. The two women immediately hushed as they saw me enter the room. I saw her sat with her eyes closed. She seemed delirious, with some crying sounds coming from her. Her body was rigid. I touched her forehead; she had a high temperature. I controlled my anger at the two ladies and firmly asked why she was sat up when she was clearly not well. I quickly put her back in bed and sponged her down to reduce the fever. She was in convulsions. I gave her some paracetamol and gently encouraged her to take a few sips of an energy drink and some rice pudding. She responded to my pleas and took a few mouthfuls. She opened her eyes momentarily. I saw that she saw me. She smiled ever so faintly. For the next couple of hours, I held her, rocking her like a baby while calling for a doctor to come and see her. In that moment, I realised something imperative that our faith teaches us: you may have stature, money, assets, influence and power...but these cannot save you. Nothing can stop this moment.

Me and my nephew, Hamza, tried to deceive each other (and ourselves) that she was still with us. 'Her body is still warm' I thought. 'That was a pulse, wasn't it? Let me check her breathing just one more time'. The paramedics arrived, and recognised me. They tried to revive a life that had gone for my peace of mind. But that was that. She had passed away quietly in my arms. She was gone. We just couldn't accept it. I cried softly as I let her go but in my heart, I realised that it was my selfishness that made me want to hold onto her. The pain that she had endured as she had been lying in that bed for four years couldn't have been easy. As always, it fell to me to organise everything and to stay strong for everyone. After those first few tears in the hospital, I jumped to action.

Later that evening, I did what I had dreaded doing all my life. In our faith, it is expected that immediate family members, such as the children, bathe the dead and perform the last rites themselves. There in my hands, my beautiful mother's head lay lifeless. As I poured water over her face and moved her head from side to side, she looked beautiful and serene, yet this proud woman was helpless like a ragdoll. We forget this certainty. We think we are invincible and undefeatable. It was a sobering moment. A true Muslim must live in constant preparation for this certainty: that death can strike at any moment and that life here is merely a blip. There can be no place for arrogance. That night, I sat with her in my bedroom, alone again in my grief. No man, no friend, no sibling around. My daughter called and I shared my pain with her on a video-call. Ridha and I cried together and bid my mother a tender, warm goodbye. Tomorrow was another day of public appearances and duty, but tonight was ours. Three generations of women: Mothers and daughters who were all different to each other yet similar in so many ways.

As I laid my mother to rest, I realised it was not a goodbye. Every day, I look into the mirror and see her in my trademark smile. Every time I articulate, she is in my delivery. Every time I write, she is in my words. She is with me in everything I do and everything I achieve.

So, until we meet again my dear mother... may you rest in perfect peace.

§

Early 2017 was marked by new experiences. My travels by road had taught me about Pakistan's landscape and people first-hand. This had allowed me to report accurately, without exaggeration. It was also how I came to love my heritage and my beautiful land more than ever. Now was the time to see more of it and do more for it.

From July 2017, I went on a political campaign style intensive tour. It was not planned to be one but my continued presence and efforts in deprived communities turned it into just that. After the Panama decision, when the sitting PM was dismissed on the flimsy grounds of not declaring receivable assets, there was suddenly a political vacuum. It made people feel vulnerable and look towards me for leadership and guidance. I was one of few familiar personalities that people had expectations of. The problem with Pakistani politics is not only that the elite rule, but also that the masses want celebrities or influential people to represent them. This is a flawed mindset. By doing this, the people create 'the electables', and discourage the growth of grassroots politics.

I love meeting people and have been told I can give decent speeches, but in my heart, I've always felt that this isn't the way forward. Rhetoric sickens me, and I did not want to take people down the same route that others have before me. Political rallies remind me of the empty promises of our political elites. I focused on social work, but eventually these events evolved into something beyond my control. In places like KP and Gilgit Baltistan, the masses, fed up with waiting for me to announce my political intentions, started imposing events on me. My social events turned into huge corner meetings with attendance of thousands of people. At the end of a gruelling schedule of five districts and two provinces, I decided to take a break from my public appearances. Instead, I began to search for a magical place Imran had once promised to take me to.

When Imran had proposed to me, he'd talked about his love for the country and its landscape. He knew my love of flowers and lavender fields, and described a place in Gilgit Baltistan which apparently had fields of bulbs even prettier than Keukenhof in Holland. He said it would be exactly like the iconic image from the song 'Dekha aik khwab tu yeh silsilay huay' (Which roughly translates to 'I had a dream and that's how it all began' from the famous Bollywood film *Silsilay*. He insisted that we get married in August so we could go for our honeymoon there, as the flowers bloomed for only two weeks. He had believed that the *dharna* would end very quickly. He had added that he would need JKT's helicopter, and I had groaned.

Now, over two years later, I would finally give myself the holiday a man had once promised. Coincidentally, Imran and PTI were linked with me again at this time. While I was on the road, news broke of a female MNA from his party who had accused him of sexual harassment. The news channels went crazy trying to get a comment from me. Ayesha Gulalai had entered on a reserve seat in 2013. Many of us had been shocked at the unfair distribution of seats. She had behaved very arrogantly with me personally after her seat had been confirmed. The last time I'd seen her was in Bannu in July 2014. I never saw or spoke to her after that. When this news came out, I finally realised why she had vanished.

I remembered how I had been outraged on the 5th of October 2014 when Arif Nizami had run a story on my possible marriage. It had been an accurate story about how Imran Khan was smitten by the television anchor Reham Khan and that his family was opposing any union. It had also mentioned a 44-year-old woman from Bannu. At the time, I thought it was just a Chinese whisper, and that the 'woman from Bannu' was also me, since I was working with the IDPs there. But when the Ayesha Gulalai accusations came out in 2017, I finally understood. The woman from Bannu had probably been Ayesha. I had immediately asked Imran why my name had been in the story. Imran had turned and said, "Because Arif said you called him". Infuriated, I said, "I have no idea who this man is. And why would I ruin my public image myself by giving him a story like that?"

Back in 2014, I had panicked about the embarrassment of my family and I being linked with a man. I had always been so careful about my conduct. Imran would pacify me by saying, "You are worrying yourself over nothing. Everybody thinks I am having an affair with Ayesha Gulalai since she wears a *chadar* like you and is in and out of Bani Gala frequently". Now the past conversations, the hints in the media, and even the possible pregnancy began to flash back to me. I wondered if this was yet another promise of a marriage. She seemed like a woman who was severely emotionally disturbed. I recalled the pictures of them both sitting in matching leather jackets in the winter of 2016, and the rumours of another Pashtun bride from Bannu. It appeared to be yet another story of a woman led down the path of 'Use, abuse and betray'.

I had no part in her leaks but apparently neither did PMLN, as I started getting messages from their key workers in the media, praising me for what they thought I had done. Towards the end of August, a group of Justice Wajih supporters from PTI urged me to meet Ayesha Gulalai but I refused. I was also aware, from Imran reading texts and emails from Asad Umar out to me during the marriage, that Justice Wajih had Asad's tacit support. It wouldn't be impossible to imagine that Asad Umar had a hand in the Gulalai incident.

I could avoid the ratings-hungry media phone calls, but it was still a slight jab to the heart. This man I had once so desperately wanted to protect was being stabbed repeatedly. Yet he still did not see how and where he was wrong. In his blind greed for the seat, Imran had never understood who was faithful to him and who was using him. Women blame themselves when men treat them unfairly or with suspicion, but a scared, wounded animal will bite you if you try to take the thorn out of its paw. Your concern will not be understood and there is no reason to feel that you could have done more. It is important to think 'You did enough. More than he deserved'.

I chose not to get dragged into a story that was not mine. I disappeared. In the middle of the night I told my entourage that I would drive from Chilas to Deosai in the early morning. The hosts panicked and made excuses. They tried to tell me that it was not safe but I stated firmly that I would be going regardless. The journey was painfully long and dreadfully uncomfortable. We travelled nonstop to reach Chillim by the evening. There were no clean toilets or hotels on the way. I miraculously found us a couple of clean and comfortable rooms in a rest house after making conversation with the local wild life protection officers. After a short rest, we set off in search of the valley of flowers Imran had once described to me. Gilgit Baltistan's beautiful, rugged landscape is unparalleled. It is also, as I discovered, nothing like Holland.

We stopped only for a moment to take in the breath-taking views of Shiozar Lake before continuing our quest to reach the valley of flowers. Deosai is a conservation area left untouched and untampered, with very strict laws to preserve its wildlife. The government had managed to save and effectively preserve the big brown bears and snow leopards of the area. Evening approached. We kept travelling. At this point, countless hours and miles into our journey, I finally realised that my ex-husband had perhaps taken liberty with the truth. The locals informed me that what I saw on the roadside were the flowers of Deosai. There was no big 'valley of flowers'. My crew made fun of me for falling for his lies again. I shook my head in disbelief at the man and his exaggerations. However, because of his hyperbolic words, I'd still managed to give myself the most peaceful, memorable, and enjoyable holiday of my life.

Girls, don't wait for a man to take you on that honeymoon. Give yourself the holiday that you will cherish for the rest of your life. Finally, I was in love with my own life and my own soul. If you can do that, then you'll find it to be far more gratifying than any relationship you will ever have.

§

The sexual harassment case was only the beginning for PTI. I watched in amazement as their lewd behaviour was called out by this woman. But all of this barely registered with me. How could it, after the things I had seen? It only brought to mind some of the bigger issues in the rich mine of depravity that had yet to be truly explored.

There were many shocking sights for me in Bani Gala, both minor and major. One of the earliest shocks greeted me as I walked into Imran's bedroom one day and found a bald elderly man, wearing only a grubby vest and *shalwar,* with curls of hair protruding out at every angle and a cigarette hanging from the corner of his mouth, going through the motion of vacuuming the rug. I backed out of the room in embarrassment. In retrospect, this was a relatively minor thing to consider shocking. If I'd had any idea what else was waiting for me, I wouldn't have cared about this.

I asked Imran to have a word with the staff so that they'd be dressed appropriately as there was a lady in the house. Instead, Imran embarrassed me by calling the servant in and announcing, "From now on, this *bibi* is your boss. Her rules will be followed". From that moment, Sajjawal had seemingly decided to make my life as miserable as he possibly could. Since he was also from Hazara, I'd tried my hardest to be friendly with him. I personally counselled his daughters on job prospects and problems in marriage. However, Sajjawal was set in his ways and used to a different lifestyle. He wasn't there for keeping surfaces clean or cooking food on time. He, like the other long-term staff, was there to cover up Imran's secret life.

Despite this, Imran had me reprimand Sajjawal for not serving his friends properly. On one occasion, Sajjawal did not serve Zakir water and soft drinks with the food, and even forgot to bring bread in with the meats. Imran told me to immediately go and sort him out for his slack service. I spoke firmly but not rudely, and the man broke down in tears. I told him there was no reason to be hysterical, and to be careful in the future. I emerged from the kitchen to find Imran just outside the door. He patted me on the shoulder and said, "Well done". I was puzzled. Why had he been eavesdropping?

The main driver, Safeer, had also been with Imran for ages. As a rather distinguished-looking man with salt and pepper hair, he was frequently eyed by Imran's male friends. He behaved more like a Member of Parliament than a chauffeur. One couldn't expect him to do so much as open car doors. Because of the limited mobility of my right arm, I ended up trapping my fingers in the heavy bulletproof car doors several times. Safeer's arrogance was well-known. He had pet names for all Imran's mistresses, as well as his sisters. Ayla Malik was his pet hate. The *maharani* (queen) had seemingly irritated more than just Imran's sisters.

Safeer, like everyone else, continually complained about the Chairman's personal and political failings. The chauffeur was just far more vocal than all the rest. His snobbery was not appreciated but I couldn't really find fault with all he was saying. The problem was that, although staff like Safeer could identify where the Leader was wrong, they ended up picking up many of his traits. Corrupt ways have a trickle-down effect.

Awn Chaudry kept bringing me complaints about Tahir, the office clerk, from the PTI Chairman Secretariat below. He insisted that Tahir was consistently taking a portion of the money from foreign transactions and currency exchanges. I raised this concern with Imran when it appeared that around PKR 30,000 would regularly be short of the expected amount. Imran agreed that the man must be cheating PTI out of money but, curiously, never took action. As time progressed, I understood why the staff were so loyal. They, and their accounts, were being used to send money. I was certainly not on board with this kind of activity, and never took a single penny on Imran's behalf (or for myself) from any benefactor in my time at Bani Gala. The cash injections were plentiful.

I kept a tab on money spent, and looked into other areas too. The more I investigated, the more discrepancies I found, and the more disillusioned I became. I found that the tax records submitted to the ECP by my husband had declared only one vehicle: a silver Toyota Prado. I couldn't see that anywhere in Bani Gala, and soon learned that Moby had taken it. Imran suggested that a new vehicle could be brought for me but I insisted that the Prado should be returned, as I preferred to drive a car my husband actually owned. That car was the only one I ever drove, and the one used to get my daughter to school. For most PTI events, Awn would drive me himself in his own white Land Cruiser. For some invitations to events, the hosts would send their cars.

Imran used the famous black, bulletproof V8 with the LEE1 registration, but the registration documents suggested it was owned by a business linked to JKT. Another white bulletproof car was provided by Aleem Khan, and a black Hilux was donated by Dr Waseem Shahzad. The fuel for both these vehicles was provided by the respective owners on a business fuel card. I started noticing that there was more petrol being claimed than being used. I kept a record, which clearly did not go down well with the staff, as I was soon asked to return the card to Safeer.

There were benefactors everywhere. I was only scratching the surface of this; I'd never be able to learn about them all. The confirmed and openly acknowledged benefactors included Anil Mussarat, Aleem Khan, Jahangir Tareen and Aqeel Karim Dhedi. Major financiers like Arif Naqvi were handled by Imran Chaudhry and Jahangir Tareen. There were also other donors I was introduced to. They were mostly of Shia or Ismaili background. All were very unhappy with Imran's continual failings. I was never told their exact names or connections but I met some of them.

On the 21st of September 2015, Jahangir Tareen's helicopter had flown some of these benefactors in. I was asked to arrange a lunch for a father and son. I can't even recall their names. The investors seemed to belong to a Memoni background, and were of East African origin. I was told they had concerns about Imran's politics and were about to withdraw funding. After Imran spent three hours wooing them back, I asked him to use the helicopter outside to attend the funeral of Captain Asfandyar. The young boy had recently been martyred at the Badahaber Airbase. The Captain had gone out of the way to save others and sacrificed his life. His death had struck a chord with Pakistanis, and his funeral was a huge affair attended by the Chief of the Army Staff and other political leaders. But Imran refused point-blank. Awn mentioned that Shah Mehmood had been waiting for over two hours in the secretariat, but Imran refused to meet him too.

Although the guests seemed lovely and enlightened, I found my husband's blatant lying about the change in KP hard to stomach. Even though I was sitting with him, he would continue to take credit for Zamong Kor, the centre I had worked so hard on. I didn't mind this, but (since he had no idea what it was all about) he kept referring to it as an orphanage rather than a development centre and academy of excellence. I didn't correct him in front of the guests. As they left the property, the older man held my hand and said earnestly to me, "I am so glad you are here now because I have been very worried about where Imran was going. I feel he will be guided by you". However, I'd understood by then that my kind of guidance wasn't what Imran was going to appreciate. He had made it abundantly clear that he would not allow anyone to raise the issues of the corruption of Chief Minister Pervez Khattak, the monetary benefits JKT received under his Government, or even Asad Umar's newly-introduced and disastrous PEDO.

In the last few months together, Imran effectively forbade me to speak of wrongdoing anywhere. He asked me to instead write such things down, so he could read if he wanted to. He categorically told me that I was not to bring complaints to him anymore or voice disappointment in the evenings. When he continually ignored my notes, I started reading bits to him as he exercised in the garden in the mornings. PTI had not taken an interest in demanding that the Western corridor of the hugely important China-Pak Economic Corridor be developed. The incumbent government had conveniently directed all energy and focus into the Eastern corridor that mainly ran through Punjab. I had revisited this issue many times with Imran but had no luck.

By the end of September, I'd managed to convince him to meet a delegation about the issue. I felt quite pleased with myself and wrote a speech and content for a press conference for him but he was simply humouring me by meeting the professor and research fellows. There was no effort to absorb the information or take any action. However, soon after the divorce, two of my recommendations were followed. One was the appointment of Dr Mehrtaj Roghani (another universally-hated lady by the leadership) to the Deputy Speaker position. The other was to give the Home Ministry to the only PTI minister actually doing some work in the provincial cabinet. Mehmood Khan had been removed from the Ministry of Irrigation earlier to accommodate the demanding coalition partners, the QWP. I thought he should have been kept on. But of course, my opinion didn't matter. Pervez Khattak had the magic wand that Imran's journo wife did not.

When I'd confronted him on the 28th of October, he'd asked me for the last time, "*Saath rehna hai ke nahin*?" (Do you want to stay or not?)

I'd said, "Will you put a stop to Jahangir Tareen's and Pervez Khattak's corrupt ways? Will you?"

The answer was a "Fuck off". And I left, never to return.

And then the day finally came. In September 2017, my sources told me that JKT would not be spared, and Imran was perhaps finished too. I personally didn't think Imran was done. They needed him for a little longer yet. Besides, the case against Imran's foreign funding looked ill-prepared. It was missing some crucial information. However, in December JKT ended up being disqualified from holding public office by the Supreme Court of Pakistan and resigned as Secretary General of PTI the next day. Ali G's introduction of Jahangir and his modus operandi all came rushing back to me. The first health minister of PTI in KP government in 2013, Shaukat Yousafzai, was forcibly removed because he questioned why the basic health units under PPIH (a company that JKT owned) were being shut down. Shaukat later revealed that Imran had whispered in his ear, "We can't offend Jahangir. Please be careful".

I had tried to protect Imran but he had chosen to remove his own wife instead. I could only wonder if my words were ringing in Imran's ears as he faced public humiliation. As my ex sat squirming in the chair in front of the anchor Kashif Abbasi, with his unreasonable defence of Jahangir Tareen, it was obvious that the advice of people like me, who had predicted IK's public political demise, was not remembered with love. Imran saw no wrong in what he was doing. But for all of us who were sincere to him, it was painful to watch him helplessly defend the indefensible. The nation sniggered. Ideological supporters like me cringed. The empty sloganeering of a man who had run on an anti-corruption agenda and vowed to promote justice in the country stood stripped naked for all to see. The frustration at being caught out was clear on his face. He had not only been harbouring corrupt men, but he was protecting corrupt men.

Whenever I would ask him to defend his own wife, he would protest about 'democracy' and 'freedom of speech'. I had to face the wrath of those who hated me. Night after night, his anchor-friends would sit on primetime TV, labelling his lawfully wedded wife a honey trap, and equating her with Monica Lewinsky. He did nothing. He also asked me not to sue anyone for defamation. But when Justice Wajih sent a 'show cause' notice to JKT, meaning he would face some sort of disciplinary action, Imran dissolved all positions and wings. It happened again after the Judicial Commission report was released. A fresh push to remove Jahangir Tareen resulted in Imran angrily shouting at party workers in a speech in August 2015. He made it clear that he was the ideology, and everyone could leave the party if they had a problem with Jahangir. No one thought it was possible for Imran to humiliate himself further. But he surprised the nation yet again by naming Jahangir's young kid as the candidate in the by-elections after his father had been disqualified. The nepotism was rewarded by a humiliating defeat for the kid at the hands of an unknown PMLN worker.

So, my analysis had been right all along: Imran was never meant to succeed. He was a pawn who was being used by everyone. In his blindness for the PM seat, he did their bidding. What people saw as a U-turn was merely Imran doing as he was told by his financiers and handlers. It wasn't that he was stupid or easily swayed: he simply had no moral direction or ideology of his own. A puppet moves where the strings pull him. A puppet cannot love as it has no heart. A puppet cannot stand firm as it has no ground to stand on. It dawned on me very late that I was in love with a man he never was.

§

I'd warned Imran many times to not use his staff's numbers to make phone calls. During the courtship, I downloaded Blackberry Messenger to stay in touch. But since I was always travelling in areas with no WIFI, we couldn't stay in touch a lot. I never carried phones with SIM cards, so I was never really contactable. But Imran had a habit of making calls of a sensitive nature from his own phone, or from Awn's. Safeer would receive calls for him most frequently. This would come back to bite him more than once. There was the famous recorded conversation leak between Karachi leader Arif Alvi and IK during the *dharna*. Imran was encouraging the protestors to force their way into the state TV offices.

Despite my many warnings, Imran carried on with his frivolous attitude. Both the drivers had a habit of informing and advising me of things IK was doing wrong. In fact, the whole household staff was politicised. It was difficult to make any journey without a constant commentary and analysis on PTI politics. After a while, I got fed up and stopped them.

In July and August, both Safeer and my own driver Wajid tried to drop hints here and there of phone calls and visits of friends who were a negative influence. Both the drivers had also told me how IK was not mindful of his decibel level, particularly on the helipad. Clearly the helicopter did not quite mask his conversations. Apparently everyone could hear what he was saying. One day, Wajid followed me to my bedroom door with a miserable look on his face.

"I really need to tell you something. IK is talking to someone on the phone. He is suggesting that this marriage is over. He asks this person for help repeatedly".

My husband had just told someone the marriage was over. For some reason, this sign flew over my head and I was still surprised at what happened in the coming months. What I did at the time was check with a friend and learn that Pakistan's Intelligence Bureau had recorded these phone calls. The calls were made to the wife of a customs officer hailing from PakPattan.

Immediately after the divorce, my ex-husband was seen wearing a large ring on his little finger that was given to him by this woman. By June 2016, this woman was making headlines again. It was not yet clear whether she or her sister was the new wife. At the end of 2017, I was told by a reporter that the same woman had taken a divorce from her husband to marry IK. The husband had wanted his younger daughter to be the one tying the knot, but the mother had beaten all the competition. The media channels hunted me down again. I refused to comment. But privately, I thought 'Could he be that unstable?' And I knew the answer to that. The dependence on *pirs*, the amulets scattered around the bedroom, the mysterious cauldrons bubbling away...this was all only one side of Imran's erratic nature.

Chapter 30

In late 2016, I finally considered putting pen to paper. However, noting down my unbelievable experiences was far from straightforward. I knew that there was a story that should be told but couldn't bring myself revisit all those memories needed to write it.

Each day I would avoid writing, even as PTI made announcements that a book was coming out by September 2016. Indeed, their constant fake news may have actually pushed me to release a book after all. But still it wouldn't come. I would wake up every night with thoughts of what I would write, and the memories I didn't want to confront would come rushing back faster than the tears that were stinging my eyes. I would dream deeply and vividly in the few hours of sleep I could steal (courtesy of Melatonin). It was the same dream: I'm back in the house in Bani Gala, trying my best to fit in, but I don't recognise anything. Family members sit outside in the garden and I peer at them through the half-open windows. Imran's hussies pull him up on the train leaving the home and I am powerless to stop him. The interior of the house is nothing like the simplicity of the exterior. It has a gaudy, ostentatious feel, and is littered with signs of the previous night's decadent indulgences.

In one dream, a friend said to me, "Take a few souvenirs with you". I'd go into his room, thinking about what I should take. But nothing in the room looked like it belonged to the husband I knew. I didn't recognise the room or the things. Like a visitor, I would touch things curiously. Scared that I would be caught prying, I would retreat, only to wake up with the realisation that I was already out of that house and that I had nothing of his. No souvenir. I never got the picture I wanted of us two looking at each other. The only thing I got was an autograph on the divorce deed. For months, I didn't open the piece of paper or even touch it with bare hands. I didn't want to touch anything he had touched. I would use a plastic sleeve to move it.

The anger of why I had become involved with him grew with time. I would drift off mid-sentence while talking, suddenly remembering something he had said. I'd just suddenly zone out of reality. I would sit in the car with my kids, singing at the top of my voice as I drove them around in the countryside, when the words of his song for me would flash through my head: 'I must have been through about a million girls...but then I fooled around and fell in love'. A million girls sounded about right, though for Imran, it was probably not necessary to limit the line to just 'girls'. As I'd found out, Imran had been through just about everything. And among his list of 'experiences', I knew that there was probably not much fond reminiscing of me.

It took me almost a year to move from thinking about writing and noting down small details to actually getting any writing done. But by late 2017, I was finally hitting my stride. My story was ready to be told.

'How did you do it all?'

That was always the first question I would be asked when I would begin to tell my story. When we were evicted out of the house in Lincolnshire, I moved us to Astwood Bank, a border town between Worcestershire and Warwickshire. The location was chosen to get the best job opportunities and the top schools. My daily trek took me from home in Worcestershire to Shropshire, and then on to Aston in Birmingham. The children went to school in Warwickshire. Before this, I'd been travelling from Lincolnshire to Birmingham every day. When we would move on, I would commute from Newbury, Berkshire, to Southampton, while Sahir would commute to Burnham, Slough. One look at a map would show how crazy these arrangements were. And all the while, I was trying to raise three young children.

I honestly don't know how I coped. I faced it like I have faced every other challenge in life. Some may say I had more grit than the average person but I think there were other key advantages. I was always blessed with great health and tons of stamina. I believe that a healthy lifestyle (a guilty pleasure for chocolate notwithstanding) kept me sane and focused. My family background also gave me an edge over others. I knew more than the average child is taught in school. Belonging to a highly educated family improved my survival abilities. I believe that it is a postcode lottery: Your success depends so much on the family you are born into. This is why I became a flag-bearer for equal opportunities.

My kids also benefited from the same sort of environment. I would be constantly sent messages by their employers or teachers telling of how competent they were compared to their peers. It meant a lot more to me because of my lifetime mission to be a good parent. And although I developed constant guilty feelings thinking about how my personal decisions had disrupted their lives or caused them pain, it was a wonderful feeling to see them grow into such good human beings. Though Sahir would accomplish many things, there was much more to him than his impeccable academic record and great writing skills. The young boy became a wholehearted cheerleader for women who were breaking the glass ceiling. My heart filled with pride whenever I saw him talk to or about women.

My greatest fear was that he would become an insecure man with a violent temper, like his biological father. But as he grew up, I saw a young man who put his mother and sisters first. I saw an undemanding man who would thank me for preparing a meal for him; a generous individual who didn't think twice about giving someone time, or spending whatever he had on others. I saw a self-contained youngster who was content with the small pleasures of life.

He balanced his love of playing music with excellent academic results, and he became the best buddy any sister could have.

The absence of a brother for Sahir was completely filled by his sisters. Although they had very different interests and lifestyles, they would overlap in numerous places. Ridha even ended up becoming a Chelsea fan like her brother, after being enamoured by new, charismatic players like David Luiz and Oscar. It was always heart-warming to see them together, especially when they were out. When Ridha found ogling eyes offensive, Sahir would tell her to walk with more confidence and not let it bother her. To see such a modern, progressive, secure man emerge out of such an insecure, uncertain start in life was both wonderful and a great relief. He was born with that nature and his tremendous abilities. All I did was ensure he had an environment where those abilities were nurtured and appreciated.

A male family friend would say to me, "I thought my mum was great but when I see your interaction with Sahir, I am so envious. I wish I could have talked to my mother like this". His mother had not been speaking to him for a full month before she tragically died. The time we have together is precious and short. As a youngster, I could not wake up as early as my dad to accompany him on his walks. And then one day, he passed away and I would never again have the opportunity to join him on those walks. It was that classic irony: when he died, I was awake and ready at 6am, preparing for work. But I could not wake up for my Daddy.

There is no magic formula for being a good parent. I just talked and listened. I gave respect to them. Children are just smaller human beings. I never regretted trusting my children. Sahir was only 13 when he started school in Stratford-upon-Avon. I gave him my bank card with £1000 of overdraft on it for emergencies. Other than occasionally buying Krispy Kreme doughnuts and a few other small luxuries in later years, Sahir never used it. He wasn't the type to abuse my trust. No instructions were given to him. The trust was implicit. I never saw that card again, and it never caused me any problems.

In Pakistan, I would be surrounded by lavish hospitality wherever I went. But what touched me most was how I was treated on my first visit to my daughter's house at university. She would not even let me pay for groceries. She wanted to host me on her student budget. It meant everything to me. I felt tears of pride well up in my eyes. It wasn't only her hospitality, but her sense of maturity and independence that I had worked to build. This girl would get her rather demanding baby sister ready for school when she was just ten years old. The two young ladies were only six years apart, but their bond would be closer than a mother and daughter.

This early sharing of responsibility was a great support to me. We all slipped into different well-defined roles right from the start, and this dynamic would never change. Had I not had the support of the older two, I couldn't have focused on making enough money like I did.

I always wanted a perfect loving home. It took me a long time to realise that it doesn't have to have a husband or father in it to be complete.

§

My mother was the epitome of grace. I could do the elegant ladylike look for only short public appearances. I was generally the embarrassing mum, who was the first one to jump on the slide or fight over who got to sit on the good swing first. As a kid, I was the performer who would be entertaining the grown-ups, from doing *Rekha* dance numbers as a skinny preadolescent in the hot summers of Peshawar, to mimicking political figures. Keeping the family entertained was my forte. My 'mother of the nation' look during my second marriage irritated my family and friends. My mum asked me sweetly after the divorce when I would start wearing colourful clothes again, and cease with the awful auntie bun. To please my mum, I would take out the most bright and colourful outfits when I would visit her. I was wearing her favourite outfit of mine, a deep shade of purple, the moment she slipped away forever in my arms.

My kids, especially my youngest one, always groaned at my refusal to age gracefully. I always took great pleasure in torturing them by being an embarrassing mum. Although they always protested, we have always been inseparable. I always wondered how they would ever move out and have relationships of their own. They were always happy cooped up in one room with me. This is perhaps also the reason that I couldn't possibly go out at all in my life and find men who would be suitable for me. My sister's sons are also still single. When her eldest son turned 32, my very religious brother joked to him that if he wasn't quick to find a girl, his aunt may get married again.

Despite the trials of my life, I never lost the ability to hope for love and laughter. I have seen kids who are scared of entering into relationships these days. Despite my disasters with men, I remained very much a little girl at heart, who would believe that she would find love one day. We must greet every day with shining bright eyes and a spring in the step. What's the point of being scared?

Life is a great adventure. Taking the safe route is unexciting. I wanted to have plenty of stories to tell my grandkids. There was more to my fun-loving nature than simply jumping on the roundabout in the playground. I always loved to explore, would drive my children across Europe. The first trip was made partly due to a desire to erase bad memories of an earlier European holiday. It's my style to not wallow in the past, but make new happy memories to replace the bad ones. That extended to my own story. I found it incredibly difficult to write about the trials I faced, since this inevitably required re-living them.

Driving myself on long journeys was always therapeutic. I felt free. The kids loved these moments so much that they refused to go on many trips in Pakistan because of the staff that would often surround them. Though the kids would get along with virtually anyone, and were always quite fond of the staff, it was a very different dynamic. One major issue was music; the girls could never sing at the top of their lungs while in the presence of the chauffeurs. They began to plan holidays in countries where we could be on our own, rent a normal car, and drive somewhere unnoticed. With the music on and mum joining in with the singing, the atmosphere was ideal for the girls. A lot of geography and history was picked up this way as well. One of the worst things parents can do is force information down a child's throat. Instead, I chose to be facilitator, and make it fun to explore. You take them on a trip so the experience is different than a book. Let them see with their own eyes. It was always better to let them ask the questions.

We stumbled onto cheese farms where the kids would learn to make my favourite Camembert, and small chocolatiers where they'd have a go at making their own chocolate. One year, I took the kids to Cyprus. We started off in a villa in Paphos, on the Western side. Even though I was unfamiliar with the country, I hired a car and we tried to explore the rest of the island, going through Limassol and trying to reach Nicosia. We also went up the Troodos Mountains to see something known as Mount Olympus. To our knowledge, Mount Olympus would have been somewhere in Greece, so we were naturally curious. After driving for several hours and seeing some truly beautiful areas, we eventually found our way to the top of the mountain and prepared to find some exciting reference to Greek mythology. Instead, we found some sort of military base. Whatever Mount Olympus was, it certainly wasn't particularly scenic or exciting (Sahir would discover years later that we had actually stumbled across a British long-range radar).

We were on our way back down the mountain when it began to get dark. I was keeping an eye out for a petrol station when Sahir asked for a drink from the boot of the car. I threw him the keys and he opened the boot to get whatever he was after. He then shut the boot, only to realize immediately that he had set the keys down next to him, and had just locked them in the boot.

He immediately went pale. It was a dizzyingly winding road with no help for miles. Sahir burst into the back and clawed at the upholstery, seeing no way to get to the keys in the boot beyond ripping the seats out. I took a different approach. Instinct took over and I wasted not even a second in shouting or panicking, instead going over to the boot and proceeding to break several nails, but it did the trick. Moments later, we were on our way. To this day, I'm not sure what exactly I did. I just shoved my nails at the lock and somehow, resolved the crisis. Sahir never forgot it, and thought it made for a great story. Anecdotes like these are far better memories than perfect pictures in an album.

Taking the kids to Disneyland Paris gave me the most beautiful memory of my life. The expressions on their faces were priceless. But once again, it was memorable for my unladylike behaviour. My kids recall their mother's commitment to getting them the full Disney experience. I had never chased after celebrities for autographs but for my little girl, I ran full-pelt after Goofy, and promptly fell on all fours, breaking my sunglasses and grazing my knees. The lengths I would go for my children...

The journo in me was hard to suppress on holidays too. I just had to interview people. As a kid, I would sit away from my parents so passengers would think I was travelling on my own, and I'd strike up a conversation with fellow travellers. Many a prospective love interest of older family members has suffered at the hands of my hard-talk style grilling. On holidays, I just preferred not to rush through places so that we could absorb the culture and soak up the experience. It's at the local grocery shop that one will often find the true essence of a place. The bakers, street vendors, and everyday people are the ones who can share the true flavour of a locale, rather than the tourist spots. On a trip to Malaysia in 2017, we all fell in love with the attentive waitress at the local restaurant in Bukit Bintang. My kids were aware of my tendency to pull entire biographies out of random people, and began glaring at me to cut my enquiries about her home life short.

Ironically, I never used this quizzing technique on my suitors, and ended up marrying whatever was available.

§

By late 2016, my efforts were bearing fruit. For the first time in years, I felt that satisfaction in my work. I received a reaffirmation of my mission. I was doing something.

I'd put my heart and soul into my charitable foundation, RKF. During my second marriage, I'd been forbidden to work through my own charity. None of my efforts or ideas were supposed to be in my name. Now a free bird, I could openly focus on my campaign for child rights. The aim (and motto) is simple: Protect the Future. I began campaigning for safe childhoods, free from abuse in all its forms. Eradicating child labour and providing educational opportunities to the most deprived in our communities became my priority. Child mortality is the main issue (followed by child abuse and joblessness among our youth). No political party or leader has addressed these issues in 70 years. Not much is different in neighbouring countries like India and Afghanistan. Instead, the general aura centres on religion and hate politics. The reality is in stark contrast to the narrative promoted on media and in political speeches. Using America and India is a convenient diversionary tactic for the hidden enemy within.

I travelled from Thar in Sindh to Chilas in Gilgit Baltistan, from Malakand in the tribal region to Gujranwala in Punjab. People embraced me with open arms everywhere I went. Once a local administration was causing procedural delays in opening a centre in the area. I told the RKF team to change location, but was pleasantly surprised when the local elders took a *jirga* (committee) on my behalf to the District Officer and persuaded him to expedite the permission.

With no political party or foreign donor behind me, the size of the gatherings I was addressing was phenomenal. In my home province, when the police and local administration were given specific instructions from the top to not provide me with support or security, they would still turn up to look after me. I have never feared death or avoided adventure but it was endearing to see locals worry about my safety and comfort. Every bit a country clod, I loved the rustic simplicity, and people reciprocated with their trust. As the trust grew over a period of two years, the expectations of me grew too.

The most amazing thing for me was the fact that people in seemingly very religious and conservative areas saw me as an individual beyond my gender. There was no trace of misogyny with them, unlike the urban pseudo-elite. Heartened, I decided to show the world what Pakistan was really like. I wanted to portray the land and the people as accurately as possible. In April 2017, I launched a YouTube channel with a series titled 'My Pakistan'. However, as soon as the 30-sec promo went out, the channel was the subject of mass-reporting and sabotage, and ended up being shut down for supposedly violating community guidelines. It took us months to have it restored but we came back stronger, and I immediately started getting international interest. People in the US and the UK were commenting on how they had never seen this side of Pakistan. I saw that I needed to do more of this. Encouraged, I thought of new ideas, like the filming of a tour across the country via train.

I'd wanted to take charge of the misguided narrative about my people since I first started in Pakistani media. We may not be perfect but we are not all terrorists. We are as wacky and fun as anyone else, and we want peace in our communities as much as anyone else. We have been misrepresented in media and by our politicians. If I was so happy, despite all that had happened to me in my personal life, it was only because of the people of Pakistan that I had grown to love dearly. I was not a feudal princess, nor a party head. I was not even a celebrity's wife, yet the respect and love I was receiving was humbling. I was not bringing overnight change but I was making people think about their actions and the choices they made. And I was doing whatever else I could too.

In our centres, we wanted to provide training to our youth and women particularly by building on their capabilities and helping them find employment. In our first three centres, we focused on teaching computer coding and gemstone cutting to locals. With community support, I want to start teaching more courses in hospitality and catering, and other courses tailored to match the opportunities that will be created once the CPEC has been fully developed. Three areas have been earmarked in KP for these pilot programs: one in Mingora, Swat, one in Kotnali near the Havelian dry port of the CPEC, and one in Malakand. A bigger set up is in the pipeline for Gujranwala, as there is a higher literacy rate there but no jobs for women who observe strict *purdah*.

Surprisingly, I got support from the community. Local Imams from the mosques would come to my office with their councillors and village elders to ask me to build schools and training centres in their areas. Finding donors and getting no-objection certificates was tedious, but slowly and steadily I made progress. The aim was to work aggressively on advocacy, which I did through my Mashoom initiative (Pashto for child). I toured the country, giving talks in universities and villages, and recruiting interns and volunteers. The response was hugely impressive. I was making a difference after all.

People who got an insight into my life would sometimes get frustrated with my approach and my lack of care for money or assets. In 2016 and 2017, as I spent more and more time and money on RKF, and very little on business prospects, a young man who worked for me and had grown up with criticism blurted out, "What do you have to show for the last two years?" I was shocked that he couldn't see that what I'd earned in those two years was more than I'd earned all my life. It was immeasurable. I had earned the satisfaction that so many families had clean water and a promise of a secure future. I had earned many a good night's sleep knowing that I had saved a few lives. I had earned the respect of not only my own children but also others who thought of me as their mother. My staff is mostly made up of volunteers. Even those on permanent positions go beyond the call of duty to look after me. The driver will come in and make me a good cup of tea. The guard will buy me clothes. My PA will insist on scheduling pedicure appointments for me. His mother cooks me my favourite dishes. My editor brings me a bag of M&Ms every day.

These are people who love me and value me as a mother, but I did not give birth to them. My assistant is one of them. Bilal Azmat came to work as an intern for a couple of weeks when he was only 21 years old, and ended up staying. He wanted to be on TV, but (while running for my endless coffees and biscuits) he became the critical and analytical journalist I wanted him to become. I am a certainly not the most understanding boss to work for. The fainthearted won't last. But Bilal stuck around. In public, he referred to me as his ma'am but in private I was like his mother. Every conversation I had with him felt like a great investment of my time as I watched him grow personally, professionally and spiritually.

I also had Sufian, who helped me by compiling notes, setting up computers and handling all my writing in utter secrecy. Speculation about my book had been everywhere in the media for over a year but no one knew the truth of exactly when I started besides my family and select few like Sufi. He bore the brunt of my dark moods when writing some of the most painful stuff. I also had my good friend Suhela, of course, who kept me company with long, pointless chatter and a constant stream of presents she felt I needed.

I had the honour of being a mentor to many other young girls and boys who came to work with me as interns. Many ended up staying, like Anzar, my super-editor, and Jalal, my central coordinator and selfie-partner. The Mashoom team became more like a big family. I tried to guide all of them; these kids had no one else they could talk to about their thoughts on religion, careers and relationships. If I manage to inspire just one youngster to stand up for the right principles, then I can consider my life a success.

I am always on the go and the journeys are long and often in unfriendly terrain. If you don't eat when food is served or go to the toilet while there is time, you may quickly find yourself in trouble. On one trip, Bilal learned bladder control very quickly when his constant requests were ignored en route to Lukki Marwat. The driver was as unforgiving on the bumpy road as I was. Poor Bilal was bursting by the time we reached the next stop. The crew were in hysterics. I told him he was welcome to go out in the wilderness but the dark, unfamiliar border area was not really an option. From his mood swings to his frequent requests for toilet stops, everything was corrected. But he didn't hate me for it. He instead learned to match my pace. He felt pain every time I was attacked online and by the media. His eyes would glisten with tears as he begged me to allow him to reply to the cyber-bullying. This loyalty is priceless to me. The truth is that I have much to show for my life.

My TV crew also stayed loyal to me through my ups and downs. I'll never forget how they carried my wheelchair up two flights of stairs to my office as I returned to work after my crash. My nephews are also on the list of those who regard me as a mother-figure. In times of crisis, they always morally and physically supported me, even more than my own siblings. When I was horrifically injured that accident, Behram would say to me, "Just hang in there. Give me one more year *khala*. Once I graduate, you'll have another son who will earn for you. You have nothing to worry about". And I knew that this child, who I had done relatively little for, meant it.

The eldest, Abubakr, was quietly supportive. While not expressive with words or flashy gestures, he is a true *dervaish* in spirit. I remember how he quietly rolled me into the operation theatre and signed the consent forms. Hamza, my brother's oldest son, made my favourite chocolate mousse for me, and fed me lovingly as I lay, unable to move. He surprised me by putting liquid eyeliner on for me. And of course, there was Yousaf. He had been around more since I moved to Pakistan, and had to bear the brunt of all my misfortunes, so to speak. From receiving me on a stretcher in the hospital to being suddenly called in by the press to comment on the wedding of the year to being shunned by acquaintances after my divorce, he put on a brave face through it all.

My accident was an eye-opener. It showed me how lucky I was. For me, the love of these children is achievement enough. The kids not only made up for my lonely childhood, but also for a life where I never really had real friends around me. I never really missed the company that a life partner could have given me. Although family had always been on top of my priority list, it never felt like a burden. I was blessed with a family that I was fond of, and could genuinely get on well with. It's a cliché to say that my children and I are more like friends than anything else, but in our case it was always true. I could never think of going on holiday with anyone but them. We always hung out and argued like friends too. It's not only because we love each other but also because my children are truly decent human beings, something other people tell me. It's shocking and somewhat tragic how rare this seems to be, and how surprising people find it. I was labelled ambitious and competitive by people who did not know me, but in truth, my only ambition was to create a loving home that my children would not want to leave. That one, essential ambition is one I think I achieved.

As a young girl with perfect, unblemished skin, I spent hours (as my young daughter does) applying face masks. I was a well-loved child from a privileged family and the most popular girl in college, yet I didn't think I was that great. I would cringe when my mother would praise me in front of teachers or in social gatherings. I was ready to settle for anyone who would ask for my hand in marriage. I did not have self-esteem issues, but I did not realise my worth either. At the BBC, I had been a School Report Mentor for four years. School Report is an initiative intended to create and nurture interest in journalism in schools. It was sad to see that even fourteen-year-old girls in England would not put themselves forward like the boys did. They would pull at their sleeves to hide their hands in them in their shyness. It hurts and shocks me to think that some young teenage girls still feel they are not as good as the boys.

Society had given me the idea that I had to be perfectly hairless, spotless and immaculate, but the men in my life did not need to be perfect at all. I remember my mother's words as I eagerly put on my rather unimpressive engagement ring as a young teenager to show off at a wedding. "*Beta*, you deserve so much better," she sighed almost inaudibly. I was shocked at her comment. Although her dissatisfaction might have been only because of my fiancée's lack of class and status, she knew what she was talking about.

I think I really understood my worth after I left Imran. At 42 years of age, I finally understood. Everyone had predicted that I would be irrelevant after the divorce. In actual fact, I found myself swamped with marriage proposals. At 44, when I had no wish to ever settle down again, and had become this go-getting woman who put her comfort and work first, I realized that I'd suddenly become very attractive to even 26-year olds.

The difference was that I didn't care anymore. I didn't care if I was seen without my eyeliner or with unkempt hair. My 'I don't live to please you' attitude was a turn on. Independence is a very attractive trait in any human being. A clingy man or woman who lives for their 'other half' is not much appreciated. I'd finally stopped caring whether anyone stayed or left. I'd had my share of shitty sex and toxic people in my life. I blocked and deleted fearlessly. My life did not revolve around pleasing everyone or being pleasant anymore. I knew what I wanted and wasn't afraid to get it for myself. I did not need to wait for someone to approach me. If I wanted to, I could grab the arm of whoever I chose. Here I was: an auntie by Pakistani standards. I am so old that even visa restrictions for Saudi Arabia do not apply anymore. According to my designer, I needed work done here and there on my eyes and jawline, but I wore the expression lines with pride.

Gone was the ladylike restraint my mother had taught us. No longer did I sit demurely. I sat more confidently. I occupied the space around me boldly. I spread my arms out wide and fearlessly. I left the self-consciousness that is drummed into girls. My body language had changed completely.

I was a woman reborn.

Epilogue

According to Plato, 'the state is what it is because its citizens are what they are. We need not expect to have better states until we have better men'.

Perhaps he had a point. Any state, and indeed the state of the world, cannot be expected to improve if its component parts do not. But he (and I) seemed to overlook something. Perhaps we don't need to focus on better men. We can use the capable women.

It's amazing how things turned out in the end, and I can't thank God enough for what he has given me. Despite all the struggles and all the pain, I was given some moments of pure beauty. It takes a monumental amount of heat and pressure to produce even the smallest diamonds. I now have more than I ever imagined, and it's because of my experiences. Without my extraordinary life, I wouldn't be where I am today. I wouldn't be in a position where I can make a real difference. I wouldn't even have freedom from the chains of society and all its players. It seems that this is what we are: simple pawns in a game of complicated rules and restrictions. For years, I was stuck in this game, at the mercy of those who knew how to play it better than I. And now, having seen the nature of life, I can never go back.

After embarking on my own journey, I ultimately exceeded the expectations of my parents, my family, and everyone who knew me. I soon eclipsed those who had held me back. I continued to move from one platform to the next, constantly leaping to new heights. Soon, I will have eclipsed everyone I have ever encountered. It might sound arrogant, but it's the simple truth. You become brave by doing brave things. You are decent based on the decent things you do. And if you stick to your principles and never give up, you will have succeeded in eclipsing all others in terms of your persona. Others may be more famous, popular and wealthy, but that is not the true measure of a person. The best people stay true to their principles and their desire to better themselves. And in time, these people will be successful.

I am ready to face any challenges that might be foolish enough to face me. My kids and I have remained the unit we always were, and we have become better equipped than ever to cut through the waves of this world.

Sahir graduated with expertise in economics and political science, and went to work in Parliament for several months. After the 2017 general election, he turned his back on that to help pull my experiences out of me and get them into book form, before getting some major job offers. Though working in the Civil Service was tempting, he eventually joined IBM, one of the biggest companies in the world.

Ridha finished school on her own, while her mother was working on a different continent. She dealt with the most stressful circumstances imaginable, and started university in London, where she is currently flying. She is studying politics, like her brother, but combined with history, a polar opposite to his more mathematical degree. She brought it all full circle by exceeding all expectations and flourishing, like her older brother. She matched him in numerous ways, and eclipsed him in countless others. Like me, she kept the train rolling, despite every attempt to derail it.

Inaya lived through the harshest circumstances of all. As a child, she knew only the toughest of times for our family. Her pivotal teenage years were dominated by issues no young adult should have to face. People have lost their way on much less. But like me, and like her siblings, she never did. She powered through year after year of school in an environment where even the teachers would mock her for her association with political leaders. She was taunted and abused from every angle, saw her friends and family turn on her, and lived through the most difficult moments of my life. Yet she remains the sharp, bright, fiery and dedicated soul that she always was. This 14-year-old began working incredibly hard to take her O-levels and finish school, without even knowing which country she would be living in and which exams she would be sitting. I knew I had nothing to worry about with her.

A lot of Sahir's time and effort has gone into prioritising his family and working on things with me. He had wanted to do an internship during his final university years but couldn't because of all the chaos brought on by my marriage. He could barely even attend lectures in the first semester of his third year, as my divorce took over our lives. But it wasn't long at all before I was getting messages about how he was wowing people in the Shadow Cabinet with his work ethic. He came back to Pakistan after the general elections in the UK, and we set up a website and online channel so we could share footage of my travels and experiences. Soon after, we set about trying to make memoirs of my complicated life. And then, despite all the distractions, he suddenly went back to the UK with a plan. Within a few short months, he told me how he had found his dream job, and started on April 4th. I started to cry and just could not stop. I remembered my first husband telling me that my son would amount to nothing, and that my approach was all wrong. I remember being told repeatedly that I was a failure as a mother. But my child had come back to me triumphant. And to top it all, his new job would start on my first husband's birthday, as if to prove a point to him and the universe. You just couldn't make it up. I could only sit there and cry as I thanked God yet again for the mysterious ways in which he worked to help me.

As for me...it's different now. Gone is the woman who would suffer in silence through all manner of physical and emotional abuse for over twelve years. Gone is the woman who would care about what people said and how people would unfairly criticise her. Gone is the woman who would sit through a year of chaos and mental torture because she finally thought love had arrived. Gone is the woman who was content to be a journalist, making money and being able to feed her family.

All that is gone...to be replaced with something far better. Telling the truth and being morally upright is never straightforward or easy, which is why only the best of us try. That honesty and decency is rare. Sometimes people will be very convincing at claiming they are decent and righteous despite showing completely the opposite with their actions. Trying to work with and change such people cost me a lot, and brought me pain. But going through it all made me realise the importance of never stopping, and never being bullied into staying silent when you see something wrong right in front of you. You need to fight.

All my life, I thought I had to change myself to find happiness and meaning. I thought I needed to be less of who I am. But it was exactly the opposite. The world wanted more of me.

My life has become one of speaking out and forcing change. That's what started the Reham Khan Foundation and its main movement, Mashoom. I saw something wrong. If no one else was going to do something about it, then I was.

I finally ditched all those things that held me back. I stopped putting up with injustice and I brought out more of those things that were always part of me.

I am still that person who loves knowledge, experiences and culture. Now, I get to travel to far-flung places and see all manner of new and wonderful things.

I am still that person who will go to extreme lengths to provide for her family. With RKF, my family just got bigger.

I am still that person who likes spending time with her best friends; my friends just grew up. They became stronger than I could have ever imagined. We are more of a team than ever before.

I was a bird that was constantly warned about flying too close to the sun, but now I choose to fly where I will. I was someone people tried to cage, but now I am an unstoppable force. And the best is yet to come.

Photographs

Practising the smile

A young Reham refusing to pose

Me with my brother, Munir Khan Nayyar, at the wedding Ijaz saw me at

Daddy with Behram and Sweety. A 15-year-old Reham in the background

Engagement, 1992

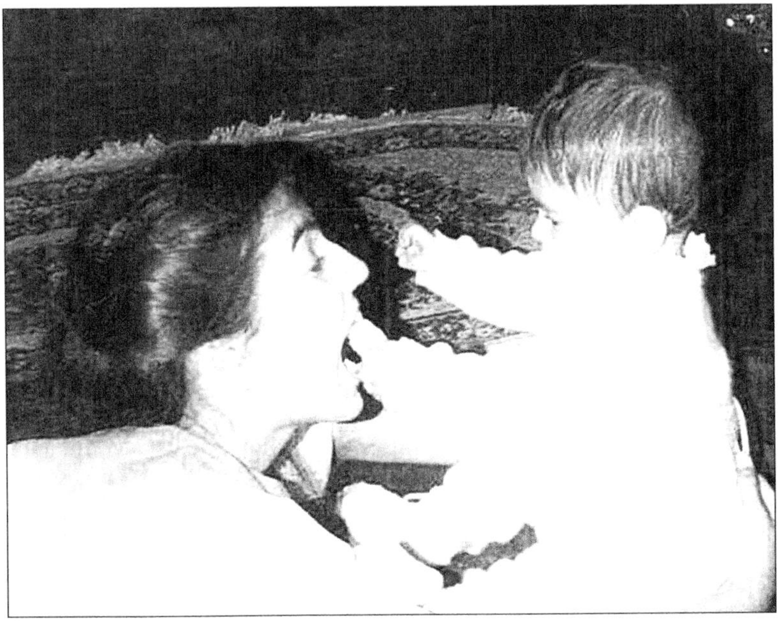

If you want my love, feed me biscuits! Abubakr and his khala

Sahir arrives. My mother holds him

Wedding, 1992

Reham, Sahir, Ijaz - 1994

Sahir and I, sunburnt at the Vatican

Mummy (wearing family jewellery) with siblings

Mummy looking regal on her wedding day wearing
Beejee's *dawni* (headpiece)

Abdul Rauf Khan with his young sons and grandparents, Ghullam Yahya Khan and Zohra *Jaan bibi*, at Governor House

My paternal uncle, Justice Abdul Hakeem Khan, Governor of KPK

Dr Sher Bahadur Khan (Khanjee)

Munir's Birthday. Sweety holds me. Daddy and Mummy in 70s fashion

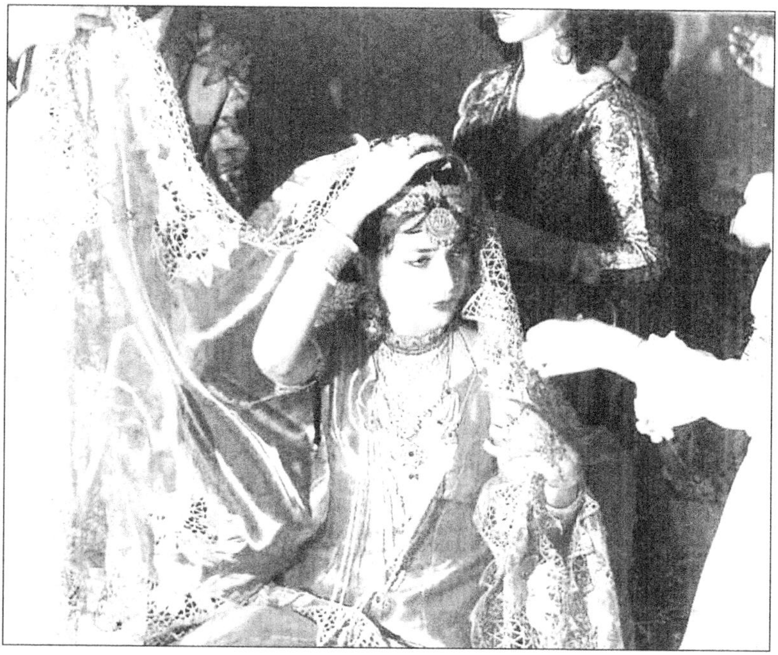

A more stunning bride, I never saw. Sweety's wedding

Sweety and Khalid wedding, with Mummy in pink

Reham and Munir kite-flying at the Ochre House in Abbottabad, 1988

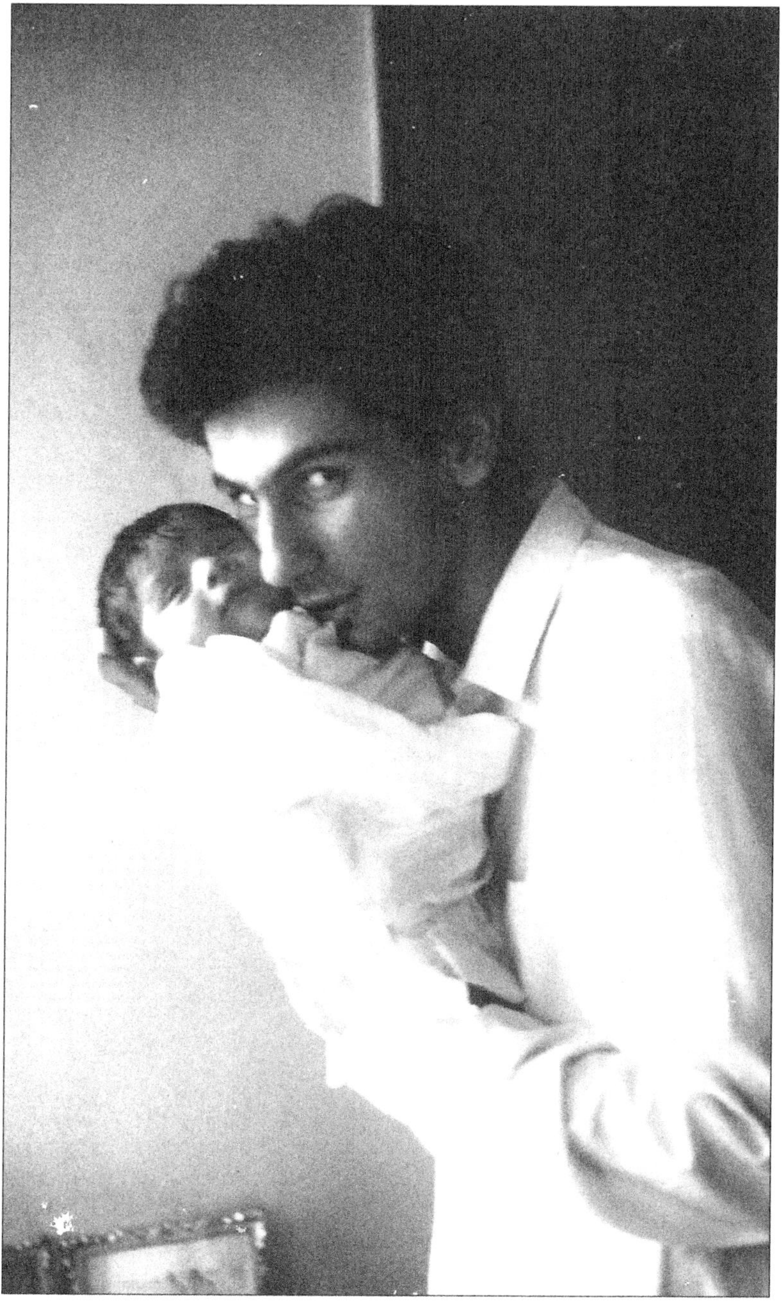

Munir with Hamza, his firstborn

Happy alone with the baby!

Hospital Accommodation, Goole, 1995

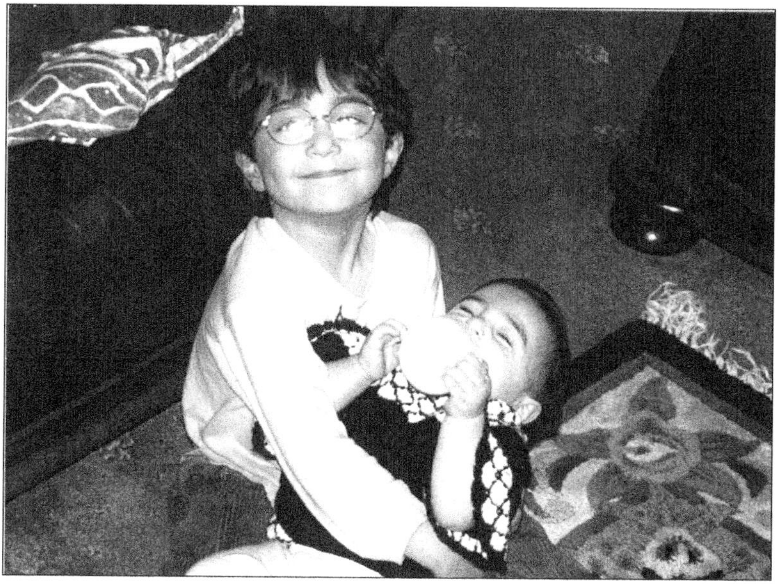

Sahir was very confident handling his baby sister

Ridha and I. North Ferriby

Ridha copying mum's cleaning style

Inaya, Ridha and Sahir in Thornton Curtis

Hollywood star Inaya

Holiday in Normandy

Disneyland Paris

Little Maximus with little Ridha

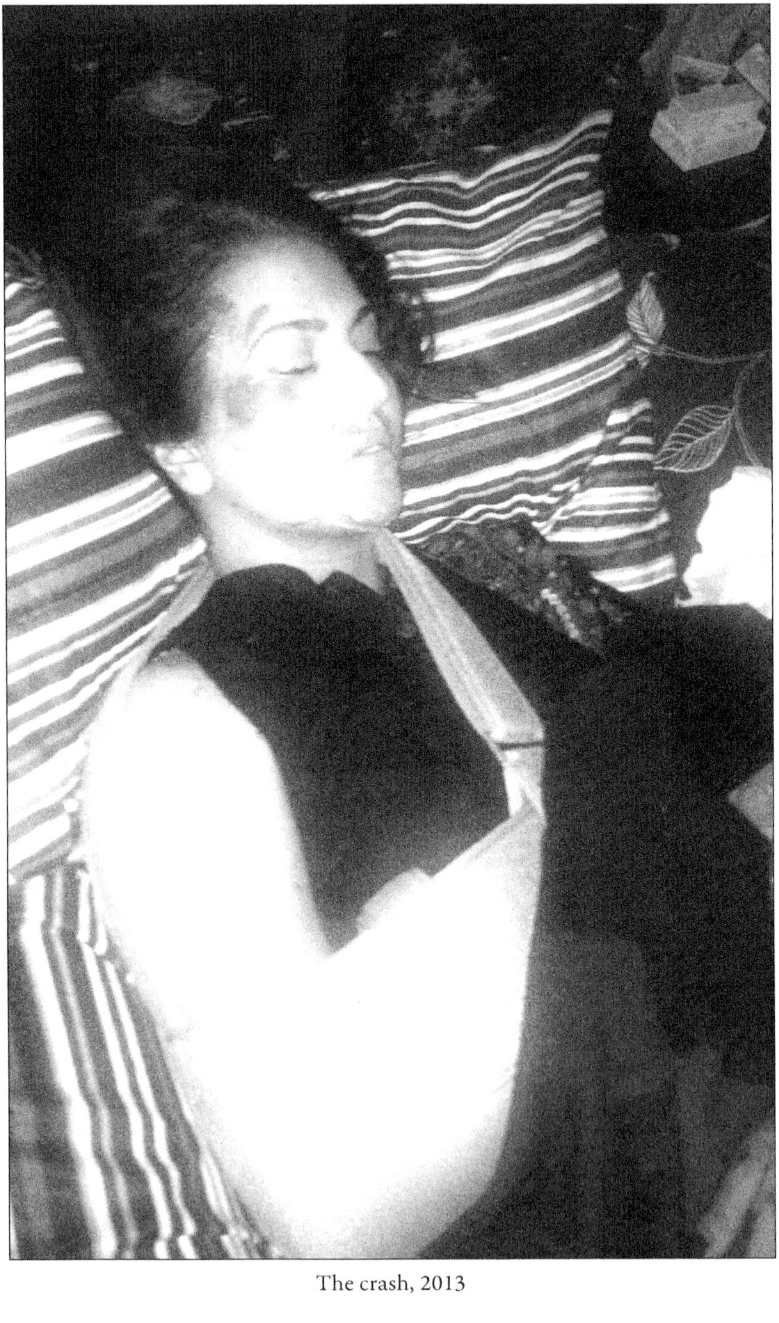

The crash, 2013

Sahir with mum and Ridha at the family wedding
which prompted fresh cyber attacks

Picture-perfect bride and bouquet

Picking wedding pictures to release

Imran putting the ring on (provided by Mufti Saeed)

Imran & I on our daily morning walk

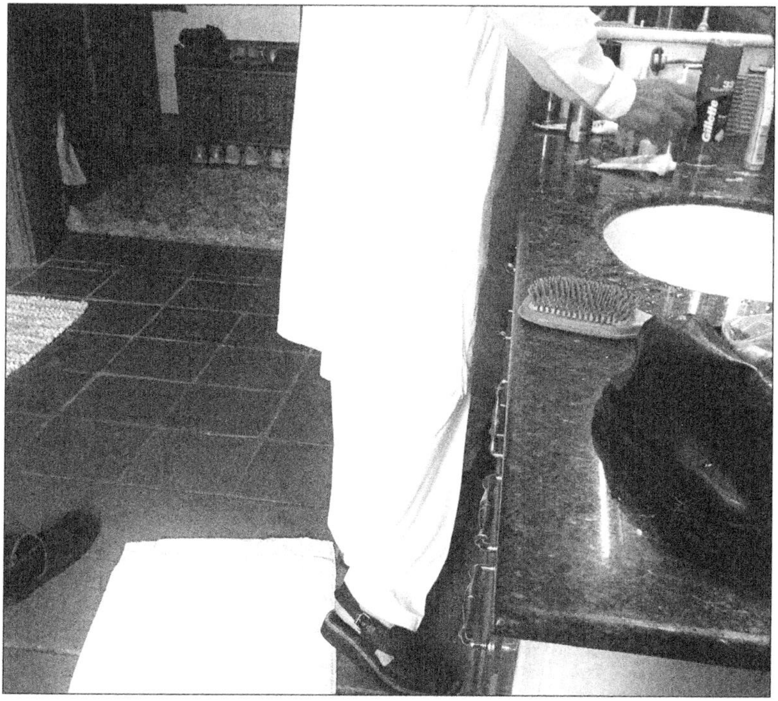

Imran getting ready

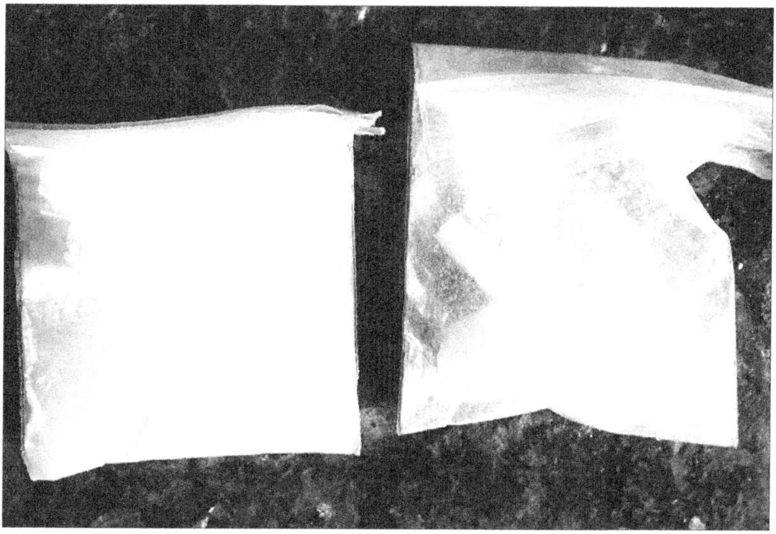

Cocaine in Imran's coat pockets

Iftar dinner with ambassadors including Richard Olson, US ambassador (sitting opposite Imran)

An angry Imran on Eid-ul-Adha 2015

Birthday hamper on Conference Rock

The birthday photo that ruffled so many feathers

Quran Khatam on Imran's Birthday. October 5th, 2015

Eid Day, Bani Gala. Sahir tries to put his arm around Imran.
Imran moves away

Imran's birthday, 2015. The cake he would not cut or eat

My son's graduation

The gang! Inaya, Abubakr, Yousaf, Reham, Sahir, Behram and Ridha

Zaitoon *bibi* (My Aunt)

Pre-production of Janaan

Malakand, 2017

Fun with the family

Hanging out with the girls in Thar

Leading from the front. Visiting Parachinar bomb blast victims,
Lady Reading Hospital

Mummy as President of Children's Academy Peshawar,
with local politicians, 1980s

Mashoom. Protect the future

Appendices

Character List

Family

Reham Khan

Sahir Khan - Eldest son of Reham Khan. Born 1st October 1993

Ridha Khan - Second child and first daughter of Reham Khan. Born 10th June 1997

Inaya Khan - Youngest child of Reham Khan. Born 8th May 2003

Extended family

Salma Khan Nayyar - Reham's elder sister, known as Sweety to her family

Khalid Khan - Sweety's first husband

Abubakr Khan - Salma's eldest son

Behram Khan - Salma'a second son

Yousaf Khan - Salma's youngest son

Mohammad Munir Khan Nayyar - Brother to Reham

Fauzia Munir - Wife to Munir Khan Nayyar

Ghullam Yahya Khan - Father to Nayyar Ramzan

Zohra Jaan - Mother to Nayyar Ramzan

Dr Nayyar Ramzan - Father of Reham Khan, known in the family as Daddy

Saeeda Nayyar - Mother of Reham Khan, known in the family as Barimummy (meaning 'The Big/Elder Mummy')

Dr Sher Bahadur Khan Pannee – Father to Saeeda Nayyar

Beejee – First wife of Sher Bahadur Khan Pannee

Saadat Sultan – Second wife of Sher Bahadur Khan Pannee. Mother to Saeeda Nayyar

Colleagues:

Umer Khalid – Close friend of the family and personal assistant to Reham Khan in 2015 to 2016

Bilal Azmat - Personal assistant to Reham Khan, volunteer for Mashoom and the Reham Khan Foundation, and close friend of the family

Wajid Ali - Staff member and driver for Reham Khan

Ali Akbar - Member of Reham Khan's TV crew

Waseem Abbasi - Member of Reham Khan's TV crew

Maria Kakakhel – Long-term friend of Reham Khan and the family

Saleha Khaqan - Reham Khan's best friend between 2003 and 2013

Khaqan Khwaja - Husband of Saleha

Others

Ijaz Rehman - Reham Khan's first husband. First cousin. Consultant psychiatrist for the NHS

Imran Khan - Chairman of the PTI and former cricketer

Jahangir Khan Tareen - Secretary General of PTI. Commonly known as JKT

Awn Chaudry - Secretary to Chairman PTI Imran Khan 2014 to present

Naeem Ul Haq - Chief of Staff, Information Secretary of PTI, 2013 to 2015

Shah Mehmood Qureshi - Vice Chairman of PTI

Pervez Khattak - PTI senior leader and Chief Minister of KPK

Ali Zaidi – President of PTI Karachi

Shah Farman – KP Minister

Atif Khan – KP Minister for Education

Faisal Vawda - PTI leader in Karachi

Imran Ismail - Senior Leader, PTI Karachi

Anila Khawaja - PTI International Media coordinator

Uzma Kardar - PTI member

Andaleeb Abbas – PTI's President of Punjab

Dr Waseem Shahzad – PTI senior member. Advisor to the Chairman and benefactor

Ayesha Gualalai - PTI MPA on a KP reserve seat

Javed Hashmi – Pakistani politician and former PMLN Cabinet Minister. Joined PTI in 2008 and held the newly-created position of President of PTI before leaving in 2013

Justice Wajihuddin – Senior retired judge and head of PTI's tribunal on intra-party elections

Malaika Raza - PTI worker

Kristiane Backer - Former MTV presenter and ex-girlfriend of Imran Khan

Moby - Close friend of Imran Khan

Zakir Khan - Former cricketer. Friend of Imran Khan

Yousaf Sallahuddin - Friend of Imran Khan. Socialite based in Lahore. Also known as 'Salli'

Zulfi Bukhari - Friend and benefactor of IK. Businessman based in London

Arif Naqvi - Investor and head of ABRAAJ Group

Amir Kiyani - Vice President Rawalpindi Punjab

Amin Gundapur - Minister KP

Imran Chaudry - Friend of IK in Dubai

Arif Alvi – MNA from NA-250 (Karachi South-II)

Safeer - Imran's Driver in Bani Gala

Sajjawal - Staff of Bani Gala

Rubina - Eldest Sister of Imran Khan

Aleema Khan - Sister of Imran Khan

Rani - Sister of Imran Khan. Wife of Hafizullah Niazi

Uzma - Youngest sister of Imran Khan

Hafizullah Niazi - Columnist and analyst. Husband to Rani

Inamullah Niazi - Potential candidate for NA-72 (Mianwali). Brother of Hafizullah

Jemima Goldsmith (formerly Jemima Khan) - British heiress and ex-wife of Imran Khan

Zac Goldsmith - Member of Parliament for Richmond as part of the Conservative Party

Sir James Goldsmith - Father to Jemima and Zac Goldsmith

Annabelle Goldsmith - Wife of the late Sir James Goldsmith, mother to Jemima and Zac

Russell Brand - British comedian and media personality, and an ex of Jemima Goldsmith
Rashid Ali Khan – Close friend of Jemima Goldsmith
Asma Rashid – Close friend of Jemima Goldsmith. Married to Rashid Ali Khan
Suleiman Khan - Eldest legitimate son of Imran Khan (with Jemima Goldsmith)
Qasim Khan - Second legitimate son of Imran Khan (with Jemima Goldsmith)
Tyrian White - Illegitimate daughter of Imran Khan (with Sita White), and adopted daughter of Jemima Goldsmith
Nawaz Sharif - Prime Minister of Pakistan from 2013 to 2017. Served twice previously
Kulsoom Nawaz – Politician and wife of Nawaz Sharif
Maryum Nawaz Sharif - Eldest daughter of Nawaz and Kulsoom
Shehbaz Sharif - Brother of Nawaz Sharif and Chief Minister of Punjab, the largest province of Pakistan
Hamza Shehbaz – son of Shehbaz Sharif
Chaudhry Nisar – Deputy Prime Minister and Interior Minister of Pakistan
General Pervez Musharraf - Leader of Pakistan from 2003 to 2007 following a coup d'etat
General Hamid Gul – Former Director General of the ISI
General Asad Durrani - Former Director General of the ISI

Commonly used terms

MNA – Member of National Assembly (of Pakistan)

MPA – Member of Provincial Assembly (of Pakistan)

PMLN – Pakistan Muslim League (Nawaz). Political party of the Sharifs (distinct from PMLQ)

PPP – Pakistan Peoples Party. Political party of the the Bhutto-Zardari family

PTI – Pakistan Tehreek-e-Insaf. Political party

Naya Pakistan – A PTI slogan meaning 'New Pakistan'

KPK or KP – Khyber Pukhtunkhwa, province of Pakistan

Punjab – Biggest province of Pakistan

Pashtun– A people who speak Pashto and live in Afghanistan and certain regions of Pakistan

ISI – Inter-Services Intelligence. Pakistan's premier intelligence agency

ISPR – Inter-Services Public Relations. The media wing of the Pakistani Armed Forces

JC – Judicial Commission, the body set up to investigate electoral rigging of the 2013 Pakistani General Election

DG – Director General

MD – Managing Director

Seat/Ticket – Nomination as a candidate in an election

Sahab or *Sahiba* – Term of respect to accompany a name

Bhabhi – endearing term that means 'brother's wife' but has the cultural significance of 'mother'

Bhai or *baji*– Meaning 'brother' or 'sister', used in endearing fashion to non-relations

Beta – Meaning 'child' in affectionate fashion

Bibi – Respectful term for a lady

Fajr/Zuhr/Asr/Maghrib/Isha – Islamic prayer timings

Sehr – Breakfast during Ramadan (start of the fast)

Iftar – Evening meal during Ramadan (end of the fast)

Istikhara – Special prayers
pir – Spiritiual advisor
nikkah – Marriage

Printed in Great Britain
by Amazon

22188929R00304